The Politics of Inflation and Economic Stagnation

LEON N. LINDBERG AND CHARLES S. MAIER
Editors

The Politics of Inflation and Economic Stagnation

Theoretical Approaches and International Case Studies

Brian Barry
David R. Cameron
Colin Crouch
Douglas A. Hibbs, Jr.
Albert O. Hirschman
Robert O. Keohane
Karl-Heinz Ketterer
Rudolph Klein
Norbert Kloten
Leon N. Lindberg
Charles S. Maier
Andrew Martin
Michele Salvati
Rainer Vollmer
John T. Woolley
Kozo Yamamura
John Zysman

THE BROOKINGS INSTITUTION
Washington, D.C.

Copyright © 1985 by
THE BROOKINGS INSTITUTION
1775 Massachusetts Avenue, N.W., Washington, D.C. 20036

Library of Congress Cataloging in Publication data:

Main entry under title:
The Politics of inflation and economic stagnation.

Includes index.
1. Inflation (Finance)—Addresses, essays, lectures.
2. Stagnation (Economics)—Addresses, essays, lectures.
3. Unemployment—Effect of inflation on—Addresses,
essays, lectures.   4. Economic policy—Addresses, essays,
lectures.   5. Economic history—1945–1971—Addresses,
essays, lectures.   6. Economic history—1971–   —
Addresses, essays, lectures.   I. Lindberg, Leon N.
II. Maier, Charles S.   III. Barry, Brian M.
HG229.P66   1985   332.4'1   84-23263
ISBN 0-8157-5264-4
ISBN 0-8157-5263-6 (pbk.)

1 2 3 4 5 6 7 8 9

THE BROOKINGS INSTITUTION is an independent organization devoted to nonpartisan research, education, and publication in economics, government, foreign policy, and the social sciences generally. Its principal purposes are to aid in the development of sound public policies and to promote public understanding of issues of national importance.

The Institution was founded on December 8, 1927, to merge the activities of the Institute for Government Research, founded in 1916, the Institute of Economics, founded in 1922, and the Robert Brookings Graduate School of Economics and Government, founded in 1924.

The Board of Trustees is responsible for the general administration of the Institution, while the immediate direction of the policies, program, and staff is vested in the President, assisted by an advisory committee of the officers and staff. The by-laws of the Institution state: "It is the function of the Trustees to make possible the conduct of scientific research, and publication, under the most favorable conditions, and to safeguard the independence of the research staff in the pursuit of their studies and in the publication of the results of such studies. It is not a part of their function to determine, control, or influence the conduct of particular investigations or the conclusions reached."

The President bears final responsibility for the decision to publish a manuscript as a Brookings book. In reaching his judgment on the competence, accuracy, and objectivity of each study, the President is advised by the director of the appropriate research program and weighs the views of a panel of expert outside readers who report to him in confidence on the quality of the work. Publication of a work signifies that it is deemed a competent treatment worthy of public consideration but does not imply endorsement of conclusions or recommendations.

The Institution maintains its position of neutrality on issues of public policy in order to safeguard the intellectual freedom of the staff. Hence interpretations or conclusions in Brookings publications should be understood to be solely those of the authors and should not be attributed to the Institution, to its trustees, officers, or other staff members, or to the organizations that support its research.

Foreword

In the mid-1970s, as policymakers and social scientists began to perceive the duration, pervasiveness, and depth of that decade's worldwide inflation, the Brookings Institution organized several conferences of international experts to investigate its causes. This volume stems from a 1978 conference that examined the political and social processes underlying the global acceleration of prices. The authors look at the pressures behind economic policy and outcomes. They consider such factors as the public commitment to the welfare state, party competition for electoral support, the connections among large trade unions, industrial leaders, and government officials, and the changing international economic power of the industrial nations. Their contributions furnish a wealth of comparative information and illustrate new approaches to understanding inflation. Several authors also raise the important issue of how political and social factors can be integrated with the traditional "economic causes" of inflation in an interdisciplinary approach.

The study is necessarily retrospective. Though inflation is still serious in Latin America and Israel, in Europe and North America it has receded and become less variable and more publicly tolerable than during the surges of the 1970s. Nonetheless, the economic difficulties of the 1970s represented the most severe problems since World War II for the nations of the Organization for Economic Cooperation and Development. Moreover, inflation has been slowed only at great cost in terms of employment and output. Many problems still linger, especially the dilemmas of industrial restructuring and the political framework that allowed inflation to develop such a head of steam in the first place. Thus, though the volume is a historical analysis that attempts to measure the fundamental causes for a decade of economic anguish, it also provides a foundation that can be used in examining current policy choices.

Leon N. Lindberg, professor of political science at the University of Wisconsin in Madison, and Charles S. Maier, professor of history and associate at the Center for European Studies at Harvard University, the editors of this volume, organized the conference at which the authors first presented their analyses. All the participants benefited from one another's critiques during the drafting stages. Outside commentators who offered valuable suggestions during and after the conference included Daniel Bell, Villy Bergström, Stephen Blank, Hugh Heclo, Carl-L. Holtfrerich, Peter J. Katzenstein, Serge-Christophe Kolm, Edward J. Nell, Mancur Olson, Benjamin I. Page, Hugh Patrick, T. J. Pempel, William Poole, Robert Solomon, Paolo Sylos-Labini, Edward R. Tufte, and Lloyd Ulman. Charles Albert Michalet, Michael Piore, and Gösta Rehn participated at early planning stages for this project, and Paul Peretz made a major presentation to the conference. The editors acknowledge with thanks these various contributions. They also wish to thank associates of the Brookings Institution who encouraged their work at many points: Henry Owen, former director of the Foreign Policy Studies program, Ralph C. Bryant, Lawrence B. Krause, Joseph A. Pechman, Walter S. Salant, and Robert Solomon.

Individual authors also gratefully acknowledge the following assistance: David R. Cameron, for comments from Hugh Heclo, Benjamin I. Page, and Steven Rosenstone; Colin Crouch, for support from the Nuffield Foundation and for comments from Michael Shalev; Douglas A. Hibbs, Jr., for support from the National Science Foundation, assistance from Richard Fryling, Larry Levine, and especially Nicholas Vasilatos, and secretarial help from Christine Aquilino and Joy Mundy; Robert O. Keohane, for comments from Thomas E. Borcherding, Peter F. Cowhey, Michael Darby, Peter Gourevitch, Ernst B. Haas, Robert E. Hall, Albert O. Hirschman, Peter J. Katzenstein, Peter B. Kenen, Helen Milner, and Marina von Neumann Whitman; Norbert Kloten, Karl-Heinz Ketterer, and Rainer Vollmer, for the collaboration of Wilem Rall as a coauthor of their early draft preparation; Andrew Martin, for assistance from members of the State and Capitalism seminar at the Center for European Studies, Harvard University, and the seminar of the Swedish Institution for Social Research (SOFI) at the University of Stockholm, and from Bo Carlsson, Lennart Erixon, Walter Korpi, Edward E. Palmer, Jeffrey D. Sachs, Michael Shalev, and especially Villy Bergström, and for support from the Ford Foundation, Harvard University, the Swedish Information Service, and SOFI; John T. Woolley, for support from the National

Science Foundation and for comments from Ralph C. Bryant and William Poole; Kozo Yamamura, for comments by Hugh Patrick, T. J. Pempel, and Takafusa Nakamura; John Zysman, for comments from Suzanne Berger, Peter Gourevitch, Peter J. Katzenstein, T. J. Pempel, Laura Tyson, and Mary Yeager.

The Brookings Institution granted permission for an earlier version of chapter 3 by Albert O. Hirschman to be published in *Essays in Trespassing: Economics to Politics and Beyond* (Princeton University Press, 1981), and part of chapter 4 by Robert O. Keohane was published in "Inflation and the Decline of American Power," in Raymond Lombra and Willard Witte, eds., *Political Economy of International and Domestic Monetary Relations* (Iowa State University Press, 1982).

Alice M. Carroll edited the manuscript and guided it through the many stages of preparation and production. Alan G. Hoden verified its factual content, and Florence Robinson prepared the index.

The project as a whole was generously supported by a grant to the Brookings Institution from the Fritz Thyssen Foundation of Cologne, while partial support to cover conference expenses was provided by the German Marshall Fund of the United States.

The views expressed in this volume are those of the authors and editors alone and should not be attributed to the organizations that helped finance this project nor to the trustees, officers, or staff members of the Brookings Institution.

BRUCE K. MACLAURY
President

April 1985
Washington, D.C.

Contents

Tables

Figures

PART ONE

Introduction

1

Inflation and Stagnation as Politics and History

Charles S. Maier

This volume seeks the reasons for the difficulties of the industrial economies that persisted from the late 1960s at least through the early 1980s. It presents not primarily the views of economists but incorporates the approaches of political scientists, historians, and sociologists. Political and historical analysis does not promise easy solutions to high inflation, painful unemployment, or the faltering of economic growth. But it emphasizes alternative perspectives—explanations rooted in party and national rivalries, the history of class relations, or the differing roles of national governments as economic factors.

Until the end of 1980, inflation remained the natural preoccupying focus for any broad inquiry into the persisting difficulties of the industrial economies during the 1970s. It is true that the sustained worldwide inflation that began in the late 1960s did not reach the hyperinflationary proportions that rendered many currencies worthless after World Wars I and II. There was no destruction of money, for instance, on the scale of the German mark's fall to one-trillionth of its prewar stable value by the end of 1923, nor of other paper monies' decline during the upheavals of war and revolution. Nor was there even an inflation on the scale of those in Argentina and Chile before their respective military coups, where prices jumped two- to seven-fold on a per annum basis, and half the years over more than two decades brought inflation rates of 50 percent or more.[1] But horror stories of catastrophic inflations elsewhere were no substitute for getting inflation under control at home. Moreover, the industrial

---

1. For selected comparative inflation rates see Charles S. Maier, "The Politics of Inflation in the Twentieth Century," in Fred Hirsch and John H. Goldthorpe, eds., *The Political Economy of Inflation* (Harvard University Press, 1978), pp. 45–46.

economies had not previously experienced inflations of the combined magnitude and duration that the members of the Organization for Economic Cooperation and Development (OECD) suffered as a group beginning in the late 1960s. Even the inflations spanning the world wars and subsequent years of reconstruction were less persistent.

The scope and momentum of the 1970s inflation was not even broken by the recession of the mid-1970s. Perhaps it was durably halted by the unemployment of the early 1980s. In any case it remained a challenge to policy and a challenge to explanation. But the larger subject of this book is the more general decline of economic performance that began in the 1960s, of which inflation was the most salient index. Performance encompasses, along with price stability, the capacity of an economy to secure the full use of human resources, continuing growth, and at least moderate advances in equity, whether these are measured by growing income equality or the opening of educational opportunity and other public goods to the less advantaged. Securing these advances as a package seemed easy for the generation after World War II and its immediate aftermath. Attaining them simultaneously now seems far more difficult. Even when the focus is on the great inflation that was the major symptom of the 1970s, the broader concern remains the fall-off of economic achievement in general.

Methodological Premise

Mainstream economic analysis has provided only a restricted analysis of the underlying problem. To state this is not to indict economics as a discipline, but to ask about its limits. The analytical advances of classical economics, with both its Keynesian and monetarist branches, required rigorous intellectual abstraction. Critics sometimes accuse economists of reducing complex psychological creatures to simple utility maximizers, but this procedure was necessary for the progress of the discipline. The task of analytical economics is not to describe reality in its texture and richness, but to provide an ideal type of how transactions might be arranged if Everyman were indeed Economic Man. This intellectual reduction meant focusing on choices, decisions to buy or sell, produce, consume, or save, that were supposedly free from constraint. In other words, economics separated politics and the market. Where economists have sought at all to incorporate political factors into economic behavior they typically have done so by conceiving them as quantifiable incentives or disincentives, governmental carrots and sticks. What is more, economic models generally presuppose an equilibrium state that could be recovered, whether static or changing at a stable rate. Economic models have proved less versatile in describing transitions from one equilibrium to another. But the student of social and political institutions cannot make that assumption. The industrial world may be precisely in a profound transition that impedes equilibrating processes. To summarize, mainstream economics has entailed a radical simplification of how choices are made. Moreover, it conceptualizes politics as an impinging exogenous variable instead of as a matrix of power relationships constantly structuring group rivalries, collective values, and even property rights. And it tends to envision recovery of a high-growth equilibrium as feasible and natural.[2]

Yet even when successful policy outcomes or predictions are used as a criterion, the dominant economic doctrines do not adequately model the process of inflation. Too often, mainstream economic explanations attribute real-world developments to either freak events or policy errors. For instance, the major OECD investigation of the inflation and recession of the 1970s suggested that "the immediate causes of the severe problems" could "largely be understood in terms of conventional economic analysis. There have been underlying changes in behaviour patterns and in power relationships internationally and within countries. But *our reading of recent history is that the most important feature was an unusual bunching of unfortunate disturbances unlikely to be repeated on the same scale, the impact of which was compounded by some avoidable errors in economic policy.*"[3]

But this approach does not suffice either to understand or to shape events. Events that must appear as random from the perspective of a deductive system became so continuous in the 1970s that they should be regarded as systemic. This study thus seeks to understand the institutional structures that generate what conventional economic analysis must accept as random events or shocks. To explain the intractability of inflation over a long period or disappointing economic performance in general requires a methodology that seeks to make these random events more endogenous. This is not to claim that no events are random, in the sense that they might not have occurred or might have happened at other junctures. The

2. See Leon N. Lindberg, "The Problems of Economic Theory in Explaining Economic Performance," *Annals of the American Academy of Political and Social Science,* vol. 459 (January 1982), pp. 14–27.

3. Organization for Economic Cooperation and Development, *Towards Full Employment and Price Stability* (Paris: OECD, 1977), p. 14. (Hereafter McCracken Report.)

outbreak of the Yom Kippur War in 1973, the oil embargo and subsequent quadrupling of oil prices were random shocks in one sense, no more to be expected than that a particular cosmic ray or meson might pass through a bubble chamber. Nonetheless, the generation of cosmic rays and mesons is a foreseeable statistical outcome. Even without the Middle East war, an informed political analysis might well have predicted that the possession of a monopoly resource by the Organization of Petroleum Exporting Countries (OPEC), a rising tide of nationalist self-awareness, old resentments at exploitation, all set against American political uncertainties at home after Vietnam as well as domestic inflation already under way, would force renegotiation of the terms on which petroleum was to be made available.

The same consideration holds for policy errors. Of course errors are committed; optimal policy is rare. Policy errors contributed to the deepening of the Great Depression of the 1930s and to the aggravation of inflation in the 1960s and 1970s. The point is that errors often express deep-seated social and ideological preferences, political-party or group commitments not easily altered, patterns of influence, business or bureaucratic arrangements learned only slowly and painful to modify. They are rarely willful experiments although they may rest upon mistaken calculations. To understand a so-called error requires explaining on what grounds the recommendation seemed likely to appeal (ideology, for example), and how it might be implemented, persisted in, and even magnified in final outcome (institutional structures).

This volume seeks to develop an understanding of how political preferences and institutional arrangements contribute to economic outcomes. It does not exclude the study of markets—of transactions supposedly free of coercion and governed by the endowments of wealth, time, and talent that each actor brings—in favor of the study of the state and rule making, which is backed up by constraint. Such a division into economic and political spheres is misleading. The inflationary process demonstrates that the state and market are connected, and the task here is to understand the institutions of political economy where politics and the market converge.

This is an assignment akin to that of institutional economics; however, in the last generation institutional economics—drawing especially on continental European thinkers—lost ground to the more analytical branch. This volume seeks to restore what was valuable in that older approach, drawing on historical interpretation, the study of contemporary social and political arrangements and values, and even linguistic and philosophical analysis. Comparison, across space and through time, is fundamental to this multidisciplinary approach. Several questions have to be untangled. The first is why all Western countries became more vulnerable to inflation or required more recession to combat it. The second is why this development apparently emerged at the end of the 1960s and not before. The third question asks why some economies were far more inflation prone than others. Each inquiry requires a different approach. To ask why the industrial economies seemed to be so vulnerable to stagnation as a group, why they seemed to become so resistant to demand management or policy-intractable, calls for looking at changes in institutions and values common to modern societies in general. Indeed sociological analyses of inflation sometimes allege causes so profound that no remedy appears possible under capitalism. The "deference politics" of an earlier era has dissolved, it is argued, and citizens demand entitlements that exceed what can be delivered.[4] Thoughtful Americans have asked whether it is democracy that might not ultimately be at fault, whether it is compatible with the renunciation of consumption needed for capital formation and economic growth.[5] Economists sensitive to the social fabric of transactions stressed labor market transformations—whether union power or stable wage policies designed to hold onto a trained work force—which tended to ratchet wages upward but rarely downward. In Arthur Okun's homely phrase, "Who threw the ratchet into the soup?"[6]

These general explanations are important, but they focus on the background factors. They cannot explain why inflation jumped at the end of the 1960s and not before. And the explanations may be too general— enough hard pounding through unemployment and workers may pull the ratchet out of the soup! The general factors must be supplemented by historically specific accounts that suggest why the institutional background

4. See John H. Goldthorpe, "The Current Inflation: Towards a Sociological Account," in Hirsch and Goldthorpe, *Political Economy of Inflation,* pp. 186–214; from a highly critical point of view, see E. J. Mishan, "The New Inflation: Its Theory and Practice," *Encounter,* vol. 42 (May 1974), pp. 12–24.

5. See Robert Lubar, "Making Democracy Less Inflation-Prone," *Fortune* (September 1980), pp. 78–86. Alfred E. Kahn, "Market Power Inflation: A Conceptual Overview," in Gardiner C. Means and others, *The Roots of Inflation: The International Crisis* (New York: Burt Franklin, 1975), p. 239, speculates that "this time is different—that we really have entered a new era of chronic, permanent inflation, at least so long as democracy and welfare-state capitalism survive."

6. Arthur M. Okun, *Prices and Quantities: A Macroeconomic Analysis* (Brookings Institution, 1981), p. 3. See also Arthur M. Okun, "Political Economy: The Lessons of the Seventies," in Arthur M. Okun and Robert M. Solomon, *Current Issues in Political Economy,* Ontario Economic Council Discussion Paper Series (Toronto: The Council, 1979); Tibor Scitovsky, "Market Power and Inflation," *Economica,* vol. 45 (August 1978), pp. 221–33.

changed when it did. In this volume, Albert Hirschman considers some of the general sociological and psychological variables that operate in many inflation-prone societies. Robert Keohane and the authors of the four country studies, on the other hand, stress particular historical transitions that have facilitated inflation and made for policy-intractability. This introduction also seeks the specifics of the decade of inflation, examining the remarkable character of the period of high growth after World War II, and asking what changed. Leon Lindberg, in chapter 2, then asks about the transformations of socioeconomic and political institutions that aggravated the vital "core rate" of inflation, especially in the case of the United States.

In questioning why inflation rates vary, explicit comparison is required. Comparison exposes those attitudes and institutions that promise more successful economic management and performance. John Zysman and Colin Crouch explicitly compare national approaches to industrial politics and coordinating of labor markets. In addition, the four case studies of national economies allow instructive contrasts. Michele Salvati's discussion of Italy helps to explain a society with deep divisions and institutional weaknesses that make coherent policymaking difficult. Japan, as presented by Kozo Yamamura, accepted periods of moderate to high inflation in return for continued growth (a finding Zysman also emphasizes). Ya-mamura does not indulge in the breathless enthusiasm for Japanese work habits and corporate loyalty that many popular studies stress. Instead he focuses on the political management of the economy and the stresses that may yet afflict it. The West German study spotlights the institutions that until recently seemed to ensure high growth and low inflation. Although unemployment as well as the structural vulnerabilities of their industry began to preoccupy the West Germans in the 1980s, it remains instructive to study the institutions that allowed effective policy coordination and labor-management consensus for so long. Finally, Andrew Martin's chapter on Sweden asks whether a high-performance, open economy can durably reconcile extensive social welfare and economic growth under capitalism.

The lessons to be drawn from the case studies are complex. By far the simplest one is that we all sail in leaky boats. Growth, equity, price stability are hard goals to pursue simultaneously and even harder to achieve over long periods. Comparison teaches no simple remedies for combining price stability and high growth, or for macroeconomic management in general. Societies are complex systems, and countless variables change from one to another; hence it is difficult to be sure which factors assure desirable results. Even when certain institutional arrangements or a commitment to values do seem to have inhibited inflation in one country, it is not easy to know whether they can be transplanted. Americans do not easily become Germans or Japanese, although some lessons may be transferable. Comparison suggests the feasibility of certain remedies in different contexts; it may provide some guidance under what circumstances industrialization strategies or incomes policy or labor-management concertation promises success in slowing inflation without renouncing growth.

Ultimately the debate about economic policy must be a reflection on ends as well as means. Individual preferences for the mix of growth, employment, price stability, and equity that a society should strive for may differ—assuming that all cannot simply be maximized at once. But a nation must come to some agreement on priorities. One of the major tasks of this volume is to demonstrate that the decision on economic *ends* and not just economic *means* or techniques must be a political act. But thinking about those priorities, asking about the costs of inflation and the costs of slowing inflation or the costs of American economic institutions in general is often obscured. In this book Brian Barry and David Cameron, as well as Douglas Hibbs and, by implication, John Woolley, address the issues of political values and choices.

Inflation is obviously a deeply troubling phenomenon to Americans, accelerating inflation even more so. But the inflation of the 1970s was the manifestation of a whole cluster of economic disappointments and institutional rigidities. Did they have to be accepted? Have they really been rendered more curable by renouncing public policy and wagering on such markets as exist? Or could economic performance more in line with earlier success have been achieved (assuming agreement) by designing a new armory of public, nonmarket guidelines? Must the rivalry among strong interest groups lead to more inflation or can it be harnessed for production and growth? These are the questions that do not allow politics to be separated from economics.

The Historical Premise

Looking back on a decade of stabilization policy, James Tobin noted in 1980 that "the tormenting issues of strategy have remained essentially the same throughout the period since the Second World War. Can the instrument of demand management achieve both monetary stability and

Table 1-1. *Average Annual Rates of Growth in Eight Countries, Various Years, 1950–80*
Percent

Country	Growth of gross domestic product[a]			
	1950–73	*1960–69*	*1970–79*	*1974–80*
Canada	5.2	5.5	4.4	2.6
France	5.1	5.5	3.9	2.8
Italy	5.5	5.8	3.0	2.6
Japan	9.8	11.1	5.4	4.9
Sweden	3.7	4.4	2.0	2.3
United Kingdom	3.0	2.9	2.3	1.3
United States	3.9	4.4	3.4	2.8
West Germany	6.3	4.6	2.9	2.7

Source: *World Business Cycles, 1950–80* (London: Economist Newspaper, 1982), pp. 22, 24, 45, 62, 65, 83, 87, 126.
a. Based on GDP stated in constant prices.

satisfactory real economic performance? If so, how? If not, what are the terms of feasible choices, and what criteria should guide them? If the macroeconomic instruments are inadequate for the goals, is it useful to supplement them with incomes policies temporarily or permanently?"[7] Nonetheless, while the "tormenting issues of strategy" may be the same, the context of economic policymaking has changed dramatically. There have been in fact two major economic phases since the initial postwar years of reconstruction. The first, extending from the late 1940s to the late 1960s, was characterized by unprecedented, sustained growth, even more rapid in Japan and continental Europe than in the United Kingdom and the United States. The second phase began with the transitional years of 1967–74—with the inflationary financing of the Vietnam War, the major European labor offensives, the dramatic abandonment of Bretton Woods, the oil price rise of early 1974, developments that initiated a troubled period of lower growth, high inflation, two major recessions, and severe structural problems in the traditional staple, manufacturing industries. In short, after a generation of growth, over a decade of relative stagnation (see table 1-1 for the growth rates of the postwar generation as a whole, for the buoyant 1960s, the 1970s reflecting the break in trend, and finally the years following the oil price increases).

The decline in economic performance affected all the industrial econ-

7. "Stabilization Policy Ten Years After," *Brookings Papers on Economic Activity, 1:1980*, p. 22. (Hereafter *BPEA*.)

Table 1-2. *Average Annual Rates of Inflation in Eight Countries, Various Years, 1950–81*

Percent

Country	Change in consumer price index[a]				
	1950–59	*1960–69*	*1970–79*	*1973–75*	*1979–81*
Canada	2.2	2.6	7.5	10.3	10.7
France	5.6	3.8	8.8	11.9	12.7
Italy	3.0	3.8	12.2	16.5	17.8
Japan	4.0	5.4	8.7	16.5	6.2
Sweden	4.6	3.6	8.4	9.4	12.2
United Kingdom	3.6	3.6	12.4	18.2	13.9
United States	2.1	2.4	7.0	9.6	11.3
West Germany	1.9	2.5	4.9	6.2	5.7

Source: International Monetary Fund, *International Financial Statistics*, vol. 37 (October 1984), line 64 and various previous issues.

a. Rates of change calculated using differences of logs.

omies although some, such as the United Kingdom and Italy, proved more vulnerable than others such as West Germany. Inflation, of course, was the salient index of economic difficulty (see table 1-2). Price rises afflicted all societies, including the United States, which in 1974 and 1979–80 suffered from double-digit inflation and lost the resistance it had earlier shared with the Federal Republic of Germany to approach the mid-level susceptibility of the OECD economies. The new inflation of the 1970s was not merely the result of oil price shocks. It incorporated a consistent increase in the core, or underlying, secular rate of price and wage increases. As Philip Cagan pointed out, what was new about the inflation of the 1970s was not that supply shocks could drive up prices, but that the core rate proved relatively impervious to the severe recessions of 1975 and 1979–80.[8] Only in the early 1980s did the core rate give signs of moderating—although at great cost in terms of the other indexes of economic performance, employment, and growth.

Following hard on inflation, unemployment rates and declining economic growth likewise revealed a common decline in economic performance. In general, as Douglas Hibbs points out in chapter 7, the United States long accepted a less proinflationary trade-off and acquiesced in higher unemployment than the other OECD countries. By the end of the

8. *Persistent Inflation: Historical and Policy Essays* (Columbia University Press, 1979). Okun, *Prices and Quantities*, p. 2, and many others make the same point.

Table 1-3. *Average Annual Unemployment Rates in Eight Countries,*
1967–73 and 1974–80[a]
Percent

Country	1967–73	1974–80
Canada	5.1	7.2
France	2.4	4.8
Italy	5.7	6.7
Japan	1.2	1.9
Sweden	2.2	1.9
United Kingdom	3.5	5.6
United States	4.5	6.7
West Germany	1.0	3.2

Source: Organization for Economic Cooperation and Development, *OECD Economic Outlook*, no. 34 (December 1983), table R12, p. 163.

a. Standardized unemployment as percent of total labor force.

1970s it was moving toward the center of the pack, catching up on inflation, being overtaken in terms of unemployment (see table 1-3).

By 1981–82 unemployment had become the outstanding policy issue in the major European economies. It contributed to the victory of the French Socialists on a reflationary economic platform in 1981; remained at record postwar rates to trouble the Thatcher government in Britain; and eroded the rule of the incumbent Social Democrats and Free Democrats in West Germany, where the coalition fell apart between prescriptions for job creation and for encouraging private-sector investment. In almost all respects the industrial economies were functioning at a far lower level of overall performance than had been the norm for over two decades.[9]

Long-lasting declines in labor productivity suggested that economic difficulties were deep-rooted in the 1970s. As Edward Denison and others documented, productivity growth slackened at the end of the 1960s and declined even more markedly after 1973–74.[10] National income per person

9. New York Stock Exchange, Office of Economic Research, *U.S. Economic Performance in a Global Perspective* (NYSE, February 1981), pp. 6–11, calculated an economic performance index by dividing annual real economic growth rates by the sum of unemployment and inflation rates (Okun's "discomfort index"). The statistics overdramatize the decline from the 1960s to the 1970s by, in effect, multiplying highly related quantities, but the order-of-magnitude results are suggestive. In Japan the index fell from 145.9 in 1960–73 to 37.8 in 1974–80, in West Germany from 123.9 to 29.0, in France from 85.5 to 18.0, in Italy from 67.2 to 13.4, in Canada from 64.2 to 16.5, in Sweden from 55.6 to 15.3, in the United States from 50.4 to 15.2, and in the United Kingdom from 43.1 to 2.2.

10. Edward F. Denison, *Accounting for Slower Economic Growth: The United States in the 1970s* (Brookings Institution, 1979); J. R. Norsworthy, Michael J. Harper, and Kent Kunze, "The Slowdown in Productivity Growth: Analysis of Some Contributing Factors," *BPEA, 2:1979*, pp. 387–421. For a more optimistic view see Gregory Schmid, "Productivity and Reindustrialization: A Dissenting View," *Challenge*, vol. 23 (January–February 1981), pp. 24–29.

employed remained essentially stagnant. Among the many reasons suggested for the long decline, changes in the age-sex composition of the
work force, declining capital investment per worker, the increasing number
of service jobs in the modern economy, the oil price increases (OPEC I
and OPEC II), and governmental regulation may all have played some
role. Whatever the reasons, the aggregate effect outran the suggested
causes. Inflation and declining productivity gains probably reinforced each
other. As productivity increases slowed, workers could no longer claim
the same wage increases without triggering an inflationary price rise.
Conversely, expectations of continuing inflation with lower real returns
on capital might have inhibited the new investment that could have
restored growth.[11]

Despite these discouraging indicators, however, the economic performance of the United States could be credited with some major accom-
plishments (although inflation may have been part of their cost). The
1970s comprised a remarkable period of job creation. If the 1982
unemployment rate was close to 10 percent, 97 millions were still working,
almost 11 million more workers than a decade earlier.[12] These new jobs
responded in part to the desire of women to enter the labor market; they
were generated in services and no longer in manufacturing. (Rudolf Klein
in chapter 8 points to the particular role of the public sector, especially
in Britain, in accommodating this trend.) The shift toward services is also
difficult to evaluate. Once welcomed as the advent of postindustrial society,
it began to arouse increasing preoccupation as factories continued to
close.

In effect, the U.S. economy absorbed new job seekers from the ranks
of women and youth into service employment that allowed for little gain
in output per worker, even as traditional industrial sectors became
obsolescent or shut down plants entirely.[13] Throughout most of the
1970s, excepting the mid-decade recession, the price of this underlying
change was higher inflation, low growth, weakened profits, and stagnant

11. This diagnosis was behind the frequent invidious comparisons of the low American savings rate
with the far higher savings of the Japanese. On the other hand, William D. Nordhaus proposed that if,
as he believed, declining productivity had largely to be attributed to an autonomous decline in technological
innovation, then higher savings were not called for; "Economic Policy in the Face of Declining
Productivity Growth," *European Economic Review*, vol. 18 (May–June 1982), pp. 131–57.

12. Bureau of Labor Statistics, U.S. Department of Labor, January 1982.

13. See Robert Bacon and Walter Eltis, *Britain's Economic Problem: Too Few Producers* (London:
Macmillan, 1978); Lester C. Thurow, *The Zero-Sum Society: Distribution and the Possibilities for Economic
Change* (Basic Books, 1980), pp. 162–67; Emma Rothschild, "Reagan and the Real America," *New
York Review of Books* (February 5, 1981), pp. 12–18; Felix Rohaytn, "Reconstructing America," *New
York Review of Books* (March 5, 1981), pp. 16–20.

personal income. Most European societies incurred the same liabilities without the job creation. Whether the trade-off was worth making, or might have been made at lower real cost, remains an open question. In the wake of the 1979–80 OPEC II oil-price increase and the policies chosen by the Republican administration, the terms of the trade-off began to change. Inflation abated, but the toll on employment climbed to a new high; in addition earlier progress toward reducing inequality was modified as a policy commitment and perhaps in terms of results as well. Different policies, it was suggested, would end the stagflation afflicting the American economy.

The difficulties of so many mixed economies at one time—some governed by Social Democrats, others by free-market conservatives— suggest that no conventional policy "fix," whether interventionist or market oriented, could easily reverse the sclerosis of the 1970s. The skepticism of a contributor to the McCracken Report that a "narrow path" to recovery really did exist between the Scylla of recession and the Charybdis of inflation was perhaps well-founded.[14] But must the Western economies be so resistant to policy intervention in general, or have the right formulas just not been found? Should the limping economy of the 1970s and early 1980s have been considered "normal" just as the growth of the 1960s once was? Perhaps the question is badly phrased. Normal is a misleading concept. The Western economies are not machines that can be tuned to operate at a certain level as inputs change and expectations evolve. As this study illustrates at many points, the Western economies are historical formations and embody evolving institutions. The factors that make for any given pattern of performance constantly alter. Whether the ambient conditions for the late 1980s and 1990s can be as favorable as those that nurtured the achievements of the 1950s and 1960s cannot be predicted. Historical examination does suggest that in the quarter century after World War II the industrial economies did benefit uniquely from a set of favorable circumstances unlikely to recur. Once those are understood, it may be possible to seek policy substitutes or at least to understand the limits of likely performance.

Postwar Consensus and Its Breakdown

Although the postwar period was filled with bitter partisan conflicts in the United States and Europe, the tasks of reconstruction can in

14. "Comments by Professor Komiya," in McCracken Report, p. 250.

retrospect be seen as having evoked an overriding consensus. In the wake of wartime destruction, restoration of output and production loomed as the highest priority. Even the Western Communist parties originally endorsed the objective of reconstruction to demonstrate their responsibility as would-be governmental partners. And although by the late 1940s the Communists had withdrawn or been thrown into opposition, authoritative labor leaders in America, Britain, and on the continent accepted the priorities of growth and productivity.

In return for the implicit collaboration, which produced more than a decade of wage restraint, labor won several fundamental objectives: first, a general public commitment to high employment policies; second, a general assurance that wages would at least rise in line with profits and productivity even if there were not to be any planned pretax redistribution; third, the development of pensions and transfers associated with the welfare state. Each of these gains meant overcoming a critical interwar weakness that had apparently contributed to the onset of the depression or to the misery of the classes enmeshed in it. These postwar bases of public policy essentially created an implicit social compact; indeed, it was largely the breakdown of the implicit compact that led to painful, more overt, and therefore more difficult attempts at renegotiations. The commitment to economic growth in the 1950s and 1960s could rally both capital and labor and thus replace earlier (and avoid later) conflicts over shares. And the reality of growth—the more than doubling of real income from 1948 to the early 1960s—made the bargain seem worthwhile.

Other forces reinforced the consensus on growth and the adjournment of a conflict over income shares. The discipline of the cold war—the negative example of East German socialism for workers in the Federal Republic, the intense anticommunism of American labor and European Social Democrats and Catholics, the concrete inducements of American aid—was a major factor. So too was the relative labor surplus released by agricultural modernization or by refugees from Eastern Europe.[15] As John Zysman emphasizes in chapter 6, the Western economies benefited from a massive one-time epochal transition from the countryside to the city. The percentage of active workers on farms dropped in the United States

15. See Charles P. Kindleberger, *Europe's Postwar Growth: The Role of Labor Supply* (Harvard University Press, 1967). For an emphasis on the role of cold war consensus, see Angus Maddison, "Economic Policy and Performance in Europe, 1913–1970," in Carlo M. Cipolla, ed., *The Fontana Economic History of Europe*, vol. 5: *The Twentieth Century* (Harvester Press/Barnes & Noble, 1977), pt. 2, pp. 442–508.

from over 12 percent to under 4 percent between the war and the 1960s; in France from 27 percent as late as 1954 to 14 percent in 1970; in West Germany from 23 percent in 1950 to 7 percent in 1976. The farms they left behind made rapid gains in productivity and output thanks to new tractors and fertilizers. The industries to which they flocked made even greater gains, so that even a modernized agriculture made less of a contribution to national income. The labor pools they augmented were deployed as reconstruction and reinvestment proceeded—rapidly enough to absorb the migrants, but not so rapidly as to create a seller's labor market. The 1950s thus saw a temporary slowing of the general twentieth-century trend toward growth of wages and salaries as a percentage of GNP.[16]

The special circumstances of the 1950s and 1960s could not have lasted forever. The population in agriculture might stabilize between 3 and 10 percent (depending on the specific society) but not much lower. The benefits of capital replacement after the destruction during World War II were likely to be disproportionate in the early years when modest reconstruction could eliminate major bottlenecks. Replacement of prewar plant; the advent of enough mass wealth to sustain the market for television, appliances, and automobiles (products, significantly enough, technologically available between the wars but hardly marketed for lack of demand); finally, the formation of social capital expressed in the rough tripling of Europeans' access to higher education in the 1960s could make investment especially potent. But in each of these spheres there had to be diminishing returns.

In addition, the political discipline imposed by the cold war became less compelling by the late 1950s. The age of Dulles and Adenauer gave way to that of the U.S. Democratic party's New Frontier, Great Society, and War on Poverty, to the German Great Coalition (1966) and the victory of the Social Democrats (1969), to the Opening to the Left in Italy (1961), and the return of Labour in Britain (1964–70). By the late 1960s the wage restraint that had prevailed for almost two decades buckled as Dutch (1964–69), French (1968), Italian (1969), and German (1970) workers sought and won major pay increases. Labor's disappointment with earlier gains where their own left-wing parties had been in power (the United Kingdom), or political frustration where the Left remained

16. OECD, *Labor Force Statistics,* as summarized in McCracken Report, pp. 290–91; Simon Kuznets, "Quantitative Aspects of the Economic Growth of Nations: IV, Distribution of National Income by Factor Shares," *Economic Development and Cultural Change,* vol. 7, pt. 2 (April 1959).

out (France and Italy) led to the highest level of militancy since the Liberation. American workers were exceptions to the unrest; Douglas Hibbs in chapter 7 discusses the lower apparent rates of political mobilization. In addition, the great conflicts in the United States over racial issues and then the war in Vietnam may have cut across class lines and reduced the salience of economic issues.

If American labor did not participate in the massive strikes at the turn of the decade, the Atlantic economies still swung into an increasingly coordinated pattern of overcorrecting economic phases. The slight recession in 1970–71 was followed by a boom (heated up by the Nixon preelection expansion) in 1972–73, with the fastest run-up of prices and capacity utilization in a decade and capped by the commodity and oil price increases. The responses to the OPEC rise of 1973–74 (from $3.00 per barrel to $11.50) may well have contributed more to inflation than the hike itself. Where countries allowed the new oil price to pass through without much intervention, the effect on prices (and then on wages as labor sought to preserve its real income) was direct. Where the government (as in the Japanese case) feared the contractionary effect of the oil levy and countered it with monetary expansion, it lost control of domestic prices. Where (as in the United States) an effort was made to control domestic price repercussions, the subsequent effort to contain the 1973–74 inflation, which tended to disguise the contractionary real effects of the changes in the terms of trade of 1973–74, precipitated the severest recession since the 1930s. By mid-1974 OECD unemployment was running at 5.5 percent (with another 0.6 percent implicit in the return of migrant workers). Unemployment, however, hardly moderated inflation. Indeed Britain and the United States sought to export their own inflationary tendencies to the strong-currency Germans and Japanese by urging them to accept a "locomotive" role on behalf of the West as a whole—that is, by seeking their more rapid and vigorous reflation. The second major OPEC price rise of 1979 only reconfirmed the renewed inflationary thrust of fiscal and monetary policies as the decade closed.[17]

Looking back at this tortuous decade of economic management, one can see that there was no more give in the system as a whole. Neither industry nor labor within the Western economies was prepared to acquiesce

17. This chronology relies on the McCracken Report, pp. 37–80. See also the country studies in Lawrence B. Krause and Walter S. Salant, eds., *Worldwide Inflation: Theory and Recent Experience* (Brookings Institution, 1977); papers prepared for the Conference on National Stabilization Policies in Industrial Countries, 1972–75, organized by the Brookings Institution, in Rome, May 30–June 3, 1977; the country studies in chapters 12–15, below.

in the sacrifice of real income implicit in the OPEC levy, and the ultimate allocation of burdens was left to the chaotic rivalry of a wage and price spiral. Nor were the petroleum producers prepared to see their new real gains frittered away by the depreciation of the dollar, and so by the end of the 1970s they reclaimed the real income that the West had started to recover since 1975. Under these strains most efforts at renegotiating explicit consensual arrangements such as the British social compacts or the German concerted action proved vulnerable and short lived.

And what a reversal by 1982 as inflation rates tumbled sharply even in Great Britain and output and employment sagged! Even a former enthusiast of monetarist remedies for inflation, such as Samuel Brittan, now felt that hopes for controlling the expansion of the money supply had proved illusory. Inflation might be in a proximate sense a monetary phenomenon, but "neglect of the international dimensions and of institutional change"[18] accelerated disinflation just as it had earlier augmented inflation. The lesson at the end of inflation confirmed what should have been the lesson during inflation as well—that some fundamental reshufflings of power, resources, and values was at work on economic outcomes.

The Changing International Monetary Structure

The process outlined testified to a second major transition that marked the 1970s, the weakening of the U.S. role in anchoring a stable international monetary system. Again, the harbingers of this development had appeared long before the outright crisis. Eisenhower had fretted about the adverse balance of trade; Kennedy had recalled servicemen's dependents from overseas; de Gaulle had refused to hold dollars as a reserve currency as early as 1965. The inflationary financing of the Vietnam War and the increase in international liquidity interacted with European labor unrest to increase inflationary pressures. The British devalued in 1967, the French in 1969 (see Michele Salvati's discussion in chapter 15); the Germans finally had to revalue in 1969 rather than be swamped with dollars; and by 1971 Washington had forced a general revaluation against the dollar with its own abandonment of Bretton Woods convertibility and temporary imposition of a 10 percent import surcharge. But even the new Smithsonian parities of December 1971 could not endure, given the advance of American inflation. By the spring of 1973 a regime of general floating—

18. "A Very Painful World Adjustment," *Foreign Affairs*, vol. 61 (America and the World, 1982), pp. 541–68, esp. p. 556.

with the European countries seeking to regroup in the "snake"—finally emerged.

These adjustments were often attended by overshooting and unwelcome domestic reverberations. Revaluation in West Germany (1969) and devaluation in Italy (1973) and Sweden (1974) produced such profit surges that they provoked major union reactions and sometimes more than compensatory rises in real wages. And while economists had often predicted that floating rates would allow national economies to shield themselves from imported inflation, the net result was more to loosen any residual international cohesion and to confirm the perverse policy effects predicted by Robert Mundell.[19] That is, would-be expansionary policies just sent money abroad to less inflationary neighbors, thus transmitting inflation rather than producing domestic expansion and by the late 1970s motivating everyone to turn to West Germany and Japan to revalue and to reflate. As the Mitterrand government learned during 1981–82, the ready transmission of inflationary pressures seemed to preclude successful Keynesianism in one country (although Keynes himself had suggested his remedies as policies that implied reducing the domestic links to the international economy). Other difficulties also arose. Countries that sought to redress their international accounts by devaluation faced higher import prices without being able to stabilize the prices of their export goods. Conversely, revaluing countries such as West Germany seemed (at least until 1980) to sustain their exports without a dent; called upon to diminish their trade balance to pull other countries out of recession, in effect they could reduce exports only when their partners slipped back into recession.

These perverse results were perhaps not the worst possible outcome. The protectionism often predicted for the 1970s did not come to pass. But the abandonment of the Bretton Woods regime seemed to make it more difficult for the soft-currency countries to use international adjustments to overcome inflation and harder for the hard-currency countries to assume inflation. In the first decade of flexible exchange rates ironically, everything remained tradable except monetary stability, which was hard to export or to import.

Underlying these dilemmas was a basic transformation in political

---

19. Robert A. Mundell, *Monetary Theory: Inflation, Interest, and Growth in the World Economy* (Pacific Palisades, Calif.: Goodyear Publishing Co., 1971). See also Rudiger Dornbusch, "Exchange Rate Economics: Where Do We Stand?" *BPEA, 1:1980,* pp. 143–85, and "The Theory of Flexible Exchange Rate Regimes and Macroeconomic Policy," *Scandinavian Journal of Economics,* vol. 78, no. 2 (1976), pp. 255–75.

organization as well as monetary regime. Robert Keohane in chapter 4 argues for the connection between global inflation and international tug-of-war between states for scarce resources. In addition, certain international constellations seemed to encourage general inflation, especially the situation that might be termed waning hegemony. This was the United States' global status in the 1970s, starkly defined by defeat in Vietnam, the loss of control over oil producers, the new restraint inherent in the Nixon doctrine, and then reticence in Angola, Iran, and elsewhere. Within the more limited sphere of international financial leadership, waning hegemony had also characterized London's role between the world wars, and, looking backward, one might even say that of Spain in the seventeenth century.

Each of these historical situations was marked by the inflationary impulses emanating from the declining power, or by compensatory efforts to reassert international financial power that required domestic deflation—a choice Britain made when it revalued the pound in 1925 and when it sought to defer devaluations from 1945 to 1949 and again from 1964 to 1967. For each of these international leaders, economic ascendancy had originally been easily achieved. Spain's was assisted by American treasure, Britain's by a lead in early industrialization, that of the United States by later technology and American insulation from wartime destruction. Preserving ascendancy is harder than attaining it. As imperial powers reach ascendancy and organize an international economy, they draw on the reserve role of their own currencies to provide the liquidity their creditor position requires. Even before World War I, London relied in part on her colonies to fund her international accounts. Between the wars she accepted some deflation but also called on the United States to share the burden of sterling by accepting some inflation. And during the 1940s Keynes's proposals for the future International Monetary Fund envisaged that strong-balance-of-payments economies would compensate weaker ones.[20] He met resistance from Washington, just as American secretaries of the treasury met resistance from de Gaulle in the mid-1960s and from the West Germans and Japanese to revaluation by the late 1970s. Only the

20. Marcello de Cecco, *Money and Empire: The International Gold Standard, 1890–1914* (Totowa, N.J.: Rowman and Littlefield, 1975); Benjamin M. Rowland, ed., *Balance of Power or Hegemony: The Interwar Monetary System* (New York University Press, 1976); Fred L. Block, *The Origins of International Economic Disorder: A Study of United States International Monetary Policy from World War II to the Present* (University of California Press, 1977); Peter J. Katzenstein, ed., *Between Power and Plenty: Foreign Economic Policies of Advanced Industrial States* (University of Wisconsin Press, 1978), esp. Stephen D. Krasner, "United States Commercial and Monetary Policy: Unravelling the Paradox of External Strength and Internal Weakness," and Stephen Blank, "Britain: The Politics of Foreign Economic Policy, the Domestic Economy, and the Problem of Pluralistic Stagnation."

United States' continued provision of political goods—namely, international military security—and the unwillingness of the strong-currency nations (West Germany, Switzerland, Japan) to accept a reserve role for their own monies prolonged the privileged role of the dollar.

International impulses to inflation thus flowed from the weakening of an economy whose currency had occupied the key reserve position. Rather than accepting austerity at home, from the late 1960s on Washington sought to persuade other countries to inflate their own economies and thus alleviate the pressure on the American balance of payments. The growing pressure on the balance of payments sprang in turn from the diffusion of industrialization first to the resurgent European economies, then to the developing nations of the third world. It also derived from political causes such as the loss of control over primary producers in the Middle East and from domestic desires to cut foreign commitments and avoid the domestic burdens such as higher taxes or much higher oil prices that would have been required to restrengthen the dollar as a reserve currency.

Inflationary impulses, in short, naturally arise from a situation where a formerly dominant power with an accepted internationalized currency seeks to prolong the reserve role of its money beyond the time justified by its earlier balance-of-payments strength. In the history of modern economies, periods of international monetary leadership have been relatively brief and few. During their existence they have, on the one hand, provided for vast increases in international trade, as in the generation before World War I and the generation after World War II. As critics have charged, they may also have helped to perpetuate the differentiation of economies into industrial leaders and underpaid primary producers. In any case, economic integration under a powerful reserve-currency economy has always been vulnerable. Periods of fragmented international exchange, bilateral trade, ad hoc payment arrangements have been more prevalent. In this respect, the 1950s and 1960s, not the subsequent disarray, have the claim to uniqueness.

The Changing Role of the State

It is impossible to be definitive about the inflationary consequences of the major change in the role of the state and public spending that characterized the years after the late 1960s. Rudolf Klein suggests in chapter 8 how difficult it is to ascribe a causal influence on inflation to public expenditure alone, and David Cameron in chapter 9 likewise contests some of the usual generalizations about the inflationary role of government. Many economists agree that much of the 1970s inflation was not impelled by government-induced excess demand, and still others suggest that modern governments must in any case validate the money demands emerging from the market arena.[21] As Klein emphasizes, government spending as a percentage of national income is primarily a measure of how social consumption and investment have been centralized; it does not have to imply changing end uses (except in wartime). The major component of increasing public expenditure has been transfer payments. This may imply taking money from relatively rich people's savings and giving it to relatively poor people's consumption. On the other hand, such transfers may have at best managed to keep constant national primary income distributions that would otherwise have grown more unequal.[22] Certainly the very large budget deficits of 1976 and 1980 followed recessions that would have generated far greater hardship without the transfers involved.

If there is a connection between public expenditure and inflationary trends, probably it does not rest on the differential consumption functions of the classes from which the money is taken and to which it is distributed. It may involve instead the strains on the economy as it goes from one level of state intervention to another. Throughout the twentieth century, public expenditure in the West has tended to increase, but in spurts. From perhaps 10–14 percent of national income before World War I, public expenditure surged to perhaps 40 percent of GNP during the war and then settled down at 18 to 22 percent in the 1920s. The Great Depression summoned forth another significant increment, which was coupled with the demands of rearmament for World War II. By 1950 public expenditure in the OECD countries stood at a median 34 percent of national income; it had risen to 41 percent by 1965 and reached 49 percent in 1973, with several of the European economies propelled over the 50 percent mark of GNP.[23] While public spending at any given level of national income may not be associated with inflation, the jump from one plateau to another—connected obviously with the world wars, but also with the

21. Basil J. Moore, "The Endogenous Money Stock," *Journal of Post Keynesian Economics,* vol. 2 (Fall 1979), pp. 49–70.

22. Thurow, *Zero-Sum Society,* pp. 47–54.

23. See G. Warren Nutter, *Growth of Government in the West* (Washington: American Enterprise Institute for Public Policy Research, 1978), p. 4; OECD, *Expenditure Trends in OECD Countries, 1960–1980* (Paris: OECD, 1972), and *Public Expenditure Trends* (Paris: OECD, 1978).

developments of the 1965–75 period—may involve strains that also are productive of inflation. (This holds for the correlation for Western countries as a group from one period to another; within any given period, the correlation between specific countries' increase in public expenditure and their respective inflation rates is less valid, as Cameron demonstrates.)

It is not possible to say that the increase in public expenditure produces inflation; Klein suggests the reverse may be just as true. Nor is it possible to correlate particular political coalitions with increased inflation. It may be that along with inflation, increased public spending testifies to underlying seismic changes in the demands placed on governments during periods of strained economic allocation. Drawing on socialist analysis of the early twentieth century, recent writers have suggested that the state budget becomes the battleground of different economic classes.[24] But the dispute is not simply between capital and labor; the state's own needs enter in. In a period of declining growth, left coalitions may defend welfare claims, while the state and the business sector struggle over the resources available for their respective programs and investments. Budgets (and deficits with inflationary consequences) can increase even when governments seek to reduce them. Programs cut under one heading can lead afflicted groups to seek benefits they might not claim otherwise. It is possible that the expansion of the state that can be accommodated without inflation during periods of growth (as during the 1960s) may contribute to the inflationary tug-of-war when growth falters. On the other hand, it may buffer society from far harsher and more direct social clashes and upheavals.

Finding specific historical and political changes that help explain the period of inflation after the late 1960s should not be read as a pessimistic message. It does point to certain epochal transformations: the new political and market power of the Western working classes, which could, however, be accommodated without inflation during a period of strong growth and indeed probably assisted in such growth; the declining international role of the United States; the diffusion of technological competitiveness to nations that were once safe markets for Western value added exports. Tranformations such as these suggest that the interval from World War

24. Rudolf Goldscheid, "Staatssozialismus oder Staatskapitalismus" (1917), in Rudolf Goldscheid and Joseph Schumpeter, *Die Finanzkrise des Steuerstaats: Beiträge zur politischen Ökonomie der Staatsfinanzen,* Rudolf Hickel, ed. (Frankfurt: Suhrkamp Verlag, 1976); James O'Connor, *The Fiscal Crisis of the State* (St. Martin's, 1973); Ian Gough, "State Expenditure in Advanced Capitalism," *New Left Review,* no. 92 (July–August 1975), pp. 53–92.

II until the late 1960s represented a confluence of uniquely favorable circumstances for the Western economies. Yet they do not necessarily consign the Western world to a continuing era of inflationary pressure or to severe recession as the price of holding inflation down. Declining productivity trends can reverse themselves as demographic variables change and technological innovation resumes a faster pace. Spokesmen for labor have recognized the need for investment and accumulation; consensus on growth may reemerge if agreement can be reached on who determines investment. Some of these issues are discussed in the concluding policy recommendations of this study.

Moreover, as growth slows, inflation is not inevitably its most serious consequence. Inflation remains, after all, a price phenomenon. Its influence on the production and allocation of real resources is not determined a priori. It can sometimes stimulate, sometimes inhibit the creation of wealth. In Brazil and in France it accompanied real growth; in Britain it seemed to make economic decline even more painful. Certainly inflation must accompany any failure to achieve the potential output that social groups expect or demand. For this reason, the inflation of the 1970s encouraged diagnoses that overexpectation must be the inevitable result of modern democracy. The history of those years does not teach that inflation is easily surmountable; far from it. But it does suggest the historical specificity of the recent era of inflation. It leaves open the possibility that not the new democratization of society or greater inter-national equality was the cause of inflation, but rather that the *transition* to these new distributions of power imposed strains tending to generate inflationary responses. Inflation, therefore, in historical perspective need not be the fatal accompaniment of mass democracy and consumer societies if they reach internal and international agreement on the allocation of their collective productive efforts. But how is that agreement to be reached? Will the marketplace alone retain enough legitimacy to be entrusted with the task of reconciling economic aspirations and resources? Will those who command fewer resources in the market seek a greater role for political review of decisions to consume and invest? That is the major domestic issue most Western electorates have confronted at the polls in recent years. This study seeks to contribute to revealing the many implications of that choice.

2

Models of the Inflation-Disinflation Process

Leon N. Lindberg

Economic theory and doctrine as well as the policymaking priorities of political elites in advanced capitalist societies have been decisively changed by the inflation and stagnation experiences of the 1970s and early 1980s. This chapter seeks to present a synthetic account of the inflation-disinflation process that is broadly consistent with the research reported in the chapters that follow and that highlights how this approach differs from conventional economic models. A more or less coherent account of inflation-disinflation does emerge in the chapters that follow. On the other hand, the view presented here would not necessarily be subscribed to in its entirety by any of their authors.

In the 1970s government policy toward inflation became the overriding preoccupation of economists, policymakers, and the public.[1] Tight fiscal and monetary policies began to bring inflation rates down in the 1980s but at the cost of deep global recession and unemployment rates not seen since the Great Depression. Even as inflation seemed at last to respond to the bitter medicine of sustained recession, it became clear that disinflation was also destabilizing. Were "solutions" to inflation to fail to produce promised results, and to weigh sharply against widely held norms of equity and fairness, the result might eventually be more radicalizing. The state budget could then become an ever more highly visible and sharpened arena of class and group conflict. How long can tacit coalitions supporting monetary and fiscal contraction hold together when consumers, producers and investors, debtors and creditors all confront the fact that disinflation

1. Fred Hirsch and John H. Goldthorpe, eds., *The Political Economy of Inflation* (Harvard University Press, 1978), p. 1, called it the "great unsolved issue" of modern capitalist society.

seems to entail not only an essentially random pattern of massive income and wealth redistributions, but also unpredictable consequences for various industries and for aggregate employment? What would be the political and economic consequences of another bout of inflation as prostabilization coalitions collapse?

The 1970s produced many surprises and "awkward facts" for standard economic doctrines about the causes of inflation and the means for its control.[2] The new, more tenacious, and persistent inflation sparked considerable learning among economists—though "different people," as Arthur M. Okun pointed out, "learned widely different things."[3]

Three broad lines of neoclassical economic argument have emerged, all of them envisaging systematically altered relations and expectations among suppliers and purchasers of goods and labor and the state that supervises their transactions. Neo-Keynesians see an inflation-prone society, rooted in the claims of organized producer groups, in implicit contracts, and in a sense of fairness in market relations and within society at large. They believe that only wage and price controls can break the price-wage spirals set off by external shocks and the like. Monetarists also see a changed price system and a price-wage spiral; but they attribute both to indecisive, erroneous, or cowardly government policy. They believe there are no economic barriers to reducing inflation, only the political barrier of finding politicians with the will to resist political pressure and special interests and to maintain slack demand in the economy long enough to squeeze out inflationary expectations. Supply-side economists tend to reject the idea of an inflationary momentum; they believe that inflation rates will drop precipitously once individuals firmly believe that a government policy of tax reductions and budget cuts will be sustained and will curb inflation.

The three views rest on similar empirical observations with respect to price behavior, the effectiveness of an activist fiscal and monetary policy, the tendency of government policies to establish floors but not ceilings, expectations and senses of entitlement, and the changing conditions of productivity, capital formation, and investment in capitalist democracies. Their interpretations of the data, however, produce significantly different

2. See Ronald A. Krieger, "Economic Stabilization," *Society,* vol. 17 (July–August 1980), pp. 73–78; James W. Dean, "The Dissolution of the Keynesian Consensus," *Public Interest,* Special Issue (1980), pp. 19–34.

3. "Political Economy: The Lessons of the Seventies," in Arthur M. Okun and Robert Solomon, *Current Issues in Political Economy,* Ontario Economic Council Discussion Paper Series (Toronto: The Council, 1979), p. 1.

pictures of how inflation is transmitted through the economy. Each implies major assumptions about how economic agents and group interests interact, how state policy responds, and how organizations and individual agents in the economy react to policy.

None of the economic models has done well in explaining price behavior in the 1970s.[4] Richard Lipsey's explanation is that the crisis in the economy is "a crisis of policy."[5] As Modigliani sees it, "the crisis is right there in the structure of the world, not in our ability to capture that structure."[6] That crisis has afflicted all theories. The inflation of the 1970s was a particularly well entrenched inertial inflation, a wholly new phenomenon that proved very difficult to control. The political and economic volatility and uncertainty associated with disinflation, the failure of interest rates to validate monetarist expectations by following inflation rates down, the stubbornness of inflationary expectations even as inflation rates drop sharply, and the failure of supply-side tax cuts to stimulate new business investment support Lipsey's contention that all economists are equally unprepared to deal with contemporary inflation or disinflation.

A Political and Institutional Analysis of Inflation

If contemporary inflation is a symptom of deeper problems in the economy and the political system, analysis of economic performance and policy from a political and institutional perspective may reveal something about the nature of inflation.[7] This volume attempts to trace the causes and mechanisms of inflation to changes in political power and social organization, in the expectations of individuals and groups, and in the interaction among collective actors in the market and the state.

Any concept of policymaking in democratic capitalist countries must

---

4. See Franco Modigliani, "Discussion of Inflation and Unemployment in a Macroeconomic Model by Ray C. Fair," in *After the Phillips Curve: Persistence of High Inflation and High Unemployment*, Conference Series, no. 19 (Federal Reserve Bank of Boston, 1978); Richard G. Lipsey, "The Understanding and Control of Inflation: Is There a Crisis in Macro-economics?" *Canadian Journal of Economics*, vol. 14 (November 1981), pp. 545–76: James Tobin, "Stabilization Policy Ten Years After," *Brookings Papers on Economic Activity, 1:1980*, pp. 19–71; Otto Eckstein, *The Great Recession: With a Postscript on Stagflation*, Data Resources Series, vol. 3 (Amsterdam: North Holland, 1978); Alan S. Blinder, *Economic Policy and the Great Stagflation* (Academic Press, 1979).

5. "Understanding and Control of Inflation," p. 546.

6. "Discussion of Inflation and Unemployment," p. 195.

7. See Leon N. Lindberg, "The Problems of Economic Theory in Explaining Economic Performance," J. Rogers Hollingsworth, "The Political-Structural Basis for Economic Performance," and Jerald Hage and Remi Clignet, "Coordination Styles and Economic Growth," *Annals of the American Academy of Political and Social Science*, vol. 459 (January 1982).

first recognize that macroeconomic choices do not, as economic models so often take for granted, represent the best attainable trade-off among inflation, employment, and the balance of payments. Rather, economic policymaking involves a continuing struggle among business, labor, and other organized interests, including the state and its various agencies, over the distribution of power and income in society.[8] The crucial factors in this struggle are the ability of interest groups or dominant coalitions to control the instruments of macroeconomic policy, and the relative bargaining strength of various parties in the market arena.

Forty years ago, Michael Kalecki took exception to Keynes's belief that government policy could guarantee full employment and stable growth by manipulating spending, taxing, and control of the money supply without infringing on established property rights or intervening in the relationships of production or in income distribution.[9] According to Keynes, government intervention to assure the economic circulation and close the "break" in the investment process would guarantee full employment, and eventually a sustained full employment would bring about a decline in income inequality and would reduce the scarcity power of capital and of rentiers.

Kalecki, however, foresaw the strains of trying to sustain full employment over a period of time and under changing economic conditions. The disciplinary effects of the fear of unemployment on factory workers would be eroded and so would the confidence of entrepreneurs as labor's increased bargaining power put strain on the price level and on the ratio of wages to profits. Changing economic conditions would confront policymakers with a choice of trading full employment for other goals such as price stability, or of intervening further in the economy. Kalecki believed that there was a deep contradiction between capitalist drive and values and the policies and institutions that would be necessary to maintain the economy on that course. The outcome would thus hinge on the distribution of political power within the state.

The second requisite of a political-institutional analysis is a specification of the institutional structure of the political economy. This necessarily implies explicit attention to the precise ways in which the incentives and

8. Stanley W. Black makes a similar argument in "Strategic Aspects of the Political Assignment Problem in Open Economies," in Raymond E. Lombra and Willard E. Witte, eds., *The Political Economy of International and Domestic Monetary Relations* (Iowa State University Press, 1982), and in "Politics versus Markets—International Differences in Macroeconomic Policies" (March 1982).

9. "Political Aspects of Full Employment," *Political Quarterly*, vol. 14 (October–December 1943).

behavior of employers and workers, investors and producers are conditioned by institutional and cultural contexts, by established relationships that prevail between the public and private sectors, and by the perceived legitimacy and competence of state authorities. The regularities posited by economic theories about the behavior of politicians and policymakers, such as an inherent tendency to an inflationary business cycle, the innate cowardice or incompetence of politicians, or the rational propensity of economic agents to systematically anticipate and seek to offset government stabilization policies may all reflect particular institutional and cultural settings.

Furthermore, policymakers do not have a free choice of instruments; some can only choose among indirect and global instruments that influence aggregate demand and the money supply, whereas others may also be able to choose instruments that influence manpower skills, prices and wages, and industrial structure. Political authorities in some nations may be able to use a coordinated set of policy instruments, whereas in others a fragmented government structure may prevent adoption of a sustained and coherent policy.

Each economic theory of inflation presupposes certain constitutional arrangements and a process for assuring these arrangements in a political democracy. Thus, if Shapiro is correct in saying that "a money system that corresponded to orthodox economic principles . . . would require an isolationist and radically decentralized and limited government,"[10] then orthodox principles either cannot readily be applied in policymaking in the United States, or those economists who propose them are promoting a radical redistribution of political and social power. From a political and institutional perspective all three neoclassical approaches to economic organization seem to see politics, collective sentiments, organizational prerogatives, and redistributive claims as intrusions on an otherwise potentially rational economic sphere. Economists seem professionally predisposed to deplore "the politicization of the economy" and to prefer market and quasi-market strategies of stabilization.

But market controls have in the past exerted a constantly destabilizing effect on the societies within which they operate. Either some external value consensus, direct or indirect state or class coercion, or remedial intervention by the state has been needed to assure aggregate demand

10. Robert J. Shapiro, "Politics and the Federal Reserve," *Public Interest,* no. 66 (Winter 1982), p. 139.

and to correct market failure.[11] The chronically unstable social and political environment of a market economy spurs defensive reactions on the part of market actors and public and group demands for state intervention. Hence the tendency for a liberal market economy to be transformed into an organized and politicized one. Firms, unions, and professional associations have long since acquired organizational and informational capacities that permit them to directly influence market exchange relations. And governments have been progressively opened up to pressure from organized interests seeking the extension of nonmarket controls.

From this perspective, the objective of inflation policy should not be to recreate market conditions but to induce organized interests to contribute to economic order in the face of the distortions and disruptions provoked by their own behavior.[12] To return to market controls may only further destabilize the system. The key to stanching inflation may be to experiment with political controls that induce a "concern for the common interest" among organized interests and state authorities and encourage them to act on the interests they share with society at large. Incomes policies, social contracts, tripartite bargaining structures, corporatist industrial relations systems, arrangements for direct representation of organized interests within the state, and institutions of indicative planning can all be seen in these conditions as implicit or explicit gropings for political control. They are also, as Black points out, "means of reducing the redistributional possibilities open to the players and thus defusing the confrontational aspects of the [policy] problem."[13]

Whatever the form taken by what Leijonhufvud calls the new monetary constitution, installing a system of behavioral rules that will guide fiscal and monetary authorities and reliably constrain and condition the behavior of economic agents and the public is a profoundly political decision.[14] A decision to legitimate some particular sets of price expectations has enormous redistributive implications and carries unknown risks for all concerned. The political process by which such a monetary constitution is reconstituted must assure the representation of all interests and conform to society's ethics of compromise, fairness, and equity.

11. John H. Goldthorpe, "The Current Inflation: Towards a Sociological Account," in Hirsch and Goldthorpe, *Political Economy of Inflation*, p. 194.

12. Colin Crouch, "Inflation and the Political Organization of Economic Interests," in Hirsch and Goldthorpe, *Political Economy of Inflation*, pp. 217–39.

13. "Politics versus Markets," p. 3.

14. Axel Leijonhufvud, "Expectations: Policymaker's Predicament," in Joint Economic Committee, *Expectations and the Economy*, 97. Cong. 1 sess. (U.S. Government Printing Office, 1981), pp. 40–47.

Establishing an Empirical Baseline

Two approaches can help in analyzing how policy has been applied in different political and social settings. The first is to disaggregate inflation into its interacting components, each of which can be traced to a proximate origin or event and to more fundamental causes. The second is to provide a typology of inflation and stabilization configurations.

The Core Rate

For the disaggregation of inflation, the concept of a core or underlying or secular rate, as distinguished from temporary shocks, allows a common benchmark. Otto Eckstein defined the "core inflation rate" as "the rate that would occur if the economy were on its long-term equilibrium growth path, free of shocks and excess demand."[15] Shocks or surges of excess demand or bottlenecks can become embedded in the core rate, however, through expectations or some other mechanism. The most striking feature of the inflation of the 1970s in the United States and elsewhere was "the deterioration of the core rate," which ratcheted upward steadily over the period. One-time shocks or blips and temporary excesses of spending became embedded in prices and wages rather than passing through the economy. From slightly over 2 percent in the early 1960s, the core rate declined, rose again, then leveled off at 4 percent in 1970, where it remained until late 1973 (see figure 2-1). In 1974–75 the core rate jumped to 8 percent, where it settled, and in 1979–80 it advanced to the 9–10 percent range.

Most commentators agree that the deterioration of the core rate originated not on the cost side of the economy but in excess-demand pressures engendered by U.S. decisions as to how the Vietnam War would be financed and in the reluctance of the United States' trading partners to change parity with the dollar.[16] President Johnson's unwillingness to raise taxes between 1965 and 1967 and an economy that was near full capacity as the war escalated produced a classic excess-demand

15. "Economic Choices for the 1980s," *Challenge*, vol. 23 (July–August 1980), p. 16. Also see Walter W. Heller, "Shadow and Substance in Inflation Policy," *Challenge*, vol. 23 (January–February 1981), pp. 5–13; Albert T. Sommers, "The Challenge of Inflation in the 1980s," in Walter E. Hoadley, ed., *The Economy and the President: 1980 and Beyond* (Prentice-Hall, 1980), pp. 34–73.

16. Eckstein, "Economic Choices"; Philip Cagan, *Persistent Inflation: Historical and Policy Essays* (Columbia University Press, 1979); Geoffrey Maynard and W. van Ryckeghem, *A World of Inflation* (Barnes & Noble, 1975).

Figure 2-1. *The Core Inflation Rate and the Consumer Price Index,*
United States, 1960–79

Percent

Source: Otto Eckstein, "Economic Choices for the 1980s," *Challenge*, vol. 23 (July–August 1980), p. 16.

inflation which slowly built up in the economy and pushed the consumer price index from 2.5 percent in 1965 to 4.5 percent in 1968 and 6.0 percent by 1970. The mild recession brought about by the Nixon administration's classic restraint policies during 1969–70 brought the CPI down to 4.5 percent in the second quarter of 1971. But high unemployment rates (6 percent) and the prospect of the 1972 presidential election, along with confusion and uncertainty about differences among various inflation measures, were instrumental in causing President Nixon to announce his New Economic Plan in August 1971 and in stimulating the so-called reelection boom of 1972. Excess-demand pressures were to some extent contained until 1973 when most of the Nixon price controls were removed.

If excess demand was the major proximate source of the 1968–71 rise in the core inflation rate and the initial stages of the 1973–74 surge, external shocks were most instrumental in boosting the U.S. consumer price index to 12 percent and the core rate to nearly 8 percent by the end of 1974. Simultaneous booms in the industrial countries in 1972 and 1973 followed by raw-materials shortages and panic and speculative buying, farm price increases after the 1972 U.S. grain sale to the USSR and the decline of Peruvian anchovy production, and above all else the OPEC oil price actions of late 1973 had a profound impact on the inflation rates in all the major industrial countries. The United Kingdom, the United States, Canada, Japan, and Italy were especially affected, with inflation rates in Japan and the United Kingdom surpassing those in the traditionally inflation-prone France. Relatively, U.S. price rises in 1973 remained among the least inflationary.[17]

The recession of 1974–75 and the waning of the shocks of 1973 helped bring about a price deceleration in most countries by the middle of 1975. In the United States the CPI leveled off and held at between 5.5 and 6.0 percent until 1978 despite unemployment rates that reached 8.9 percent in May 1975 and declined only slowly to 7.9 percent in the second half of 1976 and to 6.0 percent at the beginning of 1978. However, according to Eckstein the core inflation rate held at just under 8 percent from 1975 to 1978. In 1978 the overall rate began to accelerate again, reaching 12 percent in 1979—a surge, concentrated in a few key sectors of the economy, that falls under the heading of shock inflation. Energy prices increased at the rate of 37.4 percent in 1979 compared to 8 percent the previous year while prices of nonnecessities (all consumer goods except energy, food, shelter, and medical care) increased by 6.5 percent in 1978 and by 6.8 percent in 1979.[18] In 1980 the underlying rate of inflation, reflecting a round of wage increases, was just below 10 percent even as the economy appeared to be approaching the bottom of the recession and unemployment neared 8 percent.

Declining productivity seems to have been an important factor in the inflation in most member countries of the Organization for Economic Cooperation and Development, and particularly in the United States.

17. Cagan, *Persistent Inflation*, pp. 182–84, estimates that foreign influences raised U.S. prices in 1973 and 1974 by approximately 10.5 percentage points, although he feels they would have had much less effect on prices had the economy not already been in the zone of demand-pull pressures.

18. Gar Alperovitz and Jeff Faux, "Controls and the Basic Necessities," *Challenge*, vol. 23 (May–June 1980), pp. 22–24. See also Leslie Ellen Nulty, "How Inflation Hits the Majority," *Challenge*, vol. 21 (January–February 1979), pp. 32–34.

About 1968 "productivity became an ever lesser offset to rising wages so that unit labor costs accelerated even more than the rate of wage increases."[19] The rate of productivity increases declined slowly up to 1973, fell steeply in 1974–75, recovered to 1973 levels between 1976 and 1978, and disappeared or became negative by 1980. Most countries moved toward more restrictive policies—especially in 1974–75 and after 1979—that failed to bring about much real improvement in productivity between 1979 and 1982.

Inflation-Stabilization Configurations

Albert Hirschman observes in chapter 3 that "an effective way to write the comparative social and political history of the last thirty years of the twentieth century may well be to focus on the distinctive reactions of various countries to identical pressures of worldwide inflation." In so doing, we should keep a number of factors in mind. First, some economies are structurally more vulnerable than others to the pressures of inflation. Japan, Sweden, and the Federal Republic of Germany are far more vulnerable to oil price increases than is the United States because imported petroleum represents a much greater share of their energy supply. Western Europe generally feels the shock of changes in international interest rates and exchange rates more than the United States does because exports represent much larger fractions of gross national product in Europe. Trade competition from newly industrializing countries has a stunning impact in a country like Sweden that relies heavily on export of a few specific industrial and raw materials. Such differences in inflationary impulses complicate the task of isolating patterns of domestic structure and policy choice.

Second, because some countries entered the 1970s with higher normal inflation rates than others, it is best to base comparisons on changes in their rates of inflation. Changes in unemployment levels should also be noted as one indication of the extent to which monetary and fiscal contraction was alone relied on to combat inflation. For many analysts a discomfort index that is the sum of the inflation rate and the level of unemployment seems a reasonable approximation of the economic damage and human pain inflicted by economic change. But it is certainly debatable, considering the ambiguous evidence with respect to their distributive and

19. Eckstein, "Economic Choices," p. 17.

allocative consequences, to assume that the effect of an increase in the rate of inflation is equally as painful as the same increase in the unemployment level. The effects of both inflation and unemployment depend on many factors, including the mix of policies designed to stimulate productivity, investment, and economic adjustment. In terms of human pain, M. Harvey Brenner argues, unemployment in the United States "has a multiplier effect far exceeding the relative size of the unemployment rise."[20] Of course, the social impact of unemployment—on rates of suicide, mental hospital admissions, homicide, cirrhosis, cardiovascular- and renal-disease mortality—will vary by country, as the programs designed to provide security and status guarantees during times of economic turbulence vary. Hence social policy can be an important variable in assessing policy responses.

Finally, by the mid-1970s public opinion in most advanced countries had shifted from unemployment aversion to inflation aversion. As Douglas Hibbs, David Cameron, and Brian Barry suggest in chapters 7, 9, and 10, mass political support for incumbents actually seems to be more sensitive to growth or decline of real income than to nominal economic performance per se. Electorates in the United States and the United Kingdom seem to have equated the two, perhaps reflecting the fact that the increases in inflation rates coincided with losses of real income from 1973 onward, as well as the "information" provided to citizens in these countries by their policymakers and media. The strong political support for draconian anti-inflation policies in these countries may represent a cumulation of discontent with relatively weak general economic performance, stretching back to the 1950s and 1960s. It may also reflect the relatively weak protections offered by social programs in these countries, especially when compared with continental Europe and even Japan.

From the record of national responses to inflation, strong patterns emerge (see table 2-1). In some countries—notably the United States, Canada, the United Kingdom, and Italy—the core rate of inflation tended to ratchet upward during the demand and supply shocks of the 1970s, while unemployment levels remained relatively high. The United States and Canada, for example, moved in the 1970s from rankings at or near the bottom of the "low inflation club" to an intermediate position, joining

---

20. "Estimating the Social Costs of National Economic Policy: Implications for Mental and Physical Health and Criminal Aggression," in Joint Economic Committee, *Achieving the Goals of the Employment Act of 1946—Thirtieth Anniversary Review,* vol. 1: *Employment,* Paper 5, 94 Cong. 2 sess. (GPO, 1976), p. v.

Table 2-1. *Change in the Average Annual Rates of Change in the Consumer Price Indexes of Eight Countries, 1960–69 to 1970–79*[a]

| | Average annual rate of change in CPI | | |
Country	1960–69	1970–79	Change, 1960–69 to 1970–79
West Germany	2.5	4.9	2.4
Japan	5.4	8.7	3.3
United States	2.4	7.0	4.6
Sweden	3.6	8.4	4.8
Canada	2.6	7.5	4.9
France	3.8	8.8	5.0
Italy	3.8	12.2	8.4
United Kingdom	3.6	12.4	8.8

Source: International Monetary Fund, *International Financial Statistics*, vol. 37 (October 1984), line 64 and various previous issues.

a. Countries ranked by change, 1960–69 to 1970–79.

a cluster of countries (France, Denmark, Belgium, Norway, and Sweden) long considered inflation prone either because of the strength of labor unions or left-wing or Catholic parties, or because of the scale of their welfare spending and general tax and expenditure levels. Many countries whose normal inflation rates were higher managed to absorb the shocks of the 1970s with only modest increases in inflation and without incurring the costs of extended periods of dramatically higher unemployment rates and lost output.

Some countries (the United States, Canada, and the United Kingdom) relied almost exclusively on deliberately restrictive economic policies and recessions to wring inflation out of the system, even though these policies took a very heavy economic toll. Yet the record up to the early 1980s suggests that restrictive policies worked more effectively and at less cost in West Germany and Japan than they did in the United States and the United Kingdom. Some countries—typically smaller open economies like Belgium, Denmark, Canada, Finland, the Netherlands—that were forced by fluctuations in interest and exchange rates to accept higher unemployment rates shielded their populations with generous welfare programs or job-training programs (Canada less so than the others). Still other countries (Sweden, Norway, Japan) were able to keep rates of unemployment very low by combating inflation through strategies encouraging wage and price restraint or through manpower, investment, and industry policies aimed at the supply side of the economy.

Discomfort indexes—especially when weighted by some measure of political sensitivity to economic fluctuation, such as Hibbs proposes—suggest that macroeconomic fluctuations and policies have not been nearly as contentious and politically destabilizing in Sweden and West Germany, for example, as in the United States or Britain. This seems to reflect the means used to combat inflation and to shield the population from the consequences of those policies and from the redistributive impact of real income losses suffered by the economy as a whole. Policymakers are able to undertake long-term strategies of economic adjustment and to align the tactics of reducing the inflation rate with strategies for evolving and legitimating "a new monetary constitution." There is a danger in the United States and Great Britain that short-term fiscal and monetary tactics will undermine the political capacity of those countries to confront basic problems of economic adjustment.

Three patterns of inflation and stabilization between 1970 and 1982 emerge from data reported in this volume. The distinguishing features of the configurations outlined in table 2-2 represent the efforts of state authorities, dominant elites, and organized interests to absorb and allocate the real income losses attendant on the broad systemic changes that took place after 1973. Macroeconomic policies and confrontations within labor, product, and capital markets were the chief weapons in the struggle to assert power and determine how income would be distributed. The resources available to the players and the opportunities and constraints inherent in the institutional structure differ with each configuration. One configuration is defined as a system of open and unstructured confrontation, another as one of muted confrontation and structured bargaining, and a third as one of statist or controlled management.

In light of these configurations, how do the differing economic theories of inflation stack up?

Economic Models of Inflation

All of the main economic models of inflation—neo-Keynesian, monetarist, and supply-side—accept the argument that the core rate of inflation ratcheted upward in the 1970s because the shocks of excess demand and supply became embedded in the overall price level, and because the

Table 2-2. *Three Configurations of Responses to Inflation, 1970–82*

Item	Open and unstructured confrontation	Muted confrontation and structured bargaining	Statist or controlled management
Characteristics	Struggle for political control; policy instruments used to realize power and income claims; few means exist for limiting struggle. Dominant elites prefer recession and market controls to bargaining for new monetary constitution; some seek dramatic redistribution of income and power. Stop-go pattern; dramatic, nonlegitimated shifts in power and policy possible as a result of policy stalemate and distributional struggle.	Explicit bargaining among organized groups and the state to evolve new monetary constitution. Organized interests of labor, business, and finance highly integrated into state policymaking. Elaborate institutions to limit distributional possibilities. Preservation of collaborative relations and basic income shares a general objective. Bargaining may be protracted; inflation-employment trade-off and profit-investment dynamic depends on balance of labor and business power.	Governing elites and supporting coalition have power and legitimacy to force explicit or de facto acceptance of new monetary constitution; also have capacity to guarantee income and employment security. Shifts in political power rare; occasional anomic outbreaks of opposition.
Representative countries	United States, United Kingdom, Canada, Australia, Italy.	West Germany, Austria, Sweden, Norway, Denmark, Netherlands.	France (to 1979), Japan.
Distinctive economic performance	General, sustained loss of economic resilience; escalation of core rate of inflation; downside uncertainties and instabilities endemic in sustained high unemployment, high and volatile interest rates. Financial system increasingly dominant, industry dependent. Cost, risks, uncertainties of borrowing depress investment and growth. Company-led adjustment process.	Limited, partial loss of economic resilience; recovery under way. Escalation of core rate controlled or high employment targets maintained; investment climate and price expectations being stabilized. Controlled or institutionally managed financial system assures flow of credit for new industrial investment. Lender-borrower relations not transformed. Negotiated or tripartite adjustment process.	Limited loss of economic resilience; inflation rates normal for country. Inflation controlled, expectations stabilized, productivity improving. Flow of credit state-managed; no growth-aborting capital shortages or rationing through high interest rates. State-led adjustment process.

Economic policies and instruments	Sporadic, uncoordinated use of short-term, indirect, global instruments. Policymaking controversial and politicized. Policy reversals or stalemate endemic.	Monetary and fiscal restraint supplemented with direct, sectoral, selective policies targeted on labor quality and supply, investment guidance, industrial policy, income and status security.	Direct, sectoral, and selective policies, especially direct channeling of investment, subsidization of exports, encouragement of industrial concentration and reorganization. Monetary and fiscal policies squeeze wages and consumers.
Institutional structure			
Political parties	Weak, declining mobilizers of public. Weak or weakening left-wing party participation in government.	Strong mobilizers of public sentiment. Labor or Christian Democratic parties play significant government role.	Labor or left-wing parties seldom in government; historically weak and fragmented. Weak mobilizing capacity.
Bureaucracy	Decentralized and infiltrated, or centralized with little discretion in economy. Low autonomy.	Partial autonomy; mediator-facilitator between business and labor. Active in economy, often with low profile.	Centralized, semiautonomous economic player. Extensive discretion in economy. Organizes state-business cooperation.
Business	Firm autonomy important; trade associations weak. Decentralized private sector. No relation to financial system.	Centralized business sector; strong trade associations with legitimate authority over firms. Close relations with finance and industry.	Strongly organized, centralized. Relation to finance mediated by state; state controls credit.
Financial system	Capital market based. State monetary controls general and indirect. Targets on M1 or base. Trend toward financial deregulation.	Credit based, dominated by a few institutions. Extensive channels for tripartite allocation and bargaining over investment and credit control.	Credit based; price administered. Monetary policy controls broader aggregates, dominates bank lending or growth of bank credit.
Labor and industrial relations	Labor organizationally weak. Relations with management adversarial, conflictual. High strike activity, low institutionalized cooperation. Weak, decentralized unions and employers dominate wage bargaining. Three-year contracts dominate.	Labor strong or dominant. Unions and employers organized for wage bargaining. Relations cooperative within normal competitive roles of capitalism. Low strike activity; annual contracts dominate. Corporatist institutions for economic policy and wage-price bargaining.	Labor weak, fragmented, usually excluded. Annual bargaining; relatively low strike activity (sporadic political strikes).

relationships and expectations among suppliers and purchasers of goods and the state were systematically altered. But their interpretations of these changes and prescriptions for controlling inflation diverge widely.

Neo-Keynesian models that attribute a great deal to structural factors—the nature of markets, the role of labor, and the effectiveness of interest groups—can accommodate some of an institutional explanation. Arthur Okun's notion of explicit or implicit contract markets, in contrast to the auction markets and continuous market clearing of more orthodox theory, can account for deviations of pricing behavior from a neoclassical model. Rational economic agents know information is costly, recognize their own vulnerability, and hence establish patterns of behavior to minimize search and shopping costs. What is crucial, argues Okun, is the "sense of fairness, that sense of wages following wages, wages following the cost of living, wages being relatively insensitive to the labour market."[21] The implicit contracts that govern the market arena depend on a social atmosphere that incorporates a sense of mutual respect and a consensus on principles of fair play and good faith. Equity is then a vital lubricant of the market system, not an extraneous irritant imposed by politics. And in the state arena, which senses a new and widespread humanitarian consensus, a "modern democratic ethic just doesn't permit a bulge in costs in one segment of the body politic to be offset by a reduction of income in another segment."[22]

This neo-Keynesian interpretation recognizes that the favorable economic performance of the 1950s and 1960s in the United States left an important legacy of expectations and revised relationships among organized groups. But the inflation of the 1970s seems to owe less to the prevalence of implicit or explicit contracts, a sense of fairness and equity in labor markets, and a new humanitarianism than to the weakness or erosion of these characteristics in countries like the United States and the United Kingdom. The inflation of the 1970s may then reflect conflict more than equity. The factors stressed by Okun and colleagues are more pronounced in West Germany, Sweden, and Austria—countries that fall into the category of muted confrontation and structured bargaining. That may be why their inflation, unemployment, and productivity performance was relatively better than that of the United States during the trying 1970s and early 1980s.

21. Okun, "Political Economy," p. 4.
22. Heller, "Shadow and Substance," p. 8.

But monetarist explanations of the inflation of the 1970s hold up even less well in light of the typology described above. Monetarists in the 1970s stressed the "exaggerated sensitivity" of governments to unemployment, the "mistaken belief" in a long-run trade-off between inflation and unemployment, and a spreading awareness of the reduced effectiveness of policy instruments. They thus blamed government policy—notably the pursuit of full employment unconstrained by gold-reserve requirements—not only for the regular recurrence of episodes of excess demand, but for the persistence of the core rate itself.[23] Thus monetarists believe "there are no economic barriers to reducing inflation,"[24] only the political barriers of the "indecisiveness" of policymakers and their unwillingness to resist "political pressures" for special claims on the budget. The most stringent monetarists and public-choice theorists argue that discretionary government intervention in the economy and the welfare state itself are inherently inflationary. Governments allegedly respond to the short-term exigencies of reelection and to excessive expectations created by their own rhetorical excesses.[25] These imprudent guarantees supposedly eliminate the fear of unemployment as a vital element of the discipline of the market and dispel "the general cautionary air of business." Finally, governments fail to stop inflation once it has started, although they could if they refused to increase spending and expand the money supply. They do not do these things because inflation is useful as a means of expanding expenditures without levying higher taxes, and as a way to reallocate government spending in real terms without explicitly legislating changes.

According to monetarist analyses, some of these tendencies derive essentially from the self-interested behavior of politicians and bureaucrats or are attributes of "politics" or "bureaucracy." Bureau officials seek to maximize their budgets for reasons of public reputation, patronage, salary, and so forth;[26] bureaucracies tend to perpetuate themselves because they are spending other people's money and are never subject to a market test; they "advertise" to drum up business for services to justify ever-increasing

23. Cagan, *Persistent Inflation*, pp. 41–42.

24. Ibid., p. 248.

25. A favorite theme of the political–business cycle literature. See, for example, Samuel Brittan, "Inflation and Democracy," in Hirsch and Goldthorpe, *Political Economy of Inflation*, pp. 161–85; James M. Buchanan and Richard E. Wagner, *Democracy in Deficit: The Political Legacy of Lord Keynes* (Academic Press, 1977).

26. William A. Niskanen, Jr., *Bureaucracy and Representative Government* (Aldine-Atherton, 1971); Thomas E. Borcherding, ed., *Budgets and Bureaucrats: The Sources of Government Growth* (Duke University Press, 1977).

budget and staff size;[27] bureaucratic myopia prevents any overall budgetary control;[28] the state bureaucracy persistently makes uninformed decisions and spends "exorbitant" sums for goods it purchases;[29] policy favors short-term and concentrated benefits, deferred and diffused costs, new and expanded programs, conspicuous projects, packages of reforms and complex revenue sources, constraints on producers and taxation of market efficiency;[30] political influence supersedes market activity as the means to wealth and influence, and "poetic criteria of equity" overwhelm those of productive efficiency.[31]

Evidence with respect to these arguments is quite mixed, and it is assessed in detail in the chapters that follow. There can be little doubt that the promise of full employment and automatic stabilizers have made unemployment more tolerable. Governments in the United States and many other countries have obviously occasionally had recourse to demand stimulation beyond the point of prudence, especially during wartime (particularly if the war is unpopular) and when unemployment has proven politically threatening and no alternative policies exist to create jobs and provide new manpower skills. Governments have regularly "validated" inflation, because they feared the political consequences of not doing so. Government expenditures have grown everywhere and some countries have known persistent budgetary deficits (although this is more consistently a problem among the *low* spenders than the high spenders). Government officials, bureaus, and programs *have* displayed a certain autonomy; the logic, reigning values, and ethical criteria of the political process clearly differ from those of the marketplace. There is every reason to suspect that productivity trends, profit margins, the availability of profitable investment opportunities, and the propensity to invest are systematically related to the failures of economic policymaking in the 1970s.

Nonetheless, these problems appear most debilitating where government has intruded least and claimed the smallest fraction of resources— in countries of open and unstructured confrontation. As the inflation-

---

27. Niskanen, *Bureaucracy and Representative Government;* Borcherding, *Budgets and Bureaucrats.* See also William Mitchell, "The Anatomy of Public Failure: A Public Choice Perspective," Original Paper 13 (Los Angeles, Calif.: International Institute for Economic Research, 1978).

28. Roland N. McKean, "Divergences between Individual and Total Costs Within Government," in Ryan C. Amacher, Robert D. Tollison, and Thomas D. Willett, *The Economic Approach to Public Policy: Selected Readings* (Cornell University Press, 1976), pp. 362–68.

29. See, for example, Gordon Tullock, *Private Wants, Public Means: An Economic Analysis of the Desirable Scope of Government* (Basic Books, 1970).

30. Mitchell, "Anatomy of Public Failure."

31. Ibid.

disinflation configurations suggest, inflation was more prevalent and difficult to control and disinflation much more turbulent where policymakers have been least consistently committed to full employment (the United States, Canada, the United Kingdom); policymakers have spent far less and taxed far less (the United States, the United Kingdom, Canada as compared to Sweden, West Germany, Austria, the Netherlands, Norway, France); policymakers lacked the capacity or the will to coordinate various instruments of stabilization policy (that is, they were not just being indecisive or self-serving, or myopic); and policymakers could not make use of instruments other than monetary and fiscal policies to combat unemployment and therefore had to suffer preelectoral booms (for example, the early ratcheting of the U.S. core rate is traced to the Johnson and Nixon booms). In contrast, the countries that seem to have fared best in the difficult climate of the 1970s—those in the structured bargaining and statist categories—do not resemble the ideal government implicit in the monetarist model. Indeed, these governments have generally spent and taxed more, intervened in their economies much more extensively and regularly, and according to coherent government, or bipartite or tripartite planning, in order to correct or override purely market calculations.

Keynesian and monetarist theories do not exhaust the economic models of inflation. The supply-side and rational-expectations accounts of the economic problems of the 1970s depart in some important ways from those of the neo-Keynesians and monetarists. By and large, no basic change in the pricing mechanism is seen—the idea of a difficult-to-eradicate inflationary momentum is rejected. Also denied is most neo-Keynesian and monetarist reasoning that "systematic management of demand can alter the paths of real economic variables."[32] Supply-side models hold that government spending, social security, unemployment insurance, and regulation all increase marginal costs, especially of labor and of entrepreneural risk-taking. The essential ingredient of the supply-side and "ratex" view is the psychological premise that economic decisions by individuals and organizations are based more or less exclusively on marginal costs and on expectations of future inflation. The implication is that the economy can respond very quickly, since psychological states are much more fluid than "social conventions" or "codes of good behavior."

32. Tobin, "Stabilization Policy," p. 26. Supply-side models "reject any demand-impelled multiplicative effect of fiscal change on total income." Norman Ture, "Forecasting the Supply Side of the Economy," Hearings before the Joint Economic Committee, 96 Cong. 2 sess. (GPO, 1980), p. 62.

Aggregate monetary and fiscal policy cannot influence the economy in any systematic and predictable way because economic agents have already taken their consequences into account. Government policy will thus always be erratic and unpredictable and hence act as a persistent and principal cause of demand fluctuations. "What is needed," these theorists argue, "is a fixed policy rule, possibly embodied in a constitutional amendment that makes policy constant and predictable."[33]

Although the real world never provides unambiguous tests of economic theories, events seemed particularly unkind to the supply-side and rational-expectations story. The Reagan administration's 1981 tax cuts (Margaret Thatcher is a less pure case) did not produce the expected lightning effects on new business investment. Inflation fell only at the cost of major recession. On the other hand, government stabilization policies in some countries—in the structured-bargaining and statist categories—have apparently proved quite capable of stabilizing the expectations of economic agents, suggesting that government can predictably influence economic performance and structure, and that economic agents may develop their expectations in concert with government authorities or through government-sponsored bipartite or tripartite bargaining. These countries offer scant support for the proposition that high levels of government taxing and spending per se constrain productive investment.

A Political and Institutional Model of Inflation

Indeed, a political-institutional account for the 1970s seems to fit the empirical data far better than any of the economic models reviewed above. Such an account stresses two broad historical trends—one, elaborated in chapter 1, toward economic maturation or decline in an increasingly more competitive and intrusive international environment, and another toward political democratization in both market and state arenas. The cumulative effects of democratization became evident when the slowdown in economic growth, and thus in real or anticipated income, in advanced industrial nations revealed strikingly diminished asymmetries of power in labor and product markets and in access to the instruments of state policy. Full employment and welfare state policies and increases in literacy, organizational skills, and the like since 1945 have resulted in a more symmetrical

33. Martin Neil Baily, "Economic Models under Challenge," *Science*, vol. 216 (May 21, 1982), p. 860.

distribution of economic and political power.[34] No longer can the classical burden-bearing segments of society as easily be made to accept a disproportionate share of the costs imposed by worsening terms of trade, declining values of currencies, losses in sales of manufactured goods, and rising prices of energy and materials. Labor, women, the unemployed, low-income groups, the aged, the economically unproductive are now protected by income transfers, wage stabilizers, and indexation of pension and transfer programs. The state has become a conduit for the income and security claims of less productive groups and interests. Built-in stabilizers have made wage agreements less vulnerable to changes in global and monetary policies. Cost-of living adjustments have allowed wages to move up along with prices. And profit-led recoveries seem to have provoked unions into inflationary catch-ups. Deflationary policies have thus had their greatest impact on output and have served to concentrate unemployment in low-status groups and among the latest entrants in the labor market.

The flow of consumer expenditure has been sustained by the explosion of consumer installment debt and the proliferation of two-income families. Lower-level incomes have been protected through political pressures that have brought sharp increases in the minimum wage, reintroduced agricultural price supports, and linked income transfers to the inflation rate— the indexation of social security in 1972, then of the pensions of military and civilian government employees, was a major step in the United States. The expansion of the state into many new domains, including research and development, energy production, and delivery of health, education, and other services, has opened it to further income demands. Many professional groups—most dramatically physicians and hospitals—have succeeded in guaranteeing their incomes through such programs as medicare and medicaid. With the politicization of economic life, the ability to escape the authority and discipline of the market, to gain control of price and income and of one's economic destiny, has been generalized. Societies thus must develop new arrangements for distributing income losses and adjusting the expectations of all groups.

Accompanying the democratization of economic life has been a faster pace of economic adjustment. Policymakers must be able to recognize and interpret rapid and unpredictable changes in costs, market conditions, and power structures and adapt their patterns of bargaining to them. The

34. For a similar argument, see Tibor Scitovsky, "Market Power and Inflation," *Economica*, vol. 45 (August 1978), pp. 221–33.

economies of nations with tripartite bargaining covering wages and economic conditions—structured bargaining systems—seem to have performed much better than those that lack them. The United States, Britain, and Canada have demonstrated what Albert Hirschman describes as "the strenuous avoidance of cooperative encounter and agreement on the part of social groups." The defensive actions of "reluctant losers"—groups determined to defend their accustomed shares of the national product— probably cause inflationary spirals in these countries. In countries where confrontation is open and unstructured, political authorities have displayed minimal capacity to use instruments of policy selectively in order to minimize uncertainty and conflict with business, labor, and the public at large.

In the United States and other countries where confrontation is unstructured, groups and interests evaded economic adaptation in the 1970s and the state was too politically divided to bring about a new consensus on how the burdens of adjustment would be distributed. A classic tug-of-war or free-for-all resulted as more and more groups achieved the means to evade the market controls implied by standard fiscal and monetary contraction. Supply-side shocks and structural problems further limited the reach of aggregate demand instruments. The powerful constituencies accustomed to established income shares or freedom from government intrusion implicitly preferred inflation to policies designed to control inflation that might ratify the economic distortions already wrought by the gains of unions and lower groups.[35] Long-dominant economic groups and political interests learned to adjust to inflation by means of price surcharges and anticipatory markups, use of overseas lines of credit to circumvent monetary restrictions, new accounting practices, and the like.

The conflict was very much a free-for-all in the United States, where business seemed particularly determined to reverse trends in the capital-labor ratio and remained only partially reconciled to the integration of labor in the bargaining process and to active government involvement in the economy. Business spokesmen preached against inflation, using the issue to rally support for cutting public expenditures, for tax cuts to business, and for renewed and sustained monetary restraint. The business community was apparently able to substantially insulate itself from the

---

35. Fred Hirsch, "The Ideological Underlay of Inflation," in Hirsch and Goldthorpe, *Political Economy of Inflation*, pp. 263–84.

impact of the disciplining measures. Corporations and banks formed larger and larger units and went international in response to competition and escalating capital requirements. Inflation was fed by struggles over access to credit and investment funds—among sectors and regions, between agriculture and industry, between domestic firms and those with international affiliates, between durable and traditional consumer goods industries.

Does the contribution of government to inflation accord with the economic models? Comparison suggests not. Of course, labor, retirees, the poor, and popular majorities afflicted by deflationary policies use their access to the state arena—elections, lobbying, administrative rules—to pursue the goals they cannot achieve in the market. It is difficult to imagine they would do otherwise in societies in which democratization is "the universalistic principle of legitimation." Votes are more equally distributed than dollars, as Arthur Okun commented.[36] Moreover, welfare entitlements have become fundamental to the welfare state. In 1980 the U.S. Office of Management and Budget classified 76 percent of the budget as "relatively uncontrollable," a category that encompasses social security, trade adjustment assistance, housing subsidies, student loans, and food stamps, all programs that people have come to rely on.

Adoption of such social programs and the spending levels they entail cannot reasonably be ascribed to failures of political will, indecisiveness, or innate deficiencies of collective decisionmaking processes. Spending policies respond to a broad spectrum of pluralistic pressures that are the essence of the democratic process. Revenues, on the other hand, often lag behind spending levels so as to produce chronic deficits because the politics of taxation tends to give greater voice to narrower political coalitions reflecting elite and structural power. Balancing expenditures and taxation may be difficult because those who are unwilling to be taxed in the interest of greater equality of income and services have the capacity to resist or collude with parts of the state in so doing.

Societies vary greatly in the percentage of total income taken in taxes, in the nominal and real incidence of taxation on various population groups, in the relationship between direct and indirect taxes, in the willingness to tolerate inequalities of income, wealth, and exposure to economic adversity, and in the influence that owners of wealth exercise in the political process. But the configurations in table 2-2 suggest that

36. Arthur M. Okun, *Equality and Efficiency: The Big Tradeoff* (Brookings Institution, 1975).

there is no correlation of high rates of inflation, a tendency to deficits, and declining productivity with high levels of taxation or of public spending. Often quite the opposite. When the state fails to provide economic safeguards, the struggle moves to the market arena where it can accentuate class and group conflicts and feed the inflationary tug-of-war or free-for-all.[37] Workers who are unprotected by income supports, relocation and retraining allowances, manpower and labor market policies are virtually forced to oppose technological improvements and industrial restructuring. Several countries (notably West Germany and Austria) have been able to moderate the tug-of-war because their social policies have assured the basic security and status of their citizens and economic agents, and their monetary and fiscal policies have included measures designed to stimulate the economy, eliminate bottlenecks, and provide side payments and compensation.

Democratization of course can produce chronic fiscal and monetary pressures that feed the process of inflation but it also encourages an attack on the causes and mechanisms of the pressures once they are diagnosed.

Finally, one can look at productivity trends in light of the typology suggested above. Slumping productivity may be the result of too little investment, a lack of technological innovation, or failure to let outmoded industries die. Economies with a persistent tendency to stop-and-go economic policies, frequent and recurrent recessions, and persistence of idle capacity do not offer many attractive opportunities for profitable investment. Nor, as John Zysman suggests in chapter 6, will they provide the conditions for the acquisition of skills and cooperation between labor and capital that profitable investment opportunities depend on.[38]

In such an economy, Cameron argues in chapter 9, business may rely on recessions and improvements (from their point of view) in labor-capital ratios to increase productivity rather than on investments in new product and process technology. Firms in declining or stagnant economies (or sectors) may spend too little on, or misallocate their funds for, research and development. Government help may be the answer to their problems, but where high unemployment and selective withdrawal of income and security guarantees have been used to fight inflation, state subsidies of

37. See M. Panić, "The Origin of Increasing Inflationary Tendencies in Contemporary Society," in Hirsch and Goldthorpe, *Political Economy of Inflation*, pp. 137–60.
38. See Lester C. Thurow, *The Zero-Sum Society: Distribution and the Possibilities for Economic Change* (Basic Books, 1980), p. 83.

the profit-making activities of private entrepreneurs are unlikely to be politically sustainable.

The restorative and cleansing renewal traditionally associated with the business cycle has clearly been impeded in politicized and democratized economies. Industrial corporations have grown too large to be allowed to fail; the financial system is itself suspected of being too fragile to absorb the shocks of failures. Central banks, the insurers of financial stability, have often underwritten indiscriminate domestic and international lending. Disinvestment, as Zysman shows, has been successful where government-corporate coordination and planning have been possible, especially in redirecting investment out of sunset into sunrise industries. In nations like Japan and, for a time, France, political conditions have allowed the government bureaucracy and large corporations to work out industrial adaptations. Elsewhere, major concessions to labor, or at least its inclusion in tripartite forums, have been required. Calls for an end to government intervention have little effect, and resistance to disinvestment is unlikely to abate if government policy allows unemployment levels to rise and fails to protect the income of affected individuals.

Designing Anti-inflationary Strategies

From a political and institutional standpoint, it appears no longer possible to disconnect savings and investment decisions from the struggle over income distribution.[39] Unless the consensus in stagnant and declining economies encompasses political as well as economic strategies for stabilizing the economy, the continuing struggle over the relative shares of wages and profits can seriously hinder the flow of investment and further weaken prospects for economic growth. Supply-side and orthodox deflationary strategies seem likely to intensify these struggles.

The national experiences examined in this volume confirm that modern, democratic, capitalist economies must adapt to technological and structural changes in industry, working through large bureaucratic organizations and recognizing a broad distribution of power. The approaches that Japan, West Germany, Sweden, and Austria have taken to economic change seem to have important advantages. They counsel employment-

---

39. Andrew Martin, "Political Constraints on Economic Strategies in Advanced Industrial Societies," *Comparative Political Studies,* vol. 10 (October 1977), pp. 323–54.

oriented investment policies, active inclusion of workers in productivity and even in investment decisions at the plant level and in economic policymaking at the national level, and government participation in carrying out the strategies of industrial adaptation.

Simplistic public-private dichotomies and defensive ideologies are of little constructive use in today's organizationally complex (even sclerotic) mixed economies. Maintaining the moral and political legitimacy of political and economic systems and of political regimes should be a high policy goal, at least as urgent as properly allocating economic resources (and not necessarily inconsistent with doing so in a dynamic society). The inflation of the 1970s may paradoxically have better served these political and equity goals than would stabilization around relatively constant price levels. But the powerful public aversion to inflation seems to signal that we have reached the limits of this implicit and permissive strategy. It is critical now to search for new policies that will preserve and husband the reserves of civility and intergroup and interclass comity. The experiences reviewed in this volume scarcely support the idea that this can be done by governments' withdrawing from economic life or seriously eroding the status and security guarantees long taken as democratic rights by their citizens.

To a substantial degree, the stubborn inflation of the 1970s resulted from a complex of rationally adaptive implicit contracts, government guarantees, and institutional arrangements in both the market and political arenas. These helped assure a certain necessary predictability, a capacity to minimize information costs and to more or less accurately gauge the risks of lending, borrowing, buying, or producing in a very turbulent time. Such predictability may be indispensable in complex, interdependent political economies in which long-term relationships among citizen and government, government and business, customer and supplier, and borrower and lender are vital to economic growth and stability. Economic strategies that strip away these guarantees in the name of liberating market forces and subjecting economic and political transactions to the discipline of the market may produce a politics and economics of disinflation that is far more destabilizing than the disturbances produced by the inflation of the 1970s.

PART TWO

Collective Interests
and Policy Outcomes

The chapters in this part share a common analytical approach, which is a venerable one in political analysis. They presuppose that social outcomes derive from contending group interests and are best explained in reference to group preferences. This does not mean that social groups are always well organized or even have well-thought-out notions of their collective interest. Sometimes the groups emerge as implicit coalitions around issues or economic transformations; and of course they can always choose policies that are counterproductive to what outsiders might deem their real long-term interests. The point is that the approaches here suggest that more can be understood about inflationary processes by focusing on group rivalry than upon aggregating idealized individual preferences.

In chapter 3 Albert Hirschman seeks to generalize lessons from an area of the world where inflation has been endemic since the early twentieth century and especially since World War II. Latin America is instructive, not because the North Atlantic societies are closely comparable, but because Latin American inflation starkly suggests some of the possible social mechanisms that may be in play. Hirschman's focus is less on specific social groups than on the general patterns of economic rivalry that create a vulnerability to inflation. Robert Keohane, in chapter 4, borrows some of Hirschman's concepts to explore how political rivalry between nation states influences economic outcomes, and vice versa. Keohane stresses not groups within nations, but states as the collective actors within international systems. Obviously, as the history of the

Organization of Petroleum Exporting Countries (OPEC) demonstrates, conflicting international interests can express themselves in price rises. Keohane suggests in addition that economic tendencies originating within the several nation states of an international system can have an influence on the level of conflict that characterizes it. What is more, under some conditions generalized inflationary trends may forestall harsher expressions of rivalry and conflict.

Chapters 5 and 6 examine particular sets of collective interests. Colin Crouch spotlights the role of organized labor as an actor in the political economies of the advanced industrial societies. He is less concerned with the economic structure of labor markets—that is, with patterns of wage determination—than with the political and social integration of unions and its ramifications. Organized labor can play a more or less adversarial role; it can be treated more or less as a social "partner." Crouch discusses under what conditions these outcomes are likely and what diverse influences on wage restraint and price stability may result. Centralized unions may be more powerful vis-à-vis management, but they may be able to impose wage bargains on their own constituency that more fragmented labor organizations cannot. Political concessions to labor leaders may increase trade union power, but perhaps purchase relative wage restraint.

John Zysman, finally, looks at the interaction between industrial interests and state policymaking under the conditions posed by technological change and competition from new industrializers. A major source of inflationary pressure that conventional models of a short-run economy do not incorporate involves the costs of adjustment—sometimes protection for new industries, sometimes subsidies for ailing ones. Zysman shows that different states have dealt with these problems in more or less inflationary ways. He looks at the coalitions between public officials and business representatives to establish which patterns of adjustment have emerged and why. Moreover, he sorts out these patterns, not for a utopian world of fixed technologies, but for the uncomfortable one of continuing innovation and obsolescence.

Taken together, these four chapters suggest that the rivalry among social groups—firms and individuals facing similar market situations—and the interaction between these groups and bureaucratic agencies representing the state are crucial units of analysis. These chapters imply further that the groups in play cannot be depicted too abstractly. Merely differentiating labor and capital may not yield satisfactory analysis. Differing trade-union structures, firms in different industrial sectors, emerge as the relevant collective agents.

3

Reflections on the Latin American Experience

Albert O. Hirschman

It has long been obvious that the roots of inflation—whether in Western Europe, the United States, Latin America, or elsewhere—lie deep in the social and political structure in general, and in social and political conflict and conflict management in particular. The disputes among Keynesians, monetarists, and other economists about the causes of inflation deal with the modeling of inflationary processes that unfold among the various spheres and sectors of economic activity and, consequently, with the improvement of economic policymaking. But it would be difficult to find an economist who would not agree that underlying social and political forces play a decisive role in causing both inflation and the success or failure of anti-inflationary policies.[1]

Economic theories of inflation dominate the field not because participants in the discussion are convinced that these theories hold the crucial variables, but rather because intricate analytical structures have been developed that lend themselves to ever further elaboration, some empirical testing, and—most important—the formulation of policy advice. In contrast, much of the writing on the (undoubted) social and political roots of inflation deals with vague notions—"rising expectations," "faltering social cohesion," "governability crisis"—that are neither intellectually articulate nor politically helpful. It is possible, however, to go beyond such obvious and almost tautological assertions about the sociopolitical context of inflation. In attempting to do just that, this chapter draws on the rich experience of Latin America.

---

1. Even Milton Friedman is reported to have distinguished between the "proximate" cause (excessive increase in money supply) and the "deeper" social causes, in a seminar. See Arthur Seldon, "Preface," in F. A. Hayek, *Full Employment at Any Price?* Occasional Paper 45 (London: Institute of Economic Affairs, 1975), p. 9.

Sociopolitical Explanations of Inflation

The persistent and strong inflationary pressures that have characterized a large number of Latin American countries have given rise to two principal currents of interpretation. The well-known structuralist thesis was articulated by a relatively cohesive group of economists during the late 1950s and the early 1960s. Authorship of the other, to be called the tug-of-war thesis, is much more diffuse and spread out in time.[2] Though elements of the tug-of-war thesis are frequently found among supporters of the structuralist argument, the logical structures of the two theses are different.

The Structuralist Thesis

The structuralist thesis emerged in the late 1950s as an antagonist of orthodox thinking which insisted that inflation was merely a matter of too much money. The economists who proposed it tended to underplay the important political dimensions of the thesis, in part perhaps to make it respectable among their confreres.

The structuralist approach concentrates on what happens on the supply side in an economy that grows or attempts to do so. The early formulations of the thesis criticized the excessive aggregation of traditional growth models. Their common starting point was the observation that in developing countries certain supply bottlenecks inevitably appeared in important sectors. Such sectoral bottlenecks could result simply from the tendency of growth in these countries to be accompanied by a wide variety of imbalances and disproportionalities in their productive structures; and in one or two sectors, in particular agriculture for domestic food production and the "production of foreign exchange" through exports, it was believed that supply was especially likely to be inadequate in relation to demand.[3] Affected items either rose in price or were rationed

2. The Spanish term *empate* when used to describe the social situations underlying inflations means less a final, evenly divided outcome of a social game than a continuing pulling and hauling by major social groups with no decisive victory being scored by any—hence "tug-of-war" seems a better translation than the usual "tie," "stalemate," or "standoff."

3. See Juan Noyola Vásquez, "El desarrollo económico y la inflación en México y otros países latinoamericanos," *Investigación económica* (Mexico), vol. 6 (Fourth Quarter, 1956), pp. 603–48; Osvaldo Sunkel, "La inflación chilena: un enfoque heterodoxo," *El trimestre económico* (Mexico), vol. 25 (October–December 1958), pp. 570–99; Joseph Grunwald, "The Structuralist School on Price Stabilization and Economic Development: The Chilean Case," in Albert O. Hirschman, ed., *Latin American Issues: Essays*

in the case of foreign exchange when the exchange rate was not devalued. In either case the economy experienced a supply shock, which, in the absence of downward flexibility of other prices, was bound to impart an inflationary stimulus to the economy.[4]

The structuralist argument has a great deal in common with the one that holds—naively yet correctly—that the 1973 rise in petroleum prices, coming on top of the boom in food and raw materials prices, made a powerful contribution to the intensification of inflation in Western countries during the following years. It took this searing experience to make the structuralist position, which had dwelt in the "academic underworld" of the economics of development, respectable in the advanced industrial countries. But those who now spoke of a "new" kind of inflation appeared to be unaware of the Latin American pedigree of their theses.[5] Another idea that has a great deal in common with the structuralist thesis is that a certain structure of wages and wage differentials is "natural" or "fair" at any one time; as a result, when some wages rise, there will be considerable pressure to restore the relative position of other wage earners,[6] with a consequent general increase in inflationary pressures.

It is an underlying assumption of all these arguments that any important change in relative prices or wages is inflationary, because the maintenance of price stability under these conditions would require a compensatory drop in some prices or wages—something the monetary managers are unlikely to enforce. Of course inflation would never occur or accelerate if these managers always rose to the occasion. But it seems quite unlikely that the policymakers' determination to undertake anti-inflationary action is always identical, no matter what its cost may be in terms of unemploy-

---

and Comments (New York: Twentieth Century Fund, 1961), pp. 95–123; Dudley Seers, "A Theory of Inflation and Growth in Under-developed Economies Based on the Experience of Latin America," *Oxford Economic Papers*, vol. 14 (June 1962), pp. 173–95; Albert O. Hirschman, *The Strategy of Economic Development* (Yale University Press, 1958), chap. 9; Werner Baer and Isaac Kerstenetzky, eds., *Inflation and Growth in Latin America* (Irwin, 1964).

4. The term *supply shock* came into use much later; see Franco Modigliani, "The Monetarist Controversy or, Should We Forsake Stabilization Policies?" *American Economic Review*, vol. 67 (March 1977), p. 14.

5. James Tobin, "There Are Three Types of Inflation; We Have Two," *New York Times*, September 5, 1974, identified one as being due to "shortages and price increases in important commodities" and then said that it is ill advised to apply the classical remedies of "tight monetary policy and fiscal austerity" to this variety. This was of course exactly the point of the structuralist critique.

6. This point, argued by Michael Piore and others, has long been familiar in Latin American countries with groups of privileged and powerful workers (Chilean miners, Venezuelan petroleum workers). For an early similar argument, with respect to price profiles, see Charles L. Schultze, "Recent Inflation in the United States," in *Employment Growth and Price Levels*, Hearings before the Joint Economic Committee, 86 Cong. 1 sess. (U.S. Government Printing Office, 1959), pt. 7, pp. 2193–2205.

ment, widespread bankruptcies, social turmoil, and the like.[7] Policymakers simply do not have either lexicographical preferences or suicidal instincts of that sort.

Social and political implications grow almost naturally out of the structuralist position. For many structuralists the cause of inflation is not some, perhaps accidental, lapse of attention or virtue on the part of the monetary authorities or a misguided concentration on the "wrong" variables such as the rate of interest in lieu of the quantity of money, but some fundamental defect of the social and economic structure which presumably can only be remedied through political action. For example, if the culprit is stagnation or slow growth of food production that is in turn due to an antiquated land tenure system, then effective anti-inflationary action requires a change in that system—that is, a change in basic property and power relations. Or, if the origin of inflation lies in the power of the Organization of Petroleum Exporting Countries (OPEC) to raise the price of oil, then the best hope for avoiding a repetition of the experience is in fostering the ability of the oil-consuming countries to apply countervailing economic or political power.

The political vocation of much of structuralist theorizing becomes more obvious still when the basic reasoning involved is carried one step further. Instead of invoking a sectoral lag in output as the original cause of inflation, a generalized decline in productivity might be assumed. Provided such a decline is unanticipated it will lead to a rise in prices, in line with the most elementary notions of monetary theory. This sort of generalized structuralist explanation of inflation is rampant in the West; some attribute inflation to increasing lack of motivation on the part of workers, others to sluggishness, amateurism, or other forms of "X-inefficiency" on the part of managers, others yet to excessive state intervention and regulation or to the parasitic growth of the service sector.[8] Whereas the Latin American economists who had first advanced the structuralist thesis were in general identified with the Left, it now appears that structuralist theorizing is a game at which all kinds of believers in the need for "fundamental" reform and change can and do play. The more persistent and intractable the inflation, the more likely are all parties to come forward with their favorite "deep" diagnosis and cure, as is shown by the Latin American and subsequent Western European experiences.

7. See Hirschman, *Strategy*, pp. 160, 164; Robert J. Gordon, "The Demand for and Supply of Inflation," *Journal of Law and Economics*, vol. 18 (December 1975), pp. 807–36.

8. See Amartya Sen, "Rational Fools: A Critique of the Behavioral Foundations of Economic Theory," *Philosophy and Public Affairs*, vol. 6 (Summer 1977), p. 334.

Among the more technical economists, structuralist reasoning has often been dismissed as ideological in nature because many of its proponents insist that the abolition of inflation must be linked to a program for sociopolitical change. But this sort of ideological element should not make the structuralists' endeavor a priori suspect. After all, inflation might well be the symptom of one or several hidden social faults that had better be corrected; and these faults are more likely to be ferreted out by those who are naturally predisposed toward noticing and doing something about them, as a result of their political views and their position in society.

In practice, however, the advice of the structuralists often amounts to substituting a sociopolitical problem, such as land tenure, excessive state intervention, and so on, for the economic problem of inflation. In order to be able to ameliorate problem A, so they argue, a solution must first be found to the more "fundamental" problem B. But what if B turns out to be less manageable or solvable than A? In that case, the structuralists are in effect responsible for an escalation in the difficulty of the tasks that are being proposed to the body politic. Something of this sort appears to have happened in Latin America.[9] The structuralist strategy could be a special case of the proposition that a certain type of self-analysis can actually worsen the trouble the patient is in.[10]

A more practical difficulty with the structuralist strategy of substituting problem B for problem A has been that problem A, inflation, often became so pressing that some relief had to be found for it right away regardless of whether the remedy at hand was alleged to deal only with the symptoms of the disease. The Latin American structuralists, reluctant to forsake their doctrinal purity, condemned as "monetarist futility" the most elementary and obviously needed anti-inflationary measures in situations of hyperinflation. Because of this lack of flexibility, they rapidly lost influence in the mid-1960s, so that when the more solid among the structuralist ideas might have come into their own in the mid-1970s, they were all but forgotten.

The Tug-of-War Thesis

The explanation of inflation in terms of social conflict between groups, each aspiring to a greater share of the social product, has become the

9. See "The Turn to Authoritarianism in Latin America and the Search for Its Economic Determinants," in Albert O. Hirschman, *Essays in Trespassing: Economics to Politics and Beyond* (Cambridge University Press, 1981), pp. 98–135.

10. This idea is implicit in J. H. Elliott, "Self-Perception and Decline in Early Seventeenth-Century Spain," *Past and Present*, no. 74 (February 1977), pp. 41–61.

sociologist's monotonous equivalent of the economist's untiring stress on the undue expansion of the money supply.[11] In Latin America, during the 1950s those who held the sociological view believed that "inflation results not merely from irresponsible profligacy, from some isolated failure of will power, but represents the difficult-to-change outcome of group attitudes and conflicts. *The structuralist, on the other hand, affirms that, to eliminate inflation, not only attitudes but basic economic relationships must be altered.*"[12] The distinction is perhaps no longer so neat. To the extent the structuralist thesis considers that the difficulty various productive agents have in cooperating is the basic cause of inflation, it rejoins the sociological explanation. The structuralist thesis, however, adds an intermediate link to the causal chain—the shortfall in production. For the structuralist, inflation could be an indirect outcome of conflicting demands for higher income shares or of other conflicts.

The sociological or tug-of-war thesis has begun to resemble the structuralist position also in its policy conclusions. As it has become increasingly clear that terminating or abating the tug-of-war is more than a matter of changing attitudes, the conviction has been spreading that the institutional relations among various interest groups and between them and the state must undergo important changes. The structuralist theory makes some basic statements about causal relationships that can conceivably be tested, while the sociological theory, perhaps just because it is intuitively so persuasive, has not articulated a fine structure of distinctions, propositions, and hypotheses. But thanks in large part to Latin American contributions, elements of such a fine structure exist so that the theory is much richer than it is ordinarily given credit for.

The Redistributive Impact of Inflation and the Tug-of-War

Economists supplied the first building blocks for a more serviceable tug-of-war or social-conflict theory of inflation by inquiring into the effects of inflation on income distribution, a topic almost as old as inflation itself. At one time, it was taken for granted that inflation would make for greater income inequality. The argument emerged first in the analysis of the business cycle; the expansion of bank credit in the course of the boom

11. See Fred Hirsch, "The Ideological Underlay of Inflation," in Fred Hirsch and John H. Goldthorpe, eds., *The Political Economy of Inflation* (Harvard University Press, 1978), pp. 263–84.
12. Albert O. Hirschman, *Journeys Toward Progress: Studies of Economic Policy-Making in Latin America* (New York: Twentieth Century Fund, 1963), p. 215 (emphasis in original).

places extra purchasing power at the disposal of business, which uses it to increase investments beyond the level permitted by voluntary savings. This inflationary financing of the investment boom is equivalent to "forced savings," that is, to an expansion of investment at the expense of consumption (assuming full employment), with the curtailment of consumption being imposed on the buying public through price rises.[13]

This doctrine of forced savings was one of the first that dealt with the distributional impact of inflation. But the idea that inflation is an engine making the rich richer—and is therefore probably designed to do so—appeared during the first decade of the century, in a rather different form, in at least one country of the "periphery." Chile had been subject to recurring inflationary pressures since the 1870s and here a chorus of voices came to accuse the large, "well-heeled and well-mortgaged" landowners of being behind inflation which permitted them to repay their peso loans in depreciated paper money.[14] The thesis is in a sense the exact equivalent, for the countries of the periphery, of the forced-savings doctrine in the central, industrial countries. In both cases inflation is assumed to be a manipulation by and on behalf of ruling groups—industrialists in the center, landowners and primary products exporters in the periphery.

There is of course another possible profiteer from inflation—the state that runs a deficit and finances it by issuing paper money or by borrowing from the central bank. During the heyday of the gold standard before World War I, governments were under serious disciplines in this regard as their direct or indirect borrowings from the central bank were often subject to strict limits. The role of the state as potentially the prime profiteer from inflation became clear as these disciplines were lifted during World War I and its aftermath. The state can combine in its favor the two types of income shifts; it can extract "forced savings" for its own investment or other spending projects, and it also gains in its capacity as a large-scale debtor and distributor of fixed incomes (pensions and the like). While these gains depend largely on inflation being unanticipated, the state gains even when inflation is fully anticipated because of the need

13. Gottfried von Haberler, *Prosperity and Depression: A Theoretical Analysis of Cyclical Movements* (Geneva: League of Nations, 1937), pp. 42–44; F. A. von Hayek, "A Note on the Development of the Doctrine of 'Forced Saving,' " *Quarterly Journal of Economics*, vol. 47 (November 1932), pp. 123–33.

14. Propounded by a number of Chilean writers early in the century, the thesis was given wide circulation and the authority of "developed-country" economic thought by Frank Whitson Fetter, *Monetary Inflation in Chile* (Princeton University Press, 1931). For a critical evaluation of the Fetter doctrine, see Hirschman, *Journeys*, pp. 163–75.

of firms and households to increase their cash balances; this need is supplied by the state which thereby obtains "free" command over real resources.[15]

In many instances of profiteering the state is only a conduit; its power is used for the purpose of shunting the resources acquired through inflationary finance in this or that direction. Here the possibility arises for neglected groups to become the beneficiaries; for example, the state can decide on new transfer payments, such as social security benefits, and in this manner groups that are unable to play the inflationary game unaided can be included. Eventually such groups can become full participants in the game, either by learning how to lean on the state or by developing the capacity for independent action, as through demands for higher wages and salaries. In fact, the early annals of inflation as a mechanism necessarily leading to a more regressive distribution of income have given place to the conviction that inflation is invariably the outcome of attempts on the part of lower-income groups—frequently aided by a reformist or "populist" state—to increase their share in the national product through higher wages, increased social security benefits, and other transfer payments. The Argentine experience during the first Perón regime (1946–55) is an early example of this sort of attempted redistribution via inflation.

All major groups of society can become expert at reaping an initial redistributive advantage from inflation. This is indeed the very meaning of the tug-of-war metaphor. But once the struggle is on in earnest, it is the pattern of countermoves likely to be unleashed by the initial move that best explains the nature and dynamics of the tug-of-war.

To this topic economic analysis and particularly the monetarist school have contributed the idea that, no matter to which group the initial advantage has accrued, it is not likely to stick. This is of course an application of the equilibrium concept. Inflation is viewed as a disturbance that cannot lastingly affect the distribution of income in society, this distribution being due to the play of "natural forces." In the early 1930s and before, this thesis was asserted with respect to forced savings and to profit inflation;[16] in the 1960s it was put forward primarily to criticize the idea that unemployment could be reduced through expansionary

---

15. David Laidler and Michael Parkin, "Inflation: A Survey," *Economic Journal*, vol. 85 (December 1975), pp. 790–93.

16. See Friedrich A. Hayek, *Prices and Production* (London: Routledge, 1931).

monetary or fiscal policies at the limited cost of some increase in inflation. If this increase were unanticipated, according to the modern monetarist thesis,[17] then various categories of income receivers would be disagreeably surprised and their reactions, in combination with official policies, would make for ever more rapid inflation or for a return to the starting point—to the rate of unemployment that policymakers were originally intent on bringing down. In the process of demonstrating that policies purporting to reduce unemployment through expansionary economic policy are self-defeating, monetarists were forced to think beyond the initial redistributive impact of inflation, and that meant a step forward in the understanding of the tug-of-war.

Intersectoral Shifts in Latin America

The experience of Latin America has introduced a more diversified group of actors than economists in advanced industrialized countries generally admit. The latter have written primarily in terms of the distribution of income between profits and wages, with the state being a third potential beneficiary. In Latin American inflations after World War II, it became obvious that one group of property holders or entrepreneurs was often favored at the expense of another. For example, when, as frequently happened, inflation was combined with a fixed exchange rate and hence necessarily with import controls (otherwise mounting imports would cause intolerable balance-of-payments deficits), exporters experienced a decline in their real incomes whereas those who were entitled by the control authorities to import at the overvalued exchange rate made an equivalent gain. As Latin America's exports consisted, until the mid-1960s at least, largely of primary products whereas imports were heavily weighted with capital goods and intermediate inputs for the expanding industrial establishment, inflation tended systematically to favor new industries at the expense of primary producers.

That inflation in an open economy could have profound effects on the intersectoral income distribution no less than on the division of income

17. What I call the modern monetarist thesis emphasizes anticipated versus unanticipated inflation; see Edmund S. Phelps, "Phillips Curves, Expectations of Inflation and Optimal Unemployment over Time," *Economica*, vol. 34 (August 1967), pp. 254–81; Milton Friedman, "The Role of Monetary Policy," *American Economic Review*, vol. 58 (March 1968), pp. 1–17. The long experience of inflation in Latin America led observers to anticipate the essentials of a thesis that when formulated by advanced-country economists was celebrated as an original and capital insight; see W. Arthur Lewis, "Closing Remarks," in Baer and Kerstenetzky, *Inflation and Growth*, pp. 21–33.

between wages and profits was noted first by Brazilian economists.[18] In Brazil the shift, toward the import-substituting industries and away from coffee growers and other primary producers, was substantial and particularly protracted; effective countermoves on the part or on behalf of the coffee growers were slow in coming, one reason being that in the short run the supply of coffee does not respond much to price change (the trees are in place and bear beans which it remains profitable to harvest even when prices drop substantially). Supply reactions are considerably stronger and faster in the case of annual crops and cattle, especially when a switch to other land uses is possible. The speed with which the initial redistributive impact of inflation is counteracted by a group that is being squeezed depends of course also on the political and economic leverage of that group; this leverage depends, at least in part, on the economic damage the group can inflict on the economy by withholding its contribution; and the ability to inflict damage and to withhold depends in turn on the physical and economic characteristics of the product line in which the group has specialized.[19]

While intersectoral income shifts provoked by inflation have occasionally played a constructive role in making extra resources available to some sector with a key role in development, they have at other times been quite erratic and needlessly disruptive. Recognition of this fact lies behind the indexation experiments, particularly in countries with persistent two-digit inflation, such as Brazil. Adjusting salaries, rents, interest payments, and so forth, in line with price changes at regular, at least yearly, intervals has often been billed as part of the anti-inflationary package introduced by the military in Brazil in 1964. Actually, the device was anti-inflationary primarily to the extent that it was grossly incomplete insofar as it did not interfere with the considerable compression of real wages that occurred in the first years of the military regime. The real function of indexation was to avoid some of the more damaging intersectoral repercussions of the substantial inflation that continued to take place after 1964 (it never

18. Alexandre Kafka, "The Theoretical Interpretation of Latin American Economic Development," in Howard S. Ellis, ed., *Economic Development for Latin America* (St. Martin's, 1951), p. 21; Celso Furtado, "Industrialization and Inflation," *International Economic Papers*, no. 12 (St. Martin's, 1967), pp. 101–19. J. Markos Mamalakis attempted to show that "sectoral clashes" provide the clues to the understanding of all of Latin American history and society; "The Theory of Sectoral Clashes" and "The Theory of Sectoral Clashes and Coalitions Revisited," *Latin American Research Review*, vol. 4 (Fall 1969), pp. 9–46, and vol. 6 (Fall 1971), pp. 89–126.

19. See Albert O. Hirschman, *A Bias for Hope: Essays on Development and Latin America* (Yale University Press, 1971), pp. 11–12, and *Essays in Trespassing*, pp. 59–97.

fell below 15 percent). In this respect, indexation was fairly effective; it safeguarded the real income of exporters (through frequent minidevaluations of the exchange rate), the assets of creditors and savers (through indexing of interest rates on loans and savings deposits), and the revenues of the state (through indexing of back taxes). But the system was always a highly administered one; as time went on, it was used to award special favors to economic activities newly considered essential, by exempting them from the indexing mechanism. For example, in 1975 it was decided that medium- and long-term loans to capital goods industries from the official development bank would carry a preferential rate of interest with a ceiling of 20 percent, which was considerably below the actual rate of inflation (which was 40–50 percent). Just as the earlier combination of inflation and overvaluation of the currency, such officially arranged loopholes in the system of indexation had once again the dual effect of shifting resources toward a favored sector and of doing so in an inflationary manner.[20]

Considerable puzzlement is often expressed over the fact that in countries like Brazil where authoritarian regimes hold sway and wages are rigidly controlled, inflation remains a problem. One reason is precisely that the tug-of-war can take place not just between profits and wages, but, for example, between profits of one business group and profits of another. In authoritarian Brazil after 1964 the opening, on a large scale, of consumer credit facilities for purchasers of durable goods made possible the sustained boom of the automobile and appliance industries in the second half of the 1960s and early 1970s, somewhat at the expense of both traditional consumer goods industries and industries producing basic inputs and capital goods; then, during a new, more difficult phase beginning in 1974, machinery and intermediate goods industries were in turn showered with incentives and credit facilities.[21] As in the shift of resources from primary producers to industrial entrepreneurs, changes in priorities within the industrial sector were politically easier to accomplish through an inflationary, if selective, credit expansion than through

20. See Werner Baer and Paul Beckerman, "Indexing in Brazil," *World Development*, vol. 2 (October–December 1974), pp. 35–47; Albert Fishlow, "Indexing Brazilian Style: Inflation without Tears?" *Brookings Papers on Economic Activity, 1:1974*, pp. 261–82 (hereafter *BPEA*); papers on "Indexation, The Brazilian Experience," in *Explorations in Economic Research*, vol. 4 (Winter 1977). The information about the officially arranged loopholes in the indexing system was made available to me by various officials in 1976.

21. José Serra, "Three Mistaken Theses Regarding the Connection between Industrialization and Authoritarian Regimes," in David Collier, ed., *The New Authoritarianism in Latin America* (Princeton University Press, 1979), pp. 129–45.

noninflationary schemes such as the coupling of subsidies with taxes or of credit expansion in one direction with credit restriction in another.

The choice of an inflationary method of shunting resources to certain sectors was not always a conscious decision of policymakers. On the contrary, the combination of inflation with overvaluation of the currency as a means of diverting income from primary exporters to import-substituting industrialists was stumbled on by policymakers and grew out of arrangements that originally had very different purposes.[22] Nevertheless, if policymakers choose time and again to make resource reallocation decisions in such a way as to fuel inflation even though other methods are available, this tells something about the nature of the relations between the state and various groups of producers.

Intersectoral and Interclass Shifts: Argentina and New York City

The importance of intersectoral income shifts and conflicts in the course of Latin American inflations makes one suspect that not enough attention has been paid to these matters in the analysis of inflation in the advanced industrial countries.[23] Latin American inflations, on the other hand, have by no means been neutral with respect to the wage-profit balance. Everywhere wage and salary earners have been very much affected by the inflationary process. But since their role comes on top of the intersectoral conflicts there immediately arises the possibility of a three- or multi-cornered act, in lieu of the simple wage-profit scenario of traditional economic analysis, and with that the possibility of shifting alliances providing a key to the changing dynamics of the inflation.

In attempts to account for the course of Argentina's inflation and recurrent stop-go cycles, three principal groups have been identified—the cattle breeders and cereal growers of the pampas, the industrial bourgeoisie, and the urban masses.[24] The pivotal group is the industrial bourgeoisie; it tends to make common cause with the urban masses in a recession

22. See Furtado, "Industrialization and Inflation."

23. Charles S. Maier attempts to delineate types of coalitions that are associated with different types of inflation in "The Politics of Inflation in the Twentieth Century," in Hirsch and Goldthorpe, *Political Economy of Inflation*, pp. 37–72; his analysis is still primarily in vertical class terms even though he allows for the distinct existence and separate interests of intermediate groups, such as white-collar workers.

24. Adolfo Canitrot, "La experiencia populista de redistribución de ingresos," *Desarrollo económico*, vol. 15 (October–December 1975), pp. 331–51; Guillermo O'Donnell, "Estado y alianzas en la Argentina, 1956–1976," *Desarrollo económico*, vol. 16 (January–March 1977), pp. 523–54. O'Donnell makes a further distinction between the small national bourgeoisie and the larger, more cosmopolitan, and multinational-oriented industrialists.

when both groups can agree on a strongly expansionary economic policy and on holding down the price of Argentina's principal export product, meat, which also happens to be its principal wage good. But exports tend to decline under those circumstances and to do so fairly rapidly both because the workers, with their increasing incomes, literally eat up the country's exports and because the cattle breeders, unlike Brazil's coffee planters, can react to a price squeeze by liquidating their herds. As a result the industrialists soon experience supply difficulties for their imported inputs and capital goods. With meat prices, among others, starting to rise, the workers make demands for higher wages; soon the industrialists find their allies too demanding. At this point they join the agricultural elites and this new coalition can now agree on holding real wages down and on raising prices for agricultural output. Policies directed to this end, and to fight inflation in general, cause a recession which eventually leads to a new switch by the industrial bourgeoisie so that the play starts over again. The different phases of the play are marked by different kinds of political regimes. During the expansive, inflationary phase an uneasy coalition is maintained between populist forces and certain sectors of the business community; the military take over when these sectors become concerned about excessive inflation and ally themselves with the land and cattle owners.

This tripartite model, while synthetic, sheds new light on the social background to Argentina's inflation and stop-go cycles. It invites comparison with such experiences as New York's fiscal crisis of the 1970s.[25] In the mid-1960s the "populist" administration of Mayor John Lindsay was able to put together a strange coalition of liberal reformers, largely from the upper-middle class, black (and other minority) civil rights movements, and large commercial banks who "were quite happy to endorse deficit financing because bond and note issues provided them with healthy commissions and good investment opportunities."[26] Arrayed against Lindsay were civil service unions and strong elements of the middle and lower-middle classes. Given the institutional framework, the equivalent of inflation was spiraling indebtedness; Lindsay was politically too weak to raise taxes sufficiently or to limit expansion of expenditures to his preferred projects.[27] But like accelerating inflation, so does increasing

---

25. See Martin Shefter, "New York City's Fiscal Crisis: The Politics of Inflation and Retrenchment," *Public Interest*, no. 48 (Summer 1977), pp. 98–127.

26. Ibid., p. 109.

27. This phenomenon is discussed below as the "complementarity effect" of public spending or investment.

indebtedness cause worry to some partners of the ruling coalition. Eventually, during the administration of Mayor Abraham Beame, the banks switched sides and support from the upper-middle class weakened; joining the middle and lower-middle classes, the banking and business interests enforced a strict austerity regime whose principal victims were the black and Hispanic communities. While the city was spared a military coup, it did suffer a substantial loss of fiscal autonomy in the wake of its near default.[28]

With their parallels—as well as differences—the Argentine and New York stories are of much interest. By drawing on intersectoral cleavages, on class conflicts, and on the dynamics of inflation itself, they succeed in explaining the various phases of the inflationary policy cycle and the transition from one to another as old alliances disintegrate and new ones are being formed. In this manner, they manage to breathe a good deal of life into the tug-of-war metaphor.[29]

The Sociopolitical Interpretation of Inflationary Group Behavior

Inflation often starts or intensifies, so it seems, when a social group holds enough power or influence to command additional wealth and income for itself (or to escape participation in some loss that is suffered by the economy), but not enough to do so in a permanent way through a definitive transfer. Inflation is a means of effectuating a temporary transfer. Partial, complete, or even overcomplete cancellation of that transfer can take place, first of all, through subsequent turns in the inflationary spiral, especially when other groups use their retaliatory power and do some grabbing (or escaping) of their own. The temporarily gained advantage can also evaporate and turn into a setback in the course of a stabilization, retrenchment, and austerity program that may follow a bout of inflation.

Though inflation may be so ubiquitous, go on for so long, and seem so familiar as to be almost normal, its characteristics mark it as a rather

28. Shefter distinguishes between externally and internally imposed disciplines; "New York City's Fiscal Crisis," pp. 99–101, 124.

29. A more general approach to the understanding of multicornered inflationary maneuvering proceeds from the simple observation that individuals and groups operate in several markets; most are price takers in some markets but have, or can acquire, price-making powers in others. See Harvey Leibenstein, "The Inflation Process: A Micro-behavioral Analysis," *American Economic Review*, vol. 71 (May 1981, *Papers and Proceedings, 1980*), pp. 368–73.

unusual social game. Compare it with some of the social and political movements of the last hundred years where there was no expectation on the part of the actors that gains, once achieved, would have to be given up in short order. Take the battles for universal suffrage, for women's vote, for the right of workers to strike or to join a union, for the forty-eight- or forty-hour week, or for paid vacations. Or take, on the other hand, business demands for subsidies or tariff protection. It was a premise of all of these actions that the sought-after gains would stick—and, in the large majority of cases, they did and proved irreversible, in spite of frequently very strong initial resistance. In fact, the mobilization of social energy needed to secure these gains would probably have been impossible if there had been any expectation that the gains would be reversible—on the contrary, the expectations at the outset were ordinarily for gains much greater than those that were eventually secured.

This historical reminder serves to demonstrate that inflation, familiar as it is, does hold a genuine puzzle. Why would any social group choose an inflationary strategy of income augmentation, that is, a strategy that brings a strictly temporary improvement, but whose outcome is uncertain and may land it in a worse position? To be sure, the group may be so naive as not to realize that other groups can retaliate. But it often will realize that its initial gain will be reduced and perhaps even more than annihilated by subsequent inflation as well as by countermoves of others, and still decide that it is necessary or worthwhile to engage in the action.

Naive Inflationary Behavior and Populism

Naive behavior is likely to be the explanation primarily when serious inflation has not been experienced for some time. The belief that the economy is elastic enough to afford something to one group without taking away from others is periodically reborn, the more so as it is occasionally correct—that is, in Keynesian situations when there is both unemployment and unused capacity as a result of recession. Populist policies, which give something to popular groups without directly taking away from others, can be relatively successful in such a situation, but their very success is apt to blind policymakers to the fact that it can last for only a limited time. The sequence from initial elasticity and smooth redistributive success to increasing problems and eventual disaster, in part because of overconfidence born from the initial success, was characteristic of Argentine economic policies under the first Perón regime and of Chilean policies under Allende.[30]

The naive incapacity to visualize the power of other groups to retaliate, through demands or actions of their own, against an initial inflationary foray affects not only social groups in relation to each other. It often happens within the public sector as the government sponsors one particular program without foreseeing that other agencies will react to that program by pushing through their own demands. A government that decides to undertake a major effort in one particular sector or region will frequently find that, as a result of these highly visible favors, demands from other sectors or regions become activated and have to be granted at least in part for the purpose of putting together the political coalition that will permit the original plan to go forward. This "complementarity effect of certain public expenditures" is apparent in the official development moves in Brazil's underdeveloped Northeast. For example, when President Kubitschek gave top priority to the building of Brasília, the new capital, he found that to secure the necessary political support for this venture he had to promise funds for wholly unrelated projects in the Northeast.[31] Every dollar that a government intends to spend on a project of its own choice is thus likely to lead, via a political complementarity or multiplier, to some additional, originally unintended public spending. The size of the complementarity effect depends both on the enterprisingness of the government and on its ability to push through its own priorities without having to make too many promises or compromises in other directions— that is, on its political strength vis-à-vis claimants for public funds. A government that is both enterprising and politically weak is most likely to be overwhelmed by the unintended inflationary consequences of its development moves—not too surprising a conclusion and one that points, once again, in the direction of populist governments.

Gratification of Pseudohostility and Pseudofriendliness

Once inflation has become a fixture in the economic landscape, most groups will be aware that demands on their part for higher incomes will give rise to countermoves that will cancel much of those gains, with some probability even that they may end up in a worse position than the initial

30. See José Serra, "Economic Policy and Structural Change in Chile, 1970–73" (Ph.D. dissertation, Cornell University, 1976), chaps. 8, 9.

31. Hirschman, *Journeys*, pp. 36, 86.

one. Under such (nonnaive) circumstances, the continuation of inflationary group behavior becomes more difficult to explain.

Predominant opinion denies there is much of a problem here, alleging that, once inflation is under way and rolling, an individual group with some power over prices or wages has no choice but to behave in such a way as to contribute further to the inflationary spiral. In fact, each group that does so can justifiably claim that it is just engaging in defensive moves. Essentially this thesis of inflationary behavior rests on the prisoner's dilemma model; in the absence of some sort of deus or social contract ex machina that could produce a cooperative solution, an ongoing inflation condemns all social groups to behave in the noncooperative manner that perpetuates the inflation.

Such a denial of responsibility or of freedom of action on the part of admittedly powerful social groups takes their protestations of innocence and of powerlessness far too much at face value. For in the prisoner's dilemma model the prisoner in solitary confinement is an extraordinarily inapt metaphor for such inflationary actors as giant corporations, producers' associations, and powerful trade unions. Assuming, therefore, that such groups engage, to some extent at least, in inflationary behavior because that is what they have decided to do even though they know all about inflation, the question remains, why would they do it?

To explore the situation through a rational action model of individual or group behavior, along standard lines, suppose a group attempts to estimate the impact of an inflationary action or demand on its eventual position. This involves estimating a probability distribution with a mean or expected value and a variance. For a group to engage in any action at all the expected value must be positive—otherwise it would not be worthwhile for it to shoulder the risk that is expressed through the variance. With any given positive expected value the willingness to engage in inflationary action will depend on the degree to which the group is risk-averse. It will also depend on the group's time preference and horizon. The bigger its preference for present over future income, the more will a group be prone to engage in inflationary actions. This is so because the group is assumed to be able to obtain immediately an increase in its income through its actions or demands, an increase that is then whittled down as a result of the inflationary consequences of that increase and of the countermoves of others. Inflationary group behavior that is aware of these repercussions thus requires that willingness to take risks be combined with a short time horizon, that is, with a strong preference for present over future income. Now this combination of attitudes is not easy to find among the social groups of the real world. Low-income people are usually risk-averse, while perhaps having a short time horizon; middle- and upper-class people, on the other hand, may be willing to take risks but their time horizon tends to be long. It is therefore troublesome to account along "rational action" lines for inflationary group behavior when it is clear to everyone concerned that such behavior will only result in temporary advantages and may carry a long-term penalty.

One interesting explanation suggested by a Brazilian economist[32] is essentially an application of the Duesenberry axiom that people will always strain to get back to the highest income they have ever experienced.[33] It is one of the characteristics of inflation (without instantaneous indexation) that different groups experience their respective highest levels of income at different points in time. If there are just two groups, the highest level for group A will coincide with the lowest level for group B, and vice versa. This seesaw relationship is inevitable. Because of resource limitations it would be impossible for both A and B to reach their peak incomes at the same point in time; they can do so only alternatingly, each group reaching its peak at the expense of the other. Attempts to recapture the peaks on the part of either or both groups must lead therefore to continuing inflation.

It is also clear that only inflation permits each group to reach (in rotation) higher real income levels, even though temporarily, than it could achieve with a stable price-wage structure. Within limits people may actually prefer an income that fluctuates around an average to a stable income that would be equal to that average, provided they do not suffer intolerable hardship when their income cycle hits its low point. A reason for such preference could precisely be the achievement, be it but temporarily, of an otherwise unattainable income level, and perhaps the taste for hope-sustaining movement and variety in general.[34] To the extent that such group preferences exist, their satisfaction via inflation would constitute a latent benefit of inflation.

32. Mário Henrique Simonsen, "Brazilian Inflation: Postwar Experience and Outcome of the 1964 Reforms," in Roberto Alemann and others, *Economic Development Issues: Latin America* (Praeger, 1967), pp. 272–73.

33. James Duesenberry, *Income, Saving, and the Theory of Consumer Behavior* (Harvard University Press, 1949), p. 89.

34. See Tibor Scitovsky, *The Joyless Economy: An Inquiry into Human Satisfaction and Consumer Dissatisfaction* (Oxford University Press, 1976).

It is possible to suggest a more weighty explanation for inflationary group behavior. In a situation of high social tension and group antagonism, such behavior could come to be engaged in less for its normally expected material results—additional real income—than because it is enjoyed for its own sake. This means inverting the usual means-end relationship; the gratification of intergroup hostility that is obtained by the achievement of a highly inflationary price or wage rise can be the real benefit, to the point where it would not matter if inflation eroded, totally and in short order, the gains achieved. In Chile, for example, "various groups maintain and prize an attitude and phraseology of unbending opposition and hostility: they coexist, but are most anxious to avoid *overt agreement* and compromise. . . . The Chilean situation appears to be weighted more heavily with the avoidance of agreement, with the maintenance of a militant stance on the part of all contending groups. In a sense this stance is the desired benefit and inflation is its cost."[35]

Yet the acting out of social conflict that takes place through inflationary group behavior carries with it a certain amount of playacting. Each group knows that the others have the means to retaliate, no decisive victory is ever scored, and the division of the social product does effectively take place in the midst of what only looks like irreconcilable conflict over how it should be shared. The extent to which there is playacting can be made clear by comparison with other conflict situations. Ordinarily when there is lack of agreement over the division, say, of some treasure, booty, or spoils, the disputants either fight it out or come to an agreement before the actual division takes place. With inflation, the disputants somehow manage to have both fight and division at the same time. Looked at in this light, the fight loses some of its reality. Inflation appears now as a device that permits a society to have its cake and eat it, in the sense of having a great deal of social conflict while going about its business of generating and distributing the social product.

The matter can be put another way. In a society that is divided into groups that have roughly equal power to affect prices and wages, the distribution of income that prevails when inflation is on could quite conceivably be similar to that experienced when there is price stability. What, then, is the actual difference between these two situations? Not much, except that, with inflation, each group is able to engage in conflictive

35. Hirschman, *Journeys*, pp. 208–09 (emphasis in original).

behavior and to demonstrate its power and its antagonism to other groups. From this point it is not far to the conclusion that such demonstration is an important function of inflation, and perhaps its real motive.

Inflation then is a remarkable invention that permits a society to exist in a situation that is intermediate between the extremes of social harmony and civil war. Hence the dual performance of inflation in the arena of politics. Depending on the circumstances, it can act either as a substitute for civil war or as preface to much more serious social and political turmoil. Certainly, inflation has served as a school for social conflict; the social shadowboxing that is its earmark can turn readily enough into the real match. But at times, the deflecting of intergroup hostility into the making of inflationary demands has helped gain time for reducing tensions that, in the absence of the inflationary outlet, would have become right away much more explosive. As a commentator on the post-Franco inflation in Spain put it:

To explain the current inflation by appealing to economic factors is . . . sterile. Inflation must be understood as an expression of the open or muted conflicts between various social classes and economic groups. . . . The structure of the Spanish economy, as inherited from the past, fosters at present a propensity to social conflict which is not easily assimilated. . . . The intention to dominate the inflationary process by imposing a drastically restrictive monetary policy would mean . . . to transfer the underlying social conflict to other areas of political and social life where conflict would take a more radical form. The propensity to conflict receives after all a transitory relief through the inflation. This relief cannot be permanent because of the collateral problems which inflation generates, but in a moment of political transition and of change in the relative positions of the various social forces, inflation is the least harsh form which this struggle can take; it involves the most indirect confrontation available to each social group for the defense of its interests.[36]

This quotation is of particular interest because inflation is widely believed to pave the way for the establishment of authoritarian and repressive regimes. While it may do so, especially when hyperinflation is involved,[37] inflation can apparently also ease the difficult transition from authoritarianism to polyarchy. Like emigration or the open frontier, inflation can act as a safety valve for accumulated social and political tensions. But unlike these social mechanisms it is unreliable in this role and can change character in the middle of the play.

36. "Comentario sobre la situación económica al comenzar el segundo semestre," *Moneda y crédito* (Madrid), no. 141 (June 1977), p. 110.

37. See Hirschman, *Essays in Trespassing,* pp. 203–04.

Moreover, a social configuration that is the opposite of intergroup conflict—one that is characterized by a great deal of friendliness among different groups and particularly between them and the state—provides an equally favorable breeding ground for inflation. Where the state defers readily to all the successive demands made on it by one group or one government department after another, inflation has the function of denying part of what the state, in its weakness, has granted. To the extent that the process is understood, the state might be said to hand over to inflation the disagreeable job of saying no.

This additional interpretation explains why inflation has led a vigorous existence in several repressive, authoritarian states of Latin America that have eliminated independent trade union activity. This sort of state is precisely premised on professions of great friendliness with business groups, which are often showered with incentives and credit facilities; moreover, such a state is far from immune to pressures emanating from its own subdivisions; with powerful and power-hungry generals heading the spending ministries, the allocation of public funds can be less subject to central control than under civilian governments.

One objection may be raised against this additional interpretation coming on top of the previous one. As with the Frenchman who drinks wine with his meal only when the first dish is pâté or when it is not, so inflation seems fated to be the invariable result no matter whether hostility or friendliness pervades society and its groups. However, the attitudes that were shown to be conducive to inflation were not just any kind of hostility and friendliness; they had one specialized element in common— a certain amount of playacting. There is an element of playacting in the kind of intergroup hostility that leads to inflation, and the same holds for exaggerated or pseudofriendliness—the inability to say no to any new group demand. Especially when a country has already become closely acquainted with inflation, easy acquiescence to inflationary demands is rather like Charles Addams's friendly truckdriver on a curvy mountain road, who with an oncoming truck in sight waves on the car that is trying to pass him. Friendliness is here not so friendly after all, just as successive rounds of highly inflationary wage and price increases that stem from intergroup hostility are largely sham battles and are intimately known as such to the participants. The two seemingly opposite types of inflationary behavior thus merge into one—the strenuous avoidance of cooperative encounter and agreement on the part of social groups.

Political Disasters of Hyperinflation

Inflation is a social and political phenomenon no less for its outcome than for its causes. Some attention thus should be paid to its effects on social and political developments. One sequence from inflation to politics—the possibility that accelerating inflation contributes to political crisis and regime breakdown—has monopolized attention ever since Keynes erroneously reported Lenin to have said that there is no surer way to revolutionize a society than to "debauch its currency."[38] Even though ten years elapsed between the German hyperinflation of 1923 and the seizure of power by Hitler, it is often suggested that the two events are causally related. In the regime breakdowns or important political changes that were preceded by rapidly accelerating inflations in Brazil in 1964, Ghana and Indonesia in 1966, Chile in 1973, and Argentina in 1975, it would be more correct to consider inflation as one symptom among many of the disintegration of faltering regimes than as the principal factor responsible for their downfall. Nevertheless, in all these cases the enervating reality of hyperinflation certainly helped to signal regime crisis to a mass public.

When accelerating inflation is followed by sharp political change, the new government will ordinarily proclaim and try to maintain a strong anti-inflationary stand. While success in actually bringing inflation under control has varied considerably, one of the principal effects of inflation, and particularly of hyperinflation, is to bring to power governments that have a commitment to control inflation and will be judged accordingly, at least until some other problem such as unemployment or stagnation takes the center of the stage. In recent decades, strong inflationary policies have been characteristic of populist regimes, and anti-inflationary programs have subsequently often been carried on under the aegis of right-wing, business-oriented governments. In the great majority of cases hyperinflation has not led to revolution, but to military intervention, repression, and attempted suppression of trade union activity.[39] In fact, the one country in Latin America that experienced an anticapitalist revolution,

---

38. See Frank Whitson Fetter, "Lenin, Keynes and Inflation," *Economica*, vol. 44 (February 1977), pp. 77–80.

39. Thomas E. Skidmore, "The Politics of Economic Stabilization in Postwar Latin America," in James M. Malloy, ed., *Authoritarianism and Corporatism in Latin America* (University of Pittsburgh Press, 1977), pp. 149–90.

Cuba, enjoyed near-perfect monetary stability for many years before that event.

Political Uses of Moderate Inflation

Though moderate inflationary experiences have been much more prevalent than hyperinflation, the study of their political effects has been largely neglected. This may in part be due to a preoccupation with the consequences of hyperinflation that makes it very hard to detect situations in which the effects of inflation tend not to be disastrous and perhaps even, here and there, benign.

The structuralists see inflation as the consequence of deep-seated faults in a country's socioeconomic structure. They use the evidence of inflation to call attention to these faults and to enlarge public support for measures intended to deal with them. To the extent that this structuralist strategy would work, inflation could be credited with inducing action on a country's more hidden, but perhaps also more fundamental ills.

Now it must be said right away that inflation has hardly anywhere played that grandly constructive a role. But in a more modest way, something like the structuralists' sequence can be encountered here and there in the real world. Many years ago I asserted that moderate inflation may be helpful to a government and particularly to a finance minister who is trying to resist political pressure toward more spending.[40] Inflation is a telling proof that spending is already taking place at an excessive rate. To have a moderate inflation is thus similar to the tactic French ministers of finance used to follow when they hid away in some hard-to-identify account any extra cash they happened to have on hand—they knew that otherwise it would be impossible not to have it spent. It used to be said that one of the principal purposes of having a development plan for public investments is for a government to be able to restrain extravagant sectional demands. A moderate inflation can have the same effect, probably more persuasively. The matter helps explain the strange incapacity to reduce inflation to zero of the authoritarian, stability-oriented governments that have come to power in various Latin American countries in the wake of hyperinflation. The fact is that even in the new political environment

---

40. Hirschman, "Economic Policy in Underdeveloped Countries," reprinted in *Bias for Hope,* pp. 255–69.

there is need to keep up defenses against new highly inflationary projects and demands. And one such defense is afforded by some residual inflation.

The point can be extended. Inflation supplies not only evidence that spending must be controlled; when expenditures consistently outrun revenue the resulting inflation may have the effect of convincing the public and government that taxes must be raised to finance public investment. In the advanced industrial countries income taxation, and big spurts in taxation generally, have become possible only under the impact of major emergency and crisis, mostly in wartime. In a number of developing countries inflation has acted as an equivalent of war in setting the stage for more forceful taxation. The centerpiece of the 1974 tax reform in Colombia, for example, was a tax levied on the presumed income from all real assets. This concept, which had been proposed many times to deal with the problem of idle land,[41] was adopted only as a result of a peculiar combination of circumstances; one was the fact that the newly elected López Michelsen administration faced a serious inflationary and balance-of-payments crisis. Occasionally, the sequence is inverted. The Echeverría government in Mexico set out on a highly inflationary course after it had been frustrated, in 1971, in its project to carry out a long overdue fiscal reform. The government increased spending as though the reform had gone through. Perhaps it sought in this way to administer a lesson to the powerful business interests that had once again blocked the reform; unfortunately those who had to bear the cost of the lesson were not necessarily those for whom it was intended.

It begins to look as though the experience of inflation and the pressures that it brings could be put to certain positive uses. Beyond a threshold of tolerance, inflation certainly is the kind of pressing policy problem that increases the willingness of governments to take action, in spite of opposition from powerful interests, if there is firm expectation that the action will help restrain the inflation. In the Mexican and Colombian examples the connection between the inflationary process and the required action is particularly transparent; with public expenditures outpacing revenues in the course of the early stages of a country's economic development, the resulting inflation points directly to decisions on the expenditure or revenue side that would be helpful. Even then, decisions such as tax reform are often extremely difficult to take, but the crisis atmosphere generated by inflation may make it possible to modify

41. Hirschman, *Journeys*, pp. 117–21, 125–38.

structures that are part and parcel of the order of things under normal circumstances.

The ability of protracted inflation to raise questions about existing social arrangements was frequently noted in advanced capitalist societies in the period of high inflation. In a number of them, inflation led trade unions to change what might be called the money-power mix of their demands. Realizing that the quest for higher wages and benefits might be futile because of inflation or pressed by official policies to adhere to noninflationary guidelines, unions requested more participation in management decisionmaking as well as in firm profits as a counterpart to wage restraint.[42]

The social and political impact of inflation can thus range from the installation of authoritarian and repressive regimes that impose highly regressive income distributions to the adoption of tax reform and other measures in the direction of greater equality, participation, and democracy. "Like test-tube solutions that respond differently to the same reagent, these societies reveal their characters in divergent responses to the same stimulus."[43] An effective way to write the comparative social and political history of the last thirty years of the twentieth century may well be to focus on the distinctive reactions of various countries to identical pressures of worldwide inflation.

42. See Colin Crouch, "The Drive for Equality: Experience of Incomes Policy in Britain," and on Sweden, Andrew Martin, "Is Democratic Control of Capitalist Economies Possible?" in Leon N. Lindberg and others, eds., *Stress and Contradiction in Modern Capitalism: Public Policy and the Theory of the State* (Lexington Books, 1975), pp. 224–27, 40–55; "The Dutch Grope for a New Social Contract," *Business Week* (August 8, 1977), pp. 46–48.

43. Peter Alexis Gourevitch, "International Trade, Domestic Coalitions, and Liberty: Comparative Responses to the Crisis of 1873–1896," *Journal of Interdisciplinary History*, vol. 8 (Autumn 1977), p. 281.

4

The International Politics
of Inflation

Robert O. Keohane

It is widely agreed that inflation, in modern economies, is more the result of governmental action than a natural disaster imposed on an unwilling species by forces beyond human control. Governments choose to let inflation persist, or accelerate, because they believe that the consequences of preventing, or stopping, it would be worse. Governments rarely go so far as the colonial American revolutionaries, who required that creditors accept paper money at par under threat of physical punishment; nor do they usually relish the process as much as the Russian revolutionary economist, Preobrazhensky, who described the printing press as "the machine-gun of the Commissariat of Finance which poured fire into the rear of the bourgeois system."[1] But since the beginning of the welfare state and governmental management of their economies, they have generally preferred inflation to depression.

One way to understand governments' choices is to examine how they go about making decisions—in particular, to describe the strategies of cabinets, parties, quasi-autonomous agencies such as the Federal Reserve Board, and individual politicians, and to try to explain the coalitions that form and their outcomes. In this sort of analysis, interests and bargaining are at the center of attention. The other major way to understand choices is to focus not on the process of choosing, but on the incentives and constraints that face the choosers. Governments, like other social actors, look for opportunities in their environments, but they cannot achieve all

1. As quoted in Laurence Whitehead, "The Political Causes of Inflation," *Political Studies,* vol. 27 (December 1979), p. 572.

they wish. Decisions have opportunity costs; trade-offs among objectives are required. Rarely do the preferences of governmental leaders coincide exactly with what they decide to do. Thus the analysis of governmental choices must always take into account the incentives for, and constraints on, their actions.

This distinction between explanations that focus on the process of choice and those that emphasize the context of choice helps us to see the relationship between explanations of inflation that stress decisions by the monetary authorities and those that concentrate on constraints imposed by economy and society. No one doubts that inflation can always be explained by reference to decisions of the monetary authorities, since sufficiently restrictive monetary policies can control or even bring to an end a rise in prices. Yet this begs the crucial question, which should be particularly evident to anyone trained in economic ways of thinking— that is, what are the opportunity costs of running an anti-inflationary monetary policy? How much production, and how much welfare, will be forgone? Recognizing the importance of these trade-offs quickly leads both sophisticated monetarists and neo-Keynesians to an analysis of contemporary political economies: corporate and union power, adminis-tered prices, governmental intervention in the economy, and the attitudes, or expectations, of individuals. The statement that ultimately the monetary authority chooses the rate of inflation that it desires is meaningless apart from an understanding of trade-offs between the value of a stable price level and other values that may be competitive with price stability in the short or long run.

A major impetus for inflationary policies comes from domestic society. Clearly, as this volume and much other work indicate, domestic policies, and failures to develop coherent policies, were major elements in the inflation of the 1970s. Yet the incentives and constraints faced by a monetary authority are not limited to the society whose currency it seeks to manage and protect. Actions of other governments, transnational movements of capital, and the character of international institutions are also important. The position of a given country in the world political economy—as reflected in its ties with others, its position in the international division of labor, and the power resources at its disposal—will profoundly affect its environment for policy choice. So will the principles, rules, norms, and decisionmaking procedures that shape expectations about international economic relations—which are referred to here, as in the contemporary international relations literature, as "international regimes."[2] The political organization or disorganization of the world economy affects the trade-offs that confront national monetary authorities and may therefore affect rates of inflation.

This chapter seeks to show that an international political economy perspective, focusing on incentives and constraints affecting choice, can help to account for the double-peaked pattern of inflation observed in the 1970s, with high points in 1974–75 and 1979–80. For the countries of the Organization for Economic Cooperation and Development (OECD) taken together, inflation in consumer prices rose from an average of less than 4 percent between 1962 and 1972 to 13.6 percent in 1974, then fell to 8.6 percent in 1976 and dropped below 8 percent in 1978 before rising to almost 13 percent in 1980. By 1983, however, this measure of inflation had fallen sharply to about 5 percent.[3]

The rise in inflation rates in the 1970s, although not uniform from country to country, was general. In each of the twenty-four members of the OECD as of 1981, consumer prices rose more rapidly between 1971 and 1980 than between 1961 and 1970, and in more than two-thirds of them prices rose at more than double the earlier rate.[4] It would be very surprising if such a widespread change were merely the result of an unhappy combination of domestic social changes and national policies. Systemwide patterns may be expected, at least in part, to have systemic causes. It is therefore worthwhile to see how much of the average world rate of inflation can be accounted for on the basis of a systemic analysis. Analysts focusing on particular economies can then investigate reasons for the deviations of individual countries from the overall pattern.

This chapter argues that changes taking place in the early 1970s in the international regimes for money and oil had a profound effect on subsequent global inflation. The collapse of established rules was both effect and cause. Governments with the power to do so broke the old rules in both money and oil during the first few years of the decade; but the resulting uncertainty and sauve qui peut mentality led governments

2. See Stephen D. Krasner, ed., *International Regimes* (Cornell University Press, 1983); Robert O. Keohane, *After Hegemony: Cooperation and Discord in the World Political Economy* (Princeton University Press, 1984).

3. *OECD Economic Outlook*, nos. 20, 21, 25, 29, 34 (Paris: Organization for Economic Cooperation and Development, December 1976, July 1977, July 1979, July 1981, December 1983).

4. *OECD Economic Outlook*, no. 30 (December 1981), table 22, p. 47. Figures for consumer prices were calculated from the table for 1971–80. For figures on increases in consumer prices on a year-by-year basis between 1959 and 1976, see Organization for Economic Cooperation and Development, *Towards Full Employment and Price Stability* (Paris: OECD, 1977) (hereafter McCracken Report).

to seek national advantage in ways that directly or indirectly led to increases in price levels. Subsequent events can be interpreted in terms of Albert Hirschman's tug-of-war metaphor (chapter 3), in which inflation is considered to be the direct outcome of conflicting demands for higher income shares. As this metaphor suggests, the politics of inflation revolve around distributional issues. So do the politics of disinflation. Since inflation provided benefits to some members of the international system during the 1970s, for some countries the cure was more painful than the disease.

The Accommodation of Inflation before 1971

The prewar gold standard incorporated a set of anti-inflationary practices. Central banks, including privately owned banks that had semipublic status such as the Bank of England, tended to raise interest rates, thus depressing prices and demand, when they faced outflows of gold.[5] When domestic inflation led to gold outflows, a tendency therefore existed for this process to be halted, rather than to feed on itself. This does not mean that the gold standard prevented inflation.[6] But the gold standard did impose some constraints on the inflationary process.

A gold standard is incompatible with the modern welfare state. Under the gold standard, states had to give priority to maintaining the value of their currencies over domestic macroeconomic objectives. They thus had to be willing to force the costs of adjustment to change onto their own populations in the form of deflation and unemployment; and they had to renounce the aspiration for control over domestic money supplies. With the onset of the ambitious, interventionist welfare state, such rigor became politically impossible.

Thus the development of the interventionist social welfare state fundamentally changed the nature of liberalism at the international level. As John Ruggie has argued, the arrangements agreed to at Bretton Woods

5. This reaction was not so automatic as orthodox opinion at the time indicated; see Arthur I. Bloomfield, *Monetary Policy under the International Gold Standard: 1880–1914* (Federal Reserve Bank of New York, 1959); Peter H. Lindert, *Key Currencies and Gold, 1900–1913,* Princeton Studies in International Finance, 24 (Princeton University, International Finance Section, 1969).

6. Indeed, Richard N. Cooper has shown that prices were not stable under the nineteenth-century gold standard, in part because the rate of growth in the stock of gold varied, and in part because the connection between the quantity of gold available and the quantity of money was not as close as is often assumed; "The Gold Standard: Historical Facts and Future Prospects," *Brookings Papers on Economic Activity,* 1:1982, pp. 13–19. (Hereafter *BPEA.*)

in 1944 represented not a return to the old liberalism of the pre-1914 gold standard, but the inauguration of a liberal international economic system "embedded" in the domestic social welfare state. Multilateralism and domestic stability were now conditioned by one another, reflecting the "shared legitimacy" of a set of social objectives on which there was a considerable measure of agreement.[7]

This change had consequences for the role of money within the economies of the major industrialized countries. As Fred Hirsch and Peter Oppenheimer have put it, "money . . . became more of an instrument, less of an objective. The shock absorbers that had earlier been provided by the real economy were shifted to some degree to the financial economy. Money became more accommodative."[8] As money became more accommodative, so did the international financial system, allowing "a potentially limitless degree of freedom for national monetary policies and national price levels," but still providing "sufficient international credit support to reduce greatly the risk of precipitous collapse of currencies as the result of sudden pressures."[9]

The permissiveness of international monetary arrangements clearly had political as well as technical economic sources. Once the myth that the gold standard was automatic and natural had been punctured, and the collapse of 1931 had put an end to the British attempt to maintain the prewar value of the pound, "growth as a surrogate for redistribution" rather than sound money became the dominant conservative idea.[10] Even if deflationary conservatives had been in power in all major capitalist countries after World War II, it is highly unlikely that they could have reached agreement on an effective supranational system to enforce discipline on reluctant national governments. The United States, fearing world inflation, attempted at Bretton Woods and thereafter to put some control on expansion of international liquidity. No intergovernmental organization was established, however, that had the independent power to ensure this.[11]

7. John Gerard Ruggie, "International Regimes, Transactions, and Change: Embedded Liberalism in the Postwar Economic Order," in Krasner, *International Regimes,* pp. 195–231.

8. "The Trial of Managed Money: Currency, Credit and Prices 1920–1970," in Carlo M. Cipolla, ed., *The Fontana Economic History of Europe,* vol. 5: *The Twentieth Century* (Harvester Press/Barnes & Noble, 1977), pt. 2, p. 605.

9. "The Ideological Underlay of Inflation," in Fred Hirsch and John H. Goldthorpe, eds., *The Political Economy of Inflation* (Harvard University Press, 1978), p. 266.

10. Charles S. Maier, "The Politics of Inflation in the Twentieth Century," in Hirsch and Goldthorpe, *Political Economy of Inflation,* p. 70.

11. On U.S. policies during the 1940s and early 1950s, see Fred L. Block, *The Origins of International Economic Disorder: A Study of United States International Monetary Policy from World War II to the Present* (University of California Press, 1977), pp. 32–55.

Accommodative international arrangements can to some extent be seen as reflecting the essence of world politics—lack of institutionalized power centers with control over governments. They can also be regarded, however, as reflecting an implicit choice. Fred Hirsch has commented:

> Too weak to impose price stability on national economies, [international influences] have in effect served the second-best objective of the liberal community, of maintaining an open international economy at whatever inflation rate has to be accepted to attain this. . . . Critics who see these international monetary arrangements as embodying a ratchet effect for world inflation are probably right. But the relevant question is whether a liberal international economy could have been purchased at any more acceptable price.
>
> This international influence is essentially accommodative, opening the way to monetary accommodation domestically. It responds to the domestic tensions that produce inflation as the insurance against a still worse outcome.[12]

The inflation that was accommodated by the international financial system in the late 1960s emanated largely from the United States. Between 1965 and 1968 the Johnson administration tried to finance the war in Vietnam without a tax increase, and monetary policy was expansive from the fourth quarter of 1966 through 1968. The Nixon administration turned to monetary expansion in 1970, maintaining the policy through the third quarter of 1972, despite the consequences first for the Bretton Woods regime and then for the supposedly fixed exchange rates agreed on at the Smithsonian Institution in December 1971.[13] Between 1967 and 1972, the associated deficits in the U.S. balance of payments "increased the international monetary reserves of other countries and therewith their monetary bases without reducing the monetary base of the United States," and this "led to a vast expansion in the aggregate of national money supplies." Eighty-five percent of the increase in reserve money in West Germany, and all of it in Japan, resulted from inflows of foreign reserves.[14]

The accommodative tendencies of the international financial system of embedded liberalism help to explain the ease with which American inflationary pressures were transmitted abroad. Yet they do not entirely account for increases in the average rate of world inflation, since under a

---

12. Hirsch, "Ideological Underlay of Inflation," pp. 278–79.

13. Harold T. Shapiro, "Inflation in the United States," in Lawrence B. Krause and Walter S. Salant, *Worldwide Inflation: Theory and Recent Experience* (Brookings Institution, 1977), pp. 267–94, esp. pp. 278–82.

14. Note that an inflow of international reserves is not a *necessary* condition for an inflationary expansion of the domestic money supply. The increase in reserve money in Italy between 1967 and 1972 came wholly from domestic sources. It should also be pointed out that other international channels for the transmission of inflation, apart from this monetary channel, exist. For a discussion, see Walter S. Salant, "The International Transmission of Inflation," in Krause and Salant, *Worldwide Inflation*, pp. 167–227; quotation on pp. 185–86.

fixed-rate regime such as that of Bretton Woods, the transmitter's inflation rate may decline as the recipients' inflation rates increase. To understand international sources of inflation, beyond those facilitating transmission of price increases, it is necessary to examine the effects of the collapse of the Bretton Woods regime.

The Breakdown of Rules and National Monetary Expansion

Except for tactical maneuvers designed to prolong the life of the Bretton Woods system without seriously constraining U.S. macroeconomic policy, American administrations during the 1960s and early 1970s, when faced with choices between pursuing more restrictive macroeconomic policies or undermining the fixed-rate Bretton Woods regime, did not hesitate to do the latter.[15] Indeed, the crucial defect of the Bretton Woods regime was its inability to prevent the United States from creating fiat money in excess of the demand for it. The only significant restraints on the United States imposed by the Bretton Woods regime operated indirectly, through the ultimate threat that inflationary American policies would lead to loss of confidence, a disorderly collapse, and consequent weakening of the American alliance system and losses of U.S. prestige. Against the political and economic pressures created by the war in Vietnam, those constraints were not very effective. In the late 1960s and early 1970s, American monetary policy was inconsistent with the maintenance of the dollar's value.

This inconsistency, and the American choice of inflationary domestic monetary autonomy over the maintenance of the Bretton Woods regime, became explicit on August 15, 1971. On that date President Nixon announced that the United States would no longer exchange gold for dollars at a fixed rate, and that it would also impose a temporary 10 percent surcharge on imports.[16] Subsequently, a meeting of the major market-economy countries, at the Smithsonian Institution in December 1971, agreed to reinstitute pegged exchange rates on the basis of different parities, effectively devaluing the dollar.

15. Joanne Gowa, *Closing the Gold Window: Domestic Politics and the End of Bretton Woods* (Cornell University Press, 1983), p. 50; see also John S. Odell, *U.S. International Monetary Policy: Markets, Power, and Ideas as Sources of Change* (Princeton University Press, 1982). David P. Calleo, *The Imperious Economy* (Harvard University Press, 1982), also emphasizes American domestic politics as a source of inflation. I agree with much of this interpretation but believe that changes in international regimes, and the associated uncertainty, also played an important role in the process.

16. *New York Times*, August 16, 1971. Gowa, *Closing the Gold Window*, and Odell, *U.S. International Monetary Policy*, both discuss, at length, the American decision to close the gold window.

These events further reduced constraints on U.S. policy. Not only was the United States no longer committed to a fixed gold value of the dollar; its policymakers were on record as desiring a greater devaluation of the dollar than had been agreed to by America's partners at the Smithsonian meeting. In this context, an argument for tight monetary policy "to defend the dollar" was unlikely to be even as persuasive in 1972 as it would have been a year or two earlier. The result was continued laxity of monetary policy and a large American contribution to increased world liquidity; the U.S. official settlements deficit for 1970–73 totaled over $50 billion. As they had during the last years of the Bretton Woods regime, the enormous U.S. deficits "effectively removed balance-of-payments constraints in other OECD countries, and facilitated a massive expansion of money supplies," contributing to inflation.[17]

The paths to monetary expansion differed from country to country. Some governments (the United Kingdom, Italy, and initially France) sought expansion; others (including Japan and the Netherlands) accepted it; and still others (especially West Germany) had monetary expansion thrust upon them through the effects of capital inflows. Great Britain was perhaps the most expansionist. The Conservative government of Edward Heath felt released, finally, from the shackles of defending the pound, and able to make a "dash toward growth." When expansionary British monetary policy precipitated a sterling crisis in June 1972, Britain quickly unpegged the pound and let it depreciate. Although British and American actions were rather extreme, especially for countries previously seen as responsible leaders of the system, other governments happily or unhappily followed suit. The conditions of 1972 reduced incentives for tight monetary policies throughout the industrialized world.

The logic behind this breakdown of incentives can be reconstructed as follows. Effective anti-inflationary policies on the part of any individual country would be likely to lead to capital inflows and eventual currency appreciation, given the rapid increases in money supply taking place in the United States and elsewhere and the fragility of pegged exchange rates after August 1971. Such appreciation would have the advantage of countering inflation, but it would have been likely to lead to an exchange rate that was too high to produce equilibrium on current account. Under floating exchange rates, one would expect this to be corrected eventually by higher inflation rates elsewhere; but between 1971 and 1973 it was

17. McCracken Report, p. 56.

still expected that a new long-term arrangement for stable pegged rates would be negotiated, and that inflation would remain moderate. Under these conditions, it could be expected that countries exercising self-discipline could experience overvalued currencies for some time to come, since current exchange rates would be likely to form the basis for long-term rates. Thus as long as such a future agreement was regarded as likely (that is, until 1973 or 1974), uncertainty about future international monetary regimes may have created disincentives for internal discipline. For purposes of controlling inflation, the international monetary arrangements between 1971 and 1973 combined the worst of both worlds, incorporating the defects of both fixed and floating rates without providing the benefits of either.

Not only did these arrangements reduce incentives for restrictive policies; they actually made it more difficult for countries seeking to limit inflation to do so. Despite increasingly strict controls imposed by German monetary authorities, the Bundesbank had to take in $4.5 billion worth of foreign currencies during June and July 1972 alone; and for the entire year, the German money supply grew by about 15 percent.[18] As a result of the breakdown of the Bretton Woods regime, "more expansionary action was taken than would otherwise have been the case and, especially, more of this action took the form of *monetary* expansion."[19]

The monetary policies of the seven major OECD countries between 1965 and the end of 1978 provide evidence on the inflation-proneness of the Smithsonian arrangements. This period includes three subperiods, delineated according to the exchange rate regime: a period of relatively stable exchange rates under the Bretton Woods regime (first quarter of 1965 through the second quarter of 1971); a period of uncertainty, with the short-lived pegged rates established at the Smithsonian Institution in force throughout much of the period and with substantial official intervention taking place (third quarter of 1971 through the first quarter of 1973); and a third period of floating rates (second quarter of 1973 through the fourth quarter of 1978), ending before the Iranian revolution and the oil price rises of early 1979. Table 4-1 indicates, for each period, the number of quarters in which the seven governments engaged in monetary restraint as defined by the OECD.

---

18. Leland B. Yeager, *International Monetary Relations: Theory, History, and Policy,* 2d ed. (Harper and Row, 1976), pp. 514–15; McCracken Report, pp. 86–87.

19. McCracken Report, p. 56 (emphasis in original).

Table 4-1. *Monetary Restraint in Seven Countries, 1965–78*

Country	Exchange-rate characteristic, by period		
	Pegged rates, *1965:1–1971:2* *(26 quarters)*	*Weakly pegged rates,* *1971:3–1973:1* *(7 quarters)*	*Floating rates,* *1973:2–1978:4* *(23 quarters)*
	Number of quarters of restraint		
Canada	2.0	0.0	13.5
France	8.0	2.5	7.0
Italy	5.0	0.0	6.0
Japan	7.0	0.5	8.0
United Kingdom	17.5	0.0	10.0
United States	7.0	2.0	10.5
West Germany	19.0	2.5	6.0
	Percentage of quarters in restraint[a]		
Seven countries	36.0	15.3	37.9

Sources: Calculated from Organization for Economic Cooperation and Development, *Towards Full Employment and Price Stability* (Paris: OECD, 1977), chart 14B, pp. 83–95; *OECD Economic Outlook*, no. 26 (December 1979), chart C, pp. 30–31.

a. Unweighted average.

It is readily apparent that the *least* restraint was exercised during the period between the middle of 1971 and the spring of 1973, the period of "Smithsonian uncertainty." Restraint was much greater both under the pegged rates before August 1971 and the flexible-rate arrangements after March 1973.

This suggests that whether exchange rates are pegged or allowed to fluctuate may not be the crucial issue. This inference is consistent with economic analysis, which lends little definitive support to arguments that either pegged or flexible rates are inherently more inflationary than the alternative. Although theory suggests that countries will have greater freedom to choose their own rates of inflation under flexible rates, it provides little guidance on the question of whether flexible rates will increase the average world inflation rate. Corden and Salant both conclude that no general answer to this question can be given, since to reach a conclusion one would need additional information about national policies and how these would be altered by one exchange rate system or another.[20]

20. W. N. Corden, *Inflation, Exchange Rates, and the World Economy: Lectures on International Monetary Economics*, 2d ed. (University of Chicago Press, 1977); Salant, "International Transmission of Inflation." A report by the OECD indicates that the great *variability* in inflation rates among OECD countries after the oil price increases of 1973–74 was related to flexible exchange rates, since differences in national economic policies led to appreciation of some countries' exchange rates (reducing inflation

In other words, to understand how an international monetary regime affects inflation, one needs to examine its effects on the incentives facing governments.

Pegged exchange rates create a long-term constraint on inflationary policies if equilibrium in a country's external accounts is to be maintained without devaluation, provided that other major countries avoid excessive monetary expansion. Yet this constraint did not operate effectively in the late 1960s and early 1970s, precisely because inflation rates increased for almost all major OECD countries. In the short run, furthermore, pegged exchange rates may increase incentives to manipulate the economy in an inflationary way for political purposes, since the effects will not immediately be apparent in a depreciating currency.[21] Yet neither are flexible rates sufficient to bring inflation under control. The key issue from the perspective of monetary theory—and political economy—is not pegged versus flexible exchange rates per se, but rather how international arrangements, and changes in them, affect rates of national money supply growth in the major economies.[22] In the early 1970s it was the lack of *any* coherent regime, and the effects of a sudden breakdown of the Bretton Woods regime, rather than the existence of one regime or another, that fostered inflation. As long as the behavior of the major countries had been generally consistent with the rules of the Bretton Woods regime, these rules had affected expectations and helped governments to adjust their behavior to what others were likely to do. Their collapse brought about a significant change. Governments were not compelled to pursue inflationary policies, but some incentives not to do so had now been removed, and some incentives to do so may have been created.

---

rates as a result of decreases in import prices) and the depreciation of the currencies of others (increasing inflation rates as import prices rose). This study does not argue, however, that flexible exchange rates affected the world inflation rate. See "International Aspects of Inflation," in *OECD Economic Outlook: Occasional Studies* (Paris: OECD, June 1982), pp. 5–27.

21. Thomas D. Willett and John Mullen, "The Effects of Alternative International Monetary Systems on Macroeconomic Discipline and Inflationary Biases," in Raymond E. Lombra and Willard E. Witte, eds., *Political Economy of International and Domestic Monetary Relations* (Iowa State University Press, 1982), pp. 143–56.

22. Ralph C. Bryant, *Money and Monetary Policy in Interdependent Nations* (Brookings Institution, 1980), holds that differences among macroeconomic conditions in different countries can only exist under variable exchange rates (p. 441). Nevertheless, it is also his view that the "fixed versus flexible" exchange rate debate is misspecified, since genuinely fixed rates are impossible among heterogeneous countries governed separately, and since even flexible exchange rates cannot thoroughly insulate an economy from the macroeconomic policies of others (pp. 441, 500).

The Collapse of the Old Oil Regime and Inflation

Before the 1970s, the world oil regime was dominated by the governments of the United States and Great Britain, along with the seven major international oil companies, all of which were American, British, or Anglo-Dutch. This regime was always informal and never fully accepted by exporting countries; it helped its leading participants to cooperate, but it was not particularly popular outside that charmed circle. Under the existing arrangements, oil companies were able to set prices on the basis of what the oligopolistically influenced market would bear, subject to the sharing of revenues on a roughly fifty-fifty basis with producing countries. Oligopolistic controls kept prices well above marginal cost; but a ceiling was placed on potential profits by the ability of new entrants (often domestic private oil firms, sometimes state firms) to explore for, and sell, oil at home or abroad. In current dollars, the price of oil fell from about $3.00 per barrel shortly after the war to $1.80 during the 1950s and 1960s. Even after the price rises of 1971, the nominal price of oil was only back to its early postwar level. Since manufactured exports from the advanced industrialized countries were subject to inflation (albeit moderate compared to the 1970s), the real cost of oil fell between 1950 and 1971.[23]

Between 1970 and the end of 1973, this regime collapsed. Governments of the oil-exporting countries, banded together in the Organization of Oil Exporting Countries (OPEC), negotiated a substantial price rise in 1971, and then imposed a fourfold increase after the Yom Kippur War of October 1973. Oil companies based in the OECD area aggravated these price rises by bidding against one another for available supplies. Furthermore, there was no effective intergovernmental policy coordination—indeed, there was a competitive scramble for oil supplies—among the governments of the advanced industrialized countries. Uncertainty about the future led to a massive problem of collective action, in which each buyer of oil, in seeking to protect itself, worsened the situation for all buyers collectively.[24]

When the old oil regime collapsed, it was not replaced by a new set of generally accepted rules. The advanced industrialized countries created

23. Hanns Maull, *Europe and World Energy* (London: Butterworth, 1980), pp. 207–11.
24. Louis Turner, *Oil Companies in the International System* (London: Allen and Unwin for Royal Institute of International Affairs, 1978); Keohane, *After Hegemony,* chap. 9.

the International Energy Agency (IEA), largely as an insurance regime, designed to protect each of them against embargoes targeted on individual countries, as well as to help them collaborate in reducing their long-term demand for oil. But by the mid-1970s the limit of oil prices was set much less by the IEA's activity than by the actions of producing governments and by market forces. Producers charged what the traffic would bear.

After a period of relatively stable nominal oil prices, implying a decline in real prices (allowing for inflation), prices more than doubled in 1979, under the impact of the Iranian revolution and associated reductions in Iranian production. As in 1973–74, a competitive scramble for supplies aggravated the situation; indeed, production for 1979 as a whole actually *increased*, while consumption remained steady. Market panic meant that in that year, "the industrialised countries of the OECD inflicted on themselves one of the most disastrous events in their economic history."[25]

These oil price increases were not the result of the inherent strength of OPEC. On the contrary, OPEC was weak. Its members were unable, during the 1970s, to devise a system of production controls, nor could they exercise the collective restraint in tight markets characteristic of oligopolies with long-term time horizons and concern for their relationships with customers. Both in 1973–74 and 1979–80 OPEC's price rises followed rather than preceded increases on the spot market. Wars and revolutions led to price increases by creating expectations of shortages, even when (as in 1979) no real production shortfalls ever materialized. As in the monetary area, a major effect of the collapse of an existing regime was a dramatic increase in uncertainty. This led to uncoordinated actions by individual countries designed to protect themselves but which instead compounded the effect of worsening the situation for the group as a whole. In its attempts to combat this uncertainty, the IEA had mixed results. It was quite ineffective during the oil crisis of 1979 but may well have made a positive contribution to avoidance of a new round of price rises during the period after the outbreak of the Iran-Iraq war in the fall of 1980.[26]

In the long term the price of oil after the collapse of the old regime was limited by the effects of market forces, particularly oil discoveries outside of OPEC, by the price elasticity of demand for oil (which proved

---

25. Daniel Badger and Robert Belgrave, *Oil Supply and Price: What Went Right in 1980?* Energy Paper no. 2 (London: Policy Studies Institute and Royal Institute of International Affairs, 1982), p. 95.
26. Keohane, *After Hegemony,* chap. 10.

surprisingly great), and by the effects of the world depression or recession of 1980–83, which was aggravated by higher oil prices. The fall in oil prices in 1982–83 reflected real market constraints on the producers. In the absence of a coherent overall regime, market constraints were the best guarantees available to consuming countries that oil prices would not continue to escalate.

Clearly, the collapse of the oil regime affected oil prices. And at least in the short run, increases in oil prices spurred inflation. The McCracken Report estimates that the quadrupling of oil prices after October 1973 increased the overall price level by 2 percent, and that resulting price increases for domestically produced energy had effects of almost the same magnitude. Using an aggregate model of the U.S. economy, Mork and Hall find that the first oil shock led to an increase in the U.S. price level, in 1974 and 1975, of about 6 percent; five other models also find price effects, although estimates of magnitude vary widely. The 1979–80 oil price increases were smaller in percentage terms—crude oil prices rose by about 170 percent between 1978 and the beginning of 1981—but larger in current dollars than those of 1973–74. The OECD estimated in 1979 that the direct effects on its members' price levels of the 1979–80 oil shock would reach almost 2 percent by the end of 1980, and that the total effect, including indirect impact, would be on the order of 3 percent.[27]

These estimates, of course, beg the question of how monetary policy would react to increased oil prices. Monetarists would expect that if the long-term growth rate of monetary aggregates were not affected, the inflation rate would return to the level determined by this rate of monetary growth. And if the oil shock should prompt decisions to reduce monetary growth, its ultimate effect on prices could even be deflationary. Indeed, after the initial shock of the 1979–80 oil price increases, effects on output were more severe than effects on prices, since the major countries imposed tight monetary policies to prevent runaway inflation. The International Energy Agency estimates the combined loss of output at about 5 percent of gross domestic product (GDP) in 1980 and nearly 8 percent in 1981

27. See McCracken Report, p. 67; Knut Anton Mork and Robert E. Hall, "Energy Prices, Inflation and Recession, 1974–1975," Working Paper 369 (Cambridge, Mass.: National Bureau of Economic Research, 1979); OECD, International Energy Agency (IEA), *World Energy Outlook* (Paris: OECD, 1982), p. 64; *OECD Economic Outlook*, no. 26 (December 1979), pp. 41–45. Barry P. Bosworth and Robert Z. Lawrence, *Commodity Prices and the New Inflation* (Brookings Institution, 1982), p. 45, estimate that 80 percent of the acceleration of general inflation between 1970 and 1974 was accounted for by increases in commodity prices, particularly those of grains and oil.

for a total of over one trillion current dollars.[28] But regardless of long-run effects, which depend heavily on monetary policy, oil price increases have clear effects on the price level in the short run. Thus the collapse of the old oil regime helps to account for the double-peaked pattern of 1970s inflation.

Shifts in Power, Regime Change, and Inflation

Clearly, the collapses of the postwar international regimes for money and oil were associated with the increased rates of world inflation experienced in the 1970s. But it is not so clear that regime change played a genuinely causal role. Inflation could have had deeper political sources, of which the transformations of international regimes were merely reflections, or symptoms. From the standpoint of Realist international relations theory, indeed, it would be expected that shifts in regimes as significant as those of the early 1970s had their roots in fundamental changes in the distribution of world power. Furthermore, since the regimes that collapsed were regimes that the United States had established, a plausible hypothesis would be that their demise was produced by a decline of American power. The Realist perspective thus leads to the question of whether there is a causal link between the erosion of American hegemony and inflation, mediated by the decline of old international regimes.

Since *power* is such an ambiguous word, it is necessary at the outset to specify what is meant by it, and to indicate the sort of power analysis being assessed. Essentially, the conception is that "power resources," which some actors possess, can be used to induce others to do what they would otherwise not do because of what they perceive as the contingent actions of the powerholders. Thus an analysis of the 1970s inflation that focuses on the "decline of American power" rests on the assertion that policies of at least some governments were affected, directly or indirectly, by power relationships in which both they and the United States were involved, and that, on balance, reduction of the constraints imposed by these relationships contributed to inflation.[29]

28. IEA, *World Energy Outlook*, p. 64.

29. See Keohane, *After Hegemony*, chaps. 2, 3. I reached a more positive judgment on the utility of power models for the explanation of world inflation in an earlier version of this chapter; see Robert O. Keohane, "Inflation and the Decline of American Power," in Lombra and Witte, *Political Economy*, pp. 7–24.

Changes in the Oil Regime and the Decline of American Power

Until the late 1960s, a surplus in the balance between U.S. capacity to produce oil and American consumption gave the United States the ability to affect the price of oil, as well as to provide oil supplies to its allies in supply disruptions such as took place in 1956–57. In 1967, after the June War, Saudi Arabia threatened an oil embargo against the West, but found that its warnings were disregarded by the United States and its allies. The excess domestic oil production capacity of the United States was greater than the volume of its imports, so on a net basis the United States was more than self-sufficient in petroleum. Before each crisis, production capacity comparable to about 25 percent of U.S. consumption was not being used, while in 1956–57 the United States imported only 11 percent of its consumption and in 1967 only 19 percent. By 1973, however, U.S. excess capacity was down to 10 percent of its oil consumption, but imports amounted to over 35 percent, a substantial proportion of which came from the Middle East. Thus the United States had a net deficit equal to about 25 percent of consumption. Furthermore, between 1956 and 1973 proved reserves of domestic oil grew only slowly in absolute terms and fell in relative terms from 18.2 percent to 6.4 percent of total world reserves.[30] In the earlier crises the United States could (from the perspective of the oil-consuming countries) be "part of the solution"; by 1973, it was "part of the problem." Its fundamental petroleum resource base had been greatly weakened.

During the same period, U.S. political and military dominance in the Middle East had also eroded, under the dual challenges of Arab nationalism and increased Soviet involvement. In the 1950s the United States, along with Britain, had a virtual monopoly of great power influence in the area. The United States had been able in 1953 to engineer the overthrow of a nationalistic Iranian premier and to reinstall the shah on his throne. American and British influence was predominant in Baghdad, Cairo, and Damascus. In 1973, although the shah was still in power, he had become more assertive; and Iraq, Egypt, and Syria were all closely linked to the Soviet Union.

Other developments also strengthened the hands of the oil producers. Large increases in demand for petroleum during the early 1970s tightened

---

30. Keohane, *After Hegemony,* chap. 8; Joel Darmstadter and Hans H. Landsberg, "The Economic Background," *Daedalus,* Special Issue, vol. 104 (Fall 1975), pp. 30–32.

the oil market, putting producers in a better position. Furthermore, the relationships between producing country governments and the oil companies had changed. In the 1950s, a small number of multinational oil firms, mostly based in the United States, had controlled oil production worldwide. These firms had complex cooperative arrangements with each other and collectively dominated relations with the governments of oil-exporting countries, particularly in the Middle East. They possessed greater financial resources, more technological knowledge, and greater sophistication about the complexities of the industry than the host governments; furthermore, in extreme situations they could call on the economic or even the military power of the United States and Britain. The interests of U.S. corporate and governmental officials were usually complementary—"both were interested in seeing plentiful and secure supplies of oil flowing within the non-communist world and both preferred to deal with stable, pro-Western governments."[31]

As the structure of power in petroleum changed, so did the interests and inclinations of the companies. Aramco, for instance, was highly responsive to the demands made on it by Saudi Arabia during the 1973–74 embargo. Even before the embargo, Morris Adelman had described the companies as "tax-collecting agents" of OPEC; Anthony Sampson later asserted that they were "closer in their interests to the producing countries than to the Western consumers"; and Louis Turner declared in 1978 that "there now is a community of interests between companies and host producer governments which did not exist before the 1970s," although he warned against exaggerating this harmony.[32] For the United States and its allies, weakness bred weakness; the shift in companies' interests itself contributed to an erosion of the Western governments' positions.

The decline in American power resources was a necessary condition for the drastic nature of oil price increases. Without this erosion of U.S. strength, the Yom Kippur War and the Iranian revolution could not have led to such vast shifts in relative prices. Admittedly, the United States was not skillful in its bargaining with OPEC states, or in coordinating with its own allies, at the Teheran meetings in February 1971.[33] The

31. Turner, *Oil Companies,* p. 109.

32. Ibid., p. 139, quoting testimony of Anthony Sampson before the U.S. Senate Antitrust Committee, and p. 147. M. A. Adelman, "Is the Oil Shortage Real? Oil Companies as OPEC Tax Collectors," *Foreign Policy,* no. 9 (Winter 1972–73), p. 69.

33. G. Henry M. Schuler, "The International Oil Negotiations," in I. William Zartman, *The 50% Solution* (Anchor Books, 1976); *Multinational Corporations and United States Foreign Policy,* Hearings

subsequent decline in the value of the dollar, in which the prices agreed on at Teheran were denominated, gave oil-producing governments an additional incentive to renegotiate the Teheran Agreement, since dollar devaluation reduced the real value of their earnings and sharply reduced their share of overall profits.[34] And the Yom Kippur War made Arab members of OPEC more willing to assume the risks of an embargo. Nevertheless, had these events taken place in the context of American strength, their impact would have been much less important. After all, OPEC was only a pale shadow of a true cartel; it was weakly institutionalized and until 1982 had no agreed-upon scheme for prorationing production cutbacks. The oil crisis was not forced on the West by external forces or historical accidents. On the contrary, it was largely the result of changes in international political structure, to which American policy failures contributed.

Yet the shift in power was not a complete reversal; it did not make Saudi Arabia, or OPEC collectively, into a hegemonic power. The oil market imposed constraints on producer ability to set prices, or to establish rules to which the major company or consumer governments had to conform. This became evident in 1982–83, when oil prices fell by about 15 percent in response to an oil glut brought about by the combination of increased non-OPEC production and decreased demand, resulting both from the direct effects of oil price increases and the impact of the world depression. The continued escalation of inflation, which many people during the 1970s had feared, was limited by the restricted power of the producers and their would-be cartel.

Changes in U.S. Power and the Collapse of Bretton Woods

A bold and sweeping Realist argument could hold that the dramatic changes in the rules of the international monetary regime that took place in 1971, like the changes in the oil regime, can be explained by a decline in American power. But this contention would be at best misleading. In 1971 the United States was still by far the most important of the advanced capitalist countries. It had a vastly larger economy than any of its partners. It had much greater political and military resources than its allies. And it was ultimately able to use this power to change the rules of the international

---

before the Subcommittee on Multinational Corporations of the Senate Committee on Foreign Relations, 93 Cong. 2 sess. (U.S. Government Printing Office, 1974), pt. 5.

34. Edith Penrose, "The Development of Crisis," *Daedalus*, vol. 104 (Fall 1975), pp. 39–57.

monetary game to its advantage.[35] By 1981 the United States had managed to regain greater autonomy of policy under flexible exchange rates, without sacrificing the central role of the dollar in the system or the value of the dollar relative to other currencies. By 1983 the dollar's effective exchange rate was higher than it had been before the fateful year 1971 began. The dollar also retained its position as the major world currency for lending and settlement of transactions.

Despite its great sources of long-run, underlying strength, however, by 1971 the United States faced problems of influence in the international monetary regime. It was no longer easy or convenient for the American government (given the fiscal and monetary policies that it sought to pursue) to maintain the value of the dollar in terms either of gold or of major foreign currencies. Confidence in the dollar, which had been extraordinarily high earlier, was eroding as the result of highly publicized balance-of-payments deficits, whether measured in terms of gross liquidity or the "basic balance."[36] The situation had temporarily improved from the American standpoint in 1968, when the requirement that the United States redeem gold held by private citizens had been formally deleted and an implicit understanding apparently reached among central banks that gold redemptions would henceforward be minimal. Europeans recognized "that to press for large conversions would provoke dispute and possibly the end of convertibility."[37] Nevertheless, even though the American current account had been in surplus each year between 1960 and 1967, and was in surplus again in the recession year of 1970, the underlying trends showed deterioration.

If the United States had continued to uphold the Bretton Woods regime, it would have had to sacrifice some of the autonomy that it cherished. To maintain the value of the dollar, it would have had to adopt policies in which holders of dollars would have confidence. Otherwise, large shifts of funds into other currencies would take place, risking a disorderly collapse of exchange rate parities. This meant that as long as the United States was committed to maintaining the Bretton Woods regime, it would be susceptible to pressure by foreign governments and central banks, as well as private investors, holding large amounts of the American currency. From a political point of view, by the late 1960s, the

---

35. See Susan Strange, "Still an Extraordinary Power: America's Role in a Global Monetary System," in Lombra and Witte, *Political Economy*, pp. 73–93.

36. Block, *Origins of International Economic Disorder*.

37. Odell, *U.S. International Monetary Policy*, pp. 199–208, 177.

Bretton Woods regime had become a liability for the United States. As Robert Solomon expressed it, speaking as a former American official, "the growing economic and political strength of Europe and Japan made the Bretton Woods system obsolete."[38]

Thus the United States, precisely because it remained strong in underlying power resources, had compelling political incentives to force major changes in the rules. Only by breaking the rules could the United States maintain the freedom of action that it demanded. The breakdown of the Bretton Woods regime was not, therefore, a simple result of a decline in American power. It was, however, affected by the dual power position of the United States—the discrepancy between the sensitivity of the United States to the pressures of others within the regime and its stronger underlying position.

Conclusion: American Power, Policy, and Inflation

The collapse of the international regimes for oil and money in the early 1970s contributed to inflation by creating uncertainty and reducing incentives for noninflationary behavior by governments. In oil, the collapse of the regime was closely linked to a decline in American power; but in the monetary area, this was not the case. The collapse of both regimes, and the decline in American oil power, can be traced in considerable measure to American policy.

The erosion of American oil resources was largely a result of previous American actions. During the 1950s and 1960s U.S. oil policy was one of "draining America first," through the use first of voluntary restrictions, then mandatory oil import quotas. This policy, sought by domestic oil and coal interests, was followed despite the prescient forebodings of State Department officials, who had tried in 1945 to use a proposed Anglo-American oil agreement to increase imports of eastern hemisphere petroleum, thus reducing in relative terms the rate of exploitation in the new world.[39]

38. *The International Monetary System, 1945–1976: An Insider's View* (Harper and Row, 1977), p. 212.

39. Internal memorandum of John A. Loftus, acting chief, Oil Division, U.S. State Department, May 31, 1945 (National Archives of the United States, decimal file 1945–1949, box 5849, file 841.6363/5-3145). Loftus acknowledged that increasing eastern hemisphere production relative to that in the western hemisphere "is an objective which probably cannot be stated in precise or quantitative terms without provoking acute internal political controversy here." Loftus and other State Department officials went to great pains to conceal that this was a principal purpose of the proposed Anglo-American oil agreement, which later died in the U.S. Senate. See Keohane, *After Hegemony*, chap. 8.

Erratic American monetary policy was also costly for another valuable, but in this case intangible, political resource—the confidence of other governments in U.S. policy. Although the U.S. current account was almost exactly balanced for the decade as a whole, the pattern varied greatly from year to year. In the two years before each sharp rise in oil prices (1971–72 and 1977–78), the United States ran deficits of over $7 billion and $27 billion, respectively.[40] These were periods during which American fiscal and monetary policies lost the confidence of dollar-holders abroad as well as at home. Willingness to rely on the United States was reduced and respect for American policy declined. During the 1950s the United States had invested in power resources—building its alliances and supporting international organizations. The United States had acquired great prestige in the process, at the expense of some tangible costs. During the Johnson administration and in the two inflationary episodes of the 1970s, under Presidents Nixon and Carter, the pattern was reversed; the United States sought to avoid having to bear the costs of change, at the expense of its long-term economic and political position.

United States policy failures thus bear a substantial share of the blame for world inflation. American policies increased inflation directly by increasing U.S. monetary growth and encouraging American consumption of oil, and they did so indirectly, at least in oil, by weakening the ability of the United States to prevent or combat inflationary actions by others. The gradual decline of relative American economic resources as a result of European and Japanese growth might well have made it more difficult to maintain a stable world monetary system in any event. But farsighted U.S. policies would surely have made the problem less severe and more manageable. The decontrol of oil prices in the Carter and Reagan administrations, and the move toward tight monetary policy, begun in the last third of the Carter administration, helped to correct the inflationary excesses of previous years, although the consequences for production, employment, and the world financial system were severe.

The International Tug-of-War

Albert O. Hirschman argues in chapter 3 that inflation often results from a tug-of-war among actors who can determine the prices for their

40. OECD, *Main Economic Indicators: Historical Statistics, 1960–1979* (Paris: OECD, 1980), p. 86; Bank for International Settlements, *Fifty-Second Annual Report, 1st April 1981–31st March 1982* (Basel: BIS, 1982), p. 93.

own products more effectively than they can influence the prices they pay for the products of others. Each actor would prefer stable prices, provided that he could assure himself of his desired share of the social product under such conditions; but since he has insufficient means to accomplish this, he seeks to demand more (in nominal terms) in the hope of gaining, or at least not losing, in real terms. In this model, inflation is explained in terms of social conflict between groups each aspiring to a greater share of the social product, and by the absence of an effective government that can authoritatively allocate shares of that social product.

This tug-of-war model seems applicable to international economic relations, which take place without the benefit of effective, overarching governmental rules and enforcement procedures. Indeed, as a dominant power declines in strength, more frequent and more consequential tugs-of-war between it and others seem likely. It is therefore worthwhile to use Hirschman's tug-of-war metaphor as an interpretive device to help understand worldwide inflation. The emphasis of this account, which is meant to be suggestive and even speculative, is on patterns of interaction between OPEC and the major oil-consuming countries.

Hirschman argues that "the bigger its preference for present over future income, the more will a group be prone to engage in inflationary actions." Such groups must, however, be willing to take risks. The "high price hawks" of OPEC—such as Algeria, Iran, Iraq, Libya, and Venezuela—were not poor (which might have led them to be risk-averse), but their ambitions, relatively small oil reserves, and ability to rely on Saudi Arabia disproportionately to absorb production cutbacks gave them a preference for present over future income. They sought quick development and engaged in inflationary behavior, as Hirschman's proposition suggests that they should.

Even more suggestive for an interpretation of the OPEC-IEA relationship is Hirschman's view that "inflation is a means of effectuating a temporary transfer. Partial, complete, or even overcomplete cancellation of that transfer can take place, first of all, through subsequent turns in the inflationary spiral, especially when other groups use their retaliatory power and do some grabbing (or escaping) of their own."

Clearly the oil price rises of 1973–74 and 1979 effected a transfer to the OPEC countries. More interestingly, the 1973–74 price rise created incentives for the advanced industrialized countries, particularly the United States, not to take decisive action against inflation, since a decline in the value of the dollar allowed them, in Hirschman's words, "to do some grabbing (or escaping) of their own." The OPEC countries were unwilling to reduce the nominal price of oil, but the real price of oil could be reduced both by increases in the prices of goods sold to OPEC countries and by declines in the value of the dollar, in which oil prices are denominated. American policy during 1977–78 was in a sense the converse of OPEC's policy during 1973–74. The oil producers had increased the price of oil by supplying less of it than would have been desired at the previous price. The United States reduced the price of the currency that it "produced" (dollars) by supplying more of it. In both cases the results were inflationary.

It seems unlikely that U.S. policymakers deliberately stimulated inflation in order to reduce the real price of oil. Nevertheless, the reduction of real oil prices produced by inflation and dollar depreciation provided incentives to Western governments, and particularly to the United States, not to deal too severely with inflation, especially when policymakers' own preferences, as in 1977, emphasized growth over control of inflation. As long as Saudi Arabia was willing to tolerate declines in the real price of oil as a result of dollar depreciation, and as long as the American government was willing to tolerate a relatively rapid fall in the real value of the dollar, inflation functioned as a device that helped to avoid overt conflict over the level of oil prices.

Yet no good thing can last forever—even inflation. By 1978 a number of constituencies that had tolerated inflation as preferable to other alternatives were becoming restless. This was certainly true in the United States, but it was notably the case for two sets of foreign actors as well. By early 1978 the Saudis were apparently becoming concerned about continued dollar depreciation. King Khalid reportedly wrote to President Carter stating that Saudi Arabia might not be willing to resist efforts within OPEC to raise the dollar price of oil if the dollar continued to depreciate.[41] Since the United States required implicit Saudi cooperation to reduce real oil prices through inflation, King Khalid's dismay about the decline of the dollar threatened the continued validity of an inflationary strategy.[42]

As the Saudis became nervous about American policy, so did the Europeans and Japanese. By late 1977 the German government in particular had become openly critical of American policy. West Germany's

41. "The Dollar: Export or Appreciate," *Economist* (London) (April 1, 1978), pp. 24–26; *New York Times,* January 5, 1978.

42. Robert E. Hall suggested several of the points made in the preceding three paragraphs.

chief delegate to an OECD meeting in November said that the American "locomotive theory," by which the major economies were to pull the others out of recession, was "naive." Chancellor Schmidt warned that prosperity could not be restored by printing money but required thrift and hard work. Although the Japanese were characteristically more reticent in their public comments, they also resisted American pressure.[43] This pressure from abroad may have contributed to an emerging U.S. resolve to tighten monetary policy, although it is unlikely, in view of American displays of autonomy before and after, to have been decisive by itself. At any rate, the Federal Reserve Board took restrictive measures in the fall of 1978 and embarked on decisive action in the fall of 1979, after the second oil shock. Unlike the oil tug-of-war, the monetary disputes among the advanced industrialized countries did not lead to increased rates of price increase, but eventually may have reinforced American determination to do something about inflation.

The Aftermath of Inflation

Although inflation is often painful, it also has advantages, which become most evident when the rate of price increase falls sharply. International inflation, when accompanied by the depreciation of the dollar in 1977–78, cushioned the effects of the post-1973 oil price increases for European economies. Conversely, when the dollar appreciated in 1981–82, oil prices in many European currencies rose although dollar-denominated prices of oil were stable or even fell somewhat. Perhaps more important for the world financial system, inflation in its early years reduced the real cost to the less developed countries of servicing their debt to foreign bondholders and banks. By contrast, the tight monetary policies used to bring inflation down led to sharply increased debt service costs during a period of economic recession in the markets of the advanced industrial countries and helped to precipitate the series of debt crises and renegotiations that began in the summer of 1982.

The effects of the first few years of rapid inflation on real interest rates clearly benefited the less developed countries. According to Peter B.

---

43. Robert O. Keohane, "U.S. Foreign Economic Policy toward Other Advanced Capitalist States: The Struggle to Make Others Adjust," in Kenneth A. Oye, Donald Rothchild, and Robert J. Lieber, eds., *Eagle Entangled: U.S. Foreign Policy in a Complex World* (Longman, 1979), p. 104. For a thorough recent account, see Robert D. Putnam and Nicholas Bayne, *Hanging Together: The Seven-Power Summits* (Harvard University Press, 1984).

Kenen's calculations, interest rates on total disbursed debt as of 1973 were about 5.44 percent for higher-income less developed countries, 4.18 percent for middle-income countries, and 2.55 percent for countries at the low end of the income scale.[44] For the decade before 1973 these nominal interest rates would have led to real interest rates of about 3–4 percent for most non-oil-producing less developed countries, since the prices of their exports were increasing at only about 1.5 percent per year. But between 1972 and 1976 their export prices increased at an average annual rate of 17 percent.[45] Since most loans at that time were at fixed interest rates, long-term loans outstanding in 1972 carried substantial *negative* real interest rates through the end of 1976. The borrowing process therefore involved large real income transfers from the industrialized countries to less developed countries.

Unfortunately for the less developed countries and other borrowers, lenders eventually adjusted their expectations to ongoing inflation. Real interest rates on bonds, which were negative in 1975, subsequently turned positive, although they briefly became negative again in 1980 before rising sharply in 1981.[46] By 1982, real long-term interest rates in the United States had risen to almost 5 percent per annum, more than twice the level of the 1960s. Nominal interest rates for the OECD countries as a whole peaked at 13 percent in 1981. Since by this time loans were generally offered with variable rather than fixed interest rates, the impact on the less developed countries was immediate and severe. In Argentina, Brazil, Chile, and Mexico, interest payments on external debt alone ranged in 1982 between 35 percent and 45 percent of projected exports of goods and services. For a number of countries, debt service payments (interest payments plus *all* debt falling due) for 1982 exceeded their projected exports of goods and services.[47]

For the less developed countries, inflation early in the decade was the "invisible hand" that provided them with large resources at low or negative real interest rates. When inflation in the advanced industrialized countries

44. "Debt Relief as Development Assistance," in Jagdish N. Bhagwati, ed., *The New International Economic Order: The North-South Debate* (MIT Press, 1977), p. 77. The differences in rates are accounted for largely by the greater proportion of bank credits (at an interest rate of about 7.75 percent) in the debt structures of higher- and, to some extent, middle-income countries.

45. International Monetary Fund, *Annual Report, 1977,* p. 9.

46. BIS, *Fifty-Second Annual Report,* p. 64.

47. *OECD Economic Outlook,* no. 33 (July 1983), p. 32; Morgan Guaranty Trust Company, *World Financial Markets* (October 1982), p. 5.

was countered by tight monetary policies, however, the resulting high real interest rates thrust large adjustment costs onto the borrowers, and even threatened their ability to service their debt. Perhaps the ease of borrowing, and the low real cost, characteristic of the 1970s led them further into the "debt trap."[48] By the middle of 1982, the abrupt slowdown in the rate of inflation, combined with policies in the United States and elsewhere that brought on recession, had made the debt trap deeper and had threatened to push the banks, as well as the borrowers, into it. For many less developed countries and banks, disinflation was more painful than inflation.

Conclusion

American macroeconomic policies and the resulting balance-of-payments deficits accelerated world inflation under the accommodative Bretton Woods regime. In the early 1970s the contradiction between the desire of the Nixon administration to pursue inflationary monetary policies and the traditional value of the dollar led to the collapse of fixed exchange rates. In addition, the effects of American oil policies during the 1950s and 1960s undermined the ability of the United States to maintain the old oil regime when it came under pressure in the early 1970s.

Yet changes in international regimes also made a difference. International regimes establish expectations and help to facilitate the flow of information among governments.[49] When they change suddenly, the resulting uncertainty can aggravate the effects of some governments' proinflationary policies. After all, it was not only the United States that pursued lax monetary policies in 1972; and it was not the members of OPEC that aggravated price increases in 1973–74 and 1979 by bidding against one another for scarce oil.

Thus the inflation of the 1970s holds lessons both for American policy and for international regimes. International macroeconomic stability requires more willingness to adjust to adverse changes in international economic conditions than has often been evident on the part of the

48. Cheryl Payer, *The Debt Trap: The IMF and the Third World* (New York: Monthly Review Press, 1974); Jeff Frieden, "Third World Indebted Industrialization: International Finance and State Capitalism in Mexico, Brazil, Algeria, and South Korea," *International Organization*, vol. 35 (Summer 1981), pp. 407–31.

49. Keohane, *After Hegemony*, chaps. 4–7.

United States.[50] Forcing the costs of adjustment onto others may make political sense in the short run, but it entails adverse economic consequences later on. Yet for a big country like the United States, willingness to adjust probably depends on successful domestic macroeconomic policies, since economic failure seems to concentrate the minds of American leaders on how to impose some of the consequences of their mistakes on others. For the world economy to be stabilized during the last fifteen years of this century, the United States will have to become a source of stability again, rather than of disruption.

The inflation of the 1970s should also remind us of the value of well-functioning international regimes. Commentators often take international principles and rules for granted, and even complain about their weakness or failure to meet economists' high analytical standards. But in evaluating international regimes, we should always consider the alternatives. If international economic regimes did not already exist, they would have to be invented.

50. For a discussion of the need for coordination, see Gilles Oudiz and Jeffrey Sachs, "Macroeconomic Policy Coordination among the Industrial Economies," *BPEA, 1:1984,* pp. 1–64. See also Bryant, *Money and Monetary Policy,* chap. 25.

5

Conditions for Trade Union
Wage Restraint

Colin Crouch

Some schools of thought attribute inflation to government's maintenance of over-full employment, in response to public pressure for high employment and for a combination of high public spending and low taxation which is itself inflationary. At first sight this excludes organized labor as a cause. But labor is an important element in articulating that public pressure and may therefore be said to "cause" inflation, even if its wages pressure can have no more than a once-and-for-all effect. Inflation of this kind may be regarded as a form of class compromise. Labor has gained enough power to secure high levels of employment and public spending, the former strengthening its bargaining position with capital. But it is not able to replace capital in any way, and capital will therefore seek to retain its position in the distributive struggle. Assuming continuation of the balance of political forces that led to the original government stance on spending, taxation, and employment, the resulting strain will be borne by the price level.[1]

But a high level of inflation may lead to demands for a revision of priorities. It will certainly lead to a deterioration in the country's payments balance, pressure on its exchange rate, and possibly international indebtedness; and there will be powerful pressure on the government to deflate the economy. Thus the consequences of inflation will be a reverse for the labor movement, entailing a reduction in its political and economic

---

1. Brian Burkitt, *Trade Unions and Wages: Implications for Economic Theory* (Bradford, U. K.: Bradford University Press, 1975), remarks that the union movement has been able "to secure sufficient power to disturb the smooth operation of the capitalist system while possessing insufficient strength to achieve fundamental changes in its social ethos and power structure."

strength—that being dependent in good measure on the level of demand for labor. (For these reasons it may be rational for unions to restrain their members' pay demands—to cooperate in what Whitehead refers to as "shifting the Phillips curve back again." He has suggested that "a particular type of political initiative—one for example that systematically offended ordinary British mineworkers and provoked them to strike, could shift the Phillips curve outwards. . . . An opposite type of political management might flatter or coax miners into moderating their wage claims and to that extent might somewhat shift the Phillips curve inwards."[2])

These arguments assume that prices (and, by derivation, wages) are highly responsive to demand. But in major areas of employment today that is doubtful. An alternative approach holds that in the major industrial nations, units of capital have grown and amalgamated to produce an economy comprising a small number of oligopolistic producers and enormous barriers to new entrants (in terms of technology and minimum viable size).[3] This is not to say that there is no competition in such sectors; even where there is no competition in the strict sense, there is some restraint on prices in that all goods and services to some extent compete with each other. But these oligopolistic firms are not subordinated to the market in the same way as those in perfect competition; they have some capacity for strategy, for planning prices and output, and of course for collusion even if of a tacit kind. In their price behavior these firms have some degree of autonomy from overall levels of demand, and thus some scope for discretionary decisionmaking. They "can avoid a price fall by reducing their output; they can also avoid a price rise when demand increases."[4] In most countries, there is a similar autonomy from demand levels in the public sector.[5]

It is within the oligopolies and in the public sector that unionization in most countries is strongest; and in these sectors unions are able to bid up wages, not entirely independently of the overall level of employment but with considerably less dependence than in a perfectly competitive system. Within the oligopolies, unions have thus been able to preempt

2. Lawrence Whitehead, "The Politics of Inflation," paper presented at Nuffield College, Oxford University, 1977.

3. Organization for Economic Cooperation and Development, *Socially Responsible Wage Policies and Inflation* (Paris: OECD, 1975), p. 58.

4. P. Sylos-Labini, "Competition: The Product Markets," in Thomas A. Wilson and Andrew S. Skinner, eds., *The Market and the State: Essays in Honour of Adam Smith* (Oxford University Press, 1976), p. 227.

5. With the notable exception of France, where the state's role as an employer has declined, though from exceptionally high levels; see Pierre Dubois, *Mort de l'etat-patron* (Paris: Editions Ouvrières, 1974).

for labor at least some of the fruits of market power produced by the concentration of industry, leading to either a profits squeeze or, as prices finally rise, inflation—probably a combination of both.

At first sight, therefore, it would appear that the kind of labor movement most conducive to low levels of inflation is one so weak that it cannot affect anything. However, it is the thesis of this chapter that once a union movement represents enough of the work force to have macroeconomic effects, its contribution to restraining or exacerbating inflation will depend on the extent to which it is capable of centralized strategic action in relation to the economy as a whole. To test this thesis, this chapter examines the macroeconomic impact of the labor movement in the late 1960s and the 1970s.

Inflation and Organized Economic Interests

Social interests that are organized on a small, localized scale receive in full any gain from distortions they produce in market processes but bear only a minute proportion of the general cost; indeed, they share in the general cost of other similar actions, even if they fail to participate. Their only rational course is therefore to try to be sure of their own possibilities for gain through disruption. The position of an interest organized at a national or near-national level will be completely different, as it will experience directly the negative effects of its disruptions—it can therefore be expected to take these effects into account.

A similar argument has been developed by Olson to account for variations in national economic growth rates. His general thesis rests on the assumption that common-interest organizations, of which trade unions are an important example, will use their strength to inhibit changes hostile to their interests. However, he also points out that this will be less true to the extent that the organizations concerned are large in scope and small in number. "The incentives facing an encompassing special-interest organization are dramatically different from those facing an organization that represents only a narrow segment of society. . . . The members of the highly encompassing organization own so much of the society that they have an important incentive to be actively concerned about how productive it is; they are in the same position as a partner in a firm that has only a few partners."[6]

6. Mancur Olson, *The Rise and Decline of Nations: Economic Growth, Stagflation and Social Rigidities* (Yale University Press, 1982), p. 48.

For Olson, the above pattern is a distinct second-best solution, as he sees various ways in which encompassing organizations of this kind will embody rigidities of decisionmaking.[7] His preferred solution, certainly the one for which his book has rapidly become widely noted, seems to be a reduction in the capacity of economic interests to organize at all. However, this may be either impossible or achievable only at the expense of unacceptable costs.[8]

There is an important paradox here. Once economic interests have become organized, they will be less likely to behave in ways consistent with allocative efficiency the greater the extent to which their form of organization retains characteristics of liberal political economy. The reasons for this are as follows. The liberal political economy achieves order through the existence of a mass of atomized actors, each of which plays too small an individual part for its own autonomous decisions to have a general effect; they are forced to act in response to the laws of supply and demand. In other words, these actors do not take action with regard to any perception of a general interest; the market *impersonally imposes* on them conformity with a general interest.[9] Further, as economic actors they are confined to acting within the sphere of economic relations, producing and exchanging goods and services in order to realize a goal of profit-maximization. They have no concern for general political questions, and no sense of group or common interests; they are apolitical and amoral. If these interests then become organized to the point where they can continue to pursue maximization by wielding power to distort market forces, while otherwise remaining within a framework of competing, disaggregated, apolitical units, they acquire the characteristics of specific-interest associations which, in Olson's account, are conducive to inefficiency. If they move to his model of common-interest associations, which can take general interests into account, they do so by dropping further characteristics of liberal political economy—they become centralized, aggregated, and politicized.[10]

7. Ibid., p. 52.

8. Colin Crouch, "New Thinking on Pluralism," *Political Quarterly*, vol. 54 (October–December 1983), pp. 363–74.

9. It must of course be recognized that the only general interests that the market is able to register are those capable of being embodied in commodity form.

10. See Colin Crouch, "Inflation and the Political Organization of Economic Interests," in Fred Hirsch and John H. Goldthorpe, eds., *The Political Economy of Inflation* (Harvard University Press, 1978), pp. 217–39; Alessandro Pizzorno, "Political Exchange and Collective Identity in Industrial Conflict," in Colin Crouch and Alessandro Pizzorno, eds., *The Resurgence of Class Conflict in Western Europe since 1968*, vol. 2: *Comparative Analyses* (Holmes & Meier, 1978), pp. 277–98.

These arguments bear an interesting relation to theses of the institutionalization of conflict that were developed in the 1950s and early 1960s to describe the apparent pacification in the postwar Western world of the class conflicts that had seemed characteristic of capitalist societies.[11] These theses, like the account of a society of organized interests, recognize that, in modern industrial societies, economic and social relations are conducted through organizations that cannot be reduced to market interactions. On the other hand, they assert that a society will be stable if its inevitable conflicts, while organized, avoid central coordination. The core of institutionalization theory, like liberal economic theory, is that conflicting interests are less likely to cause major social disruption if they are disaggregated, split into several insulated parts. There is also a particular stress on the importance of industrial conflicts being separated from political ones. These arguments conflict with the thesis presented here.

Institutionalization ideas were developed against the background of the interwar years, when centralized, highly political economic-interest organizations had battled their way through enormous conflicts which often involved bloodshed and which led, in significant cases, to fascist dictatorship. Clearly, the centralization of interest organizations by itself does not guarantee conduct consistent with economic, or even basic social, stability. Several writers studying this question have considered the importance of a political variable and claim that union movements are likely to moderate their behavior if the government in office is favorable to their interests. As long ago as 1960 Ross and Hartman saw lengthy Social Democratic tenure of office as one of the reasons for the extremely low levels of industrial conflict characteristic of Scandinavian countries.[12] Hibbs has observed an inverse relation between the level of nonmilitary public expenditure and the volume of strike activity, the former variable being itself very closely related to tenure of office by labor-movement political parties.[13] He argues that in countries with high levels of public spending the locus of distributional struggles shifts to the polity; workers, less dependent on employment income for their standard of living because

---

11. See Ralf Dahrendorf, *Class and Class Conflict in Industrial Society* (Stanford University Press, 1959); Arthur Kornhauser, Robert Dubin, and Arthur M. Ross, eds., *Industrial Conflict* (McGraw-Hill, 1954); Richard A. Lester, *As Unions Mature: An Analysis of the Evolution of American Unionism* (Princeton University Press, 1958); Arthur M. Ross and Paul T. Hartman, *Changing Patterns of Industrial Conflict* (Wiley, 1960).

12. *Changing Patterns.*

13. Douglas A. Hibbs, Jr., "On the Political Economy of Long-Run Trends in Strike Activity," *British Journal of Political Science,* vol. 8 (April 1978), pp. 153–75.

of the high level of their "social wage," are less likely to bother to strike to secure wage increases. But this argument assumes a ceiling on workers' ambitions; why should they not take for granted a certain standard that is secured by state welfare, and then seek an even higher standard through wage rises? Hibbs's explanation may be more pertinent to once-and-for-all major *increases* in welfare-state measures, as in any one year these may be sufficient to satisfy all aspirations for improvements. The improvements, however, would need to be very large and to make a sizable impact on individual households' living costs, which of course is done by only certain kinds of welfare benefit. (It is, for example, unlikely that education spending or retirement pensions could have such an impact.)[14]

Headey has shown a connection between labor-movement party tenure of office and union willingness to cooperate in incomes policy.[15] Korpi and Shalev suggest that union leaders become committed to achieving their goals through cooperation with government and therefore have less need for strike action.[16]

The paradigms for all these arguments are in Scandinavia, especially Sweden. Until the Social Democratic and Labour party took a solid grasp on office in 1936, strike levels in Sweden were very high. They then began to fall steadily, to reach their almost nonexistent levels of the past few decades. But outside Scandinavia the only country largely to fit this model is Austria. The Federal Republic of Germany was characterized by low strike levels for several years before the Social Democratic party became the principal governing party in 1969. The Netherlands Labor party is a very important coalition partner in most Dutch governments, but it has never dominated an administration. The Belgian case is similar to the Dutch, though Belgian strike levels are higher. Switzerland, with the lowest strike levels of all, not only has a Social Democratic party that has to share office with equally permanent religious parties, but with its reliance on referenda it departs from the Western norm of parliamentary

14. Hibbs also argues (ibid., p. 171) that the high levels of direct taxation in countries with high levels of social spending discourage workers from seeking wage increases, as the return in real pay increases from a nominal rise is small. But the opposite conclusion is equally plausible—that is, that the higher the marginal rate of income taxation, the more fiercely will workers struggle to obtain a rise in real wages, a process for which, as Hibbs admits (pp. 172, 173), some evidence exists in the United Kingdom (see Frank Wilkinson and H. A. Turner, "The Wage-Tax Spiral and Labour Militancy," in Dudley Jackson, H. A. Turner, and Frank Wilkinson, *Do Trade Unions Cause Inflation?* [Cambridge University Press, 1972]).

15. Bruce W. Headey, "Trade Unions and National Wages Policies," *Journal of Politics,* vol. 32 (May 1970), pp. 407–39.

16. Walter Korpi and Michael Shalev, "Strikes, Industrial Relations and Class Conflict in Capitalist Societies," *British Journal of Sociology,* vol. 30 (June 1979), pp. 164–87.

government led by political parties. Taking public spending rather than labor-movement party tenure of office as the key variable helps account for Dutch exceptionalism but makes Switzerland even more of a problem.[17]

Consociation helps explain some of the exceptions. The nature of political opposition in a consociation is very different from that in an Anglo-Saxon two-party system. In consociation, a number of parties each commands an electorate, a major part of which is inaccessible to the others in electoral competition (through, for example, a religious definition of political allegiance). Further, no one party can reasonably expect to obtain an overall majority. Several parties that are not really in electoral competition with each other recognize that they must form coalitions to share in office. The pattern of coalitions can vary, as parties rise and fall in strength or suffer from internal divisions that make a spell in opposition advisable. One year's opponent may be next year's coalition partner. No party can look forward to successful long-term triumph over the others, and all must be willing to compromise with measures and attitudes favored by rivals.[18] Such a system of government may be said to have characterized Switzerland, the Netherlands, Belgium, Finland, and Austria for the first two decades after World War II.

Once labor has been admitted to the core of parties seen to make up the *ministrable* elements of a consociational political system, not only will its representatives cease to seek the overthrow of the capitalist system, but employers will also cease to entertain hopes of a nonunionized labor force. The two sides are forced to come to terms with each other on a permanent basis. This is of course part of the argument of the thesis of the institutionalization of conflict; what is being added is a political component that demonstrates to the two sides of industry the impossibility of final victory. There is, for example, little point in employers pursuing a strategy of deunionization if labor-movement parties are frequently included in governments.

The main burden in this process falls on employers. Revolutionary hopes of abolishing the employer class have played a very small part in the day-to-day activities of established trade-union movements, but the abolition of unions is a very real possibility and one employers have

17. The Netherlands has a level of public spending second only to that of Sweden. Switzerland, on the other hand, has the fourth lowest level of the countries being considered.

18. Gerhard Lehmbruch, "Consociational Democracy, Class Conflict and the New Corporatism," in Philippe C. Schmitter and Gerhard Lehmbruch, eds., *Trends toward Corporatist Intermediation* (Sage, 1980), pp. 53–61; Arend Lijphart, *Democracy in Plural Societies: A Comparative Exploration* (Yale University Press, 1977).

sometimes pursued with success. Seen in these terms, the effects of labor-movement party domination of government and of labor's admission to the consociational group may be very much the same. Both remove the "fight to the finish" from both labor and capital's political and industrial agenda. This argument helps account for the Swiss, Dutch, Austrian, and, to a certain extent, Belgian cases. It raises a new problem, however— Finland, which is consociational but exhibits a high level of conflict. The German case is partly explained; while West Germany does not have a consociational system, its federal system of government has virtually guaranteed that the Social Democratic party will dominate at least some state governments and therefore cannot be relegated to permanent opposition status. Furthermore, the unique system of codetermination through worker representation on supervisory boards and, more important, on powerful statutory works councils makes it difficult for German employers to pursue a strategy of eliminating worker representation.[19]

Perhaps most important of all is the fact that social democracy and consociationism both lead to an increasing engagement of unions (and employers' bodies) in the making and administration of policy, an arrangement that political scientists have labeled either corporatist or neocorporatist. This routine participation prevents excessive expectations being invested in individual "big deals." The sheer multiplicity of transactions reduces the risk involved in any one of them and makes it possible for concessions made on one issue to be offset against gains on another. As Lehmbruch has put it: "Corporatism will tend to be stable . . . to the degree that concessions made in one field . . . appear to yield a long-run pay-off in other domains."[20] Involvement in policy administration enables lower-level officials to perform important tasks within the framework of the centrally determined policies, reducing the need for them to find their raison d'être in rebellion.[21] This helps explain why sudden, politically highly charged incomes policy gambits in the 1970s often failed to produce long-term results.[22]

The admission of organized labor into political respectability has thus

19. This by no means implies that there is a consensus over codetermination.

20. Gerhard Lehmbruch, "Neokorporatismus in Westeuropa: Hauptprobleme in internationalen Vergleich," in Klaus Armingeon and others, "Neokorporistische Politik in Westeuropa" (Universität Konstanz, Diskussionsbeiträge nv I/1983). For an extensive demonstration of how this operates in the Austrian case, see Bernd Marin, *Die paritätische Kommission* (Vienna: Internationale Publikationen, 1982).

21. A major instance of this is the involvement of lower-level union officials in the administration of Swedish labor-market policy (Lehmbruch, "Neokorporatismus").

22. Armingeon and others, "Neokorporistische Politik."

inhibited the two sides of industry from pursuing the massive conflict that characterized centralized systems in earlier periods. It is important to note that this applies only to centralized systems. In decentralized cases there is far less scope for *either* massive political conflict *or* intensive political cooperation, and little or no scope for strategy. Even if union leaders would like to orient the actions of their unions toward central national political questions, there is little they can do about it.

If this argument is correct, the significance of labor-movement parties' participation in government is to push centralized economic interests into a cooperative rather than a combative logic; that participation does not itself directly determine that process. To a certain extent, generalization here is difficult because, so far, the admission of labor to governmental participation has been a once-and-for-all historical process. What would happen in such societies if labor were to leave office for a prolonged period? Would its gains of political acceptance survive? If labor were once again to be seen as an outsider, then a renewal of conflict could be expected. The extensive general strike in Sweden in 1980 may have been a warning that, if Swedish unions were pushed outside the political center following the loss of Social Democratic government, they would respond with centralized, strategic conflict.[23]

Disentangling the relation between organizational centralization and the strength of social democracy is difficult because their historical development was so interwoven. Labor-movement political strength has been greatest where a powerful and united union movement has mobilized the working-class electorate; in turn, powerful and united labor movements developed where employer interests were also heavily organized around a state that was taking a prominent part in industrial development because of the lateness of development or the small, open nature of the economy.[24] Indirectly and rather paradoxically, social democracy can be seen as a consequence rather than a cause of the relative weakness of market forces and the dominance of organizational and political forces in the economy.

Examining Labor's Role in a Market Economy

Within advanced capitalist democracies, two broad types of industrial relations systems can be identified—neocorporatist systems in which a

23. A similar point is made in Lehmbruch, "Neokorporatismus."
24. John D. Stephens, *The Transition from Capitalism to Socialism* (London: Macmillan, 1979), chap. 2.

centrally coordinated union movement has developed within a political context responsive to labor demands, and liberal systems in which the labor movement lacks any significant centralized coordination, irrespective of labor's political place. Ideally, liberal systems should be subdivided into a straightforward liberal grouping that covers countries (primarily Anglo-Saxon ones) in which the state has adopted a broadly liberal, noninterventionist approach toward organized labor, and a grouping based on labor exclusion that covers those (primarily in southern Europe) in which the state, while playing a fairly interventionist economic role, has rejected participation by labor's major representatives who, in these cases, are largely communist. However, the number of cases available for study and the inadequate nature of the data make it difficult to elaborate on these subtypes; the examination is thus unfortunately restricted to generalizations based on the two major types.

It is predicted that the organization of labor will lead to disruptions of the market economy, the extent of disruption depending on the level of organization, but that where labor's organizations are centrally coordinated and have achieved a secure level of acceptance within the polity, their disruptive activity will be considerably reduced. This thesis is examined against data comparing the eighteen major members of the Organization for Economic Cooperation and Development that have had extensive postwar liberal democracy experience.

The reliability and comparability of data on the eighteen countries are so uncertain, and the universe of advanced capitalist democracies so small, that the results of statistical tests can only be useful to suggest whether the theory deserves more sustained research. The data are used to estimate the strength of labor organizations, the extent of economic disruptions, and the degree of neocorporatism within the organized economic interests of each country.

Union membership figures for most countries are taken from statistical yearbooks or similar volumes; the sources and the coverage of the data vary from country to country.[25] These figures are then expressed as a

25. No regular national source of information is available in several countries. Information on Italy is from Salvatore Coi, "Sindacati in Italia: iscritti, apparato, finanziamento," *Il mulino,* vol. 28 (March–April 1979), pp. 201–42. On Austria, from Kurt Steiner, *Politics in Austria* (Little, Brown, 1972). On Belgium, from Anthony Carew, *Democracy and Government in European Trade Unions* (London: Allen and Unwin, 1976); Michel Molitor, "Social Conflicts in Belgium," in Crouch and Pizzorno, *Resurgence of Class Conflict,* vol 1: *National Studies,* pp. 21–51; Derek Torrington, *Comparative Industrial Relations in Europe* (Greenwood Press, 1978). On France, from Pierre Dubois, Claude Durand, and Sabine Erbès-Seguin, "The Contradictions of French Trade Unionism," in Crouch and Pizzorno, *National Studies;* Jean-Daniel Reynaud, "Forces et faiblesses de la négociation collective," in Jean-Daniel Reynaud and

proportion of the total dependent work force, using data from the yearbook of the International Labor Organization. Where gaps in series exist, it is assumed that trends continue across the missing years.

To estimate the extent of economic disruption, ILO data on numbers of workers involved in conflicts are expressed as a proportion of either all dependent workers or all union members. For nearly all countries the figures fail to distinguish between strikes and lockouts, and the latter are evidence of employer rather than labor militancy; fortunately, lockouts are a minor part of conflict in most countries, except perhaps West Germany. Nothing can be done to sort out strikes that may be the result of employer militancy. There are also important problems resulting from the noncomparability of countries' strike statistics. First, strike rates differ between different industries, and the distribution of industries among countries is uneven; the most important cases are the considerable differences in the relative sizes of coal mining and agriculture, the former being usually a high-strike industry and the latter a low-strike one. To a certain extent therefore international differences in conflict simply reflect variation in industrial composition.

Further, national collection standards and methods vary widely.[26] Only crude, extreme differences between countries can be distinguished. But averages over a run of years in countries' performances have a certain stability, and they are what is of interest here.

Data on inflation and unemployment form the basis of further measures of disruption, using OECD figures.[27]

Several yardsticks are used to measure the degree of corporatism in labor movements. Romanis has attempted a simple classification of both trade-union movements and employers' federations for thirteen countries, which uses the variable crucial to the hypothesis developed here: coordination (see table 5-1).[28] The distinction that Romanis makes between competitive and independent can be ignored; nor is it necessary to take account of the special cases of the two countries where union action "is

Yves Grafmeyer, eds., *Français, qui etes vous?* (Paris: La Documentation Française, 1981), pp. 241–50; Edward Shorter and Charles Tilly, *Strikes in France, 1830–1968* (Cambridge University Press, 1974). On Switzerland, from François Höpflinger, *Industriegewerkschaften in der Schweiz* (Zurich: Limmat Verlag Genossenschaft, 1976); Willy Keller, *175 Jahre Geschichte der schweizerischen und bernischen Arbeiterbewegung, 1800–1975* (Bern: Schweizerischer Gewerkschaftsbund Arbeiterbildungsausschuss, 1975).

26. Michael Shalev, "Lies, Damned Lies and Strike Statistics: The Measurement of Trends in Industrial Conflict," in Crouch and Pizzorno, *National Studies*, pp. 1–19.

27. *OECD Economic Outlook* (Paris: OECD, various issues).

28. Anne Romanis, "Cost Inflation and Incomes Policy in Industrial Countries," *International Monetary Fund Staff Papers*, vol. 14 (March 1967), pp. 169–206.

Table 5-1. *Characterization of Wage Bargaining in Thirteen Countries*

Classification and country	Bargaining by	
	Employers' federations	Unions
Uncoordinated wage bargaining		
Belgium	Uncoordinated	Competitive
Canada	Uncoordinated	Independent
France	Uncoordinated	Competitive
United Kingdom	Uncoordinated	Competitive
United States	Uncoordinated	Independent
Coordinated wage bargaining		
Austria	Coordinated	Coordinated
Denmark	Coordinated	Coordinated
Netherlands	Coordinated	Coordinated
Norway	Coordinated	Coordinated
Sweden	Coordinated	Coordinated
West Germany	Coordinated	Coordinated
Scope for union action limited by labor market situation		
Italy	Uncoordinated	Competitive
Japan	Uncoordinated	Independent

Source: Anne Romanis, "Cost Inflation and Incomes Policy in Industrial Countries," *International Monetary Fund Staff Papers*, vol. 14 (March 1967), p. 197.

limited by the labour market situation." All countries in Romanis's coordinated group have either had lengthy Social Democratic domination of government (Sweden, Denmark, Norway) or a consociational pattern (West Germany, Austria, the Netherlands). The other countries in table 5-1 can be classified as liberal.

Table 5-2 adds to the neocorporatist and liberal categories the five countries not considered in the Romanis study. Finland and Switzerland are classified as coordinated. Finland has a centralized pattern of national collective bargaining like other Nordic countries, though this centralization is not without its problems.[29] Switzerland is not as clearly coordinated as the other cases, but its industrial relations are heavily dominated by a social peace agreement in the metal industry and similar arrangements in other major industries.[30] Further, Kriesi has recently shown how an

29. Jaako Nousiainen, *The Finnish Political System* (Harvard University Press, 1971); John T. Addison, "Finnish Incomes Policy" (University of South Carolina Press, 1980); Voitto Helander and Dag Anckar, *Consultation and Political Culture: Essays on the Case of Finland* (Helsinki: Societas Scientiarum Fennica, 1983).

30. Lukas F. Burckhardt, "Industry-Labor Relations: Industrial Peace," in J. Murray Luck, ed., *Modern Switzerland* (Palo Alto, Calif.: Society for the Promotion of Science and Scholarship, 1978).

Table 5-2. *Classification of Industrial Relations Systems in Eighteen Countries*

Neocorporatist	Liberal
Austria	Australia
Denmark	Belgium
Finland	Canada
Netherlands	France
Norway	Ireland
Sweden	Italy
Switzerland	Japan
West Germany	New Zealand
	United Kingdom
	United States

informally highly centralized group of *Dachverbände* provide a form of organizational coordination in that country that, if not corporatism, is certainly a functional equivalent for it.[31] Finland and Switzerland have consociational patterns of government. Australia, New Zealand, and Ireland, on the other hand, exhibit decentralized bargaining with weak confederations. This is slightly less true for New Zealand than in the other cases, but there is nothing there resembling coordination of the German or Scandinavian type.[32]

Table 5-3 presents Schmitter's ranking of fifteen countries according to their degree of societal corporatism, which means virtually the same as my neocorporatism. It is derived from two indexes, one of organizational centralization developed by Headey,[33] and the other constructed by Schmitter from data on associational monopoly. This rank ordering confirms Romanis's account of West Germany, Sweden, Austria, Denmark, Norway, and the Netherlands as grouped toward the corporatist pole, and the United Kingdom, France, the United States, Canada, and Italy as liberal. It also confirms my allocation of Finland within the former and

31. Hanspeter Kriesi, "The Structure of the Swiss Political System," in Gerhard Lehmbruch and Philippe C. Schmitter, eds., *Patterns of Corporatist Policy-Making* (Sage, 1982), pp. 133–61.

32. For Australia, see Hugh Armstrong Clegg, *Trade Unionism under Collective Bargaining* (Oxford: Blackwell, 1976); Ross M. Martin, *Trade Unions in Australia* (Penguin Books, 1975); Kenneth F. Walker, *Australian Industrial Relations Systems* (Harvard University Press, 1970); Diane Yerbury and J. E. Issaac, "Recent Trends in Collective Bargaining in Australia," *International Labour Review*, vol. 103 (May 1971), pp. 421–52. For New Zealand, John M. Howells, Noel S. Woods, and F. J. L. Young, eds., *Labour and Industrial Relations in New Zealand* (New York: Pitman, 1974). For Ireland, Charles McCarthy, *The Decade of Upheaval: Irish Trade Unions in the Nineteen Sixties* (Dublin: Institute of Public Administration, 1973); Torrington, *Comparative Industrial Relations*.

33. "Trade Unions and National Wages Policies."

Table 5-3. Societal Corporatism Ranking in Fifteen Countries

Country	Ranking		Country	Ranking
Austria	1		Netherlands	6
Belgium	7		Norway	2
Canada	11		Sweden	4
Denmark	4		Switzerland	9
Finland	4		United Kingdom	14
France	13		United States	11
Ireland	11		West Germany	8
Italy	15			

Source: Philippe C. Schmitter, "Interest Intemediation and Regime Governability in Contemporary Western Europe and North America," in Suzanne Berger, ed., *Organizing Interests in Western Europe* (Cambridge University Press, 1981), p. 294.

Ireland within the latter group in table 5-2. However, Schmitter's ranking of Belgium above West Germany raises a question about their respective positions in the liberal and neocorporatist groupings. Switzerland's inter-mediary position in Schmitter's list leaves my allocation of that country in table 5-2 unverified. Unfortunately, Schmitter does not include Japan, Australia, and New Zealand. The role of union confederations in the latter two countries is similar to that in the United Kingdom, while Japan has a number of competing union confederations that have an extremely poor hold over individual unions and very little power.[34] Examination of these countries according to Schmitter's criteria places them at or near the bottom of his corporatism ranking, which is consistent with Romanis's labeling of Japan and my designation of the Australasian countries as liberal.

Lehmbruch has classified seven countries on the basis of institutional features. His rank ordering in table 5-4 is broadly consistent with the classifications of both Romanis and Schmitter. However, he reverses Schmitter's ranking of the Netherlands and Denmark—his qualitative account is able to recognize the large amount of cooperation among apparently rival union confederations within the Dutch consociational system, as well as the considerable tension under the surface of ostensible centralization in Denmark. It is particularly significant that Denmark, like Finland but unlike Norway and Sweden, had a union movement that

34. Kazuo Okocki, Bernard Karsh, and Solomon B. Levine, *Workers and Employers in Japan* (Princeton University Press, 1974); Tadashi Mitsufuji and Kiyohiko Hagisawa, "Recent Trends in Collective Bargaining in Japan," *International Labour Review*, vol. 105 (February 1972), pp. 135–53; Hideaki Okamoto, "Japan," in Benjamin C. Roberts, ed., *Towards Industrial Democracy: Europe, Japan and the United States* (Totowa, N.J.: Allanheld, Osmun, 1979); Taishiro Shirai, "Prices and Wages in Japan: Towards an Anti-Inflationary Policy?" *International Labour Review*, vol. 103 (March 1971), pp. 227–46.

Table 5-4. *Classification of Neocorporatism in Seven Countries*

Country	Strength of corporatism
Austria	Strong
Netherlands	Strong
Sweden	Strong
Denmark	Medium
United Kingdom	Medium
West Germany	Medium
France	Weak

Source: Gerhard Lehmbruch, "Introduction: Neo-Corporatism in Comparative Perspective," in Gerhard Lehmbruch and Philippe C. Schmitter, eds., *Patterns of Corporatist Policy-Making* (Sage, 1982), pp. 16–23.

developed from a strong craft rather than industrial base; the legacy of this survives in a significant degree of shop-floor power.

Lehmbruch's ordering of France and the United Kingdom is also the reverse of Schmitter's; that may be the result of his focus on the 1970s, during which period a rather shaky edifice of neocorporatist institutions was being erected in Britain.

Clearly, countries differ in their degree of neocorporatism; but, equally clearly, it is difficult to achieve a precise rank ordering. The extended Romanis classification in table 5-2 is used here since it has been substantiated by the two other listings, with possible queries over the positions of Belgium and Switzerland.

The Evidence

Figure 5-1 compares data on workers' involvement in industrial conflict with data on unionization of the dependent work force. For the eighteen countries as a whole, there is little evidence that disruption varies directly with the level of unionization. However, when the countries are considered separately in the neocorporatist and liberal groupings, the neocorporatist group (in italics) shows virtually no relationship between unionization and industrial conflict, while among the liberal group the relationship is strong.[35]

35. For the figures in this chapter I used regression equations to test the significance of the observed relationships. The number of cases being so small, the variation between them on some indicators being so large, and the data for some of the indicators being so approximate, it is highly misleading to give an impression of statistical precision by the use of techniques designed to deal with large samples from large universes. A simple difference-of-means test for the rate of log worker involvements per 1,000 trade union members for the two groups yielded a t-statistic of 3.9308, which is significant at the 1 percent level.

Figure 5-1. *Worker Involvement in Conflicts and Union Strength in Eighteen Countries, 1965–80*

Log of number of workers per 1,000 involved in conflict

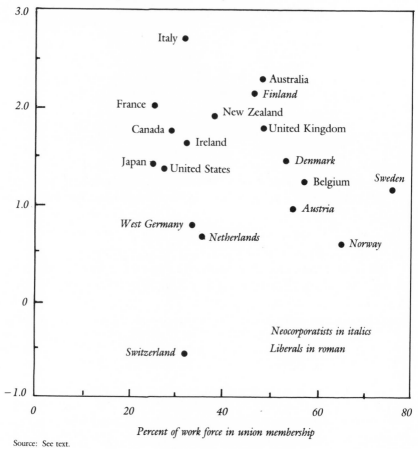

Percent of work force in union membership

Source: See text.

Belgium, however, fits comfortably in the corporatist group, though it is classified as liberal in table 5-2; but Schmitter's ranking suggested that it may be a marginal member of that grouping. Finland, in contrast, behaves like a normal member of the liberal group, though it is classified in table 5-2 as neocorporatist. One possible explanation is Finland's large and politically important Communist party, which plays an important part in the union movement. One wing of the party participates as a cooperative partner in Finnish consociationism, but the other regards itself as an outsider in Finnish political and industrial life.[36] Is it possible that a politically alienated Communist party is able to offset the effect of consociational corporatism? It is worth noting that the two other countries with a large Communist party—France and Italy—also exhibit larger than expected levels of industrial conflict. A further problem in Finland, which again demonstrates the fragility of centralization there, is the existence of interconfederal union rivalries, especially for the representation of white-collar workers—groups who have been prominent in unofficial strikes.[37]

Switzerland also gives some cause for concern. Given its relatively marginal position within the corporatist group, the extremely low position of this country on the industrial conflict scale cannot really be said to be explained primarily in terms of my hypothesis.[38]

Inflation itself is used in figure 5-2 to indicate to what extent the rise in price levels, which everywhere followed the rise in commodity prices in the mid-1970s, was exacerbated by the presence of powerful labor movements, and of neocorporatism. The inflation datum is an average of the annual rises in the consumer price index for the year with the biggest rise, one year before, and two years after. The year before the biggest rise is included in order to take account of countries in which the sharp rise was followed by a further rise rather than a drop, the years after to assess capacity to recover from an initial inflationary shock. In most cases the year of the biggest rise was 1974, in some 1975, in New Zealand 1976, and in Sweden 1977. The datum on union membership is an average for the four years preceding the four-year period of the inflation datum in each case.

Figure 5-2 reveals no obvious pattern for all countries, but as with figure 5-1 distinct patterns emerge among the neocorporatist and the liberal groups. Given the wide range of factors outside the industrial relations system that will cause differential exposure of economies to inflation, there is little reason to be concerned at slightly exceptional cases within the two groups.[39] However, as in figure 5-1, Belgium and Finland

36. Addison, "Finnish Incomes Policy"; Voitto Helander, "Self-Sustaining Corporatism? The Finnish Incomes Policy System, 1968–1982," in Helander and Anckar, *Consultation and Political Culture*, pp. 104, 107.

37. Helander, "Self-Sustaining Corporatism?" p. 96.

38. One consequence of presenting the worker involvement data in log form is to exaggerate differences between low numbers.

39. A difference-of-means test of the extent to which the inflation rate for a given level of union membership varies between the two groups is clearly inappropriate. While it can be plausibly argued that the level of conflict will vary directly with the level of union membership, to claim that the level of inflation will vary similarly is to assume one of the main hypotheses being examined here; the fact that

Figure 5-2. *Average Peak Inflation Rate and Union Strength in Eighteen Countries, Mid-1970s*

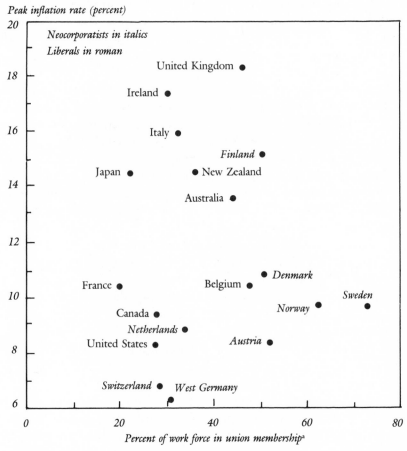

Peak inflation rate (percent)

Source: See text.
a. Immediately before period of peak inflation.

remain major deviant cases, each behaving as a perfectly conforming member of the opposite group.

It may be contended that inflation levels in the peak period were partly a function of inflation levels in earlier years, that union membership levels in the early 1970s were a response to that earlier inflation level, and that

the level of unionization tends to be highest in the corporatist countries prejudges the issue in favor of the hypothesis. A difference-of-means test simply comparing peak inflation levels between the two groups of countries yielded a *t*-statistic of 2.4737 (significant at the 5 percent level).

Figure 5-3. *Rise in Inflation Rate, Mid-1960s to Mid-1970s, and Union Strength in Eighteen Countries*

Rate of peak inflation minus inflation of 1964–67 (percent)

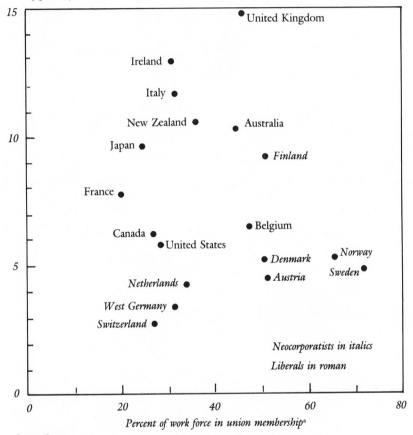

Source: See text.

a. Immediately before period of peak inflation.

the association shown in figure 5-2 is a pure artifact of this. But further inspection does not substantiate this view. Taking the inflation rate for the years 1965–68, before the period of turbulence in the Western economies which began around 1968, figure 5-3 uses the difference between that "normal" rate and the peak period rate to plot the relationship between inflation and unionization. Far from disappearing, the relationship of union strength and inflation seems considerably strengthened. This implies that the extraordinary rise in inflation during the mid-1970s, as

Figure 5-4. *Inflation and Unemployment Performance and Union Strength in Fourteen Countries, Mid-1970s*

Combined inflation and unemployment rate (percent)

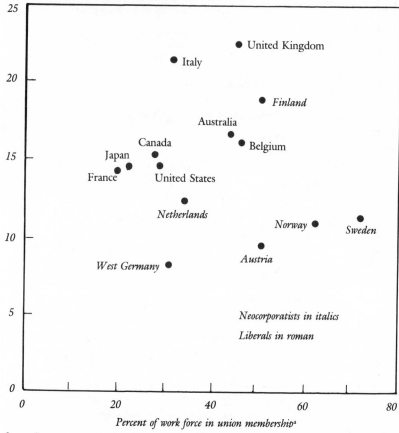

Percent of work force in union membership[a]

Source: See text.

a. Immediately before period of peak inflation.

well as the difference among national rates of price acceleration, is better explained by industrial relations forces than just by prior inflation alone.[40] This is compatible with the hypothesis that organized labor used its strength to secure short-term protection from the commodity price-rise shocks, except to the extent that neocorporatist union structures led it to

40. A simple difference-of-means test for the inflation rise between the two groups yielded a *t*-statistic of 3.9004 (significant at the 1 percent level).

pursue strategies more compatible with longer-term price stability. McCallum has suggested a further argument why this might happen.[41] Where there is social consensus (which might be secured by corporatist institutions) there will be a relatively rapid adaptation of real wages to economic developments, and therefore less inflation. McCallum uses strikes as an inverse indicator of social consensus, which relates strikes and inflation more satisfactorily than the usual assertions "strikes cause inflation" or vice versa.

Finally, figure 5-4 examines the relationship of inflation, unionization, and unemployment. Some theorists suggest a trade-off between inflation and unemployment, and unemployment is a variable closely related to union strength. The relationship between the rate of inflation I and union strength S may be expressed as

(1) $$I = f(S).$$

But union strength is a function of union membership M and other factors, among which the level of unemployment U is significant and in inverse relation:

(2) $$S = \frac{f(M)}{f(U)}.$$

Combining equations 1 and 2, the relation becomes

(3) $$I = \frac{f(M)}{f(U)}.$$

For neocorporatist union movements, the effect of their actions on the level of employment is likely to be important; a union movement with capacity for strategy will try to reduce the level of unemployment, whether by pressure on government or by restraint in its own behavior. Given that, as figures 5-2 and 5-3 suggest, corporatist union movements are likely also to be associated with lower levels of inflation than liberal ones for a given level of union membership, they can be expected to be associated with lower combined levels of inflation and unemployment:

(4) $$I = \frac{f(M)}{f(U)} \left(\frac{1}{F(C)} \right)$$

or

(5) $$I, U = \frac{f(M)}{f(C)},$$

where C is the level of neocorporatism of the labor movement.

41. John McCallum, "Inflation and Social Consensus in the Seventies," *Economic Journal*, vol. 93 (December 1983), pp. 784–805.

Given the simple category nature of the data used to assess degree of corporatism and the small number of cases, it is not realistic to test an equation of this kind. We can approximate a test by combining I and U *additively* (which of course amounts to the same as the well-known Okun index of "discomfort"). As in the previous tests, this can then be plotted against the unionization measure M, examining the neocorporatist measure C for the neocorporatist and liberal groups separately. Figure 5-4 does this, again for the peak inflation period, for the fourteen countries in the group considered in this chapter for which the OECD publishes standardized unemployment data. Apart from a poorer than expected performance by the Netherlands, the result is similar to those in the previous figures, with the same exceptions.[42]

These investigations suggest that it is worthwhile to include institutional variables corresponding to the distinction between liberalism and neocorporatism in economic equations designed to account for international differences in inflation rates. The indicators of corporatism need to be refined, to give at least a rank ordering of all eighteen countries; and the deviant cases of Switzerland, Belgium, and Finland need further study to determine whether they are instances of "decayed" corporatism or genuine exceptions. In such cross-sectional analyses there are not enough countries to justify the construction of complex equations with a large number of variables. Studies that try to trace a relationship between industrial relations variables and changes in year-to-year inflation have the advantages of a large number of units as their base and of concentrating on one country at a time, eliminating problems caused by differences in international calculations of union membership, strikes, and so forth. However, the defects of this approach are its unreality and its failure to grasp what is meant by an institutional or sociopolitical variable.[43] The factors that

42. A simple difference-of-means test for combined inflation and unemployment levels between the two groups yielded a *t*-statistic of 2.5891 (significant at the 5 percent level).

43. For arguments supporting the importance of sociological variables, see George Leland Bach, *The New Inflation: Causes, Effects, Cures* (Brown University Press, 1973); Thomas Balogh, *Labour and Inflation* (London: Fabian Society, 1970); Crouch, "Inflation and the Political Organization of Economic Interests"; John H. Goldthorpe, "The Current Inflation: Towards a Sociological Account," in Hirsch and Goldthorpe, *Political Economy of Inflation*, pp. 186–216; Roy Harrod, "The Issues: Five Views," in Randall Hinshaw, ed., *Inflation as a Global Problem* (Johns Hopkins University Press, 1972); Aubrey Jones, *The New Inflation: The Politics of Prices and Incomes* (London: Deutsch, 1973), pp. 43–45. For arguments insisting on the irrelevance of social variables, see Michael Parkin, "The Politics of Inflation," *Government and Opposition*, vol. 10 (Spring 1975), pp. 189–202; David Purdy and George Zis, "Trade Unions and Wage Inflation in the UK: A Reappraisal," in David Laidler and David Purdy, eds., *Inflation and Labour Markets* (Manchester University Press, 1974); R. Ward and G. Zis, "Trade Union Militancy

affect the number of worker involvements in strikes, let alone the number of strikes or days lost in any one year, are varied and to a certain extent arbitrary; it should not be expected that an economic variable, such as inflation, will move in any close relationship with such erratic movements. Those who set out to show that there is little connection between year-to-year variations in strike activity and inflation rates set themselves an easy task.[44] Similarly, it should not be expected that year-to-year changes in union membership levels will have rapid noticeable effects on economic outcomes.[45] Rather, institutional variables are relatively static, slow-changing factors that should be expected to affect behavior over a fairly long term. This effect is more easily measured by comparing countries with diverse institutional arrangements than by considering fluctuations over short periods of time within countries.

Comparison of a Neocorporatist and a Liberal System

By examining two cases in detail, it is possible to compare the behavior of trade unions in a neocorporatist and a liberal industrial relations system. West Germany and the United Kingdom are good representatives of the two systems.

West Germany is neocorporatist but far from an extreme example; there are strong elements of neoliberalism in its economic policy.[46] And

---

as an Explanation of Inflation: An International Comparison," *Manchester School of Economic and Social Studies,* no. 1 (March 1974), pp. 46–55; George Zis, "Inflation: An International Monetary Problem or a National Social Phenomenon?" in Michael Parkin and George Zis, eds., *Inflation in Open Economies* (Manchester University Press, 1976), pp. 1–23. David Soskice has attempted a synthesis of economic and sociological perspectives in "Strike Waves and Wage Explosions, 1968–1970: An Economic Interpretation," in Crouch and Pizzorno, *Comparative Analyses,* pp. 221–46.

44. See Ward and Zis, "Trade Union Militancy."

45. The pioneering work in this field is A. G. Hines, "Trade Unions and Wage Inflation in the United Kingdom, 1893–1961," *Review of Economic Studies,* vol. 31 (October 1964), pp. 221–52. This has been criticized by Purdy and Zis, "Trade Unions and Wage Inflation," and by Ward and Zis, "Trade Union Militancy."

46. It is important to see West Germany's social-market policies as a movement toward liberalization within an economy that had hardly known a period of liberal capitalism and had, during the Nazi period, been under an extremely high degree of political control. German governments were slow to dismantle the cartels of earlier economic regimes, and business continued to make important use of its associations in its relations with government. Andrew Shonfield, *Modern Capitalism: The Changing Balance of Public and Private Power* (Oxford University Press, 1965), chaps. 11, 12; Geoffrey Denton, Murray Forsyth, and Malcolm MacLennan, *Economic Planning and Policies in Britain, France and Germany* (London: Allen and Unwin, 1968), chap. 2; Marianne Welteke, *Theorie und Praxis der sozialen Marktwirtschaft* (Frankfurt: Campus Verlag, 1976). These factors have been of continuing importance to the role of employers' associations in industrial relations.

the main union confederation, the German Trade Union Federation (Deutsche Gewerkschaftsbund, or DGB), has nothing like the control that the central confederations in the Scandinavian countries, Austria, and the Netherlands have over their affiliates. Indeed, some observers regard German unions as weakly coordinated.[47] Be that as it may, the structure of German industrial relations and of political economy generally leads German unions to act in a highly coordinated way.

The United Kingdom is sometimes seen as an extreme case of liberalism; it has the most decentralized union movement in the industrial world, a fact reflected in the compilation of Schmitter's index. However, at certain periods (1940-51, 1961-69, 1972-79) it has been involved in some distinct attempts at neocorporatist public policy.[48] At these times the country has displayed the close cooperation between ministries and union leaders familiar in corporatist countries. It is factors such as these that account for the higher assessment of the level of corporatism in Britain made by Lehmbruch. Like West Germany, the United Kingdom is therefore a suitable case for an attempt at disentangling form and substance.

The central point of departure for a comparison is the very different level of labor-movement centralization. In the United Kingdom this was high immediately after World War II but dissipated fairly rapidly.[49] Employers' organizations had never been highly centralized, or powerful among their member firms, except perhaps during the period of corporatist rationalization in the 1930s, the British economy's sole and reluctant flirtation with cartelization. Employers' associations in Britain rarely developed the industry-level cohesion of bargaining policy, backed up by mutual support and sanctions, characteristic of their counterparts in West Germany, Sweden, and the Netherlands.[50]

From the late 1930s and throughout the war, British unions had become highly centralized, though in nothing like the tidy industrial-

---

47. See Headey, "Trade Unions and National Wages Policies." His classification of union confederations was used to construct the corporatism index in table 5-3, above.

48. Colin Crouch, *Class Conflict and the Industrial Relations Crisis* (London: Heinemann, 1977).

49. Hugh Armstrong Clegg, *The Changing System of Industrial Relations in Great Britain* (Oxford: Blackwell, 1979), chap. 2.

50. See Geoffrey K. Ingham, *Strikes and Industrial Conflict: Britain and Scandinavia* (London: Macmillan, 1974); Stephens, *Transition from Capitalism*, pp. 129–40; Peter Jackson and Keith Sisson, "Employers' Confederations in Sweden and the U.K. and the Significance of Industrial Infrastructure," *British Journal of Industrial Relations*, vol. 14 (November 1976); Tinie Akkermans and Peter Grootings, "From Corporatism to Polarisation: Elements of the Development of Dutch Industrial Relations," in Crouch and Pizzorno, *National Studies*, pp. 159–89.

union form introduced after the war in West Germany. The centralization, initially defensive in the face of mass unemployment and then prolonged for the exceptional period of wartime hostilities, never developed the infrastructure of organizational arrangements that might perpetuate it. From the early 1950s it rapidly collapsed, as in changed economic circumstances the historical shop-floor base of the British labor movememt reasserted itself. With an untidy union structure that made concerted policymaking difficult, and with very weak employers' organizations as bargaining counterparts, there was little to sustain effective strategic capacity in the unions. Shop-floor activists, especially the shop stewards, emerged again as autonomous centers of power. A plant level of bargaining grew up alongside and independent of the national level in many industries. The guardians of institutionalized bargaining—union officials, employers' bodies, and the Ministry of Labour—preferred to act as though the unofficial movement did not exist, though by the late 1960s it was by far the most active agent in industrial disputes, grievance settlements, struggles over working conditions, and, to a lesser extent, pay rises in many major industries, especially in the private sector. There was not often outright conflict between union hierarchy and stewards, but there was no integration either.

This kind of decentralization was very much a part of the liberal legacy of British economic history. The process of industrialization had been long, ad hoc, relatively unguided by the state or by organized industrial groups. There was little inherited coordination on either side of industry and a good deal of resistance to attempts at imposing it.

In West Germany employers' associations play an important part in bargaining, help employers maintain a common front against unions, and even maintain strike protection funds.[51] This is one aspect of German economic life that retains the older pattern of cartelization. The unions are similarly centralized, having been established on a simplified industrial base of sixteen (later seventeen) organizations within the DGB after the war.[52] Although bargaining is often carried out at the regional level, the union leaders who carry it out are part of a staff organized by the national headquarters. Streeck has argued that industrial unionism is conducive to solidaristic wage policy of the Swedish kind, which seeks to advance a

---

51. Lloyd Ulman and Robert J. Flanagan, *Wage Restraint: A Study of Incomes Policies in Western Europe* (University of California Press, 1971), p. 178.

52. About 85 percent of all German trade unionists are members of DGB affiliates.

common interest among a range of different kinds of workers on different pay levels, rather than an opportunist playing of the market that the organizational untidiness and decentralization of the British kind permit.[53] Further, national leaders of these large industrial unions must weigh the likely macroeconomic effects of their bargaining strategy, at least within their industry and, in the case of the larger unions which dominate the movement, the economy itself. Finally, as Lehmbruch has pointed out, the wage leadership of the steel and engineering union IG Metall (the free world's largest trade union) performs something like the function of confederal bargaining coordination, especially in the light of the centrality of the steel, machine-tool, and automobile industries to the German economy.[54]

In addition, shop-floor power in West Germany is poorly developed. One source of this lies in the system of codetermination—not so much in the oft-noted worker-director system, but in the role of the works councils, which comprise workers' representatives only. These councils have veto power over certain aspects of company operation, and the right to consultation on others. Against this, they are forbidden to engage in open conflict. They are not formally a part of union organization and in fact comprise a means whereby German employers have kept unions out of their plants; on the other hand, nearly 80 percent of their membership are normally union members whose candidature is supported by the unions.

During the late 1970s the unions began to take a more inventive approach toward the works councils, occasionally *negotiating* an increase in their rights in collective bargaining with employers as well as relying on government action to do so as in the past.[55] The relationship between the councils and the unions is therefore complex and highly interesting. On the one hand the fact that the councils have the power to achieve gains for the workers through formal, nonconflictive means reduces the volume of shop-floor conflict and makes it difficult for shop-floor activists to mobilize workers around accumulated grievances. The councils therefore

53. Wolfgang Streeck, "Gewerkschaftsorganisation und industrielle Beziehungen: einige Stabilitäts-probleme industriegewerkschaftlicher Interessenvertretung und ihre Lösung im westdeutschen System der industriellen Beziehungen," in Joachim Matthes, ed., *Sozialer Wandel in Westeuropa* (Frankfurt: Campus Verlag, 1979).

54. Lehmbruch, "Neokorporatismus," p. 18.

55. Eugen Loderer, "Erfolgreicher Kampf um soziale Besitzstandssicherung," and "Dokumentati-onen: Metalltarifrunde in Nordwürttemberg/Nordbaden 1978," *Gewerkschaftliche Monatshefte* (Cologne), vol. 29 (May 1978), pp. 257–60, 303–10.

reduce the level of militancy and also continue as a nonunion channel of representation. At the same time, the fact that their relations with the unions are very close means that they become a de facto union channel in many instances and dispense with the need for unions to develop autonomous channels of representation. Instead the unions can rely on their links with the councils to give them a shop-floor role while themselves concentrating on regional and national tasks. In this way the works councils insulate the centralized activity of the unions which is crucial to neocorporatism, while also helping them insure the ventilation of shop-floor grievances.[56]

It has also been claimed that works councillors are a moderating influence within the unions.[57] Council members often participate in the formulation of union wage claims, encouraging a policy that asserts a solidaristic norm at industry level and leaves scope for works councils to secure extra rises within the most profitable companies.

Such a system does not work perfectly. In 1969 and in the early 1970s, there were occasional shop-floor revolts, sometimes led by union shop stewards within the plant, sometimes by groups of workers (such as immigrants) whose needs had been neglected.[58] But newly active shop stewards often find themselves becoming members of works councils. Most German workers seem reasonably satisfied with the system of plant representation.[59] Almost by accident the industrial relations system has developed in a way that protects union centralization while providing a safety valve for grievances at shop-floor level.

Initially, postwar bargaining in Britain also tended to exclude unions

56. Gerhard Brandt, "Industrial Relations in the Federal Republic of Germany under Conditions of Economic Crisis," in Shigeyoshi Tokunaga and Joachim Bergmann, eds, *Industrial Relations in Transition: The Cases of Japan and the Federal Republic of Germany* (University of Tokyo Press, 1984), pp. 5–20.

57. Charles F. Sabel, "The Internal Politics of Trade Unions," in Suzanne Berger, ed., *Organizing Interests in Western Europe: Pluralism, Corporatism, and the Transformation of Politics* (Cambridge University Press, 1981), pp. 233–36.

58. Berndt Kirchlechner, "New Demands or the Demands of New Groups?" in Crouch and Pizzorno, *Comparative Analyses*, pp. 161–76; Walther Müller-Jentsch and Hans-Joachim Sperling, "Economic Development, Labour Conflicts and the Industrial Relations System in West Germany," in Crouch and Pizzorno, *National Studies*, pp. 257–306. See also Rainer Zoll, "Centralisation and Decentralisation as Tendencies of Union Organisational and Bargaining Policy," and Roderick Martin, "The Effects of Recent Changes in Industrial Conflict on the Internal Politics of Trade Unions: Britain and Germany," in Crouch and Pizzorno, *Comparative Analyses*. Wolfgang Streeck, "Qualitative Demands and the Neo-Corporatist Manageability of Industrial Relations," *British Journal of Industrial Relations*, vol. 19 (July 1981), notes more recent signs of tension.

59. Heinz Hartmann, "Works Councils and the Iron Law of Oligarchy," *British Journal of Industrial Relations*, vol. 17 (March 1979). The fact that nearly 80 percent of those eligible to vote in council elections do so is also some indication that these bodies are not mere tokens.

from direct activity in the plant; bargaining took place at the level of nationally organized unions and employers' associations, with an older historical legacy of district bargaining in certain sectors. At the plant level, activity was to be left to joint consultation committees that had no statutory base and, unlike the German works councils, conferred no power on worker members.[60] As shop-level union organization recovered its strength during the period of postwar full employment, shop stewards began to take the initiative in the settlement of shop-level grievances, developing autonomous power bases that relied on the strike threat and on the mobilization of the work force. In the industries and areas where such a pattern developed, a machinery emerged that could also take the initiative in wage demands. The new unofficial system was linked to the unions; in contrast to some of the Italian shop-floor delegates who emerged in the 1970s, British shop stewards were always union members and union activists. But their bargaining activity had little to do with union wage strategy.

Given the large number of unions, it was unlikely that pressure would be brought to bear in the Trades Union Congress on individual unions or shop-floor groups who carried on a policy that, if generally replicated, would have adverse economic consequences. By the late 1960s the existence of "two systems" of industrial relations in Britain became a common theme of criticisms of the unions both by their enemies and by some of their friends.[61] Despite a flurry of initiatives to try to integrate the two levels, the main story of the 1970s was of further growth at the decentralized level; if any integration took place it was through union leaderships giving increasing scope within their structures to shop-floor groups.[62]

The differences between British and German patterns of union organization are compounded by differences in legal systems. In West Germany there are far more legal constraints on unions than in the United Kingdom;

60. While German works councillors have no power to take conflict action, their veto rights, which are limited to a number of issues, give them considerable leverage. Clearly, they can use their power in a restricted area to gain concessions in further areas in exchange for moderation in their exercise of the veto.

61. The focal point of this debate was evidence gathered for Great Britain, Royal Commission on Trade Unions and Employers Associations, 1965–1968 (Donovan Commission), *Report*, Cmnd. 3623 (London: Her Majesty's Stationery Office, 1968).

62. This process in fact played a crucial part in breaking the temporary and partial centralization of British industrial relations during the period of the "social contract," 1976–79. It was recently decentralized groups within the health service and local government who took the initiative in the wave of strikes against pay restraint in January 1979.

but legal constraints also exist in some liberal economies with high levels of industrial disruption (for example, the United States). More important is the type of legal framework. German labor legislation has largely emerged from older legal traditions, predating the Federal Republic.[63] Perhaps most important is the restriction of the rights to form associations and to strike to the limited number of formal trade unions recognized by the state. These rights are a development of the medieval concept of corporate liberties enjoyed under state license—in contrast to the individual rights to organization and withdrawal of labor that developed from liberal legal systems of such countries as England and France. Alongside and in keeping with the corporatist assumptions of such law is the obligation of unions to maintain industrial peace, and the designation of unions, alongside employers' organizations, as bodies with a duty to help maintain social order. Such a designation, with its implied delegation to private associations of the public function of maintaining law and order, is pure corporatism and develops from an entirely different organizational tradition from the liberal concept of pressure groups each trying to maximize its advantages within a free-market competition for gain.

British labor law was, until the 1970s, as pure an instance of liberalism as German is of corporatism. The rights to strike and to unionize developed, albeit paradoxically, from individual freedoms, English common law being as individualist as the German legal conceptions are collectivist. As it became clear during the latter nineteenth century that the collectivism of labor could not be prevented, though it was clearly illegal under common law principles, governments made space for the legal development of unions by conceding to them immunities from prosecution for what would otherwise have been actionable behavior. Union and strike law thus developed negatively; there was virtually no attempt at constructing a comprehensive body of law that would allocate organized labor a set place in law and society. This was deliberate; to construct such legislation would have meant making an explicit breach with the liberal tradition in the face of an increasingly powerful movement.[64]

Significantly, it was during the 1970s, when various corporatist

---

63. Thilo Ramm, "The Legality of Industrial Actions and the Methods of Settlement Procedure," and Folke Schmidt, "Industrial Action: The Role of Trade Unions and Employers Associations," in Benjamin Aaron and K. W. Wedderburn, eds., *Industrial Conflict: A Comparative Legal Survey* (London: Longman, 1972); Johannes Schregle, "Labour Relations in Western Europe: Some Topical Issues," *International Labour Review*, vol. 109 (January 1974), pp. 1–22.

64. Lord Wedderburn of Charlton, "Industrial Relations and the Courts," *Industrial Law Journal* (London), vol. 9 (June 1980), pp. 65–94.

experiments were being launched within British industrial relations, that changes were attempted in this characteristic British pattern, most notably in the Industrial Relations Act 1971, which would have laid on unions some of the obligations characteristic of German law.[65] Equally significantly, however, that act was never capable of implementation and was repealed within three years. On the other hand it was replaced by an interesting development. As part of the corporatist social contract with the unions, the Labour government of 1974 introduced a series of acts that considerably advanced union and individual workers' rights.[66] While these did not impose the obligations and responsibilities that the German system does, they did locate British developments in a legislative framework with some corporatist implications. For the first time, union recognition became a matter for legal definition, to be administered by a tripartite Advisory, Conciliation, and Arbitration Service. Not surprisingly, given its tripartite structure, ACAS tended to give preference in recognition cases to claims by existing established unions. Given the tendency toward amalgamation and concentration in British unions, this might be thought to mark a tendency toward a limited number of large unions partly secured by legal process, albeit organized on a less unified industrial base than in West Germany.

However, it was notable that when judgments of ACAS on union recognition went before the normal law courts on appeal, the verdict was given to small, new, fragmentary unions—the latest manifestation of the tendency of the British judiciary to enforce individualistic conditions within a collectivist framework. In any case, in 1980 the new Conservative government repealed this provision of the mid-1970s legislation; it also introduced a range of new constraints on union action, but none that took a corporatist form.

The German approach to legal formalism in the definition of unions also furthers centralization by freezing the mold of organization and inhibiting breakaways. German unions thereby gain a functional equivalent of the closed shop, a major organizational advantage of British (and American) unions that is illegal in West Germany. Compulsory unionism maintains the strength of a work force against employers, but it also insulates the leadership from membership pressure (the ability to "vote with one's feet") and massively reinforces the disciplinary sanction of expulsion from union membership. If a centralized movement exists, these

65. Crouch, *Class Conflict*, chap. 10.
66. Ibid.

factors would heavily reinforce it. However, the fact that in West Germany it is difficult to organize outside the framework of formal unions means that it is very difficult to leave a union if one wants to engage in collective action—which presumably is what any worker seeking a higher level of militancy is doing.

In sum, German unions are, as a recent comparative study concluded, more bureaucratic in their administration, more centralised in policy-making and more legalistic in the way they pursue their objectives than their British counterparts. In wage policies especially, the executive committees and full-time officials in West German unions exercise a degree of authority over their members that is found in very few British unions. . . . In West Germany, power resides in individual national unions and there are clear limits on both the initiating role of the confederation and the autonomy of union members in the workplace. In Britain, the power relationship between the confederation, national unions and rank-and-file members is more complex and . . . less predictable.[67]

Neither the DGB nor the TUC has the formal role in union bargaining strategy that a confederation in the purer corporatist cases has. But the leadership of the DGB's seventeen major industry-based and internally centralized unions will encounter far fewer obstacles in the way of informal coordination in the interests of a general policy than will a movement of the British type.

More than a hundred trade unions organised around differing occupational, industrial and sectoral interests are affiliated to the TUC. Competitive multi-unionism characterises most parts of the private and public sector of employment in Britain and contributes to the more complex problems of policy-making in the TUC. More than three-quarters of the TUC's affiliated unions are not represented on the General Council and its sub-committees—a representational problem that has been exacerbated by significant changes in the occupational and industrial distribution of union membership in the last decade or so, especially the growth of public service trade unionism. The greater complexity of the internal environment of the TUC arises not only from the organisational diversity of membership, but, as one might expect, the extent to which this reflects important ideological divisions (at least, amongst union leaders) and the perception of competing interests.[68]

Only a coordinated union movement can operate in the way that Norbert Kloten, in chapter 12, describes the bargaining strategy of German unions since the aftermath of the oil crisis in 1973. The unions

67. Jon Clark and others, *Trade Unions, National Politics and Economic Management: A Comparative Study of the TUC and the DGB* (London: Anglo-German Foundation for the Study of Industrial Society, 1980), pp. 9, 10.
68. Ibid., pp. 8, 9.

are seen as either accepting in advance the implications for wages policy and unemployment of the Bundesbank's monetary stance, or of deciding to try to shift those implications by the autonomous action of their own bargaining. The strategy by no means imposes automatic cooperation with the authorities; neocorporatist unions, unlike classically corporatist ones, retain their autonomy and may use this as a bargaining counter. Their action conforms to a strategy, and that strategy can be changed and reversed if it appears to have been mistaken. This is quite different from the position of a competitive, decentralized union movement, where opposition to the authorities takes the form of an uncoordinated mass of local actions, none of which embodies an overall macroeconomic project—as occurred in the shop-floor revolts that brought down the social contract and the Labour government in Britain in the early weeks of 1979. If British unions adjusted their bargaining policy to far more modest targets in the early 1980s, it was not because they anticipated unfavorable consequences for employment levels, but because they had already been weakened by very high levels of unemployment.

It is these structural aspects of the industrial relations system that explain differences in the behavior of different union movements, not pieces of formal institutional machinery like the concerted action forum—which is so often identified as the source of the superior capacity of West Germany's industrial relations to cope with the instabilities of the 1970s. Chapter 12 makes clear that since its initial period (1967–72) concerted action has probably served as nothing more than a symbolic affirmation of a practice of mutual orientation and strategic behavior among the social partners that is supported by deeper structural factors. Ironically, the height of British admiration for concerted action (during the election campaign in 1979)[69] came at a time when German unions had been boycotting sittings of concerted action for nearly two years!

Indeed, if national forums were all that were required, the British have one in the National Economic Development Council, set up in 1961 largely for the purpose of persuading union leaders to orient their behavior toward national economic indicators[70]—at that time in supposed imitation of French rather than German institutions, though equally mistaken. In the absence of any mechanism for coordinated action at a national or

---

69. See, for example, Confederation of British Industry, *Pay: The Choice: CBI Proposals for Reforming Pay Determination* (London: CBI, 1979).

70. Crouch, *Class Conflict*, chap. 11.

industry level by either labor or capital, such devices will remain mere talking-shops.[71]

Conclusions

There does seem to be a case for taking seriously the argument that, once economic actors have become organized, the sociopolitical context most likely to be consistent with relative freedom from economic distortions will be one that encourages coordination of action and centralization of organization rather than one that tries to reproduce among organized interests situations analagous to a free market.

Transplantation of a few formal institutions of concerted action is hardly likely to change the capacity for restraint of a particular country's labor movement, for such institutions reflect factors rooted deeply in national histories. For example, it is notable that six of the liberal countries listed in table 5-2 developed in the Anglo-Saxon institutional tradition, with its individualistic legacy of common law, associated laissez-faire economic system, and low role for governments and organized capital in the early stages of industrialization. Two other low-corporatism countries, France and Italy, and in a rather different way Japan, embody a further historical pattern. The polities of these societies have long involved considerable corporatism, but in relations between capital and the government alone; labor, or at least its most important representative bodies, has been excluded from national consensus. A socialist government in France can be expected to change this pattern only if measures are taken to increase the central coordination of the labor movement.

This does not mean that nothing can be done to change the cast of a society's institutions once they have been set, but policy needs to go

---

71. It is possible that the different degrees of integration between the financial and industrial sectors of the British and German economies is relevant here. As Stephen Blank has shown ("Britain: The Politics of Foreign Economic Policy, the Domestic Economy, and the Problem of Pluralistic Stagnation," *International Organization*, vol. 31 [Autumn 1977], pp. 673–721), at crucial moments in recent economic history, British governments have supported the international interests of the financial sector (the City of London)—which has never been closely involved in the financing of British industry—at the expense of domestic manufacturing interests. The impressive array of tripartite economic consultative bodies has never embraced the financial sector or been able to affect this allocation of priorities. The relationship between German banks and industrial corporations has always been close, and this issue of the division between the two sectors has not arisen. See also Shonfield, *Modern Capitalism;* Yao-Su Hu, *National Attitudes and the Financing of Industry* (London: PEP, 1975); Susan Strange, *Sterling and British Policy: A Political Study of an International Currency in Decline* (Oxford University Press, 1971); John Woolley, chap. 11, below; Colin Crouch, "Varieties of Trade Union Weakness: Organised Labour and Capital Formation in Britain, Federal Germany and Sweden," *West European Politics*, vol. 3 (January 1980), pp. 87–106.

beyond formal institutional tinkering. One may also, on the basis of this analysis, consider critically attempts at deliberately reducing the level of corporatism in a society by, say, expelling the labor movement from the center of the political consensus, weakening the power of confederations, reducing the role of wide-ranging bargaining institutions. Unless powerful groups are prepared to try to destroy unionism completely, attempts simply to press an organized labor movement back into a form that seems more analogous to a decentralized market economy may be counterproductive; some of the conditions for stability under pure market conditions are the very opposite under conditions of organization. It was the very fact of coordination and capacity for strategy that enabled the German trade union movement, when it so chose, to respond to signals of tight monetary policy at an early stage, thereby reducing the need for that policy actually to bite deeply into the labor market. In Britain's more liberal industrial relations system the response had to wait for unemployment to rise above 10 percent.

Of course, the installation of neocorporatist structures, even if they can be successfully introduced, does not insure success in the fight against inflation or other sources of economic distortion. Corporatism places enormous reliance on the capacity of organizations to regulate their members. This capacity will often fray badly at the edges and may fail entirely. Chapters 12 and 13 describe this process as occurring in Sweden and Germany—both, however, still look considerably more stable than the frayed liberalism of the United Kingdom or Italy. As Lehmbruch has pointed out, the general shift to monetarist economic policy in the late 1970s signaled a certain loss of capacity of corporatist mechanisms to produce an "adequate" reduction in inflation.[72] Of course, as he has stated elsewhere, it was only in those cases where organizations could not provide centralized coordination (for example, in the United Kingdom and the United States) that monetarism was eventually used virtually alone.[73] Elsewhere (for example, in West Germany) a mixed strategy of the kind described by Kloten in chapter 12 was more likely.

The political supports necessary for neocorporatism are only partly known. What would happen if the association between Social Democratic power or at least consociationism and cooperative behavior on the part of centralized labor movements were removed for a lengthy period? Were

---

72. "Neokorporatismus," p. 9.
73. Gerhard Lehmbruch, "European Neo-Corporatism: An Export Article?" Colloquium Paper (Woodrow Wilson International Center for Scholars, 1982).

the Swedish general strike of 1980 and the strike for reduced working time in the German metal industry in 1984 an indication of what might become typical? It is interesting that Kloten regards the presence in office of the Social Democratic party as a factor insuring cooperation by German unions in the mid-1970s.

Finally, what are neocorporatist trade unions able to achieve for their members? The evidence presented in this chapter can be interpreted as saying that the effect of central coordination among unions is to offset the impact of the level of unionization—that is, the more centrally united is organized labor, the more are its actions compatible with the stability of that market economy against which labor started to organize itself in the first place! Such a view is of course dependent on the assumption that it is in labor's interest for the stability of the economy to be disrupted— a view that some within the labor movement do adopt. But even setting that aside, the question of what neocorporatist unions gain for their members in exchange for restraint is worth asking—from the points of view of both the workers themselves and the employers who may ask what they are conceding in exchange for this cooperative if organized labor force. To phrase the question differently, if part of the output of trade unions in liberal political economies is industrial conflict and inflation, do neocorporatist unions spend their energies achieving something more constructive?

6

Inflation and the Politics of Supply

John Zysman

Most discussions of inflation assume balanced growth or even a steady-state economy. They do not examine how sectoral changes, in which industries displace one another, or in which firms and technologies obsolesce, contribute to inflation. They may consider the macro fact of growth but not the microeconomic processes of adjustments in what is produced and how. This chapter examines how these processes of industrial adjustment can generate inflation and press special problems on stabilization policy. Some of these challenges are caused by endogenous or technological factors and some by new competition. The premise here is that growth itself exerts pressures that can lead to inflationary results, not merely from the general bottlenecks long associated with theories of structural inflation but from the political management of growth economies. The chapter addresses the issue of how diverse societies in the political management of the multitude of changes that constitute growth and the allocation of the associated costs can make their economies more or less prone to inflation.

It is difficult to establish the degree of inflation caused by sectoral shifts and problems of adjustment. The contribution to the movement of the price index made by paying an inefficient firm to manufacture overpriced steel or automobiles (overpriced in terms of world market alternatives) is not readily deduced. The contribution of government bribes to persuade hesitant enterpreneurs to invest in a modern steel factory is not easily established. Still there is a recognition that those costs—inducements to enter a sector or cushions for redundancy—are paid by society and can contribute to inflation. Industrial adjustment—

the continuing adaptation to new conditions—involves flexibility in the factory and mobility of resources between uses. Adjustment, of course, is not a bloodless or smooth process, and not surprisingly those displaced by the destruction that industrial growth entails may seek protection or assistance from government. The privileges won by those who seek change, and the protections and restrictions maintained by those who resist it, directly affect the flexibility and mobility of the economy. The pace, type, and cost of adjustment are directly affected by political choices about the management of adjustment and the institutional arrangements governing economic competition or coordination. Thus it is not simply a matter of whether change occurs, but how it occurs and who pays for it.

What this chapter seeks to explain is not the magnitude of the effects nor the technical path of transfer payments. Instead it argues that countries are more or less prone to provide such transfers, to fund them in inflationary ways, and to promote resource bidding according to characteristic social and political alignments and institutional features of the economy. There is no single set of political solutions that assures adjustment. Factory flexibility may be limited by the inability or unwillingness of small entrepreneurs to adopt competitive strategies as much as by worker resistance. The politics of adjustment, it must be clear from the outset, does not reduce to the power of labor to resist change nor can it be understood as a crisis of democracy expressed and measured by the proliferation of interest groups.[1] An analytic approach to the politics of adjustment must link the individual controversies about industrial change to national political issues and identify national approaches to adjustment and the kinds of political settlements made in the process. The sources and consequences of three types of adjustment—company-led, state-led, and tripartite-negotiated—are explored here.

Growth involves changes and adjustment, the shift of resources from one sector to another or the more productive use of resources within a particular sector. Substantial payments are usually required to induce businessmen and workers to enter new industries. The price of adjustment—the transfer cost—is the sum of payments necessary to induce the entrepreneur to assume the risk, and the laborer to accept the dislocation,

1. Organization for Economic Cooperation and Development, *Towards Full Employment and Price Stability* (Paris: OECD, 1977) (hereafter McCracken Report); Robert O. Keohane, "Economics, Inflation, and the Role of the State: Political Implications of the McCracken Report," *World Politics*, vol. 31 (October 1978), pp. 108–28; Mancur Olson, unpublished papers; Trilateral Commission, *The Crisis of Democracy* (New York University Press, 1975).

of entering a new sector. The market will provide incentives for adjustment if the gain from entering a new sector—the transfer premium—is great enough to make these payments to labor and capital. If the market is unable to cover all of the costs of adjustment, government may decide to transfer resources to industry to reduce costs of production and distribution, supplement profits, or make up for losses incurred. These subsidies may be in the form of direct payments, or restrictions such as trade barriers that allow protected firms to extract additional income from the market, or institutional arrangements and laws, such as those that protect labor against dismissal or that guarantee a market share for particular companies, that retard adjustment and permit incomes to be retained that otherwise would be lost.[2] These payments and restraints represent supply rigidities that discourage efficient use of resources, and they directly affect the costs of adjustment.

Adjustment difficulties can provoke inflation in a number of ways. If some sectors are subsidized, competitive bidding for shifting resources takes place at artificially high price levels. If protected groups are able to maintain their relative position in the market, the gains won in a growing sector will become higher costs throughout the economy. Also, the sum of subsidies and payments can add to aggregate demand without producing compensating supply. In 1978, for example, the British government spent $200 million and the Swedish government $400 million to cover the deficits of shipbuilding companies. The French directly subsidized ship costs to the sum of $200 million as well as providing modernization grants of 15 percent of new ship sale prices.[3] In France a fund of $1 billion was established for restructuring ailing industries, and government takeover of the steel industry meant that the state absorbed the $1 billion of loans that had destroyed the financial viability of the industry (a 1979 estimate put the subsidy at $2 billion a year).[4] Between 1969 and 1973, French support for the financing of exports intended to draw resources into expanding sectors was running between $600 million and $700 million.[5] And the supply consequences may be far more substantial than the actual expenditures. In 1970, for example, direct subsidies to engi-

2. Lance E. Davis and Douglass C. North, *Institutional Change and American Economic Growth* (Cambridge University Press, 1971), pp. 3–25.

3. "Spend Now, Contract Later," *Economist* (December 30, 1978), p. 48.

4. Paul Lewis, *New York Times*, August 6, 1979.

5. John Zysman, "The French State in the International Economy," in Peter J. Katzenstein, ed., *Between Power and Plenty: Foreign Economic Policies of Advanced Industrial States* (University of Wisconsin Press, 1978), p. 290.

neering industries in the advanced countries were running between $4 billion and $6 billion, but the lost production resulting from misallocation of resources that government policies brought about exceeded $50 billion.[6]

The Changed Context of Growth

If growth flags, the costs of adjustment become more inflationary. Growth rates themselves do not correlate with inflation across countries. But as the sources of growth falter, each country's performance will decline in respect to past records. Several distinct patterns of growth and inflation emerge from the records of five major industrialized countries (table 6-1). France and Japan were high growth and high inflation economies, West Germany had fast growth and low inflation, Britain had slow growth and high inflation, and the United States was a medium-to-slow-growth economy with low inflation. If growth and inflation (or growth and price stability) did not go together, what principles of growth did exist? Probably the most salient source lay in the fact that the fast growth countries were those with large agricultural sectors at the beginning of the postwar period. Although it hardly explains all gains, it allowed a major transition. As farming was mechanized, labor was freed for other uses. In France, West Germany, and Japan, patterns of land ownership remained stable; farm size increased, but as a result of death, not displacement. The position of the rural elites in the national community changed, but their place in the local order was not overturned.[7] Government grants and price supports were keyed to maintaining traditional

6. Unpublished OECD estimates.

7. In France the total number of farms decreased between 1942 and 1975 by 47 percent; farms of 20 to 50 hectares declined only slightly, and those greater than 50 hectares increased. In West Germany the total number decreased between 1949 and 1977 by 49 percent; farms of 20 to 50 hectares (and those greater than 50 hectares) increased markedly, and farms of 10 to 20 hectares declined only by 22 percent. In Japan, where the average farm size is extremely small, the total number decreased by 20 percent; farms of 2 to 3 hectares (and those greater than 3 hectares) increased substantially. Calculated from Institut National de la Statistique et des Etudes Economiques, *Annuaire statistique de le France 1977* (Paris: Ministere de l'Economie et des Finances, 1977), p. 153; Statistisches Bundesamt, *Statistisches Jahrbuch für die Bundesrepublik Deutschland 1978* (Stuttgart and Mainz: W. Kohlhammer GmbH, 1978), p. 134; Office of the Prime Minister, Statistics Bureau, *Japan Statistical Yearbook, 1978* (Tokyo: Statistics Bureau, 1978), p. 99. Dislocation resulting from industrial growth affected primarily smaller farms and nonowners, neither of which is the most politically influential component of the countryside. Indeed, governments in all three countries lavishly subsidized and protected the agricultural sector throughout the postwar period of industrial expansion. Guido Goldman, "The German Political System," in Samuel H. Beer and Adam B. Ulam, eds., *Patterns of Government: The Major Political Systems of Europe*, 3d ed. (Random House, 1973), p. 571; Philip H. Trezise and Yukio Suzuki, "Politics, Government, and Economic Growth in Japan," in Hugh Patrick and Henry Rosovsky, eds., *Asia's New Giant: How the Japanese Economy Works* (Brookings Institution, 1976), pp. 772–74.

Table 6-1. *Agricultural Employment and Inflation Rates in Five Countries, 1954–78*[a]

Percent

Country	Growth rate[b]			Agricultural employment rate[c]				Inflation rate[d]		
	1954–68	1969–78[e]	1954–78[e]	1950	1960	1970	1976	1954–68	1969–78[e]	1954–78[e]
Japan	9.6	8.2	9.1	40.3[f]	32.6	17.4	12.2	4.0	9.3	6.1
West Germany	5.5	4.6	5.2	23.2[g]	11.8	8.5	7.1	2.2	4.7	3.2
France	5.1	5.0	5.1	26.7[h]	19.8[i]	14.3	10.8	3.9	8.4	5.7
United States	3.5	3.9	3.6	12.2[g]	6.5	4.4	3.8	1.7	6.5	3.6
United Kingdom	3.0	3.0	3.0	5.1[j]	3.8[k]	3.2	2.7	3.3	11.9	6.7

Sources: Organization for Economic Cooperation and Development, *Main Economic Indicators* (Paris: OECD, 1970); United Nations Economic Commission for Europe, *Structure and Change in European Industry* (UN, 1977), chap. 3; United Nations, *Statistical Yearbook, 1960, 1966, 1967, 1970, 1977, 1978*.

a. Countries ranked by rate of growth.
b. Average annual increase in domestic production (constant prices).
c. Share of economically active population engaged in agriculture.
d. Average annual increase in consumer price index.
e. Does not include figures for two worst inflation years, 1974–75.
f. In 1955.   g. In 1950.   h. In 1954.
i. In 1962.   j. In 1951.   k. In 1961.

rural life, and the peasantry was held in place even as its destruction was assured. The shift out of agriculture, however, accounts only for a portion of gain in output;[8] it cannot be separated from the growth in investment and advances in technology.

The transition out of agriculture was, in any case, by its nature a one-time process. The political task of sustaining growth in advanced market economies now depends on a steady move out of low productivity industries and a continuing increase in the productivity of existing industries.[9] Moreover, industrial productivity must expand rapidly enough to compensate for expansion in the service sector, where productivity increases are slow.[10] Assuring "creative destruction" in sectors such as textiles and steel that must be displaced or transformed may prove even more difficult than displacing the peasants and modernizing agriculture were in the postwar years, for politically entrenched interests will have to be directly confronted rather than finessed.

Changes in industrial structure represent a challenge to patterns of ownership. Even medium-sized firms provide substantial numbers of jobs and a political and social position of importance in local communities for owners or managers that unite labor and capital in resisting change. Industrial workers are so well organized that they can adopt protective strategies that will affect not simply wages but the organization of production. Their position is reinforced by a web of protections built up over the years.

Because the gap between returns from any two industrial sectors is likely to be relatively small, protections and subsidies required to appease political unrest in weakening industries may seriously dampen market incentives for adjustment. A generation ago in the fast growth countries, agriculture could be subsidized to gain political quiescence without eliminating incentives to move or modernize. Now those countries along with the slow growth countries must face long-standing problems.

Adjustment must occur within industry. But the flexibility and mobility required for inflation-free growth may be impeded as important sectors

8. Edward F. Denison, *Why Growth Rates Differ: Postwar Experience in Nine Western Countries* (Brookings Institution, 1967), pp. 211–16.

9. United Nations Economic Commission for Europe, *Structure and Change in European Industry* (UN, 1977). See also Jean Francois Hennart, "The Political Economy of Comparative Growth Rates: The Case of France" (September 1978); Nicholas Kaldor, *Causes of the Slow Rate of Economic Growth of the United Kingdom* (Cambridge University Press, 1966).

10. Robert Bacon and Walter Eltis, *Britain's Economic Problem: Too Few Producers* (London: Macmillan, 1976), develop the case that public service expenditure slows growth and speeds inflation.

are threatened with a sharp loss of jobs or dramatic alteration in the composition of production. Workers who must move into sectors that require very different skills and offer relatively few jobs are likely to fight to hold onto their existing jobs.

The changed character of international trade in a number of sectors may also make internal adjustment difficult. In the boom years of the 1960s it was thought that specialization in production would result in trade between nations within sectors—that the United States and West Germany would exchange different types of machine tools, for example.[11] A dramatic instance of what happened is Japanese competition in the production of color television sets that virtually destroyed the American industry. In many industries, economies of scale in a few countries and stagnant levels of production in others have brought about worldwide overcapacity. But in such diverse industries as textiles, shipbuilding, and steel, excess capacity is as much due to competition from third world producers as to any drop in aggregate demand. Government efforts to maintain simultaneously employment, market shares, and prices in the face of such overcapacity can unfortunately cause threatened sectors to coalesce into an alliance for protectionist policies and resistance to industrial change.

Between 1967 and 1977 the manufactured exports of less developed countries grew some ten times, reaching a total of $44 billion.[12] By 1981 they grew to between $100 billion and $145 billion.[13] In global terms, they represented 1–2 percent of total imports of manufactured goods.[14] But the figures are less relevant than is their effect on unemployment in the importing countries (including layoffs attributed to increased productivity provoked by the imports). The massive impact of imports on regionally concentrated industries makes the transfer of capital and labor out of the affected sectors particularly difficult and magnifies the political and policy reaction. Government subsidies and supports are undoubtedly higher than they would be if the impact were diffused throughout the economy.

11. Richard N. Cooper, *The Economics of Interdependence: Economic Policy in the Atlantic Community* (McGraw-Hill for Council on Foreign Relations, 1968).

12. Between 1973 and 1977, they increased some $20 billion. Commissariat General du Plan, *Rapport du groupe charge d'etudies l'evolution des economies du tiers monde et l'appareil productif francais* (Paris, 1978); Lawrence G. Franko, *A Survey of the Impact of Manufactured Exports from Industrializing Countries in Asia and Latin America: Must Export-Oriented Growth Be Disruptive?* NPA Report 174 (Washington: National Planning Association, 1979).

13. Commissariat General du Plan, *Rapport*, p. 12.

14. Franko, *Survey*, p. 15.

In capital-intensive production sectors, where productivity is at the center of competition, overcapacity is concentrated in countries whose industries are uncompetitive. Subsidies promote expansion that results in declines and subsidies in other countries.

Firms that expand production rapidly can frequently drive costs down and may be able to gain a competitive edge. Growth of the domestic market may enable firms to invade foreign markets. That happened, for example, in the Japanese automobile sector, where production jumped from 160,000 units in 1960 to 4.5 million in 1975 and exports during the period grew to reach 45 percent of production.[15]

But expanded output and government-backed modernization do not in themselves assure competitive productivity. The benefits of expansion depend on the choices about technology and production organization a firm makes. Together, the exports of less developed countries and the problems of industrial competitiveness create a set of endangered industries that are prepared to resist adjustment.

Fear that new jobs may not be created as fast as workers are displaced and certainly not with skill requirements to fit the labor pool provides the fuel for intense political efforts to protect existing jobs. The problem is not so much the loss of jobs as it is the internal adjustment that must be faced. Increases in the advanced countries' exports of manufactured goods to less developed countries have more than matched the growth in imports; the former grew from $36 billion in 1972 to $102 billion in 1976, while the latter grew from $24 billion to $71 billion.[16] The adjustment problem is the mismatch of relatively unskilled and immobile labor in traditional industries with requirements in new export sectors.

Another problem lies in the nature of the export industries. Between 1960 and 1970 in Western Europe there were three rapidly growing industries: chemicals, electrical machinery (which includes electronics and machine tools), and petroleum. Over the decade their share of output increased from 16.86 percent to 23.52 percent of production while their contribution to employment rose from 14.0 percent to 16.7 percent.[17] New production did not mean new jobs. That problem is likely to worsen as automation becomes widespread with the advance of electronic micro-circuitry.

When adjustment entails sharp dislocation and extended unemployment

---

15. Christian Stoffaës, *La grande menace industrielle* (Paris: Calmann-Levy, 1978), pp. 64–70.
16. Commissariat General du Plan, *Rapport*, p. 12.
17. UN Economic Commission for Europe, *Structure and Change*, pp. 82–99.

in a range of sectors and communities, the result is intense political resistance to change. Eventually that means subsidies to sectors requiring protection and transfer payments to growing sectors. But if continued growth depends on a smooth shift of resources between industrial sectors and this is a politically more difficult task than in the past, can new alliances and strategies be found to contain the pressures for protection and privilege?

Officials and Firms: The Possibilities for Coalitions of Growth

Political action plays a part in the adjustment to industrial change in every country. Its effect on price levels depends on whether it is used to override existing protections and restrictions or to construct new restrictions and complicate adjustment further. Assuming that economic circumstances after World War II were roughly the same among the high growth countries, all of which saw a rapid decline in their agricultural population, and among the slower growth countries, which were entirely dependent on change within industry, the variations in each group suggest how institutional arrangements affect adjustment. Within the high growth countries the central problem in realizing new market possibilities was to move labor out of agriculture into industry; flexibility was assured by the expansion rather than the transformation of plant. In the slow growth countries the problem was very much the adaptation of industry to shifting markets and altered international positions.

Some of the battles during the process of adjustment could only be resolved by political coalitions and state control, while others could be settled purely by corporatist arrangements within industry. In those cases where industry alone cannot assure adjustment, but the state must become involved, the question first arises whether the state actively takes initiative in shaping the response to pressures for change, and second whether it will support positive adjustments toward industry positions unattainable in the market. Three types of explanations suggest themselves. The character of the adjustment problem may compel certain choices; the government's role in the economy and the policy instruments it controls may make some tactics more tempting than others; and the political volitions of those undergoing change may differ. The issue is how these several influences—market organization, institutional structure, and political purpose—combine and intertwine in a national context.

Political leadership in industrial affairs rests on very particular institutional foundations. The state must be able to impinge selectively on company choices and participate actively in the organization of industry. The critical hypothesis is that for the state to act as an economic player and exert industrial leadership, it must have discretionary and selective influence over the allocation of industrial finance—as it does in France and Japan. In Britain, creation of such a capacity has been the subject of political debate, while in the United States such a capacity has been eschewed. Yet these structural possibilities alone do not determine the uses to which the state apparatus is put. Political struggles must determine to what degree institutional resources are created or utilized. So too, business leaders will seek to draw in or keep the state out of the market. Firms must formulate strategies for coping with their competitors and their production problems, strategies that may mean either remaining competitive or seeking restrictions on market forces. Firms might try to keep government from interfering with their affairs, trusting their fate to success in the market. They might engage state support to protect their income, seek subsidies to supplement their market take, or seek help in controlling the cost of production—meaning labor costs for the most part. Or firms might seek the state as an ally in their expansion, trying to increase what they can earn in the market from new activities.

An industry or firm in decline is likely to turn to government for protection, one in ascent to seek support for its expanding efforts, while a mature and profitable sector with stable markets and a solid competitive position may simply want the government out of its hair. But competitive position alone cannot account for national differences in industry strategies. The textile industry in Britain, for example, is one of modern capital-intensive firms that have emerged in the face of cheap Commonwealth imports; in France, by contrast, natural fiber manufacturers have sought protection both from foreign imports and from domestic producers of artificial fibers.[18] In part, such differences turn on corporate capacities within national industries. They are also determined by sectoral politics, which directly affect firm strategies. A company's willingness to press a competitive advantage or its concern over market weakness depends in part on its alliances—within the sector, with other sectors, and with labor.

The important questions here are whether those seeking opportunity and profit in market changes or those fearing change and seeking insulation

18. Robert Berrier, "The Politics of Industrial Survival" (Ph.D. dissertation, Massachusetts Institute of Technology, 1978), chap. 2.

predominate, and whether either group requires government support or aid for its plans. The demands of the industry and its influence will depend on the interests of the spokesmen and the organizational platforms, since the problems and needs of firms vary widely within a sector. Trade associations that group winners and losers under a single roof cannot be expected to articulate particular interests.

Broadly cast groups are less likely to serve as instruments of state support for expansion, but otherwise their purpose will depend on the particular business interests that control the organization. Demands for help are likely to come from particular companies or smaller associations within an industry that compete with the broadly cast trade association for influence within the government.

The state has powerful means of shaping the demands made on it—everything from privileged policy access to the right to administer state policies. Bureaucrats and elected policymakers are not merely passive, of course. Their role will depend on the coalitions they build among themselves and with corporation or labor spokesmen. The more that state officials or their business allies have a voice across economic sectors, the more they can override particularistic needs. In the Federal Republic of Germany, governments have consistently resisted demands for protection and subsidy from all particular industrial sectors. In a centralized system such as France or Japan, the same bureaucrats, bankers, and politicians will have a hand in the politics of many sectors. Policies for any one sector will be shaped as much by the effect on all coalition members as by the needs of that sector.

What determines the strength or purposefulness of state officials in the adjustment coalition? In part it will be the needs of firms themselves in confronting a changing market. But here the discussion concentrates primarily on the government side of the coalition.

The High Growth Countries

In France and Japan state bureaucrats have actively sought to organize development, and they have been able to act as industrial leaders. This capacity depends on at least partial autonomy from the pressure of groups that support the government and on the ability to discriminate, especially in finance, between firms. A centralized bureaucracy, a permanent elite civil service, and limited parliamentary involvement in policymaking create the conditions for autonomy. Not only are the avenues of access controlling the influence of interest groups limited, but access is a resource the state leadership can offer to interest groups in exchange for some influence over policy, leadership, and organization. Influence in the organization of an industrial sector, however, also demands the ability to select targets and favorites. The selective allocation of credit, and institutions that permit it, provides a multipurpose and multisectoral tool vital to state-led industrial strategies. The government does not have to find specific authority to influence individual decisions or to control bureaus with authority over specific instruments. Moreover, it can operate within the framework of business decision, most directly the balance sheet, to act as a player in the market.

Possessing potent resources for intervention, the elite members of the centralized state bureaucracy in France and Japan could aggressively promote adjustment out of agriculture into industry and out of low wage into higher wage sectors. In each case the state supported newer sectors bidding resources out of traditional uses, but by means of policies that differed substantively. The French were more constrained by international agreement in their tactics and dependent on weaker and less internationally oriented companies. The Japanese sought to build self-sustaining market positions for their companies in growth industries, whereas the French sought to override the market in many instances, by sheltering chosen companies or promoting favorite projects. The Japanese, committed to growth as a systematic priority, maintained an undervalued currency for a generation, but the French had competing policy purposes and did not systematically attempt the same monetary tactic. Moreover, the French seem to have been more constrained by their uncompetitive sectors; they provided them more support and were less able to force them into competitive paths. The important contrast to those two state-led economies is West Germany.

FRANCE. The politics of growth in France served to entrench privilege at the same time that it encouraged change—subsidized privilege was set against subsidized protection. Postwar development in France was led, or at least promoted and nurtured, by a centralized state bureaucracy with links to the business and financial community. Growth in the gross domestic product was very rapid, averaging 4.7 percent a year between 1950 and 1975.[19] And, as Stephen Cohen noted in his assessment of the Fifth Republic's first twenty years, "the French economy has been transformed."[20] Boom and backwardness created powerful market incen-

19. Hennart, "Political Economy of Comparative Growth Rates."
20. Stephen S. Cohen, "Twenty Years of the Gaullist Economy," in William G. Andrews and Stanley Hoffmann, eds., *The Fifth Republic at Twenty* (State University of New York Press, 1981), p. 241.

tives to move from agriculture into industry. The shift was abrupt and sudden. Between 1949 and 1968 the average annual decline in the agricultural labor force was 3.3 percent, and between 1968 and 1974 it was 5.3 percent, which brought the sector down to less than 10 percent of the active labor force. In the first quarter of the century, by contrast, the rate averaged 1 percent and in the second quarter, which was disrupted by depression and war, there was no outmigration.[21]

The transformation was a victory of political leadership. The political strategy was to alter the economic order while buying social peace and political equilibrium by partially insulating critical groups. The price was mostly paid from growing national production, partly by the common agricultural policy, and seemingly in part by inflation. State leadership was at the center of the process. A handful of ranking government officials sought to reform the bureaucracy and alter the role of the state in the economy, and they used their power to press for modernization and growth.[22] What began in the bureaucratic citadels of the French state was managed and completed by the Gaullists.

The economy was changing, but politically potent groups in agriculture, small business, inefficient firms, and the like could impede the industrial advance, as indeed alliances had done throughout the Third Republic. The Poujadist uprising of small shopkeepers in the 1950s did, for a moment, give voice to part of the opposition. Those supporting industrial expansion had to prevent the formation of an active opposition while maintaining incentives and pressure for adjustment. The beginnings of European economic integration pushed French businessmen into seizing many market opportunities that had always been there; the Coal and Steel Community and the Common Market preoccupied many of the possible members of a coalition against growth. Such devices as agricultural supports diverted others. The Gaullists completed the job; their great achievement was to hold once powerful social groups "in line politically so they would not dismantle the growth machine. . . . Gaullism kept the dreadnoughts of the French past politically impotent,"[23] while the market displaced them.

21. Hennart, "Political Economy of Comparative Growth Rates," p. 7.
22. See Stanley Hoffmann, *Decline or Renewal? France Since the 1930s* (Viking, 1974); Charles P. Kindleberger, "The Postwar Resurgence of the French Economy," in Stanley Hoffmann, *In Search of France* (Harvard University Press, 1963); John Zysman, "The Interventionist Temptation: Financial Structure and Political Purpose," in Andrews and Hoffmann, *Fifth Republic*, pp. 252–70.
23. Cohen, "Twenty Years," p. 241.

The political victory was not simple, complete, or cheap. One tactic was to trap and immobilize the collection of interests that would have limited development, but a second range of tactics involved paying off at least some of the multitude of demands with tax privileges, subsidies, and restrictive business arrangements. Differential treatment of taxes, specialized lending circuits, and toleration of competitive agreements that sustained prices were part of the effort to preserve the traditional small business community of shopkeepers and small producers. As the social face of France altered, these groups became even more crucial politically to the conservative majority and fitted congenially into the business strategies of many larger and more advanced firms.

Labor's position was weak. The unions withdrew and were kept out of the efforts to plan the economy. Although the events of May 1968 brought substantial wage increases, the gains were lost by a devaluation the next year. (By contrast Michele Salvati contends in chapter 15 that Italian labor was able to block similar policies.) Rights to existing jobs, often embedded in elaborate layoff procedures, were stoutly defended. Labor mobility did increase, but there was not a wholesale displacement of restrictions on change. Some of the protections of the hothouse economy were available even to the politically weaker groups.

The uneasy and expensive balance of development without disruption is evident in sectors where firms committed to modernization struggled against those attempting to preserve old patterns. One series of projects, including the Concorde and the abortive attempt at a national computer industry, was a costly political attempt to buy the symbols of industrial advancement without establishing possible market conditions for the industries. In sectors such as oil, where the domestic market could be isolated and heavy capital investment was crucial to success, efforts to impose political goals on the industry worked. In entrenched sectors such as steel and textiles, where industrial reorganization and rationalization would mean displacing entrepreneurs of local or national importance and creating widespread layoffs in single-industry regions, modernization was tentative. The steel industry was reorganized, several times, when capital needs and cash crunches forced the firms to accept state initiatives. Massive new facilities were opened at seaside locations, but older, less efficient facilities were not closed because of the powerful resistance anticipated. The industry trade association remained an intermediary between the firms and the government in the decade-long negotiations that culminated in a debt-forced nationalization which the state would have liked to avoid.

In textiles, the traditionalists found themselves as allies of the Ministry of Industry in its bureaucratic fight to wrest policy instruments from the Ministry of Finance. The government acted not only to preserve small and often marginal firms, but to hold in place a very traditional nonintegrated textile industry, unique among the advanced countries. Manufacturers of artificial fibers were kept out of the textile business in exchange for a monopoly in the supply of fiber. Modernization plans were drawn upon to justify support for marginal firms, and a segmented labor force was created to provide cheap immigrant labor for uncompetitive small firms and stable, highly paid jobs for local workers. In each sector the problem of adjustment was resolved within the confines of the government's commitment to modernization, even when the outcomes proved unworkable or unduly expensive.

In effect, the myriad institutional arrangements were subsidies that permitted many to hold to the past a little longer and others to make that past part of the future. Social immobility and the effort to maintain constant relative incomes made France particularly vulnerable to inflation and contributed to an inflation rate well above the composite foreign index during most of the period between 1960 and 1974.[24] French strategy led to widely dispersed real and apparent benefits, while obscuring and muting the costs or isolating the groups damaged. Satisfying the monetary demands of all groups and letting inflation shift the resources is, however, an old trick in French politics—after both world wars the French middle classes revealed a "tendency to accept the indirect taxation of inflation rather than confront the direct levies needed to avoid it."[25]

The policy instruments to pursue hidden transfers of resources between sectors, to use inflation as a continuing tactic, certainly exist in France. The banking system is organized to control the allocation of credit, and interest rates are used to subsidize privileged loans, rather than serving to allocate capital. A network of parapublic and public banking institutions, however, permits the state to pursue specific objectives in industries and firms it considers critical. The system permits the money supply to be manipulated to satisfy what are often quite specific political or policy purposes.

Despite an elaborate rhetoric about industrial deployment and economic

24. Pascal Salin and Georges Lane, "Inflation in France," in Lawrence B. Krause and Walter S. Salant, eds., *Worldwide Inflation: Theory and Recent Experience* (Brookings Institution, 1977), pp. 545–87.

25. Charles S. Maier, "The Politics of Inflation in the Twentieth Century," in Fred Hirsch and John H. Goldthorpe, eds., *The Political Economy of Inflation* (Harvard University Press, 1978), p. 57.

liberalism, the French did little to assure positive adjustment in the late 1970s. Redeployment was left to the market, and firms left to redeploy themselves.[26] Traditional sectors continued to be protected. The financial apparatus used during reconstruction to aid expansion in critical sectors, and during the boom years to forge so-called national champions, was rolled into battle to restructure troubled firms and promote exports.[27] The policy of retiring losers and protecting the public from the consequences of company failure embraced often contradictory objectives. The large programs to rationalize the shipbuilding and steel sectors did not succeed despite massive assistance. Substantial investments were made in the aircraft industry, where the airbus was successful in the market; in nuclear production, where the French staked their domestic energy future and established a position as a major exporter; in computers, where an American multinational corporation was harnessed to French policy; and in telecommunications, where the effort to make the French telephone system respectable opened the possibility of substantially affecting the semiconductor and professional equipment sectors. In the years following the oil crisis, new initiatives were made in financing exports, particularly plant and machinery sold to Eastern Europe and the third world.

France underwent buffered change. Growth took place, but with extensive side payments in the forms of subsidy and restriction to politically potent groups. For a long time, labor was one of the political losers and dissipated what strength it had on the pursuit of protective restrictions. The groups that composed traditional France were trapped inside conservative coalitions—unable to block or control change but capable of assuring that part of the old world would be preserved. The political executive—operating with some autonomy—used a system of circular and selective credit systems both to fund change and to pay for restriction. The restrictions won in the postwar boom now constrain further adjustment and raise the price of growth. Undoing that system is the political challenge.

Those difficulties continue despite a shift to the left in 1981 and the advent of President François Mitterrand. Socialist political leaders, too, draw on the same interventionist traditions; indeed, they use outright public control more expansively. Adding the unions' voice to the policy coalition may set an even higher price on adjustment than in the 1970s,

---

26. See Suzanne Berger, "Lame Ducks and National Champions: Industrial Policy in the Fifth Republic," in Andrews and Hoffmann, *Fifth Republic,* pp. 292–310.

27. Zysman, "Interventionist Temptation."

and Socialist control of the economy cannot make the trade-offs of adjustment any less painful.

JAPAN. Japan faced the same problems of managing the decline of agriculture and avoiding a rebellion of its traditional sectors, and it faced them with a state structure and financial system much like those in France. Each bureaucracy was manned at the top by an elite corps of civil servants which had enough autonomy from day-to-day political pressure to formulate its own tactics. In each country the state exercised economic leadership because it was able to act as a player in the market by the selective manipulation of finance. As in France, agricultural groups were critical of the electoral position of the conservative governments and their interests were well tended in both countries; public expenditures for agriculture in Japan represented 1.5 percent of the gross national product in the late 1960s and in France 1.6 percent.[28]

The Japanese had a strong commitment to moving labor out of low productivity sectors into high wage industries as well as facilitating the move out of agriculture. The industrial structure that was built in the 1950s and 1960s was the result of deliberate restructuring. While light industry represented 50 percent of total industrial output in 1955, by the early 1970s heavy and chemical industries with a higher wage structure represented 70 percent of manufacturing production. "The shift resulted from measures taken by the government in the 1950s channeling resources into those industries for which there was a growing world demand. The targets were greater production of machinery, metals (especially steel), chemicals, and ships."[29] In shipbuilding, for example, the rapid delivery times that helped build Japanese dominance depended on financing of stockpiles made possible by government policy.[30] Clearly some sectors were subsidized to survive, and the massive effort was to achieve growth through sectoral transfer and modernization. This shift was supplemented by an effort to encourage new products and processes that would give a distinctive competitive advantage to Japanese firms, a task aided by the burgeoning of industrial demand.

The weight of government policy was the reverse of the French. Japan sought to promote competitive industries that could be self-sustaining in

28. OECD, *Inflation: The Present Problem* (Paris: OECD, 1970), p. 99.

29. Eugene J. Kaplan, *Japan: The Government-Business Relationship* (U.S. Government Printing Office, 1972), p. 4. This is a remarkable study based in part on studies by the Boston Consulting Group.

30. See Tuvia Blumenthal, "The Japanese Shipbuilding Industry," in Hugh Patrick, ed., *Japanese Industrialization and Its Social Consequences* (University of California Press, 1976), pp. 129–60.

the market rather than selecting projects and firms for political reasons. And the sectors of low priority were left to market forces.

The commitment to rapid development was built into the structure of the financial system, which was arranged to favor industrial lending. Critically, as Kozo Yamamura demonstrates in chapter 14, the system moved funds away from the countryside and small- and medium-sized businesses toward the city and larger firms. This allowed the Bank of Japan to firmly channel funds into the sectors and types of firms it preferred. This discretionary control of finance, combined with the powers of the Ministry of Trade and Industry, created the leverage to intervene in the development of particular sectors, to promote favored firms, and to encourage expansionist strategies.[31] There is reason to suspect that in France the effort to provide funds to growth sectors meant a general expansion of the money supply. In Japan, it appears only that the growth sectors were favored, accentuating the bidding for resources.

A case can be made that the rapid promotion of growth sectors contributed to demand-shift inflation. As the pool of surplus labor in Japan dwindled, "progressively larger wage increases were necessary to transfer labor from lower-productivity sectors to rapidly growing ones."[32] But the extraordinarily rapid productivity growth in manufacturing allowed wholesale prices to rise more slowly than in France until 1963; Japanese consumer prices, however, ran ahead of the French. Japanese industry apparently stayed that one step ahead in bidding for resources and was able to pay the bill without price increases because of increasing productivity. This pattern is consistent with the different emphases of French and Japanese policy.

Thus despite political problems and structures parallel to those in France, Japan was able to move more decisively toward growth and seemingly for many years to limit the inflationary consequences of development strategies to declining sectors. One party, the Liberal Democratic, has governed Japan since World War II and that party has been dominated by an aggressively internationally oriented business elite. The presence of expanding companies in each sector and the big business elite in the leadership of the ruling party meant that the interests of the

---

31. Laura Tyson, "The Yugoslav Banking System and Monetary Control," paper presented to Western Economics Association, June 1976, has shown how selective allocation of credit contributed to expansion of Yugoslavia's money supply.

32. Ryutaro Komiya and Yoshio Suzuki, "Inflation in Japan," in Krause and Salant, *Worldwide Inflation*, p. 309.

losers in each sector could not be articulated as effectively and would not be heard as sympathetically as in France. Growth rested on the three-pronged stand of state, party, and business. In the early 1970s, the delicate arrangement that produced rapid growth with relatively low inflation came unstuck. Yamamura argues convincingly in chapter 14, below, that structural blocks to growth emerged just as the ruling LDP needed to provide state-financed benefits to constituencies previously satisfied with the spin-offs of growth. The demands were all the more urgent because the party's weakening hold on power forced it to bid more vigorously with special favors to hold what remained of its constituencies. A reduced pace of revenue increase, the concomitant of the economic slowdown, translated those political commitments into government borrowing. In Japan, as in France, demand-shift plausibly accounts for the pattern of growth and inflation, but in Japan there was a clearer and more enduring commitment to supporting the stars of the industrial future.

WEST GERMANY.   French and Japanese examples of heavy state involvement in adjustment are in sharp contrast with German experience. West Germany more stringently than other countries avoided government support for troubled industry, as was evident in the refusal to cushion the shock of the rise in oil prices in 1973–74.[33] The transfer of real resources into exports and out of consumers' pockets was accomplished quickly; overall trade surpluses were maintained and bilateral balances brought back into the black at the same time that inflation rates were kept below those in other nations. Political virtue may, however, have to share credit for the inflation-free character of the German industrial miracle; for of all the fast growth countries, West Germany required the least transformation of its industrial structure in the postwar years.[34]

German commitment to readjustment began only in the late 1960s. At war's end, Germany needed only to expand those industries—such as machinery, vehicles, electrical products, and chemical products—that were "front runners in international trade and enjoyed constantly growing markets."[35] The startling success of currency reform in 1948 gave the Christian-Democratic government a considerable leeway. Exchange rates were kept undervalued, an effective transfer from consumers to the export sector, encouraging industry to penetrate new markets with new products.

33. Alain Cotta, *La France et l'impératif mondial* (Paris: Presses Universitaires de France, 1978).
34. Gustav Stolper, Karl Häuser, and Knut Borchardt, *The German Economy: 1870 to the Present* (Harcourt, Brace and World, 1967), pp. 219–98.
35. Ibid, p. 248.

Tax policy was structured to permit high profits to be reinvested.[36] Unlike their counterparts in Britain, the major banks shared an interest in industrial exports and were part of an alliance that supported the strategy. Growth fed on growth. Rapidly improving productivity meant that higher wages could be sustained, that the higher transfer costs could be paid, and that those displaced from one job could readily believe others would be available.

Beginning in the late 1960s West Germany's stable industries faced competition from less developed countries at the same time that wages and the value of the mark were rising. Government policy seems to have been based on assisting companies to move into defensible market niches of high-wage industries. The basic technique seems to have been support for research and development for individual projects proposed by the companies themselves. In sectors such as electrical engineering and electronics (defense spending aside) and mechanical engineering, government money became a substantial portion of the national research effort.

Project funding reflecting past government efforts, excluding nuclear, space, and defense, jumped from around half to four-fifths of the budget from the late 1960s to 1980, while indirect funding through tax incentives dropped. The research budget expanded at a rate about one and a half times the overall budget. The projects were selected by government-industry committees, not only on technical merits but also for their impact on the German competitive position and their ability to generate competitive high-wage industries.[37] The entire effort was seen as a partnership that would permit the application of big science in industrial sectors, the promotion of competitive business segments, and the development of technologies that would be crucial to long-run German development. State governments too made their investments in potential growth industries, and local alliances of business, banks, and government were established for the purpose. Unlike the case in France and Japan, labor was a systematic force in policymaking and collaborated in retraining and readjustment schemes. As one industry analyst remarked, the government aid schemes worked because of good communication between the producer groups and the segments of government. The interest group and corporate alliances built in the first phase of the German boom, when growth fed

---

36. Ibid.
37. Data in this and the next paragraph are from my interviews with U.S. government steel analysts and a private, unpublished consulting study.

itself, became policy instruments in the adjustment to a downward world cycle.

The Germans professed a tough determination to resist demands for subsidy from declining industries. Strong pressures for structural adjustment policies were sidestepped and the study groups urged by labor were set up outside government in order to keep government agencies out of involvement in industry affairs. Yet in coal, shipbuilding, and textiles there were substantial assistance programs, though in textiles probably at levels below those in France and Britain. As in France, agriculture was substantially supported, and despite modernization most farms remained small and uncompetitive, and distributors in small towns were protected against the giant department stores. Clearly some claims for subsidy and protection were met, but agriculture and small business were seen as anomalies and not the centerpiece of a web of privileged market positions. The weight of German policy is perhaps suggested in the case of steel, where despite the decline in the Saar and the Ruhr the federal government provided no subsidies to industry. Rather it encouraged local investment in mechanical engineering and assisted the search for new steel technologies that would permit portions of the industry to remain competitive.

The German government spent substantially less money on sectoral support than the French—the expenditure in the early 1970s represented 16 percent of the budget in Germany and about 35 percent in France. The amounts for regional assistance in Germany were an order of magnitude greater than in France, and the funds were channeled to growing sectors. Politically, the Ministry of Economics, which was opposed in principle to subsidy, managed sectoral and regional policy whereas government support for positive adjustment through research and development was managed through a technical ministry, not the Ministry of Industry.

German policy rested on a political consensus and producer-government alliances rather than on an explicit political victory and the exclusion of one group from policymaking. In the early years the problem was simply maintaining conditions for expansion. As growth fed on growth, the theory of social market liberalism became an ideology that made it simpler to insist on adjustment and refuse particular demands. This policy stance, first taken by the Christian Democrats, was doggedly maintained by the Social Democrats. At each critical juncture, the basic soundness of the industrial structure, plus high employment and low inflation over the longer term, and the past success of forcing market adaptations, permitted tough policies to be applied without immediate political reaction. Companies committed to market adjustment, moreover, were likely to remain competitive and require little assistance.

Whether the virtuous interaction of growth and adjustment can be maintained in the face of a real decline in crucial German export sectors is doubtful. Certainly the multitude of subsidies provided suggests that the Germans are not possessed of a unique portion of economic virtue, but in part found themselves in happy economic circumstances, which only began in the early 1980s to test their political resolve in a sustained way. Since policy rested more on a corporatist alliance of producers than on the explicit victory of a party or social group, the delicate compensation required to sustain this consensus may be difficult to make during real structural change. Or, conversely, Germany may seek to resist change and persevere in the precomputer engineering and chemical industries that were the source of former strength. Constructing a political alliance around new development to replace the consensus of interest groups formed around the successes of the 1950s and 1960s may be difficult regardless of which political parties hold power.

The Slow Growth Countries

The basic adjustment problem in the United Kingdom and the United States was to shift labor from low wage, low productivity sectors to high wage and high productivity uses. In Britain that also involved a transition away from semiprotected Commonwealth markets and the complications of a reserve currency status, a shift made more difficult by the absence of a corporatist consensus about the terms of industrial change or an enduring political victory that might have imposed the terms.

UNITED KINGDOM. After World War II, England still viewed itself as a rich and great nation, giving precedence to international finance and domestic consumption over economic growth and the nation's industrial market position. Its decision to defend the value of sterling was shared between the parties. The consequences of an overvalued currency were devastating. Imports appeared more attractive and exports less so, the exact opposite of the German and Japanese situations. British goods were vulnerable to competition abroad and new markets were hard to enter. British exports lost market share in all markets and industries, which handicapped all of British industry. At home an agreement to build the welfare state had emerged from the war, its basic goal being to achieve equality and remedy injustice. Little attention was paid to the effect of these various policies on the possibilities for growth. The debate was over the question, consumption for whom? So, unlike the thrust of policy in France, Germany, and Japan, the basic lines of policy in the United Kingdom were not oriented toward sustaining and expanding industry.

By the late 1950s a debate had begun on how to speed growth. Public expenditures (particularly for local services) grew steadily until the mid-1970s,[38] without a broad public debate over the consequences for investment and production. Savings and investment in Britain were far lower than in the faster growing economies, yet political argument seldom focused on who should save and how investment might be expanded.[39] There was amorphous support for redevelopment, but no agreement on the issue of who would lead and profit from the growth.

At the political level the debate concerned the state's role in the economy, at the producer level labor's role in the factory and in politics. The Conservatives opened the debate, creating the National Economic Development Organization in 1960 as a symbol and instrument of a new direction. Yet this roundtable modeled on French modernization committees lacked the instruments for selective intervention in industry and finance that gave the French planners and Japanese bureaucrats muscle. It included no bankers.[40] The continuing commitment to an overvalued currency, a major obstacle to growth, was supported by the banking community, but it was absent from the industrial debate. Without the bankers, however, the Conservatives had neither the intent nor the instruments to intervene in industry, and Labour's strategies pushed it to adopt the position that more competition would ease Britain's problems.

The role the state would play in industry was caught up in an ideologically oversimplified conflict between nationalization and free enterprise. Free market strategies meant reinvestment of business profits, but to leftist Labourites profits implied exploitation, inequality, and capital exports. To Conservatives, state initiatives by Labour governments implied nationalization of private property, not the effectiveness of state intervention.[41] Moreover, those Tories who had used the state during the

---

38. Ian Gough, *The Political Economy of the Welfare State* (London: Macmillan, 1979), pp. 128–52.

39. Yao-su Hu, *National Attitudes and the Financing of Industry* (London: PEP, 1975).

40. Bankers only became part of sectoral committees in 1976, and then only in a limited way.

41. See Michael Stewart, *The Jekyll and Hyde Years: Politics and Economic Policy Since 1964* (London: J. M. Dent, 1977); Michael Shanks, *Planning and Politics: The British Experience, 1960–1976* (London: Allen and Unwin, 1977).

depression to try to rationalize industry and save capitalism were pushed aside when the Liberal party transferred its constituency and part of its leadership to the Conservatives after the war.[42] With the Labour party attempting direct physical management of the economy and nationalization, free market stances made good political strategy. The conservative alliance between state and industry that led the push toward growth in Japan, France, and West Germany was difficult to envision or establish in England.

Ironically, it was Labour that adopted strategies reminiscent of conservative French governments' efforts to merge undersized companies. The Industrial Reorganization Corporation (IRC), created under the first Wilson government, was so successful in promoting mergers that a decade later, giant firms dominated industrial production to a degree not found in other national economies.[43] When the Conservatives returned to power in 1970, they dismantled the IRC, but it was reborn at the next turn of the political tables as the National Enterprise Board, a state holding company set up to invest public funds in competitive enterprise. The Industry Act of 1974 that created the NEB, like a Conservative bill two years earlier, provided a range of grants and loans intended to prop up or prod industry. Governments were driven to devise policy instruments for a state-led strategy of industrial adjustment, but their innovations were overwhelmed by circumstance and partisan conflict. State initiatives represented a challenge to financial institutions that were stoutly defended by political elements well represented in the Conservative party. Government involvement in industry's power struggles went against the entrenched Conservative belief that government ought not to discriminate between firms, or to favor one against another; but beside that principle sat the assumption that government should correct deficiencies in the market and that if the markets worked perfectly British industry would surge ahead. The alternative position—that market forces would not correct Britain's decline—was developed by Wedgewood Benn from the left of the Labour party. To reassert Britain's position in international markets, he proposed not an alliance of state and business, as in Japan and France, but a replacement of business by the state, and if necessary a withdrawal from international markets. The National Enterprise Board,

42. Nigel Harris, *Competition and the Corporate Society: British Conservatives, the State and Industry, 1945–1964* (London: Methuen, 1972).

43. S. J. Prais, *The Evolution of Giant Firms in Britain: A Study of the Growth of Concentration in Manufacturinng Industry in Britain, 1909–70* (Cambridge University Press, 1976).

which was his creation, therefore contained the broader threat of using financial involvement as a means of extending nationalization. Subsequent initiatives from the Labour left, including proposals to nationalize the banking and insurance sectors, reinforced that theme. Each political cycle, then, exacerbated the free market versus nationalization dichotomy, leaving no intellectual or political space for building a strategy by which the state could nurture private enterprise.

Britain's interventionist policies thus tended to degenerate into subsidies and protections. Under both parties, job support seemingly took precedence over industrial adjustment. Policies seemed to be aimed at defending a low-wage status quo rather than cooperating to create a high-wage future, the opposite of the German choice. Indeed, the bulk of £325 million of support in the form of loans and grants in 1973–74, before the full effects of recession had hit, went toward declining industries and backward regions, some £35 million of that to the shipbuilding industry.[44]

The real substance of policy was to provide for troubled regions,[45] a pattern shaped after World War I to support declining staple goods industries. These industries were concentrated in areas dependent on these activities for their livelihood, and efforts to cushion the producing regions became a defense of declining industry and vice versa.

The state's intervention in labor markets also supported the status quo. In Britain the bulk of unemployment funds goes into paying workers cash for lost jobs. In France and Germany, the greatest effort is placed on finding them jobs. In Britain, security of employment becomes equated with holding on to particular jobs, because there is little assurance of new jobs. "Security becomes synonymous with rigidity."[46]

Labor's role is yet another unresolved issue in British politics and industry. Unions obviously have a powerful position in the Labour party and in the councils of Labour governments. Their difficult problems are within the factory, where they are powerfully present but not as partners. Government policy if anything has exacerbated the problem and has not undone organizational and social obstacles to corporatist policies.

The labor movement in England is simply not organized or motivated to serve as a partner for cooperative industrial strategies (nor has industry

44. Vincent Cable, *Import Controls: The Case Against,* Fabian Research Series, 335 (London: Fabian Society, 1977).

45. Alan Whiting, "Overseas Experience in the Use of Industrial Subsidies," in Alan Whiting, ed., *The Economics of Industrial Subsidies* (London: Her Majesty's Stationery Office, 1976), pp. 45–63.

46. Santosh Mukherjee, *Through No Fault of Their Own: Systems for Handling Redundancy in Britain, France and Germany* (London: Macdonald, 1973).

sought such collaboration). Labor has been fragmented; shop steward power has represented a threat to more conservative central leadership, and the movement is ideologically divided. Consequently, the Trades Union Congress leadership cannot negotiate policies that uniformly blanket the membership and is pressed to defend particular interests, sometimes of small groups of workers attempting to control events on the shop floor.

The underlying problems are shifts in power and politics on the shop floor. The dramatic growth in shop-floor power—reflected in extensive plant-level bargaining and the increasing number of strikes begun at the lower levels that are given sanction by national unions—was unwittingly promoted by a Conservative government, which in essence traded a hands-off policy on internal union organization for wage restraint. In labor's two-tier bargaining system, national unions moderated their demands, leaving the plant as the focus of bargaining and thus increasing shop-floor power. Inevitably the national unions' ability to pursue policies of adjustment was reduced because the effective bargaining was out of their hands.

Efforts to alter the union structure and practices by legislation proved unworkable in the face of united labor resistance. Though Labour leaders were able to organize a series of union-supported income policies in which immediate wage gains were sacrificed for policy goals such as limiting inflation,[47] arrangements broke down because the center was unable to restrain for extended periods the initiative and autonomy of the shop stewards. Only a dramatically new set of incentives, providing evident and mass benefits, would be able to overcome the obstacles to a political deal that would lay the groundwork for unions to join a corporatist consensus. The differences within the labor movement are as serious as those that separate industry and government.

The constant change of governments and the lines of fracture within the Conservative and Labour parties make it difficult to establish either a governmental or corporatist alliance for growth. Neither side is strong enough to impose a radical redevelopment policy, and no basis for cooperation is evident. The Conservatives in power could neither control nor ignore labor, and the Labour party in power had to be sensitive to the needs and demands of finance and industry. Labor leaders' need for

---

47. See, for example, Michael Moran, *The Politics of Industrial Relations: The Origins, Life and Death of the 1971 Industrial Relations Act* (London: Macmillan, 1977); Leo Panitch, "The Development of Corporatism in Liberal Democracies," *Comparative Political Studies,* vol. 10 (April 1977), pp. 61–90.

visible benefits and businessmen's fear of statist intervention clash directly, making a coherent and intensive industrial strategy hard to conceive. Until an accommodation is reached, subsidy and protection of particular interests will mean industrial rigidity, and a resulting propensity to slow growth and bias toward inflation. The Thatcher government has set out to alter the structure and behavior of the unions. It is simply too early to know if the government will succeed.

UNITED STATES. Unlike its trade partners and despite an ideology of productivity as a solvent for social conflict, the United States in the 1960s and 1970s had no explicit policy of growth nor did it show much interest in the subject. On balance, the U.S. economy appears to be like the German economy, displaying no systematic effort to support or restrict adjustment. De facto U.S. policy has rested on the autonomy of management strategy from detailed government interference, a basic consensus on the terms of union-company conflict and collaboration, and opposition in principle to national and international restrictions on trade.

Internationally the United States used its postwar dominance to press for an open system, reaffirming that commitment in the Kennedy years. Political and economic interests pushed in the direction that ideology pointed.[48] However, as U.S. industrial preeminence slipped, that openness became politically troublesome in an increasing number of sectors, and trade policy "seemed to move simultaneously toward free trade and protectionism."[49] The underlying coherence in the United States' trade adjustment policy was the protection of corporate rights to make strategy choices. The policy was not to intervene in favor of adjustment, but to offer first aid for the pain.

Domestically, the federal government did not seek to intervene selectively or systematically at the level of the sector or firm. Indeed, there was no policy apparatus to implement the kind of selective intervention that characterized French, Japanese, and recent British initiatives. With power and authority fragmented and diffused, particular sectoral interests were able to establish fiefdoms in the government and determine the character of government's relations with the sector.[50]

The responsiveness to the needs and strategies of major firms can be seen in government policies directed at Japanese penetration of the markets

48. Stephen Krasner, "The Tokyo Round: New Rules for World Trade."
49. Michael Borrus and James Millstein, "Protecting Profits" (Berkeley, Calif., 1979).
50. See Grant McConnell, *Private Power and American Democracy* (Knopf, 1966).

of the U.S. consumer-oriented electronics and steel industries.[51] The major firms in the consumer electronics sector were multinational and responded to competition by moving production abroad and establishing joint operations with their Japanese competitors while seeking to block foreign-produced imports through a series of customs court lawsuits. In steel, quasi-tariffs such as a trigger-point pricing system provided relief against dumping. There is no evidence of a strategy to rebuild the American steel industry. In the face of intense foreign competition the pattern was one of multinational corporations pursuing free-trade policies in opposition to labor, and national companies aligning with labor to gain some degree of protection.[52]

The federal structure of the United States, combined with the enormous diversity of a continental economy, makes it hard to organize resistance to adjustment. The conflicting needs of industries that were declining in the North and emerging in the South prevented regional demands from becoming the basis for national government interventions. Another basic feature of the American economy—the competition within sectors of American businesses backed by local governments in alliance with pieces of the Washington machinery—spawned giant firms with the flexibility and financial power to move between products and markets. That corporate flexibility meant that some companies moved out of the country while others diversified themselves out of the industry. Thus a policy that simply supported the autonomy of company strategy ran into the pressing objective of maintaining competitive American firms that employed high-wage American labor.

Models of Adjustment

From the five national cases, three models of adjustment emerge—a company-led, a state-led, and a tripartite pattern. They represent different balances of initiative and power between the major producer institutions measured by the degree of company autonomy and by differences in who influences company choices and how. They suggest what producer alliances can be built with government. Each arrangement, moreover, represents a

51. James Millstein, "Towards a New Political Economy of US Trade Policy: Market Adjustment and Domestic Politics in the US Television Receiver Industry" (master's thesis, University of California, Berkeley, 1979); Michael Borrus, "The Politics of Liberal Trade Adjustment: US Policy and Decline in the US Steel Industry" (master's thesis, University of California, Berkeley, 1979).

52. G. K. Helleiner, "Transnational Enterprises and the New Political Economy of U.S. Trade Policy," *Oxford Economic Papers*, vol. 29 (March 1977), pp. 102–16.

set of systematic competences and weaknesses, a group of tasks that can be accomplished easily or only with difficulty.

In the company-led model, basic choices are made by individual companies without outside interference, and workers or communities who are damaged or displaced are left to fend for themselves or seek compensation from the government. The state's role is to assure the autonomy of company choice and compensation for the rest of society. The arrangement works when the roles of neither the state nor labor are under direct question, so that the market arrangements and compensation deals can be worked out separately in each sector. The United States certainly suggests this type of adjustment.

In the state-led model the government bureaucracy attempts to orient the adjustment of the economy by explicitly influencing the position of particular sectors, even individual companies, and imposing those solutions on labor. In both France and Japan, the twentieth-century cases of great state-led capitalist expansion, command of the nation's credit system provided a means for bureaucrats to intervene selectively as players in the market as well as to allocate capital between competing uses. State-led growth is associated with the effort to force a sharp break with the past and thus involves an explicit coalition, including elite state bureaucrats, using the powers of the state and sheltering themselves in a semiautonomous state bureaucracy. Labor groups are either explicitly excluded or unable to organize and impose claims to industrial and political power. In essence, the consequences of development and adjustment are allocated by direct political choice without the participation of labor and with the preeminent influence of the state bureaucracy.

The tripartite bargaining strategy involves an explicit and continuing negotiation of the terms of change by the predominant social partners, including labor. The location and character of this negotiation differ, depending on both political and marketplace organization. In the most full-blown form, bargains are explicitly worked out by elite representatives of the several producers and political groupings. West Germany is suggestive of this model, but its arrangements are more company based than those of the smaller European economies.

The United Kingdom represents a case of the failure to choose an approach to adjustment. The political and industrial power of labor in that country makes it impossible to move without labor's support, but unions are not organized for the task of making corporatist bargains and companies are not prepared to accept them in that role.

The Role of Politics

The central question is whether any of the approaches to adjustment, or the political choices a country makes within a particular approach, actually affects the inflation rate. Does the character of the adjustment problem establish the price consequences of adjustment?

In France and Japan—countries of high growth and high inflation—an active and selective state policy resting on an enduring political coalition that included state bureaucrats both validated restrictions to change and overrode them with privileges. Evidently either the market forces were strong enough to achieve growth despite restrictions, or the privileges supplemented those market forces. The selective allocation of credit provides a direct link between adjustment policy and the resource bidding process, and in the French example a strong argument can be made that the shift of resources toward competitive sectors was made by selectively expanding the money supply.

In the low inflation countries, the United States and West Germany, although growth problems and the approaches to adjustment differed, flexibility and mobility seem to have rested on a consensus about the privileges and position of labor, industry, and state. Of course, the two consensuses were quite different, but in neither country were the terms of adjustment called into political question.

In Britain there was no such consensus, nor was there a political coalition that could impose the terms and costs of change. The limited productivity gains, in part a result of a limited commitment to growth, undoubtedly made the resolution of conflicting social claims more difficult. The British case in fact suggests that the very existence of a stable and enduring coalition may be more important to an adjustment strategy than the composition of that coalition. A clear winner means that costs can be allocated decisively and that the institutional arrangement that establishes how firms cooperate and compete will endure or change incrementally. Thus France, where labor was a clear loser virtually excluded from policy-making, pursued more successful adjustment strategies than Britain, where the alternation of government policies left unresolved the problem of how costs would be paid or which group would end up holding the bill.[53]

53. Is it possible to find confirmation of the links between inflation and models of adjustment? One approach would be to examine the relation between the wholesale price index and the consumer price index. The basic idea is that in fast growing economies, factor cost increases could be absorbed in the

The political approaches to managing adjustment do seem to have an influence on inflation apart from the economic adjustments that countries attempt. Some observers contend that labor has become more militant or powerful, making economic management more difficult, others that the uncontrollable spread of interest-group demands encourages inflation and retards growth. The analysis here indicates that whether interest groups or producer groups serve to facilitate or impede growth depends on the producer structures, state bureaucracies, and electoral coalitions in which industrial and policy issues are resolved. The types of alliances that are built within an economy are therefore the crucial issue, and the question is whether they will retard or facilitate growth.

The basic problem is allocating the costs and benefits of industrial change. Since the context of that change has altered, governmental and industry alliances that once facilitated growth may no longer be adequate to do so. In Britain, which has failed to adopt an adjustment approach, the overriding political task is to choose and make an enduring settlement about industrial change in the late twentieth century. State-led economies face the difficulties that arise from having excluded labor from policy participation. They also rely on ad hoc interventions for particular companies without an overall vision of what their future should be. In Japan, labor does not seem likely to intrude into the heaven-made marriage of state and industry, but costly side payments have become a problem. There do, however, appear to be obstacles to continuing to provide guidance in the constant effort to move resources into more productive

---

expanding sectors without price rises, while the less capital-intensive sectors with lower productivity rates would have to pass on the increase by raising prices. The more rapid the structural change, the higher would be the ratio of the wholesale price index to the consumer price index. In the Japanese case, the demand shift pattern has been identified by Komiya and Suzuki, "Inflation in Japan." Rapid growth involving a dramatic shift in the structure of the economy was associated with a high WPI-to-CPI ratio from 1953 to 1974. In the years that followed, the pattern was broken by a slowing of growth, oil price increases, and increased public expenditures. After 1973 and 1974 the pattern began to reassert itself in a sputtering way. In Germany the pattern of WPI and CPI movements has been similar, but at a lower overall rate of inflation. Wholesale prices remained almost entirely stable over the fifteen-year period from 1953 to 1968, while consumer prices did move moderately ahead. One might argue that in the two countries where the strongest support was given to the expanding sectors vis-à-vis the lagging sectors, this demand-shift pattern can be clearly seen because fewer compensations have been provided to the losers. In France, significant structural change took place in the economy also, but declining sectors were not left to the free market. Indeed, the dependence of the whole economy on the state has led the government to press for liberal policies in the expanding sectors. Presumably, therefore, pulling resources away from these less productive sectors would be proportionately more expensive as subsidies made it easier for more groups to hold onto traditional positions or at least to slow down the transition. Growth rates in France were indeed slower, but they were not so dramatically lower nor were productivity increases so much less as to account for the differences in the WPI-to-CPI ratio. The higher rates of wholesale price increase associated with rapid growth and productivity suggest greater French toleration for restriction in its industrial sectors.

uses. The French face more serious problems, for labor must now be included in accommodations. Selective intervention now seems to be used predominantly to buffer industrial change, much in the fashion that agricultural decline was eased a generation earlier. The need for a market-based industry policy is recognized, but how to switch from a politically based market policy is not yet evident. West Germany, with its tripartite approach, has seemingly shifted policy toward state support for private initiatives—selected in consultation with the government—to enter defensible market niches in high-wage sectors and to create local and regional business, labor, and government alliances to ease the shift out of uncompetitive industries. Perhaps the good will of a generation of boom can be used to ease the adjustments of industrial crisis.

For the United States, with its company-led growth and state compensation of losers, the policy task is to prevent its inevitable shift from unchallenged industrial preeminence from becoming a continual decline. Reconstruction of war-torn economies and the catch-up of less advanced countries are no longer adequate explanations for the relative decline in U.S. economic power. British experience suggests that it is neither socialism nor a public budget that has caused that economy's malaise, but a political inability to promote growth and settle the terms of industrial change. The United States still retains an edge in productivity, which, when combined with the low total labor costs created by exchange movements, becomes a substantial competitive edge in unit labor costs. It is disturbing that among the leading industrial countries, U.S. rates of productivity increase exceed only those of Britain. In part this may be a result of the continuing backwardness of U.S. industry and the partial modernization of French and Japanese. But would the same explanations apply to Canada, West Germany, and Italy? In many sectors the United States is losing its competitive edge to product and process advances of its competitors. While the United States protests foreign governments' subsidies in trade negotiations (an appropriate and necessary concern), it shies away from the domestic implication that these aids are not simply short-run price cuts but are intended to alter the long-run position of companies and whole sectors. Global business preeminence has so far allowed the United States to avoid restriction and protection; but now a national alliance for growth and adjustment must be built. This is not simply a matter of transferring power to the government or providing additional privileges to business. It is a matter of finding forms of cooperation and collaboration that will permit industry and labor to move toward high-wage competitive strategies for American business.

PART THREE

States, Citizens,
and Public Choices

Collective interests, of course, are not the only units of analysis for understanding the formation of public policy as it affects inflation, growth, and stability. Governmental institutions deserve close scrutiny, on one hand. The voting public is important, on the other. In this part the focus switches from potential interest groups to the interaction between the state and individual citizens. The contributors have tested and modified many of the generalizations usually offered.

Rudolf Klein, in chapter 8, considers the oft-cited connection between high public expenditure and a tendency toward inflation. While the link is often asserted, it is difficult to prove; and Klein's argument is that the connection has conceptual difficulties as well. Douglas Hibbs and David Cameron, in chapters 7 and 9, respectively, examine the way that public opinion is influenced by economic outcomes and in turn shapes the priorities of policymakers. Taken together these three contributions force some rethinking of positions often taken for granted. Why should public spending have inflationary consequences if it merely replaces what the private sector would consume in the way of goods and services? How might it be said that government is responsible for inflation? Indeed, might not officials in the United States have provided less inflation than public opinion was sometimes willing to risk? What fiscal structures are more or less likely to have inflationary consequences? The conventional answers, these chapters suggest, are inadequate.

173

In this spirit, too, John Woolley subjects a very special institution to examination in chapter 11. Central bankers are potentially the guardians of the money supply. Indeed monetarists have frequently suggested that only their independence—a so-called new monetary constitution—can withstand the pressure of inflationary governments. But it is far from clear that central-bank independence is necessary for resisting inflation; nor is it clear that even independent central bankers could reliably determine the money supply. Nor is it certain that their influence is a function of their independence. While many institutions of the modern state could be tested for their role in transmitting or inhibiting inflation, the central bank role developed here seems particularly crucial.

In chapter 10, Brian Barry departs from the format followed by the others to probe recent theories rather than institutions. The prevalent explanations offered by economists who think governments are proinflationary are implicitly political. They include theories of how voters behave and how politicians respond. Barry seeks to bring out the premises and logic of some of this reasoning and frankly finds much of it flawed.

What emerges from these exercises is not a new theory of the state, the public, and the supply and demand for inflation. Rather it is an invitation to get beyond some recent clichés about the inflationary propensities of modern welfare-state democracies. Perhaps these exist, but the demonstrations made hitherto are neither conclusive nor persuasive.

7

Inflation, Political Support, and Macroeconomic Policy

Douglas A. Hibbs, Jr.

This chapter explores the connection between macroeconomic outcomes and political support for incumbent governments as they existed during the period of growing and high inflation. During most of the post–World War II period, the U.S. economy performed at higher rates of unemployment and lower rates of inflation than the economies of virtually all other capitalist industrial societies.[1] This held true during the sustained high growth of the 1960s as well as the economic disruption and stagnation of the 1970s. The sizable difference in figure 7-1 between the unemployment records of the United States and six other industrial societies— France, Italy, Japan, Sweden, the United Kingdom, and West Germany— is not an artifact of unusually good performance by one or two of the other countries. On average the U.S. unemployment rate was higher, typically much higher, than that of each of the other six (table 7-1). Nor can the unemployment performance gap be attributed primarily to measurement differences (data for all of the countries are adjusted to U.S. concepts) or to differences in the composition and rate of growth of the labor force, although the heterogeneity of the labor force is a distinguishing feature of the American economy.[2] However, even if it is granted that the natural rate of unemployment is somewhat higher in the United States than abroad, it is true nonetheless that postwar economic contractions

1. Canada is an exception, but the observations in this chapter apply with almost equal force to that country.

2. Robert H. Havemen, "Unemployment in Western Europe and the United States: A Problem of Demand, Structure or Measurement?" *American Economic Review,* vol. 68 (May 1978, *Papers and Proceedings, 1977*), pp. 44–50; Roger Kaufman, "Why the U.S. Unemployment Rate Is So High," *Challenge,* vol. 21 (May–June 1978), pp. 40–49.

Table 7-1. Unemployment, Inflation, and Monetary Growth Rates in Seven Countries, 1960–69 and 1970–80
Percent

Country	Unemployment[a]		Inflation[b]		Growth rate							
					Money supply				Excess money supply[c]			
					1960–69		1970–80		1960–69		1970–78	
	1960–69	1970–80	1960–69	1970–80	M1	M2	M1	M2	M1	M2	M1	M2
France	2.02	4.81	4.12	9.37	10.1	12.5	10.0	12.9	5.0	7.5	6.2	10.5
Italy	3.65	3.67	4.05	12.79	13.0	13.0	17.7	17.0	8.0	8.0	14.6	14.2
Japan	1.32	1.72	4.54	6.67	16.2	14.6	12.6	14.0	5.1	3.5	9.3	9.5
Sweden	1.69	2.05	3.93	8.48	3.3	7.0	11.1[d]	12.5[d]	−1.0	2.7	7.9	9.2
United Kingdom	2.97	4.94	3.06	12.79	2.9	4.9	11.5	12.8	−1.3	0.7	10.6	10.5
United States	4.74	6.28	2.50	6.62	3.6	6.5	5.8	9.2	−0.2	2.7	3.6	6.9
West Germany	0.59	2.35	3.76	5.41	7.6	12.0	8.7	9.7	2.8	7.3	7.2	8.0

Sources: Constance Sorrentino, "Unemployment in Nine Industrialized Countries," and Joyanna Moy and Constance Sorrentino, "An Analysis of Unemployment in Nine Industrial Countries," *Monthly Labor Review*, vol. 95 (June 1972), pp. 29–33, and vol. 100 (April 1977), pp. 12–24; U.S. Department of Labor, Bureau of Labor Statistics, December 1981, unpublished data table; Robert J. Gordon, data prepared for "World Inflation and Monetary Accommodation in Eight Countries," *Brookings Papers on Economic Activity*, 2:1977, pp. 409–78; *International Financial Statistics*, various issues.

a. Adjusted to U.S. concepts.
b. Rate of change of GDP deflator.
c. Average rate of change of money supply minus average rate of change of trend real GDP.
d. For 1970–79.

Figure 7-1. *Unemployment in the United States and Six Other Countries,*
1960–80

Rate of unemployment (percent)

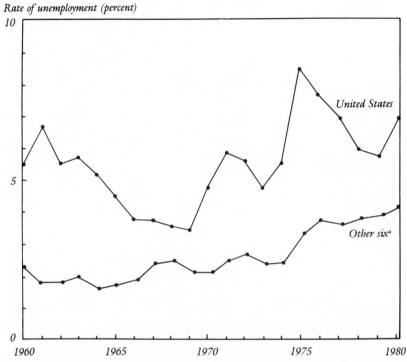

Sources: Constance Sorrentino, "Unemployment in Nine Industrialized Countries," and Joyanna Moy and Constance Sorrentino, "An Analysis of Unemployment in Nine Industrial Countries," *Monthly Labor Review,* vol. 95 (June 1972), pp. 29–33, and vol. 100 (April 1977), pp. 12–24; U.S. Department of Labor, Bureau of Labor Statistics, December 1981, unpublished data table. Unemployment rates of all countries have been adjusted to U.S. concepts.
a. France, Italy, Japan, Sweden, United Kingdom, and West Germany.

have typically been longer, deeper, and more frequent in the United States
than anywhere else.

In every year except 1968 and 1969—the peak of the inflationary surge
brought on by the Vietnam War boom—the U.S. inflation rate ran behind
that of the other six (see figure 7-2). Again, this is not due to unusual
performance by one or two of the other six. Generally, U.S. prices exhibit
greater stability during the long international boom of the 1960s, the
crushing stagflation of the 1970s, and both before and after the demise
of fixed exchange rates in 1971. The comparative inflation performance
after 1972 is particularly revealing about the aversion of officials in the
smaller, open economies to inflation, since the collapse of the Bretton

Figure 7-2. *Inflation in the United States and Six Other Countries,*
1960–80

Rate of inflation (percent)

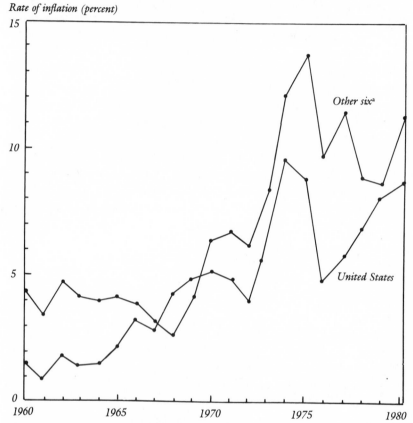

Sources: Robert J. Gordon, data prepared for "World Inflation and Monetary Accommodation in Eight Countries," *Brookings Papers on Economic Activity,* 2:1977, pp. 409–78; *International Financial Statistics,* various issues. The GNP deflator is used to compute the rates of inflation.
a. France, Italy, Japan, Sweden, United Kingdom, and West Germany.

Woods stable exchange rate system gave them more control over their
inflation rates.[3]

What explains the rather dramatic differences in rates of unemployment
and inflation between the United States and other advanced industrial
societies? The political sources of the variation are evident in governments'

3. This follows from the international monetarist theorem of open economies operating under fixed
exchange rates, which implies that the free flow of world capital prevents domestic authorities from
controlling their own nominal money supplies and, hence, their own long-run rates of inflation and
effective demand.

macroeconomic policies—monetary policy (the money supply, interest rates, exchange rate, and credit policy), fiscal policy (expenditure, taxation, the volume of subsidies, and transfer payments), direct controls (primarily wage and price controls), and occasionally rhetoric and persuasion (jawboning and appeals to a social contract). Monetary and fiscal policy instruments are governments' major macroeconomic tools. A large fraction of the economics profession, however, appears to be skeptical of the independent influence of tax and (especially) expenditure manipulations of real output and employment. Ray C. Fair has concluded that "the fiscal authority can do little about changing the output path once the money supply path is fixed."[4]

Ironically, the Keynesian position that government can favorably affect the level of real economic activity now rests heavily on an activist monetary policy. And economists generally acknowledge that "the major historical accelerations and decelerations of inflation—not only during wars and hyperinflations but also during peacetime—have been accompanied by accelerations and decelerations in the rate of growth of the supply of money."[5]

Accepting that the growth rate of the money supply is probably the single most important macroeconomic policy instrument, analysis must proceed to what causes variations in the rates. Confronted with demand shifts, supply shocks, trade union cost-push, and other inflationary pressures, the monetary authority must choose between expanding or (passively if not actively) tightening the supply of money. The former fuels inflation; the latter decreases real money balances, drives up interest rates, and ultimately reduces investment and employment. Monetary officials face the dilemma of accommodating inflationary pressure by expanding the money supply and relinquishing control over the price level in order to preserve effective demand and employment, or leaning against inflationary pressure by tightening the money supply, reducing effective demand and employment, but stabilizing the price level.[6] The first choice is sensitive to the interests of labor, especially marginal labor; the second defends the position of the financial community, rentiers, small savers, and others who are "exposed" to inflation.

---

4. "The Sensitivity of Fiscal Policy Effects to Assumptions about the Behavior of the Federal Reserve," *Econometrica*, vol. 46 (September 1978), p. 1177.

5. Robert J. Gordon, "The Demand for and Supply of Inflation," *Journal of Law and Economics*, vol. 18 (December 1975), p. 807.

6. M. W. Reder, "The Theoretical Problems of a National Wage-Price Policy," *Canadian Journal of Economics and Political Science*, vol. 14 (February 1948), pp. 46–61.

Figure 7-3. *Rates of Monetary Growth in the United States and Six Other Countries, 1960–80*

Rate of change (percent)

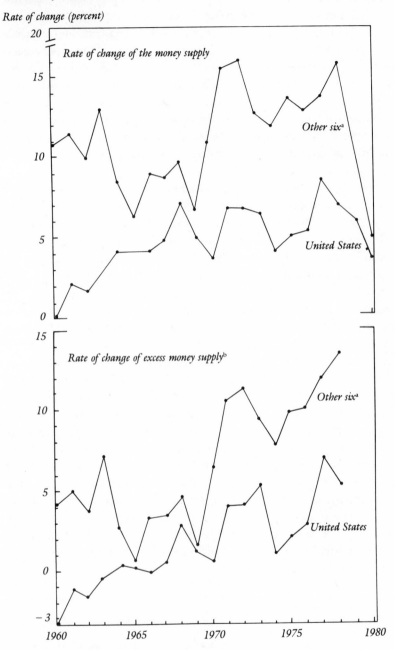

Sources: Same as for figure 7-2. Data are on M2 for France, M1 for all others.
a. France, Italy, Japan, Sweden, United Kingdom, and West Germany.
b. Rate of change of the money supply less rate of change of trend real GNP.

Figure 7-3 indicates that U.S. authorities pursued a tighter monetary policy than monetary authorities in the other six countries in 1960–80, though U.S. growth rates were in phase with the other countries' after the mid-1960s. When the rate of growth of M1 less the rate of growth of trend real GNP is used to measure monetary expansiveness, the message is the same; in every year the other six appear to have pushed their economies harder, fueling inflation in the process.[7] The data in table 7-1 confirm that with a couple of exceptions in the 1960s, U.S. monetary policy was less expansive than that of the other industrial societies. This pattern is, of course, consistent with the differences between the United States and the other six with respect to unemployment and inflation rates.[8]

The enormous supply shock of 1973–75, which originated largely in the quadrupling of petroleum prices by the Organization of Petroleum Exporting Countries (OPEC), provides a particularly stark illustration of the choices facing political authorities. The effects of the oil price rise were simultaneously inflationary and contractionary, and policymakers had to decide between accommodating the inflation, allowing nominal demand to grow at a pace sufficient to prevent sharp increases in unemployment, and pushing against the inflation at the cost of exacerbating the contraction. Figure 7-4 illustrates the range of monetary policy responses in relation to the apparent short-run impact on unemployment in the seven countries.[9] As policy activists would predict, there is an inverse association between the variables. Not surprisingly, Sweden and the United States are the limiting cases. Swedish officials reacted to the OPEC shock with a vigorous expansion of the money supply and succeeded in maintaining the volume of employment during the crisis (unemployment actually declined somewhat). A much more restrictive policy was pursued in the United States, and unemployment rose by more than 3.5 percentage points. The performance of the Federal Republic of Germany more closely resembles the experience of the United States than the rest of Europe,[10]

7. In plots of the real money supply—the rate of growth of M1 less the inflation rate—the U.S. growth rate oscillates around a mean of about 0, the other six around a mean of 4.4.

8. Differences in conventional monetary (or fiscal) policy behavior do not account entirely for international variation in unemployment and inflation; exposure to international influences, as well as legal restraints on layoffs, manpower policies, and other institutional factors also affect unemployment as well as inflation rates.

9. The results in figure 7-4 are consistent with the conclusions of James L. Pierce and Jared J. Enzler, "The Effects of External Inflationary Shocks," *Brookings Papers on Economic Activity, 1:1974*, pp. 47–54. (Hereafter *BPEA*.)

10. If the outflow of German guestworkers were included among the unemployed, the increase in the German unemployment rate would have been greater.

Figure 7-4. *Changes in Unemployment and Average Growth of the Money Supply Less Growth of Trend Real Output in Seven Countries, 1973–75*

Change in unemployment rate (percentage points)

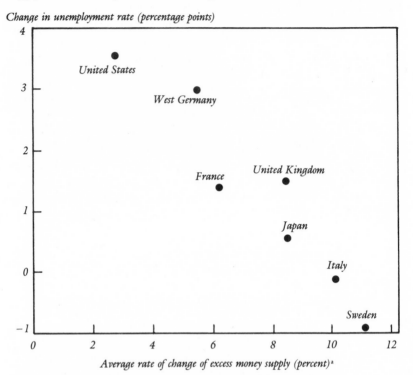

Average rate of change of excess money supply (percent)[a]

Sources: Same as for figure 7-2. Data are on M2 for France, M1 for all others.
a. Average rate of change of the money supply less average rate of change of trend real GNP.

which is consistent with the popular wisdom about German aversion to inflation.

The central political question of interest here is why some governments exhibited less monetary discipline than others by monetizing deficits and price and nominal wage increases, especially during the major episodes of inflationary pressure. Put another way, why were some governments more inclined to "supply" inflation and less inclined to "supply" unemployment than other governments? In particular, why were U.S. authorities apparently less tolerant of inflation and more tolerant of unemployment than political officials elsewhere? That question can be partially answered by investigating the demand side of the issue—the response in terms of popular support for elected chief executives or political parties that follows changes in unemployment, inflation, and real income growth.

The Economy as a Political Issue

In March 1968 Prime Minister Harold Wilson reportedly declared to the parliamentary Labour party: "All political history shows that the standing of a Government and its ability to hold the confidence of the electorate at a General Election depend on the success of its economic policy."[11] His declaration is consistent with the conclusions of many empirical studies of the impact of macroeconomic performance on public support for incumbent political parties and chief executives. Moreover, during the 1970s the state of the economy (principally, unemployment and inflation) unquestionably was the most salient issue for the mass publics of most industrial democracies.

Perhaps American authorities exhibited less willingness to accommodate inflation and push against unemployment than their counterparts in other industrial societies because mass political support for elected officials in the United States was more sensitive to inflation and less sensitive to unemployment than elsewhere. The differences between the United States and the other six countries (as well as differences among the other six) might therefore reflect, at least in part, the political response of governments to the relative weights attached to inflation and unemployment in their respective mass publics. American officials may have shown more discipline vis-à-vis inflation because demand for deflationary policies was greater.

The public's relative aversion to, or demand for, various economic outcomes in France, Great Britain, West Germany, Sweden, and the United States is estimated in table 7-2. The estimates are based on the idea that political support for an incumbent party (in parliamentary systems) or chief executive (in presidential systems) is influenced by the incumbent's cumulative discounted macroeconomic performance relative to that of its predecessor. The coefficients of statistical models based on quarterly observations from the late 1950s or 1960s through the end of 1978 are used to infer the degree of political support for the chief executive or governing party in each country.

For every country the performance variables are the rate of unemployment, the proportional changes in the rate of the rate of unemployment, the rate of growth of per capita real personal disposable income, the rate

11. David Watt, *Financial Times* (London), March 8, 1968.

Table 7-2. *Change in Support for Political Leaders in Five Countries in Response to Sustained Increases in Rates of Unemployment, Inflation, and Income Growth in the 1960s and 1970s*

Percentage points

		Change in support in response to a 2 percent increase in			
Country	Quarters covered	Real income growth[a]	Unemploy-ment	Consumer price inflation	Change in inflation rate[b]
France	1969:4–1978:4	+3.8	−2, −3[c]	...	...
Sweden	1967:1–1978:3	...	−11.5	−0.5	...
United Kingdom	1959:4–1978:4	+2.8[d]	−6.4	...	−2.6
United States	1961:1–1978:4	+5.4[d]	−4.5	−6.2[d]	...
West Germany	1957:4–1978:4	+2.1	−2.5	−1.7	...

Sources: Douglas A. Hibbs, Jr., with the assistance of R. Douglas Rivers and Nicholas Vasilatos, "On the Demand for Economic Outcomes: Macroeconomic Performance and Mass Political Support in the United States, Great Britain and Germany," *Journal of Politics*, vol. 44 (May 1982), pp. 425–62; Douglas A. Hibbs, Jr., and Henrik Madsen, "The Impact of Economic Performance on Electoral Support in Sweden, 1967–1978," *Scandinavian Political Studies*, vol. 4, no. 1 (1981), pp. 33–50; Douglas A. Hibbs, Jr., with Nicholas Vasilatos, "Economics and Politics in France: Economic Performance and Mass Political Support for Presidents Pompidou and Giscard d'Estaing," *European Journal of Political Research*, vol. 9 (June 1981), pp. 133–45.
 a. Per capita real disposable income.
 b. Rate sustained for four quarters.
 c. Measurement problems make it difficult to estimate effect.
 d. Adjusted for adverse effects of shifts in the terms of trade following the OPEC supply shock.

of inflation, and changes in the rate of inflation. For the United Kingdom a term for changes in the dollars-per-pound exchange rate is included. Exchange rate fluctuations of course were influenced by Britain's relative inflation performance.

The estimates in table 7-2 indicate that political support in the five countries is quite sensitive to movements in the unemployment and real income growth rates.[12] In all the countries except Sweden responses to an increase in the growth rate of real disposable income are positive, ranging between 2.1 and 5.4 percent. Since elections often hinge on margins of only a few percentage points of the vote, these results are not merely of academic interest. Macroeconomic management and perfor-mance obviously can have a pivotal impact on electoral shifts.

In each country, increases in the unemployment rate yield declines in political support, although in the case of France measurement problems

12. The responses to a sustained increase of 2 percentage points in the economic variables represent the political effects of changes in economic performance after all adjustment lags have worked through the underlying dynamic model. Given the rate of decay of the lag coefficients in the distributed lag regressions, sustained changes mean for practical puposes no more than six years.

with the unemployment data make it difficult to estimate unambiguously the quantitative political effects. The estimated response in Sweden is particularly large. This undoubtedly reflects the preeminence in Swedish political life of the full employment issue. Low unemployment has been the most important theme of the Swedish Social Democrats' electoral mobilization strategy since the early 1930s, and it kept them in control of the government continuously for forty-four years until their narrow defeat by the bourgeois coalition in 1976. Mass political support for British governments also exhibits great sensitivity to unemployment fluctuations, especially when evaluated relative to the political response to changes in the nominal rate of inflation. Again this probably reflects the Labour party's emphasis on low unemployment in political discourse which has generated widespread public expectations of sustained high employment.

Taken together, the general political responses to unemployment, as indicated in table 7-2, suggest that unemployment continued to have adverse political consequences deep into the 1970s, that is, even during a period that provided generous unemployment compensation and other income- and employment-contingent transfers. True, tax and transfer systems do spread the costs of unemployment more widely, and for many people loss of employment no longer poses an economic disaster. In the 1930s the unemployed and their families often went hungry; today most suffer temporary reductions in income.

However, it is no mystery why high unemployment rates tended to erode governments' mass political support. Unemployment after all represents lost real output and underutilized human resources. In the United States, for example, each extra percentage point of unemployment was accompanied by a decline of at least 2 percent in real output, which in 1980 was equal to $56 billion of unproduced output, or $700 per household. Moreover, the measured unemployment rate is just that—a rate—and a far larger fraction of the labor force experiences bouts of actual unemployment over any given time interval than the average percentage numbers might suggest.[13] In addition to households touched directly by some form of unemployment or underemployment, an even larger number will also be aware of unemployment among relatives, friends, neighbors, and work mates.

---

13. In the United States, for example, a useful rule of thumb for estimating the proportion of the work force experiencing one or more spells of unemployment during any given twelve-month period is to multiply the official average annual rate by about 3.

The estimates of the responses to inflation shown in table 7-2 indicate that the political costs of deteriorating nominal economic performance were less uniform cross-nationally than the analogous costs of higher unemployment and lower real income growth. In France and Sweden the decline in political support associated with increased consumer price inflation appeared to be negligible-to-vanishing. In these countries any adverse political consequences of inflation were transmitted through the impact of rising prices on the real income growth stream (price increases running ahead of money income growth rates) or on the unemployment rate (assuming, contrary to the Keynesian view, that high or accelerating inflation yields increased unemployment). At least until the Thatcher government the British results indicated that the electorate was not averse to inflation per se, but that changes in the inflation rate (accelerations and decelerations of prices) had important consequences for mass political support. Since the change (first difference) of the inflation rate is a reasonable (though simple) measure of inflationary surprises, this result is consistent with the view of contemporary economic theory that the pain induced by rising prices is due primarily to unanticipated bursts of inflation.

Only in West Germany and the United States did the simple rate of change of consumer prices—the inflation rate—appear to have statistically and politically significant consequences. The estimates imply that voters in these countries are averse to rising prices per se, for the models take into account the rate of change of real personal disposable income. Hence, even if money incomes kept pace with price rises, governments nevertheless suffered losses of political support as a result of inflation.

As Keynesian theorists stressed throughout the 1970s, little in conventional economic theory adequately explained this aversion to inflation. Traditionally it was argued that the principal economic costs of anticipated inflation are the resources devoted to economizing cash balances and fixed-interest-rate assets. Surely this is a trivial matter, particularly when viewed in relation to the costs of unemployment. The costs usually associated with unanticipated bursts of inflation are more extensive, but they do not provide a convincing explanation of the public's aversion to rising prices. Empirical evidence (which is thin and pertains primarily to the United States and the United Kingdom) suggests that the aggregate wage and salary income share was not affected adversely by inflation and that rising prices had no dramatic effects on the size distribution of income.[14] Unanticipated price increases tended to arbitrarily redistribute wealth from nominal creditors to nominal debtors and the aggregate amounts involved were probably large. But most people absorbed losses on some accounts (fixed price assets) and gained on others (fixed price liabilities). The aged poor, retirees whose economic well-being depends on social security or state pensions, are often thought to be more exposed to inflation than other groups. However, during the period of sustained inflation, state transfers to the old were indexed to inflation either by statute or by firmly entrenched custom in virtually all industrial societies.

To the extent that state revenue is raised by direct taxation based on progressive nominal schedules, inflation increases the effective rate of income taxation (inflationary fiscal drag) unless the authorities take compensatory action. Although discretionary tax cuts neutralized much of the potential gross transfer to the state, inflation probably has fueled a rate of growth of government revenue somewhat higher than political authorities would have achieved by making explicit real claims on the electorate.[15] The (unobservable) difference between the historical time path of effective tax rates and what would have occurred in a world of stable prices (or indexed taxes) may explain part of the public's dislike of inflation that is reflected in table 7-2.[16]

However, neither the income, wealth, nor tax effects of inflation appear large enough to explain (or, in objective economic terms, to justify) the degree of public aversion to rising prices relative to unemployment and real income growth that appeared to prevail in West Germany and the

14. See Douglas A. Hibbs, Jr., "Public Concern about Inflation and Unemployment in the United States: Trends, Correlates and Political Implications," in R. E. Hall, ed., *Inflation* (University of Chicago Press, 1982); Douglas A. Hibbs, Jr., *Economic Interest and the Politics of Macroeconomic Policy* (Massachusetts Institute of Technology, Center for International Studies, 1976); Douglas A. Hibbs, Jr., "The Mass Public and Macroeconomic Performance: The Dynamics of Public Opinion toward Unemployment and Inflation," *American Journal of Political Science*, vol. 23 (November 1979), pp. 705–31; Stanley Fischer and Franco Modigliani, "Aspects of the Costs of Inflation" (Massachusetts Institute of Technology, 1977); David Laidler and Michael Parkin, "Inflation: A Survey," *Economic Journal*, vol. 85 (December 1975), pp. 741–809; David Piachaud, "Inflation and Income Distribution," in Fred Hirsch and John H. Goldthorpe, eds., *The Political Economy of Inflation* (Harvard University Press, 1978).

15. In the United States as a result of discretionary tax cuts at the federal level, average effective tax rates increased little if at all between 1960 and 1975, fluctuating around 11 percent of adjusted personal income. See Emil M. Sunley, Jr., and Joseph A. Pechman, "Inflation Adjustment for the Individual Income Tax," in Henry J. Aaron, ed., *Inflation and the Income Tax* (Brookings Institution, 1976), p. 157.

16. If the unobserved difference between the quantity of government revenue (or spending) demanded and supplied is approximately a linear function of the inflation rate, then the observed rate of change of prices is an adequate proxy.

United States. Less tangible, psychological factors are therefore probably more important than concrete economic costs.[17] Some empirical evidence does indicate that high rates of inflation have been accompanied by high variability of the inflation rate, and such variability presumably heightens uncertainty about the future stream of prices.[18] It is also possible that people failed to credit the inflation-induced gains on fixed-interest liabilities such as home mortgages against the losses incurred on such money-valued assets as pension and life insurance reserves. Perhaps more important, they may not have understood the connection between rising wages and rising prices.[19] There is some evidence that inflation tends to be viewed as an arbitrary tax that chips away the purchasing power of nominal income increases that people believe they deserve to enjoy fully. For example, in the United States nominal personal disposable income per household rose by about 8 percent between 1975 and 1976, but the real gain was a more modest 2.4 percent because of a 5.6 percent increase in consumer prices. Some people could have had the mistaken idea that household purchasing power could have risen by 8 percent, or nearly so, if prices had not risen.

An important factor contributing to popular concern about inflation after 1973 was probably the decline in real income experienced by consumers of food, raw materials, and especially petroleum as a result of the shift in the terms of trade in favor of the producers of these commodities. It is likely that many people blamed rising prices for the shrinkage of their real incomes, even though the immediate post-OPEC surge of inflation was to a large extent merely the mechanism of a change in relative prices. Had the real loss absorbed by energy consumers taken place about a stable price level, the pain would not have been any less unpleasant, but inflation could not have been held responsible.

Political Support and Economic Outcomes

Since the macroeconomic performance variables do not all share the same metric, and because the typical level of political support for incumbents varies across political systems, it may be misleading to assess

17. For some ideas along these lines, see Arthur M. Okun, "Inflation: Its Mechanics and Welfare Costs," *BPEA*, 2:1975, p. 383.

18. Dwight Jaffee and Ephraim Kleiman, "The Welfare Implications of Uneven Inflation" (University of Stockholm, Institute for International Economic Studies, 1975).

19. George Katona, *Psychological Economics* (Elsevier, 1975).

the relative and comparative impact of inflation, unemployment, and real income growth on popular support for political authorities by direct inspection of results such as those reported in table 7-2. Another means of evaluating the relative sensitivity of political support to economic events is to compare the partial elasticities implied by the regression coefficients of the equations used to model political support. The elasticities suggest the *proportional* response of the political support ratings expected from *proportional* changes in the economic variables and are unaffected by differences of scale. Such elasticities implicitly reveal the public's marginal, proportional aversion to, or demand for, economic outcomes.

Figure 7-5 displays time plots of the estimated long-run political support elasticities for each period in the time range of the underlying regression analyses. Means of the elasticities for the 1960s and 1970s are also reported in the figures. The elasticities are interpreted in the following way. During the 1960s in Great Britain, for example, if the real variables (the unemployment rate and the real income growth rate) changed simultaneously in an adverse direction by a factor of 1 percent, on average the expected long-run proportional decline in the government's political support would equal a factor just under 0.33 percent. In the 1970s the expected long-run proportional decline in political support from the same sustained proportional movement in the real macroeconomy would have been approximately equal to a factor of 0.58 percent. If the adverse change in the macroeconomy was more like 100 percent (that is, if the unemployment rate doubled and the real income growth rate fell by a factor of 100 percent), the expected long-run proportional decline in the incumbent party's political support during the 1970s would have been a factor of about 58 percent. In other words, it is estimated that the government party's political support would have fallen on average by more than one-half.

In terms of proportional responses to proportional changes, mass political support for incumbents is considerably more sensitive to economic performance in the United Kingdom and the United States than in West Germany and Sweden. In large part this probably reflects the fact that macroeconomic performance (particularly unemployment performance) in the 1960s and 1970s was considerably better in the latter pair of countries (see table 7-1) and so proportional changes in performance constitute comparatively small absolute changes in economic conditions. And, because these countries performed so well in the 1960s and absorbed the economic shocks of the 1970s better than most others, macroeconomic

Figure 7-5. *Implied Long-run Elasticities of Political Support with Respect to Macroeconomic Outcomes in Four Countries in the 1960s and 1970s*[a]

Elasticity (four-quarter moving average)

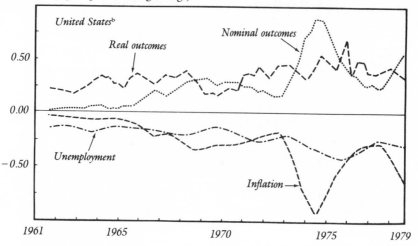

Elasticity (four-quarter moving average)

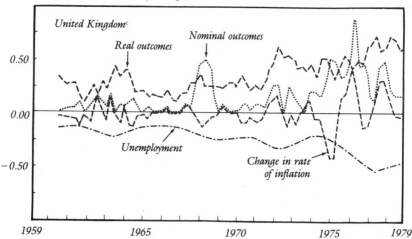

Sources: Douglas A. Hibbs, Jr., with the assistance of R. Douglas Rivers and Nicholas Vasilatos, "On the Demand for Economic Outcomes: Macroeconomic Performance and Mass Political Support in the United States, Great Britain and Germany," *Journal of Politics*, vol. 44 (May 1982), pp. 425–62; Douglas A. Hibbs, Jr., and Henrick Madsen, "The Impact of Economic Performance on Electoral Support in Sweden, 1967–1978," *Scandinavian Political Studies*, vol. 4, no. 1 (1981), pp. 33–50; Douglas A. Hibbs, Jr., with Nicholas Vasilatos, "Economics and Politics in France: Economic Performance and Mass Political Support for Presidents Pompidou and Giscard d'Estaing," *European Journal of Political Research*, vol. 9 (June 1981), pp. 133–45.

a. Each graph depicts below the 0.0 line the changing elasticity of political support with respect to changing unemployment rates and with respect to changing inflation rates. Above the 0.0 line the absolute value of the elasticity of political support with respect to real macroeconomic outcomes (unemployment and growth) is contrasted with the absolute value of support with respect to the nominal (inflation) outcome.

Elasticity (four-quarter moving average)

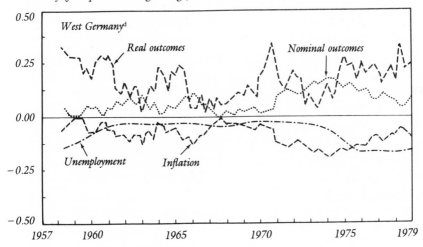

Elasticity (four-quarter moving average)

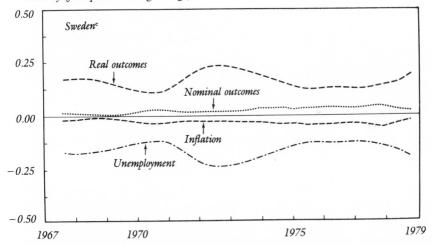

b. For 1961–69 the mean elasticity for unemployment is −0.156, for inflation −0.146, for real outcomes +0.287, and for nominal outcomes +0.146; for 1970–78 the mean elasticities are −0.282, −0.436, +0.492, and +0.436, respectively.

c. For 1961–69 the mean elasticity for unemployment is −0.162, for the change in the rate of inflation −0.010, for real outcomes +0.325, and for nominal outcomes +0.230; for 1970–78 the mean elasticities are −0.319, −0.001, +0.581, and +0.525, respectively.

d. For 1961–69 the mean elasticity for unemployment is −0.027, for inflation −0.060, for real outcomes +0.157, and for nominal outcomes +0.063; for 1970–78 the mean elasticities are −0.094, −0.116, +0.295, and +0.136, respectively.

e. For 1967–69 the mean elasticity for unemployment is −0.158, for inflation −0.012, for real outcomes +0.158, and for nominal outcomes +0.012; for 1970–78 the mean elasticities are −0.164, −0.032, +0.164, and +0.032, respectively.

policy was not so contentious a political question in West Germany and Sweden as elsewhere.

In all of the countries, except Sweden, the elasticities increase, typically quite dramatically, from the 1960s to the 1970s; in West Germany, they approximately double, implying that a given proportional change in economic performance would have had twice as much proportional impact on political support in the 1970s as in the 1960s. The elasticities of real outcome also nearly double from one period to the other in the United States and Great Britain, and in the United States the elasticities of nominal (inflation) outcome are on average about three times larger in the later than in the earlier period. This is hardly surprising in view of the favorable economic conditions of the 1960s—virtually a golden age of economic performance—and the economic stagnation (or stagflation) characteristic of later years.

In the case of Sweden it is possible to generalize only for an era of high performance that deteriorated somewhat in the late 1970s. Aside from the small bulge in 1973–74, the real elasticities for Sweden (based entirely on the unemployment rate variable) increased only negligibly because Sweden's unemployment record was so consistently favorable. Although the underlying sensitivity of political support to unemployment is sizable for the Swedish public (see table 7-2), Sweden's unemployment rate stood lower in the 1970s and exhibited a smaller relative increase from the 1960s to the 1970s than any other country's. Even though the Swedish inflation rate more than doubled from the 1960s to the 1970s, the inflation elasticities are for practical purposes negligible in both decades because, as table 7-2 indicates, political support simply was not very responsive to nominal economic outcomes in that country.

A third notable feature of figure 7-5 is that in both decades the elasticities of the real macroeconomy (unemployment and the real income growth rate taken together) are in every country larger on average than the absolute value of the nominal, inflation elasticities. In other words, viewed in terms of elasticities, mass political support for incumbents was more sensitive to real income growth and unemployment than to the economy's nominal, inflation performance, despite the fact that so much political analysis of the 1970s gives the impression that the political fortune of governments in the industrial democracies was dominated by their inflation performance records. Nevertheless, looking back, it is clear that the impact of the inflation rate, and changes in that rate relative to the rate of unemployment and to the real variables taken together, did increase markedly in the United States and Great Britain. In Britain the change came with the onset of the OPEC-induced instability of inflation rates in 1974, in the United States (and to a much lesser extent in West Germany) with the worldwide price acceleration brought on by the tight labor markets and the policy of (hidden) deficit finance associated with the Vietnam War.

In Great Britain, the United States, and West Germany the terrible recession of 1975–76 of course tempered inflation's relative impact. Nonetheless, the dramatic increase in inflation rates in the 1970s may have implanted long-lasting effects on the macroeconomic priorities of the OPEC generation, perhaps similar to those of the supposedly traumatic impact of the Weimar hyperinflation on older generations in Germany or of the Great Depression on generations of the 1930s in most industrial societies. This made the political outcomes of the 1980s take place in a different matrix. If the discomfort produced by the great post-OPEC inflation does indeed persist in the political and economic memories of the mass publics in the industrial democracies, giving rise to a sustained demand for deflation, then the thrust of macroeconomic policy for many years to come might be turned away from expansion and growth to deflation and price stability. This would represent a rather profound change in the political economies of most industrial democracies.

Is there any evidence from table 7-2 and figure 7-5 that the comparative sensitivity of U.S. macroeconomic policy authorities to inflation as opposed to unemployment reflected a distinctive aversion to rising prices in the American electorate? If the elasticities of nominal outcomes are persistently larger than the elasticities of real outcomes (or, more narrowly, if in the lower frames of the figure the inflation elasticities typically have larger negative values than the unemployment elasticities), that would provide some evidence that a chronic demand for deflation prevailed in the electorate. Policy might then be interpreted as a rational political response to pronounced public preferences in favor of greater price stability.

There is some evidence in the United States favoring this interpretation from the late 1960s on and, more dramatically, during the period following the first OPEC shock. Therefore, the U.S. response to the OPEC catastrophe (see figure 7-4) does appear to be consistent with, or responsive to, aggregate public sentiment. However, for most of the 1960s the nominal elasticities were smaller than the real elasticities; indeed, for the first part of the decade the inflation elasticities were smaller (negative) than the unemployment elasticities alone. This result suggested a political asymmetry in the sense that the expected payoff in political support from pushing harder on the real macroeconomy should have been large in relation to the political costs that would have accompanied some acceleration of prices in those periods. In short, during the early 1960s Americans probably got less expansive performance from policymakers than they were in fact willing to risk.

The institutional autonomy of monetary authorities from elected political officials in the United States may explain some of the imbalance. Monetary officials invariably give great weight to inflation (they usually are drawn from and have intimate connections with the financial community), and if given free rein they generally are unwilling to sacrifice control of the price level to push growth and expand employment. It is unlikely, however, that the Federal Reserve would (or could) have resisted vigorous and sustained political pressure to push the economy harder. Its statutory autonomy would not have survived if it had.

So part of the explanation probably resides in the fact that organized labor—in all industrial societies the key producer group mobilizing on behalf of high employment policies—was (and is) comparatively weak in the United States. A viable political base in support of greater attention to unemployment probably existed in the United States throughout most of the 1960s (and the 1950s), but in the absence of a strong trade-union movement or a political party harnessing public opinion on the issue, the latent political sentiment was underexploited. As a result, the interests of the financial community and other organized economic groups who were more concerned about inflation than high employment and rapid growth probably received greater weight in the policy process than in other industrial countries, particularly Sweden.

Although a gap also opened up between the inflation and unemployment elasticities in West Germany after the acceleration of prices in the first half of the 1970s, the magnitudes are simply too small to have been a decisive factor in the domestic political environment confronting German macroeconomic policymakers. Hence there is no evidence that the economic situation was severe enough to have produced disequilibrating political pressures. Notice, however, that in West Germany (figure 7-5) the sizable response of the elasticities of mass political support with respect to inflation, following what by international standards was a modest acceleration of prices (see table 7-1), conforms with the claimed sensitivity of the German public to rising prices. The cautious monetary policies pursued during the 1970s by the Bundesbank, which enjoys great constitutional autonomy, were apparently underpinned by considerable popular support. Part of the reason of course may be that the large foreign component of the German work force sheltered domestic labor from the consequences of contractions.

Thus throughout the 1960s most European societies were willing to risk inflation and secured policies that conformed to these preferences; West Germans, however, sought caution and got caution; and the U.S. public might well have gotten more restraint than it wished. To recapitulate, the U.S. unemployment rate seems to have been too large to be consistent with a support-maximizing policy and outcome configuration. There simply was no evidence of a broad-based demand for deflation relative to the demand for higher growth and employment.

This situation began to change in the 1970s as inflation became a major and at times dominant influence on mass political support for U.S. presidents. Deflationary policies, although painful, became politically more viable; nonetheless, contractionary policies designed to put downward pressure on the inflation rate still conferred substantial political penalties, particularly when their benefits were small and slow in coming.

Obviously by the beginning of the 1980s opinion had evolved so far that the American and British publics elected policymakers pledged to restrictive measures. Yet consistency across national lines was hardly present. The West Germans chose a Christian Democratic government in part as reaction to growing unemployment; the French turned to their Socialist party for the same reason. Incumbents were generally punished for stagflation, through the beginning of the new decade.

8

Public Expenditure
in an Inflationary World

Rudolf Klein

During the period of high inflation, public expenditure in the advanced industrial nations rose both absolutely and as a proportion of national income. It was hardly surprising that many analysts postulated a direct causal link between rising public expenditure and inflation. The aim of this chapter is less to resolve that causal link than to explore the extent to which both are explained by the same underlying societal pressures.

If there is any link between levels of public expenditure and rates of inflation, it is by no means a simple or mechanical one; when governments step on the accelerator of public expenditure, the engine of inflation does not automatically rev up. Several statistical studies have found no relation between levels of public expenditure and rates of inflation in member countries of the Organization for Economic Cooperation and Development (OECD).[1] David Cameron, in chapter 9, below, concludes that public expenditure cannot usefully be posited as a necessary or sufficient explanation of inflation. This is not to argue that public expenditure can never be *a* cause of inflation. In certain, specific circumstances the methods of financing public expenditure, whether stable or rising, can contribute to inflation—for example, if government taxation is met out of savings rather than consumption or if government borrowing drives up interest rates.[2]

1. Alan T. Peacock and Martin Ricketts, "The Growth of the Public Sector and Inflation," in Fred Hirsch and John H. Goldthorpe, eds., *The Political Economy of Inflation* (Harvard University Press, 1978); Geoffrey Maynard and W. van Ryckeghem, *A World of Inflation* (Barnes & Noble, 1975).

2. As argued, for example, by Walter S. Salant, "International Transmission of Inflation," in Lawrence B. Krause and Walter S. Salant, eds., *Worldwide Inflation: Theory and Recent Experience* (Brookings Institution, 1977), pp. 167–227.

The nature of the relationship between public expenditure and inflation is apparent in three hypotheses that converge in their emphasis on political factors. One postulates that inflation is the cause of rising public expenditure.[3] Inflation and the resulting fiscal dividend to governments permit politicians to spend more without having to raise taxes visibly or explicitly, for as nominal money incomes rise, more people automatically become taxpayers or are thrust into higher tax brackets. When inflation is the tax collector, governments may thus be under the illusion that it is possible to finance public spending painlessly. Thus the direction of causation is the opposite of that conventionally assumed.

A second hypothesis sees public expenditure as a dampener on inflation. If, as Albert Hirschman suggests in chapter 3, inflation is interpreted as a rebellion against the existing distribution of income, then government spending on transfers designed to reduce inequality might offset the demands that help to generate inflationary pressure. And if there is indeed an inverse relation between per capita social spending and inflation, as M. Panić suggests,[4] then to the extent that public expenditure helps to reduce the "aspirations gap" and acts as a solvent of social conflict, so it may succeed in lowering the rate of inflation. The third hypothesis sees inflation as the result of rising taxation.[5] As public expenditure rises so does taxation, with the effect, for example, that the take-home pay in Britain for a manual worker with two children under eleven fell from 64.5 percent to 50.6 percent of median earnings between 1971–72 and 1976–77.[6] The general result, particularly in a period of stagnant growth, will be to cut real disposable incomes. This may, however, in turn produce inflationary wage and salary settlements as trade unions demand compensatory increases designed to safeguard real, net-of-tax incomes.

Significantly, there is at least some evidence that governments have from time to time followed policies that confirm the latter two hypotheses. The 1974 Labour government in Britain explicitly acted on the assumption (the second hypothesis) that it could damp down inflationary wage claims

3. Jack Wiseman, "A Model of Inflation and the Government Deficit," in Robert Bacon and others, *The Dilemmas of Government Expenditure* (London: Institute of Economic Affairs, 1976), pp. 39–49, argues that the growth of public expenditure may be a passive consequence of inflation.
4. "The Origin of Increasing Inflationary Tendencies in Contemporary Society," in Hirsch and Goldthorpe, *Political Economy of Inflation.*
5. See Dudley Jackson, H. A. Turner, and Frank Wilkinson, *Do Trade Unions Cause Inflation?* 2d ed. (Cambridge University Press, 1975).
6. Great Britain, Central Statistical Office, *Social Trends*, no. 8: *1977* (London: Her Majesty's Stationery Office [HMSO], 1977), p. 104.

by expanding public expenditure—that there was a trade-off between the two. This was expressed in the concept of the social contract, devised jointly by the Labour party and the Trades Union Congress (TUC).[7] Subsequently, the idea of a social wage was elaborated—that is, "the recognition that personal consumption is not financed entirely out of take-home pay. In fact for every £4 of personal spending financed privately, £1 is financed by the Government."[8] A deliberate decision was thus taken to increase certain forms of public spending, such as pensions, in the expectation that this would produce wage restraint.

However, the Labour government was forced to switch policies; its 1978 white paper on expenditure accepted the need to contain the growth of public expenditure, to stabilize actual spending levels and reduce the total as a proportion of national income.[9] Subsequently, the April 1978 budget introduced considerable tax cuts (the third hypothesis). Indeed even the TUC, while continuing to press for higher spending, recognized the importance of lower taxation for its members; its report on the social contract included a table showing the beneficial effects of tax cuts on net incomes.[10] In 1979 the incoming Conservative government gave even greater priority to reducing direct taxation; as part of the new government's anti-inflation strategy, the 1980 budget cut direct taxation by £1.2 billion[11]—however, the decision to make compensatory increases in indirect taxation (translated into a rise in the retail price index) meant that there was little easing in the pressures for higher wages and salaries.

In Sweden, although public expenditure increased in the early 1970s largely as a response to trade union pressure for a new distributional order (the second hypothesis), as early as 1974 the government adopted a policy of cutting taxes as a means of buying trade union support for wage restraint (the third hypothesis). The 1975–76 budget statement claimed that tax cuts made it possible "to combine a higher real income for the individual with increased wage costs for firms that were fully compatible with the efforts to maintain international competitiveness,"[12] and the government sought to achieve its policy in 1975 and again in

7. Trades Union Congress, *Collective Bargaining and the Social Contract* (London: TUC, 1974).

8. TUC, *The Development of the Social Contract* (London: TUC, 1975), p. 11.

9. Great Britain, Treasury, *The Government's Expenditure Plans, 1978–79 to 1981–82,* Cmnd. 7049 (London: HMSO, 1978).

10. TUC, *The Social Contract 1976–77* (London: TUC, 1977), p. 9.

11. Great Britain, Treasury, *Financial Statement and Budget Report, 1980–81* (London: HMSO, 1980).

12. Sweden, *The Swedish Budget, 1975/76* (Stockholm: Ministry of Economic Affairs and Ministry of the Budget, 1975), p. 20.

1976 through three-party agreements on economic management with the two major trade union organizations. This strategy survived a change of government, after the defeat of the Social Democrats in the 1976 election. And in 1980, following the national lockout in May, the coalition government not only cut taxes for certain income brackets but also increased food subsidies.[13]

Neither the British nor the Swedish strategies proved entirely successful. Neither the original attempt to head off distributional conflict by means of increasing public expenditure nor the subsequent change of tack brought an end to inflationary pressures. This suggests that the various hypotheses, and governmental policies, that assume direct causal links between public expenditure and inflation may be oversimple. They fail to take account of the complexity of the social, political, and institutional factors that both help to explain and mediate between spending and inflation. Hence this chapter explores the factors involved in the growth of public expenditure in order to show why it may be illusory to expect to find a constant relation between levels of spending and rates of inflation.

Public Expenditure: A Problematic Concept

"The mind is easily imposed upon by the false affectation of exactness, which prevails even in the misstatements of science, and it adopts with confidence errors which are dressed in the forms of mathematical truth." So said Alexis de Tocqueville, admitting defeat in his attempts to compare the social expenditures of France and America.[14] It is a remark that should be echoed by all who try to compare public expenditure cross-nationally. For, in a crucial sense, the whole concept of public expenditure is problematic. Economists often use public expenditure figures to measure (and sometimes to condemn) the scale and scope of government activity. But this is precisely what public expenditure does not measure. For the concept fails to encompass the cost of those government activities— decisions and regulations—that are not directly financed by government. A comprehensive measure of government activity would have to include political spending, which would account for the costs to the private sector of carrying out government decisions as well as public budget outlays.

---

13. Organization for Economic Cooperation and Development, *OECD Economic Surveys: Sweden* (Paris: OECD, June 1981).

14. *Democracy in America,* rev. ed., vol. 1 (New York: Colonial Press, 1900), p. 226.

Consider a mythical country whose government decides to keep public expenditure below the 25 percent of gross national product once thought to be the maximum tolerable proportion. Instead of introducing a social security scheme or a national health service, it makes it mandatory for every firm comprehensively to insure its employees and their families. Instead of building motorways, it offers generous tax concessions to turnpike trusts. Instead of subsidizing jobs to prevent unemployment from rising, it introduces legislation forbidding companies to dismiss anyone. Instead of spending money on pollution control, it compels private industry to clean up the air and rivers it has befouled. This welfare society has virtually no welfare spending as measured in the conventional public expenditure statistics.

The society is mythical; the instances given are not. Japan has left much of the welfare role to industry; France has relied on private enterprise to build motorways; Italy has made it increasingly difficult for anyone to be dismissed; Sweden has imposed considerable pollution-control costs on industry. In the United States, the costs of social regulation (another way of describing political spending) are attracting increasing attention; indeed it has been argued that social regulation, though designed to minimize political costs, may be needlessly expensive in terms of the total demands made on the economy.[15]

The 1981 decision of the British government to shift to private employers the cost of compensatory payments to people away from work because of sickness resulted in almost totally illusory public expenditure cuts. For, in response to pressure from employers, the administration was forced to concede compensatory cuts in social security contributions of employers. The total impact on the government's financial commitments was thus negligible, though, as a parliamentary investigating committee pointed out, the effect would almost certainly be to increase administrative costs.[16] Shifting bureaucratic costs from the public to the private sector may make them less visible but does not necessarily reduce them.

The distinction between public and private spending is therefore arbitrary insofar as it ignores the role of government in determining the latter. And to the extent that countries differ in their mix of public expenditure and political spending, comparisons that rest exclusively on

15. Robert W. Crandall, "Curbing the Costs of Social Regulation," *Brookings Bulletin*, vol. 15 (Winter 1979), pp. 1–5.

16. *The Government's Proposals for Income During Initial Sickness*, H.C. 113, House of Commons, Social Services Committee, Second Report, Session 1980/81 (London: HMSO, 1981), p. xvii.

the former may yield misleading results. The problem can only be noted, not solved. Figures on political spending simply do not exist. The knowledge that they are part of the total cost of governmental activities, however, underlines the importance of caution in interpreting public expenditure statistics.

If public expenditure is seen as inflationary because of the difficulties involved in financing it through taxation or borrowing, political spending might appear to be an attractive and less inflation-prone means of providing services. But the case is far from clear-cut. For example, it is not self-evident that the economic impact on industry of introducing a payroll tax to finance social security is necessarily different from legislating compulsory contributions to private insurance schemes. Either method of financing will probably be translated eventually into higher prices for the goods produced—and may thus, in turn, generate higher wage demands—although the precise proportion of the extra costs allocated to increased consumer prices or decreased profits will vary with the elasticity of demand for the product.

But public expenditure in some areas may be seen as inflationary because of the very nature of the goods provided, because it tends to concentrate resources in "unproductive" activities.[17] Even assuming health or education costs are "unproductive" (certainly debatable in any case), whether the costs fall in the private or the public sector of the economy should not matter if the level of activity is unaffected. In the United States, for example, debate about the cost explosion in health care does not reflect a high level of public expenditure. On the contrary, government expenditure in the United States is well below the OECD average in this respect.[18] Paradoxically, while the percentage of gross domestic product devoted to public expenditure on health care is 50 percent higher in the United Kingdom than in the United States, total spending on health care in the United States (public and private) is proportionately 50 percent higher than in Britain.[19]

It cannot therefore be taken as axiomatic that a high level of public expenditure implies a high level of "unproductive" services in the community. Indeed, statistics on employment in the public sector must be treated with even more caution than those on expenditure. There is little

17. See Robert Bacon and Walter Eltis, *Britain's Economic Problem: Too Few Producers* (London: Macmillan, 1976).

18. OECD, *Public Expenditure on Health* (Paris: OECD, 1977), p. 10.

19. Ibid.; Rudolf Klein, "Costs and Benefits of Complexity: The British National Health Service," in Richard Rose, ed., *Challenge to Governance: Studies in Overloaded Politics* (Sage, 1980).

correlation between levels of public expenditure and levels of public sector manpower. For example, Sweden and the Netherlands are among the top spenders in terms of proportion of GDP devoted to public expenditure, but the proportions of their total labor force in public employment were respectively 28.8 percent and 14.6 percent in 1978; while Britain and West Germany spent roughly the same percentage of GNP on public expenditure, their respective levels of public employment were 21.3 percent and 14.5 percent.[20] The differences have nothing to do with the allocation of real resources but simply reflect the fact that in the Netherlands and West Germany such services as health are publicly financed rather than publicly provided, with the result that those employed in them are not classified as civil servants.

Similarly, the argument that an expanding state service sector sucks up labor from industry neglects the composition of the public sector labor force. As public expenditure rises, so there is a tendency for the proportion of women employed in the public sector to increase also. As of 1980 in Sweden and Norway, for example, women accounted for respectively 65.7 percent and 73.6 percent of the public sector labor force, in the United States and Japan 49.5 percent and 31.8 percent.[21] Moreover, the gross figures of public sector employment ignore the extent of part-time working. In Sweden, 34.2 percent of public sector workers are part-timers, in Britain and the United States 27.4 percent and 14.5 percent.[22] So not only is the size of the public sector labor force exaggerated by the available statistics, but there must be considerable doubt about the extent to which public employment measures the cost of resources that could otherwise be used for the output of commodities.

Indeed the expansion of many public services appears to reflect the translation of domestic services into paid public services as women take up jobs as nursery school teachers or run residential homes for the elderly, so swelling the figures of public expenditure and adding to the notional national income. (Ironically, the easiest way of boosting the growth rates of Western economies would be to turn all housewives into paid civil servants—a transfer of incomes from husbands to wives which would appear in the statistics as a sudden increase in GNP.) If the explanation for the growth in public expenditure is sought in the growth of new demands among emerging political actors, women would seem to be the

20. "Public Sector Employment Trends" (OECD Secretariat, June 23, 1980), table 1.
21. Ibid., table 5.
22. Ibid., table 6.

most obvious, followed by the blacks and other ethnic minorities in the United States. With the puzzling exception of the Netherlands, growth of public expenditure was accompanied by an increase in the participation rates for women in the period 1960 to 1975—from 35 percent to 68 percent in Sweden, from 42 percent to 53 percent in Britain, from 35 percent to 63 percent in Denmark, and from 40 percent to 59 percent in the United States.[23]

If there is a relation between increasing public expenditure and declining employment in the industrial sector, the reason for this may be the opposite of that usually assumed. The public sector may simply be filling the vacuum left by the declining ability of industry to generate sufficient jobs. If employment in industry sags—if the jobs previously available in the steelworks and shipyards migrate to Korea or Taiwan—then the state will inevitably be under pressure to become the employer of last resort. Indeed the state explicitly recognized that role in countries such as Sweden. In Britain, the Conservative administration in the 1980s continued to place high priority on reducing public sector manpower, applying tools of economic policy forged in one economic climate to a totally transformed situation. Given the costs of supporting redundant government workers on unemployment benefits, and given the revenue forgone as a result of lower tax yields from the incomes of government employees, the net financial effect of the British government's manpower reduction strategy is probably negligible. "The energies of the Ministers," Walter Eltis concludes, "are therefore now being devoted to cutting the item of public expenditure which has least to contribute to the improvement of Britain's finances in slump conditions."[24]

In discussing public expenditure it is tempting to seek an explanation for the upward trend either in the contradictions of capitalism—as in the Marxist literature[25]—or in the political competition that tends to be the hallmark of capitalist societies. But rising spending on education, social security, and health care (the programs responsible for the most dramatic increases in public expenditure) may be characteristic of all advanced industrial economies. To the extent that investment in the social infrastructure is a function of the level of industrial or technological devel-

23. OECD, *Towards Full Employment and Price Stability* (Paris: OECD, 1977), table A12, p. 292. (Hereafter McCracken Report).

24. "Do Government Manpower Cuts Correct Deficits When the Economy Is in Deep Recession?" *Political Quarterly,* vol. 53 (January–March 1982), p. 14.

25. See, for example, James O'Connor, *The Fiscal Crisis of the State* (St. Martin's, 1973); Ian Gough, *The Political Economy of the Welfare State* (London: Macmillan, 1979).

Table 8-1. Trends in Public Expenditure in Fourteen Countries, 1955–79

Percent of GDP

Country	1955–57[a]			1967–69[a]			1977–79[a]		
	Total spending[b]	Government consumption	Transfers and subsidies	Total spending[b]	Government consumption	Transfers and subsidies	Total spending[b]	Government consumption	Transfers and subsidies
Austria	29.0	12.6	11.8	36.4	14.7	14.7	46.4	17.8	19.9
Canada	25.1	13.2	6.2	33.0	17.2	8.2	40.0	20.0	12.2
Denmark	25.5	12.6	7.4	35.5	17.2	11.8	46.7	24.3	17.8
Finland	29.2	12.1	9.1	33.4	16.2	10.8	39.1	18.7	15.7
France	33.5	14.1	15.0	39.4	13.7	19.2	44.4	15.0	25.0
Italy	28.1	11.9	10.9	35.5	13.5	17.1	46.1	15.8	21.3
Japan	18.6	9.7	4.0	19.2	8.4	5.2	29.8	9.7	11.0
Netherlands	31.1	15.1	9.3	42.6	16.0	18.1	57.6	18.5	32.4
Norway	27.0	11.3	11.1	37.9	15.4	16.0	50.8	19.6	23.1
Sweden	30.2	15.6	8.2	41.3	20.2	12.3	59.9	28.4	24.1
Switzerland	n.a.	9.4	6.0	25.0	10.3	8.8	33.9	12.9	14.7
United Kingdom	32.3	16.6	7.9	38.5	17.7	11.3	43.5	20.3	15.7
United States	25.9	16.7	4.5	31.7	19.2	7.1	33.9	18.1	11.2
West Germany	30.2	12.5	12.5	33.1	14.4	13.2	43.8	19.9	18.3
OECD average (unweighted)	28.5	13.0	8.8	34.5	15.3	12.2	44.0	18.3	18.2
Standard deviation (OECD countries)	3.37	22.23	3.07	5.95	3.11	4.44	8.72	4.18	6.12

Sources: Organization for Economic Cooperation and Development, *Public Expenditure Trends* (Paris: OECD, 1978), table 2, pp. 14–15, and "Public and Social Expenditure Trends" (OECD, October 1981).

a. Three-year averages, at current prices.

b. Includes interest on public debt and investment.

opment, it would seem redundant to seek the explanation in the special circumstances of Western, capitalist politics.[26] Various comparisons of expenditure trends in capitalist and communist countries suggest that levels of spending on the welfare state are a function not of political competition or ideology but of the national income, demographic structure, and the age of the programs.[27] In other words, the point where any country, capitalist or communist, stands on the upward-moving escalator is determined more by its wealth than by its political or economic system. The large and enduring variations in public expenditure between societies may thus arise from differences in the general upward movement and variations around the trend.

General Trends in Public Spending

From the mid-1950s to the end of the 1970s, the share of public expenditure in the national income of the OECD countries as a whole rose by almost half (table 8-1). But although all the countries marched in the same direction, they traveled at different speeds. The variations around the upward trend became more pronounced at the end of the period.

Overall, this picture suggests there is a built-in secular tendency for public spending to increase as a share of national income, in line with what might be called the general sociological theories of public expenditure growth, Marxist and otherwise.[28] However, these theories do not account for the variations between or within countries at different periods.

If per capita income is used as an indicator of economic development, Switzerland and Sweden could be expected to devote a similar proportion of their national wealth to public spending. In fact, the respective figures are 33.9 percent and 59.9 percent. As table 8-1 shows, there is no consistent relation between gross domestic product and public expenditure levels. In particular, there appears to be one group of wealthy countries—

26. Daniel Bell, *The Coming of Post-Industrial Society: A Venture in Social Forecasting* (Basic Books, 1973), notes that increased spending on developing the knowledge base of societies marks a particular stage in the evolution of such societies.

27. See Harold L. Wilensky, *The Welfare State and Equality: Structural and Ideological Roots of Public Expenditures* (University of California Press, 1975).

28. See Rudolf Klein, "The Politics of Public Expenditure: American Theory and British Practice," *British Journal of Political Science*, vol. 6 (October 1976), pp. 401–32; Daniel Tarchys, "The Growth of Public Expenditure: Nine Modes of Explanation," *Scandinavian Political Studies*, vol. 10 (1975), pp. 9–31; Patrick D. Larkey, Chandler Stolp, and Mark Winer,"Theorising About the Growth of Government," *Journal of Public Policy*, vol. 1 (May 1981), pp. 157–220.

Switzerland, the United States, Canada—that are low spenders, while there are two relatively poor countries—Italy and the United Kingdom—that are comparatively high spenders. Again, Japan's level of public expenditure lags conspicuously behind her level of economic performance. Nor do rates of change in the proportion of national income devoted to public expenditure, as distinct from absolute levels, explain the differences. The elasticities of public expenditure to GDP for the period 1960–78 for the wealthy countries range from 1.43 for Switzerland and 1.45 for Sweden, at one end of the scale, to 1.19, 1.13, and 1.22 for Canada, the United States, and Japan at the other, while those for the relatively poor economic performers are 1.23 for Italy and 1.15 for the United Kingdom.[29] So, while it may be tempting to conclude from the case of Switzerland that there is a "catching up" effect among the countries with a low level of public expenditure in relation to per capita spending, this conclusion is not supported by the experience of the United States, Canada, and Japan.

Again, general theories offer a somewhat erratic guide to the pattern of change. The argument that high spending levels are associated with left-wing governments cannot be confidently translated into a prediction that center or right-wing governments will cut spending. In Britain, for example, public spending stood at 41.5 percent of GDP when the Conservatives came into office in 1979 committed to cutting the level of expenditure, the outgoing Labour government having reduced the proportion from its peak of 46.5 percent in the mid-1970s. But by 1981 the figure had risen to 44.5 percent.[30] Similarly, public expenditure in Sweden continued to rise under the coalition government that took office in 1976.[31] In short, the ideological color of governments may indicate their policy inclinations but not how those inclinations will be modified by the social, political, and economic environment prevailing at any particular time. In Sweden, for instance, the determining factor appears to have been the overarching political consensus that priority should be given to maintaining full employment.

For any political analysis of trends in public expenditure it is helpful

29. OECD Secretariat, "Public Expenditure Trends and their Relation to Social Policy," paper prepared for a Conference on Social Policies in the Eighties, Paris, October 17, 1980.

30. Great Britain, Treasury, *The Government's Expenditure Plans 1981–82 to 1983–84*, Cmnd. 8175 (London: HMSO, 1981).

31. Sweden, Ministry of Economic Affairs, *The 1980 Medium Term Survey of the Swedish Economy* (Stockholm: The Ministry, 1981).

to distinguish between government consumption and transfer payments—between the costs of the state bureaucracy and the state's activities in shuffling money from one section of the population to another. In both categories there is a general upward trend but with wide variations between different countries; again, there is no sign of convergence in the strict sense (see table 8-1). But there is a sharp contrast between the rates of growth in government consumption and in transfer payments or, as the latter have been called, socially financed private consumption.[32] Since the mid-1950s the proportion of GDP absorbed by government consumption at current prices has risen by 40.7 percent. But socially financed private consumption has risen by 106.8 percent.

The relatively slow rise in government consumption may in part be explained by the falling share of defense spending. The OECD average declined from 4.0 percent to 2.7 percent of GDP over the period, thus permitting the expansion of other programs within any given total. The fall in defense spending was particularly marked in the United States (from 9.5 percent to 5.8 percent of GDP) and in the United Kingdom (from 7.4 percent to 5.0 percent), the two heaviest spenders in the 1950s.

Again, the diversity between countries is remarkable. Four of the fourteen countries in table 8-1 spend a fifth or more of national income on government consumption, while Japan spends only a tenth. Some of the differences, of course, reflect institutional arrangements—for example, in Britain and Sweden spending on health care appears on the consumption side of the ledger, in most other Western European countries on the transfer side. Indeed, when private spending on health is added to public, there is a remarkably strong correlation between national wealth and expenditure levels[33]—which might suggest that while general societal factors explain the level, specific systems-characteristics explain the distribution of any given total as between the public and private sectors.

Because the figures in table 8-1 suggest that the government consumption sector is becoming larger relative to the rest of the economy in the scale of its activities, table 8-2 compares the growth in government consumption in current and constant prices. Current price figures measure the cost of government consumption, not the input of resources; constant

---

32. David Smith, "Public Consumption and Economic Performance," *National Westminster Bank Quarterly Review* (November 1975), pp. 17–30.

33. Joseph P. Newhouse, *Income and Medical Care Expenditure Across Countries,* Rand Paper Series P-5608-1 (Palo Alto, Calif.: Rand Corp., 1976).

Table 8-2. *Growth of Government Consumption in Fourteen Countries, 1962–79*

Percent

Country	In current prices		In constant prices	
	Gross domestic product	Government consumption	Gross domestic product	Government consumption
Austria	376	573	109	90
Canada	512	676	123	106
Denmark	580	1,002	82	122
Finland	732	1,114	94	132
France	575	656	116	81
Italy	830	1,045	98	79
Japan	909	1,166	245	142
Netherlands	529	715	104	64
Norway	509	760	109	159
Sweden	435	818	70	107
Switzerland	239	333	51	66
United Kingdom	564	685	54	47
United States	317	315	80	48
West Germany	288	423	87	86

Source: OECD, *National Accounts of OECD Countries, 1962–1979*, vol. 2 (Paris: OECD, 1981). The base year for calculating constant prices varies from country to country in the OECD accounts.

price terms allow for the so-called relative price effect[34]—that is, the fact that while wages and salaries in the public sector follow those set in industry, there is no counterbalancing gain in productivity.[35] At current prices, government consumption rose faster than GDP in all fourteen countries with the exception of the United States; at constant prices, it actually fell behind the growth of GDP in ten of the fourteen and thus declined as a proportion of the total.[36]

34. The relative price effect is also relevant to the private service sector. Its crucial role is in highlighting differences between the competitive and sheltered sectors of the economy; see Gösta Edgren, Karl-Olof Faxén, and Clas-Erik Odhner, "Wages, Growth and the Distribution of Income," *Swedish Journal of Economics*, vol. 71 (September 1969), pp. 133–60; Assar Lindbeck, "Stabilization Policy in Open Economies with Endogenous Politicians," *American Economic Review*, vol. 66 (May 1976, *Papers and Proceedings, 1975*), pp. 1–19. A two-sector model of the economy would suggest a built-in bias toward inflation, irrespective of the size of the public sector but possibly linked to the size of the service sector.

35. This has important implications also for the measurement of national income (and consequently for the figures of public expenditure as a proportion of national income). It has been calculated that in Sweden, assuming that the productivity increase in the public sector was the same as in the private sector, total production would have increased fivefold from 1950 to 1980, instead of threefold as recorded in OECD statistics. See A. Robinson and B. C. Ysander, *Flexibility in Budget Policy*, Working Paper 50 (Stockholm: Industrial Institute for Economic and Social Research, 1981).

36. This confirms the findings in Morris Beck, "The Expanding Public Sector: Some Contrary

Table 8-3. *Increases in the Constant Price Indexes of Public and Private Consumption in Fourteen Countries, 1970–78*

Country	Average annual increase (percent)		Ratio of increase in public to private consumption
	Public consumption	Private consumption	
Austria	9.0	6.4	1.40
Canada	10.7	7.2	1.49
Denmark	11.4	9.4	1.21
Finland	12.5	11.7	1.07
France	11.3	8.6	1.31
Italy	15.1	13.9	1.09
Japan	11.7	9.0	1.30
Netherlands	10.6	8.3	1.28
Norway	9.6	8.5	1.13
Sweden	11.9	9.0	1.32
Switzerland	6.9	5.5	1.25
United Kingdom	14.5	12.8	1.13
United States	7.7	6.2	1.24
West Germany	7.2	5.2	1.38

Source: OECD, *National Accounts of OECD Countries, 1950–1978,* vol. 1 (Paris: OECD, 1980), p. 82.

The relative price effect is not constant as between different countries, as the ratios of the increases in the price indexes of public and private consumption in table 8-3 demonstrate. The ratio is relatively high for Canada and Austria, but almost at par for Finland and Italy. It is tempting to seek the explanation for the differences in the relative power or militancy of public-sector trade unions. Italy's public sector is indeed characterized by a comparatively low rate of unionization (39 percent), but so is that of the United States (25 percent). And while Sweden (81 percent) and Britain (72 percent) are at the opposite end of the spectrum, their relative price ratios are not proportionately higher.[37] In any case labor is not the only input into government consumption, though it is the most important.[38] In Britain during the 1970s, for example, rising land prices were an important factor in determining the relative price effect.[39]

Evidence," *National Tax Journal,* vol. 29 (March 1976), pp. 15–21; OECD, *Public Expenditure Trends* (Paris: OECD, 1978), table 3, p. 18.

37. Richard Rose, *Changes in Public Employment: A Multi-Dimensional Comparative Analysis,* Studies in Public Policy, 61 (University of Strathclyde, Centre for the Study of Public Policy, 1980), p. 41.

38. The OECD's *Public Expenditure Trends,* p. 17, concludes that there was no general shift in pay relativities between the public and private sectors of employment, but it does not allow for such factors as the changing composition of the labor force—in particular, the high proportion of women and part-timers in the public sector.

39. Rudolf Klein, *Social Policy and Public Expenditure, 1974* (London: Centre for Studies in Social Policy, 1974).

In education in the OECD countries—where spending accounts for something like 5 percent of GDP—prices for the period from 1963 to the early 1970s rose 18 percent faster than in the economy as a whole.[40] The range was from 46 percent in the Netherlands and 32 percent in Japan to 10 percent or less in France, the United Kingdom, and Switzerland. Over the same period there was virtually no increase in the number of children at school or of real resources per pupil. Most of the increase in education's share of GDP was due to wage rises not matched by increased productivity. Moreover, there was a general tendency for the number of teachers employed to rise, as working hours became shorter and holiday entitlements longer. In manpower-intensive services like education and health,[41] an ever-increasing number of teachers or nurses is needed to deliver the same number of hours of contact with children or patients.

Education also illustrates the crucial importance of the demographic escalator. Raising the compulsory school leaving age is a policy decision, bringing children into this world a parental decision. The spending implications of the policy decision will vary as the size of the particular cohort varies. However, to make this point is only to raise a new series of questions. Why do policymakers stand so passively on the escalator? Why not cut standards when numbers increase? Why not cut the input of resources when the birth rate falls? To ask these questions is to underline the rigidities in the public sector—rigidities that are similar in character to those found in the private sector, and that are often invoked in explanations of inflation. Just as prices in the private sector tend to be resistant to downward adjustments—confounding classic theory—so commitments in the public sector tend to be resistant to downward adjustment.

The fastest growing component of public expenditure is socially financed private consumption, or transfer payments. Here the relative price effect is largely irrelevant, and the current price figures can be taken at face value. It is the "escalator effect" that is important, for it relates to those rises in public expenditure that reflect the momentum of inherited

40. OECD, *Public Expenditure on Education* (Paris: OECD, 1976), pp. 22–27.

41. Between 1971 and 1976, the number of nurses employed by the British National Health Service increased by 21.4 percent. But when these numbers are deflated to allow for changes in working hours, the effective increase was only 11.8 percent. *Spending on the Health and Personal Social Services,* HC 466-V, Ninth Report, House of Commons, Expenditure Committee, Session 1976–77 (London: HMSO, 1977), p. 66.

commitments.[42] Over the period 1962–72, the share of old-age pensions in GDP increased by almost a third in the OECD countries.[43] Of this rise, 40 percent is explained by a population increase and a further 40 percent by policy decisions to extend the coverage of existing schemes to a higher proportion of the elderly. Perhaps most surprising, rises in the real value of pensions—relative to growth in national wealth—explain only 20 percent of the growth. In other words, deliberate political decisions to improve the standards of living of the elderly relative to the rest of the population explain only a modest part of the growth in spending. Far more important was the inherited commitment to revalue pensions in line with changes in the real income of the working population and to protect benefits against erosion by inflation (with the result that in countries like Britain where the real value of working incomes was reduced in the mid-1970s, there was actually a relative increase in social security payments—an unintended consequence of a commitment made at a time when it was assumed that incomes could only go up).

But if the evidence supports the thesis that shared societal pressures help to explain the generalization of social security benefits to the whole population, there is little sign of any convergence in the level of such payments. In the early 1970s, the ratio of old age pensions to average earnings was .511 in Germany, .422 in France, .296 in Sweden, .218 in the United Kingdom, .180 in the United States, and .118 in Italy.

The escalator effect applies equally to unemployment compensation. For example, one of the main reasons for the failure of the Conservative government in Britain to carry out its commitment to cut public expenditure was the sharp rise in the social security budget in line with increasing unemployment. Ironically, the government's anti-inflation policies of tight monetary control and a strictly constrained public sector borrowing requirement generated extra expenditure demands by adding to the number of jobless. The British experience suggests that the strength of the escalator effect will depend on the nature of the constituency involved. In the case of the elderly, the Conservative government (like the Reagan administration in the United States) considered but rejected the option of snapping the link between the cost-of-living index and

42. Rudolf Klein, "Who Gets What? Problems and Prospects in the Analysis of Public Expenditures and Incomes," in Dennis Kavanagh and Richard Rose, eds., *New Trends in British Politics: Issues for Research* (Sage, 1977), pp. 105–22.

43. OECD, *Public Expenditure on Income Maintenance Programmes* (Paris: OECD, 1976), pp. 38–40.

Table 8-4. *Measures of Income Distribution and Public Expenditure in Eleven Countries, 1974–76*[a]

Country	Public expenditure as percent of GDP	Gini coefficient of posttax incomes[b]
Netherlands	53.9	0.264
Sweden	51.7	0.271
Norway	46.6	0.301
United Kingdom	44.5	0.327
West Germany	44.0	0.386
France	41.6	0.417
Canada	39.4	0.348
United States	35.1	0.369
Australia	32.8	0.354
Spain	25.3	0.397
Japan	25.1	0.336

Sources: Malcolm Sawyer, *Income Distribution in OECD Countries* (Paris: OECD, 1976), table 11, p. 19; OECD, *Public Expenditure Trends,* table 2, pp. 14–15. Date of information varies from country to country.

a. Countries ranked by level of public expenditure.

b. Rank order correlation coefficient; $r = -0.610$, $p < 0.05$.

pension levels; the elderly are a permanent, clearly identifiable constituency. In constituencies that were shifting and lacking in a clear political profile, however, the government adjusted the indexation process to allow the real value of benefits to drop marginally.

Social benefits also seem to buy a degree of posttax equality, as table 8-4 shows. Those countries with high rates of public spending appear to have a lesser degree of posttax income inequality than ones with low spending rates. But the picture is confused when the expenditure on income maintenance is compared to the proportion of the population in poverty (table 8-5). There seems to be no consistent relationship between a high rate of spending on income maintenance and the proportion of the population below a standardized poverty line. Thus the British system appears to be more efficient in directing expenditure at the target population than do the systems in the United States and Canada; and France and West Germany, which devote the same proportion of GDP to income maintenance programs, achieve very different results, with 16 percent and 3.0 percent of their populations, respectively, below the poverty line. High social security expenditure is therefore not a sufficient, though it may be a necessary, condition for closing the "aspirations gap," or for dampening social conflict.

Inevitably, the picture yielded by the evidence is shaped by the choice of countries examined. The OECD countries considered here were all

Table 8-5. *Measures of Poverty and Government Aid in Seven Countries,* *Early 1970s*[a]

Country	Income maintenance expenditure as percent of trend GDP	Percent of population below poverty line[b]
France	12.4	16.0
West Germany	12.4	3.0
Norway	9.8	5.0
Sweden	9.3	3.5
United Kingdom	7.7	7.5
United States	7.4	13.0
Canada	7.3	11.0

Source: OECD, *Public Expenditure on Income Maintenance Programmes* (Paris: OECD, 1976), table 29, p. 72. Date of information varies from country to country.

a. Countries ranked by level of expenditure on income maintenance.

b. The OECD defined as poor (ibid., p. 66) a person whose income was below two-thirds of the average disposable income in his country.

stable polities in the period under discussion; there was no successful challenge to their political systems. So it is not surprising that the pattern of growth in public expenditure is incremental in character.[44] If the analysis were focused on countries where there have been sharp discontinuities in the sociopolitical structure, the picture changes. For example, in Portugal and Greece in the 1970s, changes in the regime produced a rapid expansion of government consumption expenditures—in 1974–78 they rose at an average annual rate of 7.1 percent and 6.7 percent, respectively, in real terms, while the OECD average was 3 percent.[45]

Trying to explain the composition of public expenditure is like excavating Troy. Merely looking at the top layer may give a false impression of the nature of the civilization; public expenditure can only be evaluated in the context of its evolution over time.

Theories and Interpretations

Inflation is often explained as the outcome of conflict—a way of meeting competing demands that cannot be satisfied within the constraints of the

44. In the case of Britain, extrapolating from governmental final expenditure for 1959 to 1967 (at constant 1970 prices) yields a predicted spending total of £10.633 billion for 1976; actual expenditure was £11.049 billion (at constant 1970 prices), a difference of only £416 million. So, despite the anguished debate in the mid-1970s about public expenditure getting "out of control," there is little evidence of discontinuities in inherited trends. Figures from Great Britain, Central Statistical Office, *National Income and Expenditure 1966–1976* (London: HMSO, 1977), table 2.1.

45. OECD, *National Accounts of OECD Countries* (Paris: OECD, 1981).

available resources.[46] At first sight, it would seem that increasing public expenditure, like increasing the money supply, is a way of accommodating conflicting demands. And whether the strategy is to pump money into the economy or to raise spending on subsidies or cash-transfer benefits is a matter of political choice that will vary in different political systems. But this mode of explanation is circular; the outcome is taken as evidence of the causal processes involved. In the case of Sweden and Britain, for example, it is not at all self-evident that there has been an increase in conflict over the past decades. Although the pressure from labor organizations can be interpreted as a rejection of market-determined differentials—and thus a new source of distributional conflict—there is considerable evidence of a tenacious attachment to traditional inherited relativities.[47] On the supply side of the equation, it may be argued that the capacity of the British system to cope even with the existing level of demand has actually declined because of the falling rate of growth. If both inflation and rising public expenditure are seen as a revolt against the existing distribution of income within any given social system, does that mean there is less conflict in, say, the United States than in Sweden, although the latter is—as shown in table 8-4—a more egalitarian society?[48] Or is the impact of conflict or competing demands on both inflation and public expenditure mediated through specific political and organizational factors?

The two main components of public expenditure, government spending and publicly financed private consumption, behave in different ways, and their growth might also be expected to be responsive to different factors. In the case of government spending, theories that explain rising public expenditure in terms of supply-push (factors endogenous to the state bureaucracy) would seem to be most relevant since growth of the bureaucracy is consistent with the explanation that service providers tend to maximize their budgets and thus to expand their programs. To be sure, in some cases, the career prospects of bureaucrats may well be enhanced

---

46. See McCracken Report, p. 155; James Harvey, "Theories of Inflation," *Marxism Today*, vol. 21 (January 1977), pp. 24–29.

47. See Great Britain, Royal Commission on the Distribution of Income and Wealth, *Report No. 8: Fifth Report on the Standing Reference*, Cmnd. 7679 (London: HMSO, 1979), pp. 79–81. Much of the industrial conflict in Britain—most conspicuously, the 1974 strike by the miners—revolves around the reestablishment of traditional differentials, eroded by incomes policy.

48. It may well be that inequality is more resented in a country like Sweden, which subscribes to an egalitarian ideology, than in a country like the United States, which does not. For evidence that suggests a high degree of perceived inequality in Sweden, see Richard Scase, *Social Democracy in Capitalist Society: Working-Class Politics in Britain and Sweden* (London: Croom Helm, 1977).

if they are good at saving money[49]—in Britain the most prestigious civil servants are those who work in the Treasury and who are professional hatchet men.[50] Moreover, supply side theories do not account for the contrast between spending in current and constant prices—the relative price effect.

However, the assumption of supply-push theories that service providers are budget *maximizers* is not necessary to explain the growth of the public sector. A weaker assumption will do. This is that service providers are merely concerned to safeguard their own incomes and security—that they are defensive-minded conservatives rather than aggressive imperialists seeking to expand their services. This would help to explain, parsimoniously, both the relative price effect, discussed above, and the fact that governments find it difficult to finance new programs by liquidating existing commitments, with the result that change in the public sector tends to be additive.

Such an explanation is certainly consistent with the failure of Britain's Conservative government to check demands for higher wages and salaries in the public sector. In 1979, when Mrs. Thatcher was elected, public servants were neck and neck with other workers in terms of their relative pay. By 1981, they were earning 8 percent more than they would have got in industry.[51] On the other hand, the government had the greatest difficulty in implementing expenditure cuts that involved reductions in public sector manpower. Education illustrates the latter point, for a decline in the birth rate and in the school population gave the government an open invitation to cut.[52] It seized the opportunity by lowering expenditures by 10 percent, which involved a proportional fall in the number of teachers. But the personnel reduction was to be achieved largely through "natural wastage, early retirement and redeployment"[53] (that is, redundancies were to be avoided). Significantly, the most radical cut was in fringe activities that do not impinge on the organized power of teachers—funds allocated to providing school meals for children were halved.

49. Julius Margolis, "Comment" (on William A. Niskanen's "Bureaucrats and Politicians"), *Journal of Law and Economics,* vol. 18 (December 1975), pp. 645–59.

50. Hugh Heclo and Aaron Wildavsky, *The Private Governments of Public Money: Community and Policy inside British Politics* (London: Macmillan, 1974).

51. "Work for the Government," *Economist* (December 19, 1981), p. 52.

52. Maurice Kogan, "Education in 'Hard Times,'" in Christopher Hood and Maurice Wright, eds., *Big Government in Hard Times* (Oxford: Martin Robertson, 1981), pp. 152–73.

53. Treasury, *Government's Expenditure Plans,* Cmnd. 8175, p. 104.

Labor—trade unions and professional organizations—is an important contributor to the growth of public consumption and the problems faced by governments intent on retrenchment. The most immediate beneficiaries of the welfare state are those working in the program; in other words, the creation of a program creates an organized constituency. And the public sector tends to be the most intensively unionized part of the economy.[54] Moreover, it is likely to oppose change, if this threatens jobs, and is thus likely to become a source of organizational rigidity. This rigidity is common, in varying degrees, to all sectors of the economy in advanced industrial societies. Indeed it seems as plausible (if still only partial) an explanation of endemic inflation as of rising public consumption. Inflation can be seen as the product of the frictional problems of adjustment in societies characterized by a high degree of both turbulence (a rapid rate of technological change) and organizational rigidity. In that case, the problem reflects not the radicalization of labor—which is perhaps why no statistical correlation has been found between trade union militancy and inflation rates—but its conservatism. Thus the power of organized labor should perhaps be measured as much in its ability to resist change—for example, to prevent the euthanasia of redundant public sector programs or loss-making industries—as in its capacity to change the distribution of income in its favor.

Organizational factors are a far less plausible explanation of the increase in socially financed private consumption, whose main beneficiaries are outside the state system. Yet growth in this sector has been dramatic in most advanced industrial countries, despite attempts to reverse the trend. Emphasis on the importance of supply-push factors in the expansion of public expenditure in the United States may reflect the fact that an exceptionally low proportion of GDP there goes into transfer payments in comparison with most Western European countries (and perhaps the fact that American civil servants are more entrepreneurial in style than their European counterparts; British civil servants could more accurately be characterized as risk-minimizers than as budget-maximizers). In trying to explain this trend, demand-push theories of public expenditure growth would seem to be relevant.[55] Again, organized labor would appear to be

54. See Great Britain, Bullock Committee of Enquiry on Industrial Democracy, *Report of the Committee of Enquiry on Industrial Democracy,* Cmnd. 6706 (London: HMSO, 1977); Rose, *Changes in Public Employment,* p. 41.

55. I do not attempt to discuss theories of the political business cycle, which are dealt with elsewhere in this volume. It is generally assumed that the benefits of specific public expenditure programs will be more visible than the tax costs (see, for example, James M. Buchanan, "Why Does Government Grow?"

crucial, making demands for job preservation via public expenditure. This helps to explain the countercyclical pattern of spending increases in the 1960s, when Keynesian expenditure management was still the dominant approach in most Western countries (though it turned out to be easier to increase public expenditure in the downturns of the cycle than to reverse the trend during the upswings, a further reminder of the importance of rigidities in Western economies).

In the 1970s there was a sharp upswing in Britain and Sweden particularly, though not exclusively, in government aid to industry to prevent bankruptcies and redundancies. In Britain, for example, expenditure on various forms of support to industry and the labor market rose from £2.331 billion in 1971–72 to £3.535 billion in 1974–75 at constant prices.[56] In Sweden, outright grants on accumulated stocks to firms undertaking not to reduce employment were equivalent to 2 percent of GDP in the eighteen months up to the end of 1976.[57] Overall, therefore, the Swedish and British experience suggests that public expenditure may rise as a political response to falling profitability.[58]

Significantly, expenditure on employment maintenance survived the change of political regime in both countries. In Britain the Conservative government in its first year in office lived up to its commitment to reduce such state intervention, but by 1982 such expenditure had increased by

---

in Thomas E. Borcherding, ed., *Budgets and Bureaucrats: The Sources of Government Growth* [Duke University Press, 1977]), and that political competition generates excessive expectations among voters (see Samuel Brittan, "The Economic Contradictions of Democracy," *British Journal of Political Science*, vol. 5 [April 1975], pp. 129–59). But this is to overlook the fact that both voters' perceptions and preferences (see Paul Mosley, "Images of the 'Floating Voter': Or, the 'Political Business Cycle' Revisited," *Political Studies*, vol. 26 [September 1978], pp. 375–94) and their expectations (see Richard Rose, *Ordinary People in Extraordinary Economic Circumstances*, Studies in Public Policy, 11 [University of Strathclyde, Centre for the Study of Public Policy, 1977]) may change over time. By the late 1970s government began to compete for votes by cutting public expenditure and taxation; witness California's Proposition 13 and Britain's 1979 general election. One of the problems of the various theories developed in the early and mid-1970s is that they do not predict (or explain) what actually happened in the late 1970s and 1980s.

56. Great Britain, Treasury, *The Government's Expenditure Plans*, vol. 2, Cmnd. 6721–II (London: HMSO, 1977), table 2.4.

57. *OECD Economic Surveys: Sweden* (Paris: OECD, April 1977), pp. 12–14.

58. This conclusion is, of course, contrary to the Marxist contention that rising public expenditure is the cause of low profitability in industry through the tax system; see Mervyn A. King, "The United Kingdom Profits Crisis: Myth or Reality?" *Economic Journal*, vol. 85 (March 1975), pp. 33–54. King concludes (p. 47) that over the period 1950–73 while there was indeed "an underlying downward trend in the share of conventional gross profits before tax," there was "no long run or *secular* decline in the share of profits after tax." In other words, the tax system appears to have been used in order to maintain the level of profits, not to depress them. This might suggest that, in Britain at any rate, trade unions in the 1970s had both the economic clout to divert a higher proportion of profits to wages and the political clout to force governments to compensate for the subsequent effects on employment.

50 percent and was, moreover, considerably higher than in the last year of the previous Labour government.[59] In Sweden, expenditure on aid to industry nearly quadrupled between 1976 and 1979—rising from Kr2.443 billion to Kr10.638 billion, and thereafter falling again.[60] The trend of policy in the two countries, as reflected in expenditure figures, was not so very dissimilar, despite the one government's explicit and militant commitment to repudiating its predecessor's interventionist ideology and attempt to incorporate trade unions in the policy process, and the other's emphasis on maintaining consensus and continuity.

Organized labor has an important role also in attempts to keep the cost of living down—to insulate consumers from the effects of external shocks such as oil price rises. Governments use public spending as currency to persuade trade unions to exercise wage restraint. The economics of such a policy may be dubious, since they give an artificial stimulus to demand. But politically such increases can be seen as a sensible response to inflation. Certainly, in the mid-1970s both Sweden and Britain used public expenditure as a means of lowering expectations about future rates of inflation. Sweden in 1975 spent Kr2.6 billion, out of a total budget of Kr93 billion, on food subsidies.[61] And the British Labour government introduced food subsidies in 1974, accounting for £854 million in a total program of £58 billion.[62] It also increased expenditure designed to keep rents on municipal housing down and to compensate nationalized industries, like gas and electricity, for keeping their prices down. In the early 1980s, however, Britain's Conservative government abandoned all attempts to use subsidies as a means of influencing wage claims. Food subsidies were eliminated completely, and housing subsidies were sharply reduced. Sweden's coalition government, in contrast, not only reduced income taxes in 1980 in order to facilitate a new national wage agreement, but at the same time it increased food subsidies. Thus in fiscal 1981 the total cost of food subsidies was Kr4.5 billion, out of a total budget of Kr212 billion—although the intention was to reduce food subsidies gradually thereafter.[63]

Still, most socially financed private consumption—such as transfer payments—benefits not the members of trade unions but marginal groups in society, such as the elderly, the disabled, and the unemployed. It tends

59. Treasury, *Government's Expenditure Plans,* Cmnd. 8175, table 2.4.
60. *OECD Economic Surveys: Sweden* (June 1981), table 8.
61. Ibid.
62. Treasury, *Government's Expenditure Plans,* Cmnd. 7049, table 2.3.
63. Sweden, *The Swedish Budget, 1981–82* (Stockholm: Ministry of Economic Affairs and Ministry of the Budget, 1981).

to redistribute income across the generations and from childless to prolific couples. The explosion of public expenditure designed to benefit these groups would seem to be inconsistent with theories that see demand being generated in the political market and by organized labor.

Part of the answer to the puzzle stems from the fact that much of the growth in public spending represents the increasing cost of past commitments, reflecting demographic trends and the price of indexation, rather than new policies. And commitments undertaken during a period of optimism about future growth may reflect a miscalculation of the likely size of the national income. Equally important, the strong labor movements—and their political affiliates, like the British Labour party and the Scandinavian Social Democratic parties—tend to act as proxy groups for the less organized sectors. Their altruistic ideology is buttressed by self-interest,[64] particularly in pensions, which can be seen as deferred payments and which appear to be particularly resistant to government economy drives. If there is a link between inflation and public expenditure, it may thus run through the activities of organized labor. The wage-push theory of inflation would seem to argue in the same direction as a demand-pull theory of public expenditure, modified to take account of the role of organized labor both in the public sector and as a proxy group for the more vulnerable sections of the community.

But identification of the key role of organized labor should not be taken to mean that both inflation and the growth of public expenditure are bound to go on increasing in societies with strong trade unions. The structure of organized labor and its relation to the political system can, as Colin Crouch argues in chapter 5, modify the outcome. Imagine a country where the entire labor force belongs to the same trade union. Not only would there be no element of wage-push arising from the competition for members between various unions, but the benefits of wage restraint would be internalized. No individual union would be "providing a public good voluntarily"[65] by limiting its claims, while having

64. The history of the social contract in Britain—and the similar experience of Sweden—suggests, however, that both perceptions of self-interest and the altruistic ideology may not necessarily be shared by trade union leaders and their members. The Swedish leadership's advocacy of the social contract approach—with its emphasis on deferred benefits and redistribution—was, in practice, repudiated by the members, as Andrew Martin notes in chapter 13, below. Altruism may also be vulnerable to economic turbulence—to people's perception of their own well-being. For the British evidence that altruism declines with economic growth, see James E. Alt, *The Politics of Economic Decline: Economic Management and Political Behaviour in Britain since 1964* (Cambridge University Press, 1979); also Rudolf Klein, "Values, Power and Policies," in OECD, *The Welfare State in Crisis* (Paris: OECD, 1981), pp. 166–78.

65. Mancur Olson, *The Rise and Decline of Nations* (Yale University Press, 1982). The following discussion draws heavily on the arguments of this book.

no certainty that others would follow the same course. There would thus be no problem about pursuing the kind of strategies attempted in Britain and Sweden in the mid-1970s—with very mixed success—of buying trade union cooperation for wage restraint in return for higher public expenditure. Similarly, there would be little opposition to the termination of individual government programs; always provided that there was no net reduction in employment, it would be in everyone's interest to have a more flexible approach.

To the extent that a country approaches this kind of situation—the more encompassing its labor organization is—the more likely is a strategy of using public expenditure to buy wage restraint to be successful. The deal would not succeed if the union movement were fragmented, or if the leaders and rank-and-file had different perceptions of self-interest. The same point applies to the attitude of organized labor toward flexibility in the public sector; commitment to the status quo would be in inverse relation to the extent to which the union movement is encompassing.

But the extent to which the union movement identifies self-interest with public interest depends also on the relationship between organized labor and the political system. Here it is possible to imagine either a market or a symbiotic political relationship. At one pole, the cooperation of the union movement is bought in straight financial terms; at the other, the currency is participation in or influence over policy decisions. Moreover, the nature of the relationship is a function of the prevailing political ideology. Thus the change of government in Britain in 1979 made little change in the formal institutional arrangements for consulting trade unions. But adoption of a market perspective—and the repudiation of the idea that policies might be shaped in discussions with the trade unions—made a profound difference. Indeed the policies of the Thatcher government were shaped by the view that union self-interest and the public interest were, if anything, bound to be in conflict. In contrast, the change of government in Sweden did not mark a fundamental reassessment of the relationship between unions and the political system, even though the style and temper of the relationship was inevitably affected by the move of the Social Democrats into opposition.

The relationship between public expenditure and inflation in Western societies can thus be presented in terms of three models. In societies that approximate most closely the classic market model, and where organized interest groups are weak or fragmented, public expenditure and inflation need not necessarily move in the same direction, and either or both may be low; this will be particularly so in societies where there is an element of direct democracy (as in Switzerland) as distinct from aggregations of interests in organized groups. In societies that approximate most closely the monopsonistic model, where there are powerful and well-organized interest groups competing in the political market, rising public expenditure and inflation are likely to march in step. And in corporatist[66] societies where an encompassing labor organization is keyed into the processes of policymaking, there is likely to be an effective choice between high public expenditure and inflation.

Like all models, these fail to capture the full, shifting complexity of the real world. They suggest stability where there is flux. The same institutional framework may over time provide the setting for very different kinds of policies. Moreover, countries may commute between different models in a dialectic learning process. As Kristina Peterson suggests, "The State gradually develops corporate characteristics until a critical threshold is reached and the workers rebel. At that point, the corporate system breaks down, while the groups try different means of political expression (viz. strikes). Later, when they find that these are not as successful, they move back into the corporate pattern, stronger and more productive as corporate interest groups."[67]

Bearing these reservations in mind, the three models would still seem to be consistent with the differing patterns of the relationship between public expenditure and inflation shown in figure 8-1. Nations with a high level of public spending but a relatively low level of inflation fit rather neatly into Crouch's category of neocorporatist countries: Austria, West Germany, the Netherlands, Sweden, and Norway (table 5-2). Britain would seem to be a classic illustration of the monopsonistic model, with inflation in the 1970s running at a considerably higher rate than would be predicted on the level of public expenditure; it ranks relatively high on unionization (45 percent of the labor force) but seesaws between corporatist and confrontational policies. Italy falls, rather less neatly, into the same category; the unions are less strong than in Britain but, it can equally be argued, so are the political institutions. Both the United States and Japan would seem to approximate most closely the classic market model.

66. See chapter 5 for a discussion of corporatism. For a comprehensive review of the debate, see *Comparative Political Studies*, Special Issue: *Corporatism and Policy-Making in Contemporary Western Europe*, vol. 10 (April 1977).

67. "Corporatism and Unemployment" (Ph.D. dissertation, Northwestern University, 1981).

Figure 8-1. *Public Expenditure and Inflation Levels in Fourteen Advanced Countries, Late 1970s*

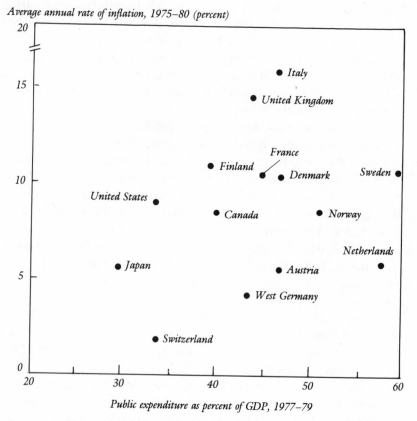

Average annual rate of inflation, 1975–80 (percent)

Public expenditure as percent of GDP, 1977–79

Sources: Organization for Economic Cooperation and Development, "Public and Social Expenditure Trends" (Paris: OECD, October 1981), and *OECD Economic Surveys: Sweden* (Paris: OECD, June 1981).

The experience of the corporatist countries is interesting in that they appear to have a lower rate of inflation for any given rate of unemployment than the monopsonistic countries. In 1980, for example, the rate of unemployment in Sweden was 2.0 percent as against 6.8 percent for Britain. This, once again, is consistent with the argument that public expenditure designed to maintain levels of employment may be a successful instrument for buying the cooperation of the trade union movement for policies of wage restraint—though not always or invariably. It may be a necessary condition but is certainly not a sufficient one.

There appear to be two political structures for dealing with the twin phenomena of inflation and rising public expenditure that correspond to the economic prescriptions offered. One is a return to the classic market system, which implies the recreation of a society that has largely vanished. This is the strategy pursued by the British Conservative government after 1979 with mixed success. Inflation indeed fell sharply, despite the failure to cut public expenditure, largely because the power of the trade unions was undermined by a socially damaging high rate of unemployment. The other is continuing advance to a corporatist form of society, which alone seems to offer the political conditions required for a negotiated wage order (though the extent to which such a corporatist society would depend on coercion, preceptorial persuasion, or bribery is an open question).[68] The middle stage appears to be a zone of instability where powerful, but politically unintegrated, monopsonistic organizations may create a situation where inflation and public expenditure may continue to flourish alongside each other.

68. See Charles E. Lindblom, *Politics and Markets: The World's Political-Economic Systems* (Basic Books, 1977).

9

Does Government Cause Inflation? Taxes, Spending, and Deficits

David R. Cameron

What causes inflation? Ronald Reagan in his first address on the economy reflected the conventional wisdom: "We know now that inflation results from all that deficit spending. . . . Bringing Government spending back within Government revenues. . . is the only way . . . that we can reduce and, yes, eliminate inflation."[1] But is President Reagan correct in attributing inflation to the imbalance between spending and revenue? And is the large majority of Americans correct in identifying federal deficits as the primary cause of inflation? Are political economists such as Buchanan and Wagner correct in asserting that "the budget deficits that emerged from the Keynesian revision of the fiscal constitution injected an inflationary bias into the economic order. Empirically, the deficit-inflation nexus is strong and is widely acknowledged in popular discussion"?[2] Is the Committee to Fight Inflation—a committee of thirteen that included two former chairmen of the board of governors of the Federal Reserve System (William Martin and Arthur Burns), five former secretaries of the treasury (Henry Fowler, Michael Blumenthal, Douglas Dillon, George Schultz, and William Simon), and an influential former chairman of the Council of Economic Advisers (Paul McCracken)—correct in linking budget deficits to inflation?

1. "Transcript of Reagan Address Reporting on the State of the Nation's Economy," *New York Times*, February 6, 1981.
2. James M. Buchanan and Richard E. Wagner, *Democracy in Deficit: The Political Legacy of Lord Keynes* (Academic Press, 1977), p. 58.

During recent decades there have been sharply rising pressures on Congress to adopt new spending programs and to expand existing programs. Pressures for spending cuts or tax increases have been much weaker. The result has been a virtually unbroken string of budget deficits over the last 20 years.... This persistent pattern of deficit financing has contributed powerfully to the impetus of inflation.[3]

Is the diagnosis of the causes of inflation made by President Reagan, the experts of the Committee to Fight Inflation, and the American public correct? Is government the problem, rather than the solution? This chapter examines a variety of hypotheses that link inflation to the fiscal policy of government. First, it considers whether inflation in the United States and other advanced capitalist nations should be attributed to the large increases and high levels of government spending that occurred in recent decades, then whether the acceleration in the rate of change in prices that characterized most of the advanced capitalist world after the mid-1960s was produced by the tendency of government to overspend—that is, to spend more than is received in taxes, thereby incurring budget deficits.

Government Spending and Inflation

Almost as many causes of inflation are advanced as there are economists—excessive demand, insufficient supply, exogenous shocks, administered pricing, decreases in productivity, increases in labor costs, increases in the market power of producers of raw materials, increases in the wage militancy of labor throughout the advanced capitalist world, sectoral alterations in the economy, compositional changes in the labor force, excessive increases in the supply of money.[4] The American public in the late 1970s gave pollsters one reply—refreshing in its simplicity—far more frequently than any other: inflation is caused by government (figure 9-1).[5] Two decades earlier, the American public apparently subscribed to a

---

3. "Text of Policy Statement by Panel to Fight Inflation," *New York Times,* June 22, 1980.

4. See Fred Hirsch and John H. Goldthorpe, eds., *The Political Economy of Inflation* (Harvard University Press, 1978); Michael J. Piore, ed., *Unemployment and Inflation: Institutionalist and Structuralist Views* (White Plains, N.Y.: M.E. Sharpe, 1979); Phillip Cagan, *Persistent Inflation: Historical and Political Essays* (Columbia University Press, 1979); David P. Calleo, *The Imperious Economy* (Harvard University Press, 1982); James Tobin, "Stabilization Policy Ten Years After," George L. Perry, "Inflation in Theory and Practice," and other overviews of macroeconomic policy in *Brookings Papers on Economic Activity, 1:1980* (hereafter *BPEA*).

5. In a national survey, 79 percent of 1,605 respondents identified federal government deficits as an "extremely important" cause of inflation; 78 percent so identified cost of oil and other energy; 74 percent, federal government "prints money"; 62 percent, business profit margins; and 46 percent, easy credit. CBS–New York Times survey, April 10–14, 1980.

Figure 9-1. *Public Perception of Government's Share of Responsibility for Inflation in the United States, 1959–78*

"Which is most responsible for inflation?"

Percent of poll respondents

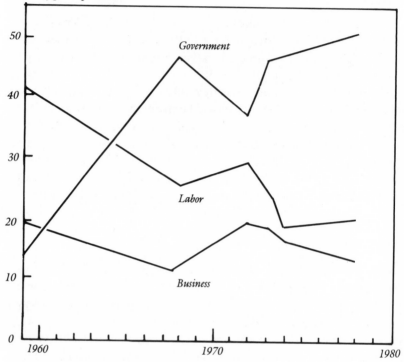

conventional cost-push view of inflation and believed that labor was responsible for increases in prices. But with an acceleration of the rate of inflation during the late 1960s and 1970s, more than half of representative national samples of citizens came to attribute responsibility for inflation to government.

The public view is not surprising given the attention devoted by business elites and the media to such reputed sources of inflation as budget deficits and government spending. One need not subscribe to Lindblom's notion of circularity,[6] for example, to suppose that the almost

6. Charles E. Lindblom, *Politics and Markets: The World's Political-Economic Systems* (Basic Books, 1977), pp. 201–15.

unanimous emphasis given by business executives to federal deficits as a cause of inflation would percolate through and shape public opinion.[7] Nor does it require heroic assumptions about attitude formation to suppose that the numerous articles on inflation in the business press— often illustrated with gushers of dollars blowing the dome off the Capitol or a cornucopia dispersing dollars from the Congress and White House— would influence public attitudes about inflation.

Primary responsibility probably still lies with government itself for making the public feel it is the cause of inflation. Time after time, political figures and public officials have suggested that the cure for (and thus by implication the cause of) inflation could be found in government fiscal policy. President Jimmy Carter in his 1976 campaign pledged to balance the federal budget, and in his 1980 economic report focused on fiscal and monetary restraint as the first line along which to fight inflation.

Moreover, it is not the mere failure to cover expenses with taxes that is blamed, but the growth of state expenditure in its own right. As Robert Gordon notes:

The steady historical increase in the share of government spending in GNP in real terms tends to increase the rate of inflation through both the demand and supply side. More government spending must be financed and, if the allocative, administrative, and negotiation costs of raising conventional taxes are taken into account, some extra money creation is optimal. . . . Further, to the extent that the higher government spending share results not from wars but rather from peacetime transfers to the unemployed and the poor, wage rates will become more rigid, which in turn will increase the political cost to incumbents of the refusal to accommodate inflation. . . . A prediction of the likely future course of inflation requires a judgment on the continuation of the past historical behavior of the share of government spending in GNP, and of the share of transfer payments to earned labor income.[8]

In a similar vein, Milton and Rose Friedman link inflation to the "rapid growth of government spending," as financed by monetizing federal debt.[9] On the other side of the ideological spectrum Heilbroner looks to the

---

7. In a survey of 1,100 business executives conducted by the U.S. Chamber of Commerce, 99 percent identified the federal deficit as a "very important" or "important" cause of inflation; 92 percent so identified union wage increases; 80 percent, social security increases; 78 percent, federal pay increases; 75 percent, increases in the minimum wage; and 10 percent, excessive corporate profits. Michael C. Jensen, *New York Times,* June 6, 1978.

8. Robert J. Gordon, "The Demand for and Supply of Inflation," *Journal of Law and Economics,* vol. 18 (December 1975), pp. 835–36.

9. Milton and Rose Friedman, *Free To Choose: A Personal Statement* (Harcourt Brace Jovanovich, 1980), p. 264.

change that profoundly distinguishes modern capitalism from the capitalism of the pre-war era—the presence of a government sector vastly larger and far more intimately enmeshed in the process of capitalist growth than can be discovered anywhere prior to World War II . . . to set the stage for an inflationary propensity where no such tendency had previously existed. . . . The assumption of political responsibility for an acceptable level of economic performance pushes government—with only brief interludes—in the direction of an expansionary fiscal and monetary policy. Governments can withstand many setbacks, but not sustained recession. Thus the political pressure builds to spend high and tax low.[10]

Similarly, Ernest Mandel argues that "in the developed capitalist countries . . . inflation first made its appearance with the hypertrophy of state expenditure caused by rearmament and war (when budgetary deficits started to be covered by use of the printing press). . . . The role of public expenditure as the main source of inflation became even more pronounced in the Second World War."[11]

Among political scientists Aaron Wildavsky, for example, has argued for a constitutional amendment to limit government spending which, he claims, "has been growing much faster than the economy" and which threatens to continue its "unabated ascent" and can only cause inflation.[12] Richard Rose and Guy Peters have similarly supported a limitation on increases. They perceive inflation to be a policy to which government resorts in order to maintain its "take-home pay" in the face of private claims in an era of reduced rates of economic growth. "Past commitments to future spending threaten to overload government, requiring it to spend more money than can be provided by the fruits of economic growth. . . . Everywhere in the Western world, politicians have reacted to the predicament of their political economy by invoking the money illusion of inflation. Inflation increases the take-home pay of citizens, and it also makes it easier to meet the costs of public policy." Eventually, however, money illusion fails to deceive. Government must then choose between continued increases in government spending, and hence reductions in take-home pay via increased taxes and a resulting threat of political "bankruptcy"—that is, loss of popular consent, increased civic indifference, and economic and institutional ineffectiveness—or the imposition of limits on government spending. Only putting the "brakes on rising costs of public policy" can resolve the dilemma.[13]

10. Robert L. Heilbroner, *Beyond Boom and Crash* (Norton, 1978), pp. 42, 44, 45.

11. *Late Capitalism* (London: NLB, 1975), pp. 413, 417.

12. *How to Limit Government Spending* (University of California Press, 1980), p. 5; he asserts that "a constitutional amendment tying public spending to economic growth will decrease taxes and lessen inflation."

13. Richard Rose and Guy Peters, *Can Government Go Bankrupt?* (Basic Books, 1978), pp. 9, 178, 219.

Figure 9-2. *Government Spending as a Share of GNP in the United States, 1948–81*

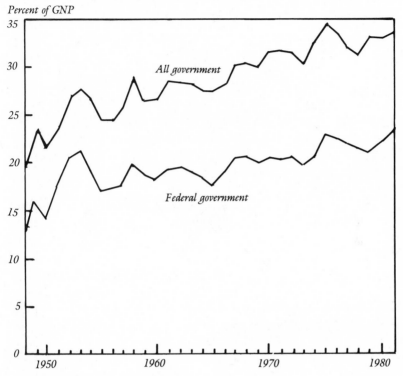

Percent of GNP

Source: *Economic Report of the President, February 1982,* tables B-1, B-75.

Growth of Government Spending

How persuasive is the argument that the acceleration in the rate of inflation in the advanced capitalist societies derives from the steady growth of government spending in recent decades? Between 1948 and 1981 the combined total expenditures of all levels of government in the United States increased by 0.33 percent of GNP per year, or about 3.33 percent of GNP per decade. Slightly more than one-half of that increase—0.19 percent of GNP per year, or about 2 percent of GNP per decade—was accounted for by the federal government.[14] While these data seem to confirm the existence of a secular trend of increasing government spending, relative to the economy, there was no dramatic long-term upward trend in spending (see figure 9-2). Virtually every increase in spending occurred

14. The measure of change is the regression coefficient when the expenditure category is regressed on time. Based on data in *Economic Report of the President, February 1982,* tables B-1, B-75.

Figure 9-3. *Government Spending as a Share of GDP in Twelve Countries, 1960–81*

Percent of GDP

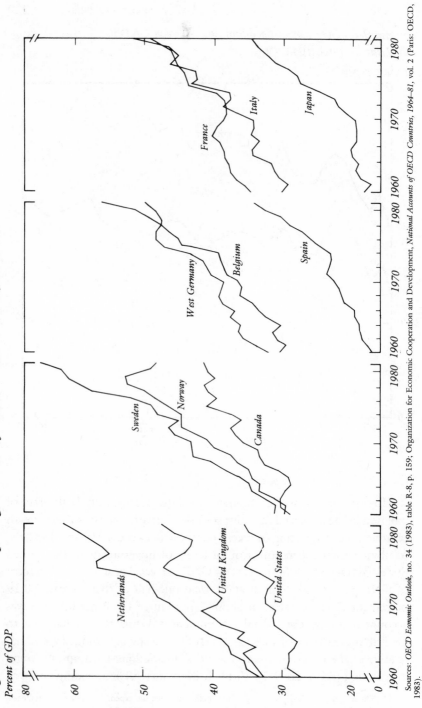

Sources: *OECD Economic Outlook*, no. 34 (1983), table R-8, p. 159; Organization for Economic Cooperation and Development, *National Accounts of OECD Countries, 1964–81*, vol. 2 (Paris: OECD, 1983).

in time of war or economic crisis, the largest during the Truman administration's war in Korea (in 1951–53), and a more modest increase during the early years of the Johnson administration's war in Vietnam (1966–67).[15] The only other years in which government spending, as a percent of GNP, increased were ones in which recessions occurred—1949, 1958, 1960–61, 1970–71, 1974–75, 1980, and 1981–82.[16] At times when the nation was not involved in war or recession, federal spending remained stable, or even decreased, as a proportion of GNP. Thus, during the late 1970s, for example—when Wildavsky was writing that "public spending has been growing much faster than the economy,"[17] and the Friedmans that there had recently been a "rapid growth in government spending"[18]—the actual level of spending of the federal government and of all government in the United States was *decreasing*.

Whether the changes over time should be characterized as minimal or significant is a matter of individual judgment. But in making that judgment, it is helpful to compare American experience with that of other countries (figure 9-3). Government in the United States spent a relatively small share of gross domestic product (GDP) in the 1960s and 1970s and that share increased more slowly than in most countries. Alarm over the extent and rate of increase in government spending may be appropriate for Sweden, the Netherlands, Norway, or Belgium (or even for Japan, Spain, or Italy among the larger nations).[19] But it hardly seems fitting for the United States. In 1979 and 1980 the average spending of all levels of government as a percentage of GDP in the Federal Republic of Germany, France, Italy, the United Kingdom, and Canada was 7–14 percentage points higher than in the United States (table 9-1). Only in Spain and Japan did government spend less than in the United States, and their rate of spending—especially Japan's after 1970—was increasing at a much greater rate than that of the United States. The rate of increase in government spending between 1960 and 1980 exceeded 1 percent of GDP per year in Sweden, the Netherlands, Denmark, and Belgium. In

---

15. On the impact of war on government expenditure, see Alan T. Peacock and Jack Wiseman, *The Growth of Public Expenditure in the United Kingdom*, 2d ed. (London: Allen and Unwin, 1967).

16. While spending appears to have *decreased* as a percent of GNP in the 1954 recession, the proportion spent in 1954 increases if the impact of the Korean War on spending in 1950–53 is removed.

17. *How to Limit Government Spending*, p. 5.

18. *Free to Choose*, p. 264.

19. For a discussion of the reasons why the growth of the public economy was unusually large in the smaller European democracies, see David R. Cameron, "The Expansion of the Public Economy: A Comparative Analysis," *American Political Science Review*, vol. 72 (December 1978), pp. 1243–61.

Table 9-1. *Government Spending as a Share of GDP in Twenty Countries, 1960–80*[a]

Percent

Country	Total government spending as a share of GDP		
	1960–61	1979–80	Increase, 1960–61 to 1979–80
Sweden	31.1	65.4	34.3
Denmark	26.0	53.8	27.8
Netherlands	34.6	61.0	26.4
Belgium	30.1	50.6	20.5
Norway	31.9	50.4	18.5
Portugal	18.2	36.0	17.8
Ireland	28.9	45.5	16.6
Austria	32.2	48.7	16.5
Italy	29.8	45.6	15.8
Switzerland	24.2	39.9	15.7
Japan	17.9	32.2	14.3
Spain	17.5	31.5	14.0
West Germany	32.7	46.7	14.0
Greece	22.6	35.1	12.5
Finland	26.4	38.4	12.0
United Kingdom	33.0	44.1	11.1
Australia	22.9	33.7	10.8
France	35.2	45.8	10.6
Canada	29.5	40.0	10.5
United States	28.5	33.0	4.5

Sources: *OECD Economic Outlook* (Organization for Economic Cooperation and Development), no. 31 (July 1982), table R8, p. 149; OECD, *Economic Survey* for various countries.

a. Countries ranked by increase in spending as a share of GDP.

all the other nations, except the United States, government spending increased by at least 10 percentage points of GDP over the two decades. In the United States the total increase represented only 4.5 percentage points of GDP.

Both in terms of the level of spending and the rate of increase in the 1960s and 1970s, the American public economy is relatively *under*developed when compared with those of the other capitalist democracies. If it is true, as Gordon, Heilbroner, Wildavsky, the Friedmans, and others argue, that the inflation derives—at least in part—from the high level and rapid increase in government spending, then the inference to be drawn from the data in figure 9-3 and table 9-1 is quite obvious. Relative to all of the other advanced capitalist nations the United States should have experienced the *least* acceleration in the rate of change in prices over the recent decades.

Politics and the Growth of Government Spending

In spite of the fact that in both the rate of increase and the level of spending the United States lagged well behind most nations, the United States in the 1960s and 1970s experienced a variety of attempts to limit spending. For example, thirty-two state legislatures called for a constitutional convention to write an amendment requiring a balanced budget (an effort spurred by the National Taxpayers Union); numerous referenda (almost always approved by voters) were held in the states to limit the increase in spending (campaigns strongly supported—although not always initiated—by the National Tax Limitation Committee); and Congress was pressed to adopt legislation to freeze federal spending as a percent of GNP or forbid, by constitutional amendment, budget deficits. Why is it that the United States witnessed so much opposition to government spending when, by any comparative measure, the level and rate of increase in spending were very modest? The answer may lie in the factors that cause spending to increase much more rapidly in some nations than in others and to reach much higher levels—often with little active resistance.

Many who attribute inflation to excessive growth of government spending relate spending increases to the inherent expansionist impulse of a government bureaucracy. Programs proliferate, Wildavsky has argued, in large part because the unintended consequences of past programs generate needs that can only be met by new programs.[20] In addition, Wildavsky claims, as do others such as William Niskanen and Anthony Downs, that public bureaucrats inevitably attempt to expand their programs and personnel, if not for more explicitly political reasons such as the attainment of ideological objectives, simply in order to enhance their status and influence.[21] The combination of program proliferation and bureaucratic entrepreneurship thus generates perpetual expansion in spending requests. And because these requests are usually subjected to incrementalist decisionmaking routines, and because the sequence of decisionmaking—at least in the American system with its separation of executive and legislative branches and with its division within the legislative branch—

20. See Aaron Wildavsky, *Speaking Truth To Power: The Art and Craft of Policy Analysis* (Little, Brown, 1979), and *How To Limit Government Spending*, pp. 20–29.

21. See Aaron Wildavsky, *The Politics of the Budgetary Process*, 3d ed. (Little, Brown, 1979); William A. Niskanen, Jr., *Bureaucracy and Representative Government* (Aldine, 1971); Anthony Downs, *Inside Bureaucracy* (Little, Brown, 1967). For a methodologically sophisticated comparative study of the attitudes of public bureaucrats, see Joel D. Aberbach, Robert D. Putnam, and Bert A. Rockman, *Bureaucrats and Politicians in Western Democracies* (Harvard University Press, 1981), chaps. 4–5.

allows subsequent appeals and reversals of previous cutbacks, they are likely to emerge as law.[22] Thus, government spending inexorably increases.

These scholars provide little assistance in explaining why nations vary so much in the rate of increase in spending and why the United States has lagged behind most other nations in the proportion of GDP spent by government. It may be true that the self-aggrandizing bureaucracy has a rapacious appetite in the United States. But why is it so much *less* self-aggrandizing and expansionist than is bureaucracy in almost every other nation?

It may be that nations vary in the scope of government spending because of differences in political organizations and institutions. One such difference may be in the ideological preferences and programmatic commitments of governing parties. As Anthony Downs had argued, "in a democratic society, the division of resources between the public and private sectors is roughly determined by the desires of the electorate."[23] And Kirschen and associates have suggested that the objectives of government in regard to such issues as growth, employment, the distribution of income, the balance of payments, and price stability vary depending on the ideological center of gravity of government.[24] For example, the ranking of macroeconomic priorities—such as the relative preference for price stability, even at the cost of unemployment, or for full employment, even at the cost of inflation—depends on whether government is controlled by Social Democratic and labor parties, Christian Democratic and other centrist parties, or conservative parties. A number of economic studies support the Kirschen argument. They suggest that cross-national differences in a variety of macroeconomic and fiscal policy domains such as inflation, employment, taxation, spending, and industrial relations over a considerable period reflect differences in the extent of control of government by leftist parties or their opponents.[25] Korpi and

22. For the classic discussion of incrementalism, see Wildavsky, *Politics of the Budgetary Process.*

23. "Why the Government Budget is Too Small in a Democracy," *World Politics,* vol. 12 (July 1960), p. 541.

24. E. S. Kirschen and others, *Economic Policy in Our Time,* vol. 1: *General Theory* (Amsterdam: North-Holland, 1964), esp. pp. 224–29. On the predisposition of leftist parties to favor, and conservative parties to oppose, such instruments of public finance as government investment, transfers to households, and subsidies to enterprises, see p. 242.

25. See Edward R. Tufte, *Political Control of the Economy* (Princeton University Press, 1978), chap. 4; Andrew T. Cowart, "The Economic Policies of European Governments, Part I: Monetary Policy; Part II: Fiscal Policy," *British Journal of Political Science,* vol. 8 (July and October 1978); Douglas A. Hibbs, Jr., "Political Parties and Macroeconomic Policy," *American Political Science Review,* vol. 71 (December 1977), pp. 1467–87; Walter Korpi and Michael Shalev, "Strikes, Industrial Relations and

Shalev, in their analysis of cross-national differences in strike activity, argue that enduring government by leftist parties tends to occur where the working class is highly unionized—primarily in a handful of industrial (rather than craft-based) unions, where the labor confederations possess significant control over collective bargaining, where the confederations have close ties to Social Democratic or labor parties, and where those parties dominate the political left and confront a fragmented nonleftist bloc.[26] An enduring dominant position in the electorate and in government, based on these several preconditions, they argue, reflects a shift in the balance-of-power resources between classes in favor of the working class—a shift that is reflected in a variety of economic policies.[27]

Does the difference among nations in the extent of control of government by parties belonging to distinct ideological groupings reflect such differences in the balance of power between classes—or, more precisely, in the magnitude of the relative *im*balance between classes in advanced capitalist societies? Table 9-2 shows the degree of control of national governments by three distinct ideological clusters of parties. Those that are defined as leftist include Communist, Socialist, Social Democratic, and Labor parties, as well as several small parties that are left of the center on a Downsian ideological continuum.[28] Those that are centrist include the Center and Liberal parties of Norway, Sweden, and Finland and the Radical Liberal party of Denmark; the German Free Democrats after 1969 (but not before 1965); the Canadian Liberal party; the American

---

Class Conflict in Capitalist Societies," *British Journal of Sociology*, vol. 30 (June 1979), pp. 164–87; David R. Cameron, "Politics, Public Policy, and Economic Inequality," paper presented at a conference on the Role of Government in the Economy, University of Wisconsin–Madison, 1981; Gösta Esping-Andersen, "From Welfare State to Democratic Socialism: The Politics of Economic Democracy in Denmark and Sweden," in Maurice Zeitlin, ed., *Political Power and Social Theory: A Research Annual*, vol. 2 (Greenwich, Conn.: JAI Press, 1981), pp. 111–40; David R. Cameron, "Spesa pubblica, sviluppo e inflazione: un'analisi comparata," *Stato e mercato* (April 1982), pp. 129–65, and "On the Limits of the Public Economy," *Annals of the American Academy of Political and Social Science*, vol. 459 (January 1982), pp. 46–62; Francis G. Castles, ed., *The Impact of Parties: Politics and Policies in Democratic Capitalist States* (Sage, 1982).

26. Their power resources model is drawn from Scandinavian—especially Swedish—experience. See Korpi and Shalev, "Strikes, Industrial Relations and Class Conflict"; Walter Korpi and Michael Shalev, "Strikes, Power and Politics in the Western Nations, 1900–1976," in Zeitlin, *Political Power and Social Theory*, vol. 1 (1980), pp. 301–34.

27. Important as this shift in the balance-of-power resources between the classes may be, it may never be great enough, in a capitalist democracy, to eliminate the dominant position of those who are owners, employers, and managers. Political and ideological conflict over this point is an enduring issue in leftist movements. See Adam Przeworski, "Social Democracy as a Historical Phenomenon," *New Left Review*, no. 122 (July–August 1980), pp. 27–58.

28. See Anthony Downs, *An Economic Theory of Democracy* (Harper and Brothers, 1957), chap. 8.

Table 9-2. *Partisan Control of Government in Twenty-one Countries, 1965–81*[a]

Percent

Country	Share of cabinet portfolios held by		
	Social Democratic and other leftist parties	Centrist and Christian Democratic parties	Conservative and other rightist parties
Austria	73	27	0
Denmark	69	6	25
Sweden	69	25	6
United Kingdom	62	0	38
Norway	61	25	14
West Germany	61	34	6
Finland	45	45	10
Portugal	32	9	59
Belgium	30	57	13
Switzerland	29	43	29
Netherlands	22	61	17
Italy	21	78	2
New Zealand	18	0	82
Australia	17	0	83
Ireland	10	18	72
France	3	14	83
Greece	1	11	88
Canada	0	96	4
Japan	0	0	100
Spain	0	26	74
United States	0	47	53

Source: *Keesing's Contemporary Archives.* Based on the proportion of cabinet seats held by each party for each month of each year.

a. Countries ranked by leftist domination of government.

Democratic party; and the Christian Democratic parties of Europe.[29] Those that are rightist include the Conservative parties of Britain and Scandinavia; the Liberals of Denmark, Belgium, the Netherlands, Italy,

29. On the centrist position of the Canadian Liberals, see G. Horowitz, "Conservatism, Liberalism and Socialism in Canada: An Interpretation," *Canadian Journal of Economics and Political Science*, vol. 32 (May 1966). Treating the American Democrats as a centrist party eliminates the potential contradiction in the notions that the Democrats' ideological center of gravity is to the left of the Republicans', and that the Democrats are not a leftist party; see Seymour Martin Lipset, "Why No Socialism in the United States?" in Seweryn Bialer and Sophia Sluzar, eds., *Radicalism in the Contemporary Age*, vol. 1: *Sources of Contemporary Radicalism* (Boulder, Colo.: Westview, 1977). Christian Democratic parties are treated as centrist because they represent in politics a position that is distinct from the ordinary left-right cleavage based on economic issues; their electoral appeal is deliberately cross-class, or "national," drawing on the religiously active of all strata; they receive a disproportionately large amount of support from the middle classes but substantial support from those in lower economic strata; and they tend to encompass a wide range of positions in regard to the role of government in the economy and considerable ideological heterogeneity regarding most left-right issues; see Cameron, "Politics, Public Policy, and Economic Inequality"; E. M. Irving, *The Christian Democratic Parties of Western Europe* (London: Allen and Unwin for Royal Institute of International Affairs, 1979).

and Austria; the Gaullists, neo-Gaullists, and Giscardians of France; the Fianna Fail of Ireland; the Progressive Conservatives of Canada; the Republicans of the United States; and the Liberal Democrats of Japan.

There are significant differences among the nations in the extent of control of government by parties of each ideological tendency. Leftist parties held more than 50 percent of the cabinet portfolios in Austria, Sweden, Denmark, Britain, Norway, and West Germany, while conservative parties in Japan, France, Australia, Greece, Ireland, Spain, and New Zealand controlled more than 70 percent of the cabinet positions between 1965 and 1981.[30] In contrast, a party of the center most frequently controlled government in Canada, Belgium, and the Netherlands.

There appears to be a strong relationship between the partisanship of government and the level and rate of increase in government spending. When the control of cabinet portfolios by political groupings in 1965–81 (table 9-2) is regressed against total government spending as a percent of GNP in 1979–80 (table 9-1), the correlation coefficient is +.60 for leftist parties, +.17 for centrist, and −.62 for rightist. And when political control is regressed against the increase in government spending as a percent of GNP from 1964–66 to 1979–80, the coefficient is +.43 for leftist parties, +.02 for centrist, and −.35 for rightist.[31] Whether government during the years since 1965 was controlled by leftist or nonleftist parties had a considerable effect on the scope of the public economy. Figure 9-4 illustrates the strong positive relationship between the proportion of all cabinet portfolios held by leftist parties over the seventeen years and the extent of government spending in 1979–80.

Nevertheless, might not the observed relationships simply reflect the fact that leftist parties happened to govern in nations that experienced severe economic slumps in the 1970s, and might not spending have increased simply to counteract economic recession, rather than for more explicitly ideological purposes? It is plausible that the deterioration in the economic performance of most advanced capitalist nations generated significant pressure for a larger economic role for government—for example, elected elites may have felt pressure for expansion in programs of social assistance. There was in fact a very strong relationship between

---

30. Control of government in the predemocratic era in Spain is classified as rightist, although in fact many members of Franco's several cabinets were "nonpartisan" technocrats. Control by the Colonels in Greece during 1967–74 is similarly classified. In contrast, the military members of the Portuguese cabinets after the revolution of 1974 are treated as representatives of the political Left, although they too were nominally nonpartisan.

31. Based on all countries included in table 9-2 except New Zealand. Results are simple product-moment correlations.

Figure 9-4. *Leftist Control of Government and Total Government Spending in Twenty Countries, 1979–80*

Total government spending as a percent of GDP, 1979–80

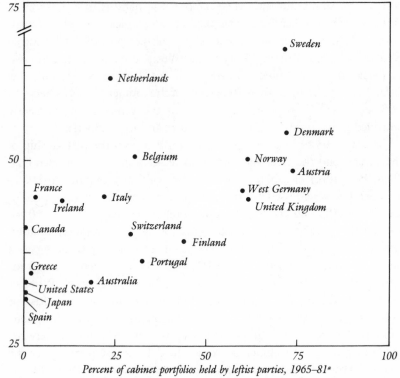

Sources: OECD, *National Accounts of OECD Countries, 1962–1980,* vol. 2 (Paris: OECD, 1982); *OECD Economic Outlook,* no. 31 (July 1982), table R8, p. 149; *Keesing's Contemporary Archives.*
a. Correlation coefficient $r = +.60$.

the magnitude of the increase in total government spending as a percent of GNP from 1964–65 to 1979–80 and the extent to which government spending on social security and social assistance increased between 1964–65 and 1978–79 (the correlation coefficient $r = +.70$).[32] Thus, perhaps 68 percent of the total increase in government spending was accounted for by social spending, broadly defined.[33] There was also a positive

32. The percent of GDP spent on social security benefits and social assistance grants was calculated from data in Organization for Economic Cooperation and Development, *National Accounts of OECD Countries, 1962–1979,* vol. 2 (Paris: OECD, 1981).
33. A regression of the increase in total spending between 1964–65 and 1979–80 upon the increase in social security and assistance spending yields a regression coefficient of $+1.48$. $(1/1.48 = 0.68.)$

relationship between the magnitude of the increase in unemployment as a proportion of the total labor force between 1965–66 and 1980–81 and the magnitude of the increase in social spending as a percent of GDP.[34] While the relationship is modest ($r = +.30$), it is much greater than that between any of the measures of cabinet partisanship and the increase in social spending ($r = +.03$ for leftist parties, $+.11$ for centrist, and $-.11$ for rightist).

Comparing the relationships between the magnitude of the increase in social spending, on one hand, and the increase in unemployment and partisanship of government on the other, the increase in *social spending*—which was closely associated with the increase in total government spending—does not appear to be a partisan phenomenon but an attempt by governments of all partisan hues to compensate for economic decline. Still, when the relationship between the measure of leftist party control of government and the increase in total government spending is compared to that between the increase in unemployment and the increase in spending, the standardized regression coefficients ($+.41$ and $+.11$, respectively) indicate that even after taking into account the spending that may have been generated as a by-product of economic stagnation, the national differences in partisan control of government remain a powerful source of the discrepancy in the growth of total government spending.

Having identified partisanship as an important source of the variation across nations in extent and rate of increase in government spending, it is possible to account for the peculiar coexistence in the United States of political hostility to spending with a relatively modest (compared to other nations) level of spending. Lacking a left-of-center political party that has organized labor as its core electorate, the United States lacks a political proponent for a large public sector. The political-economic agenda is narrower in the United States than in many nations and has its center of gravity farther to the right.[35] As table 9-2 suggests, programmatic competition and alternation in office in the United States involve an ideologically and socially heterogeneous centrist party and a conservative party. Obviously, the two parties differ in electoral base in society, as well as in macroeconomic priorities, programs, and policy objectives.[36] But

34. Rates of unemployment for fifteen countries are reported in *OECD Economic Outlook*, no. 31 (July 1982), table R12, p. 153; total unemployed (not the somewhat smaller insured unemployed) as a proportion of the total labor force for other countries was calculated from data in OECD, *Labour Force Statistics* and *Labour Force Statistics, Quarterly Supplements*.

35. Lindblom, *Politics and Markets*, pp. 208–09.

36. Tufte, *Political Control of the Economy*, pp. 71–90.

Figure 9-5. *Inflation in the United States, 1948–81*

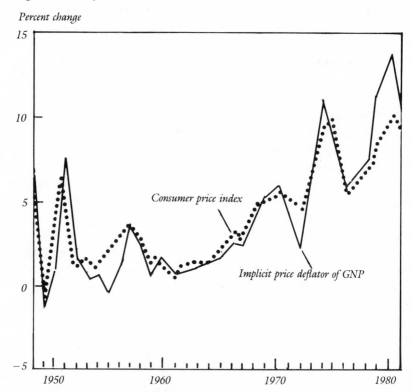

Source: *Economic Report of the President, February 1982*, tables B-3, B-55.

neither presents itself as the political arm of the labor movement and both share an aversion to a dramatically enlarged public economy.

Spending and Inflation

At this point it might be suggested that it is not the level but the steady increase in government spending that generates inflation. How persuasive is this argument? Although the rates of change in consumer prices and the implicit price deflator of gross national product in the United States have accelerated in recent years, perhaps the most striking aspect of change (see figure 9-5) is the time at which it began.[37] A long-

37. The implicit price deflator is superior to the consumer price index as an indicator because it encompasses investment goods and the goods and services of government as well as consumption. The

term gradual acceleration in the rate of change in prices began not in 1973–74, when the Organization of Petroleum Exporting Countries (OPEC) raised its prices after the Yom Kippur War, or in 1971, when President Nixon closed the gold window at the Treasury, effectively allowing the dollar to devalue, but in the mid-1960s.[38]

To what extent was acceleration associated with the increase in government spending? The trend lines in figure 9-5 bear no significant relation to those in figure 9-2 representing the levels of federal and total government spending. Occasionally, as in 1950–51, 1965–70, and 1973–75, the rate of change in prices seems to have increased simultaneously with an increase in government spending. On other occasions (1955–57 and 1977–79), however, the rate of change in prices appears to have increased while spending was *de*creasing. More generally, the yearly changes in spending were quite small, with the aggregate amount creeping upward, while the rate of change in prices fluctuated over a much wider range in the short term and moved, over time, in a pattern largely independent of the gradual upward drift in spending.

When the percent change in the implicit price deflator is regressed on the change in federal, and total, government spending relative to GNP over the 1948–81 period, there is no significant association between the two (table 9-3). The correlation coefficient of +.05 for all government indicates that the annual fluctuation in total spending, relative to GNP, explains 0.25 percent of the cumulative fluctuation in prices over the thirty-four years. The estimated effect of federal spending is also quite insignificant; the regression coefficient of +.304 indicates that the deflator increased by about 0.30 percent for every additional 1 percent of GNP spent by the federal government. This figure in combination with an estimated 0.19 percent annual increase in federal spending indicates that each year's increase in spending was associated, on average, with an invisibly small 0.005 percent increase in the price deflator.

CPI makes some peculiar assumptions about personal consumption, most notably housing. The two indexes are nevertheless very closely related (a correlation coefficient of +.96 for 1948–81) and provide nearly identical measures of the fluctuations over time in inflation. The implicit deflator is used here in the analysis of American data, but since it is not reported for all nations in all years, changes in consumer price indexes are used in cross-national analyses.

38. In fact, the acceleration in inflation in the last half of the 1960s contributed to the events of 1971 and 1973–74 that are frequently viewed as the causes of American inflation. For example, U.S. inflation in the late 1960s and early 1970s reduced the real income of the OPEC nations from all consumers in the world, and the reduction was not offset by increases in the nominal price of oil until late 1973.

Table 9-3. *Correlation of Government Spending and Inflation in the United States, 1948–81*

	Percent change in implicit price deflator of GNP		Increase in percent change in implicit price deflator of GNP	
Variable	Correlation coefficient r	Regression coefficient b	Correlation coefficient r	Regression coefficient b
	1948–81			
Increase in spending as a percent of GNP				
All government	+.05	+0.099	−.36	−0.611
Federal government	+.14	+0.304	−.26	−0.491
	1963–81			
Increase in spending as a percent of GNP				
All government	+.32	+0.751	+.26	+0.331
Federal government	+.41	+1.160	+.18	+0.270

For most of the early years of this series (in fact for all years up to 1963 except 1948 and 1951), the price deflator remained under 4 percent and exhibited no secular upward trend, in marked contrast to the later years. When the estimates are confined to the 1963–81 period, spending appears to have exerted a measurable impact on inflation—the correlation coefficient is +.32 for all spending and +.41 for federal spending. Likewise the regression coefficients indicate a stronger effect, with an increase of 1 percent of GNP in federal spending associated with an increase of the price deflator of 1.16 percent. And because the average annual change in federal spending as a share of GNP also increased in the 1963–81 period (0.24 percent), the effects of spending on inflation became more noticeable. They are still minimal, however—generating an increase in the deflator of less than 0.3 percent of inflation each year.[39]

The results of regressions in table 9-3 based on the acceleration in the rate of change of prices suggest that increases in spending were associated with *deceleration* in prices, rather than an increase in the rate of change ($r = -.26$ for federal spending). The reasons, of course, are obvious. Expenditures tend to increase most dramatically as a percent of GNP when the economy is in recession (figure 9-2). Prices, on the other hand,

39. Calculated by multiplying the average annual change in federal spending as a percent of GNP in 1963–81 (0.24 percent) and the estimated effect on the price deflator of an increase in federal spending of 1 percent of GNP (1.16 percent).

tend to increase at a slower rate—to decelerate—during and immediately after a recession (figure 9-5). The negative relationships should not be interpreted perversely—for example, as suggesting that increasing government spending represents a means of stabilizing prices. They suggest that changes in expenditures and in the rate of change in prices are only spuriously related—both changes being associated, to some degree at least, with cyclical changes in the economy.[40] There is some evidence that the acceleration in prices beginning in the early 1960s is associated with increases in government spending.[41] But with an estimated acceleration of 0.27 percent in prices for every 1 percent of GNP by which federal expenditures increased between 1963 and 1981, and an estimated average annual increase in federal expenditures of 0.24 percent of GNP, federal spending appears to have generated an average acceleration in the rate of change in prices of 0.06 percent per year.[42]

If there is little evidence that increased government spending contributed to inflation in the United States, is there any in the experience of other nations—particularly those in which government spending increased much more rapidly than in the United States? If the argument that high levels, and rapid increases, of government spending are inflationary is correct, then nations with the largest increases and highest levels of spending, relative to GDP, would have had higher rates of change in prices or higher rates of acceleration in the rates of change than nations with small increases and low levels of spending.

The data in table 9-4 provide little support for the argument. For example, Japan experienced virtually no acceleration in the rate of change in prices between the mid-1960s and early 1980s in spite of a very dramatic increase in government spending after 1970 (figure 9-3). Similarly, in the Netherlands, where spending increased rapidly to a level in excess of 60 percent of GDP, the rate of inflation accelerated by less

40. Over the 1948–81 period there was an inverse relation between the change in total government spending as a percent of GNP and change in constant-dollar GNP (the volume of goods and services) ($r = -.48$), while, in contrast, the change in the rate of change in prices covaried with the rate of economic growth ($r = +.26$). That is, spending increased most in recessions while prices increased most in periods when spending was increasing least—periods of high economic growth.

41. There was no diminution after 1963 in the propensity for spending to increase dramatically in periods of stagnation. Indeed, the relationship between the change in spending and indicators of the well-being of the economy actually became much stronger. For example, the correlation coefficient representing the change in total spending and the change in the percent unemployed was +.75 for the years after 1960 compared to +.44 for the entire period. The positive relationship in the 1963–81 analysis has more to do with the inflation rate—in particular, the fact that economic slumps in the 1970s produced smaller decreases in the rate of change of prices and produced them less immediately.

42. Calculated by multiplying the regression coefficient in table 9-3 ($+.27$) by 0.24 percent.

Table 9-4. *Average Annual Rates of Change in Consumer Prices in Twenty-one Countries, 1964–81*

Percent

| | Change in consumer prices | | |
| | | | Increase, 1964–66 |
Country	1965–81	1979–81	to 1979–81
Australia	7.9	9.7	6.6
Austria	5.4	5.6	1.9
Belgium	6.1	6.2	2.0
Canada	6.7	10.6	8.0
Denmark	8.8	11.2	5.6
Finland	9.0	10.4	4.1
France	7.9	12.6	9.7
Greece	10.9	22.8	19.9
Ireland	11.1	17.3	12.4
Italy	10.6	18.5	14.2
Japan	7.7	5.5	0.3
Netherlands	6.3	5.8	0.7
New Zealand	9.9	15.4	12.2
Norway	7.5	9.8	5.4
Portugal	14.0	20.2	15.7
Spain	12.2	15.3	6.5
Sweden	7.8	11.0	6.1
Switzerland	4.5	4.7	1.0
United Kingdom	10.4	14.4	10.4
United States	6.6	11.7	9.7
West Germany	4.3	5.2	2.1

Sources: *OECD Economic Outlook*, various issues; OECD, *Main Economic Indicators* (Paris: OECD), various issues.

than 1 percentage point after the mid-1960s. And much the same was true of West Germany, Austria, Switzerland, and Belgium. In contrast, the rate of price change accelerated by about 10 percentage points between 1964–66 and 1979–81 in the United States, Canada, France, and Britain, in spite of the fact that the four were among the nations with the smallest increases in government spending.

For the countries in table 9-4 there is no cross-nationally general relationship between high levels and large increases of government spending and high rates of change in prices and large accelerations in those rates. In fact, if any relation exists at all between spending and inflation it is *the reverse* of the conventional wisdom. Nations with the highest levels and largest increases in government spending had relatively *low* rates of change in prices and relatively small accelerations in rates of change. Thus, nations in which government spent a relatively large share of GDP in 1979–80 had, relative to other nations, low average rates of change in prices in 1979–81 and small increases in average rates of price change between 1964–66 and 1979–81 (in both cases, $r = -.29$). And those in which government spending increased most rapidly after the mid-1960s had somewhat lower rates of price change in 1979–81 ($r = -.18$) and smaller accelerations in the rate of price change ($r = -.27$). These negative relationships are certainly not strong enough to support an inference that a high and increasing level of government spending is deflationary; nevertheless, they do challenge the notion, so central to the fiscal orthodoxy in the United States (and elsewhere), that growth in government spending contributed to the acceleration of inflation that occurred throughout the advanced capitalist world in the late 1960s and the 1970s.

The Politics of Inflation

One explanation of the lack of any relationship cross-nationally between government spending and inflation involves politics.[43] Among the advanced capitalist nations, governments dominated by leftist parties tend to spend much more of the economic product than do governments dominated by nonleftist—and especially rightist—parties. The proponents of fiscal orthodoxy in the United States, who believe that high levels of spending cause inflation, might logically conclude that leftist control of government over a long period should produce relatively high rates of inflation. Such a conclusion would, of course, be consistent with the suggestion by Kirschen and associates that the primary economic priority

43. Another explanation involves the very strong covariation over time in the fluctuations in the rate of change in prices of nations whose economies are closely linked. Based on the annual first-order change in the percent change in consumer prices (that is, the acceleration or deceleration of inflation) between 1961 and 1981, there is a strong positive relationship in the movements of prices in Britain and Ireland ($r = .70$), in Sweden and Norway ($r = +.57$—the only correlation for both nations that exceeds $+.4$), in Belgium and France ($r = +.69$), in West Germany and Switzerland ($r = +.61$), in Belgium and the Netherlands ($r = +.49$), in Australia and Britain ($r = +.60$), in Canada and the United States ($r = +.32$), in West Germany and Denmark ($r = +.48$), and in the United States and Japan ($r = +.67$). While these represent only covariation and do not necessarily represent any causal relationship, they do suggest the considerable importance of processes of international transmission and diffusion of inflation. On these processes, see Robert Keohane's discussion in chapter 4, above; W. M. Corden, *Inflation, Exchange Rates, and the World Economy: Lectures on International Monetary Economics* (University of Chicago Press, 1977); Fred L. Block, *The Origins of International Economic Disorder: A Study of United States International Monetary Policy from World War II to the Present* (University of California Press, 1977); Calleo, *Imperious Economy*.

Table 9-5. *Correlation of Partisan Control of Government and Inflation across Twenty-one Countries, 1965–81*

| | Average annual percent change in consumer prices | | | | | |
| | 1965–81 | | 1979–81 | | Increase, 1964–66 to 1979–81 | |
Variable	Correlation coefficient r	Regression coefficient b	Correlation coefficient r	Regression coefficient b	Correlation coefficient r	Regression coefficient b
Percent of cabinet portfolios, 1965–81, held by						
Leftist parties	−.24	−0.0227	−.31	−0.0609	−.33	−0.0668
Centrist parties	−.36	−0.0338	−.21	−0.0416	−.18	−0.0365
Rightist parties	+.46	+0.0336	+.40	0.0609	+.39	+0.0613

of conservative governments is price stability, while that of leftist-controlled governments is full employment, with price stability being much less important.[44] Using the Kirschen framework, Douglas Hibbs reached a similar conclusion in his analysis of macroeconomic policy in some of the advanced capitalist nations.[45]

An analysis of data on twenty-one countries indicates that the argument that leftist parties are more likely to generate inflation than nonleftist parties is simply wrong—or, at the least, time-bound and true only for an era when inflation was not a significant macroeconomic problem for most nations (table 9-5). For the period 1965–81, those countries whose governments were dominated by leftist parties had lower, rather than higher, rates of change in prices and a smaller acceleration in the rate of change than those dominated either by centrists or rightists. The correlation

44. *Economic Policy in Our Time,* vol. 1, p. 227.

45. Hibbs, "Political Parties and Macroeconomic Policy," p. 1473. Accepting the inherent logic of the Phillips curve—that a trade-off exists between inflation and unemployment because a tight labor market enhances labor's bargaining power and allows it to drive up wages and thus (after some lag) prices, while a high rate of unemployment diminishes the bargaining power of labor and induces it to accept modest wage increases—Hibbs found a correlation of +.74 among twelve nations between the presence of leftist parties in government during 1945–69 and the average rate of inflation in 1960–69. However, if Hibbs had reported the regression coefficient, rather than the correlation coefficient, the effect of a year, or even a decade, of leftist representation in government on inflation would have been extremely small. Although Hibbs later reported a more modest association (generally in the range of +.3) after adding several nations and changing the measurement of the two variables in response to criticism (Hibbs, "Communications," *American Political Science Review,* vol. 73 [March 1979], p. 188), the sign remained positive and the argument remained intact—namely, that leftist parties were less averse to inflation than were nonleftist parties and that they were, when in government, more likely to generate or tolerate high rates of inflation.

between the measure of leftist party government and all three measures of price change in table 9-5 is negative. Centrist governments were similar to those dominated by leftist parties in producing relatively low rates of inflation—in marked contrast to those dominated by rightist parties. Clearly, the important political demarcation point in regard to inflation throughout the capitalist world in the 1960s and 1970s was not between leftist and nonleftist parties but between rightist and nonrightist parties.

It might be argued that these results are distorted by inclusion of Spain, Greece, and Portugal, countries that experienced protracted authoritarian rule during the 1965–81 period. The negative association between leftism and inflation and the positive one between rightist control and inflation might simply reflect the tendency for prices in these three countries to increase rapidly after the termination of authoritarianism—presumably because of the termination of restrictions on collective bargaining and on wage increases. The argument is certainly plausible, and there is in fact a strong positive correlation between the number of years a nation was under authoritarian control during 1965–81[46] and the rate of change in prices in 1979–81 ($r = +.57$) and the increase in the rate of change in prices between 1964–66 and 1979–81 ($r = +.43$). However, the inverse relation between leftism and inflation and the positive one between rightism and inflation remain when Greece, Spain, and Portugal are excluded from the analysis. The relationship between the measure of leftist control and the average change in prices in 1979–81 remains negative ($r = -.19$) as does that with the increase in the rate of change in prices from 1964–66 to 1979–81 ($r = -.28$). And the relation between the measures of inflation and rightist control remains positive; the correlation coefficients are $+.21$ for the average change in prices in 1979–81 and $+.32$ for the measure of acceleration in the rate of change in prices.

The regression coefficients in table 9-5 can be used to calculate the average effect on the inflation rate of a year (or a decade) of control by leftist, centrist, and rightist parties. Based on the increase in the average rate of change in prices between 1964–66 and 1979–81—which is superior to the other two measures—one year of government by a leftist party *reduced* the rate of change in prices by about 0.40 percent, relative to the

---

46. Greece had seven years of nondemocratic rule after 1964 (from 1967 to 1974), Spain eleven, and Portugal nine.

rate of change in nations controlled by nonleftist parties.[47] One year of government by centrist parties (in spite of the dramatic inflation in Italy under the Christian Democratic party) tended to reduce inflation on average by 0.20 percent. In contrast, every year of government by rightist parties is estimated to have *in*creased the rate of change in prices by 0.40 percent.

Enduring control of government by leftist parties between 1965 and 1981 was *not* associated with inflation, relative to the performance of prices in other nations. If anything, government by the left was associated with *stabilization* (again, relative to the performance of prices in other nations). In contrast, enduring control by rightist parties (as well as rightist nonparty officials) was associated not with price stabilization but, instead, with unusually large accelerations in the rate of change of prices. While it is true that governments dominated by leftist parties have increased the scope of the public economy and spent a larger proportion of GDP than those dominated by nonleftist, and especially rightist, parties, those increases and high levels of spending have not generated inflation. Some unidentified processes evidently are at work when leftist parties govern that dampen inflation, just as other processes that accelerate the rate of change in prices are apparently at work when rightist parties dominate government.

Budget Deficits and Inflation

American government is usually in deficit. The federal government's budget was in the red in twenty-four of the thirty-four years between 1948 and 1981 and in every year but one (1969) after 1965 (figure 9-6). Even the combined budgets of all levels of government in the United States show an obvious tendency to be in deficit—in twenty-one years from 1948 to 1981, and in all but three years (1969, 1973, 1979) after 1965.[48] At both the federal and the combined levels of government, there seems to have been a secular trend toward large deficits, relative to the size of the economy, in recent years.

47. The effect of one year of contol by leftist parties is the regression coefficient (-0.0668) multiplied by the percent of the 1965–81 period represented by a single year (100/17, or 5.882).

48. Intergovernmental transfers such as revenue sharing represent expenditures for the federal government and receipts for the states and localities. Since those transfers account for a portion of the federal deficit and a surplus at other levels of government, the most accurate measure of the surplus or deficit is one that combines all levels of government.

Figure 9-6. *Budget Deficits of U.S. Governments as a Share of GNP, 1948–81*

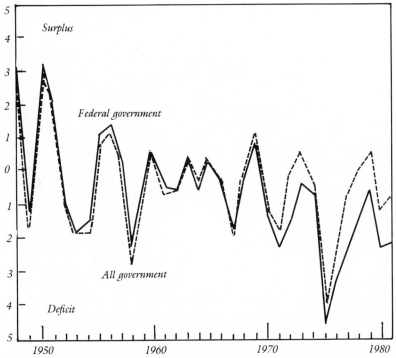

Source: *Economic Report of the President, February 1982*, tables B-1, B-75.

According to the conventional wisdom, American government suffers from an acute fiscal hemorrhage. This may well be the case if deficits are judged in terms of absolute current dollars. However, if the deficit is viewed in relation to the size of the entire economy and American experience is compared to that of other countries, a very different image appears (figure 9-7). Far from being a uniquely American problem, the tendency for government to spend more than it receives in current revenues—that is, to incur budget deficits and rely on public borrowings—is found throughout the advanced capitalist world. Indeed, the United States relies on deficits to a *lesser* degree than do most countries, including a number that are often envied for their performance in dampening inflation. For example, the average budget deficit of all government in

Figure 9-7. *Total Government Deficit as a Share of GDP in Fourteen Countries, 1974–81*

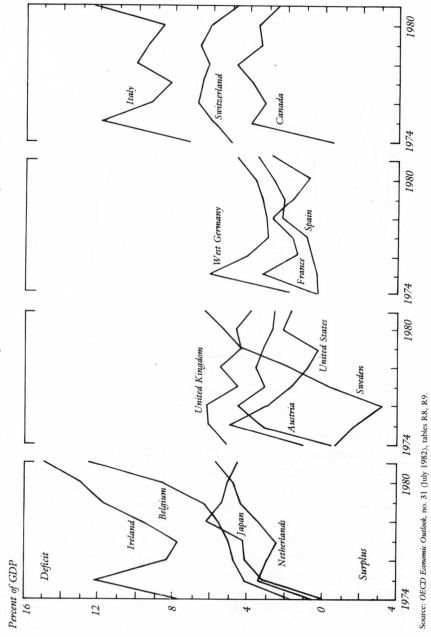

Source: *OECD Economic Outlook*, no. 31 (July 1982), tables R8, R9.

the United States was about 1 percent of the gross domestic product (GDP) after the recession of 1975, Japan's in the late 1970s exceeded 4 percent, West Germany's was 3–4 percent, Austria's about 3 percent, and Switzerland's more than 6 percent. Evidently, government in the United States was much more fiscally prudent than in those four nations. Yet they were far more successful than the United States in dampening inflation. It is true, of course, that some nations—Italy and Ireland, for example—experienced large increases in consumer prices (occasionally as much as 20 percent in one year) and very large deficits (usually in excess of 8 percent of GDP throughout the 1970s), and the former may well have been produced by the latter. But the experience of Japan, West Germany, Austria, and Switzerland, and, at the turn of the decade, Belgium and the Netherlands, suggests that large budget deficits do not inevitably generate double-digit inflation.

Most governments in the advanced capitalist world (except those in Scandinavia) were in deficit in most years between 1965 and 1980, and the magnitude of their deficits was increasing.[49] The data in table 9-6 confirm the paradoxical image in figure 9-7 of American government— an image of fiscal conservatism that is, obviously, quite at odds with the domestic rhetoric about excessive government spending, large deficits, and the need to constitutionally prescribe spending limits and balanced budgets. Thus, while the United States falls near the middle of the pack in the average size of the budget deficit of all government over the period, it incurred one of the smallest average budget deficits in 1979–80— smaller than those in seventeen of the twenty nations. And the United States was the only nation, aside from Norway, in which the magnitude of the deficit actually *de*creased between the mid-1960s and the late 1970s.[50] If, as much of the American rhetoric suggests, a balanced budget is a sign of fiscal prudence, it would appear that American government manages its fiscal affairs more prudently than almost any other government in the advanced capitalist world!

49. Even in Scandinavia—especially Denmark and Sweden—the surplus or balance in the budget gave way to unusually large deficits in the late 1970s. On Sweden's fiscal crisis, see Andrew Martin's discussion in chapter 13, below; Bengt Ryden and Villy Bergstrom, eds., *Sweden: Choices for Economic and Social Policy in the 1980s* (London: Allen and Unwin, 1982).

50. Without the very large revenues produced by its oil and gas fields in the North Sea, Norway would undoubtedly have experienced deficits in the late 1970s comparable to those in Sweden and Denmark.

Table 9-6. *Budget Deficits as a Share of GDP in Twenty Countries, 1965–80*[a]

Percent

	Budget deficit of all government as a share of GDP		
Country	Average, 1965–80	Average, 1979–80	Increase, 1964–65 to 1979–80
Sweden	− 1.1	8.4	11.2
Denmark	0.0	6.3	7.6
Portugal	2.2	8.0	7.6
Italy	6.6	9.0	6.3
Belgium	3.3	7.3	6.1
Japan	1.2	4.8	5.9
Ireland	6.4	9.0	3.9
Switzerland	4.8	6.9	3.6
West Germany	1.9	3.8	3.5
Austria	1.2	2.9	3.0
Spain	0.7	3.0	2.9
Netherlands	1.9	4.3	2.5
Australia	− 0.3	0.7	2.4
Canada	1.7	3.4	2.4
Greece	3.7	4.5	2.1
United Kingdom	3.2	4.4	1.8
Finland	− 2.2	0.4	1.2
France	0.9	1.2	1.2
Norway	− 3.0	− 2.9	− 0.2
United States	1.5	0.4	− 0.8

Source: OECD, *National Accounts of OECD Countries, 1962–80*, vol. 2 (Paris: OECD, 1982).
a. Countries ranked by increase in deficit as a share of GDP.

Deficits, Tax Burdens, and Politics

Why do nations vary so dramatically in their propensity to incur budget deficits? Since deficits are produced not simply by spending but by spending relative to revenue, a plausible explanation may involve an inability to extract revenues sufficient to cover expenditures. Colin Clark long ago articulated the idea of tax ceilings, suggesting that "25% of the national income is about the limit for taxation in any non-totalitarian community in times of peace. . . . Once taxation has exceeded 25% of the national income . . . influential sections of the community become willing to support a depreciation of the value of money [that is, willing to tolerate inflationary deficits]."[51] President Reagan suggested as much in his

51. Colin Clark, "Public Finance and Changes in the Value of Money," *Economic Journal*, vol. 55 (December 1945), p. 380. Clark was referring to the interwar period in Europe and North America.

Figure 9-8. *Government Revenues in the United States as a Share of GNP, 1948–81*

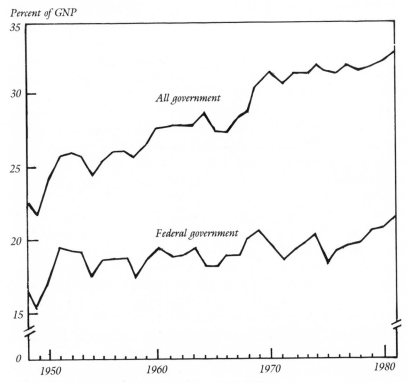

Source: *Economic Report of the President, February 1982*, tables B-1, B-75.

inaugural address and again in the 1981 address on the economy when he stated that "we've reached—indeed surpassed—the limit of our people's tolerance or ability to bear an increase in the tax burden."[52]

Was President Reagan correct in suggesting that taxes on personal income had risen so much that they had bumped up against a tax ceiling? Has the American government (and presumably others as well) extracted as much revenue as can be obtained from its citizens? Over time government revenues, as a portion of GNP, increased from roughly 22 percent in 1948 to about 32 percent in 1981 (figure 9-8). In other words, government

52. His address on the economy, February 5, 1981, provided, of course, a substantial part of the rationale for the phased reduction in tax rates enacted in 1981 that resulted in a 23 percent reduction in marginal tax rates. See William Greider, "The Education of David Stockman," *Atlantic*, December 1981, pp. 27–54.

revenues increased about 45 percent more than the economic product of the nation. However, the revenues of the federal government, which is most frequently accused of excessive taxation, display a much more modest upward trend than those of all government. Virtually all of the increase in total revenues, relative to GNP, is accounted for by the growth of the aggregate revenues of state and local governments.[53] Thus, the federal government's revenues remained in the 18–20 percent of GNP range throughout most of the period. They grew more rapidly than the economy in 1950–51, when the Truman administration increased personal income taxes to pay the additional costs associated with the Korean War, and in 1968-69 when the Johnson administration belatedly increased income taxes to cover its commitment to war in Vietnam. (These were the only two instances of a legislated increase in personal income taxes; evidently, the aversion to taxation is such that presidents believe they can introduce increases only when the nation is at war.) The increases in 1966–67, 1973–74, and 1977–81 were the product of fiscal drag associated with inflation rather than deliberate policy to increase tax rates. But what is surprising—especially in light of the alarmist rhetoric about fiscal drag and the extensive literature describing government's propensity to raise revenues via the inflation tax[54]—is the quite insignificant size of that tax. Thus, during the three periods in which the annual change in prices was highest—1966–70, 1973–75, and 1977–81—the revenues of the federal government increased by less than 2 percentage points of GNP. Moreover, those rather small increases were invariably followed by significant and frequent *reductions* of personal (and corporate) income taxes—in 1948, 1954, 1958, 1964, 1969, 1971, 1975, 1978, and 1981.[55] As a result, while the proportion of GNP extracted by all government in the United States increased, the proportion represented by the revenues of the federal government remained virtually unchanged for three decades.

53. The aggregate revenues of state and local governments, as a proportion of GNP, are represented in figure 9-8 by the space between the two trend lines. Those revenues increased from about 6 percent of GNP in 1948 to about 12 percent in 1981, or about 50 percent more than the economic product of the nation.

54. See, for example, Gordon, "Demand for and Supply of Inflation." Milton and Rose Friedman, *Free to Choose*, p. 269, succinctly describe the inflation tax: "Inflation also yields revenue indirectly by automatically raising effective tax rates. As people's dollar incomes go up with inflation, the income is pushed into higher brackets and taxed at a higher rate."

55. On tax cuts before 1979, see Herbert Stein, *The Fiscal Revolution in America* (University of Chicago Press, 1969); on the 1964 cut, see Arthur M. Okun, *The Political Economy of Prosperity* (Brookings Institution, 1970); James Tobin, *The New Economics One Decade Older* (Princeton University Press, 1974).

Figure 9-9. *Personal Taxes and Social Insurance Contributions as a Share of Total Personal Market Income in the United States, 1948–81*

Percent of personal market income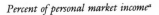

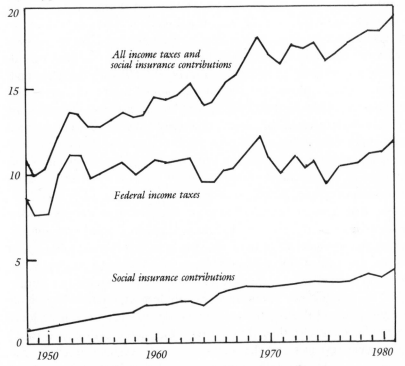

Source: *Economic Report of the President, February 1982,* tables B-22, B-23, B-76, B-77.
a. Includes the income *after* all government transfers to persons are added to the income received in the market and *before* the payment of taxes and contributions for social insurance.

The total proportion of all personal income paid in taxes to the federal, state, and local governments and as contributions for social insurance also increased markedly (figure 9-9)—from about 10 percent in 1948 to nearly 20 percent in 1981. That rate of increase was twice the cumulative rate of growth in the entire economy. Virtually none of that increase, however, was produced by federal income taxes. As a proportion of total personal income, federal income tax payments remained almost constant. Because of the frequent tax cuts, all individuals together paid in 1981 about the same proportion of aggregate personal income (10 percent) that individuals paid in the early 1950s. The bulk of the increase in total personal tax payments thus reflected the growth in social contributions and in taxes paid to state and local governments, each of which grew from about 1 percent to 4 percent of total personal income between 1948 and 1981.

The share of GNP represented by the total revenues of all government increased by about a quarter of a percent a year during 1948–81 (the regression coefficient is +.28 when total revenue is regressed on time; the coefficient for receipts of the federal government is +.09 and of state and local governments +.19). Thus, over a typical ten-year period, government revenues grew by 2.8 percent of GNP with the great bulk of that increase—about 1.9 percent—accounted for by the states and localities. Similarly, total tax payments and social insurance contributions by individuals increased by about a quarter of a percent of total personal income per year, or about 2.4 percent of total income in a decade (the regression coefficients are +.24 for payments to all government, +.05 for taxes to the federal government, +.09 for taxes to state and local governments, and +.10 for social insurance contributions).[56]

But is it true, as President Reagan suggested, that the tax burden increased so much over three decades that it encountered a ceiling, an upper limit of tolerable taxation? The data in table 9-7 cast doubt on that notion. The United States does not fall at the bottom of a ranking of the twenty-one countries on the measures of average personal taxation during 1965–80, but neither is it ranked at the top; instead, it ranks eleventh on one measure and thirteenth on the other. And its increases in personal taxation were smaller than those in ten other nations. In regard to *all* government revenues and the increase in those revenues, however, the United States appears to be something of an underachiever; with an average total government revenue of 30.6 percent of GDP during 1965–80, it ranks fourteenth among twenty nations. And it experienced the *smallest* increase in total government revenues—much less than that in Sweden, the Netherlands, Norway, Denmark, and Belgium, where revenues increased by more than 10 percent of GDP,[57] and even less than the increase in nations that were ruled by right-wing military juntas or authoritarians during much of the period. Thus, if the United States has reached a tax ceiling, it is evident that the height of the ceiling must vary considerably from country to country. In fact, it would appear that what is a ceiling in one nation may be a floor in another.

56. Calculated from data reported in *Economic Report of the President, February 1982,* tables B-1, B-22, B-23, B-73, B-76, B-77. Contributions for social insurance are included in the calculations of proportions of total personal income.

57. For a discussion of this increase, using a slightly earlier time span, see Cameron, "Expansion of the Public Economy."

Table 9-7. *Government Revenues and Taxes as a Share of GDP in Twenty-one Countries, 1965–80*[a]

Percent

Country	Total receipts of all government as a share of GDP		All personal taxes and social security contributions as a share of GDP[b,c]		All personal taxes as a share of GDP[b]	
	Average, 1965–80	Increase, 1964–65 to 1979–80	Average, 1965–80	Increase, 1965–66 to 1979–80	Average, 1965–80	Increase, 1965–66 to 1979–80
Sweden	49.7	18.8	20.3	2.4	19.8	3.1
Netherlands	47.9	20.2	17.9	4.6	11.3	2.3
Norway	46.7	16.9	16.1	3.0	16.0	3.0
Denmark	42.4	16.5	21.3	7.7	20.5	8.4
Austria	41.7	7.6	13.1	3.7	8.4	2.2
France	40.2	6.4	7.8	3.7	4.4	1.6
West Germany	39.7	7.2	15.4	4.1	10.3	2.2
United Kingdom	38.3	7.1	15.1	0.9	11.2	1.0
Belgium	37.3	12.9	14.4	10.1	11.0	9.2
Finland	36.9	6.3	15.0	3.7	15.0	3.7
Canada	34.7	8.6	14.7	6.0	10.0	4.6
Ireland	34.2	9.1	9.7	5.3	7.3	5.4
Italy	32.2	6.2	6.6	4.2	4.4	4.4
United States	30.6	5.6	13.9	3.9	9.4	3.0
Australia	29.3	6.6	11.5	4.7	10.9	4.7
Switzerland	28.8	9.6	13.8	6.8	9.8	4.3
Greece	27.5	6.7	5.8	2.7	2.5	1.6
Portugal	24.1	8.1	3.9	2.7	1.9	1.6
Spain	23.6	9.4	4.3	3.5	2.7	2.5
Japan	22.5	7.4	7.5	3.6	4.9	2.1
New Zealand	n.a.	n.a.	14.8	7.3	14.1	7.2

Sources: *OECD Economic Outlook,* no. 31 (July 1982), table R9, p. 150; OECD, *Revenue Statistics of OECD Member Countries 1965–1980* (Paris: OECD, 1981) and earlier editions.

n.a. Not available.

a. Countries ranked by average receipts as a share of GDP.

b. Personal taxes on income, wealth, and property.

c. Social security contributions by employees only.

Not only does the height of tax ceilings appear to vary across nations but, like the magnitude and extent of increase in public spending, the height seems to depend to a very large degree on politics. Whether government extracts a relatively large or relatively small share of a nation's economic product depends to a considerable degree on the ideological center of gravity of government over an extended period. Nations in which leftist parties governed for most of the time between 1965 and 1981 had higher levels of taxation—especially on personal income—than those in which conservatives dominated government. Thus there is a positive correlation between the average proportion of GDP represented by all government revenues and the measure of leftist control ($r = +.65$)

Figure 9-10. *Leftist Control of Government and Taxes on Personal Income, Property, and Wealth in Twenty-one Countries, 1965–80*

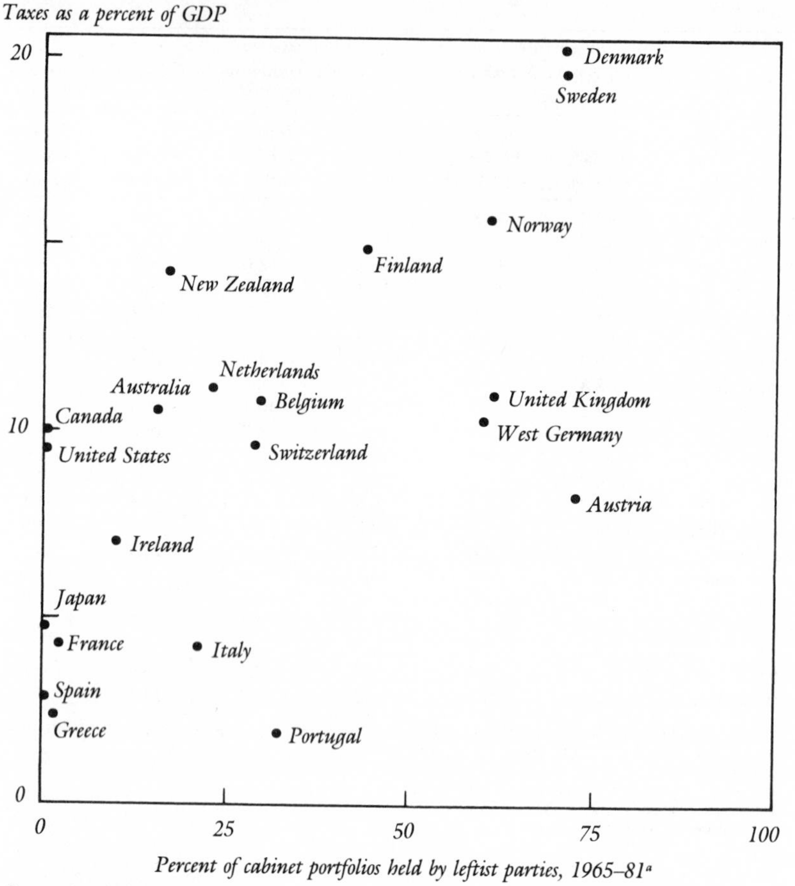

Taxes as a percent of GDP

Percent of cabinet portfolios held by leftist parties, 1965–81[a]

Sources: Same as figure 9-4.
a. Correlation coefficient $r = +.64$.

and a negative correlation between that average and the measure of rightist control ($r = -.64$; for centrist control, $r = +.16$). And in the taxes that are most visible and most explicitly redistributive in incidence—taxes on personal income—the political basis of national tax capacity is even more sharply distinguished. The correlation of leftist control with personal income taxes as a percent of GDP in 1965–80 is $+.68$ (for centrist control $r = +.04$, and for rightist $-.57$), while the correlation with the share of both personal income taxes and social insurance contributions is $+.64$ ($r = +.18$ for centrist and $-.64$ for rightist governments). As figure 9-10 illustrates, the aggregate tax burden imposed on personal incomes and wealth varies systematically with the extent of control by leftist parties. Where the left governed for more than half of the time (or dominated governing coalitions for most of the time) in 1965–81, taxes on personal income represented at least 10 percent, and occasionally as much as 20 percent, of GDP. Where leftist parties never governed, however, those taxes were often equal to less than 5 percent, and never more than 10 percent, of GDP.

Clearly if tax ceilings exist at all, they vary dramatically in height from one nation to another, depending to a considerable degree on politics. The variations in tax capacity are also closely related to variations in the average size of government budget deficits over an extended period. There is an inverse relationship between the level of taxation and the size of the deficit across the advanced capitalist nations. Thus, the higher the proportion of total government receipts relative to GDP, the smaller the budget deficit on average between 1965 and 1981 ($r = -.36$). An even stronger inverse relationship ($r = -.53$) exists between the level of taxation on personal income and the size of the deficit. While these relationships are not overwhelming, both are much stronger than that between the size of the deficit and the average level of total government spending ($r = +.04$). In other words, the propensity to incur large deficits, relative to other nations, over a long period of time has much more to do with the level of *taxation*—especially the taxation of personal incomes—than with the level of *spending*. To generalize from such cross-national relationships is hazardous, of course; however, a nation's propensity to incur deficits does seem more likely to be eliminated if taxes—particularly income taxes—are raised rather than expenditures reduced.

Given the strong relations between partisan control of government and levels of taxation and between levels of taxation and size of budget deficits, it is not surprising that the magnitude of deficits over an extended period varies with the partisanship of government. The nations in which government was usually controlled by leftist parties in 1965–81 were *less* likely to incur large budget deficits than those in which government was controlled by centrist, Christian Democratic, or conservative parties—in spite of the fact that leftist-dominated governments were much more likely to increase government spending to high levels. Thus, while there is a correlation of leftist control during 1965–81 with the level of spending in 1979–80 ($r = +.62$) and with the increase in spending between 1964–66 and 1979–80 ($r = +.43$), there is an inverse relationship between leftist control and the magnitude of the budget deficit relative to GDP in 1965–80 ($r = -.35$; the correlation of centrist control with the magnitude of the deficit is +.22 and of rightist control +.11). Evidently, enduring control of government by leftist parties allows nations to enjoy the benefits of a large and expanding public economy—for example, relatively generous provision of social security benefits, social assistance, and unemployment compensation—while avoiding whatever macroeconomic costs are produced by large deficits. How? By imposing relatively high taxes—especially taxes on personal income and wealth. The nations in which nonleftist parties usually govern are more likely to experience a smaller, more miserly public economy (especially when conservatives dominate government) *and* a chronic fiscal crisis reflected in relatively large deficits (especially when centrist and Christian Democratic parties dominate government), for they are more reluctant to levy high taxes, especially the taxes on income and wealth which fall most heavily on their upper-income supporters.

Budget Deficits and Inflation in the United States

Given the frequency of budget deficits in the United States as well as the growth in recent years in their magnitude, can the inflation of the 1960s and 1970s be attributed to the fiscal irresponsibility of government—especially the federal government? The time trends in figure 9-6, when compared with those for inflation in figure 9-5, should cast suspicion on the conventional argument that deficits cause inflation. To take but one example, the budget deficit actually diminished in each successive year between 1975 and 1979, although it was precisely in that period that inflation accelerated to its highest levels. Similarly, while the initial acceleration in the inflation of the two decades occurred in the mid-1960s, figure 9-6 suggests that budget deficits in the mid-1960s were, on average, considerably smaller than those during much of the 1950s and 1970s. In short, there seems to be little evidence of a temporal covariation between the magnitude of deficits and inflation.

Table 9-8 indicates virtually no relationship between the magnitude of the deficit of all government and the rate of change of prices in the economy over the period 1948–81 ($r = -.02$). There is a positive relationship ($r = +.23$) between the rate of change in prices and the deficit of the *federal* government; however, when inflation is defined in terms of acceleration—the increase in the rate of change of prices—it appears to be *inversely* associated with the magnitude of the budget deficit of both the federal government ($r = -.14$) and all government ($r =$

Table 9-8. *Correlation of Government Deficits and Inflation in the United States, 1948–81*

Variable	Percent change in implicit price deflator of GNP		Increase in percent change in implicit price deflator of GNP	
	Correlation coefficient r	Regression coefficient b	Correlation coefficient r	Regression coefficient b
	1948–81			
Budget deficit as a percent of GNP				
All government	−.02	−0.032	−.21	−0.348
Federal government	+.23	+0.385	−.14	−0.212
Increase in budget deficit as a percent of GNP				
All government	+.03	+0.044	−.51	−0.642
Federal government	+.04	+0.064	−.50	−0.672
	1960–81			
Budget deficit as a percent of GNP				
All government	+.27	+0.600	−.38	−0.449
Federal government	+.51	+1.030	−.38	−0.410
Increase in budget deficit as a percent of GNP				
All government	+.29	+0.510	+.23	+0.215
Federal government	+.26	+0.480	+.09	+0.094

−.21). Increases in the size of the deficit—reflecting increases in spending or decreases in revenues—relative to GNP are no more closely associated with inflation than is the magnitude of the deficit. For all government the magnitude of the increase in the deficit is unrelated to the rate of change in the implicit price deflator ($r = +.03$), and it has a strong negative correlation with the increase in the rate of change in prices ($r = −.51$). Instead of accelerating in years in which deficits increase in magnitude, the rate of change in prices has tended to *decelerate*.

For the period commencing in 1963, when inflation began to accelerate both as an economic phenomenon and a political issue, more support can be mustered for the conventional argument that deficits cause inflation. For example, the magnitude of the aggregate deficit of all government has a positive relation to the rate of change of prices in the economy ($r = +.27$) and an even stronger relation to the magnitude of the deficit of the federal government ($r = +.51$). The regression coefficients in table 9-8 indicate a one-for-one relationship between the size of the federal government's deficit and the rate of change in prices (a regression coefficient of +1.03). Similarly, there are positive—albeit more modest—correlations between the magnitude of the increase in government deficits and the rate of change in prices. But it is possible that the associations reflect only the tendency for both deficits and inflation to reach higher levels over time.[58] Examination of the relationship between measures of change in the two variables suggests that the correlations are almost entirely spurious. In contrast to the strong positive relationship between the magnitude of the federal government's deficit and the rate of change in prices, the relationship between the increase in the size of the federal deficit and the increase in the rate of change in prices is very modest ($r = +.09$). Thus, an annual increase in the federal budget deficit of 1 percent of GNP would increase prices by less than 0.10 percent.[59] Even taking the larger impact associated with the combined budget deficit of all government, the increase in prices would be less than 0.25 percent.[60]

No serious economic theory argues that deficits will in every instance be inflationary, and most hold that they might be inflationary only when the additional demand generated by the deficit fails to induce producers to supply more goods—that is, only if they occur when the economy is already operating at or near full capacity.[61] However, budget deficits are likely to be largest in precisely the opposite situation—when the economy is in recession. The decrease in revenues (because of lost production, lost sales, lost income) and increase in expenditures (unemployment compensation, company bail-outs) that inevitably occur in a recession thus cause deficits to increase (or surpluses to decrease) at precisely the time that slack in the demand for goods, services, and labor causes prices to fall (at least in theory). It is therefore hardly surprising that budget deficits are not associated with inflation, since they are likely to be largest during recessions.

Given this argument, it is necessary to control for the natural counter-cyclical movement of both deficits and prices. The comparisons of the budget deficit of all government with the Federal Reserve's index of capacity utilization in manufacturing, and the deficit of the federal government with the rate of unemployment, in figure 9-11, demonstrate the extent to which government deficits are associated with cyclical

58. This is called serial correlation.
59. Based on the regression coefficient in table 9-8 of 0.094.
60. Based on the regression coefficient in table 9-8 of 0.215.
61. And if imports are unable to fully satisfy the additional demand.

Figure 9-11. *Government Deficits, Economic Activity, and Unemployment in the United States, 1948–81*

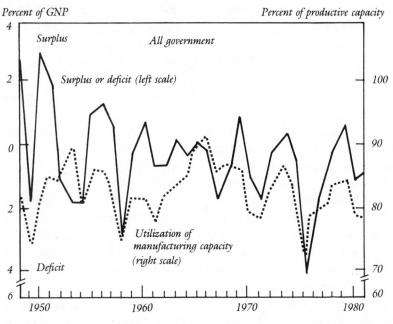

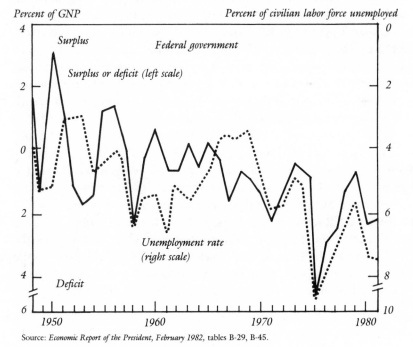

Source: *Economic Report of the President, February 1982*, tables B-29, B-45.

fluctuations in the economy. The largest deficits invariably occur in the years of recession—1949, 1954, 1958, 1970–71, 1975, and 1980. Only in 1952–53 and 1964–68 did government incur deficits while the economy was operating with relatively little slack—that is, when deficits may have generated excess demand. While the deficits in those periods were not as great in magnitude as the ones incurred in the 1970s, they were considerable when measured against the high operating level of the economy.

It must be more than coincidence that both instances occurred while the United States was involved in wars in Asia. That war is an essential element in an analysis of American macroeconomic performance is hardly a surprise. For example, it was not until 1941, the year in which the United States entered World War II, that the rate of unemployment dropped back into single digits after the Great Depression. Similarly, the two peaks in economic performance in the decades after World War II— the only two periods, for example, when the rate of unemployment dropped below 4 percent—occurred while the United States was involved in war in Korea and Vietnam.

During the Korean War, the Truman administration instituted price controls to prevent the war-induced deficits from generating inflation. Judging from the reduction in the rate of increase in the implicit deflator to less than 2 percent in 1952 and 1953, those controls were successful. Moreover, the termination of those controls did not produce a marked surge in prices—no doubt because termination coincided with the onset of recession. During the war in Vietnam, on the other hand, price controls were avoided—in spite of the obvious signs of a booming economy, such as attainment of the highest level of capacity utilization and lowest level of unemployment since World War II.[62] The deficits in the mid-1960s were not large compared to those of the 1950s and 1970s. Nevertheless, figure 9-11 suggests that fiscal policy during the Johnson administration was badly out of phase with the performance of the economy, that a purely neutral fisc would have produced a surplus equal to perhaps 1–2 percent of GNP rather than deficits, and that the actual policy therefore overstimulated the economy. And it was precisely at this time that the initial phase of the long upward acceleration in prices occurred (figure 9-5). It may be the case, then, that while deficits in general have little to do with inflation, the initial acceleration in the rate of change in prices

---

62. See *Economic Report of the President, February 1982*, tables B-29, B-45.

in the United States, in 1965–70, *was* produced by an excessively expansionist fiscal policy.

Why did the American government fail to dampen, through budget surpluses, the inflationary tendencies that would inevitably be produced by fiscal stimulation in an economy that was at the peak of its postwar boom? In retrospect, the Johnson administration's fiscal mismanagement can be attributed to four factors. The president was eager to enact John Kennedy's much-delayed tax legislation and did so in 1964, in spite of the fact that by then the economy was in a sustained boom. Not only was a federal tax cut no longer needed, it should have been replaced with an *increase* in taxes.[63] A significant reduction in income taxes could also contribute to the landslide Johnson hoped to win in the 1964 presidential election and thereby erase the memory of his predecessor and establish a mandate for his administration. Fiscal policy in the United States was excessively expansionary—in the sense of increasing the deficit, increasing expenditures, or decreasing revenues more than would occur if policy were fiscally neutral—in only two of the nine presidential election years from 1948 through 1980. In 1948 and 1964, when the incumbent was an unelected Democrat seeking to hold the office, the primary means of fiscal stimulation was a significant reduction in personal income taxes.[64] The budget was given an additional stimulus by the rapid escalation of the involvement in Vietnam in 1965—certainly not foreseen when Kennedy's advisers proposed a tax cut in the early 1960s and perhaps not anticipated even in 1964—that added literally tens of billions of dollars to government spending.[65] Thereafter, the unpopularity of the war—the expenditures for which accounted for the fiscal overstimulation in 1966–68—caused Johnson to delay the introduction of legislation (proposed by his economic advisers) to raise taxes until late in 1967.

The cumulative effect of the Johnson administration's fiscal and foreign policies (and the two cannot be separated) can be seen in figure 9-5. More than a half-decade of very low inflation ended in 1965, with the

---

63. For a discussion of the fiscal policy of the Johnson administration—a policy that was made as much *against* as with the advice of the Council of Economic Advisers—see Okun, *Political Economy of Prosperity*. Okun served as a member of the council between 1964 and 1968 and as chairman in 1968–69. For a discussion of macroeconomic policy in the early 1960s by another former member of the council, see Tobin, *New Economics One Decade Older*. Also see Stein, *Fiscal Revolution in America,* chaps. 15–17.

64. For an analytically incisive critique of the implicit arguments in the literature on political business cycles, see chapter 10, below, by Brian Barry.

65. See Okun, *Political Economy of Prosperity,* chap. 3; Tobin, *New Economics One Decade Older,* chap. 2.

rapid acceleration in the rate of change of prices in 1965–70. The enduring inflation of the 1970s and early 1980s was initiated by events that preceded by at least a half-decade President Nixon's termination in August 1971 of the convertibility of dollars into gold, and OPEC's raising of oil prices in 1973–74 in response to the Yom Kippur War and the erosion of its real dollar income.[66]

The experience of 1965–69 demonstrates that deficits may, at particular times and in certain circumstances, contribute to inflation. They did not do so throughout the 1970s for, although large, they expanded and contracted in neutral countercyclical manner, closely following the fluctuations in the economy. But during the critical mid-1960s, although not very large relative to GNP, deficits were much larger than the performance of the economy warranted and may well have initiated the acceleration in the rate of change of prices.

Budget Deficits and Inflation in Comparative Perspective

Across the advanced capitalist nations there is a very modest association between the magnitudes of budget deficits and average rates of change in prices in 1965–81. For the entire period the average rate of change in prices is slightly higher in nations in which deficits were large relative to GDP ($r = +.16$); and for 1979 through 1981 the positive association is somewhat stronger ($r = +.25$).[67] However, the regression coefficients for these years ($+0.168$ for 1965–81 and $+0.400$ for 1978–81) indicate that the budget deficits account for a very insignificant portion of the upward drift of prices. Thus, over the entire period 1965–81, an additional 1 percent of GDP in deficit, relative to that in other nations, may have added less than 0.2 percent to the average rate of change in prices, and even in the more recent period it may have contributed less than 0.5 percent to the rate of change in prices.

The weakness of the cross-national relationship is especially evident in the rates of inflation among nations that have incurred relatively large deficits—in excess of 3 percent of GDP, for example. While some of the nations in figure 9-12 with large deficits, such as Greece, Portugal, Italy, and Ireland, experienced annual increases in prices of about 20 percent in 1979–81, other nations with relatively large deficits experienced much

---

66. This argument differs in emphasis from that in Calleo, *Imperious Economy*, which concentrates on the policies of the Nixon administration and events in the world economy in the early 1970s.

67. Refers to all the countries in table 9-7 except New Zealand.

Figure 9-12. *The Size of Government Deficits and the Rate of Inflation in Twenty Countries, 1979–81*

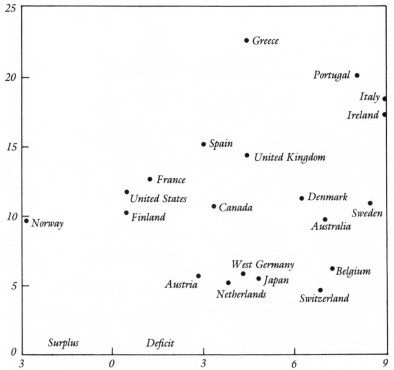

Average percent change in prices, 1979–81

Budget deficit of government as a percent of GDP, 1979–80

Sources: *OECD Economic Outlook,* no. 31 (July 1982); OECD, *National Accounts, 1964–1980.*

smaller increases. In one group in particular—Austria, West Germany, Japan, the Netherlands, Belgium, and Switzerland—prices increased by only about 5 percent a year, in spite of relatively large deficits in the range of 3–7 percent of GDP. What common attributes allowed those six countries to avoid the macroeconomic penalty conventionally associated with budget deficits? Clearly the effective exchange rate is one contributor (figure 9-13). There is an unusually strong relationship ($r = -.89$) between the extent of appreciation in a nation's currency in the 1970s and the rate of inflation. This suggests that the extent to which a nation experienced inflation or stability in prices, relative to other nations,

Figure 9-13. *Depreciation of the Currency and the Rate of Inflation in Twenty-one Countries, 1970–81*

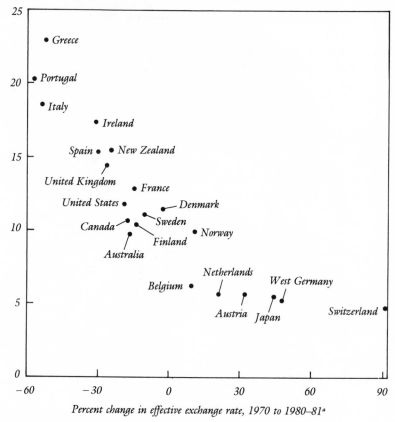

Average percent change in prices, 1979–81

Percent change in effective exchange rate, 1970 to 1980–81[a]

Source: *OECD Economic Outlook,* no. 31 (July 1982), table R16, p. 155.
a. Correlation coefficient $r = -.89$.

depended very much on its performance, relative to other nations, in the world economy over an extended period. The nations in which the effective exchange rate appreciated after the dollar devaluation of 1971, and *only* those nations, experienced single-digit inflation in the late 1970s. Whether that appreciation occurred because the nation exported enough to produce surpluses in its current accounts (Japan and West Germany) or because its currency was tied to that of a nation which did (Austria, Switzerland, Belgium, and the Netherlands—all of which linked their currencies to the deutsche mark throughout the late 1970s and early 1980s), the result was the same—an unusually small increase in prices, regardless of the magnitude of the budget deficit.[68]

If, finally, there existed a cross-nationally general relationship between budget deficits and inflation, the nations with the largest increases in the size of the budget deficit should be the ones that experienced the largest increases (that is, accelerations) in the rate of change in prices. The results of regression analysis suggest that the relationship does not exist; there is no statistical association between the size of the increase in the deficit between 1964–65 and 1979–80 and the extent of acceleration in the rate of change in prices over the same period ($r = -.02$). In short, a systematic investigation across the advanced capitalist nations reveals no more— indeed *less*—support than did the American analysis for the conventional view that budget deficits cause inflation. The notion that there is a "deficit-inflation nexus"[69] must be considered just that and nothing more—a notion, and one that lacks an empirical referent.

The Monetization of Deficits

Monetarists would argue that it is naive to believe that budget deficits are inherently inflationary, and no less naive to believe that an examination of the simple bivariate relationship between deficits and inflation would shed much light on the subject. Whether deficits contribute to inflation depends, instead, on whether they are monetized. If individuals and corporations purchase government securities with liquid assets, there would be no change in the aggregate cash balances in society. If, however, the securities are purchased by the central bank or are immediately redeemed by private purchasers—in both cases because low yields make them unattractive to investors—or if they are purchased with funds obtained from sales of nonliquid assets (stocks, real estate, savings),

68. The relatively modest increase in prices reflects the relation between a nation's currency and the U.S. dollar. Since OPEC oil has always been priced in American dollars, the effective increase in oil prices in the 1970s for any nation depends on the relation between its currency and the dollar. To the extent that a nation's currency appreciated, or depreciated less than the dollar, during the 1970s, the effective increase in the price of oil would have been less than that in the United States. More generally, to the extent that a nation's currency appreciates more than another country's, the cost of any imports priced in a common currency (for example, OPEC oil) is less to the former relative to the latter. Hence, if the two nations import and consume an equal volume of a good priced in a common third currency, the contribution of those imports to any index of inflation will be greater in the latter nation. For a discussion of the impact of international trade on domestic inflation, see Calleo, *Imperious Economy;* Corden, *Inflation, Exchange Rates;* Keohane, chapter 4, above.

69. Buchanan and Wagner, *Democracy in Deficit,* p. 58.

aggregate cash balances would increase. More liquid funds would exist in society and, with more money available, individual and corporate consumers might bid up the prices of goods and services.

According to the Friedmans,

substantial inflation is always and everywhere a monetary phenomenon. . . . If the quantity of goods and services available for purchase—output, for short—were to increase as rapidly as the quantity of money, prices would tend to be stable. . . . Inflation occurs when the quantity of money rises appreciably more rapidly than output, and the more rapid the rise in the quantity of money per unit of output, the greater the rate of inflation. There is probably no other proposition in economics that is as well established as this one.[70]

From the monetarist perspective, then, inflation is the product of an *imbalance* between the rates of growth in money aggregates (M1, M1-B, M2) and economic output. In contrast to the conclusion that American budget deficits may have been inflationary only in several years in the mid-1960s, the monetarist perspective would keep open the possibility that the far larger deficits of the 1970s were inflationary as well—in spite of the fact that the economy was operating at well below capacity during most of the decade.

To evaluate the monetarist argument—which had become, by the early 1980s, the standard operating norm of most central banks and governments in the advanced capitalist world—it is necessary to estimate the likelihood that deficits in a particular period would be monetized. Presumably, if the real yields on government securities are high—that is, above the existing rate of inflation and comparable or close to those on other debt instruments—investors would be willing to buy and hold the Treasury securities. If, on the other hand, the interest rates on new, short-term issues are low, investors would have little reason to purchase and hold them, and the securities would soon find their way to the Federal Reserve, to be converted into "printing press money" or, more precisely, bank reserves.

Figures 9-14 and 9-15 indicate that the large deficits of the 1970s in the United States may have been monetized and, as a result, may have increased aggregate liquidity and contributed to inflation. In the 1948–81 period, financial markets generally demanded that corporate bonds

70. Milton and Rose Friedman, *Free to Choose*, p. 254. See also Milton Friedman, "Nobel Lecture: Inflation and Unemployment," *Journal of Political Economy*, vol. 85 (June 1977); David Laidler and Michael Parkin, "Inflation: A Survey," *Economic Journal*, vol. 85 (December 1975); Robert J. Gordon, "World Inflation and Monetary Accommodation in Eight Countries," *BPEA, 2:1977*.

Figure 9-14. *The Size of the Federal Deficit and the Spread in Interest Rates in the United States, 1948–81*

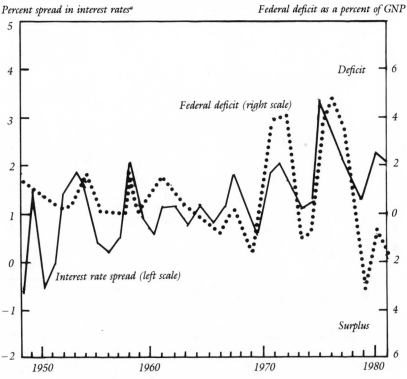

Source: *Economic Report of the President, February 1982,* tables B-1, B-67, B-75.
a. Average rate for Aaa corporate bonds minus rate for ninety-day Treasury bills (new issues).

offer about 1 percent of interest more than government securities. However, in two periods—1971–72 and 1975–77—the gap in the interest rates was unusually large (figure 9-14). It is plausible that the budget deficits in those two periods were monetized, resulting in increases in aggregate liquidity in the economy. While the inflationary consequences may have been largely neutralized by the recessions that marked the first year in both periods, they may have been significant in the later years of each—in 1972 and 1976–77. Thus, the acceleration in the rate of change in prices that began in 1973 and 1977 may be attributable to excessive increases in the money supply.

The real yield on government debt—the spread between the yield on ninety-day Treasury bills and the rate of inflation (the shaded area in

Figure 9-15. *The Real Yield on Government Securities in the United States, 1948–81*

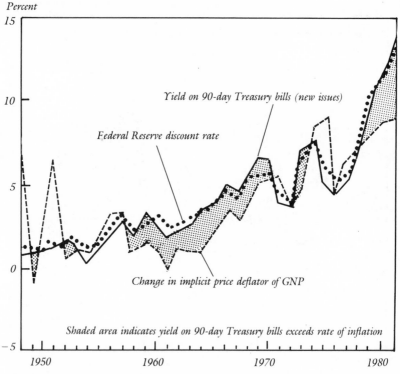

Percent

Source: *Economic Report of the President, February 1982*, tables B-3, B-67.

figure 9-15)—during 1971–72 and 1975–78 was *negative*. Purchasers of government securities were, in effect, making donations, or gifts, to the government. It seems quite probable, then, that a significant portion of the new government debt found its way into the money supply.

What institutions and policies were responsible for the likely monetization of deficits in the 1970s? Were the negative real yields the responsibility of presidents, congressmen, and their fiscal policies? Figure 9-15 suggests that, as a monetarist might argue, much of the blame must be attributed not to fiscal policy and the executive or legislative branch but, instead, to the Federal Reserve and the Nixon and Ford administrations' policies of financing the budget deficit. The yields on 90-day Treasury bills (and other government securities) followed very closely the

Federal Reserve's discount and federal funds rates.[71] While the Federal Reserve followed a responsible interest-rate policy for about a decade after the 1958 recession (responsible in the sense of charging member banks a real interest charge of 1–2 percent for their borrowings from the Fed), its policy after the late 1960s appears increasingly erratic and irresponsible. In some years—for example, 1971–72 and 1974–78—the discount rate was set so low, relative to the rate of inflation, that member banks paid nothing for borrowings and, in effect, were *paid* to borrow from the Federal Reserve. Not surprisingly, with interest rates at an abnormally low level, a marked surge in personal and commercial credit occurred in these years—a surge that fueled inflation as borrowers bid up the prices of goods and services that relied on debt financing (for example, real estate). And because the Federal Reserve kept interest rates too low— perhaps because the Board of Governors and the Open Market Committee retained fresh memories of the recessions of 1970–71 and 1973–75[72]— yields to potential purchasers of government securities were nonexistent.

In other years after the late 1960s, the Federal Reserve erred in the opposite direction. In 1979–81, for example, it raised interest rates to the highest levels of the postwar era and, more important in terms of the effect on the economy, established the highest real interest cost to member bank borrowers and, ultimately, to commercial and individual borrowers. If the real interest rate in 1980–81 was not, as Helmut Schmidt of West Germany claimed, at the highest level since Jesus Christ, nevertheless it was much higher than it had been at any other time after World War II. While those high real rates undoubtedly made government securities more attractive than they had ever been for investors (thereby insuring that the federal deficit would not be monetized), they also directly contributed to the recessions of 1980 and 1981–82 (thereby causing—because of the effect of recessions on revenues and expenditures—larger deficits).

If it appears likely that the budget deficits of the 1970s were at least occasionally monetized, did the increases in aggregate liquidity generate increases in prices? The monetarists' hallowed quantity theory, when transformed into rates of change, yields the relationship described by the Friedmans. Assuming constant velocity, or circulation, of money,[73] in-

71. For example, over 1948–81 the correlation between the Federal Reserve Bank's discount rate and the interest rate on 90-day Treasury bills is +.9997.

72. See the discussion of the Federal Reserve and its policies by John Woolley in chapter 11, below.

73. The assumption is more or less accurate for M2 although it is less valid for M1, which has displayed a long-term upward trend in velocity in recent decades.

Figure 9-16. *Changes in Prices and in the Money Supply in the United States, 1963–81*

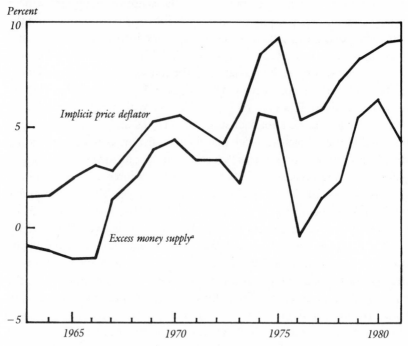

Percent

Implicit price deflator

Excess money supply[a]

Sources: *Economic Report of the President, February 1982*, table B-3; OECD, *Main Economic Indicators*, various issues.
a. Rate of change of the money supply minus rate of change of trend real GNP.

flation is a function of the difference between the rate of increase in the money supply and the rate of increase in output. In other words, $\dot{p} = \dot{v} + (\dot{m} - \dot{q})$, where $\dot{p}$ represents the rate of change in prices, $\dot{v}$ the rate of change in the velocity of money, $\dot{m}$ the rate of change in the money supply, and $\dot{q}$ the rate of change in the volume of output.

Figure 9-16 shows how the annual rates of change in prices varied with the money supply (M1), relative to the change in output, in the United States in 1963–81. The strong positive relationship between the measures ($r = +.85$) indicates that, as monetarists claim, inflation increases most rapidly when the money supply grows at a rapid rate. Of course, this does not prove that inflation increases *because* the money supply increases. But it does suggest that the monetarist perspective *may* be valid, particularly since the major accelerations in the rate of change in prices—

in 1968–70, 1973–75, and 1977–80—occurred precisely when the amount of excess money was increasing.

Robert Gordon has argued that "confirmation of the connection between money and prices is only the first and easiest step in the development of a full theory of the causes of inflation, because it leaves completely unexplained the sources of changes in money."[74] Given the close relationship between accelerations in the amount of excess money and in prices, an explanation of inflation would seem to require an explanation of why the amount of excess money fluctuates over time and why, in particular, the money supply expanded more rapidly than the economy in every year but one after 1966. If some (unknown) portion of the budget deficit of the federal government was occasionally monetized, and if changes in the money supply in excess of the growth rate in the economy were closely associated with the acceleration of inflation, was the increase in excess money therefore caused by budget deficits? The answer to this question depends on whether the magnitude of the quantity $\dot{m} - \dot{q}$ is a function of the magnitude of the federal deficit. The fluctuations in 1963–81 in excess money $(\dot{m} - \dot{q})$ are only slightly associated with changes in the size of the federal deficit $(r = +.31)$. Fluctuation in the size of the deficit accounts for no more than 9 percent of the variation in the amount of excess money (figure 9-17). In 1968–69 when the amount of excess money was increasing rapidly, the deficit was actually *de*creasing; the same was true in 1977–79. Only in a few years—1967, 1970, 1974, and 1980—did the two increase simultaneously. It would appear, then, that a theory of inflation in the United States must be built on something other than the fiscal deficits of government. The creation of excess money may be a proximate source of inflation, just as excessively low interest rates may contribute to the monetization of deficits. But the creation of excess money, like the level of interest rates, may depend much less on the fiscal policies and budget deficits incurred by the executive and legislative branches of government than on other policies implemented by other actors—for example, the financial policies of the Federal Reserve.[75]

---

74. "Demand for and Supply of Inflation," pp. 807–08.

75. On the Federal Reserve's monetary policies, see chapter 11, below; John Woolley, *Monetary Politics: The Federal Reserve System and the Political Economy of Monetary Policy* (Cambridge University Press, 1984); G. L. Bach, *Making Monetary and Fiscal Policy* (Brookings Institution, 1971); Michael D. Reagan, "The Political Structure of the Federal Reserve System," *American Political Science Review*, vol. 55 (March 1961); Nathaniel Beck, "Presidential Influence on the Federal Reserve in the 1970s," *American Journal of Political Science*, vol. 26 (August 1982). The definitive discussion of monetary policy and the constraints under which it operates is found in Ralph C. Bryant, *Money and Monetary Policy in Interdependent Nations* (Brookings Institution, 1980).

Figure 9-17. *The Size of the Deficit and Changes in the Money Supply in the United States, 1963–81*

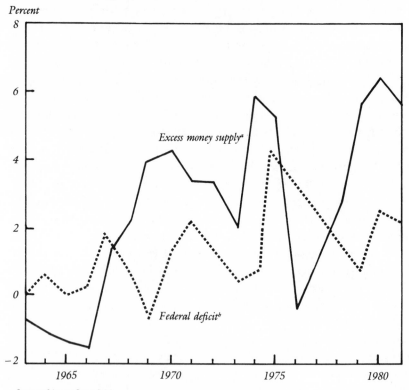

Percent

Sources: Same as figure 9-16.
a. Rate of change of the money supply minus rate of change of trend real GNP.
b. Federal deficit as a share of GNP.

Analysis of the relationship between budget deficits, money supply, and inflation in the United States indicates that an increase in the budget deficit of the federal government equivalent to 1 percent of GNP may have increased the money supply by 0.6 percent above and beyond the rate of change in economic output (the regression coefficient $b = +0.644$). An increase in the money supply of 1 percentage point more than the increase in economic output in turn may have contributed an additional 0.8 percent to the annual rate of increase in prices ($b = +0.831$).[76] Thus, an increase in the budget deficit of 1 percent of GNP may have caused

76. *Economic Report of the President, February 1982,* tables B-1, B-3, B-75; OECD, *Main Economic Indicators* (Paris: OECD), various issues.

Table 9-9. *Correlation of Budget Deficits, Changes in the Money Supply, and Inflation in Seven Countries, 1964–81*

Variable	Total deficit of all government, as a percent of GDP		Percent change in consumer prices	
	Correlation coefficient r	Regression coefficient bᵃ	Correlation coefficient r	Regression coefficient bᵇ
*Percent change in growth of excess money supply*ᶜ				
Canada	+.44	+1.081	+.37	+0.310
France	+.55	+2.262	+.65	+0.544
Italy	+.63	+1.036	+.33	+0.468
Japan	−.31	−0.728	+.36	+0.278
United Kingdom	+.60	+1.779	+.71	+0.650
United States	−.09	−0.178	+.81	+1.108
West Germany	+.58	+1.619	+.25	+0.077

Sources: *OECD Economic Outlook,* no. 31 (July 1982), tables R1, R8–R9; OECD, *Main Economic Indicators,* various issues.

a. Represents the regression of change in excess money upon the deficit.

b. Represents the regression of change in prices upon change in excess money.

c. Rate of change of the money supply minus rate of change of constant-currency GDP.

prices to rise about 0.5 percent ($0.664 \times 0.831 = 0.535$). While the figure is not negligible, neither is it very large relative to the overall magnitude of inflation in the United States in 1963–81—particularly, given the fact that federal deficits were often less than 1 percent of GNP and that only twice from 1948 through 1981 were they larger than 2.5 percent of GNP (suggesting an impact on inflation in excess of 1 percent). To a large degree, then, the conventional macroeconomic wisdom in the United States that attributes primary responsibility for inflation to the fiscal profligacy of government is badly flawed. Inflation may, indeed, be associated with unusually large increases in money—increases that may reflect policy errors by the Federal Reserve. But those increases in money cannot be attributed to budget deficits.

To what extent is it true that, as the Friedmans argue, "substantial inflation is always and everywhere a monetary phenomenon"?[77] Is inflation as closely related in other nations as in the United States to large changes in the supply of money?

The relationships in the seven largest OECD nations between changes in the magnitude of the budget deficit of all government, the supply of money relative to output, and the rate of inflation between 1964 and 1981 indicate that the American pattern is quite anomalous (table 9-9).

77. Milton and Rose Friedman, *Free to Choose,* p. 254.

In all except the United States and Japan, the relationship between the size of the deficit and the amount of excess money is strong and positive, with correlation coefficients falling in the range of $+.44$ to $+.60$ (compared with the negligible relationship in the United States).[78] In West Germany, France, the United Kingdom, Italy, and Canada, increases in the deficit equivalent to 1 percent of GDP were associated with increases in excess money of more than 1 percent—deficits in those countries *do* appear to increase the supply of money.

Table 9-9 also indicates that the American relationship between changes in the money supply, relative to output, and inflation is somewhat anomalous. No other nation fits the monetarist hypothesis that price changes reflect changes in the quantity $\dot{m} - \dot{q}$ better than the United States. The only other nations having a strong positive association between the two are the United Kingdom ($r = +.71$) and France ($r = +.65$). In West Germany, Italy, Canada, and Japan, the monetarists' quantity theory seems to account for no more than a small portion of the fluctuation in prices. Thus, while most nations display either a strong relation between deficits and excess money or a strong relation between excess money and prices, there are only two nations—Britain and France—where *both* links in the deficits-money-inflation equation are strong.

Table 9-9 suggests that the notion that deficits cause inflation—because they cause excessive increases in money which, in turn, cause price increases—is not generally true. In some nations, such as the United States and Japan, budget deficits do not generate dramatic increases in money and the explanation of inflation must search either for nonfiscal sources of increases in money (as in the United States) or for sources of inflation other than increases in money (as in Japan). In other nations— for example, West Germany, where deficits appear to generate increases in money that are not, however, the primary source of increases in prices— the explanation of inflation must look to factors other than changes in the money supply, even if deficits are monetized. Thus, while there is support for strands of the monetarist hypothesis in several nations, it appears highly unlikely that the inflation experienced throughout the advanced capitalist world—and particularly in its three largest economies (the United States, Japan, and West Germany)—can be attributed to the budget deficits of government.

---

78. Using data in *Economic Report of the President, February 1982*, rather than that in *OECD Economic Outlook*, the correlation coefficient for the United States is $+.16$.

Government Policy and Inflation

The evidence reviewed here on government spending and the propensity to incur budget deficits during the 1960s and 1970s refutes the conventional wisdom that government causes inflation. There were instances in which government contributed to the acceleration of inflation—for example, during the mid-1960s in the United States when fiscal, foreign, and monetary policies added demand to an economy that was already operating near full capacity. However, the notion that inflation occurred either in the United States or in the other advanced capitalist countries because of excessively high levels of government spending and large budget deficits receives little, if any, confirmation. The conventional wisdom about inflation is better viewed as a veiled expression of the political ideology and economic interest of some members of society than as an empirically grounded explanation.

10

Does Democracy Cause Inflation? Political Ideas of Some Economists

Brian Barry

It is not the popular movement, but the travelling of the minds of men who sit in the seat of Adam Smith that is really telling and worthy of all attention.

LORD ACTON

Since inflation has ebbed but democratic institutions have not radically changed, some economists may prefer to forget one of their major themes of the 1970s, namely, the view that inflation is the inevitable outcome of the normal functioning of democratic political institutions. But even if the economists who maintained this view are bashful, it is worth recalling their analysis and, at least retrospectively, analyzing the premises that might once again be appealed to if economic outcomes seem unfavorable. Since none of this group have themselves recanted, it seems reasonable to assume their doctrines and prescriptions still stand. These economists proposed the simple view that political authorities create or permit inflation by their control of fiscal and monetary policy. Applying the standard methodology of economics to the analysis of political phenomena, this new school of "political economists" (which is represented in this discussion principally by the work of James Buchanan and the Virginia School) went on to propose that central aspects of economic policymaking be removed from the control of elected representatives, such as governments in parliamentary systems.[1]

---

1. See William D. Nordhaus, "The Political Business Cycle," *Review of Economic Studies*, vol. 42 (April 1975), pp. 169–90; C. Duncan MacRae, "A Political Model of the Business Cycle," *Journal of Political Economy*, vol. 85 (April 1977), pp. 239–63; Richard E. Wagner, "Economic Manipulation for

Perhaps the remedy would have been worse than the disease; but to establish that, it must first be determined whether the disease—what has been termed the "democratic distemper"—was really so serious.

To decide that, three questions have to be asked. First, how important is it to ensure that inflation cannot occur? How bad are its economic, social, and political consequences? (The alternatives also have consequences.[2]) Second, is it true that representative institutions have built into them an inevitable tendency toward inflation? Third, in the light of the answers to these questions, how should the proposals for constitutional change that have been put forward be assessed? Because constitutional changes are relatively irrevocable, prudence demands that the arguments in their favor be subjected to the strictest scrutiny.

The methodological techniques that the expounders of the new political economy bring to the analysis of political phenomena constitute a serious encumbrance. Their adherence to a vulgarized Popperian methodology, particularly as represented in Milton Friedman's paper "The Methodology of Positive Economics,"[3] requires, as a matter of faith, that the assumptions used in theory-building not be subjected to direct test. A theory is taken to be true if its implications fit the facts sufficiently, and no effort is made to check the adequacy of the story it tells about the phenomena. In practice, no serious attempt is ever made to determine whether or not

---

Political Profit," *Kyklos,* vol. 30, Fasc. 3 (1977), pp. 395–410; Assar Lindbeck, "Stabilization Policy in Open Economies with Endogenous Politicians," *American Economic Review,* vol. 66 (May 1976, *Papers and Proceedings, 1975*), pp. 1–19; Michael Parkin, "The Politics of Inflation," *Government and Opposition,* vol. 10 (Spring 1975), pp. 189–202; Larry A. Sjaastad, "Why Stable Inflations Fail: An Essay in Political Economy," in Michael Parkin and George Zis, eds., *Inflation in the World Economy* (Manchester University Press, 1976), pp. 73–95; James M. Buchanan and Richard E. Wagner, *Democracy in Deficit: The Political Legacy of Lord Keynes* (Academic Press, 1977); Samuel Brittan, *The Economic Consequences of Democracy* (London: Temple Smith, 1977), pp. 223–89, "The Economic Contradictions of Democracy," *British Journal of Political Science,* vol. 5 (April 1975), pp. 129–59, and "Can Democracy Manage an Economy?" in Robert Skidelsky, ed., *The End of the Keynesian Era: Essays on the Disintegration of the Keynesian Political Economy* (Holmes and Meier, 1977), pp. 41–49.

2. "It may be true that if demand is sufficiently restricted, and unemployment correspondingly increased, collective bargaining will in time no longer operate to force up wages and prices, while other sources of inflation will prove unimportant. But restrictive policies can have other consequences that operate even more powerfully: governments may fall from power and entire societies be torn apart before inflation dies away. It is necessary, therefore, to weigh up the *total* consequences of policies recommended." Alec Cairncross, *Inflation, Growth and International Finance* (State University of New York Press, 1975), p. 14.

3. *Essays in Positive Economics* (University of Chicago Press, 1953), pp. 3–43 (Friedman does not refer to any philosopher later than John Maynard Keynes's father). See Brian Barry, "On Analogy," *Political Studies,* vol. 23 (June–September 1975), pp. 208–24; Martin Hollis and Edward J. Nell, *Rational Economic Man: A Philosophical Critique of Neo-Classical Economics* (Cambridge University Press, 1975).

fundamental assumptions should be abandoned.[4] Since it is likely that, with enough ingenuity, *some* theory can be found that will incorporate them and give rise to implications that fit the facts sufficiently, the assumptions are in effect beyond challenge.

If the orthodox methodology of contemporary economics is a cut-down version of a fifty-year-old development in logical positivist doctrine,[5] the official theory of value subscribed to by most economists is an even more antique form of logical positivism. Many economists still treat "value judgments" (statements, for example, that one form of society is better than another) as "preferences," and follow Lionel Robbins in believing that the interpersonal comparison of utilities is impossible.[6] Since Kenneth Arrow has shown that the aggregation of ordinal preferences into a "social welfare function" is impossible,[7] the only criterion left is unanimity of preferences, that is, roughly, Pareto-optimality.[8] The consequences of professing an irrationalist theory of value are that economists do not engage in open discussion of questions of value. Rather, they smuggle their values into their analyses where they are immune to rational criticism.

Economists' Evaluation of Inflation

The orthodox approach of welfare economics has had great difficulty in identifying a welfare loss from inflation at all commensurate with that often loosely attributed to it. In terms of static allocational inefficiency, the only welfare cost that can be identified is that people keep smaller cash balances than they would choose to do in the absence of inflation, because they are, in effect, losing money by holding cash. Even this is not an unmitigated welfare loss, for taxes have to be raised somehow and a tax on cash holdings (which is one way of looking at inflation) is as good a tax as any other. An economist with impeccably orthodox credentials has therefore suggested that an inflation rate of, say, 5 percent

---

4. Friedman, *Essays*, pp. 22–23, virtually admits this.

5. See Karl Popper, *Logik der Forschung* (Vienna: Julius Springer, 1935).

6. *An Essay on the Nature and Significance of Economic Science*, 2d ed. (London: Macmillan, 1969).

7. *Social Choice and Individual Values*, Cowles Foundation for Research in Economics at Yale University, Monograph 12, 2d. ed. (Wiley, 1963).

8. This, of course, brings the economists' theory of value into contact with the venerable tradition of social contract theory. The connection has been made explicit by the Virginia School. See James M. Buchanan and Gordon Tullock, *The Calculus of Consent: Logical Foundations of Constitutional Democracy* (University of Michigan Press, 1962); James M. Buchanan, *The Limits of Liberty: Between Anarchy and Leviathan* (University of Chicago Press, 1975). For a critique, see Brian Barry, "Review," *Theory and Decision*, vol. 12 (March 1980), pp. 95–106.

might be regarded as beneficial, in the "second best" world where taxation is a fact of life.[9]

Leaving aside the alleged social and political by-products of inflation, it is hard to maintain that the consequences of inflation are enormously serious, especially when that level of inflation is arrived at over a number of years so as to allow for some adjustments of expectations along the way. The difficulties with mortgage repayments, long-term leases, and so on, are not negligible, but there are expedients available for dealing with them. (There is no reason why people should not be assured a positive inflation-discounted return on their savings.) And although these expedients deal with the distributive effects of inflation only in a rough-and-ready way, the residual distributive effects seem relatively small when set beside problems like unemployment and the underemployment of resources generally, pollution, depletion of resources, and so on.[10]

Hyperinflation is another matter, in that a market economy breaks down if money has to be spent within a few hours before it loses its value. But experience suggests that there is no inexorable development of hyperinflation from ordinary inflation. In spite of quite severe inflation in most member countries of the Organization for Economic Cooperation and Development (OECD) in the 1970s, none let it get out of control and accelerate in the classic pattern of hyperinflation.

Even if the monetarists are right and there is no trade-off between unemployment and inflation in long-run equilibrium, there is no reason for expecting to get into long-run equilibrium. Meanwhile, the ill effects of anti-inflationary policies are quite certain. There are clear losers—those who would be thrown out of employment (or who would lose overtime or piecework bonuses).[11] The anxieties of being unemployed may be partially allayed by institutional change (high unemployment benefits); nevertheless, unemployment has profoundly disrupting social and psychological effects that even full replacement of income would do nothing to obviate. It is not therefore necessary to depict governments as composed

---

9. J. S. Flemming, *Inflation* (Oxford University Press, 1976), p. 112. David Laidler and Michael Parkin discuss inflation as a tax on money balances in "Inflation: A Survey," *Economic Journal*, vol. 85 (December 1975), pp. 791–94.

10. Harold T. Shapiro, "Inflation in the United States," in Lawrence B. Krause and Walter S. Salant, eds., *Worldwide Inflation: Theory and Recent Experience* (Brookings Institution, 1977), p. 290.

11. The studiously noncontroversial Congressional Budget Office suggested that in order to achieve a reduction of 1 percent in the rate of inflation by 1980 it would be necessary to cut the federal budget beginning in 1978 by an amount that would decrease GNP by 3–4 percent in each year (though the loss would decrease after peaking in 1979). U.S. Congressional Budget Office, *Recovery with Inflation* (CBO, 1977), p. 36, and table 2, p. 37.

of cynical manipulators to explain why they tended to choose economic policies that have inflation as one of their consequences. A sincere desire for the public good and a rational preference for the avoidance of certain evils in the near future rather than the avoidance of speculative evils in the distant future would have led in the same direction. The assumption underlying much of the new political economy—that the economic outcomes of democratic politics diverge sharply from those that would be brought about by a wholly benevolent dictator—is not self-evident.

Inflation as "Moral Rot"

Is there perhaps some evil of inflation so serious that economists might be justified in seeking institutional changes (such as the insulation of the central bank from political pressure) that would ensure a lower inflation rate than that produced by the workings of a competitive political system, responsive in broad terms to popular preferences? Are the citizens of the Western democracies so corrupt that their preferences can legitimately be disregarded in the higher pursuit of saving them from themselves?

To some academic economists, and to many social critics and journalists, inflation is both a reflection of and a major contributor to a general collapse of values. Buchanan and Wagner identified a "*zeitgeist*, a 'spirit of the times' . . . at work in the 1960s and 1970s," that they described as "a generalized erosion in public and private manners, increasingly liberalized attitudes toward sexual activities, a declining vitality of the Puritan work ethic, deterioration in product quality, explosion of the welfare rolls, widespread corruption in both the private and the governmental sector, and, finally, observed increases in the alienation of voters from the political process." And they contended that inflation "plays some role in reinforcing several of the observed behavior patterns. Inflation destroys expectations and creates uncertainty; it increases the sense of felt injustice and causes alienation. It prompts behavioral responses that reflect a generalized shortening of time horizons. 'Enjoy, enjoy'—the imperative of our time —becomes a rational response in a setting where tomorrow remains insecure and where the plans made yesterday seem to have been made in folly."[12] They cited in support Wilhelm Röpke's even more apocalyptic view that "inflation, and the spirit which nourishes it and accepts it, is merely the monetary aspect of the general decay of law and

---

12. Buchanan and Wagner, *Democracy in Deficit*, pp. 64–65.

respect for law. . . . Laxity about property and laxity about money are very closely bound up together; in both cases what is firm, durable, earned, secured and designed for continuity gives place to what is fragile, fugitive, fleeting, unsure and ephemeral."[13]

Similarly, the editor of the *Times* of London, William Rees-Mogg, saw inflation as part of a general twentieth-century decay: "The damage that Dr. Spock did was that he destroyed confidence in discipline for children; the damage that Freud did was that he destroyed belief in the necessity of discipline in sexual conduct; the damage of the explosion of science was that it destroyed discipline in man's dealings with nature."[14] (The remedy, according to Mogg, was God and Gold in equal doses.) He was seconded by another conservative journalist, Robert Moss, who argued that "the recent trends that are pulling us towards strato-inflation are related both to an inflation of expectations in the post-1945 consumer society, and to a loss of broader concepts of patriotism and citizenship. . . . The psychology of inflation is deeply implanted."[15]

The fact that academic economists accepted this sort of diagnosis so readily just reflects the tendency of the Friedmanite "methodology of positive economics" to divide the social realm sharply into one area where the deductive method can be put to work and another that is subject to no canons of science and is therefore open to unconstrained speculation.

Fortunately, data as well as assertions exist. A political scientist, Ronald Inglehart, has also studied the question of whether a fundamental shift in values is occuring in Western countries.[16] His findings support the notion of a generational shift in values away from hard work, self-discipline, production, public order, patriotism, and the like, toward such values as self-expression, self-realization, political participation, and concern with the "quality of life." His survey of postmaterialist attitudes in the European Economic Community and the United States in 1973 produced a close correlation between the first set of values and a high priority on control of inflation. There was a strong relation between the proportion in each category of materialist interests and in ranking by age group in the EEC countries.[17] In a simpler survey, respondents were

13. Ibid., p. 65, n. 16, quoting Wilhelm Röpke, *Welfare, Freedom and Inflation* (University of Alabama Press, 1964), p. 70.
14. *The Reigning Error: The Crisis in World Inflation* (London: Hamish Hamilton, 1974), p. 103.
15. *The Collapse of Democracy* (London: Sphere Books, 1977), pp. 69–70.
16. *The Silent Revolution: Changing Values and Political Styles among Western Publics* (Princeton University Press, 1977).
17. Ibid., p. 54.

Table 10-1. *Materialist Attitudes among Respondents to Surveys in Ten Countries, 1972–73*[a]

Country	Percentage-point spread across age groups	Percent in age group											
		19–28		29–38		39–48		49–58		59–68		Over 68	
		Materialist	Postmaterialist	Materialist	Postmaterialist	Materialist	Postmaterialist	Materialist	Postmaterialist	Materialist	Postmaterialist	Materialist	Postmaterialist
West Germany	56	24	19	39	8	46	5	50	5	52	7	62	1
France	51	22	20	28	17	39	9	39	8	50	3	55	2
Italy	42	26	16	41	8	42	7	48	6	49	4	57	5
Belgium	39	18	23	20	17	22	10	25	10	39	3	39	5
Ireland	36	24	13	31	9	41	6	37	6	45	2	51	4
Netherlands	35	27	14	22	17	28	9	40	10	41	12	51	5
Denmark	34	33	11	34	9	47	4	44	5	48	4	58	2
Switzerland	32	27	15	26	17	30	15	35	9	34	6	50	6
United States	26	24	17	27	13	34	13	32	10	37	6	40	7
United Kingdom	17	27	11	33	7	29	6	30	7	36	5	37	4

Source: Ronald Inglehart, *The Silent Revolution: Changing Values and Political Styles among Western Publics* (Princeton University Press, 1977), table 2-2, pp. 36–37.
a. Countries ranked by spread across age groups.

asked to choose the two most desirable of four aims. Two pairs (of a possible six pairs) accounted for half the responses. "Maintaining order in the nation" combined with "fighting rising prices," and "giving the people more say in important political decisions" combined with "protecting freedom of speech."[18] The first are termed materialist and the second postmaterialist; the distribution of responses by age cohort is shown in table 10-1. In the postmaterialist columns the growth of this outlook among the younger generation is striking—in West Germany and France from a negligible 1–2 percent among the oldest to 19–20 percent among the youngest age group.[19]

Suppose that the generational change is sufficiently established to be accepted. Those under thirty show a higher incidence of a complex of attitudes, including attributing a relatively low priority to fighting inflation. To that extent, the thesis of the emergence of a new *Zeitgeist* is confirmed (though even among the most susceptible age group in only a fifth or less). But there are no good grounds for accepting the assertion that inflation is a significant factor in creating and reinforcing this *Zeitgeist*. It seems to be the experience of affluence rather than the experience of inflation that is responsible for postmaterialist values. For example, France since 1948 has been persistently one of the most inflationary countries and West Germany one of the least, but both have undergone economic transformation and the two display remarkably similar profiles of age-related attitudes. It is surely reasonable to suppose that the quest for more control of one's life and for a satisfying rather than merely lucrative job will be a result of experiencing the diminishing returns of affluence and not of a change in the numeraire. A check in the rate of inflation cannot be expected to reverse the process of change in values— except insofar as the measures taken to reduce the rate of inflation produced such a decline in production and employment as to raise the priority of material goods and economic security again.

18. Ibid., p. 21.
19. Inferring a change in values from one generation to another on the basis of cross-sectional data is, of course, always suspect. Inglehart suggests that the difference in distributions of materialist and postmaterialist values between generations should be greater the more contrasting their experiences. Thus, intergenerational difference is least in Britain and the United States, neither of which has experienced defeat or change of regime in this century, and both of which were relatively wealthy countries in 1945 and have had a moderate rate of economic growth. Conversely, in Germany the older generation can remember the hyperinflation of the 1920s, the mass unemployment of the 1930s, and the ruin and chaos immediately after the war, while those in the youngest cohort have known only the prosperity of the post-1948 "economic miracle." The differences between generations in Germany are extreme. For other countries also the degree of difference between generations correlates well with difference in the life experience of the generations.

What conservatives decry as a "collapse of values" seems to be more accurately depicted as the result of two forces—a decline in respect for established hierarchies, which has been working itself out for several centuries in the West, and an extension to wider sections of the population of aspirations for autonomy and personal fulfillment. There is no reason for supposing that these profound modifications in the expectations that people hold about the conditions of cooperation with others are affected much by the experience of inflation.

It might be argued that there is indeed a causal connection that runs in the opposite direction to that so far considered. Existing industrial and governmental structures that are not going to adapt to new demands may well respond to abnormal discontent by allowing pay increases, thus buying time even at the expense of increased inflation further down the road. The big (and inflationary) pay raises for French workers that the government oversaw following the events of May 1968 constitute a clear example of this. Or inflationary responses may be the answer to the increasing difficulty of negotiating deals, as deference to authority declines, among leaders of different groups to be sold to the members of those groups. In the Netherlands, for example, the elaborate system of parceling out state functions among corporate groups has come under increasing attack and has in some matters begun to crumble. The Swiss almost carried an initiative to restrict drastically the number of foreign workers, in the face of opposition from almost every established organization, including all the political parties. In Norway, the referendum on joining the EEC produced a majority vote against, in spite of support for entry from most major organizations, including the political parties with all but a handful of seats in the parliament. In economic affairs, high-level agreements on rates of wage and salary increases have been increasingly strained—even in Sweden, normally regarded as the country in which comprehensive national bargaining is most highly developed. To the extent that trade union leaders cannot bind their followers to a program of mutual restraint, one might expect an increase in the rate of inflation, as different groups scramble for relative advantage.

If there is a causal connection running from sociocultural change to inflation, rather than the other way round, the possibility must be seriously entertained that inflation acts as a safety valve, blurring the impact of incompatible demands. Even if that is going too far, it may be that inflation is a by-product of other things that are happening and cannot be held responsible for them.

Inflation as a Cause of Regime Collapse

However unreasonable the intense feelings against change may be, they can, under certain conditions, give rise to the overthrow of a democratic system and its replacement by a regime such as that of Franco, the Greek colonels, or the Chilean junta. In this sense, it is true that inflation poses risks to the continuance of democratic institutions. Those who adhere to the idea of a collapse of values tend to conclude that nothing can be hoped for from democracy, since democratic institutions result in public policies that reflect the majority outlook. Support for some kind of authoritarian regime is a natural (if not often acknowledged) implication of their views. The tension between economic freedom (as understood by the proponents of the market) and political freedom (the freedom to publish, to organize, and to vote governments out of office) goes back over a century. Milton Friedman was not the first enthusiast for the market to endorse a collection of thugs, with his support for Pinochet. (Vilfredo Pareto was a distinguished predecessor.)

Some observers who profess to favor the continuation of democratic institutions still express fear that inflation will result in the replacement of a democratic regime by one less benign. The lesson to be drawn, however, is not that inflation and other things that arouse the violent dislike of reactionary army officers are political evils; rather, that it is important not to have an officer caste drawn from a narrow sector perpetuating an ideology in which the military stand as saviors of "the nation" from the politicians. Where such a state of affairs exists it is difficult to change it: for every Cárdenas there are many Allendes. And where it cannot be changed, or the risk of a counterstroke is too great, an honorable political leader may judge that it is better to run a hobbled democratic government than to provoke a coup. If so, then the things that are liable to result in a coup—whether they be long hair, rock music, strikes, or inflation— become things to be avoided for political reasons.

There is, however, another commonly expressed idea that inflation in a democratic system leads to massive popular discontent and thus to the collapse of the regime. The distinctive feature of the theory is that the overthrow apparently would be met with popular support, or at least acquiescence. Supporters of this hypothesis tend to rely heavily on the German hyperinflation of 1922–24 and the success of the Nazis in 1933 in securing almost half the popular vote. But the Weimar Republic, despite the fact that it was never accepted by the leaders of most of the powerful institutions and early alienated many of its natural supporters in the working class, survived the trauma of the Great Inflation. And the Nazis failed miserably in their attempts to attract support in the early 1920s. The obvious candidate for an economic explanation for their success is surely the very high level of unemployment in the early 1930s. The lesson to be drawn would thus seem to be that massive unemployment rather than hyperinflation is the serious threat to democratic institutions.[20]

None of this is to deny that hyperinflation is normally followed by the collapse of the regime under which it occurred. In this respect, the Weimar case is an exception. But the explanation is that the hyperinflation is one of the most dramatic signs of the government's failure. Hyperinflation typically occurs when government, because of war, revolution, the antagonism of powerful groups in the society, or the incapacity of its own administrative apparatus, is unable to collect sufficient taxes to finance its expenditures and therefore resorts to the printing press. It thereby buys a year or two of time, but it would be quite misleading to say that the hyperinflation led to its eventual downfall.[21]

The difficulty is one that bedevils much analysis in social science, namely, that of impossible counterfactuals. Roughly speaking, to say that A caused B is to say that, if everything else had been the same except that A had not occurred, B would not have happened either.[22] In many instances it makes perfectly good sense to pose questions about politics in those terms. For example, "Would Nixon have completed his term of office if the Watergate break-in had not been discovered?" The question can properly be posed because the possibility that the "plumbers" might have been less sloppy or the guards less vigilant is not inconsistent with the way the world works. But questions about the effects of large-scale social phenomena are liable to run into trouble.

John Stuart Mill set this point out in the course of his argument that the methods of agreement and difference are inapplicable to social phenomena.[23] His example—the effect of a protective tariff on a country's

---

20. For recognition that the collapse of Weimar followed on unemployment, but an argument that inflation had already eroded its democratic center, see Brian Griffiths, *Inflation: The Price of Prosperity* (Holmes and Meier, 1976), p. 177.

21. For an analysis on these lines of the Indonesian hyperinflation of 1965–66 (in which President Sukarno lost power), see Dudley Jackson, H. A. Turner, and Frank Wilkinson, *Do Trade Unions Cause Inflation?* (Cambridge University Press, 1972), pp. 52–54.

22. See J. L. Mackie, *The Cement of the Universe: A Study of Causation* (Oxford University Press, 1974), pp. 29–58.

23. *A System of Logic: Ratiocinative and Inductive* (University of Toronto Press, 1974), bk. 6, chap. 7. Most social scientists whom I have polled informally have the impression that Mill *advocated* the use

prosperity—is precisely the kind of association between two macro-level variables that is involved in the question about the relation between inflation and regime collapse. "Two nations which agreed in everything except their commercial policy would agree also in that. Differences of legislation are . . . effects of pre-existing causes."[24] Similarly, it does not in general make sense to ask what would have happened if everything else had been the same in a country except the inflation rate.[25]

Especially in Latin America, as Albert Hirschman points out in chapter 3, above, inflation has been widely understood as a way of accommodating conflict by displacing an explicit zero-sum conflict over the distribution of the social product into a more loosely structured scramble for competitive advantage. Of course, at some point (which has been suggested to lie at an inflation rate of about 50 percent per annum) "demands develop for drastic government action,"[26] and one consequence may well be the fall of the regime and its replacement by a more repressive one, either as a prelude to stabilization or as a reaction to the unpopularity of the government's efforts at stabilization. None of this entails the view— which members of the monetarist school are fond of attributing to others—that inflation is "caused" by conflict, as if the supply of money had nothing to do with it. To be sure, though, inflation may be a response to conflict —including in this a response by the monetary authorities.

From Interests to Preferences

It has so far been proposed that there is no objective basis for the scaremongering of those who would like to use inflation as the occasion for removing economic policymaking from the province of ordinary politics. It might be argued, however, that inflation is so unpopular with the public that the institutions of democracy must therefore have been failing in periods of high inflation. The notion that democratic institutions

---

of these methods in the social sciences! One eminent political scientist has cited "the influence of J. S. Mill's *Logic*" as one of the main reasons why "the comparative observation of unmanipulated cases could ever have come to be regarded as any sort of equivalent of experimental method in the physical sciences." Harry Eckstein, "Case Study and Theory in Political Science," in Fred I. Greenstein and Nelson W. Polsby, eds., *Handbook of Political Science*, vol. 7: *Strategies of Inquiry* (Reading, Mass.: Addison-Wesley, 1975), p. 117.

24. Mill, *Logic*, bk. 6, chap. 7, p. 882.

25. For a sophisticated contemporary treatment of counterfactuals, see Jon Elster, *Logic and Society: Contradictions and Possible Worlds* (Wiley, 1978), chap. 6. I have criticized some aspects of Elster's treatment in Brian Barry, "Superfox," *Political Studies*, vol. 28 (March 1980), pp. 136–43.

26. Jackson, Turner, and Wilkinson, *Do Trade Unions Cause Inflation?* p. 35.

are justified because they are the most efficient way of ensuring that there is some match between the policy preferences of the citizens and the policy outputs of government naturally appeals to market-oriented economists because it parallels the standard defense of a market economy.[27] The concept of consumer sovereignty—originally imported from the political vocabulary to suggest that consumers, merely by choosing how to spend their money, "control" producers—has been reimported into politics, to suggest that voters "control" elected representatives merely by deciding how to dispose their votes. In the process the concept of sovereignty in politics loses its original meaning of the power to give authoritative commands.

On the basis of the theory that political systems are to be judged by the extent to which they produce policy outcomes corresponding to the preferences of voters (ignoring the question how those preferences are to be aggregated), democratic institutions can be condemned if politicians adopt policies that bring about inflation despite its unpopularity. That opens the way for proposals to limit the fiscal and monetary discretion of elected governments so as to ensure that the citizens get the outcomes that they really want. Requirements of a balanced budget or of a fixed (and small) rate of increase in the money supply can prevent politicians from getting between the people and the outcomes they wish to have brought about. "Just as an alcoholic might embrace Alcoholics Anonymous, so might a nation drunk on deficits and gorged with government embrace a balanced budget and monetary stability."[28]

But is inflation so unpopular that its existence can be taken as evidence for the failure of democratic institutions to work as they should? Buchanan and Wagner wonder how the "ordinary democratic process" can seemingly produce "a regime of continuous and mounting deficits, with subsequent inflation, along with a bloated public sector [that] can scarcely be judged beneficial to anyone. . . . Where is the institutional breakdown?"[29] This blithely assumes that the size of the deficit, of the public sector, and of the rate of inflation are too large by "social choice" standards. Is this true? It is noteworthy that the bulk of the big increase in government

27. Arrow, *Social Choice and Individual Values*, p. 5, says that "voting and the market mechanism" can both be regarded as "special cases of the more general category of collective social choice."

28. Buchanan and Wagner, *Democracy in Deficit*, p. 159. This sample of their rhetoric is by no means atypical.

29. Ibid., p. 94. It is a consequence of the antique logical positivist faith that Buchanan is committed officially to the view that no "value judgment" can be made about any change unless everyone stands to benefit from it, or at any rate some benefit and none lose.

expenditures in the 1970s was accounted for by transfer payments rather than the government's spending a larger share of the gross national product on collective goods like defense, roads, and other public services.[30] Since transfer payments simply place spending money in the hands of different people from those who had it before tax (including social security contributions here as a tax), it may be presumed that those who receive such payments do not object, nor do those who would otherwise have to care for them or those who regard such transfers as just or as socially and politically stabilizing.

Collective expenditures raise more difficult questions. I believe that most people would find it very difficult to estimate the value to them of collective expenditures, still less of alternatives departing widely from the status quo.[31] It is conceivable (as Buchanan and Wagner apparently believe) that, in a fully informed judgment, most people would conclude that they are getting more public provision than they would be willing to pay for. But that could hardly be the case for the United States, where the lack of collective expenditure on the amenities of civilized life is painfully apparent. It would certainly be rash to assert dogmatically that the size of the U.S. budget constitutes evidence for the failure of the democratic process to give people what they want. Of course people dislike paying taxes, but they also (as the tax-cutting enthusiasts often complain) value the services the government provides.

Some people believe that if "waste" were eliminated from public expenditures, the same services could be provided with less taxation. But by the standards according to which public authorities waste billions, private consumers waste hundreds of billions. If a public authority builds a facility costing ten million dollars that turns out to be unnecessary or spends ten million dollars more than the minimum to do the job, that is excoriated as waste; if a million people spend ten dollars on dud appliances or spend ten more dollars than they needed to spend to achieve the same

30. Old age and other insurance plus public welfare payments in the United States rose from $15.3 billion (10 percent of total governmental expenditures) in 1960 to $70.5 billion (18 percent) in 1972; Michel Crozier, Samuel P. Huntington, and Joji Watanuki, *The Crisis of Democracy* (New York University Press for the Trilateral Commission, 1975), table 2, p. 69. Huntington, in ibid., pp. 71–72, notes that these transfer payments are popular with the public, which seems to cast direct doubt on the Buchanan and Wagner conspiracy theory of public expenditure. For the United Kingdom, see James Alt and Alec Chrystal, "Endogenous Government Behaviour: Overture to a Study of Public Expenditure," Discussion Paper 108 (University of Essex, Department of Economics, December 1977).

31. This makes implausible the contention of Albert Breton that political discontent occurs when people are failing to get (in their own estimation) value for money from their taxes; *The Economic Theory of Representative Government* (London: Macmillan, 1974), pp. 71–73.

end equally effectively, that is regarded as a normal incident of a market society. Of course, it may be possible for either governments or individual consumers to do better, but campaigning against "waste in government" should be recognized for what it is—campaigning against government.

The assertion that inflation "can hardly be judged beneficial to anyone" is extraordinarily implausible. To the extent that inflation is purely redistributive, there are (by definition) net gainers as well as net losers. To the extent that it has effects that do not cancel out in this way, the news is still not all bad. Against the "welfare loss" arising from people keeping smaller cash balances than they would like and the "cost" attributable to uncertainty about the future price level must be set the losses of real income and employment created by attempts to reduce inflation by the use of monetary or fiscal policy.

It may nevertheless be said that, beneficial or harmful, inflation is provably unpopular and that this is enough to condemn democratic institutions for failing to deliver the outcomes that are desired by citizens. But how exactly are the preferences of ordinary citizens for economic outcomes established? When answers to public opinion poll questions are accepted as evidence that inflation is the country's number one problem, what does that actually mean? It ought to mean that people dislike increases in the price level. But do most people have such a clear grasp of economic concepts as this requires? Such studies of popular under-standing of economic terms as have been made suggest that it would be rash to assume so. People often have a hazy idea that, in the absence of inflation, they would have been able to have their latest pay increase and keep its purchasing power through the whole of the subsequent year. Thus, a 10 percent inflation is looked on as equivalent to a 10 percent loss of real income. In endorsing the absence (or reduction) of inflation, they are opting for a state of affairs in which nominal incomes would have gone up but prices would not have risen at all or at any rate as fast as they actually had done.

The deliberate confusion of inflation with a corresponding loss of real income is pervasive. For instance, Michael Blumenthal, less than a week before his dismissal as treasury secretary, was reported to have said that inflation had "cut sharply into workers' real incomes" and to have warned that "workers should not try to make up for their loss in income because that would only result in higher prices and worse inflation."[32] Obviously,

---

32. *New York Times,* July 14, 1979.

if inflation were a gratuitous deduction from an otherwise attainable level of real income, it would be perfectly reasonable to respond by restoring the level of real income. But why should it be assumed that increases in nominal incomes would be wiped out in real terms by price increases if it makes sense to imagine that workers could have had their present money incomes *without* inflation?

Blumenthal's successor, G. William Miller (while he was chairman of the Federal Reserve Board) had similarly beclouded the relation between inflation and real income. " 'What is the social benefit for programs that are well meaning but wreck the wealth and incomes of all Americans,' Miller asked. 'An 8 percent inflation is a $160 billion tax.' "[33]

Another, more indirect way of estimating public opinion about inflation is to correlate changes in voting intentions or in support for incumbents with changes in economic indicators, as Douglas Hibbs does in chapter 7. The rates of inflation, unemployment, and change in real income (the usual aggregate indicators used in regression equations) are not, however, brute facts of experience but are mediated by newspaper and television reporting. Even inflation is an abstraction from the movements of all prices. In the absence of standard indexes, people might be aware over time of a trend in prices, but they could no more say whether the inflation rate was 5 percent or 10 percent than most people could say whether the outside temperature is 85 or 90 degrees without looking at a thermometer. Until Stanley Jevons constructed the first index,[34] nobody had apparently noticed that the rises in some prices and falls in others between 1845 and 1862 in England had not balanced out but amounted to an inflationary trend. Aggregate unemployment rates and changes in real income in a society are, obviously, even less plausibly regarded as immediate data of experience.

Scholars who analyze public opinion are well aware that the popularity of incumbents depends on more than the state of the economy. They attempt to remove disturbing factors by introducing dummy variables such as "Watergate." But when all the major changes in public opinion over a period are "explained" by political events involving the actions of incumbents or their opponents, one may wonder how much faith to have

33. Patrick R. Oster, *Chicago Sun-Times*, November 21, 1978. The notion of the whole loss of purchasing power of a given nominal income as an inflationary "tax" is, of course, to be distinguished from the more sophisticated idea of inflation as a tax on cash balances.

34. W. Stanley Jevons, *A Serious Fall in the Value of Gold Ascertained, and Its Social Effects Set Forth* (London: Edward Stanford, 1863), cited in *The Collected Writings of John Maynard Keynes*, vol. 10: *Essays in Biography* (London: Macmillan, 1972), pp. 119–22.

in assurances that the residual changes should be laid to the account of the economy. And precise claims about the way in which, say, 1 percent more inflation changes government support, other things being equal, should be viewed cautiously. They never are equal, and that is just what creates the measurement problem in the first place.

Furthermore, there is no reason for expecting that the state of the aggregate economic variables will have a fixed relation to the popularity of incumbents. Even if there is no change in the pleasantness or unpleasantness of a particular mix of those variables in people's minds, there may be a change in the degree to which they hold the government responsible for that mix. A government may improve its standing in the polls either by improving the state of the economy or by convincing people that it is doing as well as can be expected. Hence, for example, the (not wholly unreasonable) efforts of successive administrations to attribute much of the responsibility for the stagflations of 1973–74 and 1979–80 to the Organization of Petroleum Exporting Countries (OPEC). People may (as seems to have happened in Britain) continue to give a fair degree of support to governments that have presided over varying combinations of high inflation, high unemployment, and declining real income that would earlier have been a guarantee of political suicide, not because they like it but because most of the time they despair of any other government doing any better.[35]

This again, however, raises the question why politicians persist in making inflation more of a bogey than it deserves to be. If the alternative to doing better is to make people feel that what you are doing already isn't so bad, why pile on the agony in this gratuitous way? My answer is, admittedly, speculative.

There are three ways in which governments can seek to control inflation in an economy where the key economic decisions remain in private hands. The first is to deflate the economy enough that economic activity will decline to a point at which people will be glad to take jobs at any rate of pay, and prices will begin to fall. A second route, explored by Colin Crouch in chapter 5, is through neocorporatism or, more prosaically, tripartite agreement between business, labor, and government. In the United States particularly there is an obvious problem of ideological incompatibility between this kind of high-level fix and the ethos of antitrust, business unionism, and limited government. But there is also a simple problem of feasibility. The institutions do not exist; no organization

---

35. See Alt and Chrystal, "Endogenous Government Behaviour."

can speak for all workers or all employers and deliver on any deal that is struck. The roots of societal collaboration in countries such as Austria and the Netherlands go back centuries; such understandings and practices cannot be wished into existence. Moreover, it may not be an accident that the examples of successful neocorporatism are all countries with only a few million inhabitants. Perhaps the sheer size and diversity of the United States (or even Britain) rule out corporatist solutions.

The only remaining path is exhortation, and it is not therefore surprising that this is the chosen instrument of governments whose concern for popularity (or even governability) leads them to eschew the first course and whose ideological commitments or practical necessities rule out the second. But exhortation requires that the evils of inflation be painted so dramatically that people will voluntarily take less than the market will bear out of deference to the anti-inflation guidelines. Since inflation is not really evil enough to lead a rational person to pass up the chance of making a buck, creative confusion steps in to fill the gap.

To summarize, I do not believe it is realistic to hope for very exact guidance about public attitudes to inflation. But even if there were agreement that inflation *is* unpopular, does it really follow that the institutions of democracy have been failing to work as they should? I do not believe so. There has, of course, been inflation (at widely differing rates) in all the economically advanced democracies. And governments have taken harsh contractionist measures in the hopes of reducing the rate of inflation in their societies, measures that inevitably have adverse effects on employment and real income. Assuming that people care about unemployment and loss of real income as well as inflation, have governments, in general, been too lax about fighting inflation, taking as a criterion the preferences of the public? I can see no reason for thinking that, given the choices, politicians opt for more inflation than their constituents, if they understood the choices, would opt for. My own suspicion is the reverse. I cannot prove it. But I maintain that the whole presumption that underlay the economists' criticism that democracy produces more inflation than the citizens want has rested on extremely shaky foundations.

The "New Political Economy"

Economists have attempted to shore up these foundations with models of electoral behavior. But their premises, too, deserve careful scrutiny. In fact, there is not just a single theory of the effects of electoral competition on the rate of inflation, but a family of models that share certain basic features. At the core of their economic component is the idea, whose essentials can be traced back to David Hume's essay "Of Money," that an increase in the quantity of money has an initial effect of raising the level of economic activity and only later dissipates itself in a general rise in prices. At first the extra money will be used to buy and sell more at the old prices, and only later will the shortfall of supply drive prices up. "It is easy to trace the money in its progress through the whole commonwealth; where we shall find, that it must first quicken the diligence of every individual, before it increases the price of labour."[36] In modern terms, people act on expectations about future prices that are doomed to be disappointed, and it is the mismatch that makes for the increase in activity.[37] It follows, then, that the more sluggish the response of inflationary expectations to the actual experience of inflation, the more a government can stimulate the economy in a certain period (for example, in the run-up to an election) without the bulk of the inflationary effects showing until a later period.

The same analysis can be expressed using the device of the Phillips curve, a curve relating the inflation rate (on the vertical axis) and the level of unemployment (on the horizontal axis). The original Phillips curve was plotted from the observed levels of change in money wage rates against unemployment in the United Kingdom from 1861 through 1957.[38] Since the points fell on a single curve, the implication was that to every level of unemployment corresponded a unique level of increase in money wage rates, and it was hypothesized that this relationship might be accounted for by labor market conditions—the tighter the labor market, the more wages go up.[39] On the view underlying the theory of the politicoeconomic cycle, however, this idea of a single curve must be abandoned for a pair of short-run and long-run Phillips curves. In the short run, a given increase in employment is associated with a smaller increase in wages (or prices) than in the long run, so the short-run Phillips curve has a flatter slope than the long-term one. Thus, in figure 10-1, if

36. David Hume, *Essays: Moral, Political and Literary* (London: Oxford University Press, 1963), p. 294.
37. See the strikingly Humean formulation of the "new macroeconomics" in D. E. W. Laidler, *Essays on Money and Inflation* (University of Chicago Press, 1975), pp. 9–10.
38. A. W. Phillips, "The Relation between Unemployment and the Rate of Change of Money Wage Rates in the United Kingom, 1861–1957," *Economica*, vol. 25 (November 1958), pp. 283–99.
39. Richard G. Lipsey, "The Relation between Unemployment and the Rate of Change of Money Wage Rates in the United Kingdom, 1862–1957: A Further Analysis," *Economica*, vol. 27 (February 1960), pp. 1–31.

Figure 10-1. *Short-run and Long-run Phillips Curves Relating*
Inflation to Unemployment

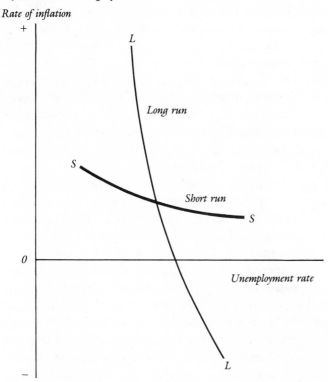

the economy is at the point where the two curves intersect, the shape of
the curves implies that the government could reduce unemployment in
the short run (by moving the economy leftward along the curve *SS*) at a
lower cost in inflation than could be sustained in the long run. Any point
below and to the left of the long-run curve *LL* designates a combination
of inflation and unemployment that is better than can be achieved in
long-run equilibrium, when expectations have had a chance to adjust fully
and behavior is in accord with those expectations.

Conversely, of course, the shapes of the curves also imply that a
government wishing to reduce inflation must accept a move to the right
along the short-run curve *SS* until expectations have adjusted to the new
conditions. Since this means moving to a point above and to the right of
the long-run curve, the analysis implies that the economy will in the short

term have a worse combination of inflation and unemployment than could be maintained indefinitely once the economy had settled down. Short-run behavior, in short, favors reduction of unemployment.

Since the long-run curve is a theoretical entity, its shape is subject to theoretical arguments. Modern monetarists suggest that it must be vertical, because at any level of unemployment except one (the "natural rate" for that economy) the rate of inflation will (in the long run) tend to go up or down. Any stable inflation rate is compatible with the same unemployment rate. The actual rate of inflation itself will be a function of the rate at which the money supply increases in relation to the real national income. While the deduction is logically impeccable, it says nothing about the world. Maybe this "long run" is never reached; that would mean, for instance, that it is never true that all contracts could be negotiated in such a way as to cancel out the rate of inflation. Even if the long run does exist, it may be measured in decades or even centuries. I therefore follow the convention of making the long-run curve steep but not vertical.

Economists who venture into formal analysis of the political system tend to assume that politicians are conscienceless seekers of power, those in office being prepared to inflict any amount of damage on their countries in order to increase, however fractionally, their share of the vote. At the same time, politicians are assumed (for the purpose of model-building) to be consummately skillful at manipulating the levers of economic policy in pursuit of the end of reelection. Voters, by contrast, are assumed to have barely any cognitive or ratiocinative capacities. They are hardly able to remember the economic record of the current government when election time comes round and have no ability to anticipate the future (or if they do then somehow this anticipation does not affect their actions). These zombies react (within the limits set by their defective memories) to past experience of inflation and unemployment rates with approval or disapproval, and also perhaps to the direction in which those rates are changing, but they do not attempt to make any estimates of their future course and respond to these.

If these are the premises, it is hardly surprising that the conclusion turns out to be that democracy is a flawed form of government. What could anyone hope for from a system characterized by a collection of rogues competing for the favors of a larger collection of dupes? Characteristically, the premises of politicoeconomic models developed by economists are baldly stated, with little discussion of their plausibility.[40] And

40. "Once it is recognized that macroeconomic policy is made by self-interested, not disinterested or other-interested politicians, a new perspective on macroeconomic policy appears, particularly if

only anecdotal evidence at best is normally adduced in support of the conclusions. Yet for no democratic country do the economists' assumptions appear to approximate the truth. Studies of national-level politicians in democratic countries suggest that they are motivated either by policy concerns or service of a personal kind to their constituents.[41] These "satisfactions of office" are derived from doing something with the office that is thought to be worthwhile. Moreover, political leaders are very often highly motivated by the thought of their reputations in history and may well be unwilling to pay a price of ignominy for doing something with predictably bad consequences in order to secure some short-run electoral gain. Even Richard Nixon, by risking further obloquy in his subsequent attempts to justify himself, illustrates the importance of reputation to politicians.

Voting studies suggest that voters try to decide which candidates would do better on the issues that they care most about and tend to vote according to the answers they come up with.[42] They also try to form estimates of the competence of alternative candidates, something way beyond the picture of voters merely responding to the "goodness or badness of the times" by voting for the ins or the outs.[43] If voters sometimes find it hard to make clear judgments about policy differences between candidates, this may reflect the reluctance of politicians to go beyond generalities. When politicians differentiate themselves clearly on an issue, the evidence suggests that voters are usually aware of it.[44]

There is no lack of evidence that voters give more weight to the more recent performance of the economy, but if they are trying to decide whether to entrust the government with another term of office, that does not seem an unreasonable thing to do. After all, for a year or even two, a government can with some legitimacy blame troubles on its predecessor, but the longer it has been in office, the better the case for judging its priorities and capabilities on the current state of the economy. Pessimistic

---

politicians believe that economic conditions can affect their survival prospects." Wagner, "Economic Manipulation," pp. 396–97. (Note: *recognized* rather than *postulated*.)

41. See Robert D. Putnam, *The Beliefs of Politicians: Ideology, Conflict, and Democracy in Britain and Italy* (Yale University Press, 1973).

42. See V. O. Key, *The Responsible Electorate: Rationality in Presidential Voting, 1936–1960* (Harvard University Press, 1966); Samuel Popkin and others, "Comment: What Have You Done for Me Lately?" *American Political Science Review,* vol. 70 (September 1976), pp. 779–805.

43. Popkin and others, "Comment," show convincingly how much George McGovern was hurt in the 1972 presidential campaign by perceptions of lack of competence following the Eagleton affair.

44. See Benjamin I. Page, *Choices and Echoes in Presidential Elections: Rational Man and Electoral Democracy* (University of Chicago Press, 1978).

analyses of democratic political economy imply that a government might find it advantageous to stage a massive deflation in its first two years if it could get the unemployment rate down again and combine it with a lower rate of inflation by election day. But I think that kind of gratuitous deflation would be remembered because it would be important information about the way the government worked. The Republicans, to give the most obvious example, were distrusted by many people for a whole generation because of what 1929–32 was taken to have told about their complacency in the face of mass unemployment.

The Political Business Cycle

The basic idea of the political business cycle can be explained using the apparatus of short-run and long-run Phillips curves. Figure 10-2 illustrates the characteristic clockwise loop that the theory seeks to explain. Starting at A, the government brings about a preelection boom, moving the economy along the short-run curve S_1S_1 to B. As expectations adapt, this favorable combination of unemployment and inflation cannot be maintained and both deteriorate (presumably after the election) to C. But suppose that C is too high in inflation to be popular electorally. The government therefore wishes to bring down the rate of inflation, which it can do only by moving the economy along the short-run curve S_2S_2 to D. This brings the economy back onto the long-run curve at A, but of course if there is time before the next election to stage a boom, it will be possible to get to B for it (assuming the intervening experience has not changed the shape of the short-run curve—an important proviso), and so the cycle is set off again.[45]

In principle the political business cycle thus generated could occur even if the voters based their decisions at election time on the experience of the whole period since the previous election, equally weighted. The driving mechanism is the possibility of producing an advantageous combination of inflation and unemployment before the election and the assumption that the long-run rate of inflation arising after the election is unpopular. However, it is clear that the motivation for government to engage in the kind of behavior depicted is enhanced if the voters discount the early years in office when judging the government's economic performance.

---

45. Compare Nordhaus, "Political Business Cycle"; Lindbeck, "Stabilization Policy"; MacRae, "Political Model"; Bruno S. Frey, *Modern Political Economy* (Wiley, 1978).

Figure 10-2. *Short-run and Long-run Phillips Curves and the Clockwise Loop of the Political Business Cycle*[a]

Rate of inflation

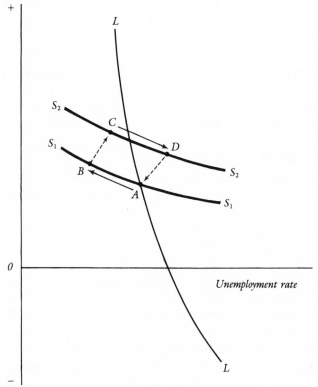

a. Solid arrows represent moves along the short-run Phillips curve brought about by government policy decisions; dashed arrows represent subsequent adjustments in the economy that shift it from one short-run Phillips curve to another.

For then the high unemployment of stage *D*, an "investment" in getting lower on the long-run curve, carries a reduced electoral penalty.

The simplest test of the notion that a political business cycle is endemic in democracies is to see whether the rates of inflation and unemployment correspond with the predictions of the model. The unemployment rate would be expected to increase as soon after an election as the government could get its policy instruments to work, and then to decline as the next election approached. Inflation is more difficult to predict; because the new government inherits inflationary pressures, the rate of inflation would increase to begin with, then decline, tapering off or even reversing itself as the election approaches.

Actual tests are a good deal cruder than this. One method compares a period before the election (one month, one year, two years, or half the interelection period, for example) with the rest of the time since the preceding election to learn whether the trend was rising or falling. Bruno Frey has checked out the hypothesis that unemployment rates are lower on the average in the two years preceding general elections in Britain and presidential elections in the United States than the rest of the time. Assuming, as Frey and Nordhaus do, that unemployment can be increased quickly after an election and will then decline steadily, the path of unemployment should be saw-toothed, and the average level in the first half of an interelection period higher than in the second.[46] Frey concludes that for Britain the reverse tended to be true if anything from the mid-1950s to the mid-1970s, while for the United States the evidence points in no particular direction. Frey also tested the hypothesis that inflation will be higher in the two years preceding an election than in the rest of the interelectoral period and found it disconfirmed.[47] However, because of the lagged relationship between unemployment and inflation that underlies the theory (and that Frey posits), it is doubtful that one should expect otherwise.

Edward Tufte claims better success with trends rather than averages of U.S. unemployment from 1948 to 1976, except in the period of the Eisenhower presidency. He claims that, excluding the 1956 and 1960 elections, unemployment was lower in November of each election year than for most of the preceding twenty-four months—results he describes as "phenomenal."[48] But during the whole of the eight years of the Democratic administrations of Kennedy and Johnson, there is no sign of any cycle—unemployment fell almost continuously month by month. The Nixon-Ford record Tufte himself describes as "mixed," which leaves only the Truman administration of 1948–52 and the Nixon "game plan" of 1968–72, both of which do show the rise and then fall in unemployment. Looking at the unemployment chart armed only with the theory of the political business cycle, it would be very hard to guess where the elections came.

William Nordhaus has tested the proposition that unemployment has a rising trend for the first half of the interelection period and a falling trend for the second half against postwar data for nine countries in which

46. See Frey, *Modern Political Economy*, p. 131; Nordhaus, "Political Business Cycle," p. 185.
47. Frey, *Modern Political Economy*, pp. 133, 134, 135, 136.
48. Edward R. Tufte, *Political Control of the Economy* (Princeton University Press, 1978), p. 21.

"a cursory examination of macro-economic policies pointed to the possibility that the three conditions for the political business cycle would be met." His conditions were "that the government be chosen in periodic competitive elections," that it "have sufficient economic control and sophistication to move the economy in the desired direction," and that voters should evaluate governments purely on the basis of the performance of the economy since the previous election. But Nordhaus was able to claim only three countries in which "the coincidence of business and political cycles is very marked," namely, the Federal Republic of Germany, New Zealand, and the United States.[49] (The other countries tested were Australia, Canada, France, Japan, Sweden, and the United Kingdom.)

Even then, his conclusions have to be treated with caution, for he misleadingly excludes results that do not negate his theory even if they do not confirm it. Nordhaus gives for each country the numbers of times the trend was downward in the second half of the interelection period (confirming the theory) and upward (disconfirming the theory) and the numbers of times in the first half the overall trend was upward (confirming the theory) and downward (disconfirming the theory). But the numbers fall far short of the number of postwar elections for some countries. The missing cases are presumably those where the unemployment rate was the same throughout or where it went both up and down in the period. But if the theory of the political business cycle predicts a rising unemployment rate and the unemployment rate does not rise, that is a negative result for the theory.

To see that this makes a difference, take the two countries where Nordhaus claims to have found "some modest indications of a political cycle," France and Sweden.[50] For France, Nordhaus claims six hits and three misses. But the nine periods add up at most to eighteen of the twenty-six years covered by his study. Thus the confirmatory experiences total at best only twelve of the twenty-six years—hardly a robust demonstration. In the case of Sweden, Nordhaus counts seven hits and five misses, and even this slender margin of success would disappear if the omitted periods were added and counted as failures for the theory.

A deeper problem is the role of caprice in deciding whether to count a set of twenty-four monthly unemployment figures as an upward trend or a downward trend or neither. Thus, in the 1946–72 period in the

---

49. "Political Business Cycle," pp. 185, 186.
50. Ibid., p. 186.

United States, Nordhaus counts 1954–56 as a success for the theory whereas Tufte does not, while Tufte counts 1960–62 and 1966–68 as successes but Nordhaus does not. Both count 1948–52 as a success, but the two-year period following the 1948 election shows a fairly symmetrical rise and fall back to the election-day level, so it hardly represents a rising trend. At any rate, it does not fit Nordhaus's hypothesis of a trend over the two years. Tufte gives unemployment as "rising" in the two years after the 1960 election, on the basis of an infinitesimal increase in the few months after the election followed by a substantial drop sustained through the whole of the second year, whereas in 1972 a fall in unemployment extending over almost a year after the election followed by a substantial rise is also described as "rising."

In another study Tufte purports to show that in twenty-seven democracies (some with rather dubious credentials), there were nineteen in which "short-run accelerations in real disposable income per capita were more likely to occur in election years than in years without elections"[51] between 1961 and 1972. However, a number of the differences appear trivial. For example, in Belgium and also in Ireland real disposable income is shown as having increased in 67 percent of election years and 63 percent of nonelection years—in both countries, two out of three election years and five out of eight nonelection years. Five-eighths represents the closest it is possible to come to two-thirds.

It does look as if there is a political-economic cycle for about half the countries. However, this is a cycle in real disposable income and not necessarily in the overall level of economic activity. It could be consistent with a uniform level of unemployment and economic growth if governments tended to raise taxes early in their term, start building roads, schools, and so forth, in time to have something to show by the next election, and tried to reduce taxes or give out increased cash benefits in their final year. The cycle would then be one of public as against private consumption.

That the two phenomena are different is suggested by the fact that Nordhaus concluded that "for the entire period a political cycle seems to be implausible as a description for Australia, Canada, Japan and the U.K.," whereas these four countries are among the most striking examples of the disposable real income cycle, the ratio of percentage increases in election years to those in nonelection years being, respectively, 75:29, 100:57,

51. *Political Control*, p. 11.

100:29, and 67:38. Conversely, West Germany, one of Nordhaus's three cases of a "marked" cycle, does not have a disposable real income cycle; disposable real income is shown as increasing in a slightly smaller proportion of election years than of nonelection years.[52] Similarly, Tufte cites a study of the Philippines describing the economy as moving in a "biennial lurch," with real income rising and falling within the electoral cycle;[53] yet the Philippines are shown in his table as not having increases of real disposable income more frequently in election years.

The Tufte data on changes in real disposable income are, therefore, suggestive in their own right but do not do anything to add to the limited support that the Nordhaus evidence provides for the theory of the political business cycle.

Politicoeconomic Models of Inflation

The theory of the political business cycle leads to the conclusion that inflation and unemployment should both rise immediately after an election, to be followed by a period of high unemployment accompanied by a falling inflation rate, and then a period of falling unemployment extending to the next election accompanied by a rate of inflation that, whether continuing to fall or starting to rise again at the end, is lower than could be combined with that rate of unemployment in the long run. No country shows this complex sequence more than occasionally, which is hardly surprising in view of the exogenous shocks to which an economy is subject. Apparently only a few show even disjointed bits of it.

Even if the theory were better supported than it is, however, it would do nothing to suggest that democracy has any built-in tendency to produce inflation. The rate of inflation, according to the theory, will fluctuate within the electoral cycle, but that is not to say either that it will fluctuate around a rising trend or, if around some constant level, whether that level will be high rather than low. The most natural expectation, assuming that vote-maximizing governments manipulate the economy for their own purposes, might seem to be that the rate will fluctuate around the level corresponding to the point on the long-run Phillips curve that is most popular with the electorate. And the clockwise loop described by the economy would cycle around that point.

52. Nordhaus, "Political Business Cycle," p. 186; Tufte, *Political Control,* p. 12.
53. Tufte, *Political Control,* pp. 13–14.

Figure 10-3. *Vote-Gathering Configurations of Inflation
and Unemployment Rates on the Long-run Phillips Curve*

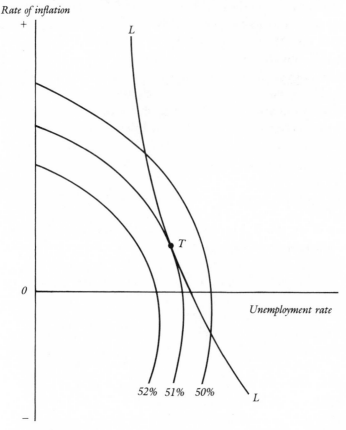

The combinations of inflation and unemployment that might gain,
respectively, 50, 51, and 52 percent of votes are depicted in figure 10-3.
On the assumption that inflation and unemployment are both disliked,
these isopsephic curves slope down to the right;[54] the further they are
from the origin, the smaller the share of the popular vote the government
will garner if it comes up to an election with the economy in that state.
The best point on the long-run Phillips curve for the government to pick
is that tangent to the highest attainable isopsephic curve—in figure 10-3
the point *T*, which gives the government 51 percent of the vote. Thus

54. I call these *isopsephic* curves rather than using the customary but barbarous term, *isovote* curves.

the rate of inflation will depend on the shapes of the Phillips and the isopsephic curves. Other things being equal, the steeper the Phillips curve the lower the inflation rate that will be chosen by a vote-maximizing government. (If the long-run Phillips curve is vertical, as monetarists claim, the most popular position attainable will be one with stable prices, assuming that isopsephic curves bend back at zero inflation—that is, if voters ask that unemployment falls if prices fall as well as rise). And, other things being equal, the steeper the slope of the isopsephic curves the higher the rate of inflation that will maximize votes. For a steep slope would mean that the voters were relatively tolerant of inflation as compared with unemployment.

The conclusion to be drawn is that voters get the rate of inflation that has the most support and that it is not necessarily high or low. And though they might prefer to do without the occasional clockwise loops of the electoral cycle, there is no evidence that the welfare losses from the part of the cycle that lies above and to the right of the long-run Phillips curve outweigh the gains from the part that lies below and to the left of it.[55] In any case, adding the political business cycle would not raise the average level of inflation or cause it to increase over time without limit. Yet economists and journalists and other commentators on current events frequently suggest that the level of inflation produced by electoral competition tends to be higher than most people want or indeed that there is some inexorable process tending to make the rate of inflation go up over time.

The Nordhaus Model

Critics, it is apparent, are often expressing disapproval for what voters allegedly want (supposedly, higher inflation) rather than solicitude for their failing to get what they want. Nonetheless, William Nordhaus has sought to make a narrower case—namely, that vote-maximizing among a myopic electorate brings about an inflation rate higher than the amount that would get the biggest majority out of all points on the long-run Phillips curve. He has tried, unsuccessfully, I believe, to formalize the idea that vote-maximizing by governments produces a level of inflation

---

55. Lindbeck, "Stabilization Policy," p. 13, says that "the experiences of recent years have shown how high the economic and social costs are during this deflationary phase of the policy cycle," but he does not mention in the same breath the gains from the good part of the cycle.

Figure 10-4. *Nordhaus Model of Vote-Maximizing Governments' Effect on Inflation*

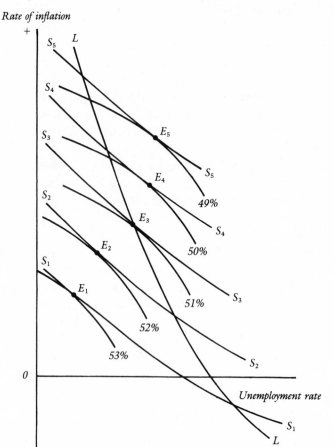

Rate of inflation

Source: William D. Nordhaus, "The Political Business Cycle," *Review of Economic Studies,* vol. 42 (April 1975), fig. 4, p. 179.

that is higher than the most popular rate.[56] His model supposes that, if the economy is on the short-run Phillips curve S_1S_1 after an election, the government picks the point E_1 on the curve that is at a tangent with the 53 percent isopsephic curve (figure 10-4). However, it cannot in fact keep the economy at any point that lies off the long-run Phillips curve, which is by definition the series of points at which any particular mix of

56. "Political Business Cycle."

unemployment and inflation can remain constant. By the time of the next election, therefore, the position will have deteriorated so that the short-run Phillips curve S_2S_2 applies. The new government will do the best it can electorally, again on the assumption that it cannot shift the short-run curve before the next election, so it will pick the point E_2. Since this too is off the long-run Phillips curve, it cannot be maintained for an extended period either, so the economy will slip to the short-run Phillips curve S_3S_3 by the next election. The point of tangency with the highest attainable isopsephic curve, E_3, now lies on the long-run Phillips curve. And the story stops there, for no government can do better than pick E_3—provided the relations between the macroeconomic variables remain the same. A government, however, can be too pessimistic as well as oversanguine. If an election is held at a time when the short-run curve S_5S_5 applies, the government will pick E_5, and be pleasantly surprised by the move to S_4S_4 and move to E_4 and thence to the improved curve S_3S_3 and point E_3.

Nordhaus also views the long-run equilibrium point E_3 as the solution to a problem in collective choice, the purely myopic point U_M (figure 10-5). It is the point that would be chosen by the biggest majority if the future were wholly discounted. If the future were not discounted at all, the point that would gain the biggest majority *on the average* over an indefinitely long period would be U_G, where the isopsephic curve V_2V_2 is at a tangent to the long-run Phillips curve. For, over a long enough period, the cost of getting to that point becomes relatively insignificant. Somewhere between U_M and U_G lies U_W, the point that would win by the biggest majority, given the "appropriate" rate of time discount. This point is taken by Nordhaus to be the "general welfare optimum."[57] Its exact location obviously depends on what is taken to be the appropriate discount rate, and Nordhaus does not discuss that question. I am doubtful of the propriety of discounting future welfare—as Sidgwick said, "the time at which a man exists cannot affect the value of his happiness from a universal point of view."[58] Economists often appear to move without adequate justification from the point that $100 now is worth more than $100 in ten years' time (which is true if only because the $100 could be invested now so as to come to more in ten years' time) to the quite different notion that the same amount of welfare has more value now than in ten years' time.

57. Ibid., p. 177.
58. Henry Sidgwick, *The Methods of Ethics,* 7th ed. (Indianapolis: Hackett, 1981), p. 414.

Figure 10-5. *Nordhaus Model of the Relation of an Economy in Equilibrium to Various Rate of Time Discounts*

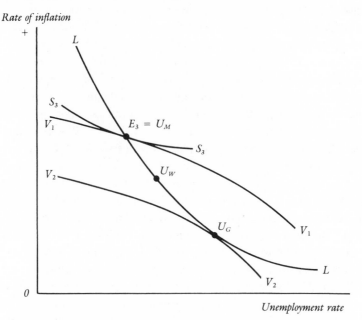

Source: Nordhaus, "Political Business Cycle," fig. 5, p. 180.

Of course, for an individual it makes sense to discount his own future welfare because the further ahead it lies the more doubtful it must become that he will be around to enjoy it. But in spite of the menace of nuclear holocaust and the possibility that a chance asteroid may destroy the earth, it seems to me that the only morally acceptable course is to attach equal weight to the interests of all generations.[59]

Still, there is a more general difficulty. Nordhaus raises the question, "In the absence of political constraints what are the optimal levels of unemployment and inflation?" What is the "appropriate criterion, or social welfare function" to use in order to evaluate the alternative possible states of the economy that might confront "a planning agency constructing a

59. Uncertainty may, however, enter into a social welfare calculation in a different and more acceptable way, namely, as uncertainty about the future course of events. If a government creates unemployment now in the hope of moderating inflation in the future, the unemployment is certain whereas the moderation of inflation is hypothetical. There is therefore some reason for discounting the future benefits, not because they are future but because they are uncertain.

medium-term plan for a mixed economy?"[60] Nordhaus suggests using the aggregate voting function, represented graphically by the system of isopsephic curves. This means in effect that the ideal planner is to try to maximize the votes for economic outcomes expressed by the aggregate voting function, discounted over time by whatever is the appropriate factor. But in general it is surely clear that vote-maximizing outcomes have no necessary connection with welfare, in any sense of welfare satisfying the condition that more of it is better than less. In a divided society, the overall vote-maximizing policy may be one that oppresses the minority in the interests of the majority, for example.

What can, however, be more plausibly claimed is that vote-maximization is an appropriate criterion for assessing the operation of a democratic political system. It can, of course, be questioned whether "giving people what they want" is something that should be asked of political leaders; and it may also be questioned whether, when some want one thing and others something else, the best form of aggregating those conflicting wants is to see what policy would get the biggest majority. Whatever the answers to these questions, it is important to know whether the forces of electoral competition can be expected to operate in some systematic way to give people what they do not want, or more specifically to give them something that would be defeated by some alternative in a straight vote. For this would suggest that there is some kind of internal flaw in democracy, that it turns out not even able to do the one thing that might be claimed for it as against other forms of regime, to give people what they want (in the majoritarian sense specified).

If a vote-maximizing welfare criterion is used in this way, then it is apparent that the future should be discounted at whatever rate the voters actually discount it. The policy U_W will thus be the one that would get the biggest majority if the voters were (contrary to Nordhaus's assumption) knowledgeable about the macroeconomic structure of the economy and thus able to compare all possible alternative policies over an indefinitely long future. Provided the rate of time discount used by most voters is neither zero nor infinity, the result arrived at by Nordhaus can be reaffirmed: U_W will lie between U_M and U_G on the long-run Phillips curve.

If the rest of his analysis is correct, then, it will have been proved that

60. Nordhaus, "Political Business Cycle," p. 175.

the tendency of electoral competition is to produce more inflation and less unemployment than the voters want. But is it correct?

The model put forward by Nordhaus to show the inflationary tendencies of democracy is independent of his model of the political business cycle. It is, indeed, incompatible with his or any other model of the political business cycle. It is also internally inconsistent. The key result reached by Nordhaus requires the assumption that, over its term of office, a government is restricted to choosing a point on the short-run Phillips curve.[61] Yet the notion of the political business cycle makes no sense unless a government can, within its term of office, shift the position of the short-run Phillips curve. Moreover, the model purporting to show the inflationary tendency of democracy incorporates a shift in the short-run Phillips curve from one election to the next, so long as the economy is off the long-run Phillips curve. Thus, the model actually requires that the position of the short-run Phillips curve shift between elections but at the same time has the government acting as if it did not.

The conclusion on which Nordhaus sets great store is that in equilibrium the "democratic outcome" is a rate of inflation that is "purely myopic . . . where the implicit rate of time preference is infinite."[62] This conclusion will obviously hold true if a government is seeking to maximize votes at the next election and can choose only points on the short-run Phillips curve. For the vote-maximizing point (by analogy with the analysis) is the point at which the short-run Phillips curve is at a tangent with the isopsephic curve. But this conclusion is completely dependent on the assumption that the government operates over its whole term of office as if it had a time horizon of zero. This is obviously not consistent with vote-maximizing behavior on the part of the government, which requires (if it does not look beyond the next election) that its time horizon begin with the number of years to the next election and decline steadily to zero on the next election day.

The model of the political business cycle depends precisely on the idea that government has foresight. It "predicts that the government will usually cut back aggregate demand after the election in order to bring down the rate of inflation, to squeeze out inflationary expectations and hence to shift down the short-term Phillips curve, as well as to reduce

61. "In a two-party system the incumbent party chooses economic policies consistent with the current short-run trade-off, but it cannot move the short-run trade-off substantially in its incumbency." Ibid., p. 178.

62. Ibid., p. 179.

the deficits in the current account, well in time before the next election, so that new expansionary actions can be undertaken again before that election without immediately running into high inflation and a large current account deficit."[63] Clearly, the government would not take unpopular actions after the election unless it was following a strategy for the whole interelection period.

Nordhaus has, in effect, produced a theory of the rate of inflation where a vote-maximizing government always expects the next election to take place tomorrow. That the economic outcome will be "completely myopic" in such conditions is a trivial consequence. Perhaps its only relevance is to cast doubt on the wisdom of Lindbeck's tentative suggestion ("a theoretical possibility") to "let the exact time of elections be determined by a random process."[64] The idea underlying this is obviously that if the government does not know when the next election is going to come, it has no incentive to run a political business cycle, because it cannot plan ahead for a noninflationary boom timed for just before the next election. But if the government reacts to this inability to plan ahead by acting all the time so as to be in the best possible position to fight an election, the result would be like that produced by Nordhaus, at any rate for governments unconstrained by any considerations except vote-maximization. More generally, the greater the time between elections the bigger the cycles would be (especially if voters discount heavily the path of the economy to its election-day position), but the shorter the period between elections the higher the average rate of inflation. Thus even on its own terms, Nordhaus's model fails because it is incoherent. It presupposes both that positions on the short-run Phillips curves (except where they intersect the long-run curve) cannot be maintained over an interelection period[65] and that governments nevertheless behave as if they could.

Inflation and Democracy

There is no reason to attribute to inflation of the kind experienced in the advanced industrial societies in recent decades any ill effects over and above the patent ones—the inconvenience of constant price adjustments,

63. Lindbeck, "Stabilization Policy," p. 13.

64. Ibid., p. 18, n. 8.

65. In fact, the slopes of the short-run curves in fig. 10-5 are if anything *flatter* than the slope Nordhaus gives for an empirically derived curve for the U.S. economy that is claimed to be a "first quarter or impact" short-run Phillips curve. Nordhaus, "Political Business Cycle," pp. 170, 171.

the uncertainty about future changes in the price level, and, to the extent that the inflation is not anticipated or compensated for by deliberate policy, a certain degree of redistribution along lines that have no particular ethical attraction. However, to the extent that the distribution of wealth and income in these societies is ethically unattractive in the absence of inflation anyway, it seems unreasonable to worry very much about a crosscutting and relatively minor form of unjust enrichment.

There is a common argument to the effect that inflation in the United States in the 1970s was particularly hard on the poor, because the highest price rises were in things whose purchase constituted a large proportion of their expenditure and that could not easily be done without. This rests on confusion between inflation and changes in relative prices. If the things the poor buy more of, like heating oil, become more expensive in relation to other things, the poor will inevitably become worse off, whatever happens to the general price level. Suppose that the overall price level had remained unchanged over a year, with a few prices going up a lot and the rest going down a little to keep the consumer price index level. The poor would be poorer to exactly the same extent as in an inflationary period. The only way of compensating for changes in relative prices is to give the poor more money. Inflation is (as so often) a red herring.

On objective grounds, there is no basis for saying that democratic institutions, by permitting inflation, can be shown to have failed and should be superseded. As for the argument that democratic institutions can be seen to have failed in terms of their own justification, because they produce outcomes that are in conflict with citizens' preferences, there is no factual evidence for the assumption, and the kind of model from which it is to be deduced rests on highly dubious premises and even then does not entail any such conclusion. Once again, therefore, the case against democracy must be dismissed.

I shall close by suggesting that for most of the economist constitution-mongers discussed in this chapter, inflation was never really the main issue anyway. The economists who make proposals to require balanced budgets, to fix the money supply automatically according to some formula, to go back to the gold standard, to make central banks more autonomous, and so on, are, for the most part, economic liberals in the nineteenth-century sense. That is, they believe that collective action carried out through the state should be kept to a minimum and that the market should determine what gets produced and who receives what income. There is, as both defenders and critics of the market have been forced to recognize over the last hundred years or so, a built-in tension between liberalism (in the nineteenth-century sense) and democracy.[66] Monetarism, and, more generally, market liberalism, is, as Ernest Gellner has written, inevitably betrayed by democratic governments.[67] For the workings of the market are not in fact conducive to the well-being of the majority of the population, and any government concerned with reelection finds itself intervening, whatever its official doctrine, to cushion people from the effects of unconstrained market forces. The demand management, guidelines, statutory controls over wages and prices, and other devices that governments use in order to try to moderate inflation are simply an aspect of this general phenomenon.

Anyone whose primary commitment is to the market must, therefore, look on the democratic state, with its inevitable tendency to regulate, make collective provision, and redistribute, with antipathy. The political problem facing that person is how to get democratic approval for tying the hands of elected governments in perpetuity. Such problems do not of course arise in nondemocratic regimes, and it is not therefore surprising that it is territories with authoritarian regimes such as Hong Kong, Taiwan, and South Korea that are often the apple of the market economist's eye.

The beauty of inflation is that it can be used as a rallying cry to sweep up people who might otherwise be chary of plans to cripple the ability of governments to make economic policy. A perfect example is James Buchanan's decade-long call for a "constitutional counterrevolution" to undo the work of the New Deal and the Warren Court.[68] Anti-inflationary hysteria is an opportunity to mobilize behind proposals that would, in calmer times, be widely recognized as reactionary twaddle. That is in the end the only reason why inflation is important.

---

66. Sir Henry Sumner Maine, *Popular Government* (London: John Murray, 1885; Liberty Classics, 1976) made the point a century ago. The quotation from Lord Acton at the opening of this chapter is from his letter of November 11, 1885, to Mary Gladstone commenting on *Popular Government*. He continued: "Maine tells me that his book, A Manual of Unacknowledged Conservatism, is selling well. It is no doubt meant to help the enemy's cause, and more hostile to us [liberals] than the author cares to appear. For he requested me not to review it." Quoted in George Feaver, *From Status to Contract: A Biography of Sir Henry Maine, 1822–1888* (London: Longmans, Green, 1969), p. 237. William Edward Hartpole Lecky, *Democracy and Liberty* (London: Longmans, Green, 1896; Liberty Classics, 1981), carried the argument further and injected a greater note of stridency. The same ideas inform the views of their descendants, the so-called Mont Pelerin group including von Mises, Hayek, and de Jouvenel.

67. "A Social Contract in Search of an Idiom: The Demise of the Danegeld State?" *Political Quarterly*, vol. 46 (April–June 1975), pp. 127–52.

68. Buchanan, *Limits of Liberty;* James M. Buchanan, *Freedom in Constitutional Contract: Perspectives of a Political Economist* (Texas A & M University Press, 1977); Barry, "Review."

11

Central Banks and Inflation

John T. Woolley

One need not read far in the economic literature on inflation to learn that inflation is ultimately a monetary phenomenon. That is, it is not easy to conceive of the conditions under which inflation could continue at a high level or could accelerate for sustained periods unless the money supply also grew or accelerated. The most vigorous statement of this position has come from monetarist economists. Some have seemed to believe that the solution to the problem of inflation is rather simple—instruct the monetary authority to control the money supply. From that point of view, monetary authorities appear to be perverse or ignorant—else why haven't they done the right thing already? A more sophisticated approach recognizes that the reasons for the behavior of the monetary authority are not obvious. Thus, for example, Karl Brunner has suggested that "one chapter on the political economy of inflation" should deal with central banks—with how they conceive of their task, and how their behavior relates to the government budget.[1]

Rather than castigating central banks for permitting inflation, students of inflation need to understand why it is that central banks do what they do. What is the role of the central bank in economic policymaking? What kinds of political constraints are there on the choices of central banks? How plausible is the widely held notion that central banks have some meaningful form of independence from politics—and, thus, behave in ways not fundamentally shaped by politics?

This chapter argues that there is a small but meaningful degree of independence that can be attained by central banks under certain conditions. However, the dominant political and economic coalition that rules

1. "Comment," *Journal of Law and Economics,* vol. 18 (December 1975), p. 851.

fiscal policy also rules in the realm of monetary policy. But inflationary monetary policy is not simply the result of monetizing budget deficits. The notion that lack of political independence of central banks leads to inflation because budget deficits are accommodated is not sufficient to account for the observed inflation of the 1970s. Accommodation of pressures for inflation need not be so narrowly conceived. Officials have many incentives to provide broad access to bank credit and to monetize wage demands, and these incentives combine in complex ways in different settings.

It is not clear that monetary policy in the United States in the 1970s was *too* accommodative. Though its inflation rates were lower than those of many other industrialized countries, the United States also had slower real growth. It is not at all obvious that the choices made in the United States were preferable to those made in other countries.

Monetary policy is typically executed by a central bank. Central banks were not created for the purpose of macroeconomic stabilization. On the contrary, in every Western setting central banks emerged as a response to needs for a central institution to serve other banks. Central banks have a long and conservative heritage. Commonly, they have been closely linked to the major financial institutions of the day, and their organizational ethos has been one stressing stability. In the context of understanding the inflation of the 1970s it is of pressing interest to know more about why monetary policy was conducted as it was.

Do Central Banks Possess Any Independence?

If central banks are fundamentally free from political constraints, then it is clear that their behavior must be considered separately from that of other political actors. However, if the policy choices of central banks are substantially constrained by other political actors, then monetary policy must be treated as a product of larger political and economic coalitions. Thus, studying monetary policy and central banks in isolation can lead to a vast overestimation of the degree to which monetary policy reflects the separate, independent preferences of a set of autonomous actors.

Many writers who are concerned about the independence of central banks would prefer that no monetary policy choices be made because of political pressure. They hope that the monetary authority will have sufficient political power to resist pressure. Commonly, this view is held by those who fear inflation and who see the central bank as being disposed to fight inflation. They welcome central bank independence—"depoliti-cization" of monetary policy—because they hope it will lead to realization of their preferred macroeconomic outcomes. Under such conditions, presumably, there would be no effective way of pressuring a central bank to accommodate government deficits, for example. On the other side are those who regard central bank independence as undesirable if it thwarts democratic control of policy even if that entails a policy considered to be suboptimal by standards of economic efficiency. Still others argue that the functional interdependence of monetary and fiscal policy requires that there be full coordination of macroeconomic policy instruments and, thus, no independence for monetary policy. This position could be consistent with the view that all economic policy choices should be relatively depoliticized.

Since the effects of monetary and fiscal policy cannot be known separately from each other,[2] one may reasonably expect monetary and fiscal authorities to be in close contact in order to learn what their counterparts are doing. One may further anticipate that they will at least occasionally be in conflict. They may disagree about how to carry out policy or about what objectives should be sought. Moreover, since both authorities control political resources, each may attempt to force the other to behave in the way he prefers. The problem confronting any outsider who attempts to understand this relationship is the limited opportunity to observe the actual bargaining relationship that exists or to know with great confidence what resources each participant uses to attempt to influence the other's behavior. Behavior that is very interesting and very important is also very inaccessible to observers.

As an initial response to this problem one can distinguish between central banks that demonstrate some minimal level of "behavioral inde-pendence" and those that do not. At a minimal level, a central bank can be considered to be independent if it can set policy instruments without approval from outside authorities, and if, for some minimal period of time, the instrument settings clearly differ from those preferred by the fiscal authority.[3] This is an explicitly political definition of independence

2. See Alan S. Blinder and Robert M. Solow, "Analytical Foundations of Fiscal Policy," in *The Economics of Public Finance* (Brookings Institution, 1974); James Tobin and Willem Buiter, "Long-Run Effects of Fiscal and Monetary Policy on Aggregate Demand," in Jerome L. Stein, ed., *Monetarism, Studies in Monetary Economics* (North-Holland, 1976).

3. See John T. Woolley, "Monetary Policy Instrumentation and the Relationship of Central Banks and Governments," *Annals of the American Academy of Political and Social Science,* vol. 434 (November 1977), pp. 170–72 (Brookings Reprint 337); Ralph C. Bryant, *Money and Monetary Policy in Interdependent Nations* (Brookings Institution, 1980), chap. 18.

of the monetary authority from the fiscal. It does not rule out the possibility that in periods of nonconflict one actor forces the other to comply. This definition means simply that for some short but meaningful period of time the resources of the fiscal authority do not guarantee that its preferences dominate in monetary policy. From such observed conflict, one infers that the monetary authority has determined its own preferred policy. Other aspects of independence can be examined as part of such an analysis, too—for example, evidence of public disagreement about fiscal policy.

Institutional Structure and Central Bank Depoliticization

Both Lindbeck and Nordhaus have suggested that depoliticizing monetary policy may be a solution to the problems of economic instability they see resulting from democratic control of economic policy.[4] While it is possible that organizational devices hold the key to depoliticizing such agencies, the evidence indicates overwhelmingly that they are only "necessary" features for central bank independence. Independence in a formal, legal sense may be better conceived of as revealing the existence of strong political support by actors other than the central bank for fighting inflation. Behavioral independence reflects the fact that the central bank controls important political resources—such as the support of a sympathetic constituency.

It is common to suppose that the degree of control of one agency or office over another depends on specific organizational form—some mechanisms increase accountability, some increase discretion. One control device commonly considered to be of crucial importance is budget approval and audit. Budget review, power of appointment and removal, definition of hierarchical responsibility, review of decisions by outside authority, limits on the scope for secrecy, and other organizational options have been widely used to try to increase efficiency, responsiveness, and coordination in government organizations.[5] Such mechanisms are important

---

4. Assar Lindbeck, "Stabilization Policy in Open Economies with Endogenous Politicians," *American Economic Review*, vol. 66 (May 1976, *Papers and Proceedings, 1975*), p. 18; William D. Nordhaus, "The Political Business Cycle," *Review of Economic Studies*, vol. 42 (April 1975), p. 188.

5. Michael Parkin and Robin Bade, "Central Bank Laws and Monetary Policies: A Preliminary Investigation," Research Report 7804 (Department of Economics, University of Western Ontario, March 1978), propose that such formal criteria as control of appointments and formal independence of governments produce lower average inflation rates. By their criterion of "diffusion of power concerning appointment of Bank directors" the Federal Reserve should be expected to be in the "most independent" category of central banks because the Federal Open Market Committee, the most important Federal Reserve decisionmaking body, includes both district bank presidents and members of the Board of

because they can be manipulated easily by policymakers. If changing such relationships predictably changes behavior, then desired central bank behavior might be reinforced or decreased through these kinds of devices.

Arthur Burns, chairman of the Federal Reserve Board, attributed Federal Reserve independence to two such factors in particular:

First, the seven members of the Federal Reserve Board serve long and staggered terms and can only be removed for "cause." This arrangement severely limits possibilities for any "packing" of the Board and enables members of the Board to act without special concern about falling out of grace politically. Second, the Federal Reserve System finances its activities with internally generated funds and therefore is not subject to the customary appropriations process. This arrangement is intended to assure that the Congressional "power of the purse" will not be used in an effort to induce System officials to pursue policies that they otherwise might consider poorly suited to the nation's needs.[6]

Burns, of course, referred to two areas long popular with reformers seeking to reduce Federal Reserve autonomy.

But comparison of the Federal Reserve with other central banks on the organizational features Burns mentioned does not reveal striking differences (see table 11-1). For example, the official length of term in office of members of central bank governing bodies varies from a high of fourteen years in the United States to a low of three years in Sweden. Two of the three central banks widely regarded as having some significant degree of independence—those in the United States, West Germany, and Switzerland[7]—are at the upper end of the range. However, while the governor of the nonindependent Bank of France has an indefinite term, the chairman of the independent Federal Reserve Board serves only a four-year term as chairman. All the members of the Swiss National Bank's directorate (the Bank Committee) serve for only four years, and district bank presidents in the Federal Reserve System, who constitute five-twelfths of the voting membership of the Federal Open Market Committee, are appointed only for five-year terms. It is not clear that the length of

---

Governors. If that were acknowledged, their already weak results would be weakened even further. For political scientists' views on the importance of organizational forms, see Harold Seidman, *Politics, Position, and Power: The Dynamics of Federal Organization,* 3d ed. (Oxford University Press, 1980); Herbert Kaufman, "Reflections on Administrative Reorganization," in Joseph A. Pechman, ed., *Setting National Priorities: The 1978 Budget* (Brookings Institution, 1977).

6. Arthur F. Burns, *Reflections of an Economic Policy Maker: Speeches and Congressional Statements, 1969–1978* (Washington: American Enterprise Institute for Public Policy Research, 1978), pp. 419–20. Subsequently, Burns advanced a more modest view of the independent role of central banks, in "The Anguish of Central Banking" (Washington.: Per Jacobsson Foundation, 1979).

7. Burns, *Reflections,* p. 420; Woolley, "Monetary Policy."

Table 11-1. *Organizational Characteristics of Six Central Banks*

Central bank	Term of office	Conditions of removal	External budget controls	External audit controls
Bank of England	5 years, governor, deputy governor; 4 years, executive directors	For cause	None	None
Bank of France (Banque de France)	Indefinite, governor, deputy governors; 4 years, Central Bank Council	Not specified	None	Banking Control Commission
Federal Reserve (United States)	14 years, Board; 4 years, chairman; 5 years, presidents	For cause	None	Limited audit, General Accounting Office
German Federal Bank (Deutsche Bundesbank)	2–8 years, Central Bank Council	For cause	None	None
Swedish National Bank (Sveriges Riksbank)	3 years, Board of Directors	Parliamentary discretion	Parliament	Parliamentary Audit Committee
Swiss National Bank (Schweizerische National Bank)	4 years, Bank Committee	For cause	None	Audit Committee, Shareholder General Meeting

Sources: Bank for International Settlements, *Eight European Central Banks* (Praeger, 1963); Hans Aufricht, *Central Banking Legislation: A Collection of Central Bank, Monetary and Banking Laws*, vol. 2: *Europe* (International Monetary Fund, 1967); *Congressional Quarterly Almanac, 1978*, vol. 34 (Washington: CQ, 1979), p. 300.

term of service can be expected to be of much significance in behavioral independence.

Only at the Swedish National Bank is it explicitly understood that the top officials may be removed at the discretion of the appointing authority. However, there has apparently been great reluctance to use this power even following apparently serious policy errors.[8] It appears to be the case that governors of the Bank of France cannot expect to retain their office if they publicly disagree with the policy of the government.[9] By one account, Leslie O'Brien was fired from the governorship of the Bank of England in 1973 after only two years of a five-year term.[10] As for the Federal Reserve System, there was speculation that Chairman Thomas B. McCabe resigned in 1951 because of outside pressure.[11] Again, it is not

8. Personal communication from Gösta Rehn.

9. The case of Olivier Wormser is a case in point.

10. Cecil Harmsworth King, *The Cecil King Diary, 1970–1974* (London: Jonathan Cape, 1975), p. 279. Elsewhere (p. 101) King suggests that O'Brien's reappointment had been understood to be for only part of a five-year term.

11. A. Jerome Clifford, *The Independence of the Federal Reserve System* (University of Pennsylvania Press, 1965), pp. 266–72.

clear exactly how important these formal components might be in behavioral independence.

As for outside budgetary control, in a 1952 study—a time that few would regard as a golden age of independent central banking—it was observed that the fifty-two central banks examined had a free hand in budgetary matters.[12] Not until parliamentary hearings in 1969 were the annual salaries paid the governor, deputy governor, and executive directors of the Bank of England publicly known. The same hearings made it clear that the bank was not subject to budgetary control by other government agencies, nor to control audits.[13] Four central banks are now subject to audit by official groups. The Swedish National Bank and the Federal Reserve are audited by legislative offices. Audits of the Bank of France and the Swiss National Bank are performed by bodies that are formally superior to the central bank but are still part of the general central bank organization. In short, the Federal Reserve does not appear to be particularly sheltered institutionally among central banks.

In recent history, major changes in the working relationships between central banks and fiscal authorities have followed not from changes in formal institutional relationships but from periods of national crisis or from a reconceptualization of the role of monetary policy. In the United States, the banking acts of 1933 and 1935 consolidated power in the Federal Reserve Board and defined a relationship for the Federal Reserve to the rest of the national government that was both more "governmental" and more removed from short-term influence by other national-level actors than had formerly been the case. An annual report to Congress was required; the secretary of the treasury and the comptroller of the currency were removed as members of the Board of Governors; funds assessed member banks were defined not to be government funds and were therefore no longer subject to Treasury audit; the Board was given new policy instruments (for example, variable reserve requirements); members' terms of office were lengthened. All of these should have increased the independence of the Federal Reserve System. Such was not the result. System policy was very passive during the period. The Federal

---

12. David L. Grove, "Central Bank Independence and the Government-Central Bank Relationship" (International Monetary Fund, Joint Bank-Fund Library, April 2, 1952), p. 40.

13. *First Report,* Parliamentary Papers, Select Committee on Nationalised Industries, House of Commons, Session of October 28, 1969–May 29, 1970, vol. 6 (London: Her Majesty's Stationery Office, 1970), pp. 14–15, 24–28, 30–31, 54–55.

Reserve helped maintain an "orderly market" for government securities—as the Treasury desired. This continued through World War II and was not a source of controversy.[14]

After the war, according to the conventional account, the Federal Reserve did not establish any scope for reasonably independent action until the early 1950s. Then, independence resulted from a negotiated agreement—the famous accord between the Treasury and the Federal Reserve—not from organizational changes. The process of achieving flexibility in monetary policy followed a long period of discussion and dispute, facilitated by congressional hearings. The clear exercise of Federal Reserve independence in 1953 was actually marked by cautious probings within a region of discretion acceptable to the Treasury.[15] Only subsequently did independence as defined here become evident.

It is the consensus of various observers of the Bank of England, including former Governor O'Brien, that the nationalization of the bank was not, in fact, the decisive change that it might have appeared to be. Rather, the Bank of England Act "in no way legislated for a revolution in relations between the Bank and the Treasury."[16] The most important change was perhaps the symbolic one of removing the Bank from "banker control" by making members of the Court of Directors crown appointments. Possibly with this in mind, one chancellor of the exchequer concluded that the act "contributed" to the evolution of the Treasury-Bank relationship.[17] More characteristic is the opinion of a permanent secretary of the treasury that "the relationships between the Bank and the official Treasury and the Bank and Ministers do not depend on anything in the Act."[18]

The case of the Bank of France is apparently similar. One observer concluded that "the changes [following nationalization] have tended to be *de jure* rather than *de facto*."[19] Another states that "nationalization did

14. Milton Friedman and Anna Jacobson Schwartz, *A Monetary History of the United States, 1867–1960* (Princeton University Press, 1963), p. 520, chap. 10; Clifford, *Independence*, pp. 152–59, 167, chap. 6.

15. Friedman and Schwartz, *Monetary History*, p. 613. See also James Tobin, "Discussion 3," Federal Reserve Bank of Boston, *Proceedings of a 50th Anniversary Symposium, Annual Report 1964*, pp. 30–33.

16. *First Report*, Parliamentary Papers, pp. 18, 20; Michael J. Artis, *Foundations of British Monetary Policy* (Oxford: Basil Blackwell, 1965), p. 31. Also see Richard A. Chapman, *Decision Making: A Case Study of the Decision to Raise the Bank Rate in September 1957* (London: Routledge and Kegan Paul, 1968), p. 85; R. S. Sayers, *Central Banking After Bagehot* (Oxford University Press, 1957), p. 35.

17. The chancellor was Roy Jenkins. *First Report*, Parliamentary Papers, p. 314.

18. Ibid., p. 1.

19. J. S. G. Wilson, *French Banking Structure and Credit Policy* (London: G. Bell, 1957), p. 286.

not bring about fundamental changes as far as the relations of the Bank and the state are concerned."[20]

The German central bank, the Bundesbank, may be suggested as an exception since it was in fact created as an independent agency after World War II. On the other hand, following World War I, the Reichsbank itself had been reorganized as an "independent" bank. In the event, that independence was no greater than that of the Federal Reserve during a period of war and crisis. Thus, twice repeating the gesture in formally establishing independence, first for the Bank deutscher Länder and then for the Deutsche Bundesbank, would hardly seem to have been decisive.[21]

Compared to the demands for cooperation during periods of crisis, the cooperation entailed by policy interdependencies, and the political resources that government controls, specific organizational features can make only a marginal contribution to central bank independence. Necessary, perhaps; certainly not sufficient.

Earlier Studies of Independence

Many economists who study macroeconomic policy have commented on the degree of coordination or independence they have perceived between monetary and fiscal policy. Several analyses using the observed movements of monetary and fiscal policy instruments to measure the degree of monetary and fiscal coordination assume that both policy instruments should move in the same direction.[22] Thus, an easing of monetary policy while fiscal policy tightens implies lack of coordination and central bank independence. Other time series analyses of monetary and fiscal policy have concluded that the overwhelming characteristic of policy in the 1960s and 1970s was the *parallel* movement of monetary and fiscal policy. Such evidence has been taken to support the conclusion

---

20. Patrice Brunet, *L'organisation de la Banque de France* (Paris: Presses Universitaires de France, 1973), p. 98.

21. M. H. de Kock, *Central Banking*, 4th ed. (London: Crosby, Lockwood, Staples, 1974), pp. 48–51.

22. George L. Perry, "Stabilization Policy and Inflation," in Henry Owen and Charles L. Schultze, eds., *Setting National Priorities: The Next Ten Years* (Brookings Institution, 1976), pp. 294–95; Alan S. Blinder and Stephen M. Goldfeld, "New Measures of Fiscal and Monetary Policy, 1958–73," *American Economic Review*, vol. 66 (December 1976), p. 792. Perry is careful to note that his measure does not demonstrate coordination, but that there was a history of informal working relations between Federal Reserve and president. Blinder and Goldfeld study impacts, not instruments, but the logic of their interpretation is analogous. Few of the studies referred to here focus extensively on questions of independence; typically they are treated in relatively brief passages.

that central bank independence is relatively small—or not exercised.[23] Still other analyses have proposed testing for independence by examining the shift points in policy. If those points coincide with presidential transitions, then it is inferred that policy is not independent.[24] Finally, it has been argued that independence can be judged from results—from different economic outcomes.

These studies are inadequate because, quite simply, they rely on assumptions about what monetary policy should have been doing without examining the actual preferences of other policymakers. In retrospect, policy may indeed have been incorrect in terms of normative economic theory. However, this does not reveal anything about the political relationships between monetary and fiscal authorities. The degree of central bank independence cannot be ascertained by examining policy instruments alone—even if both monetary and fiscal policy instruments are included. While it may be awkward for rigorous research, analysts cannot avoid the task of contrasting the preferences of one actor and the actions of the other.

To understand behavioral independence requires an understanding of the process producing movements in instruments. Policy instruments could move often in opposite directions but still be produced by a highly coordinated process. Even if policy were made by the same person it might not be possible to observe a high correlation of monetary and fiscal policy instruments. For example, Walter Heller has suggested using a tight fiscal policy with easier monetary policy as a means of tilting expansion in the direction of greater capital investment.[25] One cannot read Arthur Okun's account of economic policymaking in the period 1966–68, when monetary and fiscal policy instruments diverged somewhat, and conclude that this was a period especially marked by lack of

23. Testimony of James L. Pierce in *The Impact of the Federal Reserve's Money Policies on the Economy*, Hearings before the Subcommittee on Domestic Monetary Policy of the House Committee on Banking, Currency, and Housing, 94 Cong. 2 sess. (U.S. Government Printing Office, 1976), p. 154; James M. Buchanan and Richard E. Wagner, *Democracy in Deficit: The Political Legacy of Lord Keynes* (Academic Press, 1977), pp. 115, 116. These scholars' arguments are unconvincing even if their definitions of independence are adopted. That is, there is no strong statistical evidence for the close relationship they posit.

24. Robert E. Weintraub, "Congressional Supervision of Monetary Policy," *Journal of Monetary Economics*, vol. 4 (April 1978), pp. 341–62. Weintraub uses supplementary information about goals of fiscal policymakers to support his argument, making his analysis closer to the kind I advocate than any of the others. He relies considerably on the observed changes in monetary policy "thrust" over time in reaching his conclusion that the Federal Reserve is not independent.

25. Walter W. Heller, *The Economy: Old Myths and New Realities* (Norton, 1976), p. 163.

cooperation.[26] Indeed, in the eyes of some observers, policy during that period *should* have been headed in opposite directions.[27]

Conversely, one should not infer that a central bank had no independence just because fiscal and monetary policy instruments "tended" to move together. At the least, one would want to be assured that any of the divergences were not regarded by the participants as being very important. An observed high correlation between instruments is consistent with a monetary policy that was never quite satisfactory to fiscal authorities despite the fact that monetary and fiscal policy tended to move in parallel.

The search for shift points in the movement of an indicator of policy impact or of some intermediate policy target is much more defensible, but still it is a hazardous undertaking. The examination of shifts in policy impacts involves making the unwarranted assumption that impacts are intended and fully determined by one particular actor. Such an approach tends to ignore policy interdependencies at the very outset, which, of course, seems to be inconsistent with trying to test for the existence of independence. Searching for shift points in the movement of a possible intermediate policy target (for example some kind of monetary aggregates) also is a defective process. This approach assumes that policymakers are in fact trying to hit the chosen intermediate target—and this should be carefully justified. More damaging, this approach assumes that some sort of simple, constant decision rule is being followed by policymakers. Failure to follow that rule, as measured by deviations of the hypothesized intermediate target from the postulated ideal level, are interpreted as evidence that some other actor has exerted pressure on the central bank. This inference depends on the assumption that central bank decision making procedures are stable and rigid. This assumption is probably unwarranted. Many problems with this general approach are remediable, and the approach can provide useful information about monetary policy.[28] Still, it fails to show what is required—whether or not monetary policy is consistent with the preferences of fiscal authorities.

Finally, some observers have proposed that differences in central bank independence can be revealed by differences in the economic performance of different countries. They usually argue that the higher the degree of

26. Arthur M. Okun, *The Political Economy of Prosperity* (Brookings Institution, 1970), p. 85.

27. G. L. Bach, *Making Monetary and Fiscal Policy* (Brookings Institution, 1971), pp. 144, 145, 161.

28. James E. Alt and John T. Woolley, "Reaction Functions, Optimization, and Politics: Modelling the Political Economy of Macroeconomic Policy," *American Journal of Political Science,* vol. 26 (November 1982), pp. 709–40.

Table 11-2. *Average Rates of Change in Inflation, Output, and Money Supply in Eight Countries, 1958–80*
Percent

Country	Rate of change, 1958–67[a]			Rate of change, 1968–77[a]			Rate of change, 1978–80[a]		
	CPI	Real GNP[b]	M1	CPI	Real GNP[b]	M1	CPI	Real GNP[b]	M1
Canada	2.0	5.0	5.2	6.7	4.5	10.0	9.9	2.2	8.2
France	3.7	5.8	11.5	8.4	4.5	9.5	11.9	2.4	10.2
Italy	3.6	5.7	13.7	10.8	3.4	18.1	17.6	3.7	19.7
Japan	4.9	10.5	18.5	9.7	6.7	17.1	5.6	4.6	4.9
Switzerland	2.8	4.7	7.9	5.2	2.1	6.8	3.6	n.a.	3.6
United Kingdom	2.9	3.3	3.7	12.1	2.1	10.8	14.2	0.0	8.6
United States	1.6	4.5	3.1	6.4	2.7	5.9	11.8	2.1	7.6
West Germany	2.4	4.7	8.3	4.9	3.5	9.3	4.5	2.7	6.2

Sources: Federal Reserve Bank of St. Louis, *Rates of Change in Economic Data for Ten Industrial Countries,* October 1977, June 1978, July 1980; Federal Reserve Bank of St. Louis, *International Economic Conditions,* October 21, 1981.
n.a. Not available.
a. Annual compound growth rate.
b. For France, Italy, and United Kingdom, gross domestic product.

formal central bank independence, the better able and more likely the central bank is to resist inflation. As a consequence, inflation rates should be lower in countries with independent central banks than elsewhere. Arthur Burns, in defending the independence of the Federal Reserve, judged it "no accident that West Germany and Switzerland, which in recent years also have managed their economy better than most others, happen to have strong and independent monetary authorities like ours."[29] Burns's criterion, "economic management," is sufficiently vague that his claim is virtually impossible to evaluate. Statistics averaged over various time periods do tend to confirm that until recently the countries identified as having independent central banks have experienced somewhat lower inflation rates than have others (see table 11-2). However, statistics also show lower rates of growth in real gross national product in those countries. It is not clear if Arthur Burns meant that lower rates of growth in real GNP characterize better economic management.

This approach tells more about how observers evaluate aggregate economic performance than about central banks and their role in monetary policy. It does not tell whether or not the central bank ever acted independently. It does not reveal whether the contribution of monetary policy to "good performance" was different than it would have been were the bank not independent.

29. Burns, *Reflections,* p. 420.

Taken as a whole, these studies are contradictory and confusing. At best they provide some useful description of policy behavior, but they are inconclusive about the relationships of interest. They do not remove the need to examine the actual agreements or disagreements between fiscal and monetary authorities. Such an analysis is, unfortunately, very difficult to reduce to a summary quantitative form.

Evidence of Central Bank Independence

There appear to be relatively unambiguous instances of independent action by central banks in only two countries in recent years, the United States and the Federal Republic of Germany. Given the secrecy that surrounds central bank activities, it is possible that in other countries there have been examples of independent action. In other countries there have been instances in which central bankers have been publicly critical of fiscal policy. But whatever independence exists does not translate into policies the fiscal authorities clearly find objectionable.

By adopting widely held views about the policy preferences of monetary and fiscal authorities, one can with acceptable accuracy identify periods in which independent action by monetary policymakers is likely. In contrast to fiscal authorities, central bankers are widely assumed to be somewhat more concerned about the risk of inflation than the risks of having underemployed economic resources. However, both authorities' conceptions of acceptable performance should overlap substantially. Thus, at moderate levels of unemployment and inflation, preferences may diverge slightly, but both actors would find current economic performance to be acceptable. Under more extreme conditions, conceptions of acceptable performance would be expected not to overlap, and overt conflict should be more likely. As a result, one would expect that conflicts would be evident around the peaks and troughs in business cycles. As a period of expansion lengthens and evidence accumulates that full employment is being reached or that inflation is accelerating, central bankers, who place greater stress on evidence of growing inflationary pressure, would be ready to tighten more quickly and more firmly than would fiscal authorities. Similarly, after a downturn or in a recession, fiscal policymakers would be ready to reverse course and to begin stimulating the economy sooner than the central bankers who would prefer to continue to wring the inflationary pressures out.

Table 11-3. *Business Cycle Turning Points and Periods of Conflict between Monetary and Fiscal Authorities in the United States, Calendar Quarters, 1953–80*

	Business cycle		
	Peak	Quarters of conflict	Trough
	1953:1	. . .	1953:4
	1955:3	1953:2–4; 1957:4	1957:4
	1959:2	. . .	1960:4
	1966:1	1965:4	1966:4
	1969:1	1970:4	1970:3
	1973:2	. . .	1975:1
	1979:2	1980:4	1980:2

Sources: G. L. Bach, *Making Monetary and Fiscal Policy* (Brookings Institution, 1971); Arthur M. Okun, *The Political Economy of Prosperity* (Brookings Institution, 1970); Walter W. Heller, *New Dimensions of Political Economy* (Harvard University Press, 1966); Sherman J. Maisel, *Managing the Dollar* (Norton, 1973); documentary evidence in the Lyndon B. Johnson Library, Austin, Texas; interviews with participants in policymaking during the years 1966–78. Cyclical peaks and troughs based on index of leading indicators (see text).

The U.S. Case

For the United States, the Commerce Department's composite index of leading indicators provides a sensitive—if somewhat unreliable—measure of upward and downward movements in the economy (see table 11-3).[30] Turning points in this measure should provide an accurate indication of the timing of potential conflicts. The peaks and troughs in this series are more frequent than the recession periods defined by the standards of the National Bureau of Economic Research. These "inaccuracies" more accurately identify periods of ambiguity confronting policymakers. Periods of conflict between the Federal Reserve and the administration in the United States are also noted in table 11-3. Instances are counted as conflicts only when it is clear that both fiscal and monetary policymakers were aware that the policy instrument setting was not as the fiscal authority desired and when the instrument setting was not reversed within a very short period. Periods of high tension or public debate in anticipation of a possible policy shift are excluded if there were no clear signals of presidential displeasure, or if apparent disputes lasted only a few days and were later discounted by both sides (for example, October–November 1977). It is quite possible that when multiple

30. For data on the composite index of twelve leading indicators, see *Business Conditions Digest*, vol. 21 (January 1981), p. 10.

instruments were used, policymakers were undoing with one hand what they did with the other. This might be true for the dispute over the discount rate change in December 1965.

As table 11-3 indicates, there have been very few occasions of marked disagreement even given an expectation that disagreement would be infrequent. In interviews, members of the Council of Economic Advisers under Presidents Nixon, Ford, and Carter were unable or unwilling to cite specific instances of any significant disagreements with the Federal Reserve during their tenure.[31] Periods of conflict generally occurred very close to observed turning points. In the 1955 case, Federal Reserve policy was easier, not tighter, than the administration desired.[32] The apparent parallel between that case and reports that the Carter administration was, in mid-1979, urging the Federal Reserve to tighten further is quite interesting. One might suspect that when a turning point appears to be likely near a presidential election year, top elected officials "reverse roles" because of their desire to avoid a downturn close to the date of an election. Thus the dispute reflects a desire for recession *now* rather than later.

West Germany

Identifying cyclical reference points precisely is difficult in the case of West Germany, and the measures used refer to actual, rather than leading, cyclical movements in output and GNP. The pattern described in table 11-4 is only approximate. As expected, business cycle turning points generally coincided with times of reported disagreements between the bank and government. Conflict tended to occur during the downswing of the cycle. The freedom of action perceived by the monetary authorities may have been conditioned by international factors as well. Thus, the 1966 conflict occurred when the current account payments balance was in or close to deficit. According to Emminger, this permitted a restrictive monetary policy for domestic (inflation) reasons without risking offsetting flows of international capital.[33] Another account explains that a restrictive

31. Arthur Okun, in an interview, February 7, 1978, indicated his awareness of White House–Federal Reserve friction in late 1974 and early 1975, but Ford CEA member William Fellner, in an interview July 12, 1978, insisted that he was not aware of any such friction. The analysis presented here would have predicted conflict at exactly that time. Carter CEA member Lyle Gramley indicated in an interview June 16, 1978, that there was some disagreement on targets at the outset of 1978 and attributed that to the "cyclical phase."

32. Bach, *Making Monetary and Fiscal Policy*, p. 94.

33. Otmar Emminger, *The D-Mark in the Conflict Between Internal and External Equilibrium 1948–75*, Essays in International Finance, 122 (Princeton University, 1977), p. 20.

Table 11-4. *Balance of Payments Fluctuations and Periods of Conflict over Monetary Policy in West Germany, Calendar Quarters, 1958–78*

	Balance of payments	
Peak	Quarters of conflict	Trough
1961:1	1961:1	1963:1
1965:2	1966:2–3	1967:2
1970:1	1971:1	1971:4
1974:1	. . .	1975:2
1977:2	. . .	1978:1

Sources: Otmar Emminger, *The D-Mark in the Conflict Between Internal and External Equilibrium 1948–75,* Essays in International Finance, 122 (Princeton University, 1977), p. 35; Organization for Economic Cooperation and Development, *Monetary Policy in Germany* (Paris: OECD, 1973), p. 12; comments of Norbert Kloten, Karl-Heinz Kletterer, and Rainer Vollmer in chap. 12, below; Herbert Giersch, *Growth, Cycles, and Exchange Rates—The Experience of West Germany,* Wicksell Lectures 1970 (Stockholm: Almqvist and Wiksell, 1970); William Pollard Wadbrook, *West German Balance of Payments Policy: The Prelude to European Monetary Integration* (Praeger, 1972); Hugo M. Kaufman, "The European Monetary System and National Policy Control" (Department of Economics, Queens College, City University of New York, 1981). Some observers say that conflict between the Bundesbank and the government occurred between the third quarter of 1968 and the fourth quarter of 1969.

policy was used to offset preelection stimulus favored by the government.[34] In 1974 the Bundesbank was subject to considerable criticism for its strict policy, but as chapter 12 argues, this policy was strongly supported by the government. More recently, there have been further reports of criticism of Bundesbank policy, but there seem to have been no actions taken that were opposed by the government.

In both the United States and West Germany, open disagreement about policy instrument settings has been quite rare. There are few independent central banks; even independent central banks rarely use their independence to follow dramatically different policy from what the fiscal policymakers want. Observable behavior supports these conclusions and the notion that disagreements reflect relatively narrow differences in the definition of preferred economic performance. When policymakers disagree marginally over objectives, their differences should be expected to result in divergent courses of actions as the economy approaches full employment or is in recession—and not at other times. Central banks are least likely to demonstrate independence in periods of national crisis. Independent actions by central banks with respect to central governments are relatively infrequent—albeit often very salient to close observers. One important implication of this is that sustained periods of tight—or easy—money

34. Herbert Giersch, *Growth, Cycles, and Exchange Rates—The Experience of West Germany,* Wicksell Lectures 1970 (Stockholm: Almqvist and Wiksell, 1970), p. 25.

should be understood as government policy rather than central bank policy.

Central Bank Independence: Two Interpretations

Can these findings be reconciled with reports and documents revealing relationships that are often tense, marked by mistrust and by attempts by one actor to pressure the other? Although clear-cut conflict observable from the outside is rare, it is not necessarily the case that policymaking is primarily harmonious. If there really is no disagreement between fiscal and monetary policy authorities, why is central bank independence so carefully preserved? If there is disagreement, why, again, is central bank independence so carefully preserved? Two partially competing interpretations can be given for the findings presented above.

Underlying Consensus

One interpretation emphasizes the existence of a consensus among major policy participants that monetary policy must be protected from the pressures of "pluralistic" political processes—especially the demands of interest groups for pork-barrel benefits and protection from the costs of stabilization policy. The relationship between central bank and government is characterized as largely one of agreement—that is, it is a tacit conspiracy to keep other political actors, especially legislators, out of the monetary policy game. Formal independence—and occasional independent action—are welcomed by governments because all major actors recognize the desirability of having one macroeconomic policy instrument that can, more or less, respond solely to the technical requirements of the economy; the political costs of unpopular policy choices can to some degree be deflected onto an independent central bank and away from elected officials; and the government and the central bank agree on the undesirability of much legislative influence on monetary policy. The last factor flows naturally from the first due to the shared perception that the legislature is most likely to reflect narrow, particularistic pressures. The relationship this interpretation posits is actually a rather fragile one and contains pressures that can simultaneously undermine both the political and economic rationales that support it. However, considerable evidence can be marshalled to support this interpretation, at least for the U.S. case.[35]

35. For a particularly clear statement of this position, see Edward J. Kane, "External Pressure and the Operations of the Fed," in Raymond E. Lombra and Willard E. Witte, *Political Economy of International and Domestic Monetary Relations* (Iowa State University Press, 1982), pp. 211–36.

Historically, government in the United States has intervened in the economy to a significantly lesser degree than has been true in most Western nations.[36] In monetary policy, this is evidenced by a preference for global policy rather than selective controls. This preference was clear in the direction taken by monetary policy in the United States after World War II, and therein lie the roots of contemporary Federal Reserve independence. In sharp contrast to France and Italy and, to a lesser degree, West Germany and the United Kingdom, there was an unambiguous preference in the United States for *no* direct control over credit. This enhanced central bank independence because policy did not deliberately create new short-run distributive impacts. Legislative interest and involvement in policy have typically been high when distributive impacts are involved. Further, successfully pursuing a free market policy required sufficient autonomy from Congress to insulate against intermittent pressures for "easy money" that could be expected from the unavoidable differential burdens of interest rate variation.

Although the Federal Reserve is, technically speaking, a "creature of Congress," Congress unlike the president and the Treasury has never devised an effective means of closely influencing monetary policy. In part, to be sure, this has been due to a lack of interest and self-confidence on the part of key members of Congress. Nonetheless, by tolerating occasional public disagreements with the Federal Reserve, the president and the Treasury have been able to keep monetary policy relatively flexible, and not subject to congressional delay in changing policy direction.[37]

The specific facts of the reestablishment of the Federal Reserve's independence in the early 1950s may seem not to fit with this interpretation. The standard version is of a bitter struggle between Treasury and Federal Reserve which was settled by treaty in the accord of 1951. The settlement was encouraged by Congress, particularly by Senator Paul Douglas, rather than being resisted by Congress as this interpretation

36. David Vogel, "Why Businessmen Distrust Their State: The Political Consciousness of American Corporate Executives," *British Journal of Political Science*, vol. 8 (January 1978), pp. 45–78.

37. Evidence of this is available in commentaries on economic policymaking processes in general and the Federal Reserve in particular. Economists of various stripes mistrust and are impatient with congressional politics in economic policymaking. Okun, *Political Economy*, pp. 71, 79, 81, wrote, for example, of the case in 1966 when the Federal Reserve was there to shoulder "the thankless burden" when fiscal policy adjustment was not possible. Congressional refusal to provide flexible tax instruments for the president is another source of criticism. The problem is outlined in Joseph A. Pechman, *Federal Tax Policy*, 3d ed. (Brookings Institution, 1977), pp. 49–50. Criticism of Congress along these lines is not the special preserve of economists; various indictments are outlined in James L. Sundquist, "Congress and the President: Enemies or Partners," in Owen and Schultze, *Setting National Priorities*, pp. 583–618.

might suggest. An alternative view holds that the drama of interorganizational battle has blinded observers to more fundamental factors—that the actual increase in the flexibility of monetary policy coincided with the change from Truman to Eisenhower administrations. With a new Republican majority in Congress, Eisenhower moved to adopt a series of strong anti-inflationary policies.[38] A more active monetary policy fitted comfortably with this general policy direction.

Congressional support for Federal Reserve independence has for the most part been a symbolic exercise, defending the congressional prerogative. Members of Congress have seemed to believe that Federal Reserve independence from the Treasury enhances its responsiveness to Congress; the converse may well be true. Federal Reserve independence from the Treasury may remove a potentially effective way of defining policy responsibility more clearly.

In any case, there is much to indicate that there is more meaning to the notion of Federal Reserve independence from Congress than from the Treasury and the president. A high level of agreement between the Federal Reserve and executive branch economic policy officials has been enhanced by exchanges of personnel and by similarities in outlook which are supported by a careful process of recruitment to top positions.[39] Top policy officials in most administrations have included at least some prominent figures who have been close to the Federal Reserve.[40] Support of the Treasury for Federal Reserve independence from congressional domination has been expressed repeatedly.[41]

38. The most political account is in Clifford, *Independence,* pp. 300–03, although he accepts most of the standard account at other points. Also see Weintraub, "Congressional Supervision," p. 354; Friedman and Schwartz, *Monetary History,* pp. 623–27.

39. Of many examples, three stand out. The first post-accord chairman of the Federal Reserve, William McChesney Martin, had negotiated the agreement for the Treasury. Truman's last appointee to the Federal Reserve, James Louis Robertson, was previously a high career official with the Office of the Comptroller of the Currency, a division of the Treasury. The second post-accord Federal Reserve chairman, Arthur Burns, had served as chairman of the Council of Economic Advisers to Eisenhower and as an adviser to Nixon.

40. This has been true in both Democratic and Republican administrations. For example, under Kennedy, Dillon and Roosa (formerly vice president of the New York Federal Reserve Bank) at the Treasury were quite close in outlook to Martin at the Federal Reserve. This closeness continued under Johnson with Fowler and Deming (formerly president of the Minneapolis Federal Reserve Bank). Carter's administration included two former top Federal Reserve staffers: Lyle Gramley at the Council of Economic Advisers, Daniel Brill at the Treasury. Others who have served in both the Federal Reserve and the Treasury are Dewey Daane, Henry Wallich, Bruce MacLaury, Stephen Gardner, Frank Morris, Robert Mayo, Paul Volcker, Emmett Rice, Sidney Jones, Samuel Chase, and Peter Sternlight.

41. See statement by Treasury Secretary Douglas Dillon, in *The Federal Reserve System After Fifty Years,* Hearings before the Subcommittee on Domestic Finance of the House Committee on Banking and Currency, 88 Cong. 2 sess. (U.S. GPO, 1964), pp. 1231–32; statement of Deputy Treasury Secretary

It is clear that if this "facade of independence" interpretation is accurate, then the relationship it describes is a delicate one. In order to perform the political function of diverting criticism for unpopular policy, the central bank must be perceived to have some genuine degree of independence. It can, however, never be seen to be so independent and its policies so harsh that it provokes an attack that would destroy the illusion by formally subordinating the central bank to the executive branch. On the other hand, the more the central bank cooperates openly with the government, the less plausible it is for others to point the finger when policy tightens. Thus, the ideal relationship would be one of studied distance and intermittent squabbling. Such a process would be expected to produce policy in the long run very similar to the policy that would result from a fully subordinate central bank, subject, like the fiscal authority itself, to political pressures from various groups in society. The primary difference would be that considerable energy and inventiveness would be invested in protecting a facade of independence that primarily serves a political function.

Persistent Tension

Rather than assuming an underlying consensus between central bank and government, the second interpretation of the finding assumes a persistent tension and disagreement. One might not expect to perceive overt conflict between the two actors most of the time because differences would be negotiated quietly or a solution would be imposed by one of the actors. If relevant political resources were overwhelmingly controlled by government, no observed conflict then might be interpreted as indicating compromise on the government's terms. If this were true, of course, one would be surprised by the instances of genuinely independent action found in the United States and West Germany. Neither would one expect to see central bankers unleashing vigorous, and apparently successful, public attacks on fiscal policy proposals. Nor to find attentive elites attributing high levels of influence to central bankers.[42] These

---

Stephen Gardner, in *Financial Institutions and the Nation's Economy (FINE): "Discussion Principles,"* Hearings before the Subcommittee on Financial Institutions Supervision, Regulation and Insurance of the House Committee on Banking, Currency, and Housing, 94 Cong. 1 and 2 sess. (U.S. GPO, 1975), pt. 1, p. 604.

42. Federal Reserve Chairman Burns's criticism of President Carter's proposed fifty dollar tax rebate early in 1977 is an example of apparently successful criticism of fiscal policy. The chairman of the Federal Reserve is regularly included in the *U.S. News and World Report* annual survey identifying "the most influential individuals" in the United States generally and in particular fields.

observations, which seem to be anomalies in terms of the first interpretation, can be explained by noting that the central bank has its own political resources which may be used to support its preferred policy. What are those resources? Are those resources sufficient to account for some meaningful independence?

Central bankers possess two very valuable political resources. The first resource is expertise and a reputation for expertise. Central banks that have the capability to analyze complex economic events quickly and accurately and to maneuver adroitly in executing their policies have formidable resources. These resources are not alone sufficient to insulate a central bank from political pressure, but they may give the bank a degree of flexibility that can substantially affect policy in the short term.

The second resource is the relationship of central bankers with their natural constituency, the financial community. This relationship is one of long standing, and the resources the financial community possesses have often been effective in ordinary political commerce. There is fairly convincing evidence that central bankers work in a milieu that is significantly shaped by the interests and concerns of commercial bankers. And there is evidence that in some settings the links are strong enough that bankers can be mobilized to support central banks actively when that might be appropriate. However, it is not clear that the bankers are the first line of political support for central banks in specific controversies. Indeed, the political resources the central bank draws from this relationship exist because of the importance of the financial community in *economic* affairs—that is, this is an example of structural power. A central bank's capacity to push or pull macroeconomic policy in a conservative direction stems from the economic influence, not the political influence, of the interests the central bank represents. The interests of this constituency—representing a "sound finance" position[43]—comprise several, possibly contradictory, concerns: protecting "the value of the dollar" both from inflation and from international decline; sustaining moderate, stable economic growth; damping sharp market fluctuations that might arbitrarily inflict losses or gains on asset holders or, more importantly, undercut investor confidence; promoting the development of financial institutions that are both profitable and capable of withstanding short-term stresses

---

43. A provocative analysis of structural power in which business confidence figures prominently is Fred Block, "The Ruling Class Does Not Rule: Notes on the Marxist Theory of the State," *Socialist Revolution*, no. 33 (May–June 1977), pp. 6–28; this is also central to the analysis of Charles E. Lindblom, *Politics and Markets: The World's Political-Economic Systems* (Basic Books, 1977).

and strains; protecting the financial system from rippling panic in the event a major institution does fail; and doing all these with minimal state interference in financial markets. These concerns typically are institution-alized in central banks. The perception among the major participants in the economic system that stability is currently threatened varies from time to time, and so should support for the central bank. But there is always some sound finance sentiment that the central bank can rely on.

This support is not randomly distributed in the population of the United States. Wall Street, the financial establishment writ large, strongly supports Federal Reserve tight money as a means of combating inflation even though tight money may be against the immediate interests of parts of the financial community.[44] Positive evaluations of the Federal Reserve Board chairman among the general public increase sharply with income level, are three times as likely among Republicans as Democrats, and are twice as likely among people living in households owning stock as in nonstockholding households.[45] At various critical points, particularly involving appointments to the Federal Reserve, the question of confidence has repeatedly surfaced in the writing of financial journalists.[46] Presidents and their economic advisers are continually sensitive to the need to maintain that confidence and to avoid appearing to challenge the "principles of sound finance."[47] The Federal Reserve stands for something desirable to the groups with the greatest stake in this country's financial stability. These groups are as well identified by the label *sound finance* as any other. It is the representation of the values and preferences supported by this very important constituency that constitutes the central bank's greatest resource in negotiation with the fiscal authority.

If the central bank can claim sound finance as its constituency, and if the fiscal authority recognizes that in part it too is dependent on that constituency, then the fiscal authority has a strong incentive to be attentive

44. Sidney Weintraub, "Wall Street's Mindless Affair with Tight Money," *Challenge,* vol. 20 (January–February 1978), pp. 34–39.

45. Opinion data reported in "The Statistical Romance Covering First 14 Weeks of Fed Chairman Miller's Honeymoon" (Media, Pa.: Sindlinger and Co., 1978).

46. Concerning the appointment of Dewey Daane, see *New York Times,* October 30 and 31, and November 9, 1963; of William Sherrill, *New York Times* April 23, 1967; of William McChesney Martin, *New York Times,* March 26 and 30, 1967. The appointment of William Miller was preceded by considerable flap in the financial press about Arthur Burns's value as a generator of confidence; Charles Walker, *Washington Post,* November 10, 1977; Ira R. Allen, *Washington Post,* November 5, 1977; William Safire, *New York Times,* December 1, 1977; "After Burns the Fed Will Lean to the Left," *Business Week* (November 21, 1977), pp. 108–16.

47. John T. Woolley, *Monetary Politics: The Federal Reserve and the Politics of Monetary Policy* (Cambridge University Press, 1984), chaps. 4, 6.

to the policies recommended by the central bank. Disputes may be resolved on terms favoring the position of the central bank because the fiscal authority recognizes the need to adopt policies that engender confidence, and one expects the central bank to be strongly supportive of such policies. Periodic public disputes with the fiscal authority may reassure the sound finance constituency that the central bank retains the freedom to represent its desires and may reinforce the identity of the central bank with the sound finance constituency. Additionally, central bank independence may reinforce a credibility with sound finance that permits the bank to explain and defend all economic policies to this critical constituency more effectively than could the fiscal authority alone.

From this perspective too, the relationship of the government and central bank is fragile. Almost by definition, the sound finance community cannot mobilize swiftly and cohesively for competition in pluralist political arenas—although specific parts may well be potentially so situated—despite its continuing potential for damage in financial matters. Thus, too much obvious central bank independence again threatens to provoke a potentially damaging attack in pluralist arenas, while too little evidence of independence threatens a loss of support that would, in turn, make independent action even more hazardous. Loss of support would be particularly likely if substantial sections of the sound finance community came to share a definition of appropriate policy that the central bank believed to be in conflict with its broader "stability" mandate.

Monetary Problems as Political Problems

The most accurate view of the government–central bank relationship is a synthesis of these interpretations. If nothing else, central banks can achieve some autonomy based on expertise, and this can be exercised in negotiations over policy. However, the central bank is sufficiently vulnerable to threats from other political actors that its actions are only somewhat different from those preferred by the fiscal authority. Thus, in the short run it is possible to observe disagreements, but in the long run, policies move in the same direction—if, perhaps, on separate and parallel tracks. Monetary policy, just as much as fiscal policy, reflects the judgment of dominant political coalition members about their preferred political outcomes. If the inflation of the 1970s is "the problem," then the answer is not to be found by examining the central bank in isolation. Rather, the central bank must be viewed in its larger political and economic context.

What this means, of course, is that monetary policy choices have to be explicitly conceptualized as political choices. There are several kinds of political choices faced in monetary policy, and each kind of choice includes options tending toward more inflation. First, monetary policy plays an important role in achieving the aggregate economic performance desired by elected officials and their core constituencies. These officials and their constituencies may prefer some combination of outcomes that involve more rather than less inflation. Second, the use of monetary policy to achieve macroeconomic objectives as conventionally conceived may be constrained by a desire to avoid harming politically important but economically vulnerable groups. Protecting those groups may require tolerating inflation. These problems may be exacerbated in more open economies. Finally, policy choices in related but apparently separate arenas can constrain monetary policy or make monetary control more difficult. Thus, innovations in the financial sector that have been tolerated or promoted by policymakers for reasons apparently unrelated to economic management may have made precise economic management more difficult. To advance a social and political explanation of inflation, it is necessary to understand how policymakers might see inflation as a solution to their monetary problems or how inflation might be an undesired consequence of their policy choices.

Monetary Politics at an Aggregate Level

As conventionally viewed, monetary problems involve aggregate balances—that is, keeping interest rates, exchange rates, bank credit, and so on in some appropriate relationship to inflation, employment, economic growth, and international payments flows. There are, to be sure, important political consequences associated with these macroeconomic quantities. There is a large literature demonstrating the relationship between these quantities and government popularity and electoral success—Douglas Hibbs demonstrates in chapter 7 that this link exists. Many studies now convincingly show that citizens' evaluations of governments and their voting decisions are influenced by macroeconomic performance. However, it is far from certain that macroeconomic policy decisions are in fact guided by some narrow attempt to maximize government popularity in the short run.[48] Differences in the preferences of different electoral

48. See the review and citations in Martin Paldam, "A Preliminary Survey of the Theories and Findings on Vote and Popularity Functions," *European Journal of Political Research,* vol. 9 (1981), pp. 181–99. Also see chapter 10, above.

coalitions may partly explain differences between the policy behavior of different countries. Similarly, simultaneous decisions to adopt stimulative policies in several countries in the early 1970s may account for part of the worldwide inflationary increase observed then. Certainly, increased economic interdependence may have made it more difficult for countries to avoid importing some inflation from their neighbors. But it is not at all clear that these highly aggregate political-economic relationships are sufficient to account for most of the problems of inflation and stagnation experienced in advanced industrial countries.

Monetary Policy and Accommodation of Distributive Conflict

Political problems and political conflict typically involve distributive questions, and these are more likely to be obscured than clarified by the terminology of economic aggregates economists use to discuss monetary issues. The importance of distributive issues in political conflict immensely complicates any effort to make simple, straightforward generalizations about monetary politics in many countries because the differences in economic structures lead to different distributive consequences. Nonetheless, one can readily understand that inflation could be regarded by many policymakers as an attractive second-best choice if the alternative involves damaging some economically important or politically powerful sector. Moreover, inflation-tolerating choices may be more likely if policymakers believe that they are confronting temporary "shocks" or disequilibriums that will subside in the future. Such a belief on the part of policymakers seems to have been widespread in the 1970s.

In a few settings—for example, in France and Japan—states have sufficient power and a sufficiently broad array of policy instruments that the distributive consequence of monetary policy can be selected explicitly and with considerable precision. In such settings, credit can be directed to privileged or sheltered sectors with a high degree of success. In other countries, guaranteeing that credit is available to politically sensitive sectors is more difficult. Policy that accepts inflation in order to avoid undesired distributive consequences can be characterized as "accommodative policy."[49]

49. Robert J. Gordon, "The Demand for and Supply of Inflation," *Journal of Law and Economics*, vol. 18 (December 1975), pp. 807–36, and "World Inflation and Monetary Accommodation in Eight Countries," *Brookings Papers on Economic Activity, 2:1977*, pp. 409–77 (hereafter *BPEA*).

A quite common argument along this line focuses on government demand for credit. If government demands for loans in credit markets are increasing (for example, because of deficits), then some private borrowers may be unable to borrow at prevailing interest rates because governments, which are relatively insensitive to interest costs of borrowing, will receive available funds at the margin. When such conflicts occur, monetary authorities may wish to provide sufficient funds to accommodate some substantial portion of the demands of borrowers who would otherwise be excluded. When the economy is near full employment the result will predictably be inflation, and neither government nor the private sector will get the real value of the nominal quantity borrowed.

This is the most commonly offered interpretation of how politics affects central bank behavior and, thus, inflation. As is discussed by Rudolf Klein and David Cameron in chapters 8 and 9, there is a striking lack of confirmation for the notion that the primary source of inflation in the 1970s was in monetary accommodation of deficits. However, for at least some periods in some countries, it is clear that this kind of accommodation was significant. The most obvious and perhaps the most important example is the case of the United States and the financing of the Vietnam War in the late 1960s. The fact that this may have contributed to an increase in world liquidity makes it particularly important. No one argues, of course, that one such episode is sufficient to produce a prolonged period of continuing inflation in several countries.

A second and important kind of accommodation is a response to shocks, both real and monetary. Thus, a sudden restriction in supply of some important commodity or some rapid movement in exchange rates may have distributive consequences that policymakers wish to diminish. A sudden or sustained exchange rate increase, for example, may disadvantage or threaten the existence of a favored export industry. Returning the rate to a low level may involve tolerating a level of domestic price inflation higher than would otherwise seem desirable. In the case of a sudden supply shock, there may be a temporary burst of inflation independent of monetary policy.[50] However, policymakers may choose to respond to the shock by an accommodative monetary policy in order to shift the burden of adjustment. An accommodative monetary policy would reduce the degree to which real resources were transferred from one sector to another

---

50. Alan S. Blinder, *Economic Policy and the Great Stagflation* (Academic Press, 1979).

or from the domestic economy to a foreign economy. Something like this probably occurred in several Western European countries in response to the oil price shocks, but this seems clearly not to have happened in the United States.[51]

A third kind of distributive problem arises from the attempts by societal groups to regain lost ground following inflationary shocks or other unanticipated monetary accommodation. It is to be expected that groups within the economy will attempt to recoup their past losses. They may also attempt to avoid future losses if they expect such inflation to occur again. Under such conditions, fighting inflation through monetary policy alone—which has in several countries proven to be the only means available—requires a willingness to accept whatever pattern of distributive consequences flow from existing patterns of economic vulnerability. Sustained pressure on the most vulnerable sectors—housing, consumer durables—may be very unpopular, even more unpopular than inflation itself. In this case, political problems arise because only one effective, but rather blunt, instrument is used to fight inflation—aggregate monetary policy. With such an approach, there is no assurance that the burdens of fighting inflation are borne equitably. Indeed, in such circumstances, considerations of equity can scarcely be entertained at all, or only with considerable difficulty. At the same time, there is the certain assurance that individuals, groups, and organizations will do all they can to reduce their own vulnerability and to shift the burden of adjustment onto somebody else.

Financial Innovation and Monetary Control

One consequence of inflation, of previous financial regulation, and of previous monetary policy decisions has been financial innovation. Novel means have been developed for managing money for individuals, for corporations, and for financial institutions. This innovation has itself made anti-inflationary monetary control more difficult. In the United States, it is precisely in the era of increased inflation that a variety of financial innovations have occurred. All serve to decrease the precision of control that can be exercised by monetary authorities and thus have increased the probability that inflation-accommodating errors will occur. Indeed, recent studies suggest that this outcome may be even more likely when monetary

51. Ibid., chap. 8.

authorities are concentrating their attention on achieving monetary aggregate targets—as was true in almost every major Western country in the 1970s.[52]

Central Banks and Inflation

There can be no mistaking the fact that monetary policy choices are in fact political choices. This means that while it may be possible to depoliticize central banks by distancing them from partisan conflict, it is impossible to depoliticize the issues with which they must deal. Consider again the one interpretation of the relationship between central bank and government that proposed that central bank independence is primarily a facade and the other that such independence has some substance and is supported by important political resources. The fact that the two interpretations can largely be reconciled helps to clarify the role central banks play in fighting inflation.

There can both be substantial agreement between the central bank and the fiscal authority on most economic questions *and* be negotiation over policy stemming from the real political resources the central bank controls. The central bank not only has the resource of its identification with the sound finance constitutency, but it derives some advantage from the fact that other actors want it to act as a political "lightning rod." There is a price associated with trying to assure that difficult distributive issues are not forced on elected officials. Still, when distributive consequences arouse politically important groups or threaten economically important sectors, central banks will find it impossible not to take an accommodative stance when that is clearly sought by the government no matter how strongly the central bankers themselves feel about inflation.

Consider again the case of the United States. In the world of the 1960s, the functions the Federal Reserve was called on to perform politically and economically were generally reinforcing. That is, it could reassure its own sound finance constituency, take the heat for tight policy, and yet not confront the political boundaries that would have threatened its independence. Since most seriously contending policy options were within fairly close range of each other, independent action rarely implied a profound division of opinion or forced the choice between the sound finance constituency and the good will of elected officials.

---

52. Donald D. Hester, "Innovations and Monetary Control," *BPEA, 2:1981*, pp. 141–89.

In the course of the 1970s, the dynamics of the relationship changed. Reassuring the sound finance community became more difficult—in part because of the prevalence of monetarism,[53] and in part because one of the tasks most dear to the hearts of the sound finance constituency, fighting inflation, was not possible within the constraints of the other soundness objectives of the Federal Reserve. As stabilization policy came more and more to mean *monetary* policy, the illusion of an independent central bank became less and less plausible to attentive observers. The reservoir of support of the sound finance community was, no doubt, still there to be tapped. But the attachment to balancing the various stability goals, firmly engrained in the bureaucratic culture of the central bank, did not foster a forceful, single-minded assault on inflation, and this restraint was reinforced by an apparently growing threat from the legislature—that is, precisely in the pluralistic arena where the Federal Reserve found itself somewhat vulnerable. In addition, innovation in financial institutions, which the Federal Reserve was unwilling or unable to prevent, complicated the stabilization task. Altogether, these changes created a situation in which no policymaker, least of all a central banker, could pursue a precisely defined long-range anti-inflation strategy without imposing substantial costs on large and well-organized segments of society. In the classic pattern of "satisficing" actors, central bankers appear to have been shifting from goal to goal, trying to keep key variables within slowly widening acceptable ranges. Periodically one problem, perhaps inflation, dominated all others. Then it was that central bank independence could most clearly influence policy response.

Conclusion

Though infrequently acting independently in the terms set out in this chapter, central banks obviously can still be separately important actors. For several reasons they are probably less important, because less politically useful, in countries where they are not formally independent as well. The greater the role of the legislature in policymaking, the greater is the value of flexible and efficient policy instruments that are not subject to legislative control. And, ironically, the greater the role of the legislature in policy-making, the easier it appears to be to sustain an independent central bank

---

53. John T. Woolley, "Monetarists and the Politics of Monetary Policy," *Annals of the American Academy of Political and Social Science*, vol. 459 (January 1982), pp. 148–60.

capable of absorbing political criticism. This reflects the advantage given to defenders of the status quo in legislative processes that require repeated approval of any given proposal, such as reducing central bank independence. The liberal values underlying such separation of powers systems, especially a fear of concentrated power, provide a ready rationale for insulating major state powers from nominal control of elected officials.

At a different level, the willingness of governments to compromise with the central bank should vary inversely with the extent of nationalized industry and the ability of the state to control flows of investment capital. The greater the dependence of the state sector on private decisions regarding production and investment, the greater the usefulness of an institution like an independent central bank both to represent and to reassure the private sector.

The German case most clearly approximates these conditions favoring a prominent role for the central bank in postwar Europe. A strong bicameral legislature capable of substantial policy input was designed to fragment political power at the national level. There were, likewise, conscious efforts in the postwar years to reduce the role of the state in the economy—yet a complex system linking industry and finance persisted, with considerable influence over investment and production decisions.[54] Frequent direct contacts and a strong similarity in outlook between finance, big business, and the Bundesbank have been noted by several observers.[55]

Even in other cases such as the United Kingdom and France, the impact of central banks in policy negotiation may be substantial. In those cases, the role of the central bank should be largely determined by the nature of the consensus about the effectiveness of monetary policy in economic stabilization and by the degree to which the central bank is perceived to possess a special expertise not available elsewhere.[56] At the

54. Andrew Shonfield, *Modern Capitalism: The Changing Balance of Public and Private Power* (Oxford University Press, 1965), pp. 239–40, 246–55.

55. Fred Hirsch, *Money International* (Harmondsworth, U.K.: Penguin, 1969), pp. 319–20; William Pollard Wadbrook, *West German Balance-of-Payments Policy: The Prelude to European Monetary Integration* (Praeger, 1972), pp. 80–89; Michael Kreile, "West Germany: The Dynamics of Expansion," in Peter J. Katzenstein, ed., *Between Power and Plenty: Foreign Economic Policies of Advanced Industrial States* (University of Wisconsin Press, 1978), pp. 208–16.

56. The role of the Bank of England has apparently been affected by exactly these two factors. Changing conceptions of the efficacy of monetary policy can be delineated relative to the Radcliffe Inquiry of 1959. See H. G. Johnson and others, *Readings in British Monetary Economics* (Oxford University Press, 1972), pt. 7; Samuel Brittan, *Steering the Economy: The Role of the Treasury* (London: Secker and Warburg, 1969), pp. 47, 81; R. S. Sayers, "The British Monetary Scene since Radcliffe," in International Banking Summer School, *Monetary and Credit Policy and the Banking Community* (Oslo: Norwegian

same time, governments in these countries may have found it more difficult than in countries with nominally independent central banks simultaneously to satisfy their electoral constituencies and the sound finance constituency. Politicians may have been less able to shift responsibility for taking harsh actions. With increasing openness of economies to international disruption should come a greater likelihood that governments would welcome the economic constraints imposed by independent international actors (like the International Monetary Fund) that also stand for sound finance. This would provide both the political lightning rod and the symbol of soundness otherwise absent.

Formally independent central banks may, in fact, contribute to the capability of a country to respond to inflation. However, this result does not flow directly from organizational factors that insulate central banks from politics. Neither a central bank's organization nor its contribution to fighting inflation can be abstracted from the larger political and economic structure. Insulating a central bank politically does not mean undertaking organizational reforms so much as modifying dominant political coalitions.

Bankers Association, 1966), pp. 105–16; Lester C. Thurow and others, *Activities by Various Central Banks to Promote Economic and Social Welfare Programs,* prepared for the House Committee on Banking and Currency, 91 Cong. 2 sess. (U.S. GPO, 1971), p. 16. Recently, the technical proficiency of the Bank has been sharply questioned. See Hugh Stephenson, *Times* (London), April 4, 1977; "The Bank of England's Fall from Grace," *Business Week* (March 14, 1977), p. 61; Brittan, *Steering the Economy,* p. 28; "The Next Five Years," *Banker* (London), vol. 128 (March 1978), pp. 17–19; Stephen Blank, "Britain: The Politics of Foreign Economic Policy, the Domestic Economy, and the Problem of Pluralistic Stagnation," in Katzenstein, *Between Power and Plenty;* Frank Longstreth, "The City, Industry, and the State," in Colin Crouch, ed., *State and Economy in Contemporary Capitalism* (St. Martin's Press, 1979), pp. 157–90.

PART FOUR

Political Economies in Conflict

The four major case studies included in this part are designed to present histories of economic policymaking in their full complexity. They serve as laboratories in which to test the influence of labor unions and employers, the impact of democratic electorates and organized parties, the structure of the state and financial authorities, the challenges of a changing international economic environment. Each of these case studies, moreover, stresses the contradictions that the 1970s imposed on policymakers. They are intended to serve as studies in the difficulties of that decade, not the successes (although there were successes).

The Italian case, presented in chapter 15, is that of an inflation-prone economy highly vulnerable to its own interest groups and the impact of external events. Along with Britain, Italy suffered from the highest inflationary rates in Europe during the 1970s. (And much of the equivalent British institutional material can be gleaned from Colin Crouch's discussion of trade unions in chapter 5.) Italy is also instructive in that the relative weakness of the state must be set against the context of rapid social and economic modernization; a creaky structure based on patronage and power sharing has had to cope with the eruption of mass movements. Michele Salvati thus adopts the procedure of analyzing first the forces in the economic arena, then the contributory pressures emanating from the political sphere, finally synthesizing both in an analytical narrative.

While Italy represented a case study of a weak economy and political system—at least from the criterion of resisting inflation and ensuring stable growth—the West German example until the mid-1980s provided the opposite. In chapter 12 the authors explain what institutional and public-opinion factors helped assure that economy's continuing growth, remarkable balance-of-payments strength, and low inflation during a period when other industrial economies faltered. Outsiders often emphasized the role of the "concerted action" in which labor and business spokesmen allegedly agreed on growth priorities and allowable wage increases. Norbert Kloten and his coauthors stress less the formal structures of negotiation in the 1970s than the tacit respect on each side for what the other party could concede. Their bargain allowed growth, and continued growth facilitated further implicit bargains—a virtuous circle few other countries could achieve, especially after the levy exacted by the Organization of Petroleum Exporting Countries.

From the perspective of the mid-1980s it becomes clear that resisting inflation was not the only measure of economic success. Despite its persistent inflation and bureaucratic inefficiency, the Italian economy retained a robustness that maroeconomic statistics did not always reveal. Small producers remained vital and inventive. In contrast, the West German economy, even as it steamed powerfully ahead through the 1970s, appeared vulnerable to technological obsolescence in the new decade. Many observers worried about Germany's capacity to supplement its traditional heavy-industry strength with innovative capacity in the microchip age. The analyses of these economies were focused on inflation, but inflation alone formed only a part of overall economic performance.

So too the chapters on Japan and Sweden concentrate on the political and economic trade-offs that were so stark in the 1970s. Kozo Yamamura in chapter 14 on Japan explains the potent instruments for control of the economy possessed by state agencies, but highlights the inflationary pressures that could be posed by the diverse interests within the permanently ruling Liberal Democratic party. Sweden, also, is a country where the analyst must account for contradictory trends. In the mid-1970s squeezes on profitability, competition from third world industrializers, an adverse balance of trade seemed to dim the luster of Sweden's welfare capitalism. Andrew Martin in chapter 13 stresses the conflict of priorities between Social Democratic ideals of equality and of solidarity and the need to encourage profitable investment. This conflict was reflected in the loss of Social Democratic political control between the mid-1970s and the 1982 elections and in the impatient chafing for wider income differentiation within the Social Democratic constituency. To be sure,

Sweden has recovered from the most serious setbacks of the late 1970s, but at the cost of some compromise with the egalitarian and solidaristic ideals of earlier decades. Martin's chapter discusses how the new balance between investment and solidarity has had to be negotiated.

Obviously other case studies would have been instructive, but aspects of other countries' performance emerge in different chapters. John Zysman shows how the French were willing to go for economic growth at the cost of inflationary pressure, but his chapter does not concern the particular difficulties that the Mitterrand government faced when they sought Keynesian expansion at a time most economies were imposing retrenchment. Some of the reasons for British difficulties are implicit in the considerations adduced by Zysman, Martin in chapter 13, and Colin Crouch in chapter 5 on the unions. Illustrative material on the U.S. economy is present in every chapter, especially in Leon Lindberg's chapter 2.

Each of the case studies offers valuable lessons; but it is not clear that they can always be applied outside the home environment. Even if, entering the 1980s, Americans envied Japanese growth or German price stability, how much of those countries' social organization could they, or should they, import? Institutional forms can perhaps be borrowed; habits of cooperation or conflict may rest on a more refractory social base. Nor—as the Swedish case suggests—do the formulas of one generation work for the next. In the nineteenth century British industry and productiveness seemed irresistible; throughout the 1950s France seemed the sick man of Europe. Both characterizations proved only temporarily valid. Whether the extraordinary work ethic of Germans and Japanese can persist indefinitely is an open question. These historical reflections are meant as a reminder that even good policymaking can have unforeseen perverse outcomes, and that the cultural and political context of economic progress is highly complex.

12

West Germany's
Stabilization Performance

*Norbert Kloten, Karl-Heinz Ketterer,
and Rainer Vollmer*

Any analyst of Germany's performance in a world of inflation faces the question why the decline in the value of money in the Federal Republic of Germany was less severe than in most other countries. This question, however, is only one aspect of the inquiry into the great variation in the capacities of individual economies to maintain price stability. The wider problem requires examining those structural features of a society that may be conducive to inflation and the social processes that feed into price rises. To do this means assuming that price stability is attainable in principle in Western-type market systems, and that failure to achieve this objective is due to the maladjustment of one or more parameters of economic policy and the socioeconomic system. The question then becomes what motives—perhaps what illusions—are at work, and what obstacles preclude adjusting the parameters in accord with the objective.

The fundamental cause of inflation in a socioeconomic context is the fact that overall nominal income expectations rise higher than productive power because of the rivalries and illusions of social groups. It is significant in this connection that for individuals or groups, price stability can be considered a "collective good," which everyone benefits from whether he has made sacrifices or not.[1] Everybody is in favor of price stability, but each individual would like to avoid paying for it. Where there are public goods, there are also "free riders."[2] While this observation involves some

---

1. Gottfried Bombach, "Neue Politische Ökonomie," *List-Forum*, vol. 9 (June 1977), pp. 65 ff.
2. Ibid.

oversimplification, it gets to the heart of the problem. The rate of decline in the value of money ultimately depends on the claims society makes on the national product. This observation may be hard to incorporate in a model that is intent on grinding out high coefficients of determination (R^2); but it does bring together a range of social factors even if they do not always aggregate perfectly.

Inflation in Germany

In the three decades following the currency reform of June 20, 1948, which eliminated the monetary overhang of pent-up inflation that had accumulated in Germany during the war years, the deutsche mark lost less of its domestic purchasing power than the currencies of other industrial countries. At times during the 1960s the United States did better in the field of consumer prices,[3] and from 1975 to 1980 the Swiss inflation rate stayed below that of Germany.

Even in the initial phase, however, the D mark was not spared severe tests. The most serious arose from the Korean War. Panic buying and the hoarding of raw materials caused prices to shoot up and an already vulnerable balance of payments to deteriorate enormously. (At this time West Germany became the first major deficit case in the newly created European Payments Union.) In the fourth quarter of 1951, the year-on-year rise in the cost-of-living index reached 11 percent, a figure not even approached again after the oil crisis. This surge of inflation, however, was only brief; between 1952 and 1960 consumer prices rose by an average of only 1 percent per year (table 12-1), much more slowly than in the other industrial countries, particularly the European ones. The differences from year to year correspond to the movements of the trade cycle as reflected in the deviation of industrial production from trend (figure 12-1), which was rising steeply (table 12-2).[4] The rapid growth was accompanied by a swift reduction in unemployment, which had been very high initially (table 12-3). At the same time, the Federal Republic

---

3. Not, however, in unit values of exports.

4. The Council of Economic Experts, the Bundesbank, and other German authorities view economic cycles as fluctuations in the utilization of potential output. Because only annual figures on utilization are available, cyclical movements in the manufacturing sector—deviations of output from trend—are used to mark the cycles.

Table 12-1. *Annual Rate of Change in Price Indexes,*
West Germany, 1950–84

Percent

	Cost of living		Producer prices, industrial products	Export prices[a]	GNP deflator
Year	4-person households with employed head	All households			
1950	−6.4	...	...	...	...
1951	7.9	...	...	...	10.8
1952	2.0	...	2.4	...	4.8
1953	−1.7	...	...	...	−0.4
1954	0.1	...	−1.8	−0.5	0.0
1955	1.6	...	1.8	0.6	2.2
1956	2.5	...	1.6	3.9	3.0
1957	2.2	...	1.6	2.6	3.1
1958	2.0	...	−0.3	−1.8	3.4
1959	1.1	...	−0.8	0.7	1.4
1960	1.4	...	1.2	1.8	2.4
1961	2.3	...	1.5	0.3	4.3
1962	2.9	...	1.0	0.8	4.2
1963	3.1	2.9	0.4	1.2	2.9
1964	2.4	2.3	1.1	0.9	3.0
1965	3.4	3.3	2.4	2.2	3.5
1966	3.5	3.6	1.7	1.8	3.7
1967	1.5	1.6	−0.8	−0.4	1.4
1968	1.3	1.6	−0.7	−0.4	1.8
1969	2.1	1.9	2.0	3.1	3.5
1970	3.2	3.3	4.9	−3.5	7.3
1971	5.2	5.2	4.4	3.8	7.7
1972	5.3	5.6	2.6	3.0	5.6
1973	6.8	7.0	6.7	4.7	6.0
1974	6.7	7.0	13.3	16.0	6.9
1975	6.1	6.0	4.7	8.6	6.7
1976	4.4	4.3	3.7	4.1	3.3
1977	3.5	3.7	2.7	1.1	3.8
1978	2.5	2.7	1.2	0.0	3.8
1979	3.9	4.1	4.8	3.1	3.7
1980	5.3	5.5	7.5	7.0	4.8
1981	6.3	6.3	7.8	5.8	4.2
1982	5.4	5.3	5.8	4.3	4.7
1983	3.2	3.3	1.5	1.7	3.2
1984	2.4	2.4	2.9	3.5	1.9

Source: Federal Republic of Germany, Federal Statistical Office.
a. Based on unit values of exports.

Figure 12-1. *Production and Employment Trends in West Germany,*
1950–58

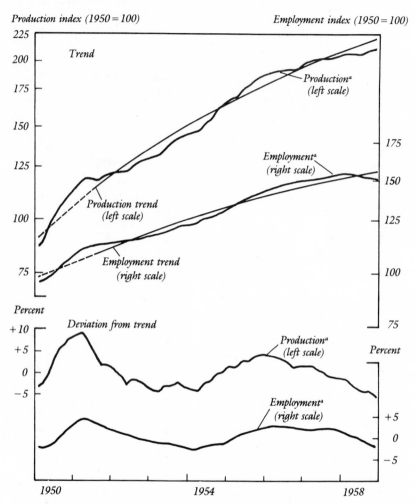

Production index (1950 = 100)   *Employment index (1950 = 100)*

Source: Helmut Schlesinger, "Geldpolitik in der Phase des Wiederaufbaus (1950–1958)," in Deutsche Bundesbank, *Währung und Wirtschaft in Deutschland 1876–1975* (Frankfurt: Fritz Knapp, 1976), p. 561.
a. Excludes construction and public energy supply.

Table 12-2. *Annual Growth Rates, West Germany, 1951–84*

Percent

Year	Gross national product[a]	Production potential[a]	Utilization of production potential
1951	10.4	. . .	. . .
1952	8.9	. . .	. . .
1953	8.2	. . .	. . .
1954	7.4	. . .	. . .
1955	12.0	. . .	. . .
1956	7.3	. . .	. . .
1957	5.7	. . .	. . .
1958	3.7	. . .	. . .
1959	7.3	. . .	. . .
1960	9.0	. . .	. . .
1951–60	8.0	. . .	. . .
1961	4.9	5.7	98.6
1962	4.4	5.6	97.5
1963	3.0	4.9	95.7
1964	6.6	4.9	97.3
1965	5.5	5.1	97.8
1966	2.5	4.5	95.9
1967	−0.1	3.6	92.4
1968	6.5	3.3	95.1
1969	7.9	3.8	98.8
1970	5.9	4.7	100.0
1961–70	4.7	4.6	. . .
1971	3.3	4.7	98.3
1972	3.6	4.9	97.8
1973	4.9	4.4	98.4
1974	0.4	3.5	96.0
1975	−1.8	2.9	92.1
1976	5.3	2.5	95.2
1977	2.8	2.1	96.1
1978	3.6	2.1	97.1
1979	4.0	2.1	99.1
1980	1.9	2.3	98.7
1971–80	2.8	3.1	. . .
1981	−0.2	2.1	96.7
1982	−1.1	1.4	94.4
1983	1.3	1.5	93.9
1984	2.6	. . .	. . .

Sources: Federal Statistical Office; German Council of Economic Experts.

a. At constant prices.

Table 12-3. *Annual Rates of Unemployment, Wage Increase, Productivity Increase, and Income Distribution, West Germany, 1950–84*
Percent

| Year | Unemployment | Wages and salaries[a] | | Productivity[a,b] | Wage share adjusted | Real net earnings per employee |
		Monthly base	Per employee			
1950	11.0	...	...	...	65.6	...
1951	10.4	...	16.3	7.7	64.4	6.3
1952	9.5	...	7.9	6.9	62.5	4.8
1953	8.4	...	5.9	5.7	63.1	8.3
1954	7.6	...	5.2	4.9	63.3	5.3
1955	5.6	...	7.9	8.0	61.7	6.0
1956	4.4	...	8.0	4.4	61.6	4.8
1957	3.7	...	5.2	3.4	61.3	3.6
1958	3.7	5.5	6.7	3.2	62.0	3.3
1959	2.6	3.0	5.5	6.4	60.9	4.8
1960	1.3	6.8	9.4	7.1	60.4	6.4
1961	0.8	8.6	10.2	3.7	62.0	6.8
1962	0.7	7.6	9.2	4.0	62.8	5.4
1963	0.8	5.2	6.2	2.7	63.2	2.7
1964	0.8	4.9	9.0	6.6	62.3	5.7
1965	0.7	7.0	9.1	5.0	62.5	6.5
1966	0.7	6.3	7.2	2.8	63.3	2.2
1967	2.1	2.9	2.8	3.2	63.2	1.5
1968	1.5	3.9	7.6	6.2	61.3	3.4
1969	0.9	6.5	9.6	6.2	61.8	5.4
1970	0.7	13.0	14.7	4.7	62.7	9.5
1971	0.8	13.3	11.8	3.0	63.6	4.0
1972	1.1	9.1	9.0	3.9	63.8	3.9
1973	1.2	10.3	12.0	4.6	64.6	0.8
1974	2.6	12.5	11.4	2.4	66.3	2.5
1975	4.7	8.5	7.2	1.6	66.1	0.5
1976	4.6	5.9	7.0	6.1	64.9	0.0
1977	4.5	6.9	6.9	3.2	64.7	2.1
1978	4.3	5.6	5.2	2.5	64.0	3.8
1979	3.8	4.8	5.5	3.1	63.5	2.2
1980	3.8	6.7	6.5	0.8	64.7	−0.3
1981	5.5	5.5	4.9	0.8	65.4	−1.4
1982	7.5	4.0	4.2	0.9	64.9	−2.2
1983	9.1	3.3	3.4	2.8	63.4	−1.0[c]
1984	9.1	2.8	3.0	3.0	62.9	−0.5[c]

Sources: Deutsche Bundesbank; Federal Statistical Office.
a. Total economy.
b. Gross domestic product per economically active person.
c. Estimated.

developed into a balance-of-payments surplus country, which it remained through the 1970s. It became clear fairly soon that Germany's stability in comparison with other industrial countries and its surplus position entailed their own danger for price stability. The first international speculation involving the D mark occurred as early as 1957,[5] and the risk of importing inflation was to become a constant problem from then on.[6]

The 1960s marked a turning point in German economic development. In 1961, unemployment fell below 1 percent for the first time. Full employment had been achieved, and growth rates diminished. The danger to monetary stability also increased, partly because new pressures for redistribution had emerged with the labor shortage. For the moment, adjustment through inflation was avoided by revaluing the D mark. But the value of money slipped from cycle to cycle.[7] Between 1961 and 1966 the average annual fluctuation, at 2.9 percent, remained appreciably higher than in the preceding decade.

Despite this definite tendency to accelerate, prices followed an unmistakable cyclical pattern, lagging some three to six quarters behind the general trend. Cyclical variations of overall demand explained the movements of the price level, as was demonstrated in the first economic setback in 1966–67. In 1967, for the first time since the war, the real gross national product (GNP) did not rise, but rather fell (albeit by only 0.1 percent). Prices and costs responded flexibly. While the growth rate of consumer prices stood at 3.5 percent at the beginning of the downswing in 1966, it decreased to 1.6 percent in 1967 and 1968, then rose to 1.8 percent in 1969. But this last price spurt could likewise at first be seen as a consequence of the sharp business cycle. After all, the situation was not one just of full employment but of overemployment, as the influx of foreign workers was increasing sharply.

Nor did a fall in foreign demand help to brake inflation. Since the D mark was undervalued, German goods failed to become less attractive to foreigners as German capacities increasingly became overtaxed. This situation was not altered much by the fiscal "substitute revaluation" of autumn 1968, or by the revaluation of the D mark just under a year later.

5. After speculation on the revaluation of the D mark took place in 1957, selecting between adjusting through inflation or revaluation remained a permanent dilemma, though it was obscured for a time by worldwide recession. The 5 percent revaluation did not take place until March 1961.

6. "The very term 'imported inflation' originated in monetary discussions in Germany in about 1954–55." Otmar Emminger, "Deutsche Geld- und Währungspolitik im Spannungsfeld zwischen innerem und äusserem Gleichgewicht, 1948–1975," in Deutsche Bundesbank, *Währung und Wirtschaft in Deutschland, 1876–1975* (Frankfurt: Fritz Knapp, 1976), p. 485.

7. Norbert Kloten and Rainer Vollmer, "Stability, Growth and Economic Policy," *German Economic Review* (Stuttgart), vol. 13, no. 2 (1975), p. 105.

Figure 12-2. *Price Movements and Economic Activity: Indexes of Cyclical Activity in West Germany, 1960–73*

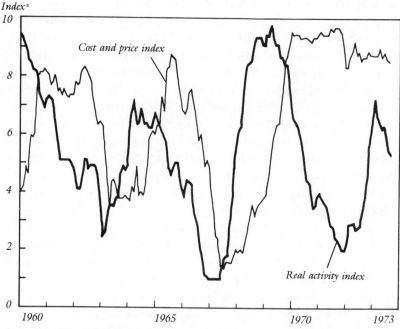

Index[a]

Source: German Council of Economic Experts, *1973–74 Annual Report*, p. 183, and for methodological explanation, *1971–72 Annual Report*, pp. 154–63.

a. Each index aggregates nine components that are assigned values between 0 and 10. Components of the real activity index include output, orders, running down of inventories, employment, etc. Components of the cost and price index include money supply, wages, wholesale and retail prices by sector, short-term credits, etc. An aggregate index lower than 5 indicates performance below a normal trend; one above 6 suggests intensity greater than the norm.

But as the overtaxing of productive capacity eased, it became clear that the pattern of inflation and thus also of the stabilization performance of the German economy had changed at the turn of the 1970s. The deterioration in the value of money had become a trend phenomenon— as the German Council of Economic Experts described it, "a process which takes place independently of the ups and downs of the trade cycle."[8] Superimposed, it emerges that the movement of the council's price and cost indicator, which had followed real developments with a relatively stable lag in the 1960s, stuck at a high level between 1970 and 1973, even though a complete business cycle occurred (figure 12-2). During that period consumer prices rose at an average rate of about 5.5 percent

8. German Council of Economic Experts, Special Report of May 4, 1973, sec. 3.

a year. The momentum of the inflationary process is particularly evident in the current rates—an annual rate of 9.5 percent in the fourth quarter of 1973, for example.

As early as the spring of 1973 Germany fell out of step with international economic developments; a downswing, the steepest in the history of the Federal Republic, began. Initially it did not appear as a downswing, partly because foreign demand increased enormously. The downturn did not become severe until the recessionary tendencies had become mutually reinforcing at the international level. West Germany experienced unemployment again, for the first time since the 1950s. Immigration of foreign workers was prohibited in the autumn of 1973, when about 2.5 million foreigners were working in West Germany. While the customary unemployment rate had been around 1 percent, it rose steeply from the end of 1973. In the winter of 1974–75 the number of unemployed persons exceeded the 1 million mark—corresponding to an unemployment rate of about 5 percent.

These developments were accompanied by a slowing of inflation. As an annual average the inflation rate was highest in 1974, at 7 percent, but this figure concealed an incipient slowdown in the pace of current price rises. This slowdown continued until autumn 1978. In October 1978 consumer prices were only 2.1 percent higher than a year before. This overstated West Germany's true stabilization performance, since there was hardly any scope for passing on higher costs in prices owing to the appreciation of the D mark. Furthermore, business was slow, so that the price level was also under cyclical pressure.

In mid-1975 a surprisingly strong economic recovery began, but good phases were soon alternating with poor ones in rapid succession. The traditional cyclical pattern of the 1950s and 1960s no longer applied, and many people spoke of a "washboard" pattern of activity (figure 12-3).

Not until the summer of 1978 did a marked improvement begin. This improvement was already discernible when at the Bonn economic summit in midyear the federal government was persuaded to launch another economic stimulation program. Capital spending picked up distinctly and employment rose. But the unemployment figure, which did not fall below 810,000 (seasonally adjusted), remained high by German standards. Even so, there was a general shortage of skilled labor. The structural discrepancies between the nature of the work on offer and the qualifications of the unemployed could hardly be overcome, at least in the short run.

The second oil price explosion—which at first tended to enhance the

Figure 12-3. *Deviation from Trend in Economic Activity, Employment, and Wages in West Germany, 1961–80*

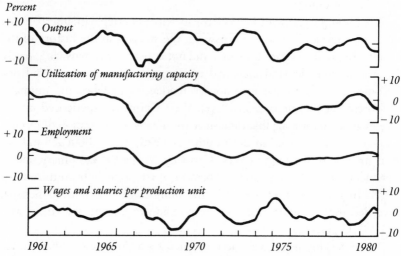

Percent

Source: Deutsche Bundesbank, *Statistische Beihefte zu den Monatsberichten,* Reihe 4, Saisonbereinigte Wirtschaftszahlen.

propensity to invest since it made a large number of energy-saving capital projects economical—created some entirely new problems for the Federal Republic of Germany, or brought some latent problems to the surface. That persistently surplus country, always suspected of pursuing an export strategy in its economic policy, suddenly showed the highest current account deficits recorded by an industrial country since the explosion (table 12-4). Moreover, West Germany had to cope with this new external challenge, as the accumulated appreciations of the D mark in 1973, 1977, and 1978 finally impaired the competitive position of German producers. The inroads that imports made into domestic markets during the 1970s provided the clearest evidence of this. This situation became more serious since government economic policy was not used to offset the new economic conditions.

The large current account deficits and the apparent helplessness of the policymakers had an adverse effect on the international standing of the D mark. As a result the German currency at times came under massive pressure, which was reinforced by a renaissance of the dollar. The exchange rate slippage of the D mark showed clear signs of overshooting. This added momentum to price rises, which were accelerating strongly anyway

Table 12-4. *Annual Change in Volume and Value of West Germany's Foreign Trade, 1951–84*

| Year | Volume of goods (percent) | | Net exports of goods and services | | Current account (billions of D marks) | Net foreign assets of Bundesbank (billions of D marks) |
	Exports	Imports	Percent of GNP	Billions of D marks		
1951	. . .	. . .	1.8	2.12	2.3	2.0
1952	. . .	. . .	2.3	3.13	2.5	2.9
1953	. . .	. . .	3.5	5.20	3.9	3.6
1954	19.7	25.7	3.1	4.98	3.7	3.0
1955	16.0	24.6	2.2	3.93	2.2	1.9
1956	15.8	10.8	3.2	6.46	4.5	5.0
1957	13.6	11.4	3.9	8.54	5.9	5.1
1958	4.6	8.7	3.7	8.65	6.0	3.4
1959	10.6	18.2	3.6	9.13	4.2	− 1.7
1960	14.4	16.6	2.6	7.93	4.8	8.0
1961	5.8	6.9	2.2	7.13	3.2	− 2.3
1962	3.3	13.1	1.2	4.30	− 1.6	− 0.9
1963	8.7	6.1	1.5	5.61	1.0	2.7
1964	10.4	12.1	1.4	5.90	0.5	0.4
1965	8.0	15.9	0.1	0.33	− 6.2	− 1.3
1966	10.5	0.6	1.5	7.42	0.5	2.0
1967	8.5	− 2.9	3.5	17.34	10.0	− 0.1
1968	14.9	16.7	3.7	19.75	11.9	7.0
1969	10.8	17.0	2.9	17.59	7.5	− 14.4
1970	14.4	19.2	2.1	14.25	3.2	22.7
1971	4.5	8.1	2.1	15.53	2.8	11.0
1972	6.5	7.4	2.2	18.48	2.7	15.2
1973	14.0	5.5	3.2	29.08	12.4	16.1
1974	10.9	− 3.9	4.4	43.44	26.6	− 9.1
1975	− 11.2	− 0.3	2.8	28.95	9.9	3.3
1976	18.6	17.8	2.5	28.63	9.9	1.3
1977	4.0	2.3	2.5	29.50	9.5	2.6
1978	3.2	6.8	2.9	37.25	18.1	12.2
1979	4.8	7.6	0.8	11.13	− 11.1	− 7.3
1980	2.0	0.0	− 0.2	− 3.10	− 28.6	− 25.7
1981	6.6	− 5.0	1.0	14.74	− 13.1	1.3
1982	3.3	1.3	2.4	38.13	8.7	2.7
1983	− 0.3	4.0	2.3	38.77	10.3	− 1.6
1984	. . .	. . .	2.6	45.87	17.9	− 1.0

Sources: Federal Statistical Office; Deutsche Bundesbank.

owing to the oil price hike. In the process, stabilization gains were lost again although inflation did not climb above 6 percent between February 1981 and February 1982.

In 1981 the pace of price rises began slackening, primarily because of a distinct improvement in the external situation. The current account moved back into surplus in the fourth quarter and the exchange rate stabilized. But domestic business activity had peaked in the spring of 1980 and unemployment was increasing steeply.

This chapter discusses the sociological and social conditions or dilemmas under which monetary stability prevailed or faltered in West Germany from 1948 to 1981.

It is helpful to consider three phases. The period from 1948 to 1969 was generally characterized by a high degree of price stability. The particular social features of the postwar period and the institutional arrangements arrived at were partly responsible for foreigners' picture of West Germany as a model of stability. But some of the distinctive social factors gradually lost their formative power in the course of reconstruction. In the second phase, during the rapid acceleration of inflation from 1969 to 1973, the claims on the national product were unmistakable; there was a general struggle over shares of the GNP, with the government an active participant. Purely economic factors such as the undermining of monetary policy by external influences added to inflationary pressures.

The German authorities succeeded in reversing inflationary expectations earlier and more effectively than authorities in most of the industrial countries after the first oil price increases of 1974.[9] Analysis of this third phase, however, is more difficult because of the second oil shock, so some uncertainty must remain whether the period from 1974 through 1981 was a political tour de force or a real improvement in the socioeconomic conditions for monetary stability.

The Period of Reconstruction, 1948–69

West Germany's relatively good record of monetary stability is often viewed as the outcome of a mysterious but typically German form of coordinated action, and foreigners are apt to inquire who is responsible for this astonishing degree of "harmonized behavior." For outsiders it is very hard to grasp that after World War II the potential unresolved

9. In terms of approximating a rate tolerable for West Germany. Other countries may have been able to curb the erosion of the value of money to a relatively greater extent than West Germany.

conflicts of interest and aim which in the last analysis form the breeding ground of inflation were much less numerous in West Germany, at least for two decades, than in most countries. This owed a great deal to the German collapse in the spring of 1945 and to the associated destruction of traditional structures.

The Reorganization of Government, the Economy, and Society

For the Germans, World War II ended quite literally in total collapse. Dramatic experience had heightened awareness of the undesirable developments of the preceding decades, of the causes of the collapse of the Weimar Republic, of the impotence of the democratic parties in the face of Hitler's seizure of power, and of the enforced conformity of German workers in the National Socialist organizations that replaced the trade unions. Germans were determined not to let such things happen again. Political sentiment was against the unstable solutions of the Weimar Republic, economic sentiment against inflation and government control.

The public still had vivid memories of the hyperinflation of the early 1920s and the later misery caused by the Great Depression. Experience of the wartime economy and postwar dislocations left an even greater impact. The government sought to counter new inflationary trends by instituting price controls and a coupon system that failed to work even during the war, let alone in the period after it. Up to the currency reform in 1948, with its drastic writing down of monetary assets, cigarettes and other articles increasingly replaced the official currency as a unit of account and often also as a medium of exchange. Aversion to bad money and official rationing determined the attitude of a generation still active in the 1970s and affected the outlook of their children.

Common experiences and common sufferings engendered a feeling now hardly comprehensible of "being in the same boat." The range of postwar tasks that had to be tackled regardless of politics was overwhelming in view of the destroyed factories, the reparations policy pursued by the Allies, and the millions of refugees. Reconstruction of factories and housing was an imperative that could not be disregarded. The acute hardship suffered by individuals and the need to build up a state practically from nothing gave rise to a yearning for "normality,"[10] and a marked

---

10. Theodor Eschenburg, "Der bürokratische Rückhalt," in Richard Löwenthal and Hans-Peter Schwarz, *Die zweite Republik: 25 Jahre Bundesrepublik Deutschland—eine Bilanz* (Stuttgart: Seewald Verlag, 1974), p. 89.

dislike of experiments.[11] The relatively low level of potential conflicts made West Germany an abnormally peaceful society well into the 1960s.[12] It also formed the basis of a solidarity that was almost taken for granted and that was the sole reason why a minimum of social security could be created quickly. The equalization of war losses and refugee aid (just as in the field of social security) and the target of overcoming the misery caused by the war militated against formation of a poor underclass.[13] Concern with reconstruction also inhibited political conflict. Tenbruck may exaggerate a little in his description of West German attitudes but he does hit upon a key factor: "Life during the fifties was virtually unaffected by public and political matters. . . . It was precisely the circumstances of reconstruction that linked the political achievements directly with the interests of all citizens, and enabled them to find common ground again in politics. Political matters therefore tended to be more or less taken for granted."[14]

There was relatively little dispute over policy among the major parties responsible for reconstruction. Thus the new constitution—the Basic Law of the Federal Republic of Germany—was adopted with little disagreement.[15] Germany's political and economic stability also made possible a modified system of proportional representation; and the constitution included a requirement that a party obtain at least 5 percent of the votes before it could enter parliament, which prevented the kind of fragmentation of political parties that had occurred during the Weimar Republic.

The general lack of animosity between parties was no doubt a result of the years of persecution and enforced absence from politics that all of the founding fathers had endured.[16] The retrospective condemnation of National Socialist rule on the one hand, and the rejection of communism, which had established itself in the other part of Germany, on the other, narrowed the political spectrum. The anticommunist consensus owed most to the Social Democratic party (Sozialdemokratische Partei Deutschlands, or SPD) between 1945 and 1949 and to the cold war.[17] The views

11. Dietrich Hilger, "Die mobilisierte Gesellschaft," in ibid., p. 113.

12. Hans-Peter Schwarz, "Ausblick: Wie wird es weitergehen," in ibid., p. 927.

13. Richard Löwenthal, "Prolog: Dauer und Verwandlung," in ibid., pp. 9–24.

14. Friedrich H. Tenbruck, "Alltagsnormen und Lebensgefühle in der Bundesrepublik," in ibid., p. 298.

15. The Basic Law came into force on September 23, 1949. It was the work of a parliamentary council composed of sixty-five representatives of eleven state parliaments.

16. Wilhelm Hennis, "Die Rolle des Parlaments und die Parteiendemokratie," in Löwenthal and Schwarz, *Die zweite Republik,* pp. 209–10.

17. Hans-Peter Schwarz, "Die aussenpolitischen Grundlagen des west deutschen Staates," in ibid., p. 47.

of the Western Allies in this matter conformed to those of broad sections of the population.

A similar consensus also prevailed concerning the regulatory ideas of economic policy in West Germany. Following the initial successes of an economy largely freed from state control, liberal concepts of economic policy were increasingly well received. The Christian Democratic Union (CDU) became the party of the future, if only because it recognized the mood of the majority of voters and understood how to mold it in accordance with the CDU's own objectives—for example, through the highly evocative picture of the social market economy.[18] The SPD, which was still opposed to the market economy, had to go into opposition; however, following the incontrovertible success of the "German economic miracle" under Ludwig Erhard, the SPD abandoned Marxist residues and the concept of nationalization in its Godesberg Program of 1959. With this program the SPD completed its transition to a national party.[19] Economic policy, including its social aspects, was thereafter hardly in dispute between the parties. This explains why Professor Schiller, the Social Democratic economics minister, rather than Kurt Schmücker (CDU), is viewed as the true successor of Professor Erhard. Thus West Germany has been spared the political alternation of nationalization and denationalization that has taken place in the United Kingdom.

The relatively strong political consensus was due in no small measure to the decision to adopt a clear-cut federal solution when reconstructing the government. In the states (the *Länder*) and municipalities the SPD had retained a governing role. After the bad experience of a strong centralized government, the architects of the constitution gave more weight to the idea of the separation and independence of the various levels of government.[20] While the federal government was given little scope for influencing the actions of the state governments, the states were given considerable leverage in the federal government through the Bundesrat, the parliamentary body that is composed of representatives of the state governments. The constitution also assigns to state governments the responsibility for any public duty not explicitly assigned to the federal government. And municipalities are constitutionally guaranteed control of local affairs.[21] One result is that the federal budget does not predominate;

18. Ibid., p. 59.

19. Susanne Miller, "Die SPD vor und nach Godesberg," in ibid., p. 391.

20. Heinz Kock, *Stabilitätspolitik im föderalistischen System der Bundesrepublik Deutschland* (Cologne: Bund-Verlag, 1975), p. 40.

21. As far as budgeting is concerned, this autonomy is essentially one of spending.

in keeping with the fairly uniform division of duties among the various levels of government, their shares of public expenditure do not differ greatly.[22] Federalism also encourages balanced regional growth because the states and cities have a stake in the establishment of industry. Regional tensions, which elsewhere tend to encourage conflict management by inflation, accordingly failed to arise and traditional conflicts decreased in intensity.[23] On the other hand, coordination problems under the federative system eventually turned out to be detrimental to stabilization policy.

Employee and employer groups likewise had no wish to return to the old structures after the war. Instead of a large number of ideologically oriented unions as in the Weimar Republic, which the National Socialists had no difficulty in abolishing because of their mutual hostility, sixteen trade unions, classified by sectors of industry, were founded and were united in the German Trade Union Federation (Deutscher Gewerkschaftsbund, or DGB) in 1949 (the federation does not include the rival salaried staff union Deutsche Angestellten-Gewerkschaft, or DAG, or two public service staff associations whose wage-negotiating powers are severely limited). The Christian Trade Union split off in the mid-1950s but it is not politically significant. Officially the DGB is not politically oriented and not linked with any political party (in contrast to the situation in the United Kingdom). However, a large proportion of the SPD members of the Bundestag and of SPD ministers and political officials are members of a trade union, and quite a number are former union officials. But there are also some trade unionists among the Christian Democrats and in the Free Democratic party (FDP).[24]

These links are not at variance with the trade unions' conception of themselves. Given the postwar attitudes, it was logical that the reemerging trade unions would seek to become comprehensive representatives of employee interests, with a full role in economic and political decision-making.[25] The DGB, the DAG, and to a lesser extent the Civil Servants Association, all consider themselves to be under an obligation to society in general, and for that reason expect to have a say. Such an attitude,

22. The federal and state governments each account for less than two-fifths of public spending and local authorities for about one-quarter. The bulk of capital spending is carried out by the local authorities.

23. M. Rainer Lepsius, "Sozialstruktur und soziale Schichtung in der Bundesrepublik Deutschland," in Löwenthal and Schwarz, *Die zweite Republik,* p. 266.

24. For example, all but 2 of the 224 SPD members of the Bundestag in 1977 were members of trade unions, while only 8.7 percent of CDU-CSU members were. Emil Peter Müller, "Die sozioökonomischen und verbändlichen Strukturen des 8. Deutschen Bundestages," Beiträge zur Gesellschafts-und Bildungspolitik des Instituts der Deutschen Wirtschaft, no. 19, 1977.

25. See Lepsius, "Sozialstruktur," p. 267.

although it does involve drawbacks, is by and large conducive to stability, as Michele Salvati makes clear in chapter 15. The trade union movement, rather like the SPD, has consistently dissociated itself from the German Democratic Republic. It aims at improving the system and not at any fundamental rejection—let alone a revolutionary overthrow—of the political and economic order in West Germany. The DGB has never left any doubt that extreme left-wing positions are incompatible with membership in a trade union. The German trade union system thus quite definitely operates within the parliamentary political spectrum.

On the employers' side, too, reorganization was necessary. In 1949 the Federation of German Employers' Associations was founded, with eleven associations covering employer functions and a profusion of subsidiary organizations.[26] At the lower level there are close links with subsidiary bodies of employers' organizations that are not mainly oriented to the employer function, such as the Federal Association of German Industry. Just as among the trade unions, there are no party ties, although an affinity to the Christian Democrats and also the Free Democrats (albeit to a progressively smaller degree) is unmistakable.

From the beginning, wage negotiations were left solely to the two sides of industry, to employees and employers. The right to collective bargaining derives from the constitutional right to form trade unions (article 9 of the Basic Law). In the 1949 Collective Bargaining Act and other legislation, trade unions and employers' associations are explicitly recognized as collective bargaining institutions. The 1949 act not only guards their autonomy but also limits and shapes the actions of the negotiating parties by codifying the areas of conflict, competences, and means of settling labor disputes. Of particular significance is the legislation that reserves the right to strike to the recognized parties and bans labor disputes initiated by relatively small groups of workers, such as are frequently observed in other countries.

Economic Policy

The key event in German postwar development was the currency reform of June 20, 1948; in the three Western zones of occupation of postwar Germany it ended a period of total price control and a comprehensive system of rationing. After a decade and a half of government

---

26. Walther Herrmann, "Arbeitgeberverbände," in *Handwörterbuch der Sozialwissenschaften*, vol. 1 (Göttingen: Vandenhoeck & Ruprecht, 1956), p. 288.

intervention, economic activity was again subjected to the laws of a market economy. Overnight, the economic situation of the individual changed. The radical difference and the overwhelming success of the currency reform were for many people conclusive proof of the correctness of liberal ideas. From the start, the free market system functioned just as had been predicted. Shops filled up with goods, money had real purchasing power again, and everywhere the signs of new economic activity multiplied. Most of the credit was given to Ludwig Erhard, the minister of economics who, acting against Allied instructions, had decontrolled the markets on the day of the currency reform. The reform and the decontrol of markets were hazardous experiments, but they were a success. The new system also triumphantly withstood its first serious tests. When West Germany became the first major deficit case in the new European Payments Union during the Korean crisis, it was offered special credit dependent on a stabilization scheme "proposed by the international monetary experts Per Jacobsson and Alec Cairncross, much of which had been prepared in November 1950 by a group of German experts. . . . This program, emphasising restrictive measures in the fields of monetary, budgetary, and fiscal policy, laid the foundations both for internal stabilization and for the subsequent balance of payments surpluses of the Federal Republic."[27] Thus, the authorities relied on the efficiency of demand management and not on state control.

In economic policy terms the currency reform was a major act of regulatory policy. Its success strengthened the conviction that economic policy should primarily be regulatory, not interventionist. The neoliberal concept evolved from rejection of the uncoordinated and often mutually contradictory government interventions between the two world wars. It shared with classical liberalism a confidence that the price mechanism can control economic activity optimally and smoothly, which explains its strong aversion to interventionist action.[28] The conditions under which the price mechanism works effectively do not, however, come about automatically. Government must create appropriate basic conditions. In particular, it must prevent the cornerstone of the system, namely, competition, from being eliminated by private economic agents. The influence

27. Emminger, "Deutsche Geld- und Währungspolitik," p. 489.
28. The most complete theoretical approach within the neoliberal school was that of the Freiburg School led by Walter Eucken and Franz Böhm. The ideas of Alfred Müller-Armack (who coined the phrase "social market economy"), Alexander Rüstow, Wilhelm Röpke, Friedrich von Hayek, and Gottfried Haberler were closely related to the Freiburg School's way of thinking. Similar ideas were developed in the United States, under Henry C. Simons, and in other countries. The organizational center of the liberal school was the Monte Pellerin Society.

that the regulatory approach to economic policy acquired owes much to the broad consensus prevailing in academic circles, which shaped generations of students and molded the ideas of the Advisory Council of the Ministry of Economics.

As a matter of fact, interventionist action was regularly taken as well, with the authorities relying mainly on monetary policy and pursuing (at least in the 1950s) a rather conservative fiscal policy. But the main characteristic of economic policy until well into the 1960s was its reliance on regulatory principles and thereafter increasingly on Keynesian doctrines (at first gradually) which the authorities attempted to reconcile with classical ideas.

DECISIONS BASED ON REGULATORY PRINCIPLES. The first of several decisions reflecting regulatory principles taken during the 1950s was the establishment of a central bank completely independent of the government, both in its staff and in its policies. When the Bank deutscher Länder was set up in 1948,[29] it was assumed that a government right to influence its actions would eventually undermine the monetary system. That bank was a two-tiered organization, including a network of independent state central banks.[30] In 1957 the dispute over a one-tier or two-tier central bank system was settled in favor of the single-tier arrangement. The Bank deutscher Länder was succeeded by the Deutsche Bundesbank.[31] Attempts to question the autonomy of the Bundesbank (half-hearted as they have been) have met with energetic resistance from all political groupings. This may be due in part to the absence of any serious disagreements between the bank and the federal government—which is not to say that monetary and fiscal policy have been perfectly coordinated. The only true test of the central bank's independence would be in a conflict of principle, when everything depends on the staying power of the parties concerned.

The remains of the two-tier system act as a built-in obstacle to a one-sided personnel policy[32]—an obstacle that also enhances autonomy in the

29. On March 1, 1948, by a law of the occupying powers.

30. The capital was owned by the state banks; their presidents were appointed by the prime ministers of the states.

31. But the main offices of the Bundesbank continued to be called state central banks.

32. The policymaking body of the Bundesbank, the Central Bank Council, is made up of the eleven presidents of the state central banks and the eight members of the Bundesbank directorate (including the president and vice-president). The president of the Republic appoints all members, those on the Bundesbank directorate being proposed by the federal government after consultation with the Central Bank Council, and the presidents of the state banks being proposed by the Bundesrat in accordance with each state's legislative instructions and after consultation with the Central Bank Council. The independence of the state central bank presidents is an important aspect of the independence of the Bundesbank.

general policy field.[33] But what has this autonomy to do with West Germany's stabilization performance? If it is legitimate for the government of a democratically organized country to feel wholly responsible for economic activity, the advantages of protecting the central bank, in its monetary decisions, from the influence of pressure groups can hardly be doubted. As Michael Parkin concluded in an analysis of twelve industrial countries, "there is strong evidence that full independence is associated with a low rate of inflation."[34]

Regulatory principles were next expressed in the Act Prohibiting Constraints on Competition of July 27, 1957. True to the neoliberal concept of competition as a government responsibility, this act ended a decades-long tradition of cartels in Germany.[35] The act came to be regarded as a basic law of competition, comparable in importance to the constitution. The German concept of economic policy saw competition as one of the prerequisites of smooth development in the private sector, which enabled inflationary tensions to be avoided.

Also in 1957, retirement pensions were linked to wages, so that they follow (with a lag) the movement of the gross earnings of the working population. This key part of the federal government's social security system has helped to keep conflicts in German society within limits. Nevertheless, the pension formula contained the seed of undesirable developments, for a wage-linked pension if wrongly handled can cause serious stabilization problems (as it did in the early 1970s).

The "economic miracle" of the 1950s was certainly fostered by West Germany's "opening to the outside world." This, too, was a decision based on regulatory principles. Germany's role in the European integration process after World War II (like that of several other European countries) was initially passive.

From the beginning West Germany was involved in economic inte-

---

33. The main duty of the Bundesbank, specified in section 3 of the Bundesbank Act of July 26, 1957, is to "safeguard the currency" and to "make banking arrangements for domestic and international payments." The Bundesbank is required to support the general economic policy of the federal government insofar as is consistent with the discharge of its duties; moreover, it is independent of the federal government (section 12 of the act). The federal government is entitled to attend meetings of the Central Bank Council (but not to vote there); and it must invite the president of the Bundesbank to attend discussions on matters affecting monetary policy. It also is entitled to postpone decisions of the council.

34. Michael Parkin, "In Search of a New Monetary Constitution for the European Communities" (1977).

35. Between the wars there were well over a thousand organized cartels in Germany. Section 1 of the act lays down the principle of prohibition. A 1973 amendment prohibits coordinated actions (section 25). In 1973, reporting requirements were replaced by the monitoring of mergers. Together with the prohibition of resale price maintenance, these measures act as constraints on competition.

gration in the heart of Europe, though not of a kind altogether in keeping with German regulatory ideas. A functional type of integration—incorporation of the participating economies in a common automatic market system through the mere return to free trade—would have conformed to German liberal thinking. But the form of integration that was chosen relied on supranational institutions with wide powers and envisaged the harmonization of national economic policies. Doubts about this approach were suppressed since the idea of political integration appeared at least as important as purely economic integration.[36]

The starting point was the Schuman Plan, under which a European Coal and Steel Community (ECSC) was established and a common market for coal, ore, scrap, and steel created, primarily by abolishing tariffs, quotas, and subsidies. When the six ECSC nations set up the European Economic Community (EEC) in 1957 the objectives were more ambitious. The treaty signed in Rome on March 25, 1957, included the free movement not only of goods and services but also of capital and labor in the countries of the community.[37] Coordination of the economic, monetary, and cyclical policies of member states was also envisaged—economic policy would be used to create conditions resembling those of a domestic market within the Community.

However, difficulties of the integration process soon emerged; one was the permanent problem of imported inflation, another a series of confrontations over stabilization concepts. West Germany's partners in the EEC (and in the Organization for Economic Cooperation and Development) showed little understanding of Germany's guiding principles. A particularly striking example was the confrontation over planning within the EEC in the early 1960s. While Minister of Economics Erhard strongly opposed the Brussels conception of medium-range forecasts and medium-term programming, which represented the Keynesianism that he so firmly rejected, a compromise agreement established that the EEC would draw up medium-term action programs in future. From then on the discussion of cyclical policy, and particularly of the role of fiscal policy, intensified in West Germany, in part because of economic developments in the 1960s. The first outcome of this discussion was the 1963 establishment of the German Council of Economic Experts. While Erhard had thought of the new council as a seconder of government policy, it in fact emerged

---

36. See Andreas Predöhl, *Aussenwirtschaft*, 2d ed. (Göttingen: Vandenhoeck and Ruprecht, 1971), p. 129.

37. The treaty came into effect on January 1, 1958.

with a far more independent role, submitting its annual report to the parliament and the public, with the government required to comment on the report to the Bundestag within a specified period. However, the council is (for good reason) not allowed to recommend particular measures of economic policy.[38]

The establishment of the Council of Economic Experts was not the only fruit of the debate over cyclical policy. A Stability and Growth Act passed on June 8, 1967, created the preconditions thought to be necessary for efficient control of the economic process; it was hailed as the stabilization "basic law" of the free market system. Expectations were optimistic for this supposedly optimum amalgam of liberal and Keynesian ideas. The act and a catalog of measures concentrate on financial policy. The monetary aspect is neglected, presumably because the Deutsche Bundesbank Act takes care of monetary policy and the instruments to be used in it. The Stability and Growth Act is very reticent in its provisions concerning incomes policy; it merely provides for guidelines to be drawn up by the federal government for "concerted action" should any of the overall economic objectives be in jeopardy.[39] It envisions early coordination of economic activity, and enactment of a Stabilization Policy Committee consisting of representatives of federal, state, and local authorities and a Financial Planning Council responsible for coordinating the medium-term financial planning of regional bodies. Both of these committees, however, are limited to issuing recommendations; they cannot mandate particular measures or interfere with independent budgeting at any level.

THE FIRST INFLATIONARY SIGNALS. Following the economic success, the first signs of excessive claims being asserted on the national product

38. The council's conceptual achievements are reflected in the measurement concepts it evolved for particular political areas such as the "cyclically neutral budget" (a sort of full-employment budget) or the "cost-neutral wages policy." Monetary policy's orientation toward quantitative control also owes a great deal to the council.

39. Outside Germany, concerted action has often been looked on as the secret weapon in Germany's successful stabilization record. But concerted action was intended to be a forum for discussion of how well the criteria of incomes policy conformed with the overall economic situation—that is, for providing "orientation" data. Reliance was to be placed on the persuasive power of information, better arguments, and the willingness of those concerned to let their actions be guided by logical reasoning. In fact, however, concerted action consisted of conferences in which the federal government discussed its program and its appraisal of the economic situation with representatives of the most important economic groups (representatives of the Bundesbank and of the Council of Economic Experts were also present). The task of this body, therefore, was exclusively that of exchanging information; it had no authority to recommend, let alone to decide on, a particular policy. In the early stages questions of wage policy were included in its agenda, but from the early 1970s the trade unions refused to discuss them.

began to emerge in West Germany by the mid-1960s. Hardly anyone allowed for the possibility of a sustained setback. High rates of growth and substantial increases in income were regarded as a matter of course. Although full employment had strengthened labor's position, the unions' wage policy was not particularly aggressive. The trade unions had shed their revolutionary programs for good, and by and large people were satisfied to see that scarcity had caused factor prices to shift in favor of wages. Despite the shift, however, the factor-weighted wage share of national income remained relatively stable (see table 12-3).

The first wave of wage increases that significantly raised costs took place in autumn 1964 and spring 1965. Although vigorous business activity may have contributed significantly to this wave, it was already possible to detect changes in behavior that reflected inflationary expectations. Government mistakes also contributed to the onset of inflationary expectations. There was reluctance to insulate the monetary system from international inflationary impulses. A further revaluation, after that of 1961, was awarded. Life in a permanent export boom was so pleasant that undesirable consequences—the structural distortions arising in the West German economy—were overlooked. Nor was that all; in 1964 and 1965 the financial policymakers shirked their responsibility for stabilization by taking almost incomprehensible expansionary measures aimed at attracting votes. Though they claimed that their balanced budget did justice to the principles of sound financial policy, they ignored the fact that disbursement of the taxes that flowed in so plentifully for cyclical reasons, and also because of the higher inflation rate, was bound to increase inflationary tensions. This fiscal stance no doubt owed a great deal to the loss of Konrad Adenauer, who retired from the office of federal chancellor. The CDU suffered a leadership crisis, especially since Adenauer's successor Ludwig Erhard, the architect of the economic miracle, was not a commanding figure in his new role. The temptation was therefore great to keep voters loyal by means of election promises.

THE CONSEQUENCES OF STAGNATION. The first slump since the war, in 1966–67, was largely caused by lack of coordination among authorities. Monetary leaders, their attention focused on the government's expansionary fiscal measures, persevered with a restrictive policy much too long. "As late as May 1966 the Bundesbank felt obliged to raise the discount rate from 4 to 5 percent although private capital spending was already stagnating. It did so because government expenditure was still too high. . . . The bodies responsible for the public budgets did not see reason until the capital market, and later also the money market, failed them."[40]

The downturn in economic activity came as a profound shock to the general public. Hardly anyone had reckoned with the possibility of a recession or even of stagnation. But the shock did at least curb inflationary claims that were beginning to be asserted on the national product. The trade unions responded to the changed economic situation with appreciable restraint, extending a large proportion of the wage agreements that were due for renegotiation ("wage pause") and concluding new agreements for longer than usual even though wage increase rates were low.[41]

Their intention was to provide employers with a stable basis for pricing. And prices did begin to respond to cyclical changes again. Still, the shock at the recession led to expansionary programs being discussed long after the trough of the cycle in spring 1967.[42] Even after the revival of foreign demand had caused a very strong upswing, private and public behavior was mainly directed toward nursing a supposedly ailing economy. A third stabilization program was still being discussed as late as 1968, when it was really high time to take corrective action against incipient inflation in line with the provisions of the Stability and Growth Act. The authorities let themselves be lulled by the low price increases, although they should have known that prices are a lagging indicator of undesirable trends. The inability to exercise control in the field of stabilization policy was reflected most clearly in the government's resistance to a revaluation, which was long overdue. Foreigners' sharply increasing claims on German productive potential were competing more and more with steeply rising domestic demand. Some overtaxing of the German economy seemed foreordained, and the government could not bring itself to carry out more than a fiscal "substitute revaluation"[43] in the autumn of 1968. This sufficed neither to

40. Karl Blessing, address on the occasion of the awarding of the Karl-Bräuer-Prize, Deutsche Bundesbank press release 25, 1967. Blessing was president of the Deutsche Bundesbank at the time.

41. In 1967, when agreements covering about 15 million wage and salary earners could have been terminated, the trade unions renegotiated agreements for only one-third of these employees. In 1968, agreements covering only one-fifth of employees were renegotiated; termination dates were on average postponed more than seven months and for eighteen months or more in the coal mining, steel, and metalworking industries. See A. Müller, "Die Tarifbewegungen 1968," *WWI-Mitteilungen*, no. 5 (1969), p. 1940.

42. The general public ascribed the rapid overcoming of the crisis to the two stabilization programs with which the Stability and Growth Act was launched. But the success of the programs was mainly based on the fact that they strengthened an upswing already in progress.

43. A 4 percent special tax on exports and corresponding tax relief on imports of nonagricultural goods.

close the steadily widening price gap between West Germany and other countries nor to contain speculation on a proper revaluation of the D mark. As the waves of speculation became more violent, monetary policy was in effect condemned to impotence. Instead of acting, Chancellor Kurt Georg Kiesinger displayed misplaced strength.[44]

Under the impact of the crisis the trade unions continued their extreme wage restraint in the spring of 1969. But government failed to curb the expansion of demand, with the result that profits rose far faster than employees' incomes as output increased while prices remained largely stable. In the course of 1969 workers became more and more convinced that they had to be compensated. The trade unions were unaware of the impending explosiveness, and the employers ignored it; no effort was made to adjust the distribution of incomes until the exasperation found vent in wildcat strikes in autumn 1969. For the first time since the 1950s the German trade unions were in danger of losing their basis of legitimacy, which had a highly adverse effect on the climate of negotiations from then on. A wave of price rises was also set in motion. The government's belated efforts, including the so-called countercyclical reserve of mid-1969,[45] made no significant impact. Economic policy appeared to be "sitting on the fence." Thus, confidence that the Stability and Growth Act really provided control of the economy soon turned out to be an illusion. The opportunities for stabilization policy presented by the downswing had been wasted. Indeed, compared with the period before 1966, the prospects for successful stabilization performance had deteriorated distinctly.

The Period of Accelerating Inflation, 1969–73

The unfortunate results of the crisis cannot explain the continuing rapid deterioration in stabilization performance after 1969. Nor does the inexorable decay of the Bretton Woods system, with its destabilizing and inflationary effects, nor—later—the oil crisis that shook the world economy

44. The views of the two partners in the governing coalition on the question of revaluation were irreconcilable. The SPD, led by Professor Schiller, the minister of economics, recommended a revaluation, but Franz-Josef Strauss (CSU), minister of finance, had Chancellor Kiesinger and the cabinet on his side. The consequence was that revaluation became an election issue. Otmar Emminger called this "a unique case of a debate on a change in the exchange rate of a major currency continuing for many months 'in the market place.'"

45. Sections 5, 7, and 15 of the Stability and Growth Act provide that, in the event of an expansion of demand in excess of economic capabilities, funds are to be immobilized at the Deutsche Bundesbank.

to the core. Social circumstances at home had also become less propitious for price stability.

The change in socioeconomic conditions was far from abrupt; there were signs of it in many industrialized countries during the 1960s.[46] Transformations in values in the second half of the decade found their most obvious expression in the unrest at universities. In other reaches of society too a feeling of disquiet (often subconscious) was fairly widespread. Everywhere the importance of economic growth was questioned. The quality of growth, it was argued, had been neglected in favor of its purely quantitative aspect. As emphasis shifted to environmental protection and limits on growth, the growing criticism of the results of events in the markets was concealed. Talk of "private riches and public poverty" was rife; the alleged incongruity between the needs and the actual supply of public goods, not least in the education sector, led critics of the status quo to assign more and more tasks to government. Claims on government began to proliferate far beyond the bounds of what had hitherto characterized the modern welfare state. But how can this underlying transformation be explained?

Perhaps society, after the season of investment, considered a season of harvest appropriate. The 1960s witnessed in a specific sense the end of the postwar period. As prosperity increased, reconstruction with its pronounced preference for the future lost value as a reason for solidarity. And as the immediate threat of cold war gave way to more relaxed relations between East and West, a further reason for solidarity lost ground. The political spectrum began to widen, and the potential for social conflict increased. Because these changes were assimilated by existing parties and associations, the impression continued to be given to the outside world that a fairly far-reaching social consensus was being maintained in West Germany. Paying heed to divergence at the grass-roots level, however, curbed the freedom of action of some of these organizations considerably.

The Change in Political Power

The combined Christian Democratic and Christian Social Unions (CDU-CSU), which had been in power continuously since 1948—albeit

---

46. Tenbruck, "Alltagsnormen," p. 300, suggests that identical technical developments brought about similar results and problems in the social sectors of many countries. His explanation does not do full justice to the problem.

in the final phase only in the Grand Coalition with the SPD—apparently lacked any intuitive feeling for these social processes of reorientation. Thus their campaign slogan of 1969, "No experiments," relied on an attitude more appropriate to the 1950s and early 1960s. The conviction gained ground well into the ranks of their supporters as well as the population at large that the CDU-CSU was unable to do justice to the wishes for modernization.[47] The SPD program, on the other hand, envisaged reform in all aspects of daily life, and the FDP promised to "part radically with old traditions." Thus all was set for a political about-face, even if the SPD and FDP gained only a small majority in the 1969 election.[48] Willy Brandt's policy statement on October 28, 1969, included an ambitious—indeed, too ambitious—program of reforms that under the slogan "We want to risk more democracy" took account of the widespread demand for broader access to economic and political advances without overlooking its counterpart, joint responsibility. His statement, however, emphasized the need for stability[49] and a sound financial policy. The first act of the new government was to carry out the long overdue revaluation of the D mark.[50] It would therefore be an oversimplification to interpret the political changing of the guard as a decision in favor of a coalition less mindful of stability.

Nevertheless, stability did finally fall victim of a "free rider" attitude—the notion that someone will act to bring about the stability that everyone favors but none is willing to make sacrifices of his own for. Such a mood could prevail because there was little fear of economic consequences. Though faith in the corrective power of the Stability and Growth Act had evaporated, confidence that the government was capable of ensuring full employment, and under SPD leadership was willing to do so, remained unshaken. The new government's stress on full employment was interpreted as a guarantee. And price rises were accepted as the unavoidable

47. Rudolf Wildenmann, "CDU/CSU: Regierungspartei von morgen—oder was sonst?" in Löwenthal and Schwarz, *Die zweite Republik*, p. 350.

48. Fear of inflation mobilized voters against the CDU-CSU owing to their firm rejection of a revaluation of the D mark. The election results of autumn 1969 were at any rate considered a victory of the Schiller voters. See Karl-Dietrich Bracher, "Die Kanzlerdemokratie," in ibid., p. 199.

49. Press and Information Office of the FRG Government, Bulletin 123, October 29, 1969. Brandt stated: "Steady economic development is the best base for social progress. It creates the climate in which private initiative, the readiness to take risks and efficiency can unfold. It ensures security of employment, and safeguards growing incomes and increasing savings against erosion by rising prices."

50. On October 27, 1969, the D mark was revalued by 8.5 percent. The formal revaluation was preceded by a short period of floating so that when the revaluation rate was determined, contact with the market forces could be maintained.

result of external influences.[51] (Little wonder, therefore, that the trade unions, still impressed by what had happened in the autumn of 1969, endeavored to meet the next crisis of legitimacy among the rank-and-file with more aggressive tactics.)

Projects for improving social security were also thrust on the government from all sides with little regard for the financial burdens they might impose. On the contrary, the heavier burden was often the basis for advancing larger wage claims.[52] Numerous groups made claims on the government in hopes of receiving more in redistribution than they had to contribute. A growing "payee mentality" tended to characterize the period and, as Ellwein noted, discussion was often dominated by those who assumed no responsibility, but led their constituencies to demand more of the state even while criticizing the state for failure to live up to the new, heightened expectations.[53]

Local authorities also had to deal with the rising expectations for public goods such as schools, kindergartens, swimming pools, parks, and the like.[54] Many local governments faced considerable pressure when they sought to adjust their charges to meet the trend of rising costs. "Red Point campaigns" often paralyzed local public transport when fare increases were imminent. Such campaigns were often accompanied by demands for free public transport, to be paid for by the local government or by the so-called perpetrators of "consumer terrorism"—namely, the retailers and department stores. In this extreme case, local authorities generally resisted, but in others they often felt compelled to give in.

Federal and state governments were also unlikely to reject the new social demands. If the new team in Bonn, moreover, was not to disavow its plans for reform so soon as to make them seem mere electioneering promises, it had to deliver some results within the parliamentary session, whether economic conditions were favorable or not. In fact the state itself had to become a participant in the struggle over the national income, which only exacerbated some of the economic difficulties themselves. The

51. A position at the rear of the international "inflation convoy" seemed to many West Germans to be a sufficient success.

52. In West Germany, moreover, the employee and the employer share equally the cost of social security contributions. Employees are not fully aware of rapidly rising costs or of the fact that employers' contributions would otherwise be available for distribution in the form of wages.

53. Thomas Ellwein, "Die grossen Interessenverbände und ihr Einfluss," in Löwenthal and Schwarz, *Die zweite Republik,* p. 486.

54. Even though considerable amounts of state and federal funds go into such projects.

inflationary process could be halted only when the connections between sanctions and erroneous policy became clear once again.

The Behavior of Government

Government behavior in this period undoubtedly contributed to the progress of inflation. Despite the high degree of utilization of production capacity, public authorities exerted an expansionary influence; the growth rates of government expenditure were all double-digit. Proposed reforms implied a larger government share in the national product. To achieve this without endangering the aim of stability, it would have been necessary to reduce private claims accordingly. Instead the state attempted to mask the cost of additional services. But the more government gave in to the claims of society, the more the payee mentality proliferated. No attempt was made to explain that any increase in public goods also demands more of the individual citizen; on the contrary, tax cuts were announced. The Work Promotion Act, for example (which came into force on June 25, 1969, before the change of government), virtually invited abuse through liberal interpretation of its conditions for benefits. In the inflationary environment, income from pensions fell behind in relative terms, which from a sociopolitical point of view was regarded as unacceptable—and probably was, to some extent.[55] Forecasts of the movement of pension insurance funds were extremely favorable,[56] and parliament responded by advancing the rise in pensions by six months and introducing a flexible retirement-age scheme. Thus transfer expenditure reinforced the inflationary exaggerations. The tendency of all levels of government to assert more claims interfered with coordination between the various levels at the very time when it was particularly necessary—and this in spite of all the provisions of the Stability and Growth Act.

In view of ample tax receipts (not least as a result of the inflation) the lower levels of government—local authorities even more so than state—could scarcely be persuaded to defer projects that appeared urgent or that constituents were demanding. Suddenly many projects were declared imperative that proved not to be when the tax flow became less favorable. Attempts to evade making a contribution toward stability—to adopt a

---

55. Pensions follow the movement of employees' earnings with a lag of three years.

56. In its annual Pension Adjustment Report the federal government forecasts trends in the receipts, expenditure, and assets of the pension insurance funds over the next fifteen years.

"free rider" attitude—are particularly understandable among local authorities because the electorate is likely to judge local politicians by what they have done for the local community, and less by what they have done toward achieving overall economic aims.[57] Local politicians will not willingly expose themselves to the reproach that they have done less to improve the quality of life than politicians in other communities.

Because the number of states is small, any attempt on their part to become a free rider is easily recognizable. Nevertheless, the states too found it hard to submit to the aim of price stabilization as long as, for example, plentiful tax revenues gave them an opportunity to contribute to the betterment of living conditions. Thus it is differences in the order of priorities that lead to problems of coordination, not—as might be assumed—differences in party or political orientation of the federal and state governments.[58] It would indeed be too risky politically for a state government to rely on its failure to act in a manner conducive to stability having a more damaging effect on the coalition in Bonn than on itself. But precisely because of the differences in priorities, those who bear a special responsibility for stabilization policy have a particular obligation in the conduct of public finance. The federal government failed to meet its responsibility for the difficult task of coordination under a federal financial system.[59] And it had largely closed the door to stabilization efforts of its own. Thus maladroitness and halfheartedness deprived any actions in the field of stabilization policy of success.

Measures were adopted too late and their impact was too weak. This fault, evident in financial policy in the 1960s, had not done much damage thanks to the more favorable stability conditions then prevailing. In 1970, precious months were wasted. Not until midyear, when the rise in prices continued undiminished, was any action taken. But the authorities shrank from applying the provisions of the Stability and Growth Act; the measures were to be tailored to the specific situation—to the detriment

---

57. Paul-Helmut Huppertz, *Gewaltenteilung und antizyklische Finanzpolitik: Ein Beitrag zur Theorie institutioneller Bedingungen der Stabilisierungspolitik in der Bundesrepublik Deutschland* (Baden-Baden: Nomos Verlagsgesellschaft, 1977), p. 154.

58. Kock proves this empirically; "Stabilitätspolitik," pp. 87–89.

59. The Council of Economic Experts caused a sensation when it suggested in a Special Report of May 4, 1973, that the federal government was "possibly making things too easy for itself by giving the state and local authorities only a growth rate for budgetary policy without at the same time publicly advocating the postponement of a number of projects in which it . . . has a considerable say. In this case stabilization policy is also a matter of public relations. It is understandable that the states do not want to be made responsible if the execution of the major reform projects, which are increasingly under the direction of the federal government, has to be delayed because the funds available are inadequate—not least owing to the ensuing burdens, which the federal government usually does not share."

of stability, as it turned out. In addition to the temporary suspension of depreciation allowances, the authorities confined themselves to introducing a refundable countercyclical surcharge on income and corporation taxes, from which—for social reasons—the lower-income groups were exempted, although they were in fact the most likely to show a demand response. As a refundable supplementary tax acts like compulsory saving, the effects on consumption were only small. But as if that were not enough, the authorities felt obliged to refund the tax (by March 1973, as promised) at a particularly unfavorable time. Worse still, to preclude the impression of a confidence trick, they were unable to raise taxes—as would have been appropriate to the situation—at the time when the refund fell due.

A stabilization program in May 1971 was also unable to curb the expansionary stimuli caused partly by the expectation of a pronounced deterioration in the economic climate.[60] Central, state, and local authorities expanded their overall expenditures by more than 15 percent in 1971, compared with 12.6 percent in 1970. This contributed to the unexpectedly early termination of the downswing, but it also fostered the acceleration of inflation. In 1972 the public budgets remained expansionary, though slightly less so than in the preceding years—nonetheless, still out of line with cyclical requirements. Even though economic developments progressed at a breakneck pace, there was no change at first in government policy in 1973. In February agreement was reached on a stabilization program, but it was ineffectual.

Government policy had taken its revenge; the authorities had kindled the inflation that reduced the value of the increase in expenditure. Thus it was not possible to raise the government's share in the national product, as had been planned, and not all promises could be kept. In the face of the rising unrest, however, it was possible to maintain the progressive wage and income tax scales that were helping financial policy.[61] In May 1973 the government introduced a second stabilization program. The financial policy measures were again more or less in line with cyclical requirements, although the Stability and Growth Act was again not brought into play. A surcharge on income and corporation taxes was imposed only on those in the higher income brackets. An investment tax

60. The program undertook to cut expenditure and reduce borrowing correspondingly (by DM1.8 billion) and also to deposit the countercyclical reserves at the Bundesbank.

61. Under a progressive tax scale, the expansion of incomes due to inflation leads to the public authorities receiving more additional revenue than consistent with the increase in taxpayers' capacity to pay.

was also introduced. At the time this was regarded as a courageous step; in retrospect it can be seen as having been too strongly directed at curbing capital investment—and this in a phase when a weakness of investment was beginning to be apparent.

But the crucial factor in a turnabout was less this stabilization program than the parallel transition to floating exchange rates. This gave monetary policy room for maneuver and opened up the possibility of easing the stability burden on financial policy.

The Collective Bargaining Process

The wildcat strikes of 1969 had a lasting effect on trade union behavior. The ambitious aims of income redistribution that the unions pursued from then on proved to their members that better results could be achieved through an organized wage policy than through individual negotiations and took the wind out of the sails of radical forces. A tight labor market facilitated the change in attitude. The trade unions' strategy now included new social claims for the less advantaged. Rises in wages were disproportionately steep in the lower-income brackets because of the introduction of so-called basic sums and the elimination of so-called low-wage categories.[62]

As early as the autumn of 1969 the metalworkers' union was able to win an 11 percent increase for the iron and steel industry. In 1970, negotiated wage rates rose by an average of 12.9 percent (in some cases by over 20 percent) and in 1971 by as much as 14 percent. Meanwhile the business cycle had passed its peak, so that progress in productivity was no longer as great and unit labor costs soared. In the economy as a whole they went up by 9.9 percent in 1970 and 9.7 percent in 1971. The trade unions' strategy of attack met with little opposition from businesses. Firms assumed that since they were working at full capacity, wage concessions could be passed on in prices. Furthermore, in view of very large backlogs of orders in 1970, businessmen felt that losses sustained through work stoppages would be more expensive than cost increases. As unions grew more confident, businessmen felt they could no longer resist claims even when it became clear that labor had made a breakthrough on the income distribution front (see table 12-3).[63]

62. A portion of the wage increase was expressed as a fixed amount for all beneficiaries, or a percentage rate was agreed on with the proviso "but not less than" a fixed amount.

63. Wage ratios of the early 1970s are often compared unfavorably with those at the beginning of

Floating the exchange rate of the D mark on May 9, 1971,[64] could have been used to stabilize real income shifts, but wage negotiations had been completed earlier in the year, and so it had little effect. Fear of recession led to a temporary period of moderation at the beginning of 1972. Comparatively small wage increases were accepted, especially in sectors sensitive to economic fluctuation. In fields where demand was steadily expanding—such as the building sector—or where experience had shown that price sensitivity was less acute, the wage increases were larger. Since, moreover, a new upswing was already under way, fear of a recession rapidly faded. The period of floating had been too short to have any really far-reaching effects. Inflation was not slowed; in fact wage increases continued to accelerate. Although this owed something to the cost pressure deriving from earlier wage rounds, the struggle over the distribution of income also entered a more acute phase under the influence of inflation. In the summer of 1973 some of the negotiated wage increases reached 15 percent. And still business put up little opposition to the demands of the unions.

Even when government economic policy changed course sharply in the spring of 1973, the risk of not being able to pass on wage concessions in higher prices apparently still seemed insignificant. When a new "profits explosion" was shifted into the realm of possibility—somewhat recklessly, as it later turned out—businesses agreed to "subsequent improvements" in the summer of 1973, so as to avoid a debacle like that of 1969. As an employer the state, too, easily conceded additional increases in pay; indeed, during this entire period its behavior was no more in accordance with the requirements of stability than that of employers in the private sector, which evoked the Council of Economic Experts' sarcastic comment that "the adequate payment of government employees [appears] to have been among the most important reform projects of recent years."[65] Inclusive of the so-called structural improvements—upgradings, bonuses, and the like—the public service was among the leaders in the expansion of incomes in the early 1970s. This made it quite manifest that the proliferating "inflation mentality" was already setting its stamp on attitudes. Wage and

---

the 1950s. But in 1950 in devastated postwar Germany comparatively much labor and little capital were involved in the production process. As the input of capital increased, the share of income accounted for by capital necessarily rose as well and the (adjusted) wage ratio fell. See German Council of Economic Experts, *1975–76 Annual Report,* par. 131.

64. The period of floating ended with the worldwide realignment in December 1971 (Smithsonian Agreement).

65. German Council of Economic Experts, *1972–73 Annual Report,* par. 338.

price rises leapfrogged upward. More than any other phenomenon, spiraling inflation was an excuse to pass the blame for undesirable developments from one side to the other in political discussions. After the shock of the quadrupling of oil prices at the end of 1973, the wish to safeguard oneself against threatening monetary erosion was almost bound to drive the struggle over the distribution of income to a new climax.

The Fresh Start

The inflation rate in West Germany reached its highest level in 1974. That was also the year in which capital and labor drifted farthest apart, and in which social consensus was smallest. In part this followed from the government's loss of authority, symbolized by the resignation of Chancellor Willy Brandt, after the discovery of a communist spy in the federal chancellery. The chancellor considered his authority undermined earlier, however, and by the end of 1973, it was evident that the program of domestic reforms that the SPD-FDP coalition had promised could not be realized. Disillusionment was reflected in the notion that only reforms that "cost nothing" would be undertaken, which tended to engender the conviction that each group must get for itself what the government had promised but was unable to deliver.

The conflict and the lack of leadership were evident at the time of the wage negotiations in early 1974, with the confrontation between the trade unions on the one hand and the federal government and the Bundesbank on the other. The dispute revolved mainly around the predicted inflation rate for 1974 and the proper economic policies to follow as a result.

At the same time the oil-producing countries' price rise meant a levy on real incomes in West Germany and other oil-consuming states. Unions resisted the new costs imposed on the domestic economy.[66] The burden, they indicated, should be shouldered by others (that is, the recipients of entrepreneurial and property income or the public sector).

Hence there was a potential conflict between employees and employers over the burden of the oil price increase, and an actual conflict between the unions and monetary authorities over the inflation rate to be tolerated in 1974 (and thus to be anticipated in the wage settlements). The question

66. See Council of Economic Experts, *1974–75 Annual Report,* par. 131 ff.

was whether the government was willing and able to reassert its authority so that inflation did not get out of hand. At the beginning of 1974 there was great uncertainty as to whether inflation in West Germany could be brought under control at all. The federal government's annual economic report for 1974 contained a single-digit projection of the rate of price rises (8–9 percent). But experience had shown that the authorities were not always able to take all the measures necessary to make their projections come true. Besides, even experts differed in their forecasts—the EEC Commission, for instance, predicted that the rate of inflation would be unlikely to be below 10 percent in any country in 1974.[67]

Representatives of the Bundesbank in particular spoke out against pessimistic forecasts of inflation. Karl Klasen, president of the bank, predicted on January 22 that the inflation rate in 1974 would amount to 7–8 percent. The bank reaffirmed on several occasions that it would do all in its power to keep the inflation rate down to single figures, which meant a continuation of the restrictive monetary policy pursued since the spring of 1973. The vice-president of the bank, Otmar Emminger, had remarked on November 30, 1973, that "additional money cannot make up for missing oil. . . . As regards demand management, we must therefore keep our foot on the brake." Only a little later (December 20) Dr. Klasen had declared "we shall not give up our firm standpoint of monetary stability," and soon afterwards had announced that the Bundesbank and the federal government were in agreement that the restrictive monetary policy should not be relaxed.[68]

The trade unions were aware that periods of monetary restriction hamper wage negotiations and force a trade-off between pressing for wage increases and preserving employment. The trade unions demanded that economic policy should switch to expansion and call off the fight against inflation. On November 23, 1973, Heinz Oskar Vetter, chairman of the German Trade Union Federation, called for an immediate relaxation of high interest rates, and on January 1, 1974, repeating this demand, he expressed the view that the inflation rate to be caught up with in the 1974 wage negotiations was higher than that of 1973. Shortly before that, the influential metalworkers' union had also declared that a general change in the course of economic policy was overdue.[69]

Collective bargaining began in January 1974; the wage round was

67. Deutsche Bundesbank, press release 12, 1974, p. 10.
68. Ibid., 6, 1974, p. 2; 91, 1973, p. 2; 96, 1973, p. 1; 3, 1974, p. 1.
69. Ibid., 89, 1973, p. 2; 1, 1974, p. 6; 96, 1973, p. 12.

started by the public service union, and it was obvious that the wage settlement there would set the pace for the other trade unions. The conflict escalated dramatically. The unions began the wage round with demands of 15 to 20 percent, while the Bundesbank and the federal government did their utmost to exercise a moderating influence. Helmut Schmidt, minister of finance, declared "15 percent more wages will put jobs at risk"; the minister of economics also warned emphatically against rises of 10 percent or more; and Karl Klasen called for a campaign of reason.[70] Chancellor Brandt appealed to management and labor in a television broadcast, saying that wage claims of 15 percent were not attainable by reasonable means. The force of his warning was, however, slightly weakened by the fact that he several times stated that he was not prepared to accept greater risks to employment.

Appeals for moderation were of no avail. The public service union (Gewerkschaft Öffentliche Dienste, Transport und Verkehr, or ÖTV) negotiated inflexibly and without regard to the changed economic climate—no doubt fortified by the knowledge that the jobs of the employees it represented were not in jeopardy. In the end it even resorted to strikes hitting the state where it was most vulnerable (public transport, garbage collection). The upshot was wage increases averaging 12–15 percent and a blow to government credibility.

These negotiations showed that the trade unions were counting either on the failure of stabilization policy or on an early switch of economic policy to an expansionary course. The *Süddeutsche Zeitung,* an influential German daily, spoke of a victory of the trade unions over the federal government, and the president of the Bundesbank declared that "on the wage front a battle has been lost."[71] Economic policymakers now faced a very difficult choice—namely, the short-term trade-off between inflation and unemployment. Should the inflation rate anticipated in the wage settlements be allowed to become the actual inflation rate, so as not to endanger employment? Or was the stabilization policy to be continued, thus making it clear to the trade unions that a wrong approach necessarily has consequences in the form of rising unemployment?

It soon became obvious which course government economic policy was going to take. On March 11, 1974 (shortly after the wage agreement for civil servants was concluded), Finance Minister Schmidt and Bundes-

70. Ibid., 8, 1974, p. 5; 6, 1.
71. Ibid., 12, 1974, p. 9; 14, 1974, p. 3.

bank President Klasen jointly stated that it was intended to keep the rate of inflation below 10 percent and that this would necessitate the continuation of the restrictive monetary policy. Dr. Klasen added that after the surge of inflation caused by the latest wage increases, the restrictive monetary policy would have to be maintained longer and applied more stringently than had originally been planned. This approach was backed by outside experts. In their 1974 spring report, the major independent German economic research institutes called for a fresh start in the field of stabilization policy; indeed, two institutes expressly demanded sanctions to prevent the parties to wage agreements from disregarding the government's objectives on yet another occasion.[72] The German Trade Union Federation thereupon accused the institutes of exhibiting a "lack of social responsibility."[73] Whether the unions acted defensively in the belief that the government could not hold inflation down, or whether they sought a redistributive gain is unclear. In any case, however, thanks to the highly restrictive stance of the Bundesbank, the actual inflation rate in 1974 was only 7 percent.[74]

As a result, the increases in real wages were larger than either the unions or employers' associations had anticipated. The consequence was a rise in unemployment (though not among the group of employees that had set the pace). Many businesses found that they could meet the strong wage cost pressure only by dismissing labor, since the price increases they could achieve proved an inadequate safety valve. At the end of 1974 the number of unemployed was approaching one million, an unusually high figure by German standards in the 1960s and 1970s. Toward the end of that year, admittedly, the growth of unemployment was fed by the incipient worldwide recession.

The events of 1974 started a controversy in West Germany. The unions blamed the Bundesbank for overdoing its restrictive policy. The Bundesbank, on the other hand, had publicly declared its unwillingness to finance any rate of inflation arbitrarily programmed by wage agreements. One thing is certain, and has been widely appreciated: unemployment in 1974 would have gone up less if the difference between the inflation rate anticipated in the wage agreements and the actual rate of inflation had

72. Ibid., 17, 1974, p. 1, 2; 21, 1974, p. 2.
73. Ibid., 21, 1974, p. 3.
74. The stringency of the monetary restriction is illustrated by the movement of the monetary base. In the spring of 1973 it was expanding at a rate of 11–12 percent, but the rate in 1974 ranged between 5 percent and 7 percent owing to the monetary restriction. Relative to preceding years, these growth rates were exceptionally low.

been narrower—in other words, if the demands for nominal income had been more moderate or if monetary policy had been less restrictive.

Return to Old Values or Mere Tour de Force?

Events from 1969 to 1973 in West Germany revealed how social and economic forces could combine to abet inflation. "Distintegrative processes in the social field," as Trappe and Hettlage express it, are "conducive to inflation."[75] And if energetic action by economic policymakers reverses part of the inflationary thrust, group claims can lead to increased unemployment (in economic terms, via an unplanned, unintended, or unforeseen rise in real wages). To reverse the trend requires a change in standards, and a new assessment of values by the responsible social groups.

To what extent did the lessons of the 1974 dispute work to bring about change? The authorities did succeed in reversing the trend of inflation rates after 1974, but the sharp appreciation of the D mark in the foreign exchange market also helped. In other words, the stabilization process was aided by the confidence that other countries placed in the D mark and thus ultimately in the social forces and political groupings in West Germany that were backing stability. After 1978, however, the situation changed again. Inflation rates again rose significantly at a time the D mark no longer enjoyed an international "confidence premium." At times, indeed, the foreign exchange market seemed to show a distinct lack of confidence.

The continuing uncertainty over monetary erosion in West Germany hampers any attempt to fit the slowdown in inflation between 1975 and 1978 into a socioeconomic context. Two contradictory positions are conceivable. If the 1974 dispute is seen as having led to a return to the values of the 1950s and 1960s, then conditions for monetary stability should have lastingly improved. According to this view, the poor performance in 1979 and later was very largely due to external pressures that had to be accepted. Inflation came from economic force majeure. If, however, socioeconomic conditions are assumed not to have changed for the better after 1974, the temporary decline in inflation rates must be viewed as simply the outcome of an economic tour de force, of a policy stance that enabled the government to reassert its authority, of a latent

75. See Paul Trappe and Robert Hettlage, "Ansätze zu einer soziologischen Theorie der Inflation," in Nello Celio, ed., *Inflationsbekämpfung unter veränderten wirtschaftlichen und sozialen Bedingungen* (Bern: Paul Haupt, 1976), p. 80.

fear that government might reimpose a sanction like that of 1974. Such a tour de force could not possibly have a lasting effect. According to this view, the stimulus imparted to inflation by the depreciation of the D mark was not to be deemed a stroke of fate, but was itself attributable to a prior loss of confidence in the D mark caused by economic policy[76]—in the last analysis to the fact that the major interest groups had not learned any lessons.

The correct assessment probably lies somewhere between these two poles. Certainly, the connection between self-regarding behavior and sanctions was restored in 1974. It was, after all, a major socioeconomic feature of the inflationary process between 1969 and 1973 that the growing demands of individuals and social groups gave rise to fewer and fewer direct consequences—time and again the direct sanction of taking action was postponed. It was possible to evade responsibility since inflation could be regarded as the outcome of the actions of others. After 1974, the idea that the government could guarantee full employment if only it wanted to had to be given up. Responsibility rested with the social groups again.

This should not, however, be construed to mean that in 1974 the economic policymakers had reckoned deliberately and from the start with the sanction of rising unemployment. It followed in part from a particular confluence of market forces, wage settlements, monetary policy, and external influences (the global recession began in 1974). Still, the combination did seem to establish a sanction for inflationary demands and reactivated socioethical standards—"basic processes," as Trappe and Hettlage call them. While no doubt far from popular, the economic policy stance was convincingly presented and displayed the courage needed to combat social and economic disintegration.[77] The fact that the stimulus came from a government led by Social Democrats, who could not easily be accused of hostility to employees or punitive measures, was certainly a help. In Chancellor Helmut Schmidt's cabinet all the Social Democratic ministers came from the trade union movement. They participated in the formulation of economic policy and in defending it before the unions' rank-and-file—proof that participation of major social groups in the government may have an integrative effect and can help implement economic restraint, provided that a substantial measure of agreement obtains on conceptual questions. Such broad-based participation, com-

76. See Council of Economic Experts, *1981–82 Annual Report*, pars. 182, 400.
77. Trappe and Hettlage, "Ansätze," p. 83.

bined with responsibility and providing in return political influence, had been a significant element in the stabilization performance of the 1950s and 1960s. Its value was not disproved even when conceptual disagreements emerged that noticeably weakened confidence in the government.

The improvement in popular understanding of the relevant relationships was also reflected in a general willingness to seek new rules for regulating the interaction between the public and private sectors. The aim was to draw the rules of economic activity in such a way that they would be acceptable to the participants—in particular to the social groups whose actions depended on official economic policy. A fresh start was to be made to restore social integration and to preserve the consensus, where it was attainable. This led to what academic circles and ministerial officials referred to as the "new assignment."

In principle, the new assignment comprised the notion that monetary policy should take the lead in macroeconomic demand management; fiscal policy should be relieved of (countercyclical) stabilization functions; and autonomous groups should recognize that price and wage decisions have direct and assignable effects on production and employment—that, for example, a more flexible response of wages is an essential prerequisite of a return to full employment. Insofar as it can be classified theoretically, this assignment was based on the neoclassical theory of the economic process. In the sociopolitical sphere it was consistent with a tendency toward a new conservatism that was common to all the political parties. The new assignment was at no time a "doctrine of salvation," such as, say, Reaganomics promised to be. Moreover, it was never realized in a pure form. But at least the leading role of monetary policy was more or less accepted. In addition, the collective bargaining system became more responsive after 1974; the trade unions implicitly conceded the mistakes made in 1974. Management and labor thereafter tried, in their wage settlements, to take account of the risks to employment and not to follow the Keynesian tradition of making government solely responsible for the employment situation. The mistakes of 1974 were not repeated, nor did the loyalty of the trade unions turn out to be linked to an early reduction in unemployment. The drastic deterioration in labor market conditions in 1981 did not result in serious conflicts (in part, of course, because of a finely meshed network of social security measures).

Even if the new assignment was never fully carried out, monetary policy assumed a new leading role after 1974. The major indication was the money-growth targets that the Bundesbank now set for each year to come. After the labor negotiations of early 1974 had foundered over the differing assumptions concerning monetary policy and expected inflation rates, the Council of Economic Experts proposed in the following November that the Bundesbank should henceforth announce its monetary stance so that unions and employers could adjust their bargaining accordingly.[78] The Bundesbank accepted the idea. While the unions do not concede a formal status to the bank's money-growth targets in wage parleys, the annual announcement unmistakably conditions negotiations. Between 1975 and 1982 inflationary expectations never got out of hand to the degree they did in 1974, although conflicts over the distribution of real income remained. When inflationary pressures grew after the second oil price increase in 1978, economic actors generally counted on the Bundesbank's capacity to limit the rise in inflation rates. By and large, the targets were accepted as a proposal that the anticipated rate of inflation should not itself figure as an issue in collective bargaining. This in turn fed back on the actual inflation rate.

So does success come from simply setting out the facts? This would be too simple an explanation. In 1974 the Bundesbank demonstrated dramatically that it can influence the inflation rate when it wants to; thus its appeals to base price and wage decisions on the inflation rate it expects are perfectly credible. The private sector can gear its behavior to the success of government economic policy and need not orient its actions to probable economic policy failures, as has happened on several occasions in Italy and the United Kingdom, for example.

The impact of the monetary targets was, however, mainly attributable to the fact that the Bundesbank chose an extremely favorable moment to start its quantitative monetary policy, whether fortuitously or not. Inflation had become intolerable to major sections of the German population; moreover, it was felt that the bank was acting strictly according to its statutory duty and was also fully supported by the federal government.[79]

78. Council of Economic Experts, *1974–75 Annual Report,* par. 316.

79. Government's concurrence implies that the higher priority given to monetary policy was not the outcome of new political pretensions on the part of the Bundesbank, and thus of a power struggle between Frankfurt and Bonn, but that it conformed to a conception that under the conditions of floating was no longer called in question. Releasing fiscal policy from its markedly countercyclical role—which was repeatedly beyond the capabilities of central, state, and local authorities—does not amount to an abdication of political power. Government authorities relied on a policy of consistency, on a medium-term orientation, which did not preclude differences in specific cases, nor prevent fiscal policy from being forced to pursue a countercyclical course for a number of years. As shown by the toleration of the overshooting of its target, the Bundesbank's monetary policy was more countercyclical in orientation than was regarded as sound and acceptable by the advocates of a stabilization policy directed toward greater consistency.

Table 12-5. *Monetary Targets of the Bundesbank, 1975–84*
Percent

| Year | Target base | Growth of money supply[a] | |
		Target	Actual
1975	Current rate	8.0	10.1
1976	Year-on-year rate of change	8.0	9.2
1977	Year-on-year rate of change	8.0	9.0
1978	Year-on-year rate of change	8.0	11.4
1979	Range of rates, 4th quarter to 4th quarter	6.0–9.0	6.3
1980	Range of rates, 4th quarter to 4th quarter[b]	5.0–8.0	5.0
1981	Range of rates, 4th quarter to 4th quarter[b]	4.0–7.0	4.0
1982	Range of rates, 4th quarter to 4th quarter[b]	4.0–7.0	6.1
1983	Range of rates, 4th quarter to 4th quarter[b]	4.0–7.0	7.0
1984	Range of rates, 4th quarter to 4th quarter[b]	4.0–6.0	4.6

Source: Deutsche Bundesbank.
a. Currency in circulation plus minimum reserves at constant reserve ratios.
b. The Bundesbank announced at midyear that it aimed at the lower limit.

At times, admittedly, the leading role of the Bundesbank seemed cast in doubt, especially in 1978 when money growth distinctly overshot its target (see table 12-5).[80] That signal failure was widely interpreted as implying that the Bundesbank no longer set any store by monetary targeting. However, the bank recovered credibility when, in 1979 and after, it set its targets in terms of a growth range, which it then at midyear sought to narrow toward the lower end. Its accuracy turned out to be high (see table 12-5), which meant that over the course of a year the supply of money in the hands of nonbanks was to be progressively reduced. There was little to criticize in the basic policy, for aligning changes in the money supply with the growth rates of potential production was recognized as an essential element of an effective anti-inflation policy. In 1981, however, the policy was carried out with such determination that the money supply was actually brought down below the level required according to the criterion of production potential. In line with the marked shortage of funds, the Bundesbank also kept interest rates high, and in 1981 they reached a historical peak for the Federal Republic.

The Bundesbank strategy in 1981 was dictated in large part, though not entirely, by external considerations. In addition to running up a large

80. The targets had been overshot in previous years, but the amount involved had generally been regarded as tolerable.

deficit on current account, the private sector exported capital from the beginning of 1980 until well into 1981. High domestic interest rates seemed necessary in light of the higher rates abroad, especially in the United States, and the pressure on the exchange rate. Domestic requirements were given a secondary priority to the interest of safeguarding the value of the D mark and of long-run employment. At the theoretical level, the Bundesbank used the arguments of a vertical Phillips curve to claim there was no long-run trade-off between inflation and unemployment.

The fact that the Bundesbank's arguments were broadly accepted by the general public, and in particular were endorsed by a Social Democratic government, illustrates how durable was the consensus reached. Even those most directly affected by the sharp rise in unemployment from the spring of 1980 onward—employees and their trade unions—confined themselves to criticism that fell short of outright confrontation. In an open letter to the president of the Bundesbank on February 28, 1980, Alois Pfeiffer, the member of the executive of the German Trade Union Federation (DGB) responsible for economic policy, asked for "more weight to be given in the policies of the Deutsche Bundesbank to the goal of full employment and economic growth." And in October 1981 he appealed to the Bundesbank "not to miss the opportunity for lowering interest rates presented by the improvement in the current account and the appreciation of the D mark."[81] This turn of phrase suggests that, at least outwardly, the DGB did not want to ignore the Bundesbank's arguments. Nor did a government considered to be friendly to labor criticize the bank. There were no public disagreements over the high interest rate policy—a situation conspicuously different from that in the United States.

Fiscal Policy and Employment

A logical consequence of the experience gained between 1970 and 1974 was a new division of labor among the elements of economic policy. Once the main thrust of combating inflation had been shifted to monetary policy, the Council of Economic Experts recommended in 1974–75 that fiscal policy should aim primarily at continuity.[82] This did not mean a

81. Deutsche Bundesbank, press release 24, 1980, p. 3; 89, 1981, p. 5.
82. Council of Economic Experts, *1974–75 Annual Report*, pars. 416 ff. The government largely adopted the recommendations in its annual economic report for 1975.

complete departure from the principles of countercyclical budgetary policy; fiscal policy might still be called on to promote expansion in times of weak economic activity and growing unemployment. Still, these were to involve exceptional and limited programs, and if fiscal policy were not to be used to quell inflation, neither would it be allowed to become routinely expansionary.

Such was the intention, but precisely the opposite took place. The programs implemented were designed in such a way that they were procyclical in some cases and fueled inflation, particularly in the construction industry; their impact on the real economy was correspondingly undermined. Moreover, there were some increases in government expenditure that the beneficiaries immediately took to be permanent, so that the possibility of reversing them gave rise to massive protests. Since taxes (particularly the income tax) were reduced on several occasions, the government found it more and more difficult to bring the expenditure side of its budget even roughly into line with its receipts. The upshot was a steep rise in government debt, which grew to proportions undreamed of since the war.

But the level of debt in itself was not the major problem. What provoked widespread disquiet among the general public and in the business community was the fact that the growth of indebtedness had obviously got out of control. Every year from 1977 to 1981 the government ran up a higher deficit. Not even in the boom years of 1979 and 1980 did the pace of its borrowing slacken.

Fiscal policymakers consequently fell into a dilemma. In 1981 the combined deficit of federal, state, and local authorities amounted to some DM80 billion, the highest level of net government borrowing in the history of the Federal Republic. A highly expansionary stimulus to business activity (far greater than in previous years) was inherent in this deficit.[83] Yet the German economy slid into a profound recession. The conditions under which government deficit spending boosts employment had apparently ceased to exist. The social and psychological repercussions of the rapid increase of public debt—the expectation of future tax increases and painful stabilization measures—detracted from the expansionary stimuli and may have more than offset them. The government's scope for further deficit spending was exhausted at a time when it was more necessary than ever before.

83. The Council of Economic Experts in its *1981–82 Annual Report,* par. 370, estimated the expansionary stimulus at almost DM50 billion.

Developments were strongly affected by programs "to foster economic activity and growth," five of which were adopted between 1977 and 1980. One, an investment program, adopted March 23, 1977, allocated DM16 billion mainly for government construction projects. A Tax Amendment Act of June 16, 1977, and an Act to Cut Taxes and Encourage Investment of October 27, 1977, provided relief for households, including the raising of children's benefits, amounting to DM8.8 billion and tax relief for businesses amounting to DM2.7 billion. On November 17, 1978, a package of measures was adopted that included cuts in direct taxes, increases in indirect taxes, promotion of innovation and investment, measures of family policy, and additional government expenditure; they increased the total burden on the public budgets by just under DM17 billion. Finally, the Tax Relief Act of July 4, 1980, extended benefits to households amounting to DM14.5 billion and to businesses amounting to DM1.9 billion for the period from 1980 to 1982.

On the receipts side of the budgets, these measures did little harm, though some of the tax cuts were self-contradictory and introduced more incongruities into the tax system. This followed not least because of the great importance attached to social factors. From the standpoint of stabilization policy, it would have been desirable to modify the tax system to encourage more growth. The various tax cuts did reverse some inflation-induced increases in tax revenue and thus contributed to a better climate for wage negotiations. A steeper rise in the tax burden would probably have led to larger pay claims by wage and salary earners and prevented any moderation in the struggle over income shares. Moreover, the programs responded to trade union concepts, though at first the unions became more critical as success in reducing unemployment failed to materialize. Nonetheless, the unions were prepared to admit that the recent crisis was rooted in structural dislocations that could not be eliminated by deficit spending alone.

On the expenditure side, budgetary management had less benign effects. If intended to reduce the government share in the national product and to increase incentives for private enterprise, the state should likewise have lowered its claims on production potential and kept the growth rates of public expenditure below those of GNP, at least during periods of favorable economic activity.[84] This did not happen. Because the fiscal

---

84. The authorities were not counting on, say, a Laffer effect. Although the ratio of overall tax revenue to the gross national product fell from 24.9 percent in 1977 to 24.1 percent in 1981, it was still higher in 1981 than it had been at the beginning of the 1970s.

policy measures served rather heterogeneous purposes, no uniform concept emerged. Each program represented the outcome of political compromise. All involved a mixture of economic stimulation, provision for growth, reform projects, and social and family policy measures. The guiding principle was always that programs should benefit the broadest possible sections of the population. Thus they departed from the Keynesian concept of gearing expenditures to bolster investment activity. And beneficiaries fought the cancellation of programs when the need to stimulate economic activity ceased to exist.

This problem was particularly clear in connection with spending cuts undertaken in the autumn of 1981 after it became evident that the federal government's deficit in 1982 might reach DM50 billion and the overall public sector deficit around DM80 billion. The package of measures finally agreed on eased the burden on the overall government budget by about DM19 billion in 1982. But debate on these economy measures almost caused the government coalition to break up while even the opposition was deeply divided before the economies it proposed had reached a total of DM10 billion. Despite the seemingly painful cuts, the federal deficit in 1982 was brought below the previous year's only by showing DM10.5 billion in Bundesbank profits as revenue.

Society obviously had no great inclination to scale down its demands on government. Yet complaints about the abuse of government benefits were increasing, and there was no lack of suggestions as to possible cuts in the major subsidy areas—but always in fields other than the advocate's. In surveying potential expenditure cuts, the government was faint-hearted and seemed disposed to put off today's conflicts till tomorrow or the day after by means of borrowing. No clear-cut fiscal policy stance was apparent.

The Response of Social Groups

Both management and labor conceded the mistakes made in the highly inflexible wage round of 1974 and were prepared to learn from them and bear a share of the responsibility for employment.[85] The trade unions did not resist adverse changes in the distribution of income between 1975

---

85. While the trade unions showed by their behavior that they were prepared to acknowledge a link between the movement of real wages and employment, the Economic and Social Research Institute of the DGB evolved a basic approach according to which high unemployment was not connected with high real wages; "Umverteilungsprogramm statt Beschäftigungsprogramm—zum Jahresgutachten des Sach-verständigenrates," in WSI-Mitteilungen, no. 1 (1977), pp. 1 ff.

and 1979 that caused wages to rise 5 percent less than they would have without the adjustments.[86] The (job-structure-adjusted) wage share declined from 66.3 percent of national income in 1974 to 63.5 percent in 1979. The changes in income distribution in 1975 and 1977 were greater than had been envisaged in the wage settlements—in 1975 because the strength of the downswing was much underrated (and not only by management and labor), in 1977 because a continuation of the upswing was expected, whereas economic activity actually slowed down.

The unions had viewed the moderate pay increases from 1975 to 1977 as advance concessions to secure fuller employment, which they saw were not paying off when the labor market failed to improve. As a more promising approach, they turned to seek steep wage increases and more government spending, even at the cost of larger deficits. In 1978 the unions were noticeably more willing to risk a conflict than at any time since 1974—probably in part because of comments by the Council of Economic Experts that led the unions to believe their efforts had been misunderstood.[87] When an effort was made to revive concerted action, the unions were unwilling to accept the continued participation of representatives of the Council of Economic Experts in the meetings. The unions claimed that the council's advice was not neutral and objective, if only because of its neoclassical stance.[88] Concerted action foundered in June of 1978 when the employers' associations instituted Constitutional Court proceedings against the Codetermination Act. The trade unions seized the opportunity to express their dissatisfaction with concerted action and walked out of the talks. Nevertheless, they remained willing to take part in other talks.

The new wage round at the turn of 1978 began with negotiations in the iron and steel and the "metalworking" (often high-technology) industries. Business conditions for iron and steel were depressed and were far more favorable in metalworking. The unions concentrated on wresting a comparatively steep rise in wages from such firms as Daimler-Benz, Bosch, and IBM, all of which enjoyed a healthy market condition. But

86. Council of Economic Experts, *1981–82 Annual Report.*

87. Council of Economic Experts, *1977–78 Annual Report,* pars. 387 ff. Commenting on the Annual Report, a DGB press release of November 22, 1977, stated: "The DGB regards it as a violation of the statutory mandate of the Council of Economic Experts if a majority of the Council's members publish, under the guise of scientific argument, assertions about alleged relationships between negotiated wage increases and economic growth rates, even though these are nothing but speculations and unproven conjectures. . . . The repeated and gross forecasting errors of the Council of Economic Experts in the past are due to its being so out of touch with reality."

88. DGB, Wirtschaftspolitische Informationen, 8, 1977, December 2, 1977.

labor also sought pay safeguards for workers shifted by reason of technological advances to lower-ranking jobs. Negotiations began in January 1978 and the unions quickly declared that they had broken down. The employers' association then appealed to the Arbitration Board, and both sides jockeyed for favorable negotiating positions.[89] The regional managers on both union and employer sides sought to keep the issue from becoming a mere political stake of the national union executive and the national employers' federation. As was expected, both sides rejected the mediation proposals, thus leading to six weeks of strikes and further negotiations, and finally to the conclusion of a new agreement providing for a 5 percent wage hike, promotion of the lowest-paid workers up one wage grade, and safeguards for individual earnings.[90] The settlement served as a guideline for the other regional negotiations and for parleys in other industries. The process illustrated the mixture of conflict, alignment for strategic position, and sensitivity to what adversaries might finally concede that characterizes industries where negotiators have known each other for years and have a good sense of what the respective bargaining agents can enforce among their own constituencies. Wage determination thus relies on a highly developed awareness of institutional and personal tolerance as well as on purely economic guidelines; indeed, without the social matrix the vaunted guidelines would be far less effective.

Hardly any of the tensions apparent in 1978 were detectable in 1979, no doubt because an upswing had resumed at long last. Unions for the iron and steel industry led off the wage negotiations in that year, calling for introduction of the thirty-five-hour week. After a sharp public debate and a rather protracted labor dispute (not least because of the threat of layoffs), pay settlements were reached without difficulty. Wage rises were moderate, though still too high from the point of view of stabilization policy. The thirty-five-hour week remained to be contested again bitterly in 1984, though many agreements lengthened paid vacations to thirty working days.

The second wave of oil price increases severely tested the social groups. The trade unions indicated at the beginning of 1979 that—in contrast to

89. Participants in negotiations before the Arbitration Board are a negotiator and two or three assistant negotiators for each party, as well as two chairmen. The chairmen, appointed for four-year terms, hold alternately the authority to cast a vote on board decisions and draft a settlement of arbitrations. The voting chairman automatically changes with each new dispute.

90. The wage agreement for the metalworking industry negotiated in April was retroactive to January; a nonrecurring wage bonus for January to March meant that the actual increase in 1978 was around 5.5 percent. Wages and salaries in the economy as a whole averaged about 5.5–6 percent higher than a year before.

1974—they were prepared to shoulder some of the transfer of real income to other countries caused by the oil price hike. Moreover, when the prices of heating oil and gasoline shot up further toward midyear and many households began to feel the pinch, the unions quickly put a stop to talk of a wage supplement. In 1980, too, they did not endeavor to recoup from business the income that had been lost to foreign countries. The fact that wages rose faster than in the two preceding years was due, rather, to West Germany's comparatively satisfactory economic performance and favorable prospects. As it turned out, real wages did not fall in proportion to the declining terms of trade. Employees' relative income position improved noticeably and business profits came under pressure.

Much the same thing happened in 1981. The trade unions aimed only at compensation for inflation. In fact, wage increases fell distinctly short of price rises. But as the upward movement of prices was mainly attributable to the soaring cost of imports caused by the depreciation of the D mark, the relative income position of employees continued to improve.

Wage policy responded to the new challenge from abroad much more flexibly than it had done in 1974. Had the response been even more flexible, adjustment to external changes might well have taken place more smoothly. But this would have imposed on wage policy the task of rectifying errors and omissions in other policy areas (energy policy and fiscal policy), whereas its primary function is to determine the appropriate level of real wages in a radically changed labor market.

Conclusion

West Germany may have represented a relative success story among Western economies, the more so as in 1984 price stability was by and large achieved, and prospects for the near future appeared to be favorable. In addition, fiscal policy returned to previous standards; the so-called structural deficit, which according to the Council of Economic Experts had amounted to DM40 billion in 1981, was eliminated almost entirely in the subsequent years. Indeed, the question has arisen whether the new government went too far in its corrective action. In any case, scope for fiscal policy has been recovered, albeit at the cost of political and social consensus. Critics have reproached the two ruling parties, the CDU and the FDP, for a regressive policy that has redistributed income upward. But this argument seems to lack validity, and it cannot conceal the fact that the political change of 1982 expressed the voters' dwindling confidence in the capability of the Social-Liberal coalition to meet present and future challenges. But the new government too has found it difficult to present convincing policies. The achievement in terms of price stability has not always been matched in other areas of policy. In spite of a considerable economic upswing, not all the challenges to continuing growth have been sufficiently mastered. In some fields of high technology, West Germany must still catch up with the leading countries. Debates over this course reflect in some way the society's indecision about how best to prepare for the future. It is precisely this irresolution that forms a major contrast to the 1950s.

13

Wages, Profits, and Investment in Sweden

Andrew Martin

Sweden's political economy combines a set of characteristics that makes the management of distributive conflict between capital and labor vital to its economic welfare. It has a small, open economy, highly dependent on foreign transactions for the levels of employment and consumption it can enjoy. With a relatively small public enterprise sector, it must rely very heavily on capitalist firms to carry out those transactions. At the same time, Sweden's labor movement has an exceptionally strong position in the state as well as market arenas. This juxtaposition of a capitalist economy and a powerful labor movement renders the country especially vulnerable to distributive conflict between capital and labor. It places a high premium on managing that conflict so that foreign demand is not jeopardized. This has in fact been possible for much of the period since World War II, contributing significantly to exceptionally high levels of employment and consumption, collective as well as private.

To the extent such management has been possible, it has apparently depended on the way in which relationships between capital and labor have been structured in Sweden. While the overwhelming proportion of production for the market is conducted by capitalist firms, trade unions covering three-quarters of the labor force organize a very large proportion of those who work in those firms. The largest of the three confederations to which the unions belong, the Swedish Confederation of Labor (Landsorganisationen i Sverige, or LO), itself accounts for about half of the labor force. The strength this gives it in the market arena is also the source of power in the state arena. The LO and its affiliates provide the principal organizational and financial resources and also the core electoral constituency of the Social Democratic party (Socialdemokratiska Arbetareparti, or SAP). This support was the crucial factor enabling the party to control the state virtually without interruption for nearly four and a half decades from 1932 until 1976. Sustained Social Democratic rule has, in turn, decisively conditioned the LO's strategy in the market arena.

During the long era of Social Democratic rule, the LO and the dominant private sector employer organization, the Swedish Employers Confederation (Svenska Arbetsgivareföreningen, or SAF), built up a highly centralized system for the private government of industrial relations. A Basic Agreement was reached by the two peak associations in 1938, primarily in order to maintain industrial peace by establishing procedures for settling disputes without strikes and lockouts.[1] In the 1950s, it was developed into a system of centralized wage negotiations. The other unions and employer organizations have been assimilated into the system, which has shaped the pattern of wage settlements throughout the economy.[2] Apart from the state's negotiations with its own employees, its direct intervention in the system is ruled out in the name of free collective bargaining. Thus, the system does not serve as a vehicle for an official incomes policy or tripartite social contract. However, the union and employer organizations acknowledge an obligation to take the economic consequences of wage growth into account, understood primarily in terms of the requirements of external equilibrium. To the extent that this happens, the system performs the function of an incomes policy that matters most for an open economy.

While the state is not a party to negotiations with the union and employer peak associations, all involved recognize that its policies significantly affect the conditions under which the negotiations take place. Thus, the willingness of unions, in Sweden as elsewhere, to exercise some measure of restraint presupposes that the state pursues policies providing some assurance that the restraint will yield benefits, acceptably distributed, to the unions' members. While unions may have sufficient power to squeeze profits so hard that there is insufficient investment to maintain employment and rising income, they have no power to assure that the investment needed to achieve the desired economic effects will actually result if the unions squeeze profits less than they would if they fully

1. Between the end of World War I and the mid-1930s, Sweden had one of the highest strike rates. See Douglas A. Hibbs, Jr., "On the Political Economy of Long-Run Trends in Strike Activity," *British Journal of Political Science,* vol. 8 (April 1978), pp. 158–60; Walter Korpi, *The Working Class in Welfare Capitalism: Work, Unions and Politics in Sweden* (London: Routledge and Kegan Paul, 1978), pp. 94–96.

2. Centralized negotiations between the LO and the SAF were abandoned partially in 1983 and completely in 1984, largely at the employers' initiative.

exerted their power in the market arena. This lack of leverage over the transformation of profits into investment is, of course, inherent in capitalist organization of investment on the basis of the private appropriation and disposition of profits.[3] If, on the other hand, the state pursues policies capable of maintaining full employment and an acceptable distribution of income, this may be regarded as providing the needed assurance. Under these conditions, unions may view wage restraint, and the risks of rank-and-file disaffection it entails, as justified. As suggested in much of the literature on neocorporatism or consensual wage regulation, such policies are more likely to be pursued when a party based on a labor movement is in office, as it was for so long in Sweden. Thus, union restraint is likely to be contingent on recurrent if not continuous control of the state by such a party.[4]

The other side to this is that the continued willingness to invest on the part of capitalist firms presupposes that the private appropriation and disposition of profits remains undisturbed, as it was throughout the years of continuous Social Democratic rule that ended in 1976. Sweden thus presented an outstanding case of what has been referred to as a social democratic class compromise. Such a compromise entails the acceptance by workers of "private profit [as] the necessary condition for the improvement of the material conditions of any group in society," while "capitalists accept institutions through which workers can make effective claims for an improvement of their material conditions." In short, "workers consent to capitalism; capitalists consent to democracy."[5] The consent to democracy includes its consequences, which in Sweden meant sustained control of the state by a labor movement party. But this was acceptable to Swedish capitalists as long as the party observed the terms of the implicit "historical compromise" struck in the 1930s which left capitalist organization of production intact.[6]

During the 1970s, however, the terms of that compromise were called into question by the LO. It began to press for new, collective institutions designed to give the state and unions a measure of control over the

---

3. Kelvin Lancaster, "The Dynamic Inefficiency of Capitalism," *Journal of Political Economy,* vol. 81 (September–October 1973), pp. 1092–1109; Adam Przeworski and Michael Wallerstein, "The Structure of Class Conflict in Advanced Capitalist Societies," paper presented at the 1980 annual meeting of the American Political Science Association.

4. See chapter 5, above, by Colin Crouch; Peter Lange and Geoffrey Garrett, "Organizational and Political Determinants of Economic Performance, 1974–1980," paper presented at the Fourth Conference of Europeanists, Washington, 1983.

5. Przeworski and Wallerstein, "Structure of Class Conflict," pp. 1, 5.

6. Korpi, *The Working Class,* pp. 80–86.

transformation of profits into investment from which they were excluded by the existing institutions for the private appropriation and disposition of profits. The new institutions, which would be set up by the state and in which union representatives would have a controlling voice, were referred to as wage-earner funds. Firms would be required to transfer to the funds a portion of profits in the form of directed issues of shares, and the funds would purchase additional shares with their income from dividends. While the funds would be introduced alongside of the existing institutions for transforming profits into investment, they would slowly but inexorably turn into the dominant mechanism for organizing that process as their accumulation of shares grew. With evident reluctance, the Social Democratic party eventually went along with the LO proposal, but only after getting the LO to accept a considerably watered-down version.[7] This did not diminish Swedish capital's intense opposition to the funds, however. Thus, the consensus over basic institutional arrangements on which the management of distributive conflict between labor and capital in Sweden had rested was breached.

Why did this happen? The answer suggested in this chapter is that the LO saw the proposed change in the institutional mechanism for transforming profits into investment as a means of coping with the increasing tension it experienced between its role in moderating wage growth for the sake of external equilibrium and its need to keep cohesion among and within its affiliated unions. The literature on consensual wage recognition has long recognized how much strain is placed on unions' internal cohesion when they participate in centralized negotiations designed to limit wage increases.[8] The LO's persistent concern with minimizing those strains led it to pursue a strategy relying on a subtle mix of government policies intended to limit both the need for wage restraint and the organizational stress posed by the restraint that it did accept.

To an increasing degree, however, LO strategy recurrently failed to guarantee the organizational cohesion the LO felt was needed. At these points the LO felt compelled to press for wage increases that threatened Sweden's foreign demand. At the same time, it became even more difficult to sustain foreign demand as the international structure of production

7. A close approximation to this version was enacted under the Social Democratic government in December 1983.

8. Lange and Garrett, "Organizational and Political Determinants"; Charles F. Sabel, "The Internal Politics of Trade Unions," in Suzanne Berger, ed., *Organizing Interests in Western Europe: Pluralism, Corporatism, and the Transformation of Politics* (Cambridge University Press, 1981), pp. 209–44.

changed, depriving a significant part of Swedish industry of the favorable competitive position it had earlier enjoyed, and as increasing instability in the world economy made macroeconomic policy more difficult.

As a result of the growing difficulty the LO experienced in reconciling the requirements of external equilibrium with those of organizational cohesion, the effectiveness of the central negotiating system in performing an incomes policy function was impaired. This was most sharply demonstrated by a wage explosion in 1975–76. But evidence of it in terms of declining profits, investment, and Sweden's current accounts position is observable since at least a decade earlier. Responding to this evidence by the beginning of the 1970s, the LO sought a way to resolve its wage policy dilemma. The result was the proposal for changes in the mechanism for transforming profits into investment that drew the LO into conflict with Swedish capital over fundamental institutional issues. This chapter attempts to show how that proposal emerged from the LO's earlier strategy and the dilemma its operation left unresolved.

The Wage Determination System

The regulation of wage growth by central negotiations among peak organizations is facilitated by some features of the organizational structure in Sweden but limited by others. Virtually all employees are covered by unions and employer associations. There is a substantial degree of centralization within these organizations, and they in turn belong to national peak organizations that are also centralized to a varying but significant extent. On the other hand, there are several peak organizations on both the employee and employer sides of the labor market. Divided along sectoral, occupational, and political lines, organizations on the same side have partially conflicting interests. Moreover, neither the peak organizations nor their affiliates are so centralized that they can gear wage growth to the requirements of external equilibrium without regard to market forces.

Employer Organization

The employer side of the labor market is divided between the private and public sectors. The former is dominated by the SAF, consisting of thirty-eight industry associations whose member firms are also "part owners" of the peak association. These firms employ slightly over half of all employees in the private sector. A little over three-quarters of all firms with five hundred employees or more belong to the SAF; they account for 14 percent of its member firms but 51 percent of the employees covered. Of the industrial associations, the engineering industry federation is the largest, covering over a quarter of SAF members' employees.[9] In addition to the SAF, there are several smaller employer associations in the private sector, in such branches as banking, the press, and consumer cooperatives.[10]

There are separate negotiating bodies on the employer side of different parts of the public sector, which employed just over 30 percent of the civilian labor force in 1975. A state negotiating agency (Statens avtalsverk, or SAV) covers roughly two-fifths of public sector employees, including those in the school system even though they are employed at the local government level. Those in state enterprises grouped in a state holding company, less than 4 percent of the sector total, are covered by a State Companies Negotiation Organization (Statsföretagens förhandlingsorganisation, or SFO). The remainder are covered by negotiating bodies of organizations of the two levels of local government, the Association of Local Authorities (Kommunförbundet) and Federation of County Councils (Landstingsförbundet).[11] Public sector employers have increasingly coordinated their negotiations through a joint body, the OASEN.[12]

Aside from the SAV, the most centralized of the major labor market organizations is the SAF. From its inception in 1902, it has had a great deal of authority over its component organizations and their member firms. According to its rules, all members must submit collective bargaining agreements to it for approval before they can go into effect. Offensive action against unions is subject to the SAF's control as well. Its executive council can order a general or partial lockout, while no member can engage in a lockout without the council's approval. Firms that are struck or engaged in approved lockouts are entitled to assistance from a fund, exclusively at the SAF's disposal, that is based on dues and assessments, if needed, equal to 2 percent of member firms' wage bills. Firms that violate the SAF's rules can be deprived of assistance, fined, or even

9. Svenska Arbetsgivareföreningens (SAF), *Verksamhet 1975* (Stockholm: SAF, 1976), pp. 5–6.

10. Lennart Forsebäck, *Industrial Relations and Employment in Sweden* (Stockholm: Swedish Institute, 1976), p. 22.

11. Ibid., pp. 22–23. See also *Statsföretag 1975* (Stockholm: Statsföretag, 1976), p. 1; Siv Gustafsson, "Lönesystem, lönestatistik och förhandlingar" (Stockholm: SAF, n.d.), pp. 60–63.

12. Olle Bolang, *Utslagen! den svenska modellen efter 1980 års storkonflikt* (Stockholm: Studieförbundet Näringsliv och Samhälle [SN&S], 1980), pp. 94–96.

Table 13-1. *Union Membership in Sweden, 1975*

Category	Thousands of workers	Percent of labor force
Labor force[a]	4,065	100
Confederations and largest unions		
LO	1,918	47
Metalworkers union	454	11
Local government workers union	340	8
TCO	881	22
Clerical and technical workers union	255	6
Local government employees union	104	3
SACO-SR	165	4
Total union membership	3,033	75

Sources: *Swedish Economy, 1977:3*, statistical appendix, p. 39; Landsorganisationen i Sverige (LO), *Verksamhets berättelse 1975* (Stockholm: LO, 1976), p. 3; Tjänstemännens centralorganisation (TCO), *Företeckning över ombud, utskott, gäster, Kongressen 76* (Stockholm: TCO, 1976), p. 10; Lennart Forsebäck, *Industrial Relations and Employment in Sweden* (Stockholm: Swedish Institute, 1976), p. 29.
a. Total labor force, excluding conscripts.

expelled.[13] Though the actual centralization of power may fall somewhat short of this formal centralization of authority, the SAF clearly has a high degree of control over wage bargaining on the employers' side.

Union Organization

The employee side of the labor market is organized by unions affiliated with the LO, which consists almost entirely of blue collar workers, and two white collar confederations, Tjänstemännens centralorganisation, or TCO, and Sveriges akademikers centralorganisation–Statstjänstemännens riksförbund, or SACO-SR. In 1975 the three covered about 75 percent of the labor force (table 13-1), a density of union coverage greater than in any other country in the Organization for Economic Cooperation and Development (OECD).

The LO, founded in 1898, is the largest of the confederations, covering 47 percent of the labor force and an estimated 95 percent of blue collar workers.[14] Its total membership was growing at an annual rate of about

13. *Stadgar för Svenska arbetsgivareföreningen* (Stockholm: SAF, 1969); T. L. Johnston, *Collective Bargaining in Sweden* (Harvard University Press, 1962), pp. 68–84; Peter Jackson and Keith Sisson, "Employers' Confederations in Sweden and the U.K. and the Significance of Industrial Infrastructure," *British Journal of Industrial Relations*, vol. 14 (November 1976), pp. 306–23.
14. Forsebäck, *Industrial Relations*, p. 30.

3 percent during the 1970s, somewhat faster than in the preceding decade. The twenty-five individual unions in the LO are organized almost entirely on an industrial basis. The metalworkers union, with a quarter of the LO's membership, was the largest until 1978 when the local government workers union overtook it.

There was relatively little white collar unionization until after World War II. Most of what there had been was brought together with the establishment of the TCO in 1944. It grew rapidly, accounting for 22 percent of the labor force, with its members distributed among twenty-two unions, by the mid-1970s. A little over half of the TCO membership was in the private sector, mostly in three unions. Of these, a union of clerical and technical workers in industry, with a quarter of the TCO's membership, is the largest. Of the TCO unions in the public sector, the local government employees union, with a little over a tenth of the membership, is the largest. The SACO-SR is a merger of two small organizations of upper-level white collar workers, predominantly in the public sector, whose combined membership was just over 4 percent of the total labor force in 1975.

Formally, the LO is not as centralized as the SAF. Nothing in the LO's rules entitles it to conduct the central negotiations with the SAF that have characterized each wage bargaining round since 1956. In each instance, negotiations have been authorized by the LO's representative council, made up of officials from all of the unions. Representatives of the LO do have the right to sit in on negotiations by its affiliated unions, and to bring issues specified in the agreements that arise at industry level up to negotiation between it and a counterpart employers association. On the other hand, individual unions are not required to submit collective agreements to the LO for prior approval, and the LO cannot levy fines or impose sanctions short of expulsion for violations of its organizational rules or policies. To all intents and purposes, affiliated unions cannot resort to a strike without approval of the LO's executive body, for the LO can deny the financial support it is otherwise obliged to give. However, about three-quarters of strike benefits members are entitled to are at the disposal of the individual national unions rather than the LO.

Underpinning the LO's authority over its affiliates is the centralization of authority within them. According to the standard set of rules prescribed by the LO, the right to decide on strike action and approve wage agreements is vested in the national union leadership. While the leadership is elected, the process is often indirect, and decisions on whether to strike or accept a contract are not subject to binding referendum—most unions have even abandoned the practice of the advisory referendum in favor of meetings of elected councils before and after negotiations.

The LO's centralization is reinforced by the fact that the SAF's control over its affiliates makes it hard for an individual union to get an employer counterpart to deviate from a central agreement. Moreover, strikes over issues covered in collective agreements are illegal as long as the agreements remain in force, and the duration and conditions for termination are specified in the agreements themselves. If not settled by negotiation, disputes over such issues go to a special labor court, consisting of union and employer nominees plus neutral jurists, set up for the purpose. This tends to make strikes a weapon that only confederation and national union leaders have at their disposal in bargaining over new agreements, providing old agreements are terminated instead of prolonged in order to preserve the "peace obligation," a restriction that again applies to local negotiations once new national agreements are concluded.[15]

In contrast with the SAF, it has been suggested, the actual centralization of power is probably greater than the formal centralization of authority in the LO.[16] However, the LO is perhaps most accurately viewed as an institutional arrangement through which member unions can arrive at and carry out a common policy. It has a great deal of moral and considerable formal authority to enforce such a policy in the face of resistance by one or two unions, but it cannot impose on its affiliates generally a policy that most do not support. This may well be true of the SAF as well. In both peak organizations, policy formation probably is dominated by the few largest component organizations, tempered by the need to draw others into consensus. On that basis, as much as the rules, the SAF and the LO have effectively acquired the power to negotiate agreements with each other and to go a long way toward securing compliance to them among their affiliates, with each increment of centralization in one providing an incentive or leverage for a parallel development in the other.

Among the white collar unions, the picture is quite different. Unlike the LO, the TCO is not a negotiating body—it was a party to the 1956

---

15. Johnston, *Collective Bargaining*, pp. 23–67, 115–65; Axel Hadenius, *Facklig organisationsutveckling: en studie av landsorganisationen i Sverige [Union Organizational Development: A Study of the Swedish Confederation of Labor]* (Stockholm: Rabén och Sjögren, 1976); Forsebäck, *Industrial Relations*, pp. 42–56.

16. Nils Elvander, *Intresseorganisationerna i dagens Sverige* (Lund: Gleerup Bokförlag, 1969), pp. 57–70; Anders Victorin, "Lönebildningsprocessen," in Lennart Brantgärde and others, *Konfliktlösning på arbetsmarknaden* (Lund: Gleerup Bokförlag, 1974), p. 173.

central agreement but to none since—and it has no comparable authority over its affiliates' action in the market arena. It serves primarily to articulate and press the white collar unions' positions concerning various public policy issues. For some time, individual TCO unions negotiated wage agreements with employer organizations. Successive moves toward joint negotiations among TCO unions in the private sector led to the establishment of a body for that purpose in 1973, a private sector salaried employees "cartel" (the Privattjänstemannakartellen, or PTK), which also includes several SACO-SR unions. Similar joint negotiating bodies, the TCO-S and the TCO-K, have been set up in the central and the local government sectors, but without any SACO-SR participation.

The LO had long sought to bring about the coordination of wage bargaining across confederal lines, while the white collar unions resisted in an effort to preserve differentials. In response to this interunion wage rivalry, the SAF shifted to a position in favor of joint negotiations. This pressure contributed to the formation of the PTK. After negotiating two separate agreements with the SAF, the PTK joined with the LO to negotiate the 1977 and 1978–79 agreements (though the PTK went on strike in 1977 without LO support). However, the PTK negotiated separately again in 1980 and 1981–82, going out on strike in the face of open LO opposition in the latter case. Coordination across confederal lines in the public sector was established for the first time during negotiations for the 1980 agreement, when the TCO-S and the TCO-K joined forces with the LO central and local government unions. However, the "gang of four," as they were dubbed, pursued an autonomous course rather than coordinating their bargaining with the private sector unions.[17]

The Wage Bargaining System

The results of the private sector central negotiations are embodied in "frame agreements" that lay down the contours of wage changes in the forthcoming contract period, varying from one to three years. Formally, these are only recommendations which the parties to the agreements are committed to urge on their affiliates. The latter, individual unions and industry associations—or companies in the case of the largest—negotiate

---

17. Forsebäck, *Industrial Relations,* pp. 20, 25–29; Christopher Wheeler, *White-Collar Power: Changing Patterns of Interest Group Behavior in Sweden* (University of Illinois Press, 1975). On Privattjänstemannakartellen (PTK), see *PTKs två första kongressperioder* (Stockholm: PTK, 1979); Bolang, *Utslagen,* pp. 14–15, 24–25.

the agreements that have the status of binding contracts under Swedish labor law. In practice, these contracts follow the general provisions of the frame agreements, translating them into detailed terms for their respective negotiating jurisdictions. Local negotiations apply the terms to individual establishments or to specific groups of workers within them. The local negotiations do not simply follow up on national agreements, however. Especially in plants where earnings depend on piecework or other performance-based payment systems, wage bargaining tends to go on continuously, informally as well as formally.[18]

The scope for interpretation and local negotiations in this multilevel bargaining system means that the increases provided for in the central frame agreements cannot completely determine the actual growth of earnings. In fact, those increases accounted for a little over half of the actual growth of earnings over the period 1956–81. The rest took the form of "wage drift"—the difference between the actual increase in earnings and the "calculated effects of the central wage agreements on average earnings."[19] Drift tends to vary with the tightness of labor markets and to some extent with profits—in other words, with the degree to which employers compete for labor.[20] This, in turn, is obviously bound to affect the bargaining power of local union officials and even individual workers.

Thus, the central negotiations provide a mechanism through which the confederations can try to resolve the conflicting claims of labor and capital in aggregate terms consistent with the long-run viability of Sweden's position in the international economy. Yet, they are limited in the extent that they can do so by the considerable degree of decentralization remaining in the wage determination system. To the extent that increases negotiated

18. Victorin, "Lönebildningsprocessen," pp. 170–90; Gustafsson, "Lönesystem," pp. 66–74; Horst Hart and Casten v. Otter, *Lönebildningen på arbetsplatsen: en sociologisk studie* (Stockholm: Prisma, 1973).

19. Nils Henrik Schager, "The Duration of Vacancies as a Measure of the State of Demand in the Labor Market: The Swedish Wage Drift Equation Reconsidered," in Gunnar Eliasson, Bertil Holmlund, and Frank P. Stafford, eds., *Studies in Labor Market Behavior: Sweden and the United States*, Proceedings of a Symposium at the Industrial Institute for Economic and Social Research, Stockholm, July 10–11, 1979 (Stockholm: Almqvist and Wiksell, 1981), p. 417. Wage drift has been described as a statistical residual, lumping together the effects of a large variety of factors (shifting proportions of workers in different pay categories, changing definitions of categories, lags between productivity increases due to improved skills or rationalization and the recalculation of piece rates, bargaining over recalculation of piece rates or the interpretation of national agreements, and informal bargaining or even unilateral offers by management, down to the workplace level, aimed at attracting or holding labor); Gösta Edgren, Karl-Olof Faxén, and Clas-Erik Odhner, *Wage Formation and the Economy* (London: Allen and Unwin, 1973), pp. 135–42.

20. See Schager, "Duration of Vacancies," pp. 396–400, 427–32.

by the peak organizations fall short of pressures for more rapid growth generated by market forces at the level of the work place, wage drift tends to close the gap. Some wage drift is regarded as unavoidable, reflecting necessary elements of flexibility and affording a kind of safety valve. But the more drift there is, the more likely that central organizations will be subjected to internal strains.

This is probably more true of union than of employer organizations, reflecting a basic asymmetry between employer and union organizations. Individual employers often have an interest in exceeding negotiated wage increases—as a means of recruiting needed labor, for example. This puts employers into competition with each other and into conflict with the organization acting for all of them, but all obviously have a common interest in keeping wage growth as low as possible. Union members, on the other hand, have a common interest in increasing wages as much as possible, and the unions' effectiveness in doing so is their principal claim to their members' support. The risk of losing support that unions incur insofar as they fail to press for the largest increases that can be won would therefore seem much greater than the risk of losing support that employer organizations incur insofar as they try to keep individual employers from exceeding increases specified in central agreements. Hence, it is primarily within union organizations participating in central negotiations that the tension between the requirements of external equilibrium and organizational cohesion arise.

The fact that there are plural organizations on each side of the labor market also limits the effectiveness of central negotiations in performing an incomes policy function. The organization of blue and white collar workers within separate confederations has tended to perpetuate status differences between them even as the actual differences in their work become blurred, at least at the edges of the occupational categories. There is also an important political difference between the blue and white collar unions. From their origins in the late nineteenth century, the LO unions have been closely linked to the Social Democratic party, together forming the Social Democratic labor movement. The TCO and SACO-SR unions are not linked to the Social Democratic or any other party. While LO members vote overwhelmingly for the Social Democrats, only a minority of white collar union members do so, while the rest spread their votes among the other four parties all the way across the political spectrum. These political differences reinforce the obstacles posed by occupational differences. On the employer side, differences in the fundamental economic position and political stakes of private and public sector employers present obstacles to common strategies, regardless of which parties are in office at national and local levels.

On the one hand, then, inclusion of almost the entire labor force in organizations characterized by a high degree of centralization provides highly favorable conditions for central negotiations capable of gearing wage growth to the requirements of external equilibrium. On the other hand, the plurality of organizations on both sides of the labor market and the elements of decentralization in wage bargaining that remain impose significant limits on the extent to which central negotiations can perform that function. Rivalry among organizations on the same side of the labor market, particularly between blue and white collar unions, reinforces the internal tensions between peak associations and their component organizations and between the latter and their members. The requirements of organizational cohesion consequently impose strong limits on the compromises the peak associations can strike between the particular perceived interests of their constituencies and the common avowed interest in sustaining the economy's international viability.

Although wage rivalry between LO and TCO unions has been increasingly important as the latter have grown, attention here is concentrated on the constraints imposed by the requirements of organizational cohesion within the LO, both because these constraints are particularly evident in that organization and because of the pivotal role it has played in the evolution of the political system as well as the wage determination system. Since it is mainly among the LO's industrial, blue collar members that wage drift takes place, the LO and its affiliates are especially vulnerable to the strains to which it can lead. At the same time, the massive weight of the LO in the labor market makes it impossible for it to neglect the consequences of its wage policy for the economy. Thus, the tension between the requirements of organizational cohesion and external equilibrium is likely to be most acute within that organization. The extent to which the central negotiation system can perform an incomes policy function would therefore seem to depend heavily on the extent to which the LO can resolve that tension.

The Functions of LO Wage Policy

Insofar as the LO's wage policy is capable of meeting the requirements of external equilibrium, it can be said to perform an incomes policy function, and insofar as its wage policy retains the support of its affiliates, it can be said to perform an organizational cohesion function. To the extent that each function is performed, the LO's wage policy provides the Social Democratic party with important forms of political support, so that the policy can be said to perform political functions as well.

External Equilibrium

Most of the participants in the system of centralized negotiations as well as most observers long shared a common view of how to decide what rate of growth of wages was necessary for long-run external equilibrium. In 1969 the rough rules of thumb accepted by both sides were given more systematic formulation in the EFO model, designed by economists of the two main union confederations and the employers confederation.[21] Their formulation was not adopted as official policy but served as a generally accepted framework within which to estimate the scope for wage increases.

The EFO model—a version of the Scandinavian model of inflation in a small, open economy developed in Norway by Odd Aukrust[22]—divides the economy into two sectors: a competitive, or C, sector produces tradable goods and services that are exported or compete with imports, and a sheltered, or S, sector, those that are not tradable. Since Sweden's standard of living depends on participation in the international economy, the requirements for the continued competitiveness of the C sector are taken as the basis for specifying the scope of increases. The essential requirement is conceived as a sufficient level of investment to keep the value of the sector product at a level consistent with external equilibrium. If the initial position is one of equilibrium, it is assumed that there will be sufficient investment in the sector to maintain its competitiveness if the relative shares of wages and profits in the sector remain unchanged. Constant shares will, in turn, be maintained if wage increases in the sector do not exceed the sum of price increases and productivity increases—in other words, that sum defines the scope for increases.

The model specifies several additional conditions or assumptions. First, the C sector is a price taker, on the assumption that prices in that sector

---

21. Edgren, Faxén, and Odhner. The model is summarized in their *Wage Formation*, pp. 11–27.
22. Published in 1966. See Odd Aukrust, "Inflation in the Open Economy: A Norwegian Model," and Lars Calmfors, "Inflation in Sweden," in Lawrence B. Krause and Walter S. Salant, eds., *Worldwide Inflation: Theory and Recent Experience* (Brookings Institution, 1977), pp. 107–53, 493–537.

are set on the international market. Second, international price movements are imported into the economy, since exchange rates were essentially fixed for most of the postwar period up to the time the model was formulated. Third, productivity growth is not significantly affected by wage changes, on the assumption that it follows a trend set by exogenous factors such as scientific and technological development.

The scope for increases in the C sector in turn defines the permissible rate of wage growth in the S sector. Thus, it is deemed essential for the C sector to act as the wage leader for the economy as a whole. Wage changes in the S sector are expected to be the same as in the C sector because standard rates are supposedly applied throughout the economy by the central negotiations and reinforced by market forces. Assuming lower productivity and standard mark-up pricing in the S sector, prices in it will rise faster than in the C sector, making the domestic inflation rate somewhat higher than the rise in international prices. This is regarded as consistent with external equilibrium as long as wage changes in the C sector remain within the scope for them defined by the model, thereby preserving competitiveness. Thus, the EFO model's target is not price stability, regarded as futile in an open economy under a fixed exchange rate regime. In addition, the C sector scope is not conceived as a norm to be satisfied in each wage round. Rather, it is understood as the main course around which the size of increases may fluctuate, as long as the long-run trend follows it.

Although the EFO model provided the framework within which wage policy was discussed for some time, attention eventually focused on inadequacies in the model, particularly as it was originally formulated. Some assumptions like that concerning the relationship between wages and productivity growth were probably wrong all along, while others no longer held. Some actors sought to discard the model while others, including the LO, called for its reformulation.[23] At this point, the EFO model's importance is that it testifies to the concern for external equilibrium shared by the LO with other actors.

Organizational Cohesion

Although the LO's affiliates have to authorize it to enter negotiations anew at the start of each round, it is hard to conceive of their not doing

23. Bengt Rydén, ed., *Stabiliseringspolitik för 80 talet: Konjunkturrådets rapport, 1980–81* (Stockholm: SN&S, 1980), pp. 8–27.

so as long as the SAF coordinates bargaining on the employers' side.[24] Yet, there have been occasions when one or more unions have decided to go it alone. In any case, agreement among the unions concerning the level and distribution of the wage increases the LO should press for— that is, the concrete formulation of an agreed wage policy—is an essential condition for the LO's coordination of their wage bargaining through central negotiations.

The general conception on which the terms of such agreements have been legitimated is "solidaristic wage policy." Its central principle is equal pay for equal work, regardless of employers' ability to pay.[25] According to this traditional labor movement norm of fairness, workers should not get different pay for the same work because of differences in firms' profitability or in demand for labor in local markets. No way of determining which jobs are equivalent, such as an economywide job evaluation scheme on which there is general agreement, has been developed, however. In the absence of that, the LO's wage policy has in practice concentrated on improving the relative position of lower-paid workers through increases that are proportionally greater the lower the wage. This low-wage bias tends to iron out differences in pay for work that is evidently similar, including differences resulting from sex discrimination as well as from variations in profitability and labor market tightness. It also tends to reduce differentials generally. Thus, solidaristic wage policy has an imprecise but egalitarian meaning, which commands wide support within the LO.[26]

The LO claims to have substantially achieved its solidaristic wage policy goals in agreements negotiated during the 1970s. Typically they provided for a general increase, in absolute cash rather than percentage terms, to

24. Karl-Olof Faxén, "Arbetsgivarorganisationer, lönepolitik och inflation," in *Erfarenheter av blandekonomin* (Stockholm: Almqvist and Wiksell, 1977), pp. 116–21. The SAF is in a powerful position to determine whether centralized negotiations will take place or not. It forced the LO unions into central negotiations in 1957 after they decided against it, and it was the SAF that blocked central negotiations in 1984.

25. This discussion is based on various LO documents, especially *Lönepolitik: Rapport till LO-kongressen, 1971* (Stockholm: Prisma, 1971), pp. 93–127, and *Löner, Priser, Skatter: Rapport till LO-kongressen, 1976* (Stockholm: Prisma, 1976), pp. 77–86, 160–227. See also Rudolf Meidner, "Samordning och solidarisk lönepolitik under tre decennier," in LO, *Tvärsnitt: sju forskningsrapporter utgivna till LO:s 75-årsjubileum, 1973* (Stockholm: Prisma, 1973), pp. 7–69; Hadenius, *Facklig organisationsutveckling,* pp. 36–122; Derek Robinson, *Solidaristic Wage Policy in Sweden* (Paris: Organization for Economic Cooperation and Development, 1974).

26. In a sample survey of LO members Leif Lewin found that 93 percent agreed that unions should strive for "equal pay for equal work regardless of the firms' ability to pay," while only 19 percent agreed that the unions should strive for a "takeover of the means of production by the people." *Hur styrs facket? Om demokratin inom fackföreningsrörelsen* (Stockholm: Rabén och Sjögren, 1977), p. 158.

all workers; additional increases, in cash terms, that are higher the more that individual workers' wages fall short of the industry average, or some norm above the average (the special low-wage increase or supplement); and a further increase designed to make up the difference between the amount by which any worker's earnings exceed the increases provided for by the first two components—that is, wage drift—and an increase, again in cash terms, corresponding to some percentage of average wage drift (this is referred to as the earnings guarantee).[27]

Quite apart from such moral force as the solidaristic norm has, the relative improvement provided by the first two components of the agreements can embrace at least a majority of LO union members. Interest in such a low-wage bias would be common to all unions to the extent that levels and dispersion of wages are roughly similar in all of them. It can be acceptable to higher-paid workers also, for all get some increase. In addition, those whose skills are in demand or who are in an advantageous position for other reasons are likely to benefit from wage drift, getting considerably more than the specified amount. But the more that wage drift counteracts the avowed intentions of the low-wage bias in the central agreements, the greater the risk that the credibility of solidaristic wage policy will be undermined, and with it the legitimacy of the LO's role. Accordingly, a substantial portion of the relative improvement in lower-paid workers' earnings must be protected against erosion by wage drift. This is precisely what the earnings guarantee is designed to do.

Groups likely to fall behind have a stake in coordinated bargaining because it builds into the wage determination system a mechanism that enables them to at least partly catch up. This makes it worth it to them to give up the right to go it alone in exchange for the earnings guarantee. Groups in the best position to gain from favorable market conditions also give up the right to go it alone in contract negotiations, but not the opportunity to make those gains through wage drift. Thus, the cost to them is not very great in terms of absolute increases in earnings, while coordinated bargaining may strengthen their position in the face of highly organized employers.

As a set of relationships among rates of increase of earnings of workers at different points in the pay scale, with different payment systems, and to some extent different unions, that individual unions are willing to

---

27. Texts of the agreements are compiled in LO, *De centrala överenskommelserna LO-SAF* (Stockholm: LO, 1979). Price index clauses in various forms began to be included during the later 1970s.

support, solidaristic wage policy provides a formula for managing distributive conflict within, and among, LO unions that allows the LO to coordinate their wage bargaining. For this agreement to be sustainable, there has to be enough slack in the system to permit some wage drift—it cannot be too centralized. Otherwise, coordinated bargaining would require workers in the best position to make gains to give up too much.

However, there can be too much wage drift, not only because it can never be fully compensated. The higher the rates of drift experienced by workers, the more evident it must be that employers are able to pay more than the LO succeeded in getting through collective bargaining. Thus, the greater the gap between the actual earnings increase and that provided in the central agreements, the lower the credibility of the LO's claim to represent the workers' economic interests.

To meet the requirements of organizational cohesion, then, the LO's wage policy has to strike a balance between specified increases and scope for wage drift that minimizes tensions within and among its affiliated unions, so as to maximize their support for its continued negotiation of central agreements.[28] A wage policy capable of solving this problem is a prerequisite for the central negotiations relied on to keep wage growth in line with the requirements of external equilibrium, as defined by the EFO model. However, the requirements of organizational cohesion can set limits on the extent to which the external equilibrium requirements can be met. The greater the tension between the two requirements, the more severe the dilemma with which the LO is consequently confronted.

Political Functions

The support that the LO provides to the Social Democratic party has been crucial to the SAP's power in the state arena. For the LO, that power has been essential to achieve goals beyond the reach of union power in the market arena, especially full employment. It has also supplied a "political alternative" to collective bargaining as a means of attaining

---

28. See LO reports for 1951, *Trade Unions and Full Employment* (Stockholm: Swedish Confederation of Trade Unions, 1953), pp. 86–87, 92–99; 1971, *Lönepolitik*; and 1976, *Löner, Priser*. In an LO survey of members, "most favored a continued combination of general increases and low wage supplements" and "a large majority also want the general increase to be the same for all specified in crowns and öre and not in percent"; LO, *Verksamhets berättelse 1974* (Stockholm: LO, 1975), p. 97. The feeling among highly skilled (and scarce) workers in the metalworkers union that equalization had gone too far was strong enough by 1983 for that union to agree with its employer counterpart in the engineering industry to engage in separate negotiations, for which the employers had been pushing for some time.

goals such as income maintenance—through legislated transfer payments instead of negotiated fringe benefits—and the strengthening of union rights—through legislation expanding the scope of collective bargaining. Thus, the party's power in the state arena reinforces and supplements the union power in the market arena on which it largely rests, while securing the conditions under which the unions are able and willing to temper the use of their power in the interest of macroeconomic policy. This, in turn, provides the party with an important form of political support. To the extent that the LO's coordination of wage bargaining contributes to the effectiveness of economic policy when the party is in office, it helps to confirm the party's principal claim for electoral support. And to the extent that the LO's wage bargaining role contributes to the unions' organizational cohesion, it enhances their effectiveness in mobilizing electoral support among their own members, who are the party's core constituency.

The SAP is one of five parties that compete for Swedish citizens' votes.[29] It and a small communist party, the Left-party communists (Vänsterpartiet kommunisterna, or VPK), are generally viewed as a socialist bloc. The other three, referred to as the bourgeois parties, make up a nonsocialist bloc. Two of the three, a liberal People's party and the Center party (formerly the Farmers party), refer to themselves as the "middle parties," to distinguish themselves from the conservatives, the Moderate Unity party (formerly the Right party).

Alone or as the dominant partner in a coalition, the SAP controlled the government virtually without interruption from 1932 until 1976, a record unmatched by any other party subject to the repeated test of free elections. That this should be the case in the country in which unions organize a larger portion of the labor force than in any other is hardly surprising. On the other hand, the high level of unionization has not given the Social Democrats a corresponding degree of political strength, principally because of political differences among the three union confederations.

The ties between the SAP and the blue collar unions are rooted in the latters' origins.[30] Founded in 1889, the party concentrated on organizing

---

29. See M. Donald Hancock, *Sweden: The Politics of Postindustrial Change* (Hinsdale, Ill.: Dryden Press, 1972), pp. 108–45.

30. See Dankwart A. Rustow, *The Politics of Compromise: A Study of Parties and Cabinet Government in Sweden* (Princeton University Press, 1955); Donald J. Blake, "Swedish Trade Unions and the Social Democratic Party: The Formative Years," *Scandinavian Economic History Review*, vol. 8, no. 1 (1960), pp. 19–44.

unions as the key to mobilizing the working class being created by the rapid beginnings of Sweden's industrialization. Unionization thus received a major impetus, but not among some nonsocialist workers; hence the differentiation of market and state arena organizations with the establishment of the LO as a separate central body in 1898. Nevertheless, the SAP and the LO continued to be identified as interdependent parts of a single Social Democratic labor movement, linked to each other in various ways at all levels.

Although they have no constitutional role analogous to that of unions in the British Labour party, LO union branches affiliated with the SAP are the core of its local organizations. Collectively, affiliated union members account for the bulk of the party's membership and much of its funds. There is considerable overlapping membership between party and union bodies.[31] A very large proportion of union activists are party activists or clearly identify themselves as Social Democrats.[32]

The electoral significance of this interpenetration is suggested by the close association between the distribution of LO member votes and total votes for the Social Democrats (table 13-2). The proportion of LO members voting for the SAP reached a peak in 1968, the year in which the party got the second of the only two majorities it ever won. Support among LO voters fell to a low in 1976, when the party lost office for the first time in forty-four years. The falling trend in LO member support was reversed in 1979, contributing to an increase in the Social Democrats' total which fell just short of bringing them back into office, and rose further to help them regain power in 1982.

While the LO unions' capacity to mobilize support for the SAP is clearly crucial to the party's electoral fortunes, it is not enough to assure victory. Six percent of LO unions voted for the communist VPK in 1973 (a more typical year than 1976), bringing the socialist majority among LO voters to over three-quarters. Sixteen percent voted for the Center party, primarily in the party's traditional rural strongholds, 4 percent for

---

31. Sveriges Socialdemokratiska Arbetareparti, *Utveckling av organisation och verksamhet* (Stockholm: Tiden, 1975), pp. 28–29; *Facklig-politisk verksamhet: Inventera-planera-genomföra* (Stockholm: Social-demokraterna, 1978). Data on party finances are curiously hard to come by in Sweden, the parties' opponents being the chief sources of estimates, or accusations, of how much money they get from various interested supporters. According to one such estimate, unions provided just under a third and the government roughly half of the funds the Social Democrats had at their disposal in the 1973 election campaign. This excludes support in kind. *Dagens nyheter* (Stockholm), August 16, 1973. Government subsidies, formally to party newspapers, are allocated in proportion to votes. Hancock, *Sweden,* pp. 110–11.

32. Lewin, *Hur styrs facket?* pp. 90–91.

Table 13-2. *Distribution of Union Members' Support among Parties in Swedish Parliamentary Elections, 1968–79*
Percent

Union confed-eration and year	Party					
	Social Democratic	VPK	Center	People's	Moderate Unity	Other
LO						
1968	81	2	8	5	2	2
1970	75	6	11	3	1	4
1973	71	6	16	4	1	2
1976	66	5	17	7	3	2
1979	68	6	10	7	7	2
TCO						
1968	46	1	14	21	13	5
1970	38	3	21	24	10	4
1973	35	3	33	12	14	3
1976	41	3	21	17	17	1
1979	37	6	14	14	27	2
SACO-SR						
1968	17	4	14	25	40	0
1970	15	3	12	30	37	3
1973	22	3	18	10	42	5
1976	12	6	27	22	29	4
1979	13	10	9	17	49	2
All voters						
1968	50.1	3.0	16.1	15.0	13.9	1.8
1970	45.3	4.8	19.9	16.2	11.5	2.2
1973	43.6	5.3	25.1	9.4	14.3	2.4
1976	42.7	4.8	24.1	11.1	15.6	1.8
1979	43.2	5.6	18.1	10.6	20.3	1.9
1982[a]	45.6	5.6	15.5	5.9	23.6	4.7

Sources: Bo Särlvik, "Sweden: The Social Bases of the Parties in a Developmental Perspective," in Richard Rose, ed., *Electoral Behavior: A Comparative Handbook* (Free Press, 1974), p. 407; Bo Särlvik, "Valet 1970," *Allmänna valen, 1970,* vol. 3 (Stockholm: Statistiska centralbyrån, 1973), p. 100; Olof Petersson and Bo Särlvik, "Valet 1973," *Allmänna valen, 1973,* vol. 3 (Stockholm: Statistiska centralbyrån, 1975), p. 84; Olof Petersson, *Valundersökningar,* report 2: *Väljarna och valet 1976* (Stockholm: Statistiska centralbyrån, 1977), p. 43; Sören Holmberg, *Svenska väljare* (Stockholm: Liber Förlag, 1981), pp. 27, 339; *Statistisk årsbok 1978* (Stockholm: Statistiska centralbyrån, 1978), p. 424.
a. Breakdown by union confederation not available.

the liberals, and 1 percent for the conservatives, adding up to a substantial nonsocialist minority.

Even if the LO were 100 percent effective in mobilizing member support, the SAP would still need support beyond its core constituency. The bulk of this additional electoral support has, of course, come from white collar employees. The political allegiances of officials and members of both white collar confederations are widely dispersed among all the parties and both are compelled to stay formally nonpartisan to avoid internal strains, although the political center of gravity is clearly to the left in the TCO and to the right in the SACO-SR. Nonetheless, in all categories of employees, union members are twice as likely to vote Social Democratic as nonmembers. More TCO voters, roughly two-fifths, have supported the SAP than any other party in recent elections.[33]

Clearly, the very high degree of unionization in Sweden contributes to the SAP's strength. But the contribution does not correspond to the degree of unionization—if it did, the party would enjoy perpetual majorities. In fact, except in 1940 and 1968, the party has had to have parliamentary support from some other party to control the government. Support from the Farmers party, informal or as a coalition partner, enabled it to govern for much of the time between 1932 and 1957. From then until 1976, except from 1968 to 1970, the SAP depended largely on the unwillingness of the small communist party to be responsible for the fall of a government supported by most of the working class.

Despite their unparalleled continuity in office, then, the Social Democrats persistently faced the need to simultaneously mobilize their core constituency and attract additional support in the electorate or parliament. Rather than try to do so by becoming a "catch-all" party,[34] it continued to claim the working class as its distinct constituency, trying to redefine its scope so as to include white collar workers. Both the LO and the party have accordingly sought to frame issues and policy positions so as to identify interests common to LO and TCO members.[35]

In the context of this electoral strategy, the support of LO union members for the SAP is crucial, and the unions themselves are clearly a vital resource for mobilizing that support. It is precisely in helping the party to make the most of this resource that the LO's wage bargaining role can perform an important political function. The LO's negotiation of central agreements on the basis of claims agreed on in advance by its component unions provides a mechanism for avoiding wage rivalry among them, or at least preventing it from breaking out in open, competitive

33. The TCO's position in the political arena is analyzed in Wheeler, *White-Collar Power.*

34. The argument that this would typically happen to labor movement parties was made by Otto Kirchheimer, "The Transformation of the Western European Party Systems," in Joseph LaPalombara and Myron Weiner, eds., *Political Parties and Political Development* (Princeton University Press, 1966), pp. 177–200.

35. See Andrew Martin, "Trade Unions in Sweden: Strategic Responses to Change and Crisis," in Peter A. Gourevitch, Andrew Martin, and George Ross, eds., *Unions, Change and Crisis: Britain, West Germany and Sweden* (London: Allen and Unwin, 1984).

bargaining. In this way, the identification of LO members with the particular unions, occupations, sectors, or even work places to which they belong, and which bargaining confined to such subconfederal units tends to encourage, can be inhibited. Instead, identification of LO members with a single, unified labor movement, of which the SAP is the political vehicle, can be fostered. Cohesion in wage bargaining can thus be expected to reinforce political cohesion, enhancing the SAP's capacity to tap union activists' energies and increasing rank-and-file receptivity to its claim, transmitted by the activists, to be the exclusive political instrument for advancing their interests.[36]

Thus, the organizational cohesion on which the LO's wage bargaining role depends can itself provide a form of political support that may be as important to the SAP as any incomes policy function which that role may perform. If so, the party as well as the LO confronts a dilemma that is indeed serious insofar as the LO is unable to carry out a wage policy capable of simultaneously meeting the requirements of organizational cohesion and external equilibrium. That the LO has in fact found it difficult to do so is suggested below.

The LO's Wage Policy Dilemma

The difficulty of reconciling the two requirements is strikingly illustrated by two successive central agreements negotiated in the mid-1970s. Moderate wage increases provided for in a one-year agreement for 1974 were certainly consistent with the requirements of external equilibrium, but at considerable cost to organizational cohesion. Much higher increases provided for in the subsequent two-year agreement for 1975–76 certainly met the organizational cohesion requirements more fully but fell far short of the external equilibrium requirements. Both agreements were affected by the exceptional instability of the international economy. But they display a pattern of satisfying first one and then the other set of requirements, each at the expense of the other, also observable in agreements since the early 1960s.

Thus, the difficulty of reconciling the two requirements has evidently

36. The importance of LO centralization for Social Democratic political strength, especially in comparison with the British case, is stressed in John D. Stephens, *The Transition from Capitalism to Socialism* (Macmillan, 1979), esp. pp. 120–28, 140–44. See also Richard Scase, *Social Democracy in Capitalist Society: Working-Class Politics in Britain and Sweden* (London: Croom Helm, 1977); Walter Korpi, *The Working Class in Welfare Capitalism* (London: Routledge and Kegan Paul, 1978).

been persistent. While the need to resolve the resulting dilemma is now recognized as more urgent than ever, the strategy for doing so to which the LO is now committed is an extension of an approach it began to develop when it first confronted the dilemma in the early postwar period.

The 1974 Central Agreement and Profit Explosion

The tension between the two requirements is clearly articulated in a wage policy report to the LO's 1976 congress. While reaffirming that "redistribution and equalization between wages and capital income" is the long-run goal, the report reiterates the need to pursue that goal within limits imposed by Sweden's dependence on participation in the international economy. To keep these limits from being breached, the redistribution "must be the result of an overall negotiated settlement and not of an economic power struggle within particular sectors or individual markets." Otherwise, intergroup rivalry—between the LO and others as well as within the LO—was likely to generate inflation that would nullify all gains and "could injure our competitiveness abroad." On the other hand, the "economic consequences" of wage increases "must not be allowed to take precedence over solidaristic wage policy." For if wage drift is allowed to fill the gap between negotiated increases and those for which there is "real scope," the resulting "tensions within as well as between different organizations' member groups" will undermine the support on which overall settlements depend.[37]

That evidently happened in 1974 (table 13-3). As it turned out, the agreed 5.1 percent increase in average hourly earnings was much lower than the increase for which there was scope. Wage drift exceeded the contractual increase by 3 percentage points, a greater difference than that during the life of any preceding agreement (although it was less than in the second year of the 1969–70 agreement). The high level of drift resulted from the surging demand and exceptionally high profits being enjoyed by Swedish industry during the international inflationary boom preceding—and contributing to—the initial raising of oil prices by the Organization of Petroleum Exporting Countries (OPEC). But there was considerable dispersion in profits, which were highest in sectors benefiting from the commodity price boom. Consequently, "the substantial drift

---

37. LO, *Löner, Priser,* pp. 81, 84, 206–07. The relationship between profits and drift is discussed in Schager, "Duration of Vacancies"; Lars Calmfors and Erik Lundberg, *Inflation och arbetslöshet* (Stockholm: SN&S, 1974), pp. 95–96.

Table 13-3. *Annual Rate of Change in Prices and in Wages and Real Earnings of Workers and Labor Costs in Mining and Manufacturing in Sweden, 1970–81*
Percent

| Year | Con- sumer pricesª | Hourly wages of industrial workers | | | Real earningsᵇ | Labor costsᶜ |
		Contrac- tual	Drift	Total earnings		
1970	7.0	3.4	7.2	10.6	3.6	12.4
1971	7.5	6.5	4.2	10.7	3.2	11.8
1972	5.7	7.4	3.3	10.7	5.0	12.3
1973	7.6	4.3	4.2	8.5	0.9	11.5
1974	10.5	5.1	8.1	13.2	2.7	17.5
1975	10.1	11.0	8.6	19.6	9.5	22.4
1976	9.4	7.8	3.6	11.4	2.0	16.8
1977	12.8	5.4	3.3	8.7	−4.1	10.8
1978	7.5	2.7	3.0	5.7	−1.8	10.7
1979	9.7	3.9	3.5	7.4	−2.3	8.7
1980	13.7	6.0	3.5	9.5	−4.2	10.2
1981	9.4	4.3	3.5	7.8	−1.6	10.7

Sources: *The Swedish Economy*, statistical appendix, various issues; Ingvar Ohlsson, LO Research Department.
a. Long-term index from December to December; 1949 = 100.
b. Change in total earnings minus change in consumer prices.
c. Index of hourly costs, including earnings, payroll taxes, other social charges, and adjustments for reductions in hours.

arising from the good profitability" was "unevenly distributed," and "much of the equalization achieved by the emphasis on low wages in the year's [agreement] . . . lost."[38] In other words, solidaristic wage policy was frustrated by the high and uneven drift.

The moderation of the 1974 agreement can undoubtedly be attributed in part to a general concern, shared by the LO, to avoid exacerbating the impact of the oil crisis. On the other hand, the contractual increases for 1974 were not lower than might have been expected. Under the 1971–73 agreement, contractual increases had exceeded drift (table 13-3), profits had been lower than throughout the preceding postwar period, and unemployment had been higher than at any time since the late 1950s. If anything, the EFO model's scope for increases might have been exceeded. In addition, there had been a considerable equalization of wages since 1970, at least within the LO.[39] Finally, earnings had exceeded consumer price increases enough to yield pretax growth in real wages of between 2 and 3 percent annually.

38. LO, *Verksamhets berättelse 1974* (Stockholm: LO, 1975), pp. 80–81.
39. LO, *Löner, Priser*, pp. 209–11.

Thus, there was little pressure for higher increases in the 1974 agreement. Soon after it went into effect, however, it became obvious to both unions and employers that the wage settlement was untenably low, and higher increases were provided for in subsequent industry-level negotiations. Nevertheless, there was a wave of wildcat strikes equivalent in magnitude to those in the winter of 1969–70, when drift exceeded contractual increases even more than in 1974.[40] The strikes were the clearest demonstration that the organizational cohesion of the LO and its affiliates had been subjected to serious strains by their conduct of wage bargaining. They therefore believed it essential to repair the damage by winning a settlement so high that it left little scope for drift. Accordingly, the next round of bargaining opened with the declaration that "wage earners as a group must take out their share of productivity growth and win back some of the [lost] share of wages in the value of output," and that "the emphasis on low wages must be intensified."[41]

These aims were largely fulfilled in the 1975–76 agreement, although the absolute level of drift was even higher in 1975 than in 1974. The result was that over the two years of the agreement, the contractual increases plus drift and payroll taxes increased hourly labor costs in Swedish industry 39 percent, the largest two-year increase since the Korean War.[42] The effect of the earlier wage explosion was easily absorbed, for it occurred at the beginning of an unprecedented period of international economic growth, in which Swedish industry started out in a very favorable position. By 1975, that growth had been disrupted and Swedish industry had lost many of its advantages, so that the later explosion had much more serious consequences.

The Impact of the 1975–76 Central Agreement

The 1975–76 wage explosion evidently contributed to a substantial deterioration in Sweden's position in the international economy. The cost gap between Sweden and its trading partners is estimated to have been as high as 27 percent, about half of it accounted for by the rise in hourly labor costs, a third by relatively lower productivity growth, and another

40. In the engineering industry, the number of worker days lost in wildcat strikes was half again as large in 1974 as in 1970, according to an SAF tabulation of August 22, 1975. The strikes following the 1974 agreement are analyzed in Bo Ohlström, *Vilda strejker inom LO-området 1974 och 1975* (Stockholm: LO, 1977).

41. LO, *Verksamhets berättelse 1974*, pp. 80–81.

42. *Swedish Economy, 1982: 2*, p. 108.

fifth by the appreciation of the Swedish crown relative to currencies outside the European monetary snake (in which the crown was tied to the rising deutsche mark).[43]

This rise in costs was bound to have a big impact on the sales and profits of Sweden's highly export-dependent industry. However, its magnitude is uncertain because of serious inadequacies in Sweden's foreign trade data. While revised balance of payments estimates covering the 1970s are available, new data on market shares and relative prices are at hand only for the second half of the decade. The old data indicated that during the three years 1975–77, Sweden lost an estimated 19 percent of its OECD area market shares, mainly because of a nearly 15 percent rise in the relative price of Swedish exports in 1975–76.[44] Revised data for 1976 and beyond indicate that in that year at least, export performance was significantly better than previously indicated. Yet, while exports of manufactured goods, other than ships, to the major OECD countries grew by 4.5 percent in 1976, total import growth in Sweden's OECD market was more than three times as high, reflecting the sharp recovery there in 1976. Thus, there was a loss of shares in that market, now estimated at 7.5 percent.[45]

The decline in Swedish industry's competitiveness was also reflected in a loss of domestic market shares. The loss of shares and successive declines in foreign and then domestic demand resulted in a deeper and much longer fall of industrial production in Sweden than in the OECD area generally (figure 13-1). The index of industrial production declined for four years in a row beginning in 1975, its only previous postwar decline having been for one year in 1952. The recovery of industrial production in 1979 and 1980 still did not bring the index back to its 1974 peak (table 13-4).

While the loss of market shares indicates that some of the cost increase was passed on in prices, taking its toll in sales, some of it was clearly translated into a fall in profits (table 13-5). From a long-time high of

43. Lars Calmfors, "Lönebildning, internationell konkurrenskraft och ekonomisk politik," in *Vägar till ökad välfärd*, Ds Ju 1979:1, Bilaga 3, pp. 130–31. A TCO economist contested the cost crisis thesis when relative unit labor costs are viewed over a longer period; Hans Engman, "Svenska löner stiger inte snabbast i världen," *TCO-Tidningen*, 20, 1977, pp. 10–11. At an earlier point, the LO's position was also skeptical; LO, *Löner, Priser*, pp. 80–81. Later LO statements reflect acceptance of the view that Sweden's relative cost position was worsened in the late 1970s and that the rapid rise in hourly wages in 1975–76 was a contributing factor; Gunnar Nilsson, chairman of the LO, in parliament, January 31, 1979. Riksdagen 1978/79. *Snabbprotokoll*, no. 77, pp. 11–12.

44. *Swedish Economy, 1978:3*, p. 38.

45. Ibid., *1982:1*, p. 56.

Table 13-4. Changes in Economic Growth Indicators for Sweden and the OECD, 1960–82
Percent

| Year | OECD, annual rate of change of GDP | Sweden, annual rate of change | | | Sweden, share of GDP | | | |
		GDP	Industrial production[a]	Industrial investment[b]	Foreign trade[c]	Payments balance[d]	Government expenditures[e]	Government revenues minus expenditures[f]
1960–64	5.0	5.2	7.6	4.8	25.1	0.2	32.6	2.1
1965–69	4.9	3.6	5.3	4.6	24.8	-0.5	39.5	3.1
1970	2.9	5.5	6.1	3.8	27.7	-0.8	44.2	4.1
1971	4.0	1.0	1.2	1.1	26.9	1.0	46.1	5.1
1972	5.5	2.1	2.4	3.9	23.4	1.3	47.2	5.0
1973	6.1	3.8	6.9	9.9	26.1	2.8	45.6	4.1
1974	0.4	4.1	5.4	10.7	32.7	-1.0	48.8	2.0
1975	-0.6	0.8	-1.7	1.6	28.4	-0.5	49.7	2.8
1976	5.2	1.5	-0.8	0.2	28.6	-2.1	52.6	4.6
1977	3.7	-2.4	-5.4	-17.1	28.4	-2.6	58.6	1.7
1978	3.9	1.3	-1.7	-21.7	27.9	0.0	60.3	-0.4
1979	3.2	4.3	6.3	3.4	31.2	-2.2	61.8	-2.7
1980	1.3	1.9	0.4	19.2	31.0	-3.5	62.7	-3.9
1981	1.4	-0.9	-3.6	-8.6	30.6	-2.6	65.9	-5.4
1982	-0.3	-0.1	-0.1	-17.0	33.0	-3.7	68.2	-7.1

Sources: Bengt Rydén, ed., *Stabiliseringspolitik för 80-talet: Konjunkturrådets rapport, 1980–81* (Stockholm: SN&S, 1980), p. 29; *OECD Economic Outlook*, no. 24 (December 1978), p. 126, and no. 29 (July 1981), pp. 138–39; data supplied by Edward Palmer, Statistiska centralbyrån, Konjunkturinstitutet; *Swedish Economy*, 1983:2, pp. 11, 52, 106, 149; *Swedish Economy*, various issues, statistical appendix; Erik Westerlind and Rune Beckman, *Sveriges ekonomi: Struktur och utvecklingstendenser* (Stockholm: Prisma, 1974), pp. 16–17, 104.

a. Index of production in manufacturing and mining; 1968 = 100.
b. Investment in plant and equipment in manufacturing and mining, in 1975 prices.
c. One-half of exports plus imports. Data before 1970 are not strictly comparable to data for later years.
d. Balance on current account for goods, services, and transfers. Data before 1970 are not strictly comparable to data for later years.
e. All expenditures of the "consolidated public sector," including consumption, investment, and transfers, by all levels of government, central and local, net of intergovernmental transfers.
f. Total revenues and expenditures of consolidated public sector.

Figure 13-1. *Industrial Production in Sweden and Selected OECD Countries, 1970–79*

Industrial production index (1975 = 100)

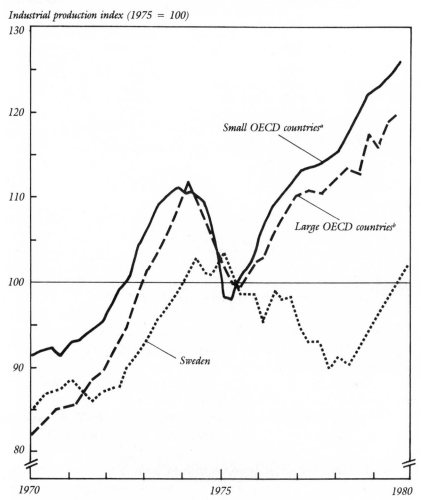

Source: Sweden, Ekonomidepartementet, *Långtidsutredningen 1980*, SOU 1980: 52, p. 268.
a. Austria, Belgium, Denmark, Finland, Greece, Iceland, Ireland, Luxembourg, Netherlands, Norway, Portugal, Spain, Switzerland, Turkey.
b. Canada, France, Italy, Japan, United Kingdom, United States, West Germany.

nearly 34 percent in 1974, the capital share fell to a low of a little under 16 percent in 1977, after averaging about 27 percent between 1956 and 1973. Pretax returns on equity in large firms became negative in 1977 after peaking at almost 15 percent in 1974 and averaging a little under

Table 13-5. *Profits in Swedish Industry, 1970–81*
Percent

Year	Capital share, C sector product[a]	Pretax returns on equity, large firms[b]
1970	25.5	11.0
1971	24.0	7.7
1972	20.7	7.7
1973	26.1	13.3
1974	33.7	14.9
1975	26.9	8.4
1976	19.3	4.5
1977	15.6	−0.5
1978	17.5	2.0
1979	26.1	8.3
1980	28.0	8.7
1981	27.5	5.0

Sources: LO, *Lönepolitik för 80-talet: Rapport till LO-Kongressen, 1981* (Stockholm: LO, 1981), p. 39; *Swedish Economy, 1983:2*, p. 127; Tiido Uutma, Bertil Hållsten, and Kjell Bengtsson, "Company Reports for 1981—A Comparison with Earlier Years," *Skandinaviska Enskilda Banken Quarterly Review*, no. 3 (1982), p. 96.
   a. Includes all allocations of income other than wages, salaries, and social charges, including depreciation and owner income. The C sector of the EFO model corresponds approximately to mining and manufacturing. The C sector capital share for years before 1970 was estimated on the basis of ratios declining from that between the revised and old national accounts data for 1970 to zero in 1951. From 1951 to 1969 the average share was 27.6 percent, the peak was 38 percent in 1951, and the low was 21.5 percent in 1967.
   b. Large nonfinancial companies listed on the Swedish stock exchange, totaling 78 in 1981.

10 percent over the preceding seven years. Thus, Swedish industry experienced the sharpest drop in profitability "at least since the 1930s."[46] The declines in production and profits were accompanied by a deep investment slump. The growth of industrial investment went down from nearly 11 percent in 1974, the highest level since 1961, to negligible levels in the next two years, and then fell 17 percent in 1977, the biggest drop in the postwar period, only to fall another 22 percent in 1978 (table 13-4).

   Swedish industry certainly seems to have been caught in a cost crisis after the 1975–76 wage explosion. The impact was much greater in some sectors than others, however, bringing to a head a structural crisis that had been in the making for some time. Many Swedish product lines, firms, and even whole sectors had been deprived of comparative advantages they once enjoyed. In part, this was the consequence of technological changes in production, transportation, and communication, and their diffusion around the world, particularly by transnational enterprise. Efforts

   46. Gunnar Eliasson and others, *Att välja 80-tal: IUI:s långtidsbedömning, 1979* (Stockholm: Industriens Utredningsinstitut [IUI], 1979), p. 208.

to exploit these changes in the older industrial countries and especially in some of the developing countries, with much lower labor costs, brought new, more competitive producers into the international market.[47]

The vulnerability of such industries as forestry and iron mining, and industries built on this raw material base such as steel and shipbuilding, had been obscured by the early 1970s boom, but when the boom collapsed the cost gap hit them very hard. Although industries like steel and shipbuilding were in trouble throughout the OECD area, in Sweden these industries suffered the additional penalties of heavy concentration on the tanker market that was destroyed by the rise in oil prices. Large portions of these vulnerable sectors could not survive the lower costs of their competitors abroad. The cost gap between Sweden and the older industrial countries suffering similar structural problems meant that expansion in the other sectors needed to take up the slack was inhibited. Thus, the cost crisis exacerbated and rendered more intractable the structural crisis.[48]

The macroeconomic manifestations of this dual crisis and of the policies pursued in response to it are apparent in the slow growth of Sweden's gross domestic product relative to the OECD average beginning in the second half of the 1960s. While GDP growth in Sweden turned down later and fell less precipitously than in the OECD area during the post–oil crisis recession, its recovery was slower. Despite a spurt that put Swedish GDP growth ahead of the OECD average in 1979, it averaged only 1.1 percent over the second half of the decade compared with the OECD average of 3.1 percent over the same period (table 13-4).

Inflation persisted along with stagnation. The annual rate of increase in consumer prices, which averaged 5.1 percent from 1963 to 1973, jumped to roughly double that level during the next four years, fell again, and then climbed to nearly 14 percent in 1980 (table 13-3). Stagnation was not accompanied by any significant increase in open unemployment, however. This is one respect in which Swedish performance was notably better than that of most of the other OECD countries. Unemployment averaged around 1.8 percent over the four recession years 1975–78 in Sweden (table 13-6) while the recession was allowed to take a much

---

47. Ibid., pp. 28–34, 318–68.

48. Villy Bergström and others, *Politik mot stagflation: Konjunkturrådets rapport, 1977–78* (Stockholm: SN&S, 1977), pp. 71–74. They conclude (p. 57), from interviews with seventeen large industrial firms, that "losses in market shares that occurred in many cases probably would have taken place even with a 'normal' Swedish cost and price development."

Table 13-6. *Labor Market Conditions in Sweden, 1970–82*
Percent

| Year | Employment, annual rate of change | | | Unemployment, as share of total labor force | | |
	Public sector[a]	Industry[b]	Total	Open[c]	Man- power programs[d]	Total[e]
1970	8.4	1.6	2.0	1.5	1.8	3.3
1971	6.7	−3.4	−0.2	2.5	2.1	4.6
1972	5.2	−1.6	0.3	2.7	2.6	5.3
1973	3.6	1.5	0.4	2.5	2.8	5.3
1974	6.1	2.1	2.0	2.0	2.5	4.5
1975	5.1	1.0	2.0	1.6	2.2	3.8
1976	4.8	−0.5	3.7	1.6	2.6	4.2
1977	4.1	−3.4	1.9	1.8	2.9	4.7
1978	5.1	−4.4	0.4	2.2	3.4	5.6
1979	5.1	0.0	1.5	2.1	3.6	5.7
1980	3.3	1.5[f]	1.1	1.9	2.9	4.8
1981	2.5	−2.9[f]	−0.2	2.5	2.7	5.2
1982	1.7	−3.2[f]	−0.1	3.1	3.3	6.4

Sources: Statistiska centralbyrån, *Statistiska meddelanden,* N 1980:4.4, app. 5, pp. 28–29, 34–35; 1980–82; *Swedish Economy,* various issues.
   a. Central and local government employees.
   b. Mining and manufacturing.
   c. Based on labor force surveys.
   d. All persons participating in training, relief work, sheltered employment, and other programs administered by the Labor Market Board; data before 1975 are not strictly comparable with data for later years.
   e. Sum of open unemployment and persons in manpower programs.
   f. Industrial employment data adjusted by linking to series for earlier years at 1979.

greater social toll in the OECD generally, with unemployment averaging 5.2 percent over the same period in twelve countries for which roughly comparable statistics are reported.[49]

Still, to accomplish this took massive public expenditures on manpower policies, employment subsidies, and rescue operations on failing companies, ranging from loans and grants to outright nationalization. The effort to cushion employment from the effects of the international economic crisis and its domestic reverberations, begun under the Social Democratic government, was vastly expanded by the successive bourgeois governments. While this kept open unemployment remarkably low, the actual employment effect can be seen as much greater if workers supported by these expenditures are viewed as having forms of hidden unemployment. Depending on which workers are counted, their addition to open

49. *OECD Economic Outlook,* no. 21 (July 1977), p. 29, and no. 25 (July 1979), p. 28.

unemployment could bring total real unemployment in 1977 to between 7 and 10 percent, or even higher if those kept from unemployment by the steel and shipbuilding rescue operations are included.[50] Estimates of the expenditures involved vary correspondingly.[51] Nonetheless, the effort to hold down open unemployment while economic growth stagnated clearly contributed to an accelerated increase in the public expenditure share of GDP, from 45 percent in 1970 to 63 percent in 1980, the highest in the OECD area. Coupled with a reversal in the growth of revenues, this resulted in central government budget deficits reaching 9.6 and 10.4 percent of GDP in 1979 and 1980, respectively.[52] Beginning in 1978, these deficits exceeded the surpluses in the social security system which had previously made the public sector as a whole a net saver, leading to growing deficits in the consolidated public sector budget.[53]

Finally, the decline in Swedish industry's competitiveness, combined with the maintenance of consumption and employment, was reflected in a balance of payments deficit estimated at 2.6 percent of GDP in 1977.[54] Although this is not especially high relative to levels in some OECD countries, it was higher than any recorded in Sweden since 1950. A fundamental disequilibrium in Sweden's external position that first emerged in the second half of the 1960s was confirmed by subsequent developments. While a combination of devaluations and highly restrictive macroeconomic policy eliminated the payments deficit in 1978, a rapid expansion of activity in 1979 was accompanied by a new payments deficit almost as large as in 1977 (table 13-4).

50. Persons in the various manpower programs raise the open unemployment totals in table 13-6 to 3.8 percent in 1975 and 5.6 percent in 1978. Other forms of hidden unemployment, including workers kept employed by the rescue operations and those who drop out of the labor force because they are discouraged or are granted early retirement because of difficulties in finding jobs, are more difficult to establish. Bergström and others, *Politik mot stagflation*, p. 31, estimate total real unemployment as close to 10 percent in 1977.

51. Funding of manpower programs plus production for inventories rose to 2.7 percent of GDP in 1977–78, compared with the previous peak of 2 percent in 1972 and an average of around 1.3 percent in the second half of the 1960s; Jan Johannesson, "On the Composition of Swedish Labor Market Policy," in Eliasson, Holmlund, and Stafford, *Studies in Labor Market Behavior*, p. 89. Transfers, loans, and share purchases to firms increased from around 0.5 percent of GDP in 1975 to a peak of 2.3 percent in 1979; *Swedish Economy, 1982:2*, p. 160. A more inclusive estimate of state support for firms puts it at 3.3 percent of GDP in 1979; Bo Carlsson, Frederik Bergholm, and Thomas Lindberg, *Industristöds-politiken och dess inverkan på samhällsekonomin* (Stockholm: IUI, 1981), p. 23. At their height, then, total manpower and industrial policy expenditures contributing to the limitation of open unemployment probably came to between 5 and 6 percent of GDP.

52. *Swedish Economy, 1982:2*, pp. 170, 156.

53. Ibid., p. 170, tables 9-4, 9-6, and similar tables in earlier issues.

54. Ibid., statistical appendix, pp. 8, 19.

As the structural problems of Swedish industry persisted, then, the economy was evidently becoming progressively less able to reach high levels of activity without running into balance of payments difficulties. Some deterioration in the Swedish economy's performance was already discernible before the 1975–76 wage explosion, but it subsequently accelerated. Sweden's economic problems are hardly unique. In some respects, however, the serious disruption of the international economy in the mid-1970s had more of an impact on Sweden than many of the other OECD countries. This was probably due in part to the particular structure of Sweden's industry, but also in part to the cost gap that opened up between Sweden and its trading partners.

Insofar as Sweden's subsequent economic problems can be attributed to the 1975–76 wage explosion, they reflect a failure of the central negotiation system to perform an incomes policy function. What drove the increase in the 1975–76 agreement up so much was the LO's determination to win an increase high enough to exceed drift and thereby ease the internal strains produced by drift that exceeded the contractual increases following the 1974 agreement. The emphasis in LO wage policy evidently shifted from the requirements of external equilibrium in the 1974 agreement to those of organizational cohesion, or, in its words, from "economic consequences" to solidaristic wage policy in the 1975–76 agreement. Such a shift was apparently not confined to the mid-1970s pair of agreements, however, for similar shifts are discernible in the pattern of agreements at least as far back as the early 1960s.

Wage Fluctuations: Pattern and Trends

Several dimensions of wage change in the continuous series of central agreements since 1956 are displayed in figure 13-2. In the top panel the space between the two curves represents wage drift. In the middle panel the curve representing that drift is above zero when the annual percentage change in contractual wages exceeds drift and below zero when it is less than drift; the horizontal lines within each agreement period indicate the average difference between contractual increases and drift. In the bottom panel the horizontal lines indicate the average share of capital in C sector value added during each agreement period.

From the 1962–63 agreement through the one for 1975–76, there is a consistent pattern of alternation between periods in which contractual increases are high relative to drift and those in which they are low relative

Figure 13-2. *Changes in Wages of Adult Industrial Workers and in Share of Capital in C Sector Value Added in Sweden, 1956–80*[a]

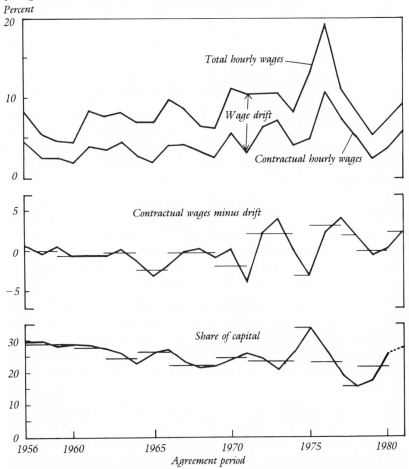

Percent

Total hourly wages

Wage drift

Contractual hourly wages

Contractual wages minus drift

Share of capital

Agreement period

Sources: Ingvar Ohlsson, Research Department, Landsorganisationen i Sverige (LO); Jan Herin, Institute for International Economic Studies, Stockholm University; LO, *Lönepolitik för 80-talet: Rapport till LO-Kongressen, 1981* (Stockholm: LO, 1981), p. 39; *Swedish Economy*, 1983: 2, p. 127. Data for 1980 estimated by adjusting measure in *Swedish Economy* to measure in *Lönepolitik*. Data for years before 1970 adjusted by ratios declining from the difference between 1970 data in revised and old national accounts to zero in 1951.
a. Horizontal line within each period of central agreement indicates average for the period.

to drift. There is a corresponding inverse alternation between periods in which profit shares rise and fall. The pattern seems to reflect the difficulty of reconciling the wage policy requirements of external equilibrium and organizational cohesion—the LO apparently tried to cope with its dilemma by switching the order of priority for the two sets of requirements from one agreement to the next.

Of course, what happened during each agreement period was affected by everything going on in the economy, including government policy. In the case of agreements that turned out to be low, government policy contributed to the failure to keep profits sufficiently squeezed to avert excessive drift. Typically, fiscal policy became restrictive too late in the course of an upswing. This permitted labor markets to become so tight and profits so high that drift reached levels threatening cohesion. Similarly, in each agreement that turned out to be high, government policy reinforced the agreement's effect in squeezing profits sufficiently to keep wage drift low. Typically, the government resorted to a sharp tightening of monetary policy to cope with the problem created or at least aggravated by fiscal policy lags, particularly when the problems materialized in the form of accelerating inflation and balance of payments deficits.[55]

Government policy was especially important in connection with the 1975–76 wage explosion. First, the pressure for large increases was reinforced by a highly expansionary macroeconomic policy. Sweden's Social Democratic government was one of the few in the OECD area that tried to offset the contractive effects of the sudden redistribution of income to the Organization of Petroleum Exporting Countries (OPEC). Most OECD governments pursued restrictive policies, apparently to keep the oil price increases from arresting the decline of inflation from its high levels in the earlier 1970s. In contrast, Sweden's government sought to bridge over the resulting recession in the OECD area, stimulating domestic demand to offset the fall in external demand. The effort was predicated on expectations about the magnitude and duration of the recession that proved much too optimistic, but these expectations were generally shared by all actors in the Swedish economic policy arena. By the time it was recognized that the recession was deeper and longer than anticipated, it was too late to keep Sweden's costs from being thrust way ahead of the much slower growing costs of its trading partners.[56]

Conceivably, the bridging policy might have worked, or at least done less damage, if the government had not pursued an exchange rate policy

55. Lars Matthiessen, "Finanspolitiken som stabiliseringspolitiskt instrument," in Erik Lundberg and others, *Svensk finanspolitik i teori och praktik* (Stockholm: Aldus-Bonniers, 1971), pp. 164–226.

56. *Swedish Economy, 1975:1,* pp. 7–8; *1975: 2,* pp. 8, 40–43. The deflationary effect of the oil price was conceived in terms of a basically Keynesian analysis applied to the international economy. The massive redistribution of income to the OPEC countries entailed in the oil price increase was understood as an excess of savings in the system as a whole, which had to be offset by an expansion of demand. To make that possible, a large balance of payments deficit in the OECD sector of the system had to be accepted, relying on borrowing from the OPEC sector to finance the deficit. Erik Lundberg and others, *Kris eller konjunkturuppgång? Konjunkturrådets rapport 1974–75* (Stockholm: SN&S, 1974), pp. 13–18.

that magnified the impact of sharply rising international prices. To blunt that impact, economists of various political persuasions urged that the crown be revalued. This would have reduced the profits of exporting firms, particularly in the raw-materials-based sectors in which drift was especially high and disruptive. A 1979 LO report characterized the failure to revalue in the first half of 1973 as the "biggest single mistake . . . in Swedish economic policy in the last 10 years." Given the breakdown of the postwar international monetary system, modification of the fixed exchange rate policy adhered to in the past, and assumed in EFO model calculations, was evidently in order. However, such modifications as did occur, apparently without attention to their macroeconomic effects, were perverse—a slight devaluation in connection with the international realignments in early 1973, followed shortly by entry into the snake, in which the crown was pulled up by the deutsche mark after Swedish costs had already been pushed up by the wage explosion.[57]

In addition, the government aggravated the effect of the 1975 agreement by settling for a two-year agreement for its own employees, setting the pattern for the rest of the public sector and the private sector,[58] and violating the EFO model norm that the private sector acts as the wage leader. Had the private sector been able to hold out for a one-year agreement, it would have been possible to correct for the misjudgments of international prospects a whole year earlier, instead of locking the Swedish economy into large wage increases for two successive years.

Especially in the mid-1970s but in the preceding years as well, international economic instability and the impact of government policy on the operation of the wage determination system had a great deal to do with the observable fluctuations in the relationship between wages and profits, and hence the degree to which the respective requirements of organizational cohesion and external equilibrium could be met in each agreement period. But these factors primarily affected the magnitude of fluctuations. The pattern itself might still have been generated by an alternation in the relative weight given by the LO to each set of requirements in successive wage rounds. While it may reflect the LO's difficulty in reconciling the two sets of requirements, however, the alternation would not necessarily prevent the central negotiation system from performing an incomes policy function over the longer run.

57. Bergström and others, *Politik mot stagflation*, pp. 18–19; *Ekonomiska utsikter* (LO) (Spring 1979), pp. 28–29.

58. See SAF, *Verksamhet 1974*, pp. 14–23, and *1975*, pp. 17–29; LO, *Verksamhets berättelse 1974*, pp. 79–83, and *1975*, pp. 48–68.

Fluctuations in wages, and in their relation to profits, are entirely to be expected, as recognized in the EFO model. What matters is the trend around which they occur. Thus, the successive agreements could offset each other, so that the long-run trend around which the relative shares of labor and capital fluctuate is constant, in conformity with the EFO model's main course. Given the analysis in that model, and the assumption that C sector output is sufficient to begin with, the investment needed to maintain external equilibrium would be assured.

This is not what happened, however. On the contrary, as can be seen in the lower panel of figure 13-2, there was clearly a downward trend in capital's share of C sector value added from the first of the central agreements. When the fluctuations became more pronounced in the early 1960s, a pattern emerged in which each new pair of low and high agreements was associated with lower profit shares than in the corresponding agreements of the preceding pair. The trend was interrupted in the 1971–73 and 1974 agreements, with the sharp rise in profits in 1973 and 1974, but was restored by even stronger movements in the opposite direction over the next two periods. On the basis of the EFO analysis, this should have led to insufficient investment in the C sector. This is essentially what was perceived to be occurring already in the second half of the 1960s.

Wages, Profits, and Investment

The 1970 *Long-Term Survey,* the government's normally quinquennial projection of economic trends and their implications for policy, pointed to current payments deficits in the boom years of 1965 and 1969–70 considerably larger than in the preceding postwar period as symptoms of a basic deterioration in Sweden's external position. Concluding that restoration of external equilibrium was the central problem of economic policy, the *Survey* estimated that industrial investment would have to grow at a rate of 6.5 percent annually over the next five years, more than twice as fast as in the preceding five years and faster than at any time since the investment boom of 1958–62.[59]

The principal obstacle to acceleration was said to be a decline in profit margins (averaging 1.2 percent per year during the 1960s) that had

59. Sweden, Ministry of Finance, *The Swedish Economy 1971–1975 and the General Outlook up to 1990: The 1970 Long-term Economic Survey* (Stockholm: Allmänna Förlaget, 1971); see pp. 98–101, 123–25.

reduced business savings to such an extent that a declining portion of investment was self-financed even though the rate of investment itself had gone down. As external financing had taken the form of borrowing, debt-equity ratios had increased, and they would continue to do so if the required investment took place without any increase in profits, making it unlikely to occur. To encourage firms to undertake as much new investment as was needed, the *Survey* concluded that "economic policy would be faced with the task of promoting the supply of risk-bearing capital, besides taking various measures to stimulate investment propensity in private business."[60]

The *Survey*'s diagnosis suggests that the central negotiation system had indeed been failing to perform an incomes policy function, at least as understood in terms of the EFO model, for some time before the 1975–76 wage explosion. The cumulative decline in the share of profits in the C sector product had apparently had the consequences for investment and external equilibrium that could be expected.

But the EFO model's norm of constant shares could be misleading. A similar decline in the profit share is observable in many countries with differing wage determination systems. If wage pressure had much to do with it, it may have been more by way of the close approximation to full employment common to those countries over most of the postwar quarter-century. On the other hand, the very growth that underpinned full employment may have built up confidence that the growth would last, thereby reducing risk premiums and increasing the optimum debt-equity ratio. Required rates of return for investment in real capital could thus have declined with reinforcement from increasingly favorable tax treatment of profits and from the combined effects of inflation and interest deductions on the real rate of interest on loan capital.[61]

Management's willingness to bid up wages to attract labor might have increased correspondingly. If so, the profit share corresponding to a given rate of wage drift would have gone down along with the declining profit share. In such a situation the LO would have to get larger contractual increases to reduce drift by the same amount as in the past. Since declining

---

60. Ibid., pp. 153–57, 163.

61. Eliasson and others, *Att välja 80-tal,* p. 195; T. P. Hill, *Profits and Rates of Return* (Paris: OECD, 1979); Jeffrey D. Sachs, "Wages, Profits, and Macroeconomic Adjustment: A Comparative Study," and William D. Nordhaus, "The Falling Share of Profits," *Brookings Papers on Economic Activity, 2:1979,* pp. 275–78; and *1:1974,* pp. 198–204. The tax treatment of company profits in Sweden is analyzed in Jan Södersten, "Bolagsbeskattningens verkninger," in *Beskattningen av företag,* Slutbetänkande av företagsskatteberedningen, bilagor, SOU 1977:87, pp. 107–93.

shares of profits would lead to higher contractual increases, the EFO norm of constant shares would understate the scope for increases, and declining profit shares would not necessarily have the consequences anticipated. In fact, it has been argued that, at least until 1976, there was "no long-term trend for profitability . . . neither rising nor falling," as opposed to the profit share, and that the relationship between equity capital and total capital had not been weakened as much as alleged.[62]

The central negotiation system in that case should not be seen as having failed to perform the incomes policy function expected of it, at least until the mid-1970s crisis. The eruption of the crisis clearly created a new situation, however. Confidence in sustained growth could hardly have survived "the wave of instability that swept over the market economies during 1973–76," as Bergström and Södersten point out. They conclude that in the 1980s "either an upward shift in the average level of profitability over the business cycle, or institutional intervention in the economic system in order to achieve central goals concerning the balance of foreign trade will presumably be required."[63]

Even if their claim that profitability was maintained under the earlier conditions is correct, however, it still does not necessarily follow that the central negotiation system was performing the incomes policy function expected of it in the period before the "wave of instability." Sweden's position in the international economy might still have been eroding in that period, and the operation of the wage determination system might have been contributing to that erosion. This might even have been the case if the EFO model's norm of constant shares had been satisfied, for the model could be misleading in the opposite direction, understating rather than overstating the requirements for external equilibrium.

Generally, changes in productivity are believed to be the result of rationalization and structural change aimed at maintaining profitability in the face of increasing wage pressures—the reverse of what the EFO model postulates. Instead of being autonomous, technological development is assumed to respond to the demand for labor-saving technology, and investment to be concentrated on such technology instead of capacity expansion. As product lines and firms with the least productivity and profitability are abandoned, productivity in the C sector as a whole would increase. But if the surviving product lines and firms do not expand

---

62. Villy Bergström and Jan Södersten, "Nominal and Real Profit in Swedish Industry," *Skandinaviska Enskilda Banken Quarterly Review*, nos. 1–2 (1979), p. 54.
63. Ibid., p. 58.

sufficiently to offset the abandonment of others, the net result might be insufficient growth in the value of C sector output to maintain external equilibrium. This, according to some analyses, including the 1980 *Long-Term Survey*, is exactly what happened in Sweden, especially after the profit squeeze intensified in 1967–68 (figure 13-2).[64]

One frequently cited measure of the decline in the size of the C sector is the sharp drop in labor input in industry. After remaining roughly constant from 1950 to 1966, total hours worked fell by nearly a quarter between 1966 and 1978. The effects of this reduction on employment were offset largely by a rapid expansion of the public sector.[65] While this expansion certainly reflected the explicit political priority placed on increasing the provision of collective services, some analysts attribute it to an "ultra-Keynesian" policy of maintaining full employment regardless of how wages affect employment in the private sector.[66] Although the resulting increase in the service component of consumption could contribute to external equilibrium because its import content is low, the accompanying growth of total consumption could still mean greater demand for tradable goods than could be met consistently with balance of payments equilibrium by the declining C sector, giving rise to a structural disequilibrium in the payments balance.

Thus, there are arguments pointing toward contrasting conclusions about the effectiveness with which the central negotiation system met the requirements of external equilibrium before the 1975–76 wage explosion.[67] The most plausible view seems to be that it had fallen significantly short of doing so since at least the mid-1960s. On this view, the system's failure to perform the function of incomes policy in the mid-1970s reflected inherent limits in its capacity to do so, so that only the magnitude of the 1975–76 wage explosion is to be explained by the exceptional conditions under which the system operated at the time. The requirements of organizational cohesion that the LO has to meet seem to be among the

---

64. Sweden, Ekonomidepartementet, *Långtidsutredningen 1980*, SOU 1980:52, pp. 42, 265–66. Rydén, *Stabiliseringspolitik*, p. 67.

65. *Långtidsutredningen 1980*, p. 266.

66. Hans Tson Söderström and Staffan Viotti, "Money Wage Disturbances and the Endogeneity of the Public Sector in an Open Economy," in Assar Lindbeck, ed., *Inflation and Employment in Open Economies*, Studies in International Economics, vol. 5 (North-Holland, 1979), pp. 71–98.

67. See the critique of Bergström and Södersten by Lars Bertmar, "Profit Measurement: A Chaotic Picture," and their reply, "Have Profits in Industry Really Declined?" *Skandinaviska Enskilda Banken Quarterly Review*, nos. 3–4 (1979), pp. 105–17, 118–21. See also Bengt-Christer Ysander, "Vägen till treprocentsekonomin—en kommentar till långtidsutredningen," *Ekonomisk debatt*, 1 (1979), pp. 47–49; Lennart Erixon, "Lönsamhetskrisen i svensk industri," *Häften för kritiska studier* 13, 6 and 7, 1980.

most important of these limits. While the LO apparently shifted the emphasis in its wage policy from organizational cohesion to external equilibrium requirements in successive bargaining rounds, the successive agreements do not seem to have offset each other. Low agreements permit profits and investment in the C sector to recover, but the succeeding high agreements prevent profits from reaching and remaining at levels at which there is sufficient investment in the sector to maintain external equilibrium over the long run. The cumulative squeeze on profits results in declining industrial investment and a growing structural disequilibrium in Sweden's external position.

Although the central negotiation system was probably kept from performing the function of an incomes policy by the LO's recurrent response to the imperative of organizational cohesion, the latter was nevertheless subjected to strain as a result of the LO's recurrent response to the requirements of external equilibrium. Solidaristic wage policy was apparently being implemented with increasing effectiveness in high agreements, but its vulnerability in the low agreements may also have been increasing. One symptom was the wave of wildcat strikes that began at state-owned iron mines and spread through a large part of Swedish industry during the winter of 1969–70. While discontent over nonwage issues was an important precipitant, the gap between contractual increases and what employers could pay, reflected in wage drift more than twice as high as contractual increases during the second year of the 1969–70 wage agreement, was clearly decisive.[68] Thus the LO's wage policy dilemma was apparently becoming more acute. The issues posed by the 1970 *Long-Term Survey* and the wildcat strikes dominated its 1971 congress. The LO responded in two distinct ways—by pressing for forms of institutional intervention in the savings-investment process aimed at making it easier to reconcile an increased supply of equity capital with solidaristic wage policy, and for changes in the industrial relations system aimed at enlarging the unions' role in dealing with workplace issues.

The LO Response

Swedish employers had long been successful in enforcing their claim that most work-place issues are managerial prerogatives, hence not subject

68. Svante Nycander, *Kurs på kollision: inblick i avtalsrörelsen, 1970–71* (Stockholm: Askild och Kärnekull, 1972), pp. 25–27; Edmund Dahlström and others, *LKAB och demokratin: rapport om en strejk och ett forskningsprojekt* (Stockholm: Wahlström och Widstrand, 1971), pp. 203–09.

to collective bargaining. The famous paragraph 32 in the SAF's rules even required that member associations and firms include in all collective agreements with unions a clause "stipulating the right of the employer to engage and dismiss workers at his own discretion; to direct and allot work; and to avail himself of workers belonging to any organization whatsoever, or to none." Though in many plants the union voice, particularly concerning dismissals, became substantial, the SAF insisted on preserving the principle of managerial prerogative.

The unions had not pressed the issue, rationalizing their exclusion from participation in production decisionmaking as a safeguard against the danger of "double loyalty." This position, reaffirmed at the LO's 1966 congress, was abruptly reversed in 1971 after the wildcat strikes convinced union leaders that collective bargaining had to be extended to work-place issues to stem the erosion of union authority. Adoption of a policy statement on Industrial Democracy at the 1971 congress marked the opening of an offensive to achieve this goal. Given the SAF's resistance, the LO fell back on the legislative alternative. The TCO took a similar position, providing the Social Democratic government with an opportunity to claim white collar as well as blue collar workers as its constituency by championing interests defined as common to both. A stream of legislation on employment security, the work environment, and trade union rights followed, culminating in a 1976 law on "joint determination" that entitled unions to engage in collective bargaining on the whole range of work-place and enterprise decisions that the employers had ruled out of bounds.[69]

The changes that the LO sought in the institutions for organizing the savings-investment process were less a departure from its earlier position than an extension of an approach it had already adopted in the early postwar period. The approach is akin to what Keynes described as the "socialisation of investment." Speculating about the problems of maintaining full employment after it had been restored by the expansionist policy he prescribed to overcome mass unemployment in the 1930s, he anticipated that over the long run a "comprehensive socialisation of investment will prove the only means of securing an approximation to full employment."[70] The LO had taken a first step in that direction in response to the wage policy dilemma with which it was first confronted

69. See Martin, "Trade Unions in Sweden."
70. John Maynard Keynes, *The General Theory of Employment Interest and Money* (Harcourt, Brace, 1936), pp. 375, 378–79.

at the beginning of the full employment era that had evidently been established after World War II.

When mass unemployment did not return as expected and inflation proved instead to be the most salient economic policy problem, Sweden's Social Democratic government won the LO's agreement to freeze wages at existing levels in 1949 and 1950 in exchange for the reinstatement of wartime price controls and food subsidies. This was the only instance of anything like an official incomes policy in Sweden. After the 1951 wage explosion, triggered by the worldwide Korean War inflation, the government called for renewed wage restraint. This time, however, the LO refused, setting forth its reasons and elaborating an alternative policy for maintaining noninflationary full employment in a policy statement, "Trade Unions and Full Employment," adopted by its 1951 congress.[71]

The 1951 statement acknowledged that noninflationary full employment could not be maintained by demand management alone. However, it rejected reliance primarily on wage restraint because this would threaten the unions' organizational cohesion. Union restraint in negotiating wage contracts would still not prevent wage drift—the local wage increases that employers would concede in a tight labor market. And the more drift, the more tension between workers who stood to benefit and those less advantaged, and the more "discord between the different unions" that "will inevitably prove disastrous ... to trade-union solidarity." This argument has underlain all subsequent LO wage-policy positions.

As an alternative the 1951 statement proposed what became known as the Rehn model, after one of the economists who formulated it. The Rehn model envisaged the differentiation of an overall labor market into partially separated sectors. General fiscal policy must be more restrictive than it had been previously, keeping demand high enough to maintain employment in most of the economy but not in the least profitable activities. The threat of unemployment in these lagging sectors would be met not by general fiscal stimulus that would intensify inflationary pressures in the most profitable activities but by selective manpower measures—for example, retraining, information, financial support.

Provided that the government pursued the prescribed combination of fiscal and manpower policies, the LO undertook to coordinate the unions' wage bargaining on the basis of solidaristic, or standard rate, wage policy.

---

71. LO, *Fackföreningsrörelsen och den fulla sysselsättningen* (Stockholm: LO, 1951). This account draws on Martin, "Trade Unions in Sweden."

Wage levels would be sought that would place weaker firms under a profit squeeze, forcing them either to enhance efficiency or to shut down, while the more profitable firms would have enough leeway to expand. Wage policy would thus reinforce the process of structural change in the economy. To be sure, this strategy implied some wage restraint for the unions in the more profitable sectors. But standard rates were expected to squeeze profits enough to restrict the scope for drift. This was essential for the LO to coordinate wage bargaining and thereby avert the interunion wage rivalry that could be an autonomous source of inflation.

However, standard rates high enough to inhibit wage drift might in fact squeeze profits so hard that expanding firms could not grow sufficiently to offset the contraction of declining firms. The LO policy statement of 1951 did not address this crucial issue explicitly, but its principal author, Gösta Rehn, repeatedly did so. Expecting the profit squeeze to reduce business saving, he proposed to offset it by increasing public-sector saving, preferably by building a surplus into the pending national pension reform. This was in fact done when the supplementary, or AP, pension system was established in 1960.[72] This institutional change in the savings-investment mechanism can be understood as a limited step toward the socialization of investment.

As long as sufficient aggregate savings were thereby assured, the Rehn model evidently assumed that investment would take care of itself, its composition guided by the differential profitability that solidaristic wage policy would preserve. But it could not be taken for granted that private firms would continue to invest at the required rate despite the curtailed profits collective savings were designed to offset. Although the question was posed when the Rehn model was originally formulated,[73] the issue remained academic for almost two decades. Economic policy began to approximate the Rehn model only by the early 1960s when an investment boom was still strong. Only by the end of the 1960s did industrial investment again appear as problematic.

As the 1970 *Long-Term Survey* pointed out, collective savings did increase more than enough to offset the decline of business savings during the 1960s, primarily by virtue of the large surplus in the AP pension

72. See Hugh Heclo, *Modern Social Politics in Britain and Sweden: From Relief to Income Maintenance* (Yale University Press, 1974), pp. 227–53; *Kapitalmarknaden i svensk ekonomi: betänkande av kapital-marknadsutredningen,* SOU 1978:11 (Stockholm: Ekonomidepartementet, 1978), pp. 441–88.

73. Erik Lundberg, "A Critique of Rehn's Approach," in Ralph Turvey, ed. and trans., *Wages Policy under Full Employment* (London: William Hodge, 1952), esp. p. 67.

fund.[74] But what was channeled to industry was in the form of loan capital, while the need, argued the *Survey,* was for equity capital. The LO faced the issue at its 1971 congress when a metalworkers' resolution asked "how increased resources can be provided for investment without having negative effects on the distribution of wealth." The metalworkers' motion conceded the need for more equity capital but rejected any solution that relied on private profits and therefore contributed to the concentration of wealth and power among the few "who dominate ownership in banks and industry." Other motions and a wage-policy report also called for alternative mechanisms for capital formation, again on the ground that the existing mechanism tended to undermine solidaristic wage policy.[75]

The LO sought such alternatives along two main lines. The first eventually led to legislation establishing a new unit in the AP system, the so-called Fourth Fund, which went into operation in January 1974 and was authorized to purchase industrial shares. Although limited to about 5 percent of the pension fees during the year, the amount was still almost as large as the average annual equity capital raised during the 1960s in the small Swedish stock market, which excluded international transactions. The limit was doubled in 1976, by which time the Fourth Fund had shares in twenty-six firms and representation on the boards of six of them, including Volvo. In 1979 the fund was voted an even higher limit, although its holdings in any one company were restricted to 10 percent.[76]

The second line along which the LO proceeded was to design new institutions for organizing collective savings at the level of the firm by turning a portion of retained profits into collectively held shares. This so-called Meidner plan, named after Rudolf Meidner, the economist who headed the LO committee which prepared the proposal and a coauthor of the 1951 statement embodying the Rehn plan, was adopted by the 1976 LO congress. It called for transferring a portion of pretax profits, say, 20 percent, earned by large firms into shares directed to wage-earner funds that would be administered by the unions. The new shares would constitute new equity capital, available to the firm for investment, and

---

74. Aleksander Markowski and Edward E. Palmer, "Social Insurance and Saving in Sweden," in George M. von Furstenberg, ed., *Social Security Versus Private Saving* (Ballinger, 1979); *Kapitalmarknaden,* SOU 1978:11, pp. 441–88.

75. LO, *Kongressprotokoll 1971* (Stockholm: LO, 1971), pp. 815–18, 859–97; LO, *Lönepolitik: Rapport till LO-Kongressen 1971,* pp. 100–02.

76. See *Näringslivets försörjning med riskkapital från allmänna pensionsfonden,* SOU 1972:63, pp. 15–24; *Kapitalmarknaden,* SOU 1978:11, pp. 452–54; *Bilaga 4, Industrins tillväxt och langsiktiga finansiering,* SOU 1978:13, p. 116; Regeringens proposition 1978/79:165, pp. 124–30.

would be exempt from corporate taxation in the same way as profits allocated to the so-called investment reserve system. But instead of accruing to private shareholders, returns on the new shares would accrue to the union-run funds. These profits were not to be distributed to individual workers but used to purchase additional shares and to support a variety of educational services and the staff needed to underpin the workers' rights to work-place participation and enterprise decisions. Voting rights of the shares would also go to the funds, which would eventually, according to the plan, gain controlling shares in the firms.[77]

These two initiatives addressed the dilemma left by the original Rehn model in significantly different ways. In principle, the Fourth Fund does not alter any effect the AP system may have had on the squeeze on profits, depending on how much of the payroll tax that finances it is shifted back onto wages. Instead, the Fourth Fund was designed to get the AP's collective savings back to industry as equity rather than loans, which firms would presumably find more attractive for financing investment. But investment might still fall short if standard rates high enough to minimize wage drift continued to squeeze profits as much as before.

The wage-earner funds, however, would offer the possibility of relaxing the profit squeeze. The funds would weaken the link between company profits and shareholders' income in the same way that solidaristic wage policy was designed to weaken the link between profits and wage earners' income. Other things being equal, profits plowed back into investment would increase private shareholders' wealth less with the funds than without. To the extent that wage settlements permitting increased profits consequently did not imply a corresponding transfer of wealth to private shareholders, the settlements would not have the "negative effects on the distribution of wealth" to which the 1971 metalworkers' motion objected. Moreover, preempting some company profits for the wage-earner funds would also diminish the scope for wage drift.

The changes called for by the LO in the early 1970s went further toward the socialization of investment than the confederation policies of the early 1950s. They portended a more far-reaching transformation than the establishment of collective saving through the introduction of the AP system, which had already aroused business opposition as an alleged effort

---

77. LO, *Kollektiv kapitalbildning genom löntagarfonder: rapport till LO-kongressen 1976* (Stockholm: Prisma, 1976). For the main text, see Rudolf Meidner, *Employee Investment Funds: An Approach to Collective Capital Formation* (London: Allen and Unwin, 1978).

to take over the capital market.[78] The Meidner plan implied that private ownership would ultimately be replaced by something like "social enterprise without owners," the alternative to both capitalist and nationalized enterprise foreseen by Ernst Wigforss, the Swedish Social Democrats' principal theorist and architect of Keynesian budgetary policy at the beginning of Social Democratic governance in 1932.

Organized business and the bourgeois parties mounted a sustained offensive against the Meidner plan, reminiscent of the battle over the pension plan. They charged that the new plan would create a "trade-union state," which they incongruously sought to identify with the Soviet-style dictatorships of Eastern Europe.

The strident opposition to the wage-earner funds could perhaps have turned them into the kind of politically polarizing issue with which the pension reform provided the Social Democrats, helping them to reverse their postwar electoral decline and strengthen their parliamentary position in the early 1960s. However, the party's leadership avoided taking a position on the Meidner plan. The fact that the LO had taken a clear stand in favor of it made it impossible for the party to reject it, but the leadership's misgivings about its economic as well as electoral implications made it unwilling to embrace it either. Its equivocation on the issue may have done it as much or more electoral damage as outright endorsement might have. In any case, the small margin by which the party lost office in the 1976 election, following a decline over the preceding two elections, could as well be attributed to any of several other issues, including the party's pro–nuclear-energy position which was dramatically attacked by the Center party leader, Thorbjorn Fälldin.[79]

After 1976, the Social Democratic leadership evidently concluded that there could be no solution to the problem of investment without some form of wage-earner funds. Joint LO-party committees eventually hammered out a mutually acceptable form of the funds that might be technically feasible and politically viable. The version adopted by the 1981 LO and party congresses was considerably watered down compared with the original Meidner plan. It did preserve the principle of collective rather than individual share ownership, with trade union participation in administering the new shareholding institutions. The profit-sharing element

78. Åke Ortmark, *Maktspelet i Sverige* (Stockholm: Wahlström och Widstrand, 1967), pp. 123–30, 200–08.
79. Martin, "Trade Unions in Sweden."

was curtailed, however, and the whole scheme was tied to the AP system.[80] Rather than acquiring shares primarily in the form of directed issues corresponding to a share of profits, the funds would now purchase shares on the market or from firms with money supplied them by the AP fund from two sources. The main one would be a 1 percent increase in the AP payroll tax. The other would be an excess profits levy taking 20 percent of "surplus profits"—those exceeding some specified "normal" rate of return. Insofar as the payroll tax was shifted to wages, a portion of the labor share would be shifted to capital, but the associated increment to wealth would accrue to the funds, through purchased equities, rather than to private shareholders. Such a shift would occur to the extent that unions accepted the reduction in the labor share rather than compensating for it by increased wages—that is, to the extent that the scheme made a corresponding degree of wage restraint possible. The excess profits levy would supposedly make such restraint less vulnerable to disruption by high profits and associated drift.

The funds would, in turn, be required to make payments to the AP system equivalent to some rate of return on the capital supplied to them by the system. This requirement resembled one that the minority Liberal government imposed on the Fourth Fund in 1979 requiring it to pay back 80 percent of its earnings to the rest of the AP system.[81] Indeed the 1981 version of the wage-earner funds scheme might well be viewed as a larger and more elaborate Fourth Fund, preserving the AP system's capacity for collective savings and identifying pension payments as the primary stake individuals have in the scheme. The most recent version thus represented an ingenious extension of the Rehn model, which goes further than the original toward the socialization of investment, but not so far as the 1976 version.

This retreat did not diminish controversy over it, however. Organized business and the bourgeois parties stepped up their offensive on the issue in an effort to make the 1982 election turn on it. Because the balance could readily be tipped either way by the positions taken by TCO unions, they were subjected to particularly intense pressures. The divisions within and among them, with different TCO unions coming down on opposite sides of the issue, made it impossible for the confederation to commit

80. *Arbetarrörelsen och löntagarfonderna: rapport från en arbetsgrupp inom LO och socialdemokraterna* (Stockholm: Tidnes, 1981).

81. Regeringens proposition 1978/79:165.

itself one way or the other, even though its reports on the subject reflected the logic of the LO position.[82]

Incumbency in office provided the bourgeois parties with an important resource in their campaign against wage-earner funds. Thus, they were able to introduce tax breaks expected to enlarge the constituency for individual forms of share ownership and erode support for collective forms, especially among employees. This was part of a broader pattern of policy that operated to reinforce the reprivatization of savings, marking a reversal of the evolution toward the socialization of investment under the preceding Social Democratic governments. The new pattern of policy implied an alternative strategy for solving the problem of investment. If the analysis here of the dynamics of the wage determination system is substantially correct, the prospects for success of such a strategy were not very promising. In fact, the governments in office between 1976 and 1982 were not able to cope effectively with the problem of investment.

Economic Policy, 1976–82

Any government coming into office after the 1976 election would have soon been confronted by the dual crisis into which the economy was slipping, even though its full dimensions still took some time to emerge. One of the central tasks of economic policy would be to reduce the cost gap and keep it from opening up again. This was a necessary if not sufficient condition for overcoming the structural problem. Only to the extent that Sweden's overall relative cost position was restored could there be enough expansion of internationally competitive production to replace the production that could no longer be competitive. This was bound to be a difficult condition to meet, given the dynamics of the wage determination system.

Short-run Strategy and the Long-run Problem

Although the new bourgeois government defined the cost gap as the central economic problem as soon as it came into office, its response took shape slowly. Not only did the government take some time to recognize

---

82. Lars Nabseth, director of the Federation of Swedish Industries, declared that the funds threatened "the very vitals of Swedish industry" and "would completely revolutionize our economic system"; *Viewpoint,* vol. 4 (September 1982). This was mild by comparison with some of the attacks on the proposal. For additional discussion, see Martin, "Trade Unions in Sweden."

the full extent of the problem, but its options were narrow. Many of the government's supporters looked to it to restore the "effectiveness of markets" which the Social Democrats had allegedly impaired—by credit market regulations since the early postwar period, by industrial policy measures since the late 1960s, and by labor legislation most recently.[83] But the political constraints against the kind of drastic turn toward the market taken by the Thatcher and Reagan governments in Britain and the United States were compelling. Sweden's first bourgeois government in nearly half a century had to reckon with a cohesive opposition that still provided a credible alternative government. Hence the new government could not afford the political risks of appearing less concerned about full employment or the economic security of those outside the labor market than the Social Democrats. Moreover, there was division within as well as among the three bourgeois parties over how much of a shift away from previous policies was desirable. At the same time, the bourgeois parties could hardly be expected to pick up where the Social Democrats left off and take further steps toward the socialization of investment. However, the recovery of profits and investment had a long way to go before they posed the issue to which those steps were a response.

Given the political conditions limiting the Fälldin government's options and the increasing severity of the economic crisis, the main thrust of the government's effort was to improve Sweden's relative cost position without allowing open unemployment to increase. This was attempted by combining devaluation and austerity with large expenditures to maintain employment.

Devaluation would work only if its export price effects were not offset by firms trying to restore margins by raising prices and by unions trying to preserve real wages by increases compensating its domestic inflationary effects. The government assumed that only the latter was a problem. It rejected the idea of a "social contract" approach that some urged on it, but which had in any case been ruled out by both sides of the labor market. Instead, the government counted on a combination of economic policies to diminish both the capacity and the desire of the unions to press for compensatory increases, and on stiffened employer resistance to such increases.

83. See *Vägar till ökad välfärd*, esp. pp. 121–58; Erik Dahmén, "Does the Mixed Economy Have a Future?" in Bengt Rydén and Villy Bergström, eds., *Sweden: Choices for Economic and Social Policy in the 1980s* (London: Allen and Unwin, 1982), pp. 108–23.

The devaluation was carried out in three installments. A small initial devaluation in October 1976 was not combined with any major policy changes, and even the January 1977 budget was essentially expansionary. However, devaluations in April and August, accompanied by withdrawal from the snake, were parts of packages marking a major shift in economic policy. The brakes were put on domestic consumption and prices were temporarily frozen, then subjected to advance notification before increases. The scope for lower export prices created by devaluation combined with reduced domestic demand was expected to improve export performance, while the price restrictions limited the devaluation's inflationary effects at home and hence the pressure for compensatory wage increases. In addition, the government sought to reduce labor cost pressures on export and domestic prices directly by eliminating the general payroll tax (not the AP contributions and other social charges). Since this would have been expansionary in the absence of offsetting budget measures for which there was little room, it was delayed and spread over two installments at the beginning and middle of 1978.[84]

At the same time, to blunt the employment effects of its restrictive policy, the government continued, expanded, and added to the array of programs that had been introduced by its predecessors. This included the long-established retraining and temporary employment activities run by the manpower policy agency, as well as the investment reserve system, through which companies gained the tax-free use of profits they had earlier set aside in blocked accounts. Also included were more recent measures encouraging "labor hoarding," such as wage subsidies for firms that kept on workers who would otherwise be laid off to produce for inventories and undergo "training," and employment security legislation that made layoffs and dismissals difficult. On top of this, the new government vastly increased expenditures to keep companies in trouble from going out of business. In addition to providing loans, loan guarantees, and grants, it bought up a number of the companies, especially in steel

---

84. The rationale for the devaluations and contractive measures is set forth by Lars Wohlin, under secretary of state for economic affairs, in "Första årets ekonomiska politik," *Ekonomisk debatt,* 6 (1977), pp. 334–45; "Åtstramningspolitiken—ett steg på vägen till balans," and "Skatter och ekonomisk tillväxt," *Ekonomisk debatt,* 7 (1978), pp. 507–18, and 7 (1979), pp. 442–52. The most relevant policy statements are "Regeringens ekonomiska åtsträmningspaket," press release, April 4, 1977, and "Regeringens stabiliseringsprogram, hösten 1977," press release, August 29, 1977. *Swedish Economy* includes accounts of economic policy measures; descriptions and analyses of policy are included in the SN&S Konjunkturrådetsrapport.

and shipbuilding, introducing a degree of "ashcan" or "lemon" socialism without precedent in the decades of Social Democratic rule.

This short-run strategy for dealing with the cost crisis seemed to accomplish its intended effects to a considerable degree. The unions' militancy and bargaining power may not have been dampened as much as they might have been by a marked rise in open unemployment. Nevertheless, the redistribution of income from labor to capital implied by an effective devaluation was accommodated by the wage determination system. This was accomplished to a limited extent by a central agreement for 1977 and to a much greater extent by one for 1978 and ten months of 1979. Contractual increases in industrial workers' hourly earnings rose by about 12 percent, to which drift added under 10 percent, bringing the total to around 22 percent from 1977 through 1979. Since the cumulative rise in consumer prices was 30 percent, industrial workers took a cut in real, pretax income of over 8 percent. About 70 percent of the jump in real wages during 1975–76 was thereby offset, reducing the average annual growth rate of real wages for 1975–79 to around 0.7 percent. By keeping nominal wage increases significantly lower than they would have had to be to compensate for the devaluation's domestic price effects, the wage determination system evidently permitted much of those effects to be absorbed by a cut in real wages, preventing a price-wage spiral that could easily have dissipated the devaluation's intended external price effects.

Thus, with the help of what the budget minister called "the responsible agreement reached in the private labor market in 1978,"[85] the government had apparently managed to bring off one of the few effective devaluations among the many that have been attempted. Much of the increase in Sweden's unit labor costs relative to trade-weighted OECD averages since 1973 had been eliminated by 1979.[86] Some of the improvement in costs was used to reduce relative export prices and some to restore margins.[87]

85. Regeringens proposition 1978/79:150, app. 1, April 23, 1979, p. 6.

86. LO, *Lönepolitik för 80 talet: Rapport till LO-Kongressen, 1981* (Stockholm: LO, 1981), p. 45. Estimates vary with differences in weighting systems.

87. Bergström and others, *Politik mot stagflation*, pp. 55–58; *Swedish Economy, 1982:2*, p. 146. Revised data for the period before the wage explosion are not available to estimate how much of the rise in Sweden's relative export prices and subsequent loss of market shares was reversed. The new data show some recapture of shares, especially in 1978, and a new small loss when Sweden's relative export prices increased by 3.5 percent in 1979 after declining by 6 and 5.5 percent, respectively, in the preceding two years.

The rise in exports that did occur contributed to some recovery of production. Manufacturing profits turned up in 1978 and continued to rise, more slowly, in 1979. By 1979, capital's share in C sector value added was back up to 26.1 percent from its 1977 low of 15.6 percent. None of this was enough to keep the decline of industrial investment from accelerating to 22 percent in 1978, while a rise of 3 percent in 1979 is ascribed entirely to public sector firms (table 13-4). Private industrial investment did turn up during 1979, so that in 1980 it registered its first year-on-year increase since 1974.[88]

Thus the government seemed to make some headway in coping with the cost dimension of Sweden's crisis. How well it came to grips with the structural dimension is a matter of controversy. It has been argued that the government relied on excessively restrictive macroeconomic policy to make devaluation work, resulting in extremely low capacity utilization, deepening the collapse of investment, and thereby retarding the adaptation of Sweden's industrial structure to apparently irreversible changes in the basic pattern of comparative advantage. In addition, because the government relied more on massive subsidies to failing companies than on manpower policy programs, open unemployment was limited in a way that tended to lock labor into noncompetitive production rather than facilitating its transfer into competitive production when demand for labor there increased, as it did in 1979.[89] Moreover, the pattern of policy with which the cost gap was reduced in the short run left unsolved the problem of preventing a new deterioration in Sweden's relative costs, which would choke off the process of structural change.

There was widespread apprehension during 1979 that wage pressures would increase as capacity utilization and profits rose. To be sure, there seemed little likelihood that the sequence of inflationary boom and deep recession in the international economy that left Sweden's economy stranded in the mid-1970s would soon be repeated.[90] On the other hand, the apparent tendency of the wage determination system to squeeze profits

88. *Swedish Economy, 1981:1*, p. 119.

89. Bengt Rydén, ed., *Mot nya förlorade år? Konjunkturrådets rapport,* 1979–80 (Stockholm: SN&S, 1979), pp. 8–20; Carlsson, Bergholm, and Lindberg, *Industristöds-politiken,* pp. 90–95; Sven Grassman, "Perspektiv på devalveringarna" and "Skämt och allvar i den ekonomisk-politiska debatten," *Ekonomisk debatt,* 5 (1978), pp. 302–14, and 8 (1978), pp. 607–11.

90. See Nils Lundgren, "Årets finansplan," *Ekonomisk debatt,* 1 (1979), p. 72; Grassman, "Perspektiv," p. 310; Bengt Pettersson and Clas-Erik Odhner, *Veckans affärer,* May 23, 1979; Bergström and others, *Politik mot stagflation,* pp. 78–79; Per-Olof Edin, *LO-Tidningen,* 27 (1978), p. 7; Gunnar Nilsson, speech in parliament, January 31, 1979.

in the alternation between low and high agreements was cause for apprehension. The pattern of alternation was interrupted after the 1975–76 agreements, with the 1977 and 1978–79 agreements each successively lower. Though the 1977 agreement provided for much lower contractual increases than the preceding one, the relationship of those increases to drift was more characteristic of a high agreement. Perhaps the wage explosion agreement had been so high that it could not be fully offset in the next. Only the 1978–79 agreement could be said to be a low one, though even during the life of the latter, wage drift did not exceed contractual increases (table 13-3). The level of drift was evidently held down despite low contractual increases by the persistence of high hidden unemployment and low profits, together with intensified efforts by the SAF to keep its members from exceeding contractual increases. In effect, the pattern was simply stretched out over the two agreements following the one for 1975–76.

Had the stretchout been continued by another low agreement for 1980, the recovery of industrial investment might have reached a level at which it could make a dent in the structural problem. Moreover, it might have been sufficient to replace the vicious cycle of declining utilization leading to declining capacity by a virtuous cycle in the opposite direction, easing the cost problem by increasing productivity and pushing back the inflationary frontier of full capacity utilization. Before the 1980 round of wage negotiations, however, there was another election.

The 1979 election returned the bourgeois parties to power, but just barely. Their electoral margin over the socialist bloc dropped from nearly 4 percentage points to a mere 0.2 percent and their parliamentary majority fell from eleven to just one seat. They had been damaged by division over nuclear energy, which precipitated the break-up of the three-party coalition government headed by Fälldin and its replacement by a minority Liberal party government. But this issue had been taken out of the election campaign when the Three Mile Island incident in the United States led to a decision to hold a referendum on nuclear energy in the spring of 1980.[91] The wage-earner funds issue had also been blunted by its relegation to an official commission of inquiry. Unemployment was the one issue on which the bourgeois parties would have been most vulnerable but they made sure that their opponents would be deprived of that issue. In fact, government policy reinforced the effect of the international recovery,

91. Olof Petersson, *Regeringsbildningen 1978* (Stockholm: Rabén och Sjögren, 1979).

fueling a pre-election boom that brought open unemployment down to 1.8 percent in the last quarter of the year.[92]

Thin as their margin was, then, the bourgeois parties retained control of parliament and, with the nuclear issue shelved, formed a new coalition government, headed again by Fälldin. Taking up the task of rectifying the structural disequilibrium in Sweden's external position begun by the two preceding governments, the second Fälldin government faced the test of creating the conditions under which the wage determination system would permit the recovery of industrial investment to continue. It did not meet the test.

A Missed Opportunity?

The 1980 wage agreement turned out to be a high one. What was different about it was that it was reached only after the largest work stoppage in Sweden since a 1909 general strike. Strikes and lockouts involving a quarter of the labor force brought the economy to a standstill for ten days in May 1980.[93] The agreement that brought the stoppage to a close resulted in contractual increases of 6.1 percent. With wage drift of 3.5 percent, the total increase in adult industrial workers' average hourly earnings in 1980 was 9.5 percent (table 13-3).[94] The direct loss of industrial production attributed to the general work stoppage, together with a subsequent strike by a breakaway dockworkers union, is estimated at between 1.5 and 2.0 percent on an annual basis. "The total loss of exports . . . is estimated at around 2 percent, while the loss in the case of raw materials seems to have been somewhat higher."[95] Unit labor costs rose, but more of the increase was accounted for by a drop in productivity growth than by the increase in hourly labor costs.[96]

Because the increase in unit labor costs was apparently not greater than in Sweden's trading partners, it did not reopen the cost gap.[97] But some

92. *Swedish Economy, 1981:1,* statistical appendix, p. 40.
93. See Martin, "Trade Unions in Sweden."
94. The amounts involved are more than usually uncertain because the available data on drift are tentative and also subject to different interpretations, depending on how increases negotiated in December 1979, in accordance with a price clause in the 1978–79 agreement, are estimated and allocated between 1979 and 1980. Adding a 2 percent increase resulting from the December 1979 agreement to a 4 percent increase resulting from the May 1980 agreement comes to a 6 percent total increase in contractual earnings between 1979 and 1980. This estimate seems the one most consistent with data for preceding years.
95. *Swedish Economy, 1981:2,* p. 56.
96. Ibid., pp. 138–40.
97. TCO, *Lönepolitikens samhällsekonomiska förusättningar* (Stockholm: TCO, 1982), p. 57.

argued that Sweden's relative costs had to be reduced further in order to permit sufficient investment in internationally competitive production to solve the underlying structural problem.[98] Total industrial investment, public and private, is estimated to have fallen 8.5 percent in 1981, after having risen 19 percent in 1980.[99] The recovery of industrial investment could hardly have been sustained in the face of the serious new downturn in the OECD area generally, no matter what happened to Sweden's relative cost position, but it might have been reversed less quickly and less sharply had it not been for the massive work stoppage and the size of the wage increase.

Could the government have averted the damage done in the 1980 wage round by acting differently? Given its composition, it could hardly have been expected to make institutional changes that would have weakened the link between profits and both shareholders' and wage earners' income along the lines urged by the LO. Besides, the problem such changes were designed to address had not yet reappeared with any intensity. But the government might have been able to create the conditions for something approximating a low agreement in 1980 if it had kept inflation from accelerating as fast as it did, and if it had been more effective in limiting the impact of inflation on workers' real disposable income. Inflation probably exerted more upward pressure on wage demands than drift did in the 1980 wage round, for the price threshold for reopening negotiations was crossed but drift did not exceed contractual wages. This suggests that the increases in nominal wages could have been lower than they were.

One thing the government would have had to do was pursue a more restrictive macroeconomic policy than it did in the course of 1979. Whether the government was attempting to engineer a political business cycle or not, it apparently lost control of the upswing to which it contributed during the year. This is suggested by the rapid acceleration of inflation by the end of the year, when it reached the highest monthly rate since the Korean War. Although the new jump in oil prices in 1979 received much attention, it accounted for less than a fifth of the increase in the consumer price index.[100] Gross domestic product grew by 4.3 percent in 1979, the fastest growth since 1970, and unemployment declined from 2.4 percent in the first quarter to 1.8 percent in the last.

98. Rydén, *Mot nya förlorade år?* p. 83.
99. *Swedish Economy, 1981:1,* p. 119; *1982:2,* p. 126.
100. Ibid., *1980:3,* pp. 94–95.

The stimulative effect of fiscal policy during the year is estimated at 3.8 percent of GDP, higher than in any of the preceding five years. The other side of this fiscal stimulus was a central budget deficit that rose from 8.5 percent of GDP in 1978 to 10.5 percent in 1979. Insofar as excessively expansive fiscal policy contributed to overheating the economy, it presumably played a part in the sharp deterioration in the balance of payments from virtual equilibrium in 1978 to a deficit of 2.2 percent of GDP in 1979.[101] This wiped out any possibility for using revaluation as a stabilization policy instrument, as the LO urged in 1979.[102] The possibility may not have been very great, and business opposed the policy, but Sweden's inflation rate lagged behind the OECD average at the time and might have allowed some revaluation.

Another thing the government would have had to do was limit the impact of inflation on real disposable income by making the distributive effects of tax measures more egalitarian than they were. Marginal tax rates were reduced directly and a system of indexation introduced as of 1979. These measures, LO economists complained, and others confirmed, were so constructed as to yield higher real income gains, not only in absolute but also in percentage terms, the higher the taxpayer's nominal income. High nominal wage increases were necessary simply to prevent lower-paid workers from falling further behind higher-income recipients.[103] The LO's demands and the increases won might have been lower if the distributive bias of the tax measures had been corrected. But then the measures would not have met the expectations of the bourgeois government's supporters, particularly in the conservative party.

There were other things the government could have done to keep the 1980 wage bargaining round from taking the course it did. Preoccupied with the coming nuclear referendum and hampered by the difficulties of policymaking in a coalition, the government failed to make its economic policy intentions clear in advance of the wage negotiations, depriving the negotiating parties of an important element in their calculations. After the negotiations were under way, lack of coordination within the government led to further confusion. Thus private sector employers may have had the mistaken impression that the government would support them

---

101. Table 13-4; *Swedish Economy, 1980:2,* pp. 148, 162, and statistical appendix, p. 40.

102. *Ekonomiska utsikter* (LO) (Spring 1979), p. 28.

103. Axel Hadenius, *Spelet om skatten: rationalistisk analys av politiskt beslutsfattande* (Stockholm: Norstedt, 1981); LO, *Verksamhets berättelse 1979,* pp. 56–57; *Dagens nyheter* (Stockholm), October 28, 1980.

in taking a very hard line against union wage demands. The bourgeois parties' return to office had apparently encouraged them to do so already, and once open conflict broke out, the SAF's chairman declared its general lockout to be an "investment in the future."[104] It did not pay off, however. Like the Social Democratic government in 1975, the second Fälldin government violated the principle of letting the tradable-goods-producing private sector be the wage leader. It made a settlement in the public sector that was larger than any either the public or the private sector unions had expected to win and then pressured the SAF to accept the terms in the private sector. Having failed to avert the breakdown of industrial peace, the government was then unwilling to risk the blame for prolonging the dispute and leaving the country without essential supplies and services.[105]

It is difficult to avoid the conclusion that in a number of ways the government might have been able to create the conditions for a more favorable outcome of the 1980 wage round, and that it missed a genuine opportunity to extend the recovery of Sweden's economy. As a result of its failure to do so, economic policy was essentially back to square one—in some respects better than in 1977 but in others worse.

Even if it was not enough to restore relative costs to what they were before the 1975–76 agreement, the 1980 agreement did not create a cost problem on anything like the scale of that following the mid-1970s wage explosion. On the other hand, for several years investment in internationally competitive production had been low. Reflecting the persistence of the underlying structural problem, the balance of payments and central government budget deficits were far larger in 1980 than in 1977. Moreover, the international economic environment was more unfavorable. Although the OECD recovery had slowed down in 1977, area GDP growth that year was more than twice as high as in 1980, 3.7 percent compared with 1.3 percent. In both years the government turned toward a highly restrictive macroeconomic policy.[106] Since this occurred in 1980 just as activity in the OECD area was turning down, the setback to industrial investment and threat of increased open unemployment was bound to be aggravated.

Up to that point, then, the bourgeois governments had not brought

104. Anders Broström, ed., *Storkonflikten på den svenska arbetsmarknaden 1980* (Stockholm: Arbetslivscentrum, 1981), p. 37.

105. Bolang, *Utslagen*, pp. 50–54.

106. Regeringens proposition 1980 U:1; "The Economic Policy Statement," in *The Swedish Budget, 1980/81, 1981/82,* and *1982/83; Swedish Economy, 1982:2,* pp. 206–12.

the basic problems of the Swedish economy much closer to solution. In particular, they had not found a way to make the dynamics of the wage determination system more consistent with the sustained investment on which the necessary structural adaptation depended. A low agreement for 1981–82 was very rapidly and quietly reached by the LO and the SAF in early 1981.[107] This was to be expected from the normal operation of the wage determination system quite apart from the strong desire to avoid a repetition of the 1980 experience. By the time that two-year agreement ran out, however, economic policy would very likely be confronted once more with the problem of making the wage determination system operate in such a way as to permit a recovery of industrial investment to continue. How the problem would be met would be decisively conditioned by the outcome of the election that was to take place before the next round of central negotiations.

No matter what happened in the election, the structure of personal income taxation was not likely to be as much of an obstacle to moderate nominal wage increases as it was in 1980. An agreement on changes in the tax structure was made between two of the parties in the second Fälldin government, the Center and Liberal parties, and the opposition Social Democrats. It was bitterly opposed by the conservatives, leading to their withdrawal from the coalition and its replacement by a third Fälldin government, a middle party coalition. The agreed tax package was turned into legislation which the LO and the TCO regarded as reasonably satisfactory.[108] Even if the bourgeois parties returned to office after the next election, the legislation was unlikely to be repealed, despite the conservatives' objections to it.

But the problem to which wage-earner funds were addressed was likely to be crucial to the next wage round. And in this connection, the election outcome would undoubtedly make a difference. A Social Democratic victory would presumably open the way to further steps toward the socialization of investment along the lines of the party-LO design for wage-earner funds. A return to office by the bourgeois parties, on the other hand, would certainly bring further movement in the direction of the reprivatization of investment, or, more precisely, of savings, since it

107. LO, *Verksamhets berättelse 1981;* SAF, *Verksamhet 1981.* A strike by the PTK, aimed at preserving differentials relative to LO members, threatened another major stoppage. But intense pressure, not least from the LO, brought it to an end consistent with the LO-SAF agreement.

108. Hadenius, *Spelet om skatten.*

was only at the savings end of the savings-investment process that Social Democratic policy had brought about any significant socialization by 1976. There were essentially two lines along which the bourgeois governments subsequently fostered the reprivatization of savings—by doing very little to arrest the decline of the AP system as a mechanism for collective savings, and by enacting measures making private share ownership more attractive.

Reduction in the growth in the AP system's surplus was built into it from its inception. Revenues were supposed to substantially exceed payments during the long transition to a fully operating pension system. Then growth in the surplus would slow down and the surplus could even decline, depending on whether the payroll tax continued to be raised.

The rapid growth of the AP fund in its initial years made it the single largest source of lending in the organized credit market, accounting for over 40 percent of net lending at its peak in 1970 and 1971.[109] While the government made some changes in the AP's funding and increased the Fourth Fund's capacity in the face of opposition by organized business, its main thrust was to directly stimulate the flow of private savings into equity capital by various tax breaks, including credit on income invested in mutual funds and tax exemption on all income from such investments. Companies were authorized to set up funds for purchasing their own shares on behalf of employees.[110] Several large companies already had employee share ownership schemes, and many others set up such schemes, some of them even offering their employees interest-free short-term loans to enroll in the schemes. Largely on the basis of such loans, there was a rapid growth in participation during the first half of 1981. The response to the new measure contributed to a marked rise in prices on the Swedish stock exchange.[111] The resulting increase in household share purchases came close to what the 1980 *Long-Term Survey* said would be necessary for industry to raise sufficient equity capital for the required rate of investment.

Prospects for the schemes' economic success were evidently not their only attraction for the companies. When the conservative economics minister had broached the idea in 1977, it was understood to be an

---

109. See Markowski and Palmer, "Social Insurance"; *Kapital marknaden,* SOU 1978:11, pp. 441–88.

110. Regeringens proposition 1980/81:45.

111. *Sweden Now,* 3 (1981), p. 11. Nineteen eighty-one turned out to be the Stockholm stock exchange's "best year since the 1930s." *Sweden Business Report,* February 2, 1982, pp. 2–3.

alternative to the LO's proposal for collective share ownership and had even been referred to as a "bourgeois Meidner fund."[112] And as the measure went through parliament, the Social Democrats and the LO attacked it as simply a political tactic designed to undercut support for wage-earner funds while leaving the fundamental inequality in the distribution of wealth and power essentially unchanged. Although such tactical aims were disavowed in public, they were acknowledged in private, and it was obvious that the companies involved had joined the government in an effort to erode support for wage-earner funds.

There was thus a clear divergence in the directions in which the Social Democrats and the bourgeois parties were moving in dealing with the savings-investment process. During the 1982 election campaign, however, neither the attacks on wage-earner funds nor the measures calculated to build support for the private savings alternative succeeded in turning wage-earner funds into a winning issue for the bourgeois parties. That issue ranked low among voters' concerns. Instead, the economy's continuing troubles were the dominant issue. The Social Democrats concentrated on them, citing them as prime evidence of the bourgeois parties' incapacity to govern. The outcome was a solid victory for the Social Democrats, who returned to office with three seats more than the bourgeois parties' combined total, and an overall socialist majority of twenty-three. If the necessary condition for making the wage determination system's operation consistent with a sustainable recovery of industrial investment is further movement toward the socialization of investment, that condition now seemed likely to be met.

Conclusion

The requirements of organizational cohesion within the LO limit the extent to which it can pursue a wage policy consistent with the requirements of external equilibrium, which thereby limits the capacity of the central negotiation system to perform the function of an incomes policy. To preserve its ability to engage in central negotiations on behalf of its affiliates, the LO has to pursue a wage policy capable of retaining their support. In effect, it has to be a policy through which distributive conflict among the affiliates and their rank-and-file members can be effectively

---

112. *Dagens nyheter* (Stockholm), September 28, 1977.

managed. This, in practice, is what defines the specific content of "solidaristic wage policy."

For the credibility of this wage policy to be preserved, the actual distribution of earnings must recognizably approximate the distribution agreed to by the LO's affiliates. No matter how successful the LO may be in embodying the policy in the central agreements that are translated into industry contracts, however, the contracts do not fully determine the actual distribution of earnings. It is also shaped by local bargaining which, in the context of varying payment systems and market forces, results in various amounts of wage drift. The more drift there is, the greater the discrepancy between the intended and the actual distribution, intensifying strains within and among the LO unions, and diminishing the effectiveness of the confederation's wage policy as a basis of support for its wage bargaining role. Accordingly, the LO is driven to press for contractual wage increases that squeeze profits sufficiently to limit the scope for drift, reducing employers' willingness to offer or concede various kinds of increases that enter into drift. Managing distributive conflict within labor, in other words, depends on maintaining the intensity of distributive conflict between labor and capital.

Yet, a persistent squeeze on profits threatens to result in insufficient investment to maintain the viability of Sweden's international economic position, and with it the levels of employment and consumption, public as well as private, in which the union membership's interests ultimately lie. Since the early postwar period, then, the LO has felt compelled not only to squeeze profits but also to seek ways of averting the consequent threat to investment. Initially the LO concentrated its attention on the role of profits as a mechanism for accumulating a financial surplus to divert resources from consumption to investment—that is, at the savings end of the savings-investment process—but it eventually became concerned also with the role of profits in making decisions at the investment end of the process. This has led the LO to seek changes in the institutions by which a surplus is accumulated and channeled into investment.

These changes transfer some of the claims to control as well as to the wealth associated with increments to capital from private shareholders to collective institutions of various forms, in which there is union participation in varying degrees. Such changes are designed to increase government and union control over income not captured for workers through negotiated wage increases and thereby maximize the utilization of that income for the needed industrial investment while minimizing its availability for nonindustrial investment or personal consumption, either by shareholders or, through drift, by workers.

This response to the problem of reconciling the requirements of external equilibrium and organizational cohesion points to very exacting conditions for managing distributive conflict between labor and capital. Labor movements must have some assurance that wages forgone through negotiated agreement to limit wage growth will actually be translated into the investment needed to maintain full employment. If that assurance could be provided by government policies to maintain full employment by conventional aggregate demand management, supplemented perhaps by manpower policies, then this condition might be met without disturbing the consensus over basic institutional arrangements that management of distributive conflict between labor and capital by agreement seems to presuppose. Although such policies have been pursued vigorously in Sweden, they have apparently not provided sufficient assurance.

In the absence of sufficient assurance that wages forgone through negotiations will not be diverted from industrial investment to consumption by either shareholders or workers, the LO seems to have been unable to limit wage growth through its participation in central negotiations without jeopardizing its own and its affiliates' internal cohesion. To meet this second condition for managing distributive conflict, then, the LO has been driven to press for policies it believes can bring it closer to meeting the first condition. Those policies encroach on the capitalist institutions through which the savings-investment process has been organized, however. Thus, the effort to manage conflict over distributive issues has drawn the LO into conflict with Swedish capital over more fundamental institutional issues.

14

The Cost of Rapid Growth and Capitalist Democracy in Japan

Kozo Yamamura

From 1981 through 1983, Japan's price levels were largely stable. The wholesale price index remained virtually unchanged and the consumer price index rose only 10 points. The Japanese must continue, however, to be concerned, as they were in the 1970s, with persistent inflation or with the threat of rapid inflation in their economy.

In assessing the future risks of inflation what is crucial is not the short-term price stability resulting from the sluggishness of economic performance in the early 1980s and the net annual capital export of almost $20 billion, part of which was induced by high interest rates in the United States. Instead what is crucial is the politicoeconomic vulnerability of the Japanese capitalist democracy, which as this chapter seeks to demonstrate, continues to face serious long-term risks of rapid inflation that for political reasons will be extremely difficult to avoid.[1] These risks are not of recent origin but were inherent in the very process of rapid growth.

1. Serious political analysis of the Japanese economy is a very recent undertaking. Thus, Takafusa Nakamura and others, "Nihon keizai wa antei kido ni noreruka?" *Ekonomisuto*, August 18, 1975, p. 68, observed that "economists not only acknowledge they are ignorant of politics but are almost proud of that ignorance." In *Nihon keizai shimbun*, September 19, 1978, Moto'o Kaji, an economist, strongly advocated the necessity of political economic studies which "yet remain untouched" in Japan. And Komiya, whose able analysis of postwar inflation in Japan focused on the "economic causes," had only the following to say on strong political pressure exerted for deficit spending in the 1970s: "The government was then under strong pressure from various political groups demanding increased expenditures as well as the tax reduction. Investment in social overhead capital and housing, expansion of public welfare programs, improvement of the national social security system, and reduction in the personal income tax were considered as urgent tasks for the government. The fear that the yen revaluation would cause a prolonged recession helped to loosen the government's purse strings." Ryutaro Komiya and Yoshio

The Era of Rapid Growth

Between 1955 and the mid-1960s, Japan's politicoeconomic machinery worked like a marriage made in heaven for conservative politicians, business leaders, bureaucrats, and most Japanese. The machinery's product is well known—the political dominance of the Liberal Democratic party (LDP) and rapid economic growth, the rewards of which were shared by all. Growth was accompanied by only a modest, by Japanese standards, inflation in the consumer price index, and the wholesale price index showed a downward trend chiefly as a result of the rapid increase in productivity (see table 14-1).

The machinery worked well because of the fundamental consensus on the need for and desirability of rapid economic growth; because the elite structure of conservative politicians, leaders of the business community, and bureaucrats provided effective leadership for growth; because an educated populace was willing to work diligently and to save; and because international political and economic conditions were favorable.[2] Of course,

---

Suzuki, "Inflation in Japan," in Lawrence B. Krause and Walter S. Salant, eds., *Worldwide Inflation: Theory and Recent Experience* (Brookings Institution, 1977), p. 322. For discussion of the role of politics in postwar Japanese economic growth, see John Creighton Campbell, *Contemporary Japanese Budget Politics* (University of California Press, 1977); Haruhiro Fukui, "Economic Planning in Postwar Japan: A Case Study in Policymaking," *Asian Survey*, vol. 12 (April 1972), pp. 327–48; Chalmers Johnson, "Japan: Who Governs? An Essay on Official Bureaucracy," *Journal of Japanese Studies*, vol. 2 (Autumn 1975), pp. 1–28; Chalmers Johnson, "MITI and Japanese International Economic Policy," in Robert A. Scalapino, ed., *The Foreign Policy of Modern Japan* (University of California Press, 1977), pp. 227–79; T. J. Pempel, "Japanese Foreign Economic Policy: The Domestic Bases for International Behavior," *International Organization*, vol. 31 (Autumn 1977), pp. 723–74; T. J. Pempel, "The Bureaucratization of Policymaking in Postwar Japan," *American Journal of Political Science*, vol. 18 (November 1974), pp. 647–64; T. J. Pempel, ed., *Policymaking in Contemporary Japan* (Cornell University Press, 1977).

2. See Hugh Patrick and Henry Rosovsky, eds., *Asia's New Giant: How the Japanese Economy Works* (Brookings Institution, 1976); Kazushi Ohkawa and Henry Rosovsky, *Japanese Economic Growth: Trend Acceleration in the Twentieth Century* (Stanford University Press, 1973); Hugh Patrick, ed., *Japanese Industrialization and Its Social Consequences* (University of California Press, 1976); Kozo Yamamura, ed., *Policy and Trade Issues of the Japanese Economy: American and Japanese Perspectives* (University of Washington Press, 1982); Takafusa Nakamura, *The Postwar Japanese Economy: Its Development and Structure* (University of Tokyo Press, 1981); Michael K. Blaker, ed., *Japan at the Polls: The House of Councillors Election of 1974* (Washington: American Enterprise Institute for Public Policy Research, 1976); Hans H. Baerwald, *Japan's Parliament: An Introduction* (Cambridge University Press, 1974); Ezra F. Vogel, ed., *Modern Japanese Organization and Decision-Making* (University of California Press, 1975); Haruhiro Fukui, *Party in Power: The Japanese Liberal-Democrats and Policy-making* (Australian National University Press, 1970); J. A. A. Stockwin, *Japan: Divided Politics in a Growth Economy* (London: Weidenfeld and Nicolson, 1975); Nathaniel B. Thayer, *How the Conservatives Rule Japan* (Princeton University Press, 1969); Robert E. Ward, *Japan's Political System*, 2d ed. (Prentice-Hall, 1978).

Table 14-1. *Annual Changes in Prices, Wages, Rate of Growth, and the Balance of Payments, Japan, 1953–83*

Year	Wholesale price index (percent)	Consumer price index (percent)	Rate of growth, in 1965 prices (percent)	Balance of payments, current account (millions of dollars)
1953	0.7	6.7	5.7	− 205
1954	− 0.7	6.5	6.4	− 51
1955	− 1.8	− 1.1	8.6	227
1956	4.4	0.4	8.3	− 34
1957	3.0	3.1	8.2	− 620
1958	− 6.5	− 0.4	5.3	264
1959	1.0	1.1	9.3	361
1960	1.1	3.5	14.0	143
1961	1.0	5.4	15.6	− 982
1962	− 1.6	6.8	6.6	− 49
1963	1.8	7.5	10.2	− 779
1964	0.2	3.8	14.0	− 480
1965	0.8	7.7	4.6	932
1966	2.4	5.0	10.1	1,254
1967	1.8	4.0	13.5	− 190
1968	0.9	5.3	14.2	1,048
1969	2.1	5.4	12.1	2,119
1970	3.7	7.9	10.6	1,970
1971	− 0.8	6.2	6.8	5,797
1972	0.8	4.6	8.7	6,624
1973	15.9	11.7	10.2	− 136
1974	31.3	24.5	− 1.8	− 4,693
1975	2.1	10.4	3.4	134
1976	5.3	9.4	5.7	4,682
1977	2.9	8.6	5.1	− 11,050
1978	− 2.6	3.8	5.1	16,536
1979	7.3	3.6	5.3	− 8,754
1980	17.8	8.0	4.6	− 10,746
1981	1.4	4.9	3.5	4,776
1982	1.8	2.7	3.3	6,850
1983	− 2.2	2.0	. . .	21,024

Sources: Bank of Japan, *Economic Statistics Annual,* various issues; Japan, Economic Planning Agency, *Annual Report on National Income,* various issues.

this success, with the fruits of rapid growth which were shared and distributed, kept the machinery purring for further success.[3]

After the Korean War boom had convinced the Japanese of the possibility of growth, they began, with characteristic zeal, and little disagreement, to devote all of their abilities and resources to achieving rapid economic growth. "There were no politics in the sense of the competitive advocacy of the fundamental goal of society,"[4] and rapid economic growth became "a war to be won, the first total war in Japanese history for which all of the nation's resources were mobilized *voluntarily.*"[5]

Three groups assumed the leadership in formulating economic policies. One was the Liberal Democratic party (LDP), whose long-standing probusiness policies were an important asset in the minds of a majority of voters who saw them also as pro–economic growth policies.[6] The opposition parties were occupied with ideological concern for the distribution of a still small pie, but most of the voters were beginning to enjoy a larger share of a pie that was growing in size.

The second leadership group was the *zaikai,* "the group of major industrial and financial leaders who spend a significant portion of their time in activities that relate to the economy in general and the society at large, generally through active participation in one or more of the four major economic organizations."[7] The *zaikai*—the major source of LDP finances and the direct beneficiary of the LDP policies for rapid economic growth—is by no means a monolithic structure, but on matters relating to obtaining growth-promoting (probusiness) policies, it had little difficulty in achieving a consensus and presenting a united front to the LDP. And in these matters its views were representative of a much more widely based interest group, the owners of small and medium-sized firms, farmers,

3. See Hugh Patrick and Henry Rosovsky, "Japan's Economic Performance: An Overview," in Patrick and Rosovsky, *Asia's New Giant,* pp. 1–61.

4. Seizaburo Sato, Shumpei Kumon, and Yasusuke Murakami, "Datsu-hokaku jidai no torai," *Chuo koron* (February 1977), p. 82.

5. Eisuke Sakakibara and Yukio Noguchi, "Okurasho-Nichigan ocho no bunseki," *Chuo koron* (August 1977), p. 110.

6. Chitoshi Yanaga, *Big Business in Japanese Politics* (Yale University Press, 1968); Fukui, *Party in Power,* pp. 58–61.

7. Gerald L. Curtis, "Big Business and Political Influence," in Vogel, *Modern Japanese Organization,* p. 39. Prime Minister Eisaku Sato's famous slip of the tongue in 1965 to the effect that he owed his newly acquired leadership of the LDP (thus, the premiership) to the support of the *zaikai* surprised no one. Yanaga, *Big Business,* p. 33, remarked that the "zaikai's power of life and death over governments has been dramatically demonstrated time and again. Candidacy for the premiership is unthinkable without its tacit approval, and the Prime Minister's days are numbered if his policies or methods no longer meet with its approval."

and others who made their wishes known to the LDP through their financial contributions and, more important, through their votes.

The last of the three groups was the rigorously selected, competent bureaucrats in the government ministries. Those of the Ministry of Finance (MOF) and the Ministry of International Trade and Industry (MITI)—regarded as the cream of Japan's bureaucracy because of the exceptionally keen competition the graduates of the elite universities must face when entering these ministries— were most responsible for making and carrying out the highly growth-oriented policies of postwar Japan. While other ministries had been weakened by the purges and reorganizations of the 1945–48 period, the MOF and MITI had remained basically intact.[8] Assessments differ as to the degree of initiative assumed by these bureaucrats in Japan's pursuit of rapid economic growth, but there has been fundamental agreement that the bureaucrats have a great deal of power.[9]

In pursuit of this growth, the overriding goal of Japan's monetary policies was to provide financial resources to firms and industries that were adopting capital-intensive new technologies, in order to increase and enhance their competitive abilities in the international market or to provide, at a lower cost, the rapidly increasing amount of capital goods required by rapid economic growth. To achieve this goal, a generally smoothly functioning money market was created on the strength of a few key laws passed by the LDP-dominated Diet, and then administered effectively by the officials of the MOF and the Bank of Japan.[10] The legal linchpin of the policy was the Temporary Interest Rate Adjustment Act of 1947, which exempted the collusive fixing of short-term loan and deposit rates among banks from antimonopoly prosecution. This law, which proved not to be temporary (though it grew to be less rigidly

---

8. Sakakibara and Noguchi, "Okurasho-Nichigan," p. 102. When over 2,000 high-ranking bureaucrats were purged by the Supreme Command of Allied Powers, the MOF and MITI lost the fewest of their senior officers.

9. For discussion of their power, see Eugene J. Kaplan, *Japan: The Government-Business Relationship* (U.S. Department of Commerce, 1972); Ezra F. Vogel, *Japan as Number One: Lessons for America* (Harvard University Press, 1979); Johnson, "Japan: Who Governs?"; Campbell, *Contemporary Japanese Budget Politics;* Pempel, *Policymaking in Contemporary Japan;* Pempel, "Bureaucratization of Policymaking in Postwar Japan"; Phillip H. Trezise with Yukio Suzuki, "Politics, Government, and Economic Growth in Japan," in Patrick and Rosovsky, *Asia's New Giant,* pp. 753–811.

10. See Henry C. Wallich and Mabel I. Wallich, "Banking and Finance," in Patrick and Rosovsky, *Asia's New Giant,* pp. 249–315; Hideo Kanematsu, "Sekai keizai no hendo to Nihon no taigai keizai seisaku," and Eisuke Sakakibara, "Henbo suru Nihon no kinyu shisutemu," *Gendai keizai,* vol. 29 (Winter 1977), pp. 120–43, 64–68; Sakakibara and Noguchi, "Okurasho-Nichigan."

enforced), provided MOF officials with the power to determine the rate structure in the money market.

Before 1965, when the trade deficit turned into a surplus and deficit spending first occurred, increases in the money supply required for meeting the needs of the expanding economy came primarily in the form of increases in credit advanced by the Bank of Japan. This meant that, rather than through deficit spending and a trade surplus which were the principal means of increasing liquidity in the U.S. and West German economies, the Bank of Japan was in a position to determine the quantity and terms of liquidity in the economy by regulating the amount of loans it made to the banks and by adjusting discount rates and reserve requirements.

As a legacy of the policies adopted during the 1930s and as the result of the decision of the Supreme Command of Allied Powers not to subdivide the giant *zaibatsu* banks, Japan had a two-tiered banking system, made up of thirteen large city banks in the urban centers and a network of local and rural banks and credit and savings institutions elsewhere. A 1950 law, which imposed stringent requirements on the sale of bonds, made borrowing from banks more attractive than the issuance of bonds. The issuance of bonds, therefore, became limited to several government-controlled financial institutions, and the government-owned Industry Promotion Bank accounted for the bulk of the bonds sold. Moreover, Japan's capital market was insulated by the Foreign Exchange and Trade Control Law of 1949. Though the law was enacted as a temporary measure to cope with problems of a "dollar shortage," it remained unchanged until 1962, when minor revisions were made under foreign pressure to liberalize Japanese international trade restrictions.

Given these highly favorable institutional characteristics of the capital market and the eagerness of the officials of the MOF and the Bank of Japan to use their legal and extralegal powers of persuasion, backed by their power to allocate loans, the money market was effectively adminis-tered for the purpose of achieving rapid economic growth. Demand for capital by industry was high, stimulated by the below-equilibrium loan rate set by the MOF. The large city banks, faced with this demand, sought to borrow all the Bank of Japan was willing to lend them. Since raising equity capital was difficult and relatively unattractive (because the capital market was thin, costs of loans at the administered rates were lower than the cost of paying out competitive dividends, tax laws favored loan capital, and issuing bonds was difficult and unattractive), firms chose to rely on bank loans, and banks in turn had to rely on the Bank of Japan. Under such circumstances, the Bank, and thus the MOF, could readily exercise its power to guide—meaning to determine which industries and, in some instances, even which firms were to be the recipients of bank loans.

An important fact of this "guided disequilibrium" policy was that the system strongly favored the largest banks and the largest firms. Small and medium-sized firms that would have been willing and able to pay the prevailing high rate of interest despite the policy (because of the high profitability of capital) were often denied access to loanable funds in the hands of small and medium-sized banks, their traditional source of capital. Because loans to smaller businesses were not looked on with favor at the Bank of Japan and were riskier and more costly to administer than loans to large firms,[11] the loanable funds (deposits) in the small and medium-sized banks flowed through the call market to the city banks, which lent them to the major firms in rapidly expanding industries.[12] The difference between a theoretical equilibrium loan rate and the government-controlled rate these large firms paid, multiplied by the total amount of the loans to these rapidly growing firms, constituted a massive subsidy provided by savers.[13] With an insulated capital market, Japan's policymakers could pursue their own independent policy goals regardless of changing conditions in the world money market, and the prevailing high rate of interest eliminated the risk that capital would leave Japan in search of higher returns abroad.

During the period of rapid economic growth, the budget typically offered no problems. It was "superbalanced," often generating a surplus, because of MOF officials' inclination to underestimate revenues that kept on rising more rapidly than did the gross national product (the elasticity of revenue to changes in the GNP was around 1.3).[14] As revenues rose, the LDP government was in a position to enjoy a larger budget year after year, thus enabling it to cut taxes almost every year. It was able to increase expenditures in a variety of growth-promoting programs yet keep total government expenditures (excluding local government) at about 14–15 percent of GNP, the lowest among the industrial economies.

11. These are general statements and there are exceptions. Also the de facto rate ceiling could be evaded by illegal means or by evading the MOF guidance (such as requiring a compensatory balance from a borrower), but these entail obvious costs.

12. Gardner Ackley with Hiromitsu Ishi, "Fiscal, Monetary, and Related Policies," in Patrick and Rosovsky, *Asia's New Giant*, pp. 201–02.

13. Koichi Hamada, Makoto Sakurai, and Yukitada Ishiyama, "Teikinri seisaku to shotoku bunpai," *Gendai keizai*, vol. 26 (Spring 1977), pp. 28–43.

14. Joseph A. Pechman and Keimei Kaizuka, "Taxation," in Patrick and Rosovsky, *Asia's New Giant*, pp. 346–49; Ackley with Ishi, "Fiscal, Monetary, and Related Policies," pp. 210–29.

Two basic principles appear to have guided Japanese budgetary policy. First, the principle that tax schedules (including rates, brackets, exemptions, and deductions) should be adjusted annually (predominantly downward) in order to keep total tax revenues (national and local) at or near 20 percent of national income. Second, arising from recommendations of the Dodge Mission of 1949 and the memory of inflation caused by the deficit spending of the 1930s, the principle of a balanced budget, which "came to mean that the central government should not borrow (other than temporarily) from the Bank of Japan nor issue marketable bonds."[15]

The character of the budget, in comparison with that of the United States, changed little during the 1960s (as shown in table 14-2). While there were sizable percentage changes in the disposition of external affairs, national debt, and pensions categories, the rise merely reflected extremely small expenditures in the base year of 1961. The most significant change in absolute amount and percentages was in the agriculture, commerce, and industry category, which is readily understandable given the policy emphasis of the LDP. The contrast with the pattern of change in the U.S. budget allocation for the same period—the years including the War on Poverty and the Great Society—is striking.

In deciding the total budget size and expenditures for each category, the opposition parties, outnumbered by the LDP in the budget committees and on the floor of both houses of the Diet, were no more than vocal critics to be tolerated by the confident majority. As late as 1971, the minister of justice observed in an unguarded moment that "in the budget committee meetings, opposition party members dozed with their feet on a heater, and passing budget bills was no more difficult than pushing jello through a sieve." Though the remark cost him his cabinet position, it nevertheless reflected the LDP view of the budgetmaking process; the anger of the opposition committee members was "aroused because it was so true."[16]

In such circumstances, the MOF bureaucrats, who virtually monopolized the data and expertise necessary in drafting the budget, exercised extensive control over the making of the budget. As long as the MOF observed the basic policy goals of the LDP and paid heed to the pet projects of the powerful members of the LDP Party Affairs Research Council, the officers of the Budget Bureau of the MOF could remain in

15. Ackley with Ishi, "Fiscal, Monetary, and Related Policies," p. 212.
16. Kazuyoshi Kitaoka, "Itcho en genzei kobosen no uchimaku," *Chuo koron* (May 1977), p. 191.

Table 14-2. *Distribution of Funds in the Budgets of Japan and the United States, 1961 and 1969*

Percent

Category	Share of budget		
	1961	1969	Change, 1961–69
Japan			
National administration	7.9	6.7	−15
Local government	18.9	21.4	13
National defense	8.6	7.2	−16
Disposition of external affairs	1.2	0.3	−75
Preservation and development of natural resources	18.7	16.3	−13
Agriculture, commerce, and industry	8.7	11.7	25
Education and culture	12.4	11.4	−8
Social security	14.5	15.8	9
Pensions	5.4	3.7	−32
National debt	2.3	3.8	65
Reserves	0.9	1.1	22
Other	0.5	0.5	0
United States			
National defense	47.0	41.2	−12
International affairs and finance	3.7	1.9	−49
Space research and technology	0.9	2.0	122
Agriculture and rural development	3.6	3.2	−11
Natural resources	1.6	1.2	−25
Commerce and transportation	5.0	4.4	−12
Community development and housing	0.4	1.2	242
Education and manpower	1.3	3.5	169
Health	1.0	6.3	530
Income security	20.4	20.7	2
Veterans' benefits and services	5.2	4.2	−22
Interest	7.9	8.7	10
General government	1.5	1.6	7

Source: John Creighton Campbell, *Contemporary Japanese Budget Politics* (University of California Press, 1977), pp. 6–7. Figures are rounded and may not add to 100.

the driver's seat in budgetmaking. As two Japanese authors—one a former officer of the MOF—observed, "until the mid-1960's, the decision-making power was almost totally in the hands of the bureaucrats. . . . And politics could intrude into the decision-making system only partially and in limited ways. Politicians played the role of cheerleaders for various ministries and were no more than go-betweens between pressure groups of local interest groups and the Budget Bureau."[17] Such a perception of the power of the MOF officials resulted primarily because "high growth tends to minimize disagreement between the party and Finance Ministry over the total size of the budget, and creates enough 'slack'—revenue surpluses—so that party demands can be granted without depriving programs which others might see as more vital."[18] "Budget priority" is not fighting language when most can get what they want.

The rapid economic growth provided wage earners with a steadily rising income, taxpayers with frequent tax cuts, and consumers with more durable goods. The LDP campaigners and the government in its white papers had no difficulty in presenting massive amounts of data demonstrating the success of their policies. Such data were hardly necessary, however, to show both white and blue collar workers that a rapidly growing firm employed more people, promoted its employees faster, and provided more employee benefits in housing, health care, and recreational facilities. For the Japanese, whose memories of the deprivation suffered during the 1940s were still fresh, the worth of the total economic war being waged was more than amply proved by the department stores bulging with consumer goods, the children in college, the Tokyo Olympics, and the ownership of color television.

Even the small minority who, for a variety of reasons, failed to share in the material and psychic rewards believed that their children could, through hard work and a little luck, pass the entrance examinations to better schools and join the ranks of the more affluent and respected in society. What Hirschman called the tunnel effect[19] was working with great efficacy in Japan during these rapid growth years because of the homogeneity of society and of the open competition to enter prestigious universities and the largest firms. As the Japanese saying goes, "those who persevere receive their just dues." Just as long as the tunnel effect worked and most shared in what rapid growth was providing, the political leaders of the total war could count on popular support for their war efforts where it mattered most, at the polls.

To be sure, there were a few important exceptions to this rosy picture—coal mining, cotton textiles, and agriculture. Each demanded various types of assistance and subsidies, but the most important among them for the

17. Sakakibara and Noguchi, "Okurasho-Nichigan," p. 129.
18. Campbell, *Contemporary Japanese Budget Politics,* p. 142.
19. Albert O. Hirschman, "The Changing Tolerance for Income Inequality in the Course of Economic Development," *Quarterly Journal of Economics,* vol. 87 (November 1973), pp. 544–46.

LDP was the nation's farmers, the most dependable and faithful supporters of the party. Their products were receiving a decreasing share of consumers' income, and they required a special, politically provided subsidy. This subsidy was readily provided to rice growers—over 90 percent of the farmers—in the form of government purchase of rice at politically determined, above-market prices, and to others in the form of import quotas on butter, meat, citrus fruits, and many other agricultural products. The cost of subsidizing the rice growers was not small, but with rapid economic growth providing steadily increasing revenues, there was little difficulty in finding the funds needed.[20] And, most consumers, whose real wages were steadily rising, did not oppose the subsidies and the high prices of the products protected by import quotas.

Finally, international political and economic conditions were extremely favorable for Japan's pursuit of rapid growth policies. The cold war, the Korean War, and the increasing political instability in Southeast Asia continued to assure that Japan would remain, in the eyes of the United States, a member of the Free World to be protected and favored. And the political favors had cash value. With the United States providing initiative and persuading sometimes reluctant European allies, Japan was admitted to membership in the General Agreement on Tariffs and Trade in 1955, and discrimination against Japan under articles 14 and 35 of the GATT soon ceased; Japan's admittance to membership in the International Monetary Fund (IMF) and the Organization for Economic Cooperation and Development (OECD) followed. Japan's sins of the 1930s were reluctantly forgiven and the barriers to Japanese exports were rapidly reduced. In pursuit of its policy in Asia and with its economy still strong, the United States was most generous to Japan and opened its market to Japanese goods with virtually no restrictions. Problems concerning what the United States believed to be the excess of imports of Japanese textile products in the late 1950s were still no more than minor irritants for that prospering economy, with its strong dollar.

There were many things pointing to minor discord within the elite structure in Japan—the increasing trend toward electoral victories by opposition parties in the major cities, occasional signs of difficulties in the monetary mechanism and in budgetmaking, and increasing European irritation with rapidly proliferating Japanese exports. Nevertheless, Japan's

---

20. Michael W. Donnelly, "Setting the Price of Rice: A Study in Political Decisionmaking," in Pempel, *Policymaking in Contemporary Japan*, pp. 143–200.

politicoeconomic machinery remained basically sound and continued to work well, with the LDP controlling both the lower and upper houses. The economy was growing at a real rate in excess of 10 percent, and inflation during the 1960s averaged only 5.4 percent.

Fortunately, growth was rapid enough to eliminate unemployment of any magnitude, and industries could draw on a labor reserve to keep the pace of growth without raising real wages above the level justified by the increase in productivity.

Unlike the situation in most other countries, inflation showed no tendency to accelerate in the late 1950s and in the 1960s. Possible reasons were that, because unemployment was not a significant problem in Japan (given its institutional structure), political pressures to "risk a little more inflation" in order to minimize the human and social costs of unemployment were negligible; moreover, throughout most of the period the existence of large labor reserves in agriculture and other traditional sectors helped to protect from excessive demand-pull pressures the average unit labor cost, which, in modern economies, serves essentially as the basic standard of value.[21]

Another reason contributing to the price stability was the labor unions' commitment, in essence, to the total war. While the Marxist leaders were dissipating their energy in political grandstanding and ideological conflict (in part because they had not been able to overcome the ideological splits of the prewar years), unions with no powerful national federation acted singly as enterprise unions on matters of substance pertaining to wages and work conditions.[22] Those in the most organized sector of the economy, large industrial firms, traded the guns of labor disputes for the butter of higher wages, and more butter was forthcoming as long as these firms could grow without work stoppages. Japan's permanent employment system and the seniority-based wage system provided additional assurance that the unions would prosper, rarely reaching for their guns.[23]

Contributing also to price stability, of course, were both the steady increase in productivity and the absence of imported inflation. Productivity increases (which were achieved through the adoption of new technology), a fixed exchange rate, stable prices abroad,[24] and Japan's efforts to achieve equilibrium in its international balance of payments kept the Japanese

21. Ackley with Ishi, "Fiscal, Monetary, and Related Policies," p. 243.
22. Walter Galenson with Konosuke Odaka, "The Japanese Labor Market," in Patrick and Rosovsky, *Asia's New Giant*, pp. 627–55.
23. Nathan Glazer, "Social and Cultural Factors in Economic Growth," in Patrick and Rosovsky, *Asia's New Giant*, pp. 876–86.
24. For example, wholesale price indexes as proxies of prices of traded goods in the United States, Japan's largest trading partner, remained relatively stable during the 1960–65 period.

wholesale price index of 1965 at 104, in comparison to 100 in 1958.[25] This in turn helped to keep the rate of inflation down during these years, despite the aggressive growth policy to expand effective domestic demand by Premiers Ikeda and Sato. The government preferred to help the economy run by means of reduced interest rates or tax cuts and was persuaded only with some difficulty to make the economy trot by adopting a tight money policy only when international payment conditions forced it to reverse gears (the overheating of the economy often sharply increased imports, especially of raw materials). Maintaining a moderate level of inflation in this fashion was a potentially risky balancing act depending on continuing productivity increases and favorable international factors. But as long as it succeeded, the politicoeconomic machinery thrived on its success.

The Problems of a Large Industrial Power

By the mid-1960s, several parts of that machinery were beginning to foreshadow major problems to come. The recession of 1965, described by MITI officials and by journalists as a structural recession,[26] was an important signal. A sharp drop in the real growth rate, from 14.0 percent in 1964 to 4.6 percent in 1965, was felt more deeply than the 1958 recession during which the rate had fallen to 5.3 percent from 8.2 percent in 1957. The Ministry of International Trade and Industry and many economists ascribed the difficulties of 1965 to a "too rapid pace of investment activities" or "overheating" in such major industries as specialized steel products, cement, ammonium sulphate, electrical machinery, and several others.[27] The ministry was confident that a momentary slowdown in the rate of investment in these industries, which were suffering from structural difficulties (that is, temporary excess capacity), could be solved in a short time since demand, both domestic and international, was expected to continue to increase. Sharing the MITI view, the Ministry of Finance chose to cope with the recession by reducing

25. Japan, Economic Planning Agency, *Keizai yoran, 1982* (Ministry of Finance Printing Office).

26. For a MITI perception of the structural problem, see Seiji Hoshida, "Kyoku ryoku kajo-ron o haisu," *Toyo keizai* (July 2, 1965), pp. 8–12.

27. See Martin Bronfenbrenner, "Economic Miracles and Japan's Income Doubling Plan," in William W. Lockwood, ed., *The State and Economic Enterprise in Japan: Essays in the Political Economy of Growth* (Princeton University Press, 1965), pp. 523–53. Kozo Yamamura, *Economic Policy in Postwar Japan: Growth Versus Economic Democracy* (University of California Press, 1967), pp. 70–109, analyzes the tendency of the rapid growth policies of this period to promote excess capacity.

interest rates and significantly increasing the government budget in order to stimulate the economy. Because of the sharp fall in government revenues resulting from the recession, increasing the budget meant that the government had to resort to deficit spending for the first time in the postwar period. The easy money policy and this deficit spending caused the CPI to rise by 7.7 percent in 1965, the largest increase in fifteen years.

Though they were put through at the cost of inflation, these policies appeared effective. Excess capacities were soon eliminated, aided by the boost these policies gave to domestic demand and, with productivity continuing to increase and the value of the yen fixed at a level that more and more economists believed undervalued the yen, international demand began to climb again. The economy was back on the rapid growth track.

However, 1965 should have warned the policymakers that the Japanese economy like the cyclist being made to carry an increasingly heavy burden would have to pedal harder and harder in order to avoid falling. Few had asked whether the continuing progrowth policy would further increase total capacity and thus the risk of another round of structural recession. Japan seemed able to pedal on with ever-increasing vigor. Domestic demand was again strong and the increasing productivity continued to capture a larger share of the world market, which was rapidly expanding due to the prosperity of the world economy and especially that of the U.S. economy of the Great Society and the Vietnam War.

The average growth rates for the next four years (1966–69) were normal—above 10 percent. Capital investment resumed its former pace and exports climbed steadily, led by electronic products, steel, heavy machinery, and automobiles. With the growth rate and tax revenues rising again, the LDP-MOF pledge to reduce dependency on government bonds could still be honored. Though the dependency rate—the proportion of government expenditures financed by the deficit—rose to 14.9 percent and 13.8 percent for 1966 and 1967, it was steadily reduced to 4.2 percent by 1970. And the CPI for the 1966–69 period rose only about 5 percent per year. Takeo Fukuda, a fiscal conservative and former chief of the Budget Bureau of the MOF, remained finance minister. During the second half of the 1960s, *Ekonomisuto* and *Toyo keizai,* the leading economic weeklies, carried only a small number of articles on the dangers of inflation, most of them discussing the relative merits of the demand-pull and cost-push theories. Statistics on growth, investment, exports, and prices appeared to indicate that battles, planned and led by the LDP, the able bureaucracy, and the major firms, were still being won in the total war for rapid growth with tolerable, mild inflation.

It was becoming evident, however, that the ground on which the complex politicoeconomic machinery had functioned so well was undergoing a major shift because the costs of rapid growth were becoming increasingly apparent and were more readily felt. One of these costs was the pollution of both air and water, which increased rapidly throughout the 1960s. It caused a wide variety of debilitating and sometimes fatal illnesses, and the destruction of nature was evidenced by destroyed fishing grounds, polluted streams, and dying forests. Another cost was the real and perceived sacrifice imposed directly on consumers as the result of LDP policies. Consumer movements led by housewives accused the oligopolistic television-set producers of exporting their products at a significantly lower price than they charged in the domestic market for identical products. These consumers then went on to challenge the high prices of rice, beef, butter, and many other commodities that were in effect set politically, either directly (as in the case of rice) or indirectly, by import quotas imposed on cheaper imports.[28] Price fixing by numerous legal and MITI-administered extralegal cartels and by extensive legal retail price-maintenance practices also came under heavy attack; the elite structure frequently found itself challenged.[29]

There were other signs of a ground shift. A sizable minority of Japanese began to feel that even with continued economic growth, their relative income and social status was not changing as they had hoped. The wage levels of employees of small and medium-sized firms, though rising, continued to remain below those of their counterparts in the largest firms; temporary employees of large firms worked on a semipermanent basis without the benefits and protection of company unions; more and more blue and white collar employees failed to climb the ladder of success because they had attended the wrong schools; even the seemingly successful salaried men of large firms found themselves commuting to work for two or more hours a day on crowded trains, between their high-pressure offices and their small, cramped houses. This undoubtedly was one of the

28. Kozo Yamamura, "Structure Is Behavior: An Appraisal of Japanese Economic Policy, 1960 to 1972," in Isaiah Frank, ed., *The Japanese Economy in International Perspective* (Johns Hopkins University Press, 1975), pp. 68–81.

29. Yasumasa Kuroda, "Protest Movements in Japan: A New Politics," *Asian Survey*, vol. 12 (November 1972), pp. 647–52; Maurine A. Kirkpatrick, "Consumerism and Japan's New Citizen Politics," *Asian Survey*, vol. 15 (March 1975), pp. 234–46.

Table 14-3. *The Decline of the Liberal Democratic Party's Dominance of the Japanese Diet, 1960–83*

Year	LDP representation in lower house			
	Number elected	Percent of total membership	Thousands of votes received	Percent of total vote received
1960	296	63.4	22,740	57.56
1963	283	60.6	22,424	54.67
1967	277	57.0	22,448	48.80
1969	288	59.2	22,382	47.63
1972	271	55.2	24,563	46.85
1976	249	48.7	23,653	41.32
1979	248	48.5	24,084	44.17
1980	284	55.6	28,262	47.88
1983	250	48.9	25,982	45.76

	LDP representation in upper house (percent of total vote received)	
	National constituencies	Local constituencies
1962	46.4	47.1
1965	47.2	44.2
1968	46.7	44.9
1971	44.4	43.9
1974	44.3	39.5
1977	35.9	39.5
1980	42.5	43.3

Sources: Michael K. Blaker, ed., *Japan at the Polls: The House of Councillors Election of 1974* (Washington: American Enterprise Institute for Public Policy Research, 1976), p. 148; Philip H. Trezise with Yukio Suzuki, "Politics, Government, and Economic Growth in Japan," in Hugh Patrick and Henry Rosovsky, eds., *Asia's New Giant: How the Japanese Economy Works* (Brookings Institution, 1976), p. 778; *Asahi shimbun,* December 7, 1976, and December 20, 1983.

major reasons why a rapidly increasing number of the salaried men were now deserting the LDP.

The desertion was reflected in the declining share of seats held by the LDP in both legislative chambers. In the elections for the lower house, votes for the LDP fell from 57.56 percent of the total cast in 1960 to 47.63 in 1969. Similarly, shares of LDP votes in the local constituencies of the upper house dwindled. Only in the national upper house constituencies did the LDP manage to hold its own (see table 14-3). However, thanks to the nonproportional electoral system which favored the LDP's candidates from agricultural electoral districts and penalized the opposition candidates in the larger electoral districts in urban centers, this decline in the LDP votes did not immediately threaten LDP control of the legislature.

In 1969, for example, the LDP still held 288 out of 473 seats (59.2 percent) in the lower house. Also aiding the LDP was the fact that the opposition was fragmented and the major contender, the Japan Socialist party, was in a virtually constant state of internal disunity because of frequent leadership and ideological struggles and received only about 30 percent of the votes in 1969.

The decline in support for the LDP was not caused by a relative deterioration in the economic position of the dissatisfied. In fact, their relative position was improving—income distribution became more equal across various income classes throughout the 1960s, and the progressivity in the burden of tax incidence remained virtually unchanged during the second half of the decade.[30] Also, surveys administered by the prime minister's office showed that around 85 percent of Japanese believed, during the second half of the 1960s, that their living standard was either rising or remaining at least the same as in the previous year.[31]

The cause for the increasing defection of those who had once voted LDP was a perceived deviation between the promise inherent in the rapid growth and the reality of pollution, inadequate social welfare and housing, increased traffic accidents, success in entrance examinations that seemed to depend on parents' ability to pay the high costs of private tutoring, and the numerous obvious favors that continued to be granted to industry, in the name of economic growth, by the LDP government. For the LDP to remain in power, it had to cling to the votes of as many people as possible, especially the blue and white collar workers, whose rising expectations were remaining unfulfilled. The political dominance of the LDP could continue only as long as it retained a sufficient number of supporters in its political camp and could continue to rely on the support of the farmers, big business, and the owners of small and medium-sized firms plus the successful self-employed and the professionals.

It was against this background that the LDP-controlled Diet rapidly increased social welfare expenditures during the 1965–69 period. With this heavy additional burden on a budget strained by an equally pressing need to stimulate the economy, the result was deficit spending. Total social security expenditures in the budget—covering public assistance,

---

30. Hiromitsu Ishi, "Wagakuni shotoku kaisobetsu zeifutan-ritsu no jittai," *Gendai keizai*, vol. 29 (Winter 1977), pp. 106–19; Hiromitsu Ishi, "Sozei kozo no antei koka," *Keizai kenkyu*, vol. 26 (January 1975), pp. 22–23; Akira Ono and Tsunehiko Watanabe, "Changes in Income Inequality in the Japanese Economy," in Patrick, *Japanese Industrialization*, pp. 363–89.

31. Japan, Prime Minister's Office, *Kokumin seikatsu ni kansuru seron chosa*, annual issues.

social security payments to the retired and the aged, social welfare programs, public health services, and various payments to the unemployed—nearly doubled, increasing from ¥545.8 billion in 1965 to ¥994.3 billion in 1969. The largest increase, from ¥155.1 billion to ¥343.7 billion for national health programs, reflected the government's decision to pay a larger proportion of the total medical costs of persons in the program. The share of social security expenditures within the budget remained relatively stable, at the 14–15 percent range, because the budget itself was increasing sharply in absolute magnitude.

As the increasing political importance of the farmers to the LDP was demonstrated in each election, the LDP became ever more active in providing them with higher prices for their rice and with other measures designed to increase their income. The fiscal burden of these politically necessary measures rose steadily, as consumption of rice declined while productivity and total output increased,[32] and the base on which parity was calculated—the real income of wage earners—rose. In short, the government had to make up an increasingly large gap between the supported price and the market price, which the LDP was reluctant to raise for fear of incurring further wrath from the consumers, on a steadily increasing total output of rice. And the market price was in fact the price that resulted from the policy of limiting imports of cheaper rice from abroad.[33]

The price of rice paid by the government to producers per 150 kilograms rose from ¥16,375 in 1965 to ¥20,640 in 1969. The price hike for the 1967 harvest was the largest of these years, raising the 1966 price of ¥17,850 to ¥19,493 (or by 9.2 percent), principally because the general election of the lower house in 1966 took place as the price was being determined.[34] Over the five-year period the total outlay for this subsidy rose from ¥120.5 billion to ¥295.0 billion. The subsidy went from 32.56 percent of the total budget of the Ministry of Agriculture in 1965 to 38.63 percent in 1969 and was the major reason that the ministry's annual expenditures increased from ¥3,700 billion to ¥7,688 billion over that period.[35] By 1969 the subsidy accounted for nearly 5 percent of the total national budget.

32. The total output of rice rose from 12.7 million tons in 1965 to 14.0 million tons in 1969.

33. Donnelly, "Setting the Price of Rice," pp. 167–80.

34. Japan, Ministry of Agriculture and Forestry, *Poketto norin suisan tokei* (Government Printing Office), annual issues.

35. Association for Publication of Agricultural Statistics, *Nihon nogyo nenkan* (Ie no Hikari Kyokai), annual issues.

Industry continued to receive its accustomed share of LDP concern. During the second half of the 1960s, the LDP and MITI, both anxious to keep the economy growing, had little trouble finding reasons for adopting probusiness policies. Mergers among the largest firms increased, with little or no opposition from the Fair Trade Commission (FTC), and both the recession and rationalization cartels increased in number, as did extralegal cartels created through the "administrative guidance" of MITI.[36]

Typifying the LDP policy was its sanction of the merger between Fuji and Yawata, Japan's largest and third largest steel manufacturers. When the request for the merger was presented to the FTC, strong objections were raised by academic economists, the opposition parties, consumer groups, and journalists. However, the LDP and MITI argued that the firms would realize economies of scale in research and development efforts, in the distribution of products, and in the adoption of a larger and more efficient productive capacity. Given the political pressure from MITI, various industries, and key members of the LDP, the FTC had little choice but to grant permission to merge.[37]

Most of the government provisions for economic assistance to business that had been in effect during the 1953–65 period were continued and, in most instances, applied even more generously in the late 1960s, and by 1969 the debt-to-equity ratio had risen to 80.4 from 76.2 in 1965. The largest firms had little difficulty in obtaining their capital at a relatively low disequilibrium rate in the money market.[38] In addition, a growing number of measures aided small and medium-sized firms; government expenditures to aid technological development approached ¥100 billion per year by the end of the 1960s,[39] and movement toward liberalization of barriers against imports and foreign investment was slow.[40]

As the LDP pursued measures intended to reduce the defection of wage earners to opposition parties and to protect its traditional political base, those very policies were causing troublesome structural problems in some industries; reinforcing trends of price rigidity for some manufactured products; intensifying international difficulties (trade balance and trade

36. Yamamura, "Structure Is Behavior," pp. 67–100.

37. Ibid., pp. 81–83.

38. Ibid., p. 71.

39. Calculated from Japan, Science and Technology Agency, *Kagaku gijutsu hakusho* (Government Printing Office), annual issues. See Merton J. Peck with Shuji Tamura, "Technology," in Patrick and Rosovsky, *Asia's New Giant,* pp. 532–34.

40. Kanematsu, "Sekai keizai," pp. 131–34; Lawrence B. Krause and Sueo Sekiguchi, "Japan and the World Economy," in Patrick and Rosovsky, *Asia's New Giant,* pp. 417–28.

conflicts, exposure of the capital market, risks of imported inflation); and tightening the labor market. The structural problems were becoming increasingly difficult to avoid in several industries where growth depended on ever-increasing investments in export-oriented and capital goods.[41] Rapid growth, which was increasing industrial capacity at an annual rate of 15 percent, depended on near-capacity production of capital goods and uninterrupted sale of capital and consumer goods both in Japan and abroad. And, an important reason contributing to the near-capacity operation of industries had been Japanese exports, which continued to increase by 14 percent each year, twice the rate of the increase in world trade.[42] Japan had somehow to overcome the arithmetic fact that a 10 percent increase in the late 1960s was, in absolute terms, much larger than a 10 percent increase on the much smaller base of the late 1950s.

In shipbuilding, electronics, machinery, iron and steel, and several other major industries, new technology had enabled the Japanese to match or surpass the productivity of Western competitors by the end of the 1960s, but fewer and fewer industries could count on this means of shortening the life of the capital goods they were rapidly accumulating. Yet under the terms of the MITI guidance, firms were in many cases advised to invest in new capacity to maintain their market shares. The result was a consistent tendency toward excess capacity.[43]

To blunt the burden of collective excess capacity, more industries asked for, and were granted, permission to form cartels to agree on prices and rates of capacity utilization. The inevitable result was a further concentration of the market structure and downward rigidity in the price of many manufactured products. The cartel prices of capital goods produced by large firms in several major, highly concentrated industries tended to raise the price of domestic consumer goods both directly and indirectly. And price rigidity in consumer products and services also began to become

41. Edward F. Denison and William K. Chung, "Economic Growth and Its Sources," in Patrick and Rosovsky, *Asia's New Giant,* pp. 67–125.

42. Krause and Sekiguchi, "Japan and the World Economy," pp. 398–402. "In a Japan heavily dependent on imported raw materials, economic growth could not proceed without increases in imports, and exports are needed to pay for them. Furthermore, export competitiveness became a goal of government policy and private investment behavior. Since the industries that are able to export are also the ones with the highest rates of productivity increase, economic growth has been generated in practice through structural shifts toward industries that export a sizable portion of their output. In addition, although foreign demand at times of cyclical recoveries has been of great importance in encouraging output, most of the time Japanese growth has been stimulated by domestic demand." Ibid., p. 398.

43. Richard E. Caves with Masu Uekusa, "Industrial Organization," in Patrick and Rosovsky, *Asia's New Giant,* pp. 486–89; Kozo Yamamura, "Success That Soured: Administrative Guidance and Cartels in Japan," in Yamamura, *Policy and Trade Issues,* pp. 77–112.

increasingly apparent as a growing number of cartels was authorized among small and medium-sized firms and among retail stores.[44]

In the second half of the 1960s, Japan's position in the international economy entered a new phase. No longer a small economy struggling to balance its trade, Japan had become a large industrial power with a consistent trade surplus. This was a new experience and a source of mounting problems for policymakers. The trade surplus tended to exert pressure on aggregate demand while the monetary authority was less than fully effective in sterilizing the increments in the surplus. As a result, the rate of increase in the supply of high-powered money continued to climb.[45] Part of the difficulty arose from liberalization measures that Japan had been forced to accept since the early 1960s. Japan's effort to carry out a tight money policy proved less effective as its short-term rate went higher, attracting short-term capital from abroad, and other policies to force the economy to trot caused imports to decline, thus aggravating the trade surplus. In addition, a clear trend toward inflation became unmistakable during the mid-1960s in Japan's largest trade partner, the United States, making the task of the Japanese monetary authority even more difficult.

An obvious solution to these developments that were threatening price stability in Japan would have been a revaluation of the yen. But this option, strongly advocated by academic economists, had few supporters. Export industries and the industries competing against imports—whose political muscle was considerable—opposed revaluation. The Bank of Japan, which might have been expected to push for revaluation because of the declining value of the foreign currency reserves it held, officially continued to stand against revaluation.[46] An important reason for this was that the MOF compensated for any losses suffered by the Bank due to depreciation of the foreign currency reserve and the Bank, which in effect was controlled by the MOF, continued to follow the MOF's wishes, which in turn reflected the wishes of the LDP and its industrial supporters.

Neither the wage earners nor the opposition parties supported revaluation either. Real wages had risen by 10 percent per year in 1968 and 1969 after a few years of lagging increases, and wage earners were fearful that revaluation would bring about a stagnant economy and a slower rate

44. Yamamura, "Structure Is Behavior," pp. 83–88.

45. Yasukichi Yasuba, "Imported Inflation and the Upward Revaluation of the Yen, 1965–1974," in Jacob S. Dreyer, ed., *Breadth and Depth in Economics: Fritz Machlup—The Man and His Ideas* (Lexington Books, 1978), pp. 225–26.

46. Ibid., p. 227.

of increase in wages. Reflecting this sentiment, the opposition parties spoke out against revaluation. The only clear losers from the continuing inflation were the savers, but their voices, unarticulated and unorganized, remained muffled. At any rate, a large portion of the savers were wage earners whose gains from the growing economy often more than compensated for their losses in savings. Thus, as late as the summer of 1969 when the wholesale price index was rising at an annual rate of 2.1 percent (as against a 0.9 percent rate a year before) and reserves were increasing at an accelerating rate, the outcries of economists to stop the welfare losses occurring from the undervalued yen failed to sway the nation's decisionmakers. Japan's trade surplus continued to increase, causing the governments of the very recipients of the welfare gains—the United States and other trading partners of Japan—to complain bitterly. In the United States, protectionist sentiments were rising, and Japan's steel producers were forced to adopt voluntary quotas. But Japan hoped somehow to weather the difficulties and cling to the strategy that so far had served so well.[47]

Another fundamental change that became obvious during the second half of the 1960s was the increasing tightness of the labor market. Japan had been meeting the need for growing amounts of labor by shifting labor from less productive to more productive sectors and had benefited from the baby boom of the immediate postwar years, but her labor reserves were exhausted. The ratio of placements to new openings—often used by Japanese labor economists instead of unemployment figures— had declined steadily from 73.7 percent in 1956 to 31.8 percent in 1966, and in 1969 it stood at 19.3 percent.[48] The wage differential between the large- and small-firm sectors was significantly narrowed, and at the entrance level for middle school and high school graduates, more and more small and medium-sized firms were being forced to pay wages even higher than those paid by the largest firms. The tightening labor market was "pulling up earnings of underprivileged workers such as those in small firms, the unskilled and females."[49] More and more wage settlements were stated in absolute amounts rather than percentages, further contributing to the wage equalization. As the number of bankruptcies among small and

47. Kanematsu, "Sekai keizai," pp. 129–34.
48. Japan, Ministry of Labor, *Rodo hakusho* (Government Printing Office), annual issues.
49. Galenson and Odaka, "Japanese Labor Market," in Patrick and Rosovsky, *Asia's New Giant*, p. 606.

medium-sized firms rose, the increased burden of wage costs was cited as the primary cause.

After nearly two decades of rapid growth, the politicoeconomic machinery was showing signs of faltering. The war was no longer total. Even the continuing good news of productivity increases and rapid growth with moderate inflation could no longer summon unquestioned enthusiasm for the war effort.

The Demand Gap in the 1970s

In the latter 1970s the prolonged recession triggered by the oil crisis did not transmit the increasing deficit spending into rapid inflation. But policymakers, who had just undergone the experience of galloping inflation during 1973–74 (including a 24.5 percent increase in the consumer price index),[50] were understandably concerned with the risks to price stability that the deficit presented. However, there was little they could do to reduce the accumulating red ink. The problems faced by the LDP and the bureaucracy were multiplying because of worldwide recession and because, in a fundamental sense, Japanese leaders were forced to face the consequences of policies that had been adopted to wage the total economic war of the preceding two decades. Japan was discovering that it was extremely difficult to sustain rapid growth. Though Japan continued to do well relative to other industrial nations, her growth rate declined and the optimism that it would somehow continue to grow rapidly could no longer be maintained.

Just as the LDP's economic hand lacked strong cards, so did its political hand. In both houses of the Diet the percentage of the total votes it garnered fell. And in the 1976 election some LDP candidates had to compete against the New Liberal Club, a splinter party created by six former LDP members of the Diet. As a result, Takeo Fukuda was elected prime minister by a margin of only one vote in the Diet. All this meant that, for the LDP to remain in power, the party had to redouble its efforts to stem the desertion of votes.[51]

These economic and political trends were the direct cause of steadily rising deficit spending during the decade. The prolonged recession after

---

50. Given the central goal of this chapter and the intent of this section, the causes of the galloping inflation of 1974 are not analyzed here.

51. *Asahi shimbun*, December 7, 1976, and July 15 and 27, 1977.

1973 provided a potent economic rationale for it and the declining political strength of the LDP worked to accelerate the pace. A shortfall in demand equal to around 20 percent of total capacity (or about 10 percent of GNP) and amounting, for example, to about ¥20 trillion in 1978 (as against the GNP of ¥210 trillion) reduced investment and increased unemployment and the trade surplus (by reducing imports). To reduce that demand gap, Japan could have increased exports, consumption, private capital investment (mostly housing), current government expenditure, and investment. Increases in exports could not have been adopted as a measure to stimulate the economy, however, because of the existing large trade surplus and a high risk of further antagonizing Japan's trade partners.[52] During the early 1970s, tax cuts were relied on, but the high propensity of the Japanese to save (22.8 percent of disposable income in 1978) made them an ineffective means of closing the demand gap. The government therefore chose to increase deficit spending. Even at ¥10 trillion, deficit spending was considerably less than the personal savings of well over ¥22 trillion in 1977–78; with corporate borrowing at less than ¥0.5 trillion and capital exports not exceeding ¥4 trillion,[53] deficit spending was a politically easy prescription to adopt and readily justifiable on economic grounds. And few could fault the economic logic of the prescription within the perspective of the 1974–78 period.

Vocal demand for deficit spending came from the leaders of the *zaikai,* whose pressure on the LDP to stimulate the economy grew increasingly more intense in the 1970s, especially after the oil crisis of 1973. The voices of the troubled iron and steel, shipbuilding, chemical, and other industries grew louder, demanding large deficit spending to close the demand gap. The *zaikai* and industrial interests have a powerful influence because their contributions to any one of several faction leaders within the LDP help to determine the outcome of the election of the party's leader. It was no accident that Premier Tanaka, who adopted a vigorous stimulation policy, was well funded and had little difficulty in maintaining a large coalition within the party. And Mr. Fukuda was certainly fully aware that the tenure of Premier Miki (his predecessor) was only slightly more than a year partly because of what the *zaikai* believed to be Miki's excessive caution in stimulating the economy.

The demand gap had to be reduced or closed if the LDP was to prevent

52. Hisao Kanamori, "Nihon keizai e no shohosen," *Voice* (Tokyo) (November 1978), pp. 40–49.
53. Ibid., pp. 43–46.

further desertion of the wage-earning urban voters. The party, having dominated postwar politics, could hardly deflect the blame for the mounting economic problems. Wage earners who criticized the costs of rapid growth during the 1960s disliked the slow-growing economy even more because it meant slower increases in real wages, slower promotions, less desirable employment, and, above all, a potential threat to their jobs. The rapid inflation of the early 1970s added fuel to their discontent. That there was virtually no increase in real wages in 1974 was a rude shock to Japan's wage earners, who in the preceding decade had become accustomed to annual increases of almost 10 percent.

Neither could the LDP afford not to stimulate the economy, since unemployment, especially threatening to older workers (more of whom voted for the LDP than did their sons), grew in magnitude and became a major political issue by 1976. However large the costs of subsidizing "home leave," a form of short-term layoff practiced by many large industrial firms, and of aiding the "reorganization" of major bankrupt firms (especially when these firms, usually in such industries as shipbuilding and iron and steel, are geographically concentrated in the electoral districts of LDP members), the LDP could ill afford not to be generous. Just as a recession is detrimental to a party's chances of staying in power in the United States, the effects of slow growth in Japan, if prolonged, could be fatal to the LDP's majority party status.

A changing public perception of the quality of life was unmistakable. The pattern of answers to the question "Do you think the general quality of your life [considering income, environment and other factors] is about the same as the past year, has improved, or has worsened?" changed visibly after 1973, the year in which rapid inflation began and economic growth decelerated. The proportion viewing the quality of their life as having improved declined from about 30 percent in the second half of the 1960s to about 10 percent, while the proportion of the respondents who felt the quality of their life had deteriorated nearly doubled from the 10–13 percent range in 1976 to the 21–24 percent range in 1977.[54]

Farmers continued to press their demands, and the LDP had no choice but to cater to the wishes of this group in exchange for their votes. That the farm votes were as crucial to the LDP as the *zaikai*'s financial contributions can readily be seen in the results of the 1976 Diet election (table 14-4). The LDP was able to obtain only low percentages of the

54. *Kokumin seikatsu ni kansuru seron chosa*, annual issues, 1969–77.

Table 14-4. *Share of Votes and Number of Seats Won by Each Party in the 1976 Election of Japan's Lower House, by Type of Constituency*

Party	Metropolitan[a]		Urban[b]		Semiurban[c]		Semirural[d]		Rural[e]	
	Percent of total votes	Number of seats	Percent of total votes	Number of seats	Percent of total votes	Number of seats	Percent of total votes	Number of seats	Percent of total votes	Number of seats
Liberal-Democratic	17.76	35	14.89	46	39.38	39	48.95	56	44.09	64
Socialist	13.90	22	19.96	31	12.48	13	19.33	24	21.10	34
Clean Government	15.80	26	5.22	10	7.42	7	5.19	5	2.69	4
Communist	6.57	11	0.73	1	1.04	1	0	0	0.61	1
Democratic-Socialist	7.86	12	10.35	9	3.38	4	2.70	3	1.34	2
New Liberal Club	7.80	10	0.50	1	5.97	3	0	0	0	0
Other	1.27	3	1.69	4	0.66	1	5.79	5	4.54	7

Source: Blaker, *Japan at the Polls*, p. 40.

a. Based on 15,420,754 votes (21.91 percent of the nationwide vote) cast in Tokyo, Kanagawa, Kyoto, Osaka, Hyogo; LDP winners received 3.89 percent of the nationwide vote.

b. Based on 13,582,825 votes (19.29 percent of the nationwide vote) cast in Hokkaido, Saitama, Chiba Aichi, Hiroshima, Fukuoka; LDP winners received 2.87 percent of the nationwide vote.

c. Based on 7,569,337 votes (10.75 percent of the nationwide vote) cast in Aomori, Miyagi, Ishikawa, Shizuoka, Nara, Wakayama, Yamaguchi, Ehime, Kochi, Nagasaki, Okinawa; LDP winners received 4.24 percent of the nationwide vote.

d. Based on 8,075,530 votes (11.47 percent of the nationwide vote) cast in Gumma, Niigata, Gifu, Mie, Okayama, Kagawa, Kumamoto, Oita, Miyazaki, Kagoshima; LDP winners received 5.62 percent of the nationwide vote.

e. Based on 10,310,605 votes (14.64 percent of the nationwide vote) cast in Iwate, Akita, Yamagata, Fukushima, Ibaragi, Tochigi, Toyama, Fukui, Yamanashi, Nagano, Shiga, Tottori, Shimane, Saga, Tokushima; LDP winners received 6.46 percent of the nationwide vote.

total votes cast in metropolitan and urban constituencies, as opposed to well over 40 percent in semirural and rural constituencies. Out of the total of 249 LDP members of the Diet (including 9 who were elected as independents), 120 came from the latter constituencies. Nearly 60 percent of the Diet seats were allocated to these constituencies, and the LDP candidates were elected on less than 50 percent of the votes cast in both semirural and rural constituencies.

These "agricultural" LDP members owed their seats to the voters of rural electoral districts whose votes constituted at most 12 percent of the total votes cast. Each farm vote, in short, was worth more than two nonfarm votes. All this is even more dramatically shown in the fact that while one LDP candidate from semirural Niigata prefecture was elected with 37,107 votes, a Communist party candidate from urban Osaka who received 114,662 votes failed to be elected.[55] This is the key to the farmers' seemingly disproportionate ability to demand and get subsidies. It is also the key to the reluctance of the Japanese to permit increased imports of American agricultural products.

Pressures continued in 1977 and 1978 from rice farmers who every year came to Tokyo en masse during the summer and early fall to petition the Diet members they had elected and to demonstrate in the city streets. Their slogan for 1977 was to the point: "Let's cash in on the support we gave them in the upper house election [of 1977]." A large number of farmers came from distant prefectures because they were aware that the Rice Price Deliberation Council, a government-appointed body, had not been able to agree on the price to be paid to farmers because of the opposition to higher rice prices voiced both by council members who represented consumers and by members who were neutral ("men of learning and experience on agricultural matters").[56] Farmers were well aware that political pressure is a deciding factor in determining the price of rice.

The necessity of continued stimulation was not exclusively a domestic matter. By late 1977, a growth rate of 7 percent was an international promise made by Prime Minister Fukuda to the Americans who were, more than in preceding years, insistent on a growing Japanese economy that could buy more American goods. Because of the importance of the American market in Japan's continued growth and in maintaining the

55. *Asahi shimbun,* December 7, 1976.
56. ibid., July 15 and 27, 1977.

Table 14-5. *Distribution of Funds in Japan's Annual Budget, 1971–77*
Billions of yen and, in parentheses, percent of total

Category	1971	1972	1973	1974	1975	1976	1977
National administration	636.1	803.5	900.3	1,195.7	1,358.9	1,534.6	1,661.7
	(6.65)	(6.73)	(6.09)	(6.26)	(6.51)	(6.22)	(5.82)
Local government	1,986.5	2,410.6	3,255.2	4,219.9	3,398.0	3,972.9	4,968.9
	(20.77)	(20.20)	(22.02)	(22.09)	(16.28)	(16.11)	(17.42)
National defense	693.6	813.4	960.8	1,234.2	1,396.9	1,535.6	1,705.9
	(7.25)	(6.81)	(6.50)	(6.46)	(6.69)	(6.22)	(5.98)
Disposition of external affairs	23.6	25.2	20.2	23.6	19.8	6.6	1.6
	(0.24)	(0.21)	(0.13)	(0.12)	(0.09)	(0.02)	(.005)
Preservation and development of natural resources	1,791.7	2,478.8	2,385.6	2,792.2	3,148.7	3,365.8	3,788.7
	(18.73)	(20.77)	(16.14)	(14.61)	(15.09)	(13.65)	(13.28)
Agriculture, commerce, and industry	1,117.9	1,340.7	1,989.5	2,389.3	2,370.9	2,652.3	2,780.8
	(11.69)	(11.23)	(13.46)	(12.50)	(11.36)	(10.75)	(9.75)
Education and culture	1,099.6	1,310.3	1,587.4	2,237.6	2,707.5	3,058.1	3,430.1
	(11.50)	(10.98)	(10.74)	(11.71)	(12.97)	(12.40)	(12.02)
Social security	1,495.7	1,880.0	2,483.1	3,526.4	4,135.6	4,807.6	5,691.9
	(15.64)	(15.75)	(16.80)	(18.46)	(19.82)	(19.50)	(19.96)
Pensions	331.2	367.8	483.8	589.9	759.0	987.7	1,162.0
	(3.46)	(3.08)	(3.27)	(3.07)	(3.63)	(4.00)	(4.07)
National debt	320.6	454.3	684.9	847.0	1,102.4	1,843.0	2,348.7
	(3.35)	(3.80)	(4.63)	(4.43)	(5.28)	(7.47)	(8.23)
Reserves	...	...	...	...	200.0	290.0	286.6
					(0.95)	(1.17)	(1.00)
Other	64.7	47.7	27.4	44.0	60.7	79.2	116.0
	(0.67)	(0.39)	(0.18)	(0.23)	(0.29)	(0.32)	(0.40)
Total	9,561.1	11,932.2	14,778.3	19,099.8	20,860.9	24,650.2	28,514.3

Source: Japan, Ministry of Finance, *Final Budget Report*, various years.

LDP's (and especially Premier Fukuda's) political power, all efforts had to be made to keep this international promise.

The cost of the LDP efforts to prevent an acceleration of the mounting discontent of the wage earners and to retain the support of the *zaikai* and the rural voters can be best seen in the national budget of these years (table 14-5). The total budget rose sharply during the 1971–77 period, the annual increase averaging 20.15 percent in contrast to an annual average growth rate of 15.31 percent in nominal GNP. Contributing to the growth of the budget were steady increases in all expenditure categories except disposition of external affairs. The most visible increase was for social security. Its share of the budget rose from less than 16 percent in 1971 to nearly 20 percent in 1977. In absolute amounts it became the largest item in the 1977 budget, while it was third largest in the former. As seen in table 14-6, this expenditure grew most rapidly among the seven largest categories of expenditures. The jump of 42 percent seen between 1973 and 1974 resulted because the LDP government sharply boosted its social welfare programs in 1973, in what it termed "the first year of the Welfare State." The government raised the monthly payment to the aged and the retired; substantially increased the coverage of social welfare programs to include more of the aged, the retired, and the sick than previously; and boosted the share of the payments made by the government under the provisions of the national health programs.[57] The steady increases in pensions in tables 14-5 and 14-6 also reflect the LDP policy goal of preventing further erosion of its political base.

Much of the increase in the local government, preservation and development of natural resources, and agriculture, commerce, and industry categories was due to the LDP intent to stimulate the economy. More than half of the expenditures in the first two categories were made in order to help boost the economy rather than to meet the administrative needs of local governments or merely to preserve natural resources. The growth of defense expenditures, too, reflected at least in part the LDP desire to stimulate the industries that were most directly affected by increasing the military procurements. As table 14-6 shows, the average annual growth rate of all of these expenditure categories exceeded 15 percent. Approximately one-third of the rapid increase in the agriculture, commerce, and industry category was due to the steady increase in the

57. Akira Fujita, "Wagakuni zaisei-kozo no henka," *Gendai keizai*, vol. 29 (Winter 1977), pp. 26–41; Japan, Economic Planning Agency, *Keizai hakusho* (Ministry of Finance Printing Office, 1973), pp. 195–202.

Table 14-6. *Annual Growth Rate of Japan's Budget, by Expenditure Category, 1972–77*

Percent

Category	Annual growth						Mean growth, 1972–77
	1972	1973	1974	1975	1976	1977	
National administration	26.31	12.04	32.81	13.64	12.92	8.28	17.67
Local government	21.34	35.04	29.63	−19.47	16.91	25.06	18.09
National defense	17.24	18.12	28.45	13.18	9.92	11.09	16.33
Disposition of external affairs	6.77	−19.84	16.83	−16.10	−66.66	−75.75	−25.79
Preservation and development of natural resources	38.34	−3.75	17.04	12.76	6.89	12.56	13.97
Agriculture, commerce, and industry	19.93	48.39	20.09	−0.77	11.86	4.84	17.39
Education and culture	19.16	21.13	40.96	21.00	12.94	12.16	21.23
Social security	25.69	32.07	42.01	17.27	16.24	18.39	25.28
Pensions	11.05	31.53	21.93	28.66	30.13	17.64	23.49
National debt	41.70	50.75	23.66	30.15	67.18	27.43	40.15
Reserves	. . .	. . .	. . .	. . .	45.00	−1.17	21.91
Other	−26.27	−42.55	60.58	37.95	30.47	46.46	17.77

Source: Japan, Ministry of Finance, *Final Budget Report*, various years.

rice price and other subsidies. The total subsidy to rice producers alone rose from ¥292 billion in 1971 to ¥909 billion in 1977, as the supported producers' price went from ¥21,305 per 150 kilograms to ¥41,100, an annual average increase of 15.5 percent as against an average rate of increase in the CPI of 12.6 percent.

But the 1970s were unlike the golden 1960s when tax receipts were rising rapidly. The slowed pace of economic growth meant smaller increases in revenues. For both economic and political reasons, taxes needed to be cut and were in fact reduced in 1970–71, 1972, and 1976. The LDP, faced with rising expenditures, had only one course left to follow—deficit spending. Aided by the ease with which justification could be provided for deficit spending—to rescue Japan from economic stagnation—and by the fact that the opposition parties, too, were eager to see increases in social security expenditures and the recovery of the economy, the dependency ratio, which had been reduced to 4.2 percent in 1970, rose again rapidly to the 11–16 percent range during the 1971–74 period and then to a fraction short of 30 percent in both 1976 and 1977 (table 14-7). As minister of finance, Fukuda had vowed in 1966 that the unhealthy, high bond dependency ratio of over 10 percent would be looked on as a temporary evil,[58] but in 1977 as prime minister he had little choice but to promote a deficit three times the unhealthy level of 10 percent. The pain of promoting such policies was eased considerably, however, by Western leaders who in 1976 and 1977 impressed on him the crucial imperative that the Japanese economy perform the role of locomotive in pulling the world out of stagflation.

Pressure to increase spending continued into fiscal 1978, and in late 1977 the Fukuda cabinet had no recourse but to increase the total budget by more than 20.3 percent, even though it meant that Fukuda's already once-revised promise to limit the bond dependency ratio to 30 percent had to be exceeded by 7 points. The major cause for this jump, of course, was the sharply increased stimulation expenditures. Expenditures in local government and in the preservation and development of natural resources—two categories of budget items that contributed both directly and indirectly to stimulation of economic activities—rose by 34.5 percent, to ¥5.45 trillion, over the same expenditures in the 1977 budget.[59]

Another major factor contributing to the size of the 1978 budget was the social security item, which seemed almost to have a life of its own.

58. Campbell, *Contemporary Japanese Budget Politics*, p. 239.
59. *Asahi shimbun*, September 12, 1977; *Japan Times Weekly*, December 31, 1977.

Table 14-7. *Annual Issues of Bonds to Finance Japan's Government,*
1965–83

Year	Total bonds issued (billions of yen)	Dependency ratio (percent)[a]	Long-term bonds outstanding (billions of yen)[b]
1965	197.2	5.3	745.7
1966	665.6	14.9	1,476.1
1967	709.4	13.8	2,213.5
1968	462.1	7.7	2,732.8
1969	412.6	5.9	3,135.5
1970	347.2	4.2	3,652.0
1971	1,187.1	12.4	4,773.1
1972	1,950.0	16.3	6,552.1
1973	1,766.2	12.0	8,306.9
1974	2,160.0	11.0	10,515.8
1975	5,280.5	25.3	15,809.6
1976	7,375.0	29.9	22,955.3
1977	8,480.0	29.7	30,355.3
1978	10,985.0	37.0	43,617.1
1979	13,471.9	33.9	52,284.4
1980	14,170.2	32.2	71,906.9
1981	12,899.8	27.2	83,629.8
1982	14,345.0	30.2	97,851.2
1983	13,345.0	26.5	111,196.2

Sources: MOF, *Zaisei Kin'yu Tokei Geppo,* no. 301 (May 1977); Prime Minister's Office, Statistics Bureau, *Nikon Tokei Geppo,* annual issues; Bank of Japan, *Economic Statistics Annual* (March 1984); *Japan Times Weekly,* January 7, 1978. Figures are for fiscal year, April 1–March 31.
a. Percentage of government revenue financed by issuing bonds.
b. Includes bonds issued to capitalize government-controlled lending agencies.

The principal causes for its growth were the escalator clauses in the allowances provided under the old age and retirement programs and the national health plans. Also, the number of people covered under these programs was increasing rapidly with the aging of the Japanese population. The MOF, of course, was aware of this demographic fact but was ill prepared for the politically motivated relaxation of some of the procedures used in calculating allowances and pensions.[60] In the 1978 budget, social security amounted to ¥6,781 billion, an increase of well over ¥1 billion from 1977.

The rapid increase in the once strongly resisted deficit spending was significant because it was accelerating the trend of change in the workings

60. Fujita, "Wagakuni," pp. 34–37.

of Japan's money market, distinctively increasing the continued risk of high inflation. By the end of 1978, increased deficit spending left nearly ¥ 44 trillion ($220 billion when calculated at the rate of 200 yen to the dollar) of government bonds outstanding in the money market, and one consequence of this was to threaten the ability of the MOF and the Bank of Japan to control the money supply effectively.[61] The suddenly increased supply of bonds had created conditions in which a strong political will— perhaps a much stronger will than the LDP, intent on political survival, could muster—would be required to control the amount of liquidity within the economy. Japan's unique methods of selling government bonds, adopted as an integral part of the disequilibrium policy, made the risk of rapid inflation extremely high. During the 1974–77 period, the Bank of Japan allocated nearly 90 percent of the government bonds to the major city banks, just as it had done since the early 1970s. Though some of the banks were less than enthusiastic, they bought the allocated bonds partly because they had a sufficient amount of idle funds (due to economic conditions) and partly because they could depend on the Bank of Japan for additional funds when corporate demand for loans increased (as economic conditions improved).

Until 1976, this method of digesting bonds encountered no major difficulty, aided as it was by the frequent consultation between Bank of Japan officials and the officers of the city banks. Contributing to this seemingly smooth digestion of the bonds was the fact that the Bank was able to buy back a sufficiently large proportion of the bonds within a year, reducing the burden of holding the bonds on these banks. (By law, the Bank of Japan cannot buy back government bonds from private holders unless they have been held for at least one year.) That is, while the total amount of bonds outstanding was ¥ 10 billion or less and the price of bonds was unlikely to fall below the face value, there was no problem in this buy-back arrangement since the Bank of Japan could buy back bonds from holders by using a part of the normal increase in the money supply or by reallocating funds that could otherwise have been made available to banks.

As the total amount of bonds rose rapidly after 1975, however, the MOF and the Bank of Japan had to be increasingly more persuasive in

61. See Fumimasa Hamada, "Akaji kokusai jidai no kinyu seisaku," *Ekonomisuto* (October 28, 1975), pp. 18–23; Akira Fujita, "Kodo seicho shuen go no fisukaru porishii," *Toyo keizai* (February 17, 1977), pp. 106–26; Sakakibara, "Henbo suru," pp. 54–68; Masaru Yoshitomi, "Takamaru kajo ryudosei infure no kiken," *Ekonomisuto* (March 23, 1976), pp. 29–34.

allocating them to the large city banks and also had to be much more active in selling bonds to small and medium-sized banks, securities firms, and private holders. By the end of 1977, the major banks were clearly unhappy (as some openly stated) because of the relatively low interest rate of the bonds (an increasing risk of capital loss which could result from the decline in the bond price) and because the Bank of Japan, not wanting to sharply increase the banks' cash on hand, was now buying back a rapidly decreasing proportion of the bonds outstanding.

But the bonds were still being digested during 1977 and into the first half of 1978, thanks mostly to the sluggish economy that was suffering from structural problems. There were as yet no visible signs of crowding out, and the increasingly uneasy bankers could still be persuaded to hold more bonds. Many economists, the *zaikai,* and even opposition parties continued to argue for stimulation throughout 1978, assuming that if the economy recovered and the demand gap were reduced, the bond issues could be reduced or even ended.

The picture, however, began to change perceptibly as a large amount of government bonds began to appear in the market as a result of the large deficit spending of fiscal 1978. Despite the super-easy money policy in effect during 1978, the banks became distinctively more reluctant to buy even the reduced allocation of long-term (ten-year) bonds yielding below-equilibrium returns. They no longer doubted that the amount of bonds they held had become too large, reducing their ability to make more lucrative loans in the near future to large firms, but they became extremely fearful of both a fall in the prices of the bonds they held and an increasing possibility that the Bank of Japan would not be able to buy back a sufficient amount of bonds or advance funds to the banks to provide them with the desired liquidity as the economy began to recover.

The banks, however, could not demand immediate liberalization of the money market. Liberalization, which would force the government to sell the bonds in the market at competitive rates of interest (thus eliminating the allocation to the banks), would also mean a huge capital loss on the large amount of bonds they already held. Of course, the MOF was not anxious to liberalize the money market because to do so would increase the costs of bonds and force the MOF-controlled long-term credit banks to compete in the bond market against the government bonds. The most the MOF could do, under the circumstances, was to adopt the temporary solution of issuing more bonds of shorter maturity (three and five years) at slightly improved terms—bonds that the banks would be more willing to buy and hold. Fortunately for the government, the economy in 1978 was still in the very early stages of recovery, and the shorter maturity and improved terms seemed sufficient to cause banks and other financial institutions to absorb these bonds. Moreover, an active public campaign to sell the bonds to private individuals was also waged with moderate success.[62]

However, this meant that the bonds were still being placed at below-equilibrium rates, making it even more difficult to liberalize the rate structure in the future. For if the LDP wished to protect the interests of the major bond holders (the politically powerful large city banks) and to continue to minimize the costs of the increasing amount of bonds to the government, it had an increased incentive to retain the disequilibrium policy. The super-easy money policy of 1978 may not have been totally unrelated to the problems facing the bond market and to the continued issuance of an increasingly large amount of bonds.

So long as the amount of bonds was limited and the economy remained sluggish, this unique modus operandi allowed the MOF to continue to preserve the disequilibrium policy, minimizing the cost of the government bonds. But the total amount of bonds was sharply increasing and economic conditions in 1978 were showing signs of improvement. Finally, in August, the price of ten-year bonds fell below the face value, clearly indicating that some change must be made in the habit of allocating a large portion of new issues to major banks at the administered rate. By fall, it was evident that the outstanding bonds had grown much too large to be conveniently retired without entailing significant inflationary pressure. The amount of bonds reaching maturity would begin to increase steadily beginning in 1981 and would reach a peak in 1987 (assuming that no more short-term bonds were issued during the ensuing years) of ¥8.4 trillion, or an equivalent of more than $40 billion.[63] The MOF officials, most familiar with the increasing rigidity of the budget, began to vigorously advocate an increased tax, a form of value added tax, and many began to advocate liberalization—decontrol of the money market to dismantle the disequilibrium policy—on grounds that the risk of

---

62. The observations in the preceding paragraphs are based on extensive discussions with Japanese bankers, economists, and officials during January and February of 1979.

63. Japan, Ministry of Finance, *Koshasai tokei geppo* (MOF Printing Office), various issues; Masataka Nakajima, "Genkaku na kinri taikei ga konpon genri," *Nihon keizai shimbun,* September 19, 1978.

inflationary pressure would be minimized if the government bond rates were subjected to free market forces and the holders of the bonds were free to buy and sell at market-determined rates of interest. Important reasons advanced for the need for liberalization were that it would enable the Bank of Japan to adapt its open-market operation to the conditions of the money market; widen the market for government bonds (if interest rates and prices were determined by market forces, more would be willing to buy and hold more bonds); and eliminate the risk of inflation by not forcing the government to increase the money supply in order to maintain the bond prices.[64]

Liberalization was not likely to be carried out, however, because of the MOF's reluctance to increase the costs of bonds and to be placed in the position of forcing the long-term credit banks to compete in the bond market against the government bonds. And liberalization would be detrimental to the interests of the largest banks and other financial institutions with considerable political power. Furthermore, the sharply differing reactions of large and small banks, securities companies, long-term credit banks, and other segments of the financial community indicated that any attempt to dismantle the long-practiced policy would not be an easy task even for the most determined of political leaders.

The MOF's reluctance to liberalize is the more entrenched because there is no Federal Reserve in Japan with an independent mind of its own, and a Japanese "Accord of 1951" is unlikely to occur. The MOF is sensitive to the wishes of the LDP, and the Bank of Japan is widely regarded as no more than a bureau of the MOF.

Even with liberalization, the risk of inflation remains extremely high if bonds continue to be issued. If the amount of bonds issued continued at the 1978 level and the economy continued to recover, the rate of interest on the bonds in a liberalized market would be pushed upward as the demand for funds increased. Newly issued bonds would yield a higher interest rate than earlier bonds in order to be competitive in the money market. The major financial institutions holding large amounts of older bonds would attempt to monetize them, but buyers would demand lower prices for the older bonds. The larger the amount of older bonds outstanding, the larger would be the rise in the rate of interest and the fall in the price of bonds. This would hold true because most of the outstanding bonds would be long-term ones held by the relatively small

64. Shoken Torihiki Shingikai Kihon Mondai Iinkai, *Nozomashii koshasi-shijo no arikata ni kansuru hokokusho,* memorandum, October 18, 1977, pp. 21–22.

number of city banks, which in the liberalized money market would no longer be in a locked-in position.

The Bank of Japan would be forced to buy back the bonds in order to prevent further declines in the price of older bonds and further increases in the interest rate of the bonds. The larger the amount of bonds the Bank of Japan had to buy back, the higher the risk of inflation would be.

Policymakers and especially the MOF chose not to face these troublesome problems in 1978. The MOF continued to issue a rapidly increasing number of three- and five-year bonds so that banks would be coaxed into buying and holding them. Though this meant readjusting the whole range of the rate structure, the MOF raised the interest rate for bonds slightly in order to cope with the decline in the price of the outstanding bonds.

As debate on the budget for fiscal 1979 began, the new premier advocated an inexpensive government, citing the increasing threat of inflation and a need to curtail the growth of the government; the MOF called for immediate adoption of a value added tax; and the *zaikai*, the opposition parties, and high-level American visitors demanded, each for reasons of their own, a budget that could stimulate the Japanese economy. Many government officials and economists had become more cautious of the continuing deficit spending because of the inflationary effects that the outstanding bonds were having and because of clear indications that the economy was recovering. However, the budget that passed the Diet by 249 to 235 votes was almost 13 percent larger than that of the preceding year and the dependency ratio—the proportion of the total expenditures to be financed by deficit—reached 39.6 percent. The social security category of the budget rose by 12.5 percent, and the various stimulation expenditures by 20 percent, but the cost of the government debt jumped by 26.6 percent. The national debt accounted for 10.6 percent of the total fiscal 1979 budget and was only slightly smaller than the expenditures for education and culture (table 14-5). In 1971, the share of debt financing in the budget was only 3.35 percent, as against 11.5 percent for education and culture.[65] A major daily newspaper, questioning the wisdom of the MOF's intention to allocate ¥11.70 trillion of ten-year and five-year bonds to the major city banks, observed with alarm that "converting at 200 yen to the dollar, the U.S. deficit for 1979 is about 12 trillion yen and West Germany's for 1978 was about 3 trillion yen. . . . Japan's 15.27 trillion yen makes her the largest deficit nation in the world."[66]

65. *Toyo keizai* (January 27, 1979), p. 46.
66. *Asahi shimbun*, January 29, 1979.

The Threat of Inflation

The pattern of deficit financing that was established in the 1970s changed little in its fundamental characteristics even into the 1980s. To be sure, the political leaders became seriously concerned with the steadily accumulating national debt. It was this concern that led Prime Minister Ohira to advocate just before the 1980 election an increase in excise taxes on consumer goods and impelled Prime Minister Suzuki to promise in 1981 that he would propose a budget plan to end deficit spending within four years. But both of these expressions of good intentions proved not only unsuccessful but also politically costly. The voters reacted to Ohira's prescription for reduction of the deficit in no uncertain terms (table 14-3). And Suzuki had to yield the premiership to Nakasone principally for failing to be able to prepare a budget that might make at least a "down payment" (to borrow an American president's expression) toward a balanced budget in four years. Learning from these politically costly errors, Nakasone was only willing to assert that he would attempt, but not promise, to end deficit spending by the end of the 1980s.

Nakasone's promise, more empty than cautious, reflects the political and economic reality in a Japan that is unlikely to be able to reduce deficit spending significantly in the near future. While economic performance and thus tax revenues are not likely to improve appreciably in the coming years, the aged and wage earners—two of the largest voting blocs—can hardly be neglected. This means that social security expenditures should continue to rise despite the efforts of the LDP and the MOF to slow the rate of increase. A principal reason for a steady escalation of this expenditure has been and will continue to be a rapid increase in the number of persons covered by old-age pensions and by two types of social security programs for the retired. The number that stood at only 2.7 million in 1965 rose to 9.5 million in 1977 and will climb to 12.5 million by the end of the century. Wage earners, as do their counterparts in other industrialized economies, will continue to demand a larger transfer income in the forms of higher medical benefits, more generous unemployment compensation, and the like, in addition to retirement pensions. They should also demonstrate as a group more tolerance for deficit spending and inflation in the belief that it would still increase their share of income. Also they could continue to call for economic stimulation, even at the cost of inflation and its likely regressive effect on income distribution.[67] Increasingly more concerned about job security, they would be more willing to pay the price of inflation to remain employed.

Neither can the loyal supporters of the LDP—farmers and the *zaikai*—be slighted by the budgetmakers. This means that expenditures for agriculture could continue to contribute significantly to the deficit. Even more important, this means that the *zaikai*'s demands must also be met. In both cases, the LDP will be compelled to proceed cautiously because of the political cost that could result from appearing too generous to its core supporters. But for the LDP to retain power, it must continue to test the limits of political tolerance of the opposition parties to secure the authorizations needed to benefit farmers and *zaikai* either directly or indirectly.

The LDP must also continue to cope with increases in several other budget items that will be, for political reasons, no easier to trim. Revenue-sharing programs with local government are virtually impossible to reduce because the expenditures for these programs are legally mandated and will increase with tax revenues.[68] The cost of debt will be even more burdensome as the deficit accumulates and because liberalization of the capital market continues to reduce the MOF's ability to control the interest rates that must be paid to bondholders.

All of the trends cited above and other demands—including the American pressure to boost Japan's military spending—that have contributed to the deficit hitherto should continue to produce significant deficit spending. There is no appreciable indication that the trend of deficit spending of the 1970s is being reversed. Instead one observes that despite the best efforts of the LDP, the dependency ratio—the proportion of deficit spending to the total budget—remained around 25 percent during the 1980–84 period (table 14-7). As a result, Japan accumulated a total national debt of ¥122 trillion (approximately $530 billion) or the equivalent of three times the total government revenues of 1984. If measured in comparison to GNP, Japan's national debt is not much smaller than that of the United States.

Furthermore, in assessing the risk of rapid inflation in coming years,

67. Hiroshi Niida, "Infureishon no saibunpai koka," *Gendai keizai*, vol. 26 (Spring 1977), pp. 6–27.

68. Shigeto Tsuru, ed., *Gendai Nihon keizai* (Asahi Shimbunsha, 1977), p. 91.

one must also be mindful of recent political developments. In the Diet elections of December 1983 the LDP lost thirty-six seats and its own majority. It was compelled to form for the first time since 1955 a coalition with the New Liberal Club that won eight seats. No one can be certain whether or not LDP strength will continue to slip in future elections. But political prospects for the LDP will not encourage it to reduce the deficit measurably, let alone achieve a balanced budget. And in discussing the future risks of inflation, one must finally note that a resource-poor Japan is at constant risk of "importing" inflation and that, for a variety of reasons, Japan is unlikely to see in the near future a sharp increase in the value of the yen—as occurred in 1977 and 1978—such as might contribute to price stability.

In the early 1980s, the LDP government partly succeeded in slowing the growth of annual deficit. The rates of increase in social welfare expenditures were somewhat moderated. However, because the government was unable to enact any significant measures to increase revenues (including a widely discussed but politically costly increase in excise taxes), the deficit continued to mount. At the end of 1984, the total deficit bonds outstanding reached ¥133 trillion and the proposed 1985 budget included debt costs (interest payments for the bonds) in excess of ¥10 trillion, a sum for the first time exceeding the total proposed expenditures for all social welfare programs. The dependency ratio of the proposed budget— the proportion of the total expenditures to be financed by deficit—stood at 22.25 percent, further reducing the likelihood of erasing the deficit in the 1980s.

Should the economy begin to grow rapidly—say, at a rate over 5 percent per year—would the risk of rapid inflation be reduced? Most who are familiar with the political and economic realities of Japan, or for that matter of the United States and other industrial democracies, feel confident in answering this question in the negative. Such a growth rate, especially if sustained, would sharply increase the likelihood of "crowding out" in the capital market. The LDP, or even a more left-leaning coalition government, would be unlikely to possess sufficient political courage to resist the demand, likely to arise from both industry and labor, to monetize the debt—that is, to adopt an easy-money policy. Recall that in Japan, the central bank is far less immune to political pressure than, for example, the Federal Reserve can be. Note also that in a buoyant economy the unions will cease to be docile and wage levels would rise more rapidly. And finally one can predict with some confidence that the LDP or a coalition that enjoyed increasing tax revenues would be unsuccessful in resisting political temptation to spend even more. In short, whether in a sluggish or a vigorous economy, accumulating deficit is like accumulating arms. Deficit spending is often declared to be undertaken for the benefit of all and to preserve the existing politicoeconomic system. But as more deficit is accumulated, cost mounts for all and all must live under an increasing threat of rapid inflation; it becomes an armament against oneself.

The Tolerance for Inflation

The risk of rapid inflation in Japan is neither evidence of the failure or incompetence of the LDP nor a result of inherent weaknesses in Japan's capitalist democracy. The policies adopted by the LDP and the ministries which it commanded were policies supported, in the final analysis, by a majority of the voters. The LDP adopted various progrowth policies, including the disequilibrium rate structure, to wage the total war. And the rapidly increasing deficit, too, was a result of LDP efforts to respond to political pressures.

The policies that increased and continue to increase the threat of rapid inflation must be seen as the outcome of political decisions made by a political party whose primary goal is the retention of political power. That does not absolve the LDP and its ministries of policy errors (which can, for example, aggravate inflation). But what is a policy error to an economist, having no political constituency to please, can very well be an action that a political party in power chooses as a viable alternative given the political and economic pressures it faces.

The problems and malfunctions attributed to the politicoeconomic machinery of Japan are readily observable, if in different forms and with varying consequences, in all other capitalist democracies. In evaluating the Japanese machinery, it is therefore useful to ask whether it worked better or worse than that of other capitalist democracies. And whether it will work better or worse in the future.

If *better* means achieving rapid growth with stable prices relative to the performance attained in other capitalist democracies, then Japan's record compares exceedingly well with those of other industrialized economies. For the economic growth Japan has achieved, her inflation has been mild. Whether Japan's politicoeconomic machinery will continue to work better than that of other capitalist democracies is a much more difficult question. There is little doubt that the growth rate of the Japanese economy will remain slow, but it could continue to be high compared to that of other industrial nations. Whatever the precise rate of inflation may be in the coming decades, the factors that contribute most to the risks of rapid inflation are the weakened political power of the LDP, various legacies of the earlier progrowth policies, and the changed realities of the international political economy.

Japan must cope in the coming decades with an increasing amount of government bonds outstanding; with the intensification of the politico-economic reactions of trade partners, in the event that the trade surplus remains large; with wage pressures on the costs of production, which are likely to rise as the economy begins to grow; with a slowed rate of increase in productivity; with the structural changes required by rising resource costs; and with changing patterns of domestic and international demand. In the political arena the LDP seems likely to retain power, either as a weakened majority party as it was until 1982 or as senior partner in a coalition as it subsequently became. This will mean increased pressure for deficit spending and less ability to cope with the pressure.

Whether or not Japan performs better than others hinges not on the growth rate but on how much higher Japanese inflation is above the moderate range, and at what level other nations are able to control their inflation. Japan could be rated as performing better even if her inflation rate should reach that of most other industrial nations, as long as her economy continues to achieve a higher growth rate than others.

Just as the record of inflation was an outcome of the workings of the Japanese political and economic machinery, the risk of inflation and the likelihood of rapid inflation are products of Japan's polity, democractic and capitalist. If rapid inflation is "a historical situation," as Goldthorpe suggests,[69] in Japan it is the result of politicoeconomic desires and pressures that acted on each other under the rules adopted in the rapid-growth decades. The majority continue to prefer inflation to changing the rules governing the political and economic costs. For the Japanese, after a century of rapid growth with moderate inflation, tolerance for more than moderate inflation is higher than that, for example, of Americans. In Japan, as in other industrial societies, the inflation to come is a price that must continue to be paid for preserving the politicoeconomic system preferred by most.

---

69. John H. Goldthorpe, "The Current Inflation: Towards a Sociological Account," in Fred Hirsch and John H. Goldthorpe, eds., *The Political Economy of Inflation* (Harvard University Press, 1978), p. 216.

15

The Italian Inflation

Michele Salvati

Among industrialized market economies Italy had one of the highest rates of inflation in the 1970s. Until the discipline of fixed exchange rates ended, its inflation was roughly comparable with that of France, West Germany, and the United Kingdom, countries that are similar to Italy in terms of size, trade relations, and social and institutional arrangements. The inflationary experiences of these highly interconnected economies from 1967 through 1979 are contrasted in table 15-1. Roughly speaking the 1967–72 period was one of uniformly increasing inflation; 1972–76 witnessed an inflationary explosion in Italy and the United Kingdom; and in 1976–79 the four countries had varying degrees of success in their stabilization policies.

The first period is not the most revealing time span for singling out the uniqueness of the Italian wage and cost spurt around the turn of the decade.[1] After 1969, labor costs rose exceptionally quickly, thus placing profit margins under a pressure that exploded once the ceiling of the fixed exchange rate was removed early in 1973. Nevertheless, the different national inflationary experiences remained largely uniform until the 1973 world boom. Thereafter divergence became a major characteristic. It was only after 1972 that the Italian (and British) rates of inflation shot up well above the European average. But this was a novel experience, for throughout the 1950s and 1960s the Italian economy demonstrated a fairly good record of price stability.

Omitting the wage and price boom of the early 1960s with which the "Italian miracle" ended, the only noticeable inflation between 1956 and

1. For the 1969–74 period, the annual growth of labor costs per unit of output for Italy was 12.5 percent; the United Kingdom, 11.9 percent; West Germany, 8.4 percent; France, 7.4 percent.

Table 15-1. *Average Annual Changes in Price and Cost Indicators for Four Countries, 1967–79*

Percent

Indicator and years[a]	France	Italy	United Kingdom	West Germany
	Average annual change			
Wholesale industrial prices				
1967–72	4.5	3.8	6.1	2.5
1972–76	10.3	21.7	18.7	6.7
1976–79	7.7	13.3	14.5	2.8
Consumer prices				
1967–72	5.6	3.9	6.5	3.7
1972–76	10.6	15.8	15.9	6.1
1976–79	9.6	15.3	12.6	3.5
Export unit values				
1967–72	4.7	3.4	5.9	1.2
1972–76	12.5	22.8	20.5	8.2
1976–79	8.1	14.2	12.7	2.8
Labor costs per unit of output				
1967–72	4.0	7.1	7.4	4.7
1972–76	11.9	19.4	17.6	5.5
1976–79	7.8	12.8	11.9	3.3
	Change over period			
Exchange rate with reference to U.S. dollar				
1967–72	−4.4	6.6	2.4	19.8
1972–76	3.0	−50.3	−27.5	26.3
1976–79	19.1	8.1	30.7	26.7

Sources: Organization for Economic Cooperation and Development, *Main Economic Indicators, Historical Statistics, 1964–73* (Paris: OECD, 1984); International Monetary Fund, *International Financial Statistics, 1983*; Italy, National Institute of Economic and Social Research, *Review*; Bank of Italy, *Relazione annuale,* various issues.

a. In order to link the average annual changes, the final year of each time period is used as the base year for the next period.

1967 (table 15-2) was that of consumer prices, due to both the wage- and income-transmission mechanism that Scandinavian economists have highlighted and, perhaps, to special inefficiency in the service and state sectors (beyond any lower rate of labor productivity owing to technological reasons). Wholesale industrial prices rose very slowly, as did labor costs, while the unit value of exports—admittedly only a rough indicator of export prices—actually decreased. Between the mid and late 1960s Italy ran a sizable surplus on current account coupled with falling export prices. Thus, throughout most of the 1950s and 1960s, Italy played the same role of world price moderator commonly attributed to West Germany.

What went wrong in the 1970s? A major component of the explanation lies in international factors—the Johnson boom in the United States, the

Table 15-2. *Average Annual Changes in Price and Cost Indicators for Four Countries, 1956–67*

Percent

Indicator and years[a]	France	Italy	United Kingdom	West Germany
Wholesale industrial prices				
1956–61	5.0	−0.3	2.0	0.1
1961–64	2.1	3.6	1.3	1.4
1964–67	1.0	0.7	2.0	1.7
1956–67	3.1	1.1	1.8	1.3
Consumer prices				
1956–61	6.1	1.6	2.3	1.8
1961–64	4.3	6.0	3.2	2.7
1964–67	2.6	3.3	3.7	2.8
1956–67	4.6	3.2	2.9	2.3
Export unit values				
1956–61	5.8	−1.7	1.5	0.6
1961–64	2.0	1.7	2.0	0.0
1964–67	1.0	−1.3	3.2	0.7
1956–67	3.4	−0.7	2.1	0.4
Labor costs per unit of output				
1956–61	2.8	0.7	2.6	3.4
1961–64	2.8	5.4	0.3	2.5
1964–67	0.7	−2.3	2.9	2.0
1956–67	2.2	1.1	2.0	2.7

Sources: Same as table 15-1.

a. In order to link the average annual changes, the final year in each time period is used as the base year for the next period.

expansion of official and private international liquidity at the turn of the decade and after, the collapse of the Bretton Woods system, the primary-products boom of 1972–73, the fourfold increase in the price of oil at the end of 1973. Another part of the story can be accounted for only by internal factors, and it is on these that this chapter concentrates. Some analysts claim that to focus on domestic determinants is to deny the role of the more general and international determinants. "Is it not stretching the imagination too much . . . to regard the upsurge of inflation after 1968 as being the outcome of some vaguely specified struggle for higher shares in national income in such widely differing economies as Britain, Japan, New Zealand, Italy, etc.?"[2] On the contrary, it does not require much imagination to exclude social and political factors—"the vaguely

2. James A. Trevithick, *Inflation: A Guide to the Crisis in Economics* (Penguin, 1977), pp. 102–03.

specified struggle"—from the causes of inflation and thus reduce it to a few easily detected ingredients. Indeed, such a view usually reduces the inflationary mixture to a single ingredient, the supply of money. As a reaction against a one-sided cost-push analysis this popular opinion is understandable. But there is nothing that makes full recognition of the common international factors theoretically inconsistent with acceptance of the view that social and political forces, varying from country to country, are also crucial to the inflationary process. The variety of responses, even among industrialized and highly interconnected economies, is just as striking as the general intensification of the inflationary trend in the 1970s.

This chapter is almost exclusively concerned with those explanatory factors that economic models usually bury in the exogenous variables or in the very forms of the equations. Still, it is not possible to locate the social and political links of the causal chain without a theory about the economic ones, so a rather traditional version of the Keynesian inflationary process is assumed. The flexibility and openness that it allows with respect to the "demand for inflation"[3] make it especially suitable as a basis for sociological explanation. In particular, it both recognizes the relevance of a wage push and says nothing about it, leaving large scope for specific historical analysis.[4]

Obviously such a general and powerful paradigm as the monetarist one can always be adapted to account for the demand side of the inflationary process. But the idea that the working of the labor market may lead to a demand for inflation—independent of economic policy mismanagement or changes in the structure of the market itself—is extraneous to the monetarist philosophy. If this idea were accepted, it would imply that an important sector of the economy cannot be properly understood through a market model. That is precisely what appears to be true of the Italian wage and conflict explosion after 1970. No convincing explanation can be found if the complex world of industrial relations must rest on the Procrustean bed of a market model.

---

3. Robert J. Gordon, "The Demand for and Supply of Inflation," *Journal of Law and Economics*, vol. 18 (December 1975), pp. 807–36.

4. Social scientists would object that this statement leaves their disciplines only a residual, noneconomic explanatory role. See John H. Goldthorpe, "The Current Inflation: Towards a Sociological Account," in Fred Hirsch and John H. Goldthorpe, eds., *The Political Economy of Inflation* (Harvard University Press, 1978), pp. 186–216.

The Legacy of the Past

The Italian inflation, insofar as it arose from internal conditions, was just one of the consequences of a deep-seated social and political crisis that had been maturing for a long time and was well advanced in the middle of the 1960s. Social analysts generally hold that in a democratic capitalist polity the state has to balance the two broad imperatives of a political and social consensus (achieved in part through social transfers and welfare) and of growth (requiring investments and maintaining profits and competitiveness).[5] But periods of social and economic transformation seem also to require a third imperative, a capacity for adaptation or rationalization so that under changing conditions the imperatives of consensus and growth can be progressively reconciled.

The Italian political system did not satisfy this third imperative. That is, it failed to create and sustain a social, economic, and political environment that might accommodate changes in the balance of forces between social groups so that consensus and growth could continue to be fostered simultaneously.

The Strategy of the 1950s

From the viewpoint of both growth and consensus the strategy of the 1950s and early 1960s was a political masterpiece. In a country in which peasants and traditional middle classes had exerted major influence and in which a Catholic culture still played a large role even in urban, industrial areas, a conservative and confessional Christian Democratic party was able to confine working-class political forces to a role of hopeless opposition. Unions were still weak and split along political lines. Their feebleness, along with residual unemployment, effectively moderated wage demands and gave management a dominant role in every aspect of industrial relations. To the ideological conservatism and the heavy reliance on the Catholic hierarchy of the late 1940s and early 1950s new instruments of control were added as the state machine extended its scope. Instead of being dismantled, the nationalized industrial sector grouped under the Istituto per la Ricostruzione Industriale, or IRI—largely a legacy of

5. James O'Connor, *The Fiscal Crisis of the State* (St. Martin's, 1973); Ian Gough, "State Expenditure in Advanced Capitalism," *New Left Review,* no. 92 (July–August 1975), pp. 53–92.

Mussolini's salvage operations in the 1930s—was slowly but continuously extended. To manage special programs for land reform, for combating unemployment, for attempting, above all, to ameliorate the southern problem, new state agencies were created that were endowed with relatively ample resources and thus offered extensive networks of patronage. State intervention in the South was a fairly efficient means of winning political consensus. But it did not succeed in stimulating autonomous economic development. And when the pools of unemployed in the North began to dry up, a large influx of young migrant workers from the South postponed any labor shortage well into the 1960s.

Italy's political masterpiece effectively excluded workingclass and left-wing parties from participation in government and unions from partici-pation in industrial relations. A buyer's labor market meant that the very legitimacy of the trade unions could be contested in the daily management of shop-floor relationships. But this extreme conflict between a predom-inantly communist and socialist labor movement and the rest of society—a "clash between civilizations"—could not last long beyond the early 1960s.

Just as the cold war heavily influenced the ideological balance of Italian politics in the 1950s, so did the new détente of the 1960s. At the same time, a tight labor market was beginning to develop in Italy and the electoral axis was slowly drifting to the left. After the victory of the conservative forces in the 1948 elections, the ideological mobilization and electoral support for Christian Democracy and its minor allies slowly eroded. Sometime in the late 1950s or early 1960s a choice had to be faced—in which direction to extend parliamentary support of the govern-ment. Moving to the right was precluded by the extremism of the Monarchists and Neofascists. The abortive attempts to build a coalition with these forces in 1960 met strong resistance within the Christian Democratic party itself, not to mention its Republican and Social Democratic allies, and obviously among the Socialists and Communists who protested in the streets. This opposition permitted only extension toward the left, which meant splitting the "unnatural" alliance between Socialists and Communists, regaining Nenni's Socialist party for the "democratic camp," and forming the first Center-Left government under Aldo Moro in 1963.

With the relaxation of ideological tension, the strengthening of the working class in the labor markets, and the shift to the left of the political equilibrium, a crucial element of the strategy of the 1950s was crumbling.

Control of wage demands and of work effort remained a prerequisite for achieving growth. But if control by means of excluding the Left from influence could no longer serve, other sources for seeking wage restraint and work discipline had to be found. Seeking this new legitimation should have been the main purpose of the Center-Left strategy, if the socioeconomic imperatives and especially the rationalization imperative were to be met. Such an attempt, however, ran counter to the basic features of the previous political masterpiece.

During the period in which the organized labor movement had been effectively excluded, a fairly simple relationship between private industrial interests and the Christian Democratic leadership had grown up. The government provided economic assistance to various sectors when needed and assured political stability, favorable labor-market conditions, and unrestrained market freedom, while private industry furnished financial and electoral support and accepted a substantial public incursion into the manufacturing sector. There was no conscious model of economic planning and growth behind this extension of public ownership. The public firms fully accepted the choices of the market. But one of the driving forces was that of providing the party in office with a source of financial power and patronage that was independent of large industry and private capital.[6] Extension of the state sector aimed less at creating a favorable framework for growth than at defending threatened economic activities, even to the point of shoring up the state's corporate organizations. This was also the case in the interventions on behalf of the two most important segments of the traditional middle classes—peasants and shopkeepers.[7] Such state encouragement, of course, could work counter to economic modernization, as often did the aid fostered in the South, where public contractors, state-subsidized firms, and even welfare recipients proved a burden for public finance and economic development.[8]

In Italy the priority of assuring growth was often overlooked in the process of preserving consensus. If interest-group participation in the

6. This is one of the most controversial issues in postwar Italy; see Eugenio Scalfari and Giuseppe Turani, *Razza padrona: storia della borghesia di stato* (Milan: Feltrinelli, 1974); Giorgio Galli and Alessandra Nannei, *Il capitalismo assistenziale* (Milan: Sugar Co Edizioni, 1976); Piero Barucci, *Ricostruzione, pianificazione, mezzogiorno: la politica economica in Italia dal 1943 al 1955* (Bologna: Il Mulino, 1978); Pasquale Saraceno, *Intervista sulla ricostruzione, 1943–1953* (Bari: Laterza, 1977).

7. See Giovanni Mottura and Enrico Pugliese, *Agricoltura, mezzogiorno e mercato del lavoro* (Bologna: Il Mulino, 1975).

8. See Arnaldo Bagnasco, *Tre Italie: la problematica territoriale dello sviluppo italiano* (Bologna: Il Mulino, 1977).

shaping of public policy is not kept within bounds, sooner or later there may be negative repercussions for economic growth. The peasant problem, for example, could probably have been solved in a way that would not have produced in the early 1970s a deficit of $4 billion in the trade balance for agricultural products—not to speak of the massive direct and indirect subsidies annually poured into the agricultural sector. And in general the network of influence between interest groups and state policymakers often just led to a simple allocation of public funds according to short-run pressures, without reference to long-term planning or objectives. As state intervention and state regulation of the economy grew, the political leadership became less able to control the large patronage network that had emerged. Increasingly the patron-client relationship between the political leadership and interest groups resembled a feudal exchange among vassals that allowed little service for the sovereign. Identification of state intervention with rational planning is particularly misleading for the Italian case.

The inability of Italy's leaders to establish a hierarchy of priorities according to a long-run program that simultaneously seeks to maximize social consensus and industrial growth has deep historic roots. The country's industrial interests have never succeeded in rallying a large enough base of support to establish ideological hegemony over the conservative side of the political spectrum.[9] The state, therefore, has always been crucial in mediating industry's conflict with the nonindustrial conservative elites (landowners, the church hierarchy) and providing a source of legitimacy during the transition to an industrial society. State support for industry and the persistent influence of nonindustrial interests within the political elite are characteristics that Italy shares with other latecomers among the industrial nations. What distinguishes Italy, though, has been the relative weakness of industrial interests in the balance of forces *within* the conservative camp itself. Thus while conservative leadership continued to prevail, it did not guarantee any priority to industry.

In the postwar period Christian Democracy thus cannot be considered the political arm of business interests in the same way that the Japanese Liberal Democratic party was.[10] Even when the Christian Democratic

9. Giampiero Carocci, *Storia d'Italia dall'unità ad oggi* (Milan: Feltrinelli, 1975); Giuliano Amato, *Economia, politica e istituzioni in Italia* (Bologna: Il Mulino, 1976).

10. See Giorgio Galli, *Il bipartitismo imperfetto: comunisti e democristiani in Italia* (Bologna: Il Mulino, 1966); Giancarlo Provasi, ed., *Borghesia industriale e democrazia cristiana* (Bari: De Donato, 1976).

leadership provided a favorable milieu for private enterprise, as during the 1950s, it maintained a distance from industry and a connection with other, potentially conflicting interests such as commerce and agriculture, which were more influential than in the Japanese case. Nor did the Christian Democratic regime ever try to develop a competent bureaucracy conversant with the problems of a complex economy and able to work together with its managerial counterpart in industry.[11] Two of the legs of the Japanese tripod therefore were rather shaky in the Italian case.

The Center-Left

The Italian government thus had to face a balance of forces within the political elite that other conservative coalitions (for example, in France and Japan) managed to avoid. In Italy it was necessary to incorporate at least part of the opposition within the parliamentary majority. The ideological distance between government and opposition, the limited political concessions and economic resources that conservative forces were willing and able to devote to the reformist incorporation of workingclass interests, and the objective difficulty of some of the issues to be tackled, especially the southern problem, made these projects especially arduous and subject to delay.

Radical political memories take a long time to decay even when the elites of opposed political parties have opted for reconciliation. Ideology is hard to dismantle, certainly for the Communists, but also for conservatives. The political history of Italy since the beginning of the Center-Left coalition has been full of obscure maneuvers on the part of the Far Right, some even verging on attempted coups d'état. Moreover, any wooing of the political representatives of the working class requires substantial concessions in terms of social welfare policy or wage increases. The main feature, however, of the political masterpiece of the 1950s, the density of the interests encrusted around the Christian Democrats with the patronage system it had developed, did not permit such concessions, even when macroeconomic conditions might have allowed, as in the mid-1960s. Within the political elite there were few men in the early 1960s who clearly understood what the stakes of the Center-Left involved, and what might be the consequences of its failure. Even within industry, recognition of the need for a social contract had to wait until Gianni Agnelli of Fiat

---

11. See Sabino Cassese, *Questione amministrativa e questione meridionale* (Milan: Giuffrè, 1977).

became president of Confindustria—the employers' peak association—long after labor relations had exploded in the early 1970s.[12]

Late to recognize the need for a strategy of consensus toward labor, business interests were hardly more successful in dealing with the government. The relative distance between private industry and the political elite widened during the 1960s. Private capital's opposition to the emergence of the Center-Left was certainly one of the factors that contributed to the failure of a strong version of that experiment (that is, one that really tackled fundamental reform), but this hostility simultaneously cost industry influence over economic policymaking.

As a program for basic social and economic reform the Center-Left remained limited; patronage, interest groups, and bureaucracy handicapped structural change. Still, as a political solution, this narrow coalition worked out quite well during the 1960s. The inclusion of the Socialist party in the government alliance solved the problem arising from the leftward shift of the electorate. It provided the short-term advantage—later a heavy liability—of introducing an element of division within the labor movement. The wage boom of the early 1960s was suffocated by a sharp monetary restriction in the winter of 1963–64. The weakness of the unions, the rise of productivity and of unemployment, served to moderate wage demands quite effectively until the end of the decade in spite of the first impact of quasi-full employment. Investment did fall in 1964 and 1965 and failed to rally greatly afterward; but exports provided a sufficient stimulus for growth, although restrictive monetary and fiscal policies prevented full recovery of employment and capacity utilization until the end of the 1960s. Since exports led growth and internal demand remained under control, no problems arose for the balance of payments. Large surpluses were earned on current account and only net capital outflows equilibrated the total balance of payments and impeded revaluation of the lira.

In the long term, this success meant trouble. The enthusiasm for economic planning of the first Center-Left years was rapidly dampened by the interests who felt threatened by reformist policies.[13] The only major reform implemented was the nationalization of the electricity-producing sector. A stronghold of private capital was thus dismantled,

---

12. See Guido Carli, ed., *Sviluppo economico e strutture financiarie in Italia* (Bologna: Il Mulino, 1977).

13. See Giorgio Ruffolo, *Rapporto sulla programmazione* (Bari: Laterza, 1973); Manin Carabba, *Un ventennio di programmazione, 1954–1974* (Bari: Laterza, 1977).

which meant in fact that the Socialists lent their support for ideological reasons to a policy that ended up giving the Christian Democrats another powerful source of influence. However, the real reforms needed were not carried out. These would have required first and foremost a more balanced geographical distribution of industry in order better to utilize existing fixed social capital (housing, schools) and to reduce the strains arising from internal migration. Insofar as migration was to continue, reforms should have included regional planning, urban development, and public services (housing, transport, and social services) to increase the welfare of immigrants and low-income citizens. Finally reform would have entailed a strategy of attention toward the unions and industrial relations in general. Instead, political leaders tended to content themselves with the fact that management had regained the upper hand in labor markets and that tranquility had returned to industrial relations after the disturbances of the early 1960s. But the latter were just a premonition in fact of what could happen later.

Toward the end of the 1960s a few signs began to reveal that the narrow or limited version of the Center-Left strategy was not working well. Seller's market conditions were once again established in the industrial markets of the North. A wave of high pay settlements at the local level—following national wage agreements that were far lower—contributed a significant wage drift. The Socialists, dissatisfied with the meager results of the narrow version of the Center-Left, continued to press for a more active policy of reform and greater public expenditure. Their participation as a junior partner in the political spoils system, moreover, was not yielding them significant electoral dividends. The party felt squeezed between the Christian Democrats and the Communists, who continued to control the dominant sector of the labor movement and effectively capitalized on the social tensions created by the absence of an effective reformist policy.[14]

With widespread dissatisfaction among the rank-and-file, the political divisions among the three large union confederations—Communist, Socialist, and Catholic—became less important. The parliamentary debate over pension reform in 1968 provoked mobilization of all the unions on a common platform. And by its very nature the unrest at the plant level,

14. The Communists' platform in the 1970s was at least as moderate as the Center-Left program that they criticized in the 1960s. The Center-Left success in the 1960s, however, appeared divisive, and only its failure and inability to secure wage restraint allowed a possible future governmental role for the Communists.

which had started in 1967 and climaxed in 1969–70, could not be channeled and divided along political lines. The local officials of the three union confederations moved toward a common front and pressed their national organizations toward unified policies.

The stage was thus set for much greater trade union influence over the formation of economic policy. Nevertheless, public policy remained predicated on moderate wage demands and on the efficacy of monetary policy in preserving restraint. The political framework, the policy instruments, the ideology, and the institutional maturity that would have been necessary for any more direct participation of the unions in shaping a noninflationary incomes policy simply did not exist. After the initial, highly ideological discussions of the early 1960s, the whole issue of union participation in an incomes policy had simply been abandoned (together with most discussion of planning and reforms) since the slack labor market itself served to moderate wage demands. All that existed instead by the end of the decade was, on one side, the grievances and the radical attitudes of a segment of society long excluded from participation and, on the other, a political leadership inadequate to impose policies for growth that might resolve conflicting demands.

The Market Arena at the Height of Inflation, 1969–79

The arena in which firms confront their employees is the central one for understanding the exceptional intensity and the timing of Italian inflation. Around the turn of the 1970s, labor markets and industrial relations became the focus for a sharp change, and economic policy—indeed government policy as a whole—was unable to deal with the new conditions without resorting to inflation.

The "Hot Autumn" and Its Consequences

The decade from 1969 to 1979 was one of industrial turbulence. But while the labor unrest contributed to inflation, it did so only through certain channels. Wage-wage or Scandinavian inflationary reasons were relatively insignificant. The central influence is to be seen in the general wage push, its effects on productivity, and the consequences for profits.

WAGES: RELATIVITIES. In an an industrial relations system with centralized, nationwide bargaining, where union federations cover whole economic sectors in industry and in other branches of the economy and, in turn, are linked to a powerful central confederation, a solidaristic policy is built into the very structure of national bargaining. Diffusion of inflation is easy since all unions try to extend to their own activity what has been won in other economic sectors.

Within industry, unions vigorously pursued such a solidaristic policy in the 1970s. Wage and salary increases, and nonwage clauses too, were very similar in all collective agreements. Wage differentials between industrial sectors, between plants of different size, between geographic regions, between men and women—all those differentials that seemed to violate the "equal pay for equal work" principle of solidaristic policy—diminished significantly. The trade unions' conscious emphasis on solidaristic policy in the two wage rounds of 1969 and 1973 brought about a major narrowing of pay differentials even before the onset of double-digit inflation.[15] After 1973 inflation added its overall leveling effect to the whole structure, particularly following the 1975 agreement on wage indexation (the *scala mobile*) between the employers' and the unions' confederations.[16]

The reduction of intersectoral wage differentials within industry, due to a policy that consciously ignored differences in productivity among sectors, probably increased inflation along the lines of the Scandinavian model. But even the most productive segments of the tradable goods sector were hit by a wage push that far exceeded productivity increases. Whatever the diffusion process within industry might have added to

15. The coefficient of variation for wage differentials by sectors fell from 23.6 percent in 1969 to 19.7 percent in 1973, and for regional differentials fell from 11.8 percent to 10.5 percent (regional "wage cages"—which set minimum wages in seven different regional values—were abolished in a general agreement between unions' and employers' peak associations early in 1969). The ratio between average compensations of women and men went up, in the same period, from 70.2 percent to 74.3 percent. Carlo Dell'Aringa, *Egualitarismo e sindacato: l'evoluzione dei differenziali retributivi nell'industria italiana* (Milan: Vita e Pensiero, 1976), pp. 51–94.

16. After a transitional period, from January 1975 to February 1977, each percentage-point increase in the cost-of-living index was to be met by an increase in monthly compensation by a fixed sum, equal for all wage and salary earners. Lower salaries would increase more than the cost-of-living index and higher salaries less, tending to equalize incomes. Among industrially advanced countries, the Italian agreement provides an unusually high degree of indexation: also its fully automatic nature is rather uncommon. See A. Romanis Braun, "Indexation of Wages and Salaries in Developed Economics," *IMF Staff Papers*, vol. 23 (March 1976); Isidoro Franco Mariani, "Gli aspetti tecnici della riforma dell'indennità di contingenza," *Rassegna di statistiche del lavoro*, vol. 27 (1975), supplement; Luigi Spaventa, "Salario protetto dal meccanismo di scala mobile a 'punto pieno,'" Gino Faustini, "Indicizzazione dei salari e inflazione in Italia," R. Filosa and I. Visco, "L'unificazione del valore del punto di contingenza e il grado di indicizzazione delle retribuzioni," Franco Modigliani and T. Padoa-Schioppa, "La politica economica in una economia con salari indicizzati al 100 o più," and A. Roncaglia and others, "Commenti a un recente studio di Modigliani e Padoa-Schioppa," *Moneta e credito*, vol. 29 (December 1976), vol. 29 (September 1976), vol. 30 (March 1977), and vol. 31 (March 1978).

inflation, the common wage push was the principal factor. Industry, moreover, was the epicenter of the inflationary push and actually produced more inflation in relative terms than the sheltered and less productive branches of the economy. The process of diffusion, if anything, slowed inflation down in the economy as a whole. In the 1969–76 period, per capita monetary income from wages and salaries increased 3.5 times in industry as a whole (5.6 million employees in 1976), 3.1 times in the private tertiary sector (3.7 million workers), and 1.9 times in the public sector (2.8 million workers).[17]

The absence of independent craft or local unions removes a major institutional impetus for the wage-wage spiral. To yield a positive response, rank-and-file grievances about relativities must either produce a change in national union policy on minimum rates or be satisfied through local bargaining. But neither seemed to serve as a relevant channel for wage-wage inflation in Italy. Because of its very nature the grievance mechanism acts too ponderously to intensify wage-wage inflation. National industrial unions do not quickly change their minimum rate policy because of local grievances about relativities unless rank-and-file dissatisfaction threatens to lead to serious revolt. But this process takes time and cannot spark a real mechanism of wage-wage inflation. Moreover, Italian unions in the 1970s, in addition to solidaristic goals, pursued an explicit egalitarian policy by seeking flat pay increases for all workers. And inflation and wage indexation strongly reinforced the union policy, producing an unprecedented squeeze in the wage differentials established according to skills and professional qualifications.[18]

There is no evidence to suggest any reaction against such a policy. Local bargaining might in theory have accommodated an effort to reestablish differentials. But although officers and lay workers' representatives at the local level are more sensitive to rank-and-file grievances than

17. National accounts data; Italy, Ministero del Bilancio e della Programmazione Economica, *Relazione generale sulla situazione economica del paese, 1971; 1976.* Wages and salaries in agriculture (1.1 million workers in 1976) were an exception, having increased more than four times. But there was a deep structural change, from part-time to full-time work, in agriculture, so that it cannot be compared with the other sectors, where full-time work is the rule. Likewise, in a few nonindustrial sectors, per capita labor income increased more than for industry as a whole, the most commonly discussed being banking, where salaries are abnormally high (in comparison with other sectors and relative to bank employees' salaries in other industrial countries), and the number of employees is relatively large (roughly 300,000).

18. Between 1969 and 1973 the coefficient of variation of wage differentials by professional qualification (traditionally divided into seven classes by the Ministry of Labor) fell from 19.0 percent to 15.0 percent (13.9 percent in 1974), and the ratio between the average compensation of workers and employers in industry increased from 53.2 percent to 63.7 percent (69.0 percent in 1974). See Dell'Aringa, *Egualitarismo,* pp. 51–94.

the national leadership, they are also part of a centralized wage-setting mechanism. Thus the pressure to conform to national guidelines is stronger than in more decentralized systems of industrial relations, such as the British one. At least during the early 1970s, the egalitarian policy of the unions enjoyed strong rank-and-file support; nor was it resisted by better paid workers until large gains had been secured for all.[19] Finally, there seems to have been an inverse relationship between the intensity of wage push at the nationwide bargaining level and the amount of wage drift at the local level. Certainly between 1969 and 1976 when there was a major increase in nationally contracted minimum rates, there was the least margin for improvement, and thus scope for regionally induced spirals, at the local level.[20]

The distortion of pay and income structures created by the explosion of wages in industry cannot therefore itself be considered an autonomous source of the 1970s inflation. But the upheaval of relativities contained a strong potential for future inflation. In the spring of 1979 state employees' unions obtained both substantial salary increases and an indexation mechanism close to that for industrial wages. Within industry itself, skilled workers and employees sought high local bargains, well above the relativities set at the national level. Self-employed farmers and retailers were relative losers in the inflationary wave, since the slack of consumer demand prevented greater increases in agricultural prices and retail margins. The causal role of wage and income relativities, within industry and between industry and other branches, seemed to be changing by the end of the decade.

WAGES: THE BIG PUSH. The rates of change of wages in manufacturing (both nationally contracted minimum rates and observed average earnings), of consumer prices, and of the values of seasonally adjusted unemployment rates in figure 15-1 portray the main ingredients of a naive Phillips curve. The wage profile is dominated by the three large wage rounds of 1969–70, 1973, and 1976.[21] National industrial agreements, if not postponed

19. See Alessandro Pizzorno, "Political Exchange and Collective Identity in Industrial Conflict," in Colin Crouch and Alessandro Pizzorno, eds., *The Resurgence of Class Conflict in Western Europe since 1968*, vol. 2: *Comparative Analyses* (Holmes & Meier, 1978), pp. 277–98; Ida Regalia, Marino Regini, and Emilio Reyneri, "Labour Conflicts and Industrial Relations in Italy," in ibid., vol. 1: *National Studies,* pp. 101–58. The post-1971 union policy of *inquadramento unico* (a common pay hierarchy from unskilled worker to lower-level management) skillfully mediated between the most egalitarian demands and the differentials sought by skilled workers and employees.

20. See Michele Salvati, "Slittamento salariale e sindacato con particolare riferimento all'industria metalmeccanica, 1954–69," *Rassegna economica*, vol. 34 (November–December 1970), pp. 1397–1442.

21. The same profile can be detected in strike statistics; hours lost for strikes usually reached a peak immediately before the signing of the agreement.

Figure 15-1. *Change in Wages, Employment, and Consumer Prices in Italy, 1968–78*

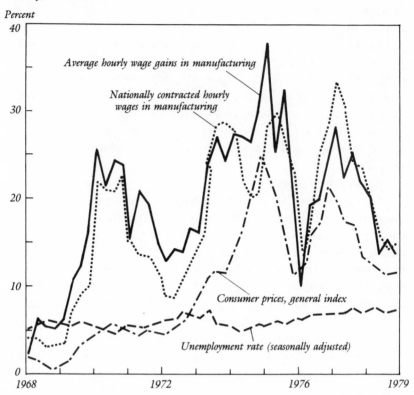

Source: Italy, Ministry of Labor, Istituto Centrale di Statistica.

or anticipated, last three years.[22] Normally the whole or the largest portion of the agreed wage increase takes place when the contract is signed. Agreements for a large part of the industrial work force usually fall due around the same time, coinciding with the date of contract renewal for the larger, stronger, and more militant section of the industrial working class, the metal and engineering workers. The really large wage gains, averaging 17–18 percent, were earned in the first round, between 1970

22. F. Modigliani and E. Tarantelli, "Forze di mercato, azione sindacale e la curva di Phillips in Italia," *Moneta e credito*, vol. 29 (June 1976), pp. 165–98, use anticipation or retardation in the renewal of the contract as a measure of union strength. Their reformulation of the Phillips curve to fit Italian experience takes account of both institutional aspects of the Italian industrial relations system and the segmented nature of Italian labor markets.

and 1972, when consumer prices were rising at a fairly constant rate of 5 percent. Increases were still substantial in the second wage round, but they became rather modest thereafter.[23]

The first wage round is also the one that remains most difficult to explain along traditional lines (as a function of unemployment and of consumer prices). After the January 1975 agreement between unions' and employers' confederations on full wage indexation, the link between wages and prices became institutionally determined. But even before that date the influence of consumer prices on wages was clearly visible and was operating both through the partial indexation system then prevailing and through union action.

The difference between the rate of change of actual and nationally contracted wages is a possible measure of wage drift. Drift is relevant both before and after the 1969–70 wage round and after the 1973 one. Before the earlier round, drift was due to the outburst of local bargaining which, in a tighter labor market, was extending the modest gains of the national agreements of the mid-1960s. After the 1969–70 round, drift arose out of the process of entrenching the unions at the shop-floor level. The favorable economic situation also permitted a significant outburst of local agreements after the 1973 round. From 1975 on, the high wage increases at the national level—due to the 1975 indexation agreement and the 1976 wage round—as well as the deteriorating economic situation did not leave much room for further drift.

None of the variables normally adopted in wage equations can explain the movements in Italy. Naive or sophisticated Phillips curves simply do not fit the first wage round; equations that introduce some indicator of conflict or union strength, or quite simply a dummy, serve better.[24] But using a dummy amounts to giving up the task of explanation, while indicators of conflict or of union activity—however sophisticated[25]—

23. The yearly rate of growth of real wages (nationally contracted rates deflated by the CPI) was 10.8 percent between 1969 and 1972, 7.6 percent between 1972 and 1975, and 5.2 percent between 1975 and 1978. In comparison with other countries, the growth of real wages in Italy is even more striking than the inflation of money wages, far exceeding what productivity and terms-of-trade development might have sanctioned.

24. See George L. Perry, "Determinants of Wage Inflation Around the World," *Brookings Papers on Economic Activity, 2:1975*, pp. 403–35. (Hereafter *BPEA*.)

25. See Modigliani and Tarantelli, "Forze di mercato"; Paolo Sylos-Labini, "Forme di mercato, sindacati e inflazione," in *Rassegna economica*, vol. 34 (November–December 1970), pp. 1339–94, who regresses hours lost for strikes against unemployment; Douglas A. Hibbs, Jr., "Trade Union Power, Labor Militancy and Wage Inflation: A Comparative Analysis" (MIT, Center for International Studies, April 1977), who relies on indicators of strike frequency and strike volume (workers out multiplied by days lost).

Table 15-3. *Annual Rate of Change in Labor Costs in Italian Industry,*
1971–79[a]

Percent

Year	Value added	Employ- ment	Produc- tivity	Labor cost per employee	Labor cost per unit of output
1971	0.7	0.0	0.7	10.9	10.1
1972	4.3	−1.0	5.5	11.3	5.4
1973	10.4	1.5	8.2	21.8	12.1
1974	5.1	2.3	2.7	22.5	19.3
1975	−9.2	0.0	−9.1	22.3	34.6
1976	10.0	−0.1	10.2	23.3	11.9
1977	1.5	−0.1	1.6	21.0	19.1
1978	2.0	−0.3	2.4	13.6	11.0
1979	4.9	0.6	4.3	20.8	15.8

Source: Bank of Italy, *Relazione annuale, 1978.*
a. Excludes construction.

simply suggest that they have something to do with the increase of money
wages but do not explain why workers suddenly get more militant or
unions more powerful.

PRODUCTIVITY AND UNIT COSTS. During the 1970s the Italian economy revealed one of the extreme instances of the labor productivity cycle
that came to prevail in all industrialized countries. Employment remained
practically constant during recessions and thus labor productivity oscillated
with output (see table 15-3). Hourly productivity showed the same profile
although with lesser intensity. Since wages followed a course hardly
influenced by output and employment, labor costs per unit of output
were also subject to wild oscillations, opposite in sign to those of
productivity.

Now the way in which labor statistics are collected tends to exaggerate
the stickiness of employment and hours and, as a consequence, the cyclical
swings of productivity and unit costs.[26] Still, there can be little doubt
that a significant change occurred between the 1960s and the 1970s.
During the 1964–65 downturn, not only were average hours massively
reduced, but employment followed suit almost immediately. Although
hours worked started to recover at the lower turning point of the output
cycle, employment continued to decrease for another year. The net

26. Employment data are fairly biased toward the large productive units, in which inflexibility is
strongest. When dualism is a relevant feature of the industrial structure as in Italy, the swings of
employment and hours during the cycle in the small firms sector may be heavily underestimated.

consequence of this behavior was that no significant productivity cycle appeared.

It is difficult to explain the difference between the two decades unless the changing balance of forces in the work place is taken into account. Firing became more difficult, and even the extended role of the *cassa integrazione*[27] did not allow firms to adjust hours to output as much as they used to. Further, the greater strength of the workers and the unions at the work place, besides compelling firms to stabilize employment during the cycle, influenced the average relationship between hours and output, tending to shift productivity downward after 1970. Overtime, internal mobility, rates for piecework, the pace and rhythm of assembly-line labor, and work effort in general became the stakes of bargaining in the factory and were no longer unilaterally determined. Firms complained bitterly over the ensuing loss of productivity, and, in fact, the stagnation of productivity between the end of 1969 and the second half of 1971 seems difficult to account for simply in terms of short-run economic influences.

To summarize, labor's power influences not only wages but productivity. In its turn productivity reacts on employment and employment on labor-market conditions and, in this way, on one of the major prerequisites for labor strength. In other words, if short-run productivity is not independent of the balance of forces between labor and employers, a strong labor force may prevent the weakening of the labor market, at least if the depression engineered by macroeconomic policy remains moderate.

PROFITS. Profits in industry were squeezed in the 1970s by the inability of firms fully to index prices to unit costs, the low rate of capacity utilization, and the growing debt burden. The last factor became significant after 1973, whereas the importance of the first greatly diminished after that date, when the lira was allowed to float.[28]

27. Roughly "wage stabilization fund," partly financed by employers (by levying a small proportion of the total wage bill) and increasingly by the state. The *cassa*, which roughly pays 90 percent of the hourly rate of wage to workers on short time, originated as a wartime institution used to stabilize wages in factories forced to interrupt production because of destruction or raw material shortages. It has been extended to apply to employees of factories whose production has been interrupted that are unlikely to reemploy the same number of workers again. Practically, the *cassa integrazione* is a coverall form of unemployment subsidy for workers who are not formally fired because the formal unemployment subsidies are ridiculously low.

28. Floating exchange rates, however, are not a sufficient condition for complete profit margin indexation in the short run. If a deflationary policy is adopted and levels of activity are low, the rate of exchange is usually stabilized or even improves, thus making it difficult to increase prices when the manufacturing sector is very sensitive to foreign competition. The rate of exchange does not react immediately to comparative unit costs, but to balance-of-payment deficits and surpluses, and the current balance usually improves when the economy is depressed.

Although it is easy to distinguish logically between those forces that act on the profit margin and those that affect the overall level of economic activity (with total profits being the product of the two), activity and margins are hardly independent. The connection is established by the behavior of short-run labor productivity and by the inability or unwillingness of firms to adjust prices to short-run variations of unit costs.[29] Unit costs rise quickly in a recession, and since firms do not increase prices proportionally, they compound the losses of reduced margins and lower volume. The contrary is true, obviously, when activity increases. This means that the amplitude of profit swings during the course of the business cycle is greater than the swings in output or employment.

Between 1970 and 1972 profits were squeezed both because prices could not be raised in proportion to costs (demand was low and the exchange rate was still fixed) and because volume was low. Late in 1972 the economy recovered sharply and so did productivity. Together with the devaluation of the lira, the surge in demand allowed a rapid increase in prices, and only the very high wage concessions in 1973 prevented the profit share from rising more than it did.

The cyclical pattern of profit shares is a far more reliable measure than is their long-run behavior. The graph of total value added in manufacturing less labor costs in figure 15-2 indicates that a sharp profit squeeze took place with the advent of the 1970s, as does the graph of the utilization of productive capacity. No further fall seems to have occurred after 1972, at least if factor-cost data are taken into account.[30] Given the dependence of gross profit on overall sales and the size of a firm's labor force, it is no surprise that industry has been insistent in its concern about the overall level of economic activity and the need for labor mobility—the latter a euphemism for layoffs and firing. Nor is it surprising that it has demanded reduction of the interest burden, which in the mid-1970s climbed to unusually high proportions of gross profits.

As in many continental countries, the dependence on borrowed funds is higher in Italy than in economies with a highly developed capital market, such as Britain or the United States.[31] Indeed dependence on

29. See Kenneth Coutts, Wynne Godley, and William Nordhaus, *Industrial Pricing in the United Kingdom* (Cambridge University Press, 1978); Italian data are provided in Paolo Sylos-Labini, "Review Article: Industrial Pricing in the United Kingdom," *Cambridge Journal of Economics,* vol. 3 (June 1979), pp. 153–63.

30. When value added is reckoned at market prices, a further increase in the labor share appears after 1973. But this increase has been roughly compensated by the decrease of indirect taxes.

31. For a brilliant account of the logic of the continental financial system, see Alexandre Lamfalussy, *Les marchés financiers en Europe: essai d'interprétation economique* (Paris: Presses Universitaires de France, 1968).

Figure 15-2. *Profit Margins in Italian Industry, 1969–78*

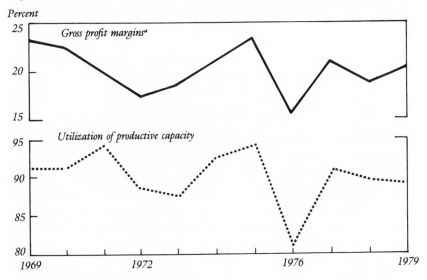

Source: Bank of Italy.
a. Total value added in manufacturing less labor costs.

credit is greater in Italy than in other European countries and it increased in the mid-1960s and the 1970s despite the relatively low investment rate.[32] When the whole interest-rate structure was pushed up by inflation and restrictive monetary policy, firms with very high debt-equity ratios and those that had been pursuing ambitious investment targets in the boom years 1973–74 found themselves in a critical situation.[33] Financial

32. See L. Izzo, "Cause dell'evoluzione della struttura finanziaria dell'economia italiana," in Franco Bernabè, ed., *Struttura finanziaria e politica economica in Italia* (Milan: Franco Angeli, 1976); Francesco Cesarini, *Struttura finanziaria, sistema creditizio e allocazione delle risorse in Italia* (Bologna: Il Mulino, 1977); Marcello de Cecco, "Banca d'Italia e 'conquista politica' del sistema del credito," in Giancarlo Mazzocchi and others, *Il governo democratico dell'economia* (Bari: De Donato, 1976).

33. Short-term rates jumped from 8.3 percent in 1973 to 14.4 percent in 1974, reaching 17.25 percent in 1976. Long-term rates and the average actual burden of debt (ratio of interest payments to financial debt) followed the same profile, though with lower intensity: 8.7, 11.7, 14.5 percent, and 7.3, 10.5, and 14.5 percent, respectively; based on data on roughly 800 large firms; AREL, "Secondo rapporto sulla ristrutturazione finanziaria" (Rome, June 1978), p. 8. Subsidized long-term credit, an increasingly important financial source for industry in the late 1960s and early 1970s, has always been very cheap (6.5 percent in 1975 and 1976) but was also very scarce during the financial crisis of 1974–76. Special credit agencies finance themselves by issuing bonds placed on the public sector and, increasingly, on commercial banks. When a restrictive monetary policy is in force, the residual willingness of the public to hold bonds directly is further reduced, and the ability of banks to absorb new issues is limited by the constraints that are set on overall credit expansion; a sharper trade-off is then present between the various uses of bank credit, leading industry to complain that its demands, both through special credit agencies and directly to the commercial banks, are crowded out because of the priority given to the public sector.

leverage worked in reverse as the interest rate on borrowed capital exceeded the rate of profit on total capital.[34] It is easy to understand why profit margins, net of interest payment, were generally so low in 1975. The sudden increase in the average debt burden had to be met out of total gross profits which had already been squeezed by the fall in demand and the rise of direct costs accompanying it.[35]

The Changing Balance among Unions, Government, and Employers

The Italian wage explosion at the turn of the 1970s was a national instance of a wider inflationary pattern common to most industrialized countries. It was, however, an extreme instance in terms of the intensity and duration of the wage push. Even more, it was distinctive in the way it transformed the system of industrial relations and some of its most critical economic outputs, such as productivity and wage differentials. In Italy, as in the Federal Republic of Germany, France, and other Western European countries, the end of the 1960s was characterized by full employment and a diffuse resentment on the part of workers and unions who wanted a share of the benefits of the boom.[36] But how did it happen that in West Germany and France the wage explosion could be somehow kept under control, whereas in Italy it was allowed to persist and to develop much more intensively?

A good part of the explanation must be sought in the different economic policy, indeed just plain policy, pursued by Italian authorities. Admittedly the problem they had to tackle was different in kind and in intensity from the one confronting their foreign counterparts, and it was more difficult to solve in a noninflationary way. In no other industrially advanced

---

34. See B. Ingrao, "Un'indagine sulla struttura finanziaria delle grandi imprese italiane," document 4 (Rome: Centro di Torre Argentina, 1978); M. Onado, "Il sistema finanziario e le imprese" (Università di Modena, Istituto Economico Aziendale, 1978); Giorgio Ragazzi, "Contabilità dell'inflazione e redditività 'reale' delle imprese italiane," and Onorato Castellino, "Ancora sulla redditività 'reale' delle imprese italiane," *Rivista di politica economica*, vol. 66 (December 1976) and vol. 67 (July 1977).

35. This is the final assessment of the official *Relazione sullo stato dell'industria italiana* (Ministero Industria, Commercio e Artigianato, 1977); it implies that firms follow the kind of long-run pricing policy that ignores increases in costs due to abnormally low levels of demand.

36. Both monetarists and Keynesians seem to agree that the Johnson boom of the late 1960s and the U.S. balance of payments deficit are the chief villains in the inflationary outburst among industrially advanced countries at the turn of the decade. For a discussion of differences in international experience, see Robert J. Gordon, "World Inflation and Monetary Accommodation in Eight Countries," *BPEA*, 2:1977, pp. 409–68; David Soskice, "Strike Waves and Wage Explosions, 1968–1970: An Economic Interpretation," in Crouch and Pizzorno, *Comparative Analyses*, pp. 221–46.

European country were unions so organizationally weak, nor participation limited to so restricted a stratum of politicized and professionally qualified workers. Nowhere else was shop-floor bargaining over wage and working conditions so removed from actual union practice. Paradoxically these relative weaknesses—the limited union coverage of the labor force and the restricted scope of local bargaining—were to become powerful causes of disequilibrium. And in few other countries were conditions so favorable for a radical change. Effective full employment was regained—after the deflationary policies of the mid-1960s—in the industrial labor markets of northern Italy around the end of the decade. This was a common situation in Europe. What was less common was that full employment was obtained through massive internal migration. The harshness of working and living conditions, the unfamiliarity with industrial discipline that immigrants faced, in comparison to the local labor force, was no greater in northern Italy than in other countries that utilized immigrant labor. However, citizenship allowed the Italian migrants far greater possibility to voice the resentment arising out of these conditions.[37]

A second important difference from other countries arose from the distinctive relationship between the unions and the political system. The obvious contradiction that had been developing in Italy in the 1960s between the practical conduct of industrial relations, which relied on deflationary discipline and the exclusion of unions, and the political role that the unions had acquired in the Center-Left coalition did not exist in France, where the unions had no direct political sponsor in the dominant Gaullist coalition. Neither did it exist in West Germany, where worker interests were not only fully represented by the Social Democratic party at the governmental level but, by virtue of codetermination, enjoyed institutional recognition in the system of industrial relations.

LABOR MARKETS. Also, an important structural feature of Italian labor markets—namely, dualism—contributed to the tensions in the labor market that developed in the late 1960s.[38] Regional dualism lay at the origin of

37. Bruno Trentin, leader of the powerful socialist and communist union of metal and engineering workers (FIOM), rightly insists on this point in *Da sfruttati a produttori: lotte operaie e sviluppo capitalistico del miracolo economico alla crisi* (Bari: De Donato, 1977). See also Alessandro Pizzorno, "Le due logiche dell'azione di classe," in Alessandro Pizzorno, ed., *Lotte operaie e sindacato in Italia: 1968–1972,* vol. 6 (Bologna: Il Mulino, 1978).

38. See Michele Salvati, *Sviluppo economico, domanda di lavoro e struttura dell'occupazione* (Bologna: Il Mulino, 1976); Massimo Paci, *Mercato del lavoro e classi sociali in Italia: Ricerche sulla composizione del proletariato* (Bologna: Il Mulino, 1973); Paolo Leon and Marco Marocchi, eds., *Sviluppo economico italiano e forza-lavoro* (Padua: Marsilio, 1973).

the large flows of internal migration, which took place in the absence of effective regional development policies, especially under conditions of high activity in the industrial areas. Even when total employment in industry was not increasing much, in the mid and late 1960s, firms solved many of their mobility problems by using migrant workers.[39] Throughout the 1960s the immigrant work force generally substituted for local labor, men replacing women, young workers replacing older ones. Immigrants were particularly numerous in the centers of rapid employment growth, and many new large factories were almost completely staffed with immigrant labor. Whether the final net replacement of local labor by immigrant labor occurred mainly because of demand factors or supply factors,[40] the fact remains that the restrictions set on eligibility for work in the large factories—young, but not too young, male—made immigration an essential source of supply. Indeed by the end of the 1960s the available pool was beginning to create serious supply problems.

Industrial and organizational dualism is another characteristic of Italian labor markets. In part it overlaps with regional dualism since small, traditional firms and cottage industry are more widespread in the poorer regions. In part, though, what is involved is a Japanese type of industrial organization that flourishes in the very regions where large firms are concentrated, with the small firms linked to them through subcontracting. And partly it is due to the intensive growth of relatively autonomous small firms in labor-intensive sectors in a few regions of northeastern and central Italy.[41] These small firms absorb local pools of labor, disproportionally recruiting very young and old men and women, sometimes linked to their company by time-honored organizational devices such as the putting-out system. Labor's resistance to geographic mobility, a large proportion of traditionally weak components of the work force, the small scale of plants, and the traditional nature of labor organization have always kept unionization less developed, wages lower, work conditions poorer, and cyclical elasticity of employment larger than in bigger firms. The labor-cost advantages, coupled with the limited incentive of economies of scale in the small-firm sector, have always guaranteed a surprising vitality in such a markedly dualist industrial organization. Indeed, the

39. Employment in industry averaged 5,988,000 in 1963 and about 6 million at the peak of the boom, and was only slightly higher in 1969 (6,005,000).

40. See Salvati, *Sviluppo economico*.

41. See Bagnasco, *Tre Italie*.

small-firm sector was actually expanding as unions succeeded in improving the conditions for workers in the large firms.[42]

The attraction for migrant labor of better wages in northern Europe, the extension of the old-age pension system, the increase in family income in the South due to various transfer programs, and the rapid increase in school participation for the younger age groups, along with the traditional dualism, created a tight market for unskilled or semiskilled labor in the late 1960s and early 1970s even as pools of unemployment and under-employment persisted and the labor force participation rate apparently declined.[43]

By the end of the 1960s a young, increasingly nonlocal, unskilled or semiskilled labor force had become a central feature of employment in the large factories of the North. The hardship of their living conditions and the unfamiliarity with industrial work hit immigrants with particular intensity; however, all workers felt the absence of social services and of a long-range housing policy, and the unchecked managerial control of working conditions. These conditions were perceived as contradicting the permissive political climate of the Center-Left governments. Unions still were rather restricted in scope, for the tight labor market of the early 1960s had been too brief, the organizational weakness and the political divisions too great, to effectively extend union participation to the rapidly growing sectors of unskilled and semiskilled labor.

This meant that a rapidly growing segment of the labor force, only recently formed and with origins largely different from the traditional working class, remained largely outside the union movement. This was no longer the case in industrially more mature countries where recruitment of labor for industry was largely completed, where the national work force had long since adjusted to the conditions of industrial labor and was increasingly moving toward the tertiary sector, and where unions had already forged links with all segments of the working class. What the absence of a traditional union role, coupled with a new, militant work

42. This probably happened both after the wage boom of 1962–64 and after 1969. The problems of *decentramento produttivo* and *ristrutturazione* have caused great concern in the unions. See *Rassegna sindacale* (January–April 1977); Augusto Graziani, ed., *Crisi e ristrutturazione nell'economia italiana* (Turin: Giulio Einaudi, 1975).

43. The president of the Central Statistical Office attributed the fall in the participation rate to the improvement of family income. That interpretation provoked an outburst of research on labor markets that revealed the inability of statistical sources to catch various forms of employment in the secondary labor market in an urban-industrial context.

force and a seller's labor market produced was not merely the normal pressure for higher wages, but a struggle for a new collective identity.[44] It was this very mobilization that helps explain the qualitative difference between the Italian "hot autumn" of 1969 and similar episodes of labor unrest and wage explosion around the turn of the decade.

THE RESHAPING OF ITALIAN UNIONISM. The slow growth of productivity in the years from 1969 to 1972 was a function both of the intensity of the labor struggle and of the new forms it was assuming, especially as control of the work process became a central stake for the unions. Firms bitterly complained about the heavy losses due to the cheap forms of struggle invented by the workers—sudden, brief, but disruptive stoppages in sensitive factory sectors, checkerboard strikes, and the like. Nonetheless, the more lasting effects on productivity derived from the loss of management's unilateral power over the work process. Conflict took on an expressive dimension not normally present in the instrumental strategy of a fully recognized actor in the industrial relations system, and control of the labor process remained a long-sought demand of the common workers who were the major participants.

Both features—the militance and the search for control—encouraged development of shop-floor participation. The persistence and strength of local bargaining was a major result. Thousands of local units sprang up during the conflict, which the unions were ready to see recognized in national contracts and which they uneasily but on the whole successfully linked to their federal organizational structure. The continuous shop-floor mobilization meant the persistence of substantial wage drift, even on top of high national agreements and at a time when firms faced reduced profit margins.

Egalitarian demands were another result of the conflict. The sharp contraction of wage differentials and the initial absence of reaction from the relatively advantaged workers were striking, but not surprising in light of the collective enthusiasm that sparked the search for a new social identity. Skilled workers and even white collar employees were deeply involved in a social process that was transforming the role of labor, and in the initial phase they largely endorsed egalitarian wage demands. With the ebbing of collective élan, of course, more self-interested demands began to move to the forefront.

"Riding the tiger"—the phrase current at the turn of the 1960s—

44. Pizzorno, "Political Exchange" and "Le due logiche."

catches the imperative of control that every organization sought to impose on its members; on the other hand, it obscures the promotional role that the unions played both in the early stages and later in extending and consolidating the labor protests. After the disappointing wage negotiations of 1966, unions were caught between the dissatisfaction of their members on one side and the absence of any political rewards for their moderation on the other. This was a period in which the Center-Left government lost any reformist initiative, the economy was following its usual export-led path of growth, large surpluses were being earned on current account, and employment in industry still remained much lower than at the end of 1963.

Weak unions normally seek to strengthen their organization as a major objective. At the end of the 1960s the disappointing results of the Center-Left strategy and worker dissatisfaction made the organizational objective particularly urgent. In 1968—a crucial year—parliamentary elections revealed that the Socialists were the major losers in the stalemate of reform; as a condition for rejoining a Center-Left coalition, they demanded the resumption of reformist initiatives. Economic conditions were good, employment increasing, and there were diffuse feelings of social dissatisfaction that exploded with the student movement.

For the unions this was a movement of intense activity, both at the national level and on the factory floor. Nationally they were involved in two large struggles—one against employers for the abolition of regional wage cages (stipulating wages according to cost-of-living differentials), and the second on behalf of legislation to increase minimum pensions and to reform welfare. At the local level they were also eager to exploit booming business conditions and massively exercise for the first real occasion their rights to bargain. When the new wage round came at the end of 1969, their internal cohesiveness had improved and new activists had been encouraged. The unions also carried the conflict outside their traditional strongholds and implanted their organization in factories and regions where they had earlier been weak.

This organizational offensive proved to be incompatible with strong control and moderation of wage demands. Both in 1969 and in 1973, wage demands and, in general, all demands entailing costs for industry were set at a very high level when reckoned in real terms (albeit more so in 1969 than in 1973, when inflation was already a problem). And both in 1969 and in 1973 the margin for maneuver that unions left for bargaining at the political level was minimal. The main problem for the unions was to satisfy the demands of the rank-and-file and local militants. They were prepared to expend all their bargaining force vis-à-vis the employers rather than engage in the sort of unproductive negotiations in the political arena that had frustrated them during 1966–68 and again during 1970–72 when they had sought housing, health, education, and other reforms without real success. In 1973, moreover, the unions faced a ministry—in the centrist Andreotti government—that was hostile and weak; they thus had no reasons for moderating demands.

OSCILLATIONS IN UNION STRATEGY. During their advance after 1968 the unions engaged increasingly in negotiations with the government over issues such as reform of the health system, housing, pensions, and social services. But the attempt to bypass the political system through direct negotiations between interest groups—albeit major interests who claimed a historical right to represent general constituencies and public concerns—encountered reluctance from the very political parties that spoke for the labor movement, and finally it broke against the same obstacles that had already frustrated these parties.[45]

The failure of a centralized reformist policy, the inability to replace parties as political brokers, and the increasing difficulty after 1973 of winning further advances on wages and working conditions led to the move toward investment control that characterized many industrial agreements and local contracts between 1973 and 1976. The unions returned to their traditional field of negotiations vis-à-vis employers and peak associations, but seeking new objectives—recognition of the union right to be consulted about investment projects and company policy in general. Union power, it was hoped, could be used to obtain goals, such as a territorially more balanced distribution of investment, that seemed difficult to achieve through economic policy and centralized negotiations.[46]

But the nature and scale of the problems increasingly favored centralized bargaining. Little except a rather bland right to information could be obtained in terms of investment policy at the local and sectoral level if

45. This was especially true for the 1969 wage round when tension was high not only because of industrial strife and the student movement, but also because of the extreme Right's bombing of a Milan bank at the Piazza Fontana on December 12, which killed twelve people and aroused strong national reaction. The contract was signed on December 21. On Labor Ministry mediation, see Gino Giugni, *Il sindacato fra contratti e riforme, 1969–1973* (Bari: De Donato, 1973), pp. 19–21, 166–67; Gino Giugni and others, *Gli anni della conflittualità permanente* (Milan: Franco Angeli, 1976), chap. 5.

46. Beyond the permissive attitude of the Ministry of Labor during December 1969, the unions won a favorable "workers' statute" the following May that enlarged union rights and allowed judges more power to curb management resistance to labor. See Emanuele Stolfi, *Da una parte sola: storia politica dello statuto dei lavoratori* (Milan: Longanesi, 1976).

the firm or sector were plagued by a low degree of capacity utilization. Rather the effort to preserve employment became the major item on the union agenda. And for the general issue of employment and the level of the real wage, government policy became the major stake. Thus peak associations became the protagonists of union policy. No ambitious effort to replace parliamentary parties as political mediators for general reform efforts remained feasible. The major issue had become the basic trade-off between the defense of jobs on one side, the level of the real wage and labor mobility on the other.

Political developments were driving in the same direction. The political situation was evolving so as to favor involvement of union leaders in an effort at wage restraint. The early 1970s were not yet ripe for a political bargain in which long-term advantages for the labor movement, political and institutional as well as economic, could be exchanged for wage restraint. And the unions, still trying to consolidate their organization among the rank-and-file, were reluctant to call for moderation. In addition the continuing exclusion of the Communist party—by far the dominant political force in the working class and the unions—impeded the process. But conditions were changing; the reorganization of the unions was near completion, the economic situation was deteriorating enough to render dramatically urgent the need to revive the economy under noninflationary conditions, and the Communists were coming closer to government than they had ever been since 1947.

The Socialist party's objections to governing together with the Christian Democrats made it impossible to return to the relatively stable formula of the Center-Left. The Center-Left collapsed in 1972, and a new effort in 1974 foundered on the same obstacles that had destroyed the earlier one. Under such conditions, especially after the parliamentary elections of 1976, the Communist party demand for participation, voiced since 1973, came to be heard with greater receptivity. A byzantine formula allowed the party to become a part of the governing majority without participating in the cabinet itself. This halfway participation had important influences on the behavior of the union leadership in 1977–78.

The presence of the parties in the government that have the strongest ties with the unions is not usually a necessary or a sufficient condition for winning union efforts at wage restraint. But certainly it favors such efforts. In particular the prize that seemed available for the Communist party—its definitive political legitimation—was significant enough to justify the costly and unpopular effort of an open commitment to wage restraint. With the two working-class parties aligned on a similar call for moderation, faced with a grave threat of unemployment, it is easy to understand how the head of the major trade union confederation pledged a concrete political bargain—wage restraint in return for protecting employment and for other institutional and normative advantages. It is harder to determine to what degree the notable slowdown of local negotiations after 1976 should be attributed to this union political design or to the deterioration of business conditions. What is certain is that the leaders of the CGIL (the socialist and communist union confederation) did nothing to exploit favorable conditions at the local level or in particular industrial sectors to press wage claims more defiantly—and this at the cost of considerable tension both from their own rank-and-file activists and those of other unions.

GOVERNMENT AND EMPLOYERS. As the unions grew more forceful both in the labor market and as allies of the Left parties, the employers' front grew weaker and the government less capable of holding a balance. The ultimate reason lay in the discrepancy between the parliamentary participation that was conceded the workingclass constituency and the wider involvement of labor interests that would have been required to give the unions a stake in wage restraint.

Government had always played an important mediating role in the wage rounds. Major agreements were signed often after tiring sessions between union and employer representatives at the Ministry of Labor with the minister participating. The Budget Ministry, the Bank of Italy, and other government agencies stood ready to furnish calculations on the inflationary consequences of high wage settlements. Still, in contrast with the practice in other countries where the authorities pressed for noninflationary settlements, the Italian Ministry of Labor in 1969 and 1973 never weighed in as an independent third partner. The ministry limited itself to moving the two parties closer toward agreement—playing the role more of mediator than of arbitrator—as if concerned less with the terms of agreement than the social tensions present in the absence of a pact.[47]

47. Since the economy was booming and devaluation of the lira was allowing profit margins to rise, the resistance of private industry to high wage increases was low. The first agreement signed in the cycle of negotiations was in the public sector, and public industry was given specific concessions (credits and capital allowances) by the government. The 1973 wage round is typical of the additive way of solving conflicts, through concessions to all the parties involved, without reference to available resources. In the 1969 wage round, no concession or compensation was given to private industry as a whole. The year following was characterized by restrictive monetary and fiscal policy and by a stable exchange rate; wage concessions brought a net loss for industry, attributable to the stronger presence of union interests in

The left-wing pressure within the 1969 government, which led to endorsement of union demands, was an important element in determining the state's role.[48] In the 1973 wage round the very weakness of the centrist Andreotti cabinet produced a similar result, since the government, which had previously let the lira float downward and prices rise, could not tolerate further social and political conflict.[49]

The intensity of the stagflationary crisis that set in after 1973 forced the government to move toward the more substantive intervention common in other industrial societies. The change, however, was slow and hesitant, for the underlying weaknesses remained, indeed were made more acute by the Communist party's demand for government participation. The agreement on wage indexation of January 1975 represented an issue resolved largely between private partners, the employers' and workers' peak associations. The government did little to influence a solution that might have massive inflationary consequences. The episode, though, that was most revealing of both the government's persisting weakness and its effort to shape a new interventionist role was the January 26, 1977, agreement between unions and Confindustria on the reduction of labor costs. The government and the political parties pressed these negotiations, which the unions felt compelled to accept, to determine labor's share of sacrifices that crisis conditions were imposing on all economic classes. Labor's major objective was to preserve the indexation system, then under heavy attack. In exchange the unions made concessions on overtime, internal mobility, the increase in working days, and other issues. Government spokesmen felt that these directly negotiated concessions were too meager and proposed to transfer some of the firms' social security burden to indirect taxes whose resultant increase was not to be included in the cost-of-living index used for calculating indexation. Nor were firms that gave in to higher wage demands to be allowed the reduction in social security contributions. Unions and left-wing parties reacted strongly against these latter provisions and managed to have their provisional enactment repealed by parliament.[50]

On the part of the employers, the 1970s saw a transition by Confindustria—belated if repentant—from an attitude of hostility and weakness

---

the government coalition and the different economic situation. A profit squeeze of that intensity, however, can be obtained only once and could not be repeated in the 1973 wage round.

48. See Bank of Italy, *Relazione annuale, 1976*, pp. 121–23; C. P. Cella, "L'azione sindacale nella crisi italiana," *Annali* (L. Einaudi Foundation, Turin).

49. Regaglia, Regini, and Reyneri, "Labour Conflicts," p. 142.

50. See *Rassegna sindacale*, nos. 62–63 (September–December 1976), *Contrattazione*, January 1977.

vis-à-vis the unions to an effort to stabilize a new and costly code of industrial relations.[51] Both attitudes represented a relatively slight resistance to union demands, the first because it was feeble, the second because of the price that finally had to be paid to negotiate new rules of the game. The combined hostility and weakness of the employers' association that extended throughout most of the 1970s originated in the basic characteristics of Italian capitalism, though in the later years they derived from the post–Center-Left relationship between the government, especially its Christian Democratic component, and the representatives of industrial capital. Even before the Center-Left, the development of the public sector meant a continuous source of friction with the government, a friction that is absent in other national situations where (as in West Germany or Sweden) public intervention in industry is slight, or where (as in Japan and France) it is massive but carried on with a greater degree of sympathy with the objectives of private capital. The Center-Left increased the tension with its nationalization of electricity firms, new taxes on dividends, as well as the new role that the Socialists played in formulating economic policy. Even after the resignation of Antonio Giolotti, the Budget Ministry and the Planning Office remained in Socialist hands. This had little effect on macroeconomic outcomes but made it difficult for big business to exert the influence on government policy that equivalent agencies elsewhere facilitate (for instance, the French Commissariat du Plan).

The stance of private capitalists toward the Center-Left had ambivalent results. Big business constituted one of the major forces that inhibited the reformist thrust, but the employers' association became so isolated from the political trends that it was seldom able to stand up to the unions. The Center-Left was an inevitable transition for Christian Democracy and for the democratic development of the Italian political system. Confindustria's opposition, therefore, resulted in a relative loss of contact with the political world and in growing difficulty in sustaining the network of relationships between big business and government leaders that constituted the most effective instrument for promoting an economic policy favorable to industry. Instead, elements of the governing parties strengthened privileged relationships with the state enterprises or established perverse relationships with a narrow segment of big "go-go" firms—economically

---

51. See Alberto Martinelli, "Borghesia industriale e potere politico," in Alberto Martinelli and Gianfranco Pasquino, eds., *La politica nell'Italia che cambia* (Milan: Feltrinelli, 1978); Donato Speroni, *Il romanzo della Confindustria* (Milan: Sugar Co, 1975); Scalfari and Turani, *Razza padrona*.

important but managerially reckless—that ended in the collapse of speculative enterprises in Sardinia and elsewhere.[52]

The employers' association and the major private capitalists were slow to understand the error they committed in distancing themselves from the political developments of the Center-Left, and slow to reverse course once they did understand. And as often occurs in cases of delayed reaction, overshooting was hard to avoid. Few industrial associations among the advanced capitalist governments would have conceded such a favorable agreement for the unions as the *scala mobile* of January 1975 and few governments would have ratified it.

The State Arena

Insofar as government accommodates inflation, it is illuminating to analyze the state in ways parallel to those used in examining the market. As the levier of taxes and the agency responsible for the major goals of social cohesion and harmony, the state faces different groups of citizens, who try to resist its authority, shift tax burdens among themselves, and win more public resources than their rivals. During the 1970s the state arena, where public resources are collected and distributed, grew enormously; the rules according to which collection and distribution take place became less transparent and less accepted; and the intensity and results of the conflict over public resources became vital for the management of the economy. Moreover, the same interest groups and classes contesting in the market arena were present in the state arena where they continued their confrontation with the weapons and procedures appropriate to politics.

In the state arena, as in the market and for many of the same reasons, the 1970s were characterized by a break in the old rules and by a collapse of authority. In the market, however, the confrontation is more direct and the trade-offs clearer; the product is more measurable in terms of physical output, and inflation sets in almost directly if monetary demands are too strong—indeed inflation is the expression of those demands. In the state arena no well-defined limit can be set on the expansion of output, and no general, immediately visible connections can be established between growth of state expenditure and inflation. On the other hand, state resources are placed directly in the hands of the political elite, and

52. See Scalfari and Turani, *Razza padrona*; Galli and Nannei, *Il capitalismo assistenziale*.

distribution is sensitive to changes in the political balance of forces. When inflationary pressure derives not only from the shift from a buyer's to a seller's market, but is accompanied by a shift in the political equilibrium that tends to work in the same direction, the political elite cannot use state power for compensating and stabilizing the thrust deriving from the market. Instead it becomes one of the protagonists in the development of inflation.

No attempt is made here to assess whether and how much the growth and structure of state expenditure and receipts and the amount and financing of public sector deficits contributed to the Italian inflation of the 1970s. The purpose of this section is rather to provide some evidence that in this period the state arena was in a condition of turbulence that paralleled that of the market and to show how the government lost its grip on the main magnitudes of the budget.

The Failures of Taxation

Public expenditure as a proportion of gross domestic product had remained fairly stable around 35 percent during the late 1960s. But in three years, between 1970 and 1973, it jumped 4 points (table 15-4), or 6 points in the more relevant, enlarged accounts.[53] This was an exceptional occurrence among market economies; in the Federal Republic of Germany, one of the countries in which public expenditure increased most during the early 1970s, the share of public expenditure grew in the same period only 2.8 percent. Italian growth from 1974 through 1976 was again very rapid, though not exceptional. In 1975, the severest recession year since the war, public expenditure grew rapidly everywhere because of the fall in national income and the deliberate public policies called upon to reflate.

A second exceptional feature of the Italian experience was the slow growth of government income. Receipts remained practically stable until 1973 as a share of GDP and started to grow only afterward, especially after 1974. Almost everywhere else (save the United Kingdom) receipts

---

53. The corrected—actually always enlarged—version of public expenditure (and of public borrowing) includes the accounts of agencies for which the state bears a final financial responsibility that are excluded in the usual accounting conventions—for example, hospitals and public utilities. Insofar as receipts from these activities do not cover costs and deficits are finally financed by the state, there is a politically determined transfer of resources to the users of the services they provide. See Franco Reviglio, *Spesa pubblica e stagnazione dell'economia italiana* (Bologna: Il Mulino, 1977), and "Spesa pubblica e sviluppo negli anni '80," *Note economiche*, special issue (November–December 1982). The corrected figures for 1970, 1973, and 1975, respectively, are 37.9, 43.6, and 50.3 percent for expenditure and −4.9, −9.2, and −16.7 percent for net borrowing.

Table 15-4. *Annual Expenditure, Receipts, and Net Lending of National Government in Four Countries, 1970–79*

Percent of GDP

Country and category	1970	1973	1975	1979
France				
Expenditure[a]	38.6	38.2	43.1	45.2
Receipts	40.0	38.6	40.3	43.7
Net saving	4.3	3.8	1.1	1.4
Net lending	0.9	0.9	−2.2	−0.6
Italy				
Expenditure[a]	33.3	37.2	41.9	44.2
Receipts	30.4	30.5	31.6	35.7
Net saving	0.2	−3.9	−7.1	−5.3
Net lending	−3.5	−7.0	−11.7	−9.4
United Kingdom				
Expenditure[a]	38.0	39.6	45.8	42.7
Receipts	40.7	36.4	40.6	39.0
Net saving	7.5	1.8	−0.4	−1.1
Net lending	2.5	−3.5	−4.9	−3.2
West Germany				
Expenditure[a]	36.1	38.9	45.5	44.6
Receipts	37.5	41.2	40.8	42.9
Net saving	5.9	6.1	−0.8	2.0
Net lending	0.3	1.2	−5.8	−2.9

Source: OECD, *National Accounts of OECD Countries, 1963–80*, vol. 2 (Paris: OECD, 1982).
a. Current disbursements plus gross capital formation and other disbursements on capital account.·

grew in proportion with expenditure, at least with current expenditure, save in the slump year of 1975. Under normal economic conditions, even without a boom, current receipts cover current disbursement and leave a margin for public savings. Italian state deficits, on the other hand, did not arise merely from cyclical vagaries; instead, there was a deeper imbalance that emerged at the beginning of the 1970s.

The result was disproportionate public dissaving. Current disbursements exceeded current receipts; negative savings appeared as early as 1971 and grew without interruption thereafter—a development that occurred in no other OECD country. This meant further an unusually high Italian level of current borrowing. The proportion of net borrowing for the enlarged public sector had reached 16.7 percent of GDP in 1975 (representing a deficit of about 35 percent of the state budget), a figure that Italy had not even reached during wartime, and commentators suggested that the country had lost the third world war. Financial needs this massive can be met only by creating money or crowding out private borrowing. There is no need, therefore, to seek ideological motives to understand private industry's campaign against state expenditure and state deficits.

Along with Ireland, Italy had the lowest yield of taxes plus social insurance contributions as a share of GDP in the European Community. That was certainly too low with respect to state expenditure, which was roughly in line with the European average. Along with France, Italy also had the lowest yield of direct taxes in the Community (although by the late 1970s and early 1980s fiscal drag would alter the situation dramatically). Indirect taxes and social insurance contributions accounted for a disproportionate share of tax revenue. Since the former was not grossly out of line with the European average, it was the share of the latter that was excessive.[54] Furthermore, administrative inefficiency and a more fragmented productive structure seem to have produced greater tax evasion in Italy than elsewhere in the Community.

There were changing political reasons, too, for national tax difficulties. The difficult and unstable political conditions of the early 1970s further impaired the already meager fiscal authority of the state. In those years in particular, the growing influence of the Left and elaboration of the tax reform bill made fiscal maneuvering an especially delicate issue. Revising the Italian tax structure required a direct confrontation with powerful and highly organized interest groups (with the unions in the case of indirect taxes on consumer goods, and with the business association in the case of social security contributions). But precisely in that period the authority of government was declining vis-à-vis the interest groups.

What is more, a tax yield that is disproportionately dependent on indirect excises and social insurance contributions cannot be increased without provoking higher inflationary pressures than would a structure in which direct taxes have a greater weight, for indirect taxes are more

---

54. See Antonio Pedone, *Evasori e tartassati* (Bologna: Il Mulino, 1979); F. Cavazzuti, *Il modo della finanza pubblica* (Milan: Feltrinelli, 1978), from which the following data are drawn. In 1975, indirect taxes plus social security contributions due from employers were 69.0 percent of total fiscal revenue in Italy, whereas they were 51.0 percent in West Germany, 45.9 percent in the United Kingdom, and 44.0 percent in the United States (in 1974). Direct taxes in 1975 amounted to only 23.9 percent of revenue in Italy, by far the lowest share among industrially advanced countries. As a percent of total tax receipts, the yield of indirect taxes (31.7 percent) was roughly in line with the European average in 1975 (35.8 percent in the United Kingdom, 32.5 percent in West Germany, 28.6 percent in Sweden, 29.5 percent in Belgium). It was the yield of social security contributions (44.4 percent) in 1975 that was completely out of line (35.7 percent in West Germany, which was already exceptionally high in comparison with the European average). A detailed comparative analysis extending to 1983 is contained in P. A. Vagliasindi "Livello ed evoluzione delle entrate e spese correnti della P. A.," in Istituto di Economia e Finanza, University of Rome, *Studi di finanza pubblica*, vol. 7 (Rome: Iacelli, 1984).

readily displaced into price increases. Although fiscal reform was near completion at the beginning of the 1970s, the fear of adding a further inflationary push in already inflationary conditions helped to inhibit increases in social insurance levies, indirect excises, and public utility rates.

The change from one tax structure to another came at a moment when the bureaucracy was already in disarray owing to a particularly disruptive strike and an ill-conceived law that encouraged early retirement of the most experienced officials. Continuing changes in fiscal laws and regulations, even after the initial years of reform in 1973 and 1974, kept yields below their potential level.[55] Nevertheless, tax yields started to rise vigorously in 1975, especially because of the heavy increase in direct taxes. Whether returns would continue to increase remained questionable, however. Because of tax evasion among small firms and independent entrepreneurs, the burden of direct taxation fell disproportionately on wage and salary earners, while inflation had moved taxpayers out of rather mild rates into more burdensome ones. Italy thus entered prematurely the political situation familiar in Britain and the Nordic countries (where direct tax receipts, however, had reached far higher levels). Workers and salaried employees were beginning to react against direct taxation and the unions were starting to bargain for wage increases and reduction of taxes. In short the postreform fiscal structure generated its own inflationary pressures.

The Nature of Public Expenditures

Spending on the traditional functions of the state, the last five categories in table 15-5, hardly kept pace with the nominal growth of GDP. The increase in the share of public expenditure in GDP is almost completely explained by the first four categories, and since the fourth (interest charges) is a consequence of the past debt, of the increase in interest rates, and of the new net borrowing, most of the increase arises from three items: pensions, health, and transfers to firms. The first two are straightforward, functional categories, the third a catchall for almost every new state objective—from regional policy to employment policy, from industrial policy to subvention of publicly provided services.

PENSIONS AND HEALTH: EXPANSION WITHOUT REFORM. Over 60 percent of the rise in the share of the public sector's expenditure occurred in the pensions and health categories, two areas of public expenditure

55. See Pedone, *Evasori*, chap. 4; "È fallita la riforma tributaria?" proceedings of a conference held in Pavia, October 27–28, 1978.

Table 15-5. *Distribution of Public Expenditure in Italy, by Category, 1970 and 1975*

Percent

Expenditure category	Share of total public expenditure		Contribution to increase in expenditure as a share of GDP, 1970–75
	1970	1975	
Pensions and family allowances	24.1	26.3	3.3
Health	12.6	15.5	2.6
Transfers to firms	12.6	13.9	1.8
Interest on public debt	4.9	7.0	1.5
Subtotal	54.2	62.7	9.2
Education and culture	14.0	11.9	0.3
Defense	6.3	4.2	−0.4
Public security	2.7	2.0	0.0
Justice	0.8	0.8	0.0
Unclassified[a]	22.0	18.4	0.4
Total	100.0	100.0	9.5

Source: Franco Reviglio, *Spesa pubblica e stagnazione dell'economia italiana* (Bologna: Il Mulino, 1977), table 39, p. 118.

a. Mainly central and local government administration.

that differ profoundly in institutional character and in the structure of interests and of groups involved in them. Beyond the common resistance of both the pension and health bureaucracies to change, pensions involve a pure distributive problem. Pensions are given in money, and the question is simply who pays (and how much) and who receives (and how much). The health system provides services and involves the question of the interests and attitudes of the doctors who provide those services. Both areas, however, were inflation-prone. Demands for higher and more equitable pensions and for better health services became very strong in the late 1960s. Projects of reform had long been discussed in both fields, and failure to implement them was responsible for a good share of the Socialists' dissatisfaction with the meager results of their participation in the first phase of the Center-Left experiment. The rapid increase in public expenditure in the early 1970s can be explained in large part by the Left's pressure for a more activist government attitude.[56]

Simultaneously, public health care systems faced a cost explosion all around the world, for many of the same, deep-rooted reasons—the limited scope for cost-reducing technical progress, the difficulty of distinguishing between essential and nonessential services, and the problem of the doctors

56. Alberto Predieri, ed., *Il parlamento nel sistema politico italiano* (Milan: Comunità, 1975).

with their ambiguous intermediary position, since they both help to create demand and satisfy it.[57] The number of doctors per capita, the frequency of visits and prescriptions, the consumption of drugs in Italy were all among the highest in the world; yet according to indexes of public satisfaction and to more objective indicators, Italy's health care was among the poorest in the industrialized countries. There was agreement among most parties on the corrective measures needed, including a nationalized public health system to replace the fragmented system of private insurance, with the final financial responsibility lying with the state; much stronger control over doctors' prescriptions and visits (and incomes); and limitation of public funding to the "really useful" core needs. Doctors, with the best of both worlds, strongly resisted a reform of this kind. They were free to exploit the private segment of the market (which is always vital because of the poor quality of the public one) and they could increase the public segment as they liked, since, at zero price, consumer demand is practically inexhaustible. Compensation per visit was low, but the time and effort devoted to patient visits were also minor, and a high revenue resulted from multiplying their number.[58]

The activist attitude of the late 1960s did not tackle these basic problems. The hospital reform law, or Mariotti law as it was known for the Socialist minister of health, simply tackled a partial problem, and in such a way as to unleash a very fast increase in costs.[59] Undoubtedly, the hospital administrative structure had to be changed. As of 1968, hospitals were still mainly organized as charities; doctors' compensation, except for department heads, was ridiculously low, and nonmedical personnel were insufficient and badly paid. The Mariotti law made hospitals public bodies,

57. See David Alan Ehrlich, *The Health Care Cost Explosion: Which Way Now?* (Bern: Hans Huber, 1975).

58. The relatively favorable economic situation of Italian doctors (both in international comparison and in relation to other professions at home) led to an overcrowded profession. And their number was increasing rapidly since there were no admission examinations and no *numerus clausus* in the faculties of medicine.

59. The Mariotti law was not only an additive response to interest-group demands, but it was an example of the Italian tendency to decentralize decisions without assigning financial responsibility. Hence the financial crisis of local administrations (in comparison with Naples or Rome, New York is an example of sound finance). See Piero Giarda, "Il finanziamento della spesa degli enti locali," in Emilio Gerelli and Franco Reviglio, *Per una politica della spesa pubblica in Italia* (Milan: Franco Angeli, 1978), pp. 131–52; for later developments, see F. Cavazzuti and S. Giannini, *La riforma malata* (Bologna: Il Mulino, 1983). But hospitals accounted only for roughly two-fifths of the increase in public expenditure for health between 1970 and 1975; even more important was the increase in expenditure due to private visits and prescriptions. After 1975 the growth of expenditure for hospitals was rather brutally choked (see Antonio Brenna, *Il sole—24 ore* [Milan], October 15, 1978), whereas the expenditure for visits and prescriptions continued to increase. See Antonio Brenna, "La spesa per la sanità," in Gerelli and Reviglio, *Per una politica*, pp. 85–107.

with their administrative councils elected by local public administrations. Staff increased very fast and, because of union pressure, wages also rose. No limit, however, was put on expenses; hospital administrative councils determined day rates each year simply by estimating total costs and dividing by the estimated total number of patient-days, then passed the costs on to insurance funds and finally to the state.

In this way everybody ended up happy. The government and its political parties could show just before the elections that they had completed a long-awaited reform. The unions won more jobs and higher wages for nonmedical personnel. Local political elites of every party gained another large source of patronage and power. And doctors—especially young doctors—were given well-paid and interesting work (private practice is rather discredited in Italy). The only minor drawback of the reform was that hospital costs trebled in five years.

Pension reform worked in much the same way. Extensive plans for reorganization had long been available.[60] The most important change in the 1970s was extension of the public pension system to peasants, retailers, and artisans, which was typical of the political orientation of the dominant elite. Moreover, for all self-employed workers, in contrast to wage earners, contributions were set at a nominal level, so that the state really paid these pensions. Furthermore, the very costly and peculiar Italian disability insurance allowed pensions out of all proportion to prior contributions and imposed only very loose medical controls on the loss of working capacity. By the 1960s, disability pensions had become a form of generalized family income support, which was particularly widespread in the southern regions and often had little to do with any real loss of working capacity. On the whole, the pension system of the 1950s and 1960s worked as a mechanism of transfer of payments from the general taxpayer to the "traditional" lower middle class and from North to South.[61]

The activist phase of government and the deep involvement of the unions led to introduction of a minimal social pension for all old people,

60. A reform project, *Riforma della previdenza sociale*, presented by a parliamentary commission (chaired by M. A. Coppini) and accepted by the National Council on Economy and Labor (CNEL), proposed a tax-financed, common pension system plus a few large, contributions-based, complementary systems; *Osservazioni e proposte sulla previdenza sociale* (1962).

61. See Onorato Castellino, *Il labirinto delle pensioni* (Bologna: Il Mulino, 1976); G. Morcaldo, "Analisi della struttura dei trattamenti pensionistici e della sua evoluzione," in *Contributi alla ricerca economica*, no. 7 (Rome: Bank of Italy, 1977); Onorato Castellino, "La spesa per le penzioni," in Gerelli and Reviglio, *Per una politica*, pp. 183–201. The difference between benefits and contributions (hence, the transfer from general funds) was L447 billion in 1976 in the case of dependent workers, whereas it was L2.26 trillion (roughly 1.5 percent of GDP) for the traditional lower middle classes (peasants, artisans, retailers).

an increase in the level of pensions for salary and wage earners,[62] and indexation of pensions in general.[63] The outcome was an increase in the total number of pension recipients from roughly 11.5 million in 1969 to 15.5 million in 1976, a growth of 2.5 times of the average amount paid, and a price elasticity due to indexation that was close to one for most pensions and greater than one for a fraction of them. Most pensions continued to be inadequate, but the increase in public expenditure for this purpose and the deficits of the pension funds were impressive. The striking thing in international comparisons is Italy's inability to increase contributions or other taxes in proportion to its expenditures on pensions, and the favorable treatment given the self-employed. Both the Socialists within the government and the unions outside failed to face the need for a reform in the structure of the system[64] and in the distribution of the new pension burdens. The urgency of winning quick and tangible results for their constituencies produced at the end a typical bargain in which left-wing forces defended the interests of wage earners and the Christian Democrats the interests of the traditional lower middle class. Since nobody wanted to antagonize anybody, significant concessions were made to all the interest groups concerned, and few legislators gave thought to the long-run financial consequences of the legislation.

TRANSFERS TO FIRMS OR SUBSIDIES TO CONSUMPTION? It might appear that a policy of major state investment lay behind the increase of state transfers to firms from roughly L2 trillion in 1970 to over L7.5 trillion in 1975.[65] But such a conclusion would be misleading. The pursuit of growth in a proper sense justifies only a fraction of this expenditure. In fact, the difficulties of resisting interest-group demands were compelling the political elite to shorten its horizons. Direct state investments, for instance, already low on an international scale in 1970, remained roughly constant as a percentage of GDP through 1975.

62. Pensions were linked to the pay of the last years of work, which is normally greater than the average pay a worker receives in his lifetime. Such a rule tends to favor nonmanual workers, whose incomes continue to grow during their working lives.

63. Social pensions and pensions of independent workers were fully indexed to the cost of living. The indexing system applied to the lower range of workers in the firm sector implied a price elasticity roughly equal to unity; the system for those in the upper range, linked to the progression of minimum wages, implied a price elasticity greater than one in the immediate future. Indexation of public employment pensions also moved to reach unity at the end of 1978. See Morcaldo, "Analisi."

64. See Amato, *Economia*, p. 168.

65. Antonio di Majo and Francesco M. Frasca, "Spesa pubblica e produzione per il mercato," in Carli, *Sviluppo economico*, pp. 345–92, esp. p. 385. The figures are obtained by lumping together all sums passed to private, profitmaking firms, from loans to capital subscription. See Giorgio Brosio, "I trasferimenti alle imprese," in Gerelli and Reviglio, *Per una politica*, pp. 153–82.

Payments to local public utilities and to nationalized services accounted for roughly half of state transfers to firms in 1975, whereas they were slightly more than one-fifth of a much lower total in 1970.[66] The real explosion in state transfers to firms was in covering the deficits of local utilities and nationalized public services such as state railways, public motorways, and the National Electricity Board. Local utilities and the nationalized services roughly split the funds from this half of the transfers budget. Subsidies to the public utilities overwhelmingly serve a consumption purpose. If half of the advantages of subsidization of nationalized services are assumed to have accrued to firms, then approximately two-fifths of what appears to have been transfers to firms really entailed public consumption.

The roughly three-fifths of the total that represents a proper transfer to firms comprises a very mixed bundle. From a functional point of view it includes all kinds of disbursements made to firms for long-run policy objectives—basically, for industrial and agricultural policy and for regional policy. From the perspective of the recipient, the major share went to state firms and to a group of large private companies—especially in the chemical sector—that were disproportionately involved in the state's regional policy and that had developed those feudal bonds of give-and-take with the political elite.[67] Indeed the dominant cause for the increase in transfers was the financial crisis into which the traditional group of state and state-assisted firms, and a few new sectors, had plunged. As usual, stockholders, managers, and the unions all pleaded for state assistance, the former to retain their investments or positions, the latter to defend employment; and, as the figures suggest, their demands were met. Whether this time-honored intervention of the Italian state in the private sector (IRI thus originated during the crisis of the 1930s) should be considered a growth objective is questionable. In a formal sense, perhaps; in this case, however, there was no conscious planning, farsightedness, or independent assessment on the part of the political elite of the long-run needs for survival and growth.[68]

---

66. See Brosio, "I trasferimenti alle imprese," p. 159.

67. There is increasing speculation that state-owned and state-assisted firms did not really aid industrialization of the South but primarily served the interests of the political and managerial elite. See Scalfari and Turani, *Razza padrona*; A. Graziani, "Il mezzogiorno nell'economia italiana oggi," *Inchiesta* (September–October 1977).

68. Procurement policy and tax policy in Italy are much less important than in the United States. The real industrial complex in Italy is state owned, and company taxation is lower and profits lower than in the United States, or in West Germany. See P. Bosi, "The Political Economy of Profit Taxation in

Inflation and Short-Run Economic Policy

If the conflicts in the market and state arenas are accepted as the source of the wage and productivity movements, of the magnitude and structure of state expenditures, receipts, and deficits, it is difficult to envisage a different pattern of short-run demand management and monetary policies that might have consistently reduced the rate of inflation without also handicapping the attainment of other economic and noneconomic objectives, such as investment, employment, output, and redistribution. The path that macroeconomic policy had to tread was a narrow one and unavoidably entailed a high dose of inflation, even had no mistakes been made.

Suppressed Inflation: 1969–72

Nineteen seventy-three marked the watershed of the Italian inflationary process. Although an acceleration in the relevant price series could be detected between 1969 and 1972, it remained moderate and in line with what was happening abroad. Certain imbalances had emerged in both the state and market arenas, but until 1973 it was the difficulties of the market arena that were really preoccupying.

HOW THE HOT AUTUMN WAS TACKLED. Faced with the labor upheaval and the crisis of industrial relations at the turn of the 1970s, the treasury and the Bank of Italy reacted with the nonaccommodating medicine that had proved so successful in 1963–64. A restrictive monetary policy (though not so sharp as that of the winter of 1963–64) was enacted in the second half of 1969 and lasted through most of 1970. Just as in 1964, a deflationary fiscal package was implemented in August 1970. But from a strictly economic point of view, the underlying situation was different. While investments had been growing vigorously in the late 1960s, no real excess demand was present in 1969–70. The balance of payments on current account was largely positive, and the deterioration of the overall balance was due to differential interest rates and political concerns that were provoking massive capital outflows.[69] From the

Italy," paper prepared for a conference on the Comparative Politics of Capital Formation, Center for European Studies, Cambridge, Massachusetts, February 3–5, 1978.

69. Effective measures against capital flight were not taken until 1972; they were reinforced in 1973 and 1974. The reluctance of policy authorities to enact regulations stemmed from their doubts about

viewpoint of social and political conditions, the differences between 1970 and 1964 were even greater. This time a restrictive policy—certainly not a rather gentle one—could not do the job.

The fear of inflation was one of the driving forces behind the nonaccommodating policies of 1969–70; documents of the time are full of explicit statements of the objective of price stability. Price stability was not deemed to be in contradiction with objectives of investment and employment.[70] If the restrictive measures were successful in moderating wage demands and labor turmoil, a vigorous export surge might be expected as a consequence of lower domestic demand. This would have produced the usual virtuous circles on which previous booms had been based and would have facilitated a long period of growing output and productivity and thus of profit margins (even without price increases).

If this was the policymakers' design, they badly miscalculated the depth of the changes occurring in the system of industrial relations. Moreover, timing was unfortunate if they were banking on an export boom, since the policy coincided with the slowdown of world trade due to the cooling off of the American and West German economies.[71] The exhaustion of the investment boom in late 1969, the moderate growth of exports, the countercyclical fiscal package of August 1970 confined the economy to a low growth path even before the slackening of world trade in 1971. Industrial production virtually stagnated between the second quarter of 1970 and mid-1972—an almost unprecedented experience since postwar

efficacy (admittedly long-run effectiveness in an open economy may be low, but short-term impact can be substantial). But also the authorities believed that capital mobility is a corollary of free trade, and the way to avoid capital flight is to preserve the conditions in which capitalists see no need for it.

70. For the continuing investment objective, see Governor of the Bank of Italy, "Final Considerations," *Relazioni annuale, 1970* and *1971*. Governor Guido Carli's stress on investment was rather exceptional; see G. Nardozzi, "Accumulazione di capitale e politica monetaria: il punto di vista della Banca d'Italia," paper presented at the conference *Economisti e politici*, 1945–1978, University of Pavia, September 28–30, 1978.

71. This was not the only cause for the relatively modest development of Italian exports between 1969 and 1972 (and up to 1974). Between 1963 and 1966—the first years of the previous export-led cycle—world trade in manufactured goods increased by 36 percent, and the Italian share grew from 5.9 percent to 6.9 percent; between 1969 and 1972 world trade increased by 26 percent, and the Italian share remained roughly stationary (National Institute of Economic and Social Research, *Review*). One explanation for this worse performance focuses on industrial relations, price increases, and supply constraints of a short-run nature; another suggests a long-run weakening of the non–price competitiveness of Italian exports due to the changing structure of world trade or relative lack of investments at home. The second line of reasoning seems rather difficult to conform. The factors it stresses seem empirically founded, yet Italian exports showed a rather spectacular recovery, in real terms, in 1975 and afterwards. See F. Onida, "La collocazione dell'Italia nel commercio internazionale," *Giornale degli economisti,* vol. 36 (November–December 1977); Massimo Roccas, "Problemi relativi alla impostazione di una politica commerciale a medio termine per l'Italia," in Carli, *Sviluppo economico,* pp. 407–63.

reconstruction.[72] Nor did this stagnation help much to moderate wage demands and restore a balance of power more favorable to employers, whose profits were hit both by the sharp increase in unit costs and by slackening demand. (Indeed, despite a continuous exodus of capital and the disturbed international monetary conditions of the early 1970s, the domestic slack and the favorable current account balance alleviated the pressures against the lira that had begun to appear in 1970, and the ceiling set by foreign competition prevented firms from raising prices in proportion to costs. This was the major force that held inflation in check until 1973; but it did so only at the cost of protracting a serious imbalance for the firms' sector.)

The governor of the Bank of Italy in his "Final Considerations" in May 1971 observed with pride that a speculative attack against the lira had been successfully repulsed and the speculators had been inflicted a heavy loss. By then, however, he could no longer ignore that the speculators' defeat of 1970 was just a preliminary skirmish. If developments did not change, the speculators might lose a few more battles but would eventually win the war. Only the depressed state of the economy and the resulting current account surplus gave the Bank its ammunition against the speculators. These conditions could not last forever. If costs continued to rise faster at home than abroad and if ultimately reflation had to be pursued, no admissible policy would prevent a major fall of the lira and a rapid increase of inflation.

Were there alternatives to the self-defeating strategy that was pursued between 1969 and 1972? What seems feasible when economic factors alone are taken into consideration often becomes historically implausible when social and political factors are taken into account. What finally occurred seems far more inevitable. Certainly a harsher set of monetary and credit curbs that really "taught a lesson" would have stiffened the resistance of employers against wage concessions and would probably have choked the élan of the collective movement. But if restrictive measures were to be chosen, then the conditions of the turn of the decade really required an overdose. Yet these very conditions precluded a stabilization maneuver of the intensity of 1963–64. No technical justification could be advanced for a massively restrictive policy, and its naked political

---

72. From the third quarter of 1970 onward, money supply increased rapidly. The budget had a more expansive effect in 1971 and especially in 1972, though not sufficient to counteract the fall of investment and the modest development of exports. As was commonly observed, liquidity was there but the horse did not drink. See Michele Salvati, *Il sistema economico italiano: analisi di una crisi* (Bologna: Il Mulino, 1975), pp. 66–69.

purpose would have been sharply at odds with the political balance of forces then prevailing.

A COMPARISON WITH FRANCE. A more plausible technical strategy, however, and one that did not fly in the face of the political balance of the late 1960s, was to be seen just across the frontier. Faced with a similar situation—the beginning of an economic boom and a violent explosion on the part of labor—French authorities took two immediate steps to restore the confidence of employers. The first was to call a general election, which resulted in a plebiscitarian victory for de Gaulle. The second was to keep the economic boom going, maintaining an abundant credit supply for industry. Despite the massive wage concessions embodied in the Grenelle agreements after the 1968 explosion, the confidence of capital was restored; and because credit was available and high demand continued, output and investment remained high. Partially as a consequence of price increases, but even more as a result of compensatory productivity gains, the wage increases were absorbed and profits proved satisfactory even by the end of 1968. Obviously there were problems for the French balance of payments, partly because of growing trade deficits, and even more because of capital outflows, since speculators rightly anticipated that despite de Gaulle's opposition the franc would be devalued and the deutsche mark revalued. French policymakers imposed some restrictions in the winter of 1968–69 and further deflationary measures later in 1969—less to restrain output than to make room for the foreign demand that was expected to revive after the devaluation of August 1969. The maneuver worked better than its authors anticipated, with the result that just after the quasi-revolutionary upheaval of May 1968, the French economy experienced the greatest boom of its history, which lasted until the world recession of 1974–75.[73]

This "masterpiece" (but also stroke of luck) was carried out right in front of Italian authorities and indeed with just the right time lag— between the French May (1968) and the Italian hot autumn (1969)— required for them to learn its advantages. They must have carefully considered the French strategy. Journalists and economic experts close to the Christian Democrats and the Socialist party later (too late for full

73. See Michele Salvati, "May 1968 and the Hot Autumn of 1969: The Responses of Two Ruling Classes," in Suzanne Berger, ed., *Organizing Interests in Western Europe: Pluralism, Corporatism, and the Transformation of Politics* (Cambridge University Press, 1981); Susan Strange, *International Monetary Relationships*, vol. 2, of Andrew Shonfield, ed., *International Economic Relations of the Western World, 1959–1971* (Oxford University Press, 1976), pp. 323–32; Valerie Giscard d'Estaing's speech of May 12, 1970, to the National Assembly, in *Allocutions ministerielles* (Service de l'Information du Ministère des Finances).

effectiveness) publicly proposed adopting an analogous course, but both parties were hostile.

If devaluation was resisted until it was impossible to avoid it, this was not because of technical incompetence but because of political conditions. The unions and the left-wing parties were opposed because they calculated that it meant both reduced real wages and a recapitulation of the pattern of export-led growth that they also criticized. Moreover, the Christian Democratic constituency had much to lose from inflation, especially the pensioners, peasants, artisans, and savers who would not have gained correspondingly from higher output. Business interests and the unemployed would have gained, but the former were not united enough to prevail and the latter were not really organized to influence policy.

In addition, the French had devalued in mid-1969 with several quarters of booming world demand still before them. An Italian devaluation would have occurred in the more disturbed international conditions of the early 1970s, just before the short recession of 1971. If, as some argue, the Italian economy was already less competitive, foreign trade results would have been less favorable than they had been for the French. And while productivity in Italy was stagnating because economic activity was depressed, what was occurring at the shop-floor level in Italy was very different from what had been occurring in France. French workers used full employment only to press hard for a wage settlement; Italian workers were seeking to alter a pattern of industrial relations more profoundly. Thus if productivity were not to rise in Italy and if supply constraints had been present, the outcome of an Italian devaluation might have proven far less favorable than it had in France. And even productivity increases could have hardly offset wage increases of the magnitude obtained in 1973; effective compliance of the unions on the devaluation-plus-reflation strategy would have had to be negotiated. No need for the overt compliance of the unions was present in France, where the parties linked to the working class remained excluded from the government coalition— indeed where the probusiness orientation had been strengthened by the elections and the advent of Pompidou in 1969.

Open Inflation and Drugged Recoveries: 1973–76

Up to 1973, inflation can be viewed in the framework of a rather simple model with wages, costs, and prices on one side, and determinants of economic activity on the other. After 1973 the model must be expanded, for the exchange rate became important in the inflationary process, and state expenditures and deficits emerged as a central concern of policymakers.

Even if some version of the purchasing power parity doctrine is accepted to explain the behavior of exchange rates in the long run, an inverse causal relationship may prevail in the short term. That is, too low a level of the exchange rate may lead to higher internal prices, thus fulfilling the predictions of the speculators and justifying ex post the "wrong" rate that speculators and policy authorities hit upon. If this is true, expectations, capital movements, J-curve effects, and monetary policy can acquire an independent causative role and add their inflationary effects to that of social forces. The existence of such perverse effects or vicious circles is widely denied, probably because these forces would provide an excuse for inflationary developments that are really caused by lax domestic policies.[74] But in the Italian case, evidence exists that overshooting occurred and a vicious circle developed, especially during the foreign-exchange crisis of 1976.[75] Still, even if overshooting complicated the tasks of Italian authorities and accelerated inflation, it probably remained a second-order factor. The first-order causes remain the "original" inflationary pressures of the market and state arenas, or (for the period after 1973) the exogenous terms-of-trade shocks. After the explosion of 1973–74, inflation remained at a high level because, in spite of the adverse terms of trade and the loss of real national income that resulted, workers still sought to defend the real gains that they had earlier won through high money-wage bargains. The growth of productivity was not sufficient to permit a defense of real wages together with a significant reduction of inflation.

DRUGGED RECOVERY 1. After two and a half years of stagnation, recovery started in the second half of 1972. The impulse flowed from every sector of internal demand—from investments (first through a restocking of inventories with strong speculative motivations, later by a real boom in fixed capital formation); from state expenditure; from consumption (both because of an increase in disposable income and a reduction in the propensity to save). This was the first boom since the

---

74. For an admission of the relevance of the vicious circle, see Organization for Economic Cooperation and Development, *Towards Full Employment and Price Stability* (Paris: OECD, 1977), and for a contrary opinion the reservations of Professor Komiya in ibid., pp. 249–55. See also "The Vicious Circle Thesis: A Fixed Rate Fallacy," American document 18, Report to the Working Group No. 3 of the Economic Policy Committee (OECD, 1976); U.S., *Economic Report of the President, January 1977*, pp. 119–23.

75. See G. Falchi and M. Michelangeli, "Interazione fra tasso di cambio ed inflazione," *Contributi alla ricerca economica*, no. 7 (Rome: Bank of Italy, 1977), esp. pp. 66–71.

mid-1950s not led by exports. The consequences were soon visible as the balance of current account turned negative at the very beginning of 1973. The worsening, however, was by no means dramatic, and the real trade results were probably much better, because the monetary data concealed a significant capital outflow (carried out by an underinvoicing of exports and an overinvoicing of imports). Still, when taken at face value, which is what counts in these situations, and when the strongly negative capital account is considered, it is understandable that keeping the lira within the European snake was an impossible task. Thus the currency was allowed to float in the spring of 1973, and it started depreciating immediately.

Monetary policymakers then had to face the difficult task of financing a fairly large treasury deficit, of providing financial means for the long-awaited boom in fixed capital formation, and simultaneously of controlling the strong inflationary pressures developing.[76] Powerful forces were generating the deficit, and investments obviously had a high priority after a long period of stagnation. Consequently, really tough monetary and fiscal restrictions were taken only in the second quarter of 1974. This meant that the Italian economy was still at a high activity level when the oil crisis struck and when major trading partners had already initiated restrictive policies. The immediate consequences were a huge deficit in the current account balance, and a very large foreign debt.

This phase of "drugged recovery," as it was immediately labeled because of its strong inflationary and speculative aspects, favored business interests, especially export-oriented industry, for high turnover and devaluation together enhance profits by increasing margins as well as volume.[77] Still, profits had suffered badly on both accounts for a fairly long time. It was natural for the pendulum to swing in the opposite direction. Political coalitions can find themselves either in the stop or in the go phases of the business cycle. The preceding government had also pursued an expansionary policy. But it was the coincidence of the Center experiment of Andreotti and Malagodi with the world boom of 1973 (and probably not the nature of the government alone) that made the difference. If a special political explanation must be sought, what needs to be accounted for is less the 1973 boom in itself than its unusual protraction, a mistake that was to cost heavy external debt.

76. See Francesco Masera, "Fattori operanti sull'economia italiana nel biennio, 1973–1974," *Moneta e credito*, vol. 28 (June 1975), pp. 145–76.

77. For two interpretations, see A. Graziani, "La strategia della divisione," *Quaderni piacentini*, no. 56 (July 1975); Galli and Nannei, *Il capitalismo assistenziale*.

DRUGGED RECOVERY 2. Another major mistake led to the renewed slump of the lira early in 1976, when the recovery from the 1975 depression was just beginning (drugged recovery 2). It was widely held, both within and outside government circles, that liquidity creation at the end of 1975 was excessive and that interest rates had been allowed to fall below the level that was safe for restraining capital outflows.[78] Policy authorities replied officially that there was no way to finance the treasury and to provide liquidity for industry (large sectors were on the verge of bankruptcy) without also provoking a speculative attack against the lira, given the divergent cost patterns between Italy and her main competitors. The defense is not wholly convincing. If a readjustment in exchange rates had to occur, it hardly justifies the violent speculation and overshooting of the exchange rate that took place in the first half of 1976. Whatever the pressures for an ample money supply emanating from the state and market arenas, and whatever technical difficulties lay in the way of engineering a recovery without unleashing an excessive speculative wave, it is still hard to believe that the Bank and the treasury did not have the power or the technical means to allow a gentler slide of the lira and thus to avoid the violent corrective credit squeeze of mid-1976. On the other hand, it is even harder to understand why policy authorities might have intentionally engineered such a foreign-exchange crisis.[79]

Although this latter view is hardly plausible in the circumstances of late 1975 and early 1976, it is not entirely unfounded. Though they rarely admit it in an explicit way—and understandably so, since it runs counter to their most sacred institutional goal—monetary authorities may feel compelled to allow inflation if they believe that an increase in profits can assist activity and investments. The Italian monetary authorities, at least during Guido Carli's governorship of the Bank of Italy, always expressed unusual concern about the distribution of income in industry. The link between profits, on the one hand, and investments and activity, on the other, can be justified in a number of ways. In his annual reports, Carli never supplied a consistent theoretical explanation but he stated the relationship again and again. Even when fixed exchange rates severely

78. See the authoritative publication of the Banca Comerciale, *Tendenze monetarie*, April 30, 1976; R. Parboni, "Il destino della lira," *Politica ed economia* (June–July 1976); Guido Carli, *Corriere della sera* (Milan), February 15, 1976; Emilio Colombo, *Corriere della sera* (Milan), October 8, 1977.

79. An anonymous article, "Il terrorismo valutorio," in *Il manifesto*, January 25, 1976, argued that policy authorities wanted both to let profit margins increase and to show that a noninflationary recovery was impossible if money wages kept growing so fast. The most careful study of the whole episode is that of A. Tasgian, *L'imposta e il deposito previo sugli acquisti di valuta* (Milan: F. Angeli, 1983).

limited the impact of monetary policy on inflation, Carli insisted that he must and could do something to restore a "proper" ratio between prices and costs. With floating exchange rates and a greater freedom to pursue an autonomous inflationary path, the governor's conviction might have played a role in facilitating the large liquidity supply of 1973–74; his 1973 report explicitly attributed restoration of higher industrial profits to Bank policy.

It is more difficult to believe, however, that such priorities could have survived the inflationary outburst of 1974–75. Whether higher prices and profits can stimulate greater activity and investment and remain within a tolerable limit of inflation depends on given inflationary expectations and on the short-run price elasticity of wages and unit costs. The elasticity of wages with respect to prices had just been pushed up by the indexation agreement of January 1975; consumer prices at the end of 1975 were increasing about 15 percent per annum, but unit costs were growing much faster. Increased inflation, therefore, was easily foreseeable. It could hardly be doubted that a large supply of liquidity and a marked fall in interest rates would end up by financing an outflow of capital and speculative purchases of all sorts, and not a sound development of activity and investments. With inflation already so high, a major foreign-exchange crisis and a powerful outburst of price increases would immediately demand sharp, deflationary measures, as actually happened. Even if a downward adjustment of the exchange rate was one of the Bank's objectives, a violent upsurge of inflation was certainly not; something must have gotten out of hand for the monetary authorities during the winter of 1975–76.

DEMAND FOR AND SUPPLY OF INFLATION. A convulsive pattern of large monetary accommodations and sharp credit restrictions characterized Italian economic policy during the mid-1970s. This did not help much to moderate a rise in prices and unit costs that was more rapid than in all the other major European countries, save Britain. The comparison with the West German outcome may be suggestive. Even the Federal Republic followed a fairly unstable policy between the end of the 1960s and the oil crisis (making Switzerland the least inflation-prone European economy). In West Germany, as in Italy, the wage explosion at the turn of the decade was met by a deflationary package. The same medicine was applied two years later as soon as the 1973 boom began to stir a new wave of industrial conflict and high wage demands. But differences from Italy can be noted both on the supply side of inflation and on the demand side. On the supply side, German authorities adopted restrictive measures as early as mid-1973, even before the oil crisis, and generally pursued a less accommodating policy. The real differences, however, lie on the demand side. Depressions in economic activity seem much more effective in slowing wage increases and in reducing labor militancy in West Germany than in Italy. The growth of money wages and unit costs was significantly reduced in West Germany as a consequence of the restrictive measures taken in 1970 and 1973. This did not happen in Italy. In the middle of the worst recession after postwar reconstruction, in 1975, Italian unions still managed to obtain the most effective indexation mechanism working in Europe, and one that immediately imparted a powerful upward thrust to money wages.

Both the demand for inflation—the thrusts from the market and the state arenas—and the supply of inflation—the inability of policy authorities to avoid accommodation of monetary demands—are relevant in this account. Exclusive concentration on either blade of the scissors would badly miss the point. Technical and political forces seeking a moderate and constant money supply were present in Italy as everywhere else. Indeed a policy of this kind was practiced from mid-1976 to mid-1978. But, faced with a wage push as strong as the one of the early 1970s, a really tough and constantly maintained nonaccommodating line would have had political consequences that Italian governments could not accept. In the last analysis, they could not accept such policies because the political orientation of the Italian governments shifted in tandem with the explosion of demands in the market and state arenas. Both changing political equilibrium and new demands were consequences of a deeper transformation in underlying social forces. Indeed, what is really worth noticing is less the propensity of the Italian authorities to monetary accommodation than their continuing predominant commitment to deflation.

An Effort at Stabilization: 1976–79

This restrictive orientation emerged most clearly after the crisis of the lira in the early months of 1976. Following the most urgent measures taken to shore up the currency in the crisis, a coherent stabilization program, comprising fiscal and credit restrictions, was launched in the second half of the year. The governor of the Bank of Italy spelled out the thrust of these interventions in his report at the end of May: the priorities of economic growth and full employment had to be sacrificed to the objectives of attaining a surplus on current account, repaying the debts contracted in the previous two years, and stabilizing the exchange rate, thus damping down at least some of the inflationary pressures.

Two aspects of Italian economic development during 1977 and 1978 deserve emphasis. From the political point of view, what was striking was less the policy reversal that followed the exchange-rate crisis—a change of course largely imposed by the gravity of the crisis—than the coherence and continuity of the new stabilization policy and its remarkable success compared with earlier oscillations. Income did, in fact, grow less than the average for the other European countries, and unemployment hovered around 1.5 million, or about 7 percent of the labor force, as of early 1979. But the objectives that had been assigned priority were satisfied beyond all expectations. The exchange rate was stabilized, foreign currency reserves grew enormously, a major part of the debts was repaid, and the surplus on current account for 1978 was one of the largest for the Common Market countries.

An exceptional recovery of exports contributed significantly to the economy's response. Just as the disappointing export performance after 1969 was unforeseen, so was the recovery of the traditional elasticity of exports in respect to the depression of internal demand largely unexpected. The authorities worriedly emphasized that much of the result derived from the traditional sectors and those with high labor intensity—sectors, that is, that seem slated for structural decline in a situation of rising labor costs. Some analysts further stressed that the unique elasticity of response was not really the result of more vigorous entrepreneurship, or a greater mobilization of capital and labor, or increased flexibility of industrial relations in the major firms, but derived instead from a more intensive exploitation of the peripheral economy—the small businesses and the subcontractors of unskilled labor. Nevertheless, the real transfer of resources demanded by the new terms of trade was carried out, even if after a delay and even if the means by which the transfers were effected might plausibly cause concern about the solidity and continuity of the competitive recovery that emerged.

The fulcrum of the entire stabilization strategy carried out by the Bank of Italy was its exchange-rate policy. This policy consciously sought an intermediate course between two divergent objectives—an anti-inflationary goal that would have required raising the value of the lira even at the cost of export competitiveness and business incomes, or a goal of maintaining exports and company profitability, but thereby making the exchange rate more dependent on internal costs. In fact, since the trend of unit costs at home did not permit linking the lira to the strong currencies of Western Europe, the Italian exchange rate remained anchored to the dollar through 1977. This allowed prices for imported primary products to be stabilized and it maintained competitiveness for manufactured exports, which were prevailingly directed to strong-currency countries. The lira, however, was cast loose from the dollar in 1978, and the balance of payments and the state of reserves appeared favorable enough by the end of the year to allow the monetary authorities to support the political decision to adhere to the European Monetary System (EMS).

Although this international agreement clearly favored their major institutional policy goals, the hesitation of the monetary authorities is readily understandable. While their stabilization measures were fully successful in terms of external constraints, no equivalent success was attained in controlling domestic prices. The decline in inflationary tensions was much slower. Even in 1978 consumer prices accelerated at a rate (12–13 percent) almost double that of the other major European economies, and money wages increased about 15 percent. Given the modest increment of labor productivity (which stagnated in 1978 except during the final quarter), this meant an increase in unit costs for industry on the order of 12 percent. To stabilize a fixed exchange rate with a country such as the Federal Republic of Germany, Italy's principal trading partner, where unit costs increased only 2 percent in 1978, represented a decision that even a central bank must have deemed risky and perhaps counterproductive. Not even the wide band of permissible variation—and Italy negotiated a relatively high one in the EMS—would suffice if such divergences were prolonged.

For few decisions of economic policy would it be so vital to reconstruct the parallelogram of forces as for Italy's joining the European Monetary System. The official declarations of the protagonists suggest that uncertainty and diversity of views persisted up to the last moment. The factor that seems to have overcome the resistance of the political and administrative elite was the conviction that the political conditions had in fact been established to attempt another and more decisive application of the anti-inflationary strategy.

Everyone who participated in or influenced the decision must have been aware that the step was risky and could work out favorably only if it were possible to control the major sources of inflation—wage pressure, above all, but also government expenditure and the deficit to the degree that it influenced monetary conditions, credit policy, and investment. Still, beyond the favorable economic circumstances at the end of 1978 (ample reserves, the surplus on current account, a greater growth of productivity owing to the autumn recovery, and finally, the stronger inflationary pressures in Italy's trading partners), monetary authorities could also take comfort from the political situation.

The government enjoyed broad parliamentary support, the unions had behaved with moderation since 1976, and even the Communist party was expressing implicit approval of the severe policies pursued by the Bank of Italy. What is more, the minister of the treasury had proposed a clear stabilization program in September—the so-called Pandolfi Document— and despite the stringent limits that this would have clamped on wage increases, the reaction of the left-wing parties and of the trade union federations did not seem to preclude its becoming the baseline for policy in the coming years. Assuming this was the case, participation in the EMS might be sustained for a long period.

The economic situation became far more sombre, however, after the 1979 oil price hike. But the internal political and social situation, above all, had made it more difficult to institute any anti-inflationary strategy that required a broad social consensus. The attempt to contain all the demands unchained on the Left during the preceding ten years by installing an emergency government coalition based on all parties seemed to have failed. Traditional political and ideological cleavages, but above all the difficulties put in the way of the reforms and concessions that might have served to win the Left for an incomes policy, had exhausted the reservoirs of consensus. A strategy of consensus, however, is not the only means of reentry from an inflationary explosion. The history of Italy and of other countries as well includes numerous cases in which reentry took place by means of a stabilization crisis based far less on consensus, with victors and defeated clearly distinguished, and with sharply unequal costs.

PART FIVE

Conclusions and Policy Implications

16

Alternatives for Future Crises

Charles S. Maier and Leon N. Lindberg

What lessons does the great inflation of the 1970s offer? Inflations, as Robert Keohane comments in chapter 4, are not "natural disasters." National societies retain some degree of freedom in submitting to or resisting inflation. They can undergo greater or lesser degrees of the price rises that were so dislocating for over a decade. This study is built on the premise that economies are institutional arrangements responsive at least in part to political and social choice. Centralized decisions as well as "the invisible hand" can affect the output of goods, the allocation of time and labor, and the movement of prices.

Having choices does not make policymaking easy. There are several orders of difficulty. First, the alternatives are often painful. The cost of not undergoing inflation may itself be a great one. Second, it is hard to measure the pain. How do countries choose between the discomfort caused by, say, 10 percent inflation or 7 percent unemployment?[1] Nonetheless, societies may arrive at a consensus that some choices are less optimal than others. Some waste more human and material resources; they impose welfare costs that may not be necessary. The point is to secure the least unfavorable trade-off, to move, in the economists' jargon, to the utility curve farthest from the origin. Charting those curves in the technical sense—that is, measuring the numbers—remains the task of the economists. But there is a further order of difficulty. An economy does

---

1. Too many economists in the 1960s assumed blithely that inflation imposed no real welfare losses except for the shoe leather worn down in carrying checks from savings banks to commercial banks. Perfect knowledge or perfect indexation might have neutralized the effects of inflation. Too often, however, those checks went from the savings accounts of the vulnerable into the money markets of those less exposed. No aggregate welfare losses, of course—except for the undermining of confidence in the future that must underlie all economic activity.

not always respond to policy choices even if rational ones are decided on. Government is only one actor in a capitalist mixed economy, though a powerful one. In the noncommunist world, economic choices are left in the hands of many actors, whose response to policy is not always predictable.

This conclusion draws on the ideas developed in this volume to clarify policy choices primarily in light of the political values they presuppose. The inflation of the 1970s, after all, constituted part of a broader failure of economic activity either to respond to public policy intervention or to surge ahead under its own steam with the vigor of the 1960s. Inflation was only the most preoccupying flaw of an economy afflicted as well by persisting unemployment, low growth, and flagging productivity. Again, two different types of problems can be distinguished. There were the continuing difficulties that undermined vigorous ongoing macroeconomic performance, namely, high unemployment and continuing inflation—in short, persistent stagflation. Some of these difficulties had abated in the United States by 1983, but preoccupations continued about prospects for a durable recovery. And even if the United States economy had responded vigorously in the early 1980s thanks to an unavowed Keynesianism, massive American budget deficits contributed to forestalling needed investment and recovery elsewhere.

Beyond the difficulties of ongoing demand management a second order of problem intervenes, that of structural decline with its attendant need for economic transformation. Moving resources from industries with excess capacity to newer sectors has caused painful problems of adjustment in Western Europe and America. It is no longer enough to seek a static plateau of macroeconomic performance without encouraging qualitative industrial transformation. Otherwise no gains in terms of price stability or employment can be rendered durable in today's world.

Inflation made overcoming each problem more difficult. More precisely viewed, inflation was one expression of each problem. It revealed that macroeconomic management was no longer so easy a task in the 1970s; keeping an economy at high employment entailed heavier doses of inflation. Indeed, in the recession of the mid-1970s significant inflation hardly dented unemployment. But inflation also resulted from structural problems. It was part of the cost of moving workers into new sectors, or of subsidizing those who for good reasons or bad had to be kept in the old ones, as John Zysman points out in chapter 6.

But these problems are not insuperable. Even if the rapid growth of the 1950s and 1960s rested on unique circumstances, achieving satisfactory macroeconomic performance should be attainable, given the possibilities of technological innovation. Overcoming structural dilemmas may involve more difficulty and human pain. Workers rooted in family and community life are not just an infinitely malleable "input" to be described as labor. In an earlier era the transition from a level of agricultural employment at 50 percent of a work force to one under 10 percent involved ugly political conflicts and it continues to demand significant subsidies. There is no reason to think that less stress and strain will be needed in the shift from smokestacks to silicon and services.

Still, most of the difficulties are political as much as they are economic. The issue of who must shoulder the costs mobilizes interested groups and individuals to seek help from government. Public policy is likely to respond not merely to economic dilemmas as such, but to the alignments of the political system.

Three Sources of Inflation

Recent commentators have distinguished economic from sociological approaches to explaining inflation.[2] Most of the contributors to this study work along the lines suggested by Leon Lindberg in chapter 2, which proposes a political and institutional approach. What separates these three views of the inflationary process?

The Economists' View

Economists, who dominate the discussion, start by analyzing inflation in terms of a self-enclosed system of transactions that follows the logic of utility-maximizing behavior. The economic analysis of inflation stands on its own terms as formally self-sufficient. This study seeks to place economists' analysis within a more general framework of social and institutional analysis. While economists recognize the role of political and social forces, they often shelve them among a world of exogenous phenomena that are left unanalyzed. When the action of government officials or organized interests comes into play as a source of inflation,

2. For a good statement of the debate, see Fred Hirsch and John H. Goldthorpe, eds., *The Political Economy of Inflation* (Harvard University Press, 1978).

the economist tends to describe their behavior as itself a type of maximizing response. The economist asks less what produces group attitudes than how they are mediated through money and prices. This volume offers alternative perspectives to supplement the economists' models.

On the other hand, economists often make wider claims about politics and society than they explicitly claim. Each of today's major economic doctrines also presupposes a model of society and politics. Economists must in effect practice sociology and political science without a license. On this terrain noneconomists can appropriately question them. How well are they practicing these social sciences? How plausible are their visions of society?

Monetarist theories, for example, deny the importance of collective economic actors, such as labor unions or oligopolies, in directly contributing to inflation. Only political authorities cause inflation by increasing the money supply beyond what "natural" rates of employment and growth can justify. They do so either because they cannot stand up to powerful interests—including the state bureaucracy itself—or they seek to woo electorates with the spurious promise of revving up the economy. Monetarist theories may be formally elegant, but, as Lindberg and Barry ask in chapters 2 and 10, is their implicit model of the social and political system correct or fully compatible with political democracy? Troubling questions arise. Why should citizens be so rational as economic actors and so misguided as voters? *Homo oeconomicus* and *zoön politikon* seem totally different creatures in the monetarist world. Why should labor unions and other collective interests be powerless to produce inflation in the market, but capable of pressuring authorities into inflation through the political system? Furthermore, why should unions be denied the power to produce inflation in the market but then assigned the task by unyielding central bankers of making their members swallow wage stability or take responsibility for unemployment?

In contrast, neo-Keynesian theories attribute a great deal of importance to interest groups and administered pricing. Prices do not recede when demand slackens; firms persist in mark-up pricing; workers allegedly take their time searching for alternative jobs in the welfare state. "Invisible handshakes" seal prices and wages whose stability allows needed expectations for doing business to persist. This neo-Keynesian view of a "sticky" social underpinning to the market is far more akin to the analysis proposed by the contributors to this study. Nevertheless, neo-Keynesians still tend to concentrate on how collective interests influence economic outcomes more than on the structure of these interests in the marketplace or in the political system.

Rational expectations analysis, finally, presupposes a universe of rational economic actors who respond to the rules of the economic game that are signaled by government. If government suggests that inflation is to be permitted, economic participants will behave accordingly and thus help to ensure the outcome even more strongly. The question that this analysis raises is whether in fact political systems do signal unambiguous rules. Might not the very rules of the game be subject to political rivalry which renders them conflicting and uncertain? Does rational-expectations analysis really allow for the number of regulating principles in contention? It is questions such as these that make the economic approaches to inflation not necessarily true or false, but incomplete. Underlying each economic theory is a model of politics and society often at odds with the policy advice that its advocates are suggesting.[3]

The Sociological Approach

In contrast to the economists' focus, the sociological approach tries to account for underlying value changes that influence economic behavior but that must be explained in their own terms. Sociological explanation usually ascribes inflation to such factors as increased political democracy or affluence. These supposedly undermine society's willingness to defer consumption. The citizen of the modern welfare state is less inclined to accept the disparities in labor and wealth that allowed wage restraint and savings.[4] Disillusioned observers have suggested that the affluence of the later twentieth century has undermined incentives to labor, to saving, and to the healthy austerity on which capital accumulation rests. Inflation is the expression of a new hedonism. Democratic and wealthy economies claim more goods and services than they are willing to work and save for. Brian Barry cites some of these theories in chapter 10. For commentators who are less critical of modern society, it is still the case that the incentive system of capitalism, based as it is on material improvement, must ultimately undermine the rugged, entrepreneurial values on which

---

3. For an even more stringent requirement of economic theory, that its core propositions and not just its implicit model of society be testable (that is, potentially falsifiable), see Mark Blaug, *The Methodology of Economics* (Cambridge University Press, 1980).

4. See John H. Goldthorpe, "The Current Inflation: Towards a Sociological Account," in Hirsch and Goldthorpe, *Political Economy of Inflation*.

572   *Charles S. Maier and Leon N. Lindberg*

its success rested. Capitalism does not have the ethical legitimacy to ward off its own moral entropy.[5]

The difficulty is that these theories, which are cast largely in terms of changing values and norms, provide little foothold for policy guidance. While they may account for inflationary trends in general, they do not explain the onset of inflation at a particular time. They also find it hard to account for the decline of inflation. If the general thrust of democratic society and the welfare state is to unleash inflationary trends, why should inflation ever come down?

The Political and Institutional Approach

Thus the contributors to this volume generally rely on a third approach to account for inflation. They tend to share with adherents of a sociological view the belief that inflation cannot be understood adequately as an economic outcome apart from political rivalries and social structures. But they find it more revealing to probe how changes in values have specific results, how they may be accelerated or altered by the political process. Political analysis thus concentrates on the transactions between office-holders and citizens or among organized social groups and between those groups and the state. Albert Hirschman, in chapter 3, comes closest to the sociological approach. But even Hirschman is not attributing inflation to global trends in modern society. Instead he suggests that inflation arises out of a continuing tug-of-war among interest groups, each of which finds it more advantageous to make a claim on national income even if its grab will stimulate the claims of rivals. In fact, Hirschman suggests, inflation may allow for a sort of acting out of conflict without bloodshed in societies that have deep social cleavages. The point is that underlying social structures and attitudes must be explained through patterns of institutional behavior.

If most of the authors represented here concentrate on political analysis, they are still skeptical of many political-economy theories that purport to relate political and economic outcomes. Brian Barry, for instance, criticizes the notion of the electoral business cycle. Many of the cases chosen to "prove" its existence for the 1960s and 1970s do not allow for the cases

5. For the critical view, see E. J. Mishan, "The New Inflation: Its Theory and Practice," *Encounter*, vol. 42 (May 1974). For the view of capitalism as a system undermining its own value system, see Joseph A. Schumpeter, *Capitalism, Socialism, and Democracy* (Harper and Brothers, 1942); Daniel Bell, *The Cultural Contradictions of Capitalism* (Basic Books, 1976).

that did not substantiate the cycle. And in any case, by the end of the 1970s, as Rudolf Klein mentions, voters were choosing candidates who promised effective anti-inflationary policies, not just incumbents allegedly stimulating the economy.

Not only the theory of the electoral cycle is challenged here, however. David Cameron has effectively questioned the premise that big government causes inflation. Cameron's correlations suggest that countries committed to extensive welfare systems and income transfers are often more responsible about covering their deficits and thus less inflation-prone than countries with less bountiful systems of public assistance. Rudolf Klein undercuts the idea that government causes inflation with a less empirical, more theoretical approach. Klein argues that state expenditures are usually responsive to wide social demands; government spending and job creation are often "endogenous," and much of the growth of service-sector jobs financed by government spending or government transfer payments corresponded to women's entry into the labor market. Indeed, the mix of demands in a modern society is remarkably stable. Some societies assign this spending to private agencies—Japan internalizes much of its welfare bill within the firm. Finally John Woolley's discussion of the role of central banks indicates that the idea of bank independence as a barrier to inflation is also riddled with difficulties. Banks are independent where political actors find it useful to keep them so. They serve as a lightning rod to divert criticism from political leaders who want restraint but not the blame for tight money. And they also fill a talismanic function, reassuring the business community that sound finance will be respected by government. In this view the central bank forms part of what Thurman Arnold once called the folklore of capitalism.

The contributors to this volume thus tend to be skeptical about the received wisdom that attributes the blame for inflation to government. They also contest the frequent indictment of labor unions as an inflationary factor. As Colin Crouch argues in chapter 5, not unions per se, but fragmented and decentralized unions seem to press wage claims with little regard for price stability. Once labor is organized on a national level, so that union confederations must reflect about the consequences of their demands for the economy as a whole, more restraint can be expected. It is unclear in any case whether unions cause inflation or merely try to catch up with rising prices. But insofar as they can be autonomous contributors to inflation, they are less likely to become such if they are freighted with national responsibility.

Thus this volume represents a dissent from some of the basic notions blaming big government or big labor for inflation. But this is not to say that political and institutional factors do not play the crucial role in generating inflation. Economic outcomes cannot be understood without considering the organization of unions and business interests—whether peak associations or powerful firms—government bureaucracies, political parties, prevailing ideological alignments, traditions of state intervention, and distributions of power internationally. As Lindberg points out in chapter 2, only an analysis of these sorts of variables can account for the failure of the economies of the Organization for Economic Cooperation and Development to respond in the 1970s according to the models offered by traditional economic theory. But the task is to summarize the relationships between these political and institutional variables and the performance of the economy. From the institutional analysis of inflation and stagnation, what sort of intervention promises desirable outcomes in terms of price stability, high employment, equity, and growth? This volume does not provide a simple formula, but it does offer a framework for thinking about which alternatives might work (and which have not worked) under differing political and social conditions.

Three Models for Economic Policy

Several of the authors suggest that in effect three stages of social and political organization help determine to what degree a national economy is inflation-prone. Crouch proposes in chapter 5 that where unions are still fragmented and small, labor's contribution to inflation is insignificant. As unions develop, compete against each other, and strive for immediate wage gains, inflationary pressure increases. In a third stage, however, as labor organizations become large enough so that they perceive the general fate of the economy as a direct concern, unions and working-class parties will act as a source of restraint. Crouch refers to Olson's discussion of organizations that are "encompassing" enough so that they themselves must share the cost of inflation[6]; their leaders can no longer believe that they can remain untouched either by the price rises that may follow from their claims or, if their demands are not accommodated by the monetary authorities, by the resulting unemployment. Where labor parties can

---

6. Mancur Olson, *The Rise and Decline of Nations: Economic Growth, Stagflation and Social Rigidities* (Yale University Press, 1982).

participate in government coalitions, all the more impetus exists to push economic interests from a "combative" to a "cooperative" logic.

Crouch writes in terms of the inflationary pressures that can arise from wage bargaining, from the labor-market arena directly. Klein's chapter 8 applies the same notion to the political arena and public expenditure. In societies closest to the model of the liberal market, public expenditure and inflation have no close relationship. In societies where there are well-organized, competitive interests, "rising public expenditure and inflation are likely to march in step." And in societies with encompassing labor organizations or working-class parties that are brought into policymaking, high public expenditure may well diminish inflationary pressures, since labor spokesmen can restrain direct wage gains in exchange for more state welfare or just greater political influence.[7]

These analyses suggest that twentieth-century economies have undergone a certain evolution. While any description of stages must be oversimplified, the OECD economic systems can still be seen as moving from a phase characterized by the model of the liberal market to a stage of competitive pluralism characterized by large unions and corporations and by administered pricing, and then in some countries to a quasi-corporatist order where public authority has sought to supervise consensual bargaining among the organized interests. Of course, most real economies embody elements of all three phases at once. Many older economies had a high degree of government intervention and concertation in the very early stages of development. Most contemporary economies still have sectors far more responsive to the rules governing the classical market. Nonetheless, for thinking about policymaking the idea of three modal organizations is a useful one. It suggests that the policy approaches that may be useful for one level of economic organization may be less workable at another.

Reliance on the Market

Each stage of economic organization described above tends to be associated with a set of corresponding policies. On the one hand, these

---

7. Alessandro Pizzorno has formalized the concept of *political exchange* to suggest that unions and parties can use the power of social disruption to extract concessions that their power in the labor market itself might not pry loose. By extension the concept suggests that labor leaders are often prepared to accept wages lower than the maximum their market power might extract in return for a greater political role. See "Political Exchange and Collective Identity in Industrial Conflict," in Colin Crouch and Alessandro Pizzorno, eds., *The Resurgence of Class Conflict in Western Europe since 1968*, vol. 2: *Comparative Analyses* (Holmes & Meier, 1978), pp. 277–98.

policies—ranging from laissez-faire to demand management to nationalization and economic planning—embody efforts to secure high performance. On the other hand, supporters often advance economic policies less for reasons of performance than of political preference, that is, to help buttress one stage of economic organization or another. Neoliberals (in the United States, neoconservatives) seek to restore the market as the major regulating force. For many of them, to be sure, the desired market is a one-sided arrangement since they rarely challenge oligopolies and administered pricing. Neo-Keynesians try to ensure cooperative behavior among the large interest groups that they believe must remain a permanent feature of the economic landscape. Post-Keynesians and Social Democrats look toward evolving a higher degree of public coordination of interest groups.

Reliance on the market, indeed a major effort to restore the scope of the market, became the dominant policy thrust in the United States and Great Britain in the early 1980s. What successes and what shortcomings can be attributed to this approach? Inflation came down in both countries, but at the cost of the most serious economic recession since the 1930s, a slump that compelled labor to concessionary wage bargaining and left a residue of long-term unemployment.

Significant differences between American results and those in Britain, moreover, reveal that even where governments are prepared to rely on a severe recession to end more than a decade of pass-along inflationary expectations, the medicine is not always effective. The earlier recession of the mid-1970s, after all, did not really work in either country. Perhaps authorities did not allow it to cut a long or deep enough swathe. The governments of the early 1980s were willing to impose the remedy with more resolution.[8] Still, even as it underwent its harsh slump, the American economy continued to produce jobs, some 20 million from 1973 to 1984.[9] Some of these jobs represented lower-quality, less qualified

---

8. Thomas Sargent has argued that from the viewpoint of changing expectations, the Thatcher experiment was not really resolute enough. By not cutting government expenses more drastically, the British authorities did not reverse long-standing beliefs that inflation must continue. He contrasts Thatcher's half-hearted effort with the earlier successful stabilization of Raymond Poincaré in 1926. "Stopping Moderate Inflation: The Methods of Poincaré," in Rudiger Dornbusch and Mario Henrique Simonsen, eds., *Inflation, Debt, and Indexation* (MIT Press, 1983), pp. 54–96. It could also be argued that in climbing out of the recession the Reagan administration was hardly relying on the market alone. Continuing major budget deficits coupled with capital inflows from abroad to finance the adverse American balance of trade, massive public expenditure on armaments, all contributed to the recovery of 1983–84.

9. See Leslie Wayne, "America's Astounding Job Machine," *New York Times,* June 17, 1984.

employment, and some represented involuntary part-time assignments. But, in Britain, employment was just plain contracted and unemployment had risen to nearly 13 percent by 1984. Efforts to cut public spending yielded little result, and public-sector borrowing remained high. Government policies appeared to incur recession without the redeeming features of economic growth and restructuring, unless these processes were percolating slowly at a subterranean level.

Why these discrepancies? Krause and Caves's study of the British economy in the 1970s had already suggested that the process of economic adjustment was very difficult; over 80 percent of nominal increases in the gross domestic product in the decade after 1968, for example, had been dissipated into inflationary price rises.[10] Conversely, the subsequent efforts to lower inflation took a heavy toll in real economic activity and did not just roll back price levels. British society seemed to have structural impediments that frustrated reflationary and deflationary policies alike.

The different results in the two countries suggest that American economic conditions still approximated the market model more than did the British. Rates of effective unionization remained far lower in the United States than in the United Kingdom, approximately 25 percent against 50 percent of the respective work forces. The scope for decentralized entrepreneurial vigor seemed more persistent in America than in England and in many other European societies. The demand for services in a wealthier United States remained higher so that as employment fell in industry and manufacturing, new jobs appeared in the service sector, whereas in Britain the process of substitution remained far more halting. In short, a wager on the market, on what Schumpeter once called "creative destruction," could produce more effective results in terms of braking inflation and creating jobs in the United States because its social and economic organization was perhaps still more fluid than that elsewhere. Capacities for improvisation and innovation still seemed to distinguish American society.

But this is not to deny the shadow side of the American performance. First of all, it remains indeterminate how much of the recovery depended on capital resources drawn from abroad. By virtue of the role of the dollar, the United States could still play on an imperial economic edge denied to other economies. The mechanisms, as Robert Keohane's chapter 4 explains them, had weakened, but they had not disappeared. American

10. Richard E. Caves and Lawrence B. Krause, eds., *Britain's Economic Performance* (Brookings Institution, 1980), p. 8.

recovery might stimulate other economies but it could also divert their resources to North America. From abroad, this process appeared exploitative. Second, policies were carried through with less concern for welfare and equity than in other societies. Nonwage labor costs rose more sharply in Europe than in America during the 1970s. They contributed to the rigidities of the European economies, to the Europeans' inability to lower the real-wage bill after the second oil-price levy on national incomes to the degree that American firms could. In turn, the more refractory costs of labor in Europe may have contributed to slower recovery.[11] But European labor remained protected from the vicissitudes of the market to a greater degree than its American counterpart. Layoffs remained more difficult; welfare could be dismantled less quickly; there was probably less of a regressive redistribution of income in the early 1980s. European administrations could not advise their unemployed workers to move to the Sunbelt where allegedly new jobs awaited.

To sum up, reliance on the market seems to work to the degree it does only where the social and political preconditions of the market effectively persist. They remain valid in the United States only in part, and more in citizens' expectations about what government should or should not provide than in the actual organization of economic transactions. Still, they probably do persist on the ideological level in the United States more than elsewhere. Corporations and pressure groups lobby to evade the market, but individual Americans largely accept its legitimacy, although their allegiance might falter if prosperity faded. In effect, this loyalty allows for capitalist flexibility, but at the cost of a trade-off in terms of equity that European societies—those ruled by Conservatives as well as Social Democrats—no longer tolerate. In Europe the role of labor is too institutionalized to have allowed the infringements on the welfare state that the United States could impose in the early 1980s. As Douglas Hibbs's chapter 7 suggests, labor interests have found weaker electoral expression in the United States than in Europe.

How each observer judges the balance of results will depend on his political and economic values. What the entrepreneur describes as a rigidity the labor spokesman sees as a justifiable protection. In any case, where these guarantees are defended by stronger unions and working-class parties, it is doubtful that resolute market policies will produce the flexible response they continued to manage in the American situation.

11. See Jeffrey D. Sachs, "Real Wages and Unemployment in the OECD Countries," *Brookings Papers on Economic Activity, 1:1983,* pp. 255–89.

Reliance on Pluralism

Throughout the 1970s most Western societies followed what can be called a pluralist approach to deal with inflation and stagnation. Policymakers have accepted the fact that free-market determination of prices and output is confined to certain spheres of economic life. Most transactions are heavily influenced by collective or group behavior. Firms follow administered pricing; labor unions seek to preserve real wages even in the face of slack employment; both capital and labor have an interest in not pushing their social partner to the wall, and both have an interest in wresting subsidies or other concessions from the state. In return state actors need to rely on unions and industry as the executors of general economic policy. Price levels, employment, investment, and growth emerge out of a matrix of implicit or explicit social compacts.

This view of the modern economy effectively underlies neo-Keynesian approaches to policymaking. Neo-Keynesians enshrined an image of institutional stickiness when they accepted Phillips-curve analysis in the 1950s and 1960s. Phillips-curve explanations implied that institutional behavior precluded perfect adjustment to price stability and full employment simultaneously. Phillips-curve approaches also sanctioned a neo-Keynesian interventionism that seemed so triumphant in the 1960s. For the neo-Keynesian approach suggested that if a trade-off had to be accepted, it was still a relatively favorable trade-off and one that could be manipulated to lower unemployment without severe costs in terms of inflation.

As the terms of the trade-off worsened from the late 1960s and inflation rates increased, neo-Keynesian analysis showed signs of difficulty. Monetarists could argue that Phillips-curve analysis had been flawed from the outset, that there was no stable trade-off and trying to purchase higher employment would just yield continuing inflation. Neo-Keynesian economists, however, were compelled to examine the sorts of market "imperfections" that undermined the outcomes they predicted. Increasingly they had to explore the sociopolitical underlay of economic transactions to discover why adjustments were so sticky, why wages and prices behaved in so ratchet-like a fashion. Arthur Okun's exploration of the institutional bargaining between employers and workers that protected investment in social capital at the cost of price flexibility was one of the most sophisticated of these quasi-sociological explanations.[12]

12. Arthur M. Okun, *Prices and Quantities: A Macroeconomic Analysis* (Brookings Institution, 1981).

The difficulty was that no matter how sophisticated, the pluralist analysis of the economic process did not lead to effective policies for braking inflation. Keynesian and neo-Keynesian approaches seemed better designed for stimulating employment than reining in prices. Neo-Keynesian policies for price stabilization took interest-group behavior as a given but sought to appeal to a common interest in price stability. In the United States the Nixon administration followed a brief statutory wage freeze (phase 1) and an effort at publicly scrutinized wage and price rises (phase 2) with less binding frameworks for collective bargaining (phase 3).[13] The Carter administration sought to rely on voluntary price controls and advanced proposals for real-wage insurance or tax incentives for firms that kept prices stable. Western European governments of the late 1960s and early 1970s likewise sought to institute social compacts between unions and employers and to offer working-class parties a greater policy voice in exchange for urging wage restraint. In Italy from 1976 to 1980, the Communist party entered into a consultative arrangement with the predominantly Christian Democratic cabinet and provided implicit political support for the central bank's stabilization policy. In Sweden and in Britain a series of social compacts highlighted anti-inflationary efforts. Still, in every country where these measures were tried, they proved frail instruments. By the end of the 1970s voting publics tended to lose patience with the incumbent governments that sought to persist with them.

In effect, neo-Keynesian policies did not have the bite that their own analytical premises suggested was really required. Albert Hirschman's chapter on the lessons from Latin America suggests some of the reasons. In the short run, unions or corporations might reason, they would still be better off by seeking immediate gains, by trying to appropriate a larger share of national product through an inflationary settlement. On the next round they might lose, but not quite as much and not immediately. In an inflationary environment, however, restraint meant certain sacrifice. Neo-Keynesians proposed that a web of voluntary restraints and compensations would lift economic actors by their own bootstraps out of this world of prisoner-dilemma games and would reestablish price stability as a tenable public good. But as Crouch suggests, this intermediate stage of economic organization—in which oligopolies and unions were powerful

---

13. See Craufurd D. Goodwin, ed., *Exhortation and Controls: The Search for a Wage-Price Policy, 1945–1971* (Brookings Institution, 1975).

enough to compel inflationary settlements, but not so encompassing as to feel the equivalent cost of indulging in them—provided an unstable basis for voluntary incentives. Inflation, in effect, had led to a neo-Keynesian impasse.[14] By the end of the 1970s some societies—for example, the United States and Great Britain—would try to return to the arbitrary discipline of the labor market. Others would consider enlarging the role of interest-group participation so private actors would have a more self-evident stake in price stability. This means, in Crouch's language, moving from the logic of conflict to that of cooperation.

Efforts at Democratic Coordination

The neo-Keynesian impasse arose because reliance on group incentives to achieve wage and price stability proved insufficient. The diagnosis was convincing, but the medication weak. Reliance on the market, on the other hand, has incurred high unemployment and regressive transfers of income. Effectiveness of market discipline, in any case, may be limited at best to societies with a relatively apolitical working class. What is the nature then of the third policy approach?

If there is to be an alternative to smashing unions, forcing concessionary wages as an anti-inflationary strategy, and eroding the welfare state, then economic policy must move beyond the limited neo-Keynesian incentives and ad hoc social compacts of the 1970s. Different initiatives are possible.

One institution familiar to students of political economy and especially of labor markets in Scandinavia, Austria, the Netherlands, and West Germany involves what is often labeled neocorporatism. Neocorporatism, or sometimes just plain corporatism, has shed its association with the spurious fascist effort to organize the economy in industrial sectors across class lines. In its post–World War II context it refers to the policy of involving spokesmen for labor, for business, and the state in tripartite consensual wage bargaining.[15] In a more general sense, as Lindberg and Zysman make clear in chapters 2 and 6, it refers to the enlisting of

14. The term Keynesian impasse is owed to John H. Goldthorpe, "Problems of Political Economy after the End of the Postwar Period," in Charles S. Maier, ed., *Changing Boundaries of the Political* (Cambridge University Press, forthcoming).

15. The literature on corporatism is extensive. For recent useful surveys, see Philippe C. Schmitter and Gerhard Lehmbruch, eds., *Trends toward Corporatist Intermediation* (Sage, 1980); Suzanne Berger, ed., *Organizing Interests in Western Europe: Pluralism, Corporatism, and the Transformation of Politics* (Cambridge University Press, 1981); Colin Crouch, *Class Conflict and the Industrial Relations Crisis: Compromises and Corporatism in the Policies of the British State* (London: Heinemann, 1977); John H. Goldthorpe, ed., *Order and Conflict in Contemporary Capitalism* (Oxford University Press, 1984).

producer groups to work with public officials in setting economic priorities and coordinating economic policies in general—wage levels, investment targets, regional development, job training, and the like. Crouch's chapter summarizes the characteristics of corporatist systems and argues that they have enjoyed a better record on wage stability than the noncorporatist economies. The study of West Germany in chapter 12 shows how German unions accepted a national framework for wage bargaining in which it was understood that wage increases had to be kept within the limits justified by expected real economic growth. West Germany had a formal corporatist framework only during the years of the "concerted action" from 1967 to 1977, but the formal tripartite framework made less difference than the highly disciplined structures of collective bargaining that persisted throughout the postwar era. German unions, moreover, have remained yoked into cooperative structures through the institution of codetermination (adopted in 1951 and extended in 1972). Codetermination provides for a worker voice in plant matters, including hiring and layoffs, as well as union representation on the firm's supervisory board of directors.[16] A whiff of codetermination came to the United States when in 1980 the head of the United Auto Workers, Douglas Fraser, was placed on the Chrysler board as a condition of its government-guaranteed loan. But American and British unions have generally shied away from assuming codetermination responsibilities, while Anglo-American employers have also rebuffed the concept. The major exception is agriculture, where farm federations and dairy boards have long been involved in policy formation and implementation.

Corporatist arrangements can extend beyond the range of the plant or firm or even national wage-determination bodies. In Austria and in Scandinavia spokesmen for the differing political parties and unions effectively partition a multitude of industrial and agricultural boards that run under the aegis of the state and have extensive planning responsibilities. On the other hand, not all formal institutions for tripartite consultation really constitute effective corporatist institutions. The social contracts in Britain, for example, often represented patchy agreements and did not produce a deep-rooted coalition for wage restraint. Britain's economic landscape was littered in the mid-1970s with James Callaghan's social contracts. In addition the Trades Union Congress accepted tax concessions

16. For a summary see Walther Muller–Jentsch, "Industrial Relations in the Federal Republic of Germany," in Ezio Tarantelli and Gerhardt Willke, eds., *The Management of Industrial Conflict,* European University Institute Publication 8 (Florence: Le Monnier, 1981), pp. 105–22.

in return for wage restraint between 1974 and 1978, but these arrangements proved ephemeral. Likewise, the major proposal for a British version of German codetermination, the Bullock Report of 1977, remained a dead letter.[17]

Corporatist institutions are not, therefore, readily imported, as if they were some turnkey technology of industrial pacification. In those countries where they have subsisted over long periods, they are grounded in a host of indigenous conditions rooted in history.[18] Corporatist structures have built on earlier economic interventions by mercantilist states, as in Sweden or Prussia, or on patterns of group accommodation worked out to negotiate long-term religious cleavages, as in the Netherlands. Corporatist structures have proved most durable, moreover, in small countries where citizens readily understand how necessary wage and price stability is for international competition. Andrew Martin's chapter on Sweden describes a situation where the labor movement, despite its strong commitment to social democracy and equality, remains acutely sensitive to the need to retain a competitive industry.

Moreover, even if they proved feasible for the United States, corporatist initiatives would require careful scrutiny. Corporatist arrangements can be exclusionary at the same time they seek to widen the elements of political and economic consultation. While they may admit working-class spokesmen into decisionmaking forums, they can also strengthen the influence of established and conservative unions at the expense of more marginal workers, the nonunionized, the unskilled, women, racial and ethnic minorities. They could also become narrow protectionist coalitions, resistant to industrial change. On the other hand, joint labor and entrepreneurial forums seem to offer a way beyond a destructive zero-sum conflict or harsh social confrontation.

Moreover, corporatism in the narrow sense is not the only framework for widening the circle of economic decisionmaking. If the social under-

17. For British developments in this period, see Andrew W. J. Thomson, "Industrial Relations during the Period of the Recession, 1974–1978," in Tarantelli and Willke, *Management of Industrial Conflict*, pp. 27–63; for other country studies, see Robert J. Flanagan, David W. Soskice, and Lloyd Ulman, *Unionism, Economic Stabilization, and Incomes Policies: European Experience* (Brookings Institution, 1983); Peter Lange, George Ross, and Maurizio Vannicelli, *Unions, Change, and Crisis: French and Italian Union Strategy and the Political Economy, 1945–1980* (London: Allen and Unwin, 1982); Peter Gourevitch and others, *Unions and Economic Crisis: Britain, West Germany, and Sweden* (London: Allen and Unwin, 1984).

18. See Charles S. Maier, "Preconditions for Corporatism," in Goldthorpe, *Order and Conflict;* Peter Katzenstein, *Corporatism and Change: Austria, Switzerland, and the Politics of Industry* (Cornell University Press, 1984), and *Small States in World Markets: Industrial Policy in Europe* (Cornell University Press, 1985).

pinning of modern economies suggests (as several chapters propose) that a logic of cooperation is more fruitful in the long run for achieving growth and stability, more inclusive involvement of labor representatives and citizen groups is probably necessary. While such collaboration has evolved most easily in small, open economies, Americans have also become acutely aware that even so massive an economy as their own is relatively open and vulnerable.

The last great negotiation of collective economic roles took place from the Great Depression through World War II. The economic growth of the decades after 1945 presupposed an underlying social compromise. The post-1945 settlement was forged out of the experiences of mass unemployment, fascist suppression of labor, wartime destruction, and the reaction against communism. Business representatives and conservative parties in the West tempered their earlier resistance to social security measures, collective bargaining, and demand management. In return, working-class spokesmen dropped their demands for extensive nationalizations and old-style socialism. They effectively left the control of investment in the hands of the industrial managers, bankers, and bureaucrats who had traditionally been in charge, and they settled for assurances of welfare and high employment. This Keynesian compromise formed the social and political underpinning of the high growth of the 1950s and 1960s. Only with the stagflation of the 1970s was this settlement really challenged on the Left and the Right.

The prolonged economic difficulties of the 1970s suggested that the Keynesian compromise might no longer assure the effective functioning of contemporary industrial economies. Conservatives have argued that the terms of the Keynesian settlement had cumulatively unleashed the growth of inflationary state expenditure and wage claims. They defined their task as one of reversing the rot that set in with the 1930s and was aggravated with the 1960s. But again, their solution presupposes a restoration of market mechanisms that contemporary society may not sanction beyond the latest upsurge of the business cycle.

It is our view that the Keynesian compromise does indeed require renegotiation, but not reversal. The former division of social functions granted working-class spokesmen and legislative representatives a say in the distribution of income, but it entrusted management and state bureaucrats (as in Japan and France) with control of investment. Inflation and stagnation, however, have undermined the legitimacy of that compromise. Even if it be patched together for another decade, the conservatives have a point. It may not generate the social cohesion to contain inflationary trends, and it may prove unable to call forth the willingness to save and invest that stimulated earlier growth. Andrew Martin's study of Swedish developments is revealing in this respect. It suggests that Swedish unions and the Socialist party themselves recognized the Swedish need for industrial renewal and investment. But in return for labor's contribution they have sought a more collective form of saving and investment that broadens the traditional channels of private profits. The Swedish solution, whose painful evolution has been shaped by many political cross-pressures, is not necessarily a model for other economies. Politically it presumes a Social Democratic party that cannot be durably excluded from governance. Still, for many of the industrial nations, it is hard to justify the direction of investment as a prerogative of private capital, especially when in an age of industrial transformation so many jobs are at stake. Not only is the division of the national product—that is, the state budget, the tax burden, and income transfers—a subject of public debate. The direction of investment becomes a policy arena as well.

Inflation and the Resumption of Growth

Considered together, the chapters in this book suggest that the problem of inflation is never resolved without tackling the broadest questions of political control of the economy. Inflation involves a diminishing valuation of the future with respect to the present. The clear images of next year's gains that justify this year's restraint fade into haze and remoteness. During the depression, Keynes argued that Western society had overvalued savings and had undervalued consumption. The judgment constituted part of his intellectual ambivalence about middle-class priorities. He looked forward to the euthanasia of the rentier and an end to the scarcity of capital, which he felt was artificial in any case. But industrial nations moved out of an era of depression, and they have learned again that the need for savings and investment is imperative, especially as the international division of labor changes rapidly and the OECD nations no longer enjoy the advantages of cheap energy and unchallenged technological leadership. If Keynes faced long-term deflation, the long-term inflation of the 1970s testified to, and increased, the difficulties of designing a new strategy for reinvestment and growth.

These difficulties, the contributors to this book suggest jointly, went deeper than mere control of the money supply or budget deficits. If Lindberg's, Klein's, Cameron's, Crouch's, Martin's, and Salvati's chapters are credited, then inflation did not arise from the "overburdening" of democracy by the welfare state. Countries could, to be sure, try to roll back wages and reduce trade union power or Social Democratic welfare schemes by the weapon of recession. Or they could try to expand the forums of economic decisionmaking by opening up political debate about the goals of growth and seek to win a new consensus for saving and investment. In either case the inflation problem rightly understood is the counterpart of the investment challenge. The resumption of growth in most cases rests on the ebbing of inflation and in turn makes overcoming inflationary pressure all the easier.[19] A contest over shares can be transformed into a sharing of national-income dividends.

All economic doctrines, except for those that presuppose unavoidable "crisis," tend to agree on this possibility. They differ of course in their prescriptions. This volume seeks to evaluate the political as well as the economic promise of these prescriptions, not for this year, but for the long term.

What are the *political* elements of a strategy for growth? Certainly they will vary from country to country. In Austria, West Germany, Scandinavia, and the Netherlands, the cadres of corporatism may serve to forge a social consensus for investment. France and Japan may well be able to build on the partnerships between state technocrats and industrial constituencies that they have long relied on. If it proves necessary to open up the consultative process to working-class spokesmen, then a formula may emerge that provides corporatism with a technocratic face. In Britain and the United States, where corporatist impulses are weaker, national legislatures seem a more appropriate instrument. The alternatives of economic policy—how much investment, what sort of investment, what provisions for disinvestment—need to be placed before elected representatives. National commissions that group labor and industrial leaders may help formulate alternatives, but they are unlikely to substitute for legislative debate. Planning insulated from local and national representation is hard to sustain in the United States, a country hospitable to technocracy only

19. There are situations where inflation can be used to transfer the resources a society needs for investment and growth. Price movements do not formally determine the way real economic quantities change. In Brazil during recent decades, for example, inflation at times probably facilitated development. But in already developed industrial societies, where growth and investment rest in part on middle-class and working-class savings and require political stability, an inflationary strategy for growth seems politically unfeasible. Inflation and a continuing struggle over national income shares produce a vicious circle that chokes off growth and aggravates the difficulties—"the English disease" of the 1970s.

in wartime and, on a more regular basis, in the relationship between government and the military and defense-related industries.

Certainly in any national investment policy, we believe, the concept of investment must be broadened from its traditional association with hardware. Social capital formation is as crucial as investment in physical plant—all the more so as the role of services increases. The task of regenerating devastated urban areas requires ultimately a work force trained not merely in specific, vulnerable skills, but adaptable to a broad range of work demands. As the Swedes have recognized, this requires high investment in job training and retraining, constant microeconomic intervention as well as macroeconomic demand management. It also requires that management comes to understand that its own best interest will lie not in making job tasks more routine, or seeking cheaper sources of labor abroad, but in organizing more flexible plants and assignments. Just preaching the end of Taylorism is not a sufficient policy, however. Tax incentives and research and development contracts may also have to be shaped to encourage a longer-term concept of returns from the firm than now prevails.

This sort of agenda may seem far more inclusive than the traditional checklist for combating inflation. In fact, America's inflationary symptoms may well have been suppressed for a time. Nonetheless, inflation and stagnation formed part of a larger challenge that still grips Western societies. As this volume emphasizes throughout, the dilemmas of the 1970s were simultaneously political and economic. Inflation and stagnation emerged from, and then helped intensify, a major questioning of the division of labor both within the industrial nations and between these nations and the newer developing regions of the world. Class and political compromises that had allowed a generation of postwar growth could no longer command the consensus they earlier had. Growth may not become so spectacularly rapid again. On the other hand, for the last century or longer economies have usually been able to generate real increments of wealth and welfare. Predictions at each stage of industrialization that technological unemployment must finally outweigh new possibilities have not yet come to pass.

No matter what the promise or problems arising out of technological innovation, the conditions for economic progress remain ultimately cultural and political. Only political frameworks provide the legal buttresses that make working for the future a credible activity. Efforts to depoliticize the marketplace tend to be spurious. They usually entail a one-sided buttressing of profits and managerial prerogatives. Nor is it likely in an age of mass parties, television, and welfare entitlements that any effort at depoliticization promises success over the long run. A primary lesson of the inflation of the 1970s—a lesson too from the continuing difficulties of economic restructuring—is that every economy is a political economy in the fullest sense. Societies can experiment with strategies of exclusion, of reducing the voice of political actors; or they can attempt strategies of inclusion and democratization, that is, of expanding the economic role of citizens; or they can seek to muddle through in the hope of another round of prosperity. The 1970s, however, seemed to exhaust the virtues of neo-Keynesian muddling; and for the early 1980s Americans sanctioned an effort at selective depoliticization. The remainder of the decade will test whether this approach can continue to command enough enduring support to prevail. When it no longer does, Americans must think seriously about the reconstruction of political economy on a more open and democratic basis.

Contributors

BRIAN BARRY *California Institute of Technology, Pasadena*

DAVID R. CAMERON *Yale University, New Haven, Connecticut*

COLIN CROUCH *London School of Economics and Political Science, United Kingdom*

DOUGLAS A. HIBBS, JR. *Harvard University, Cambridge, Massachusetts*

ALBERT O. HIRSCHMAN *Institute for Advanced Study, Princeton, New Jersey*

ROBERT O. KEOHANE *Brandeis University, Waltham, Massachusetts*

KARL-HEINZ KETTERER *University of Karlsruhe, Federal Republic of Germany*

RUDOLF KLEIN *University of Bath, United Kingdom*

NORBERT KLOTEN *Deutsche Bundesbank, Federal Republic of Germany*

LEON N. LINDBERG *University of Wisconsin, Madison*

CHARLES S. MAIER *Harvard University, Cambridge, Massachusetts*

ANDREW MARTIN *Massachusetts Institute of Technology, Cambridge*

MICHELE SALVATI *University of Turin, Italy*

RAINER VOLLMER *Landeszentralbank, Baden-Württemberg, Federal Republic of Germany*

JOHN T. WOOLLEY *Washington University, St. Louis, Missouri*

KOZO YAMAMURA *University of Washington, Seattle*

JOHN ZYSMAN *University of California, Berkeley*

Index of Names

591

General Index

601